INDIA
A HISTORY
IN OBJECTS

INDIA
A HISTORY
IN OBJECTS

T. RICHARD BLURTON

Thames
&Hudson   The British
Museum

Contents

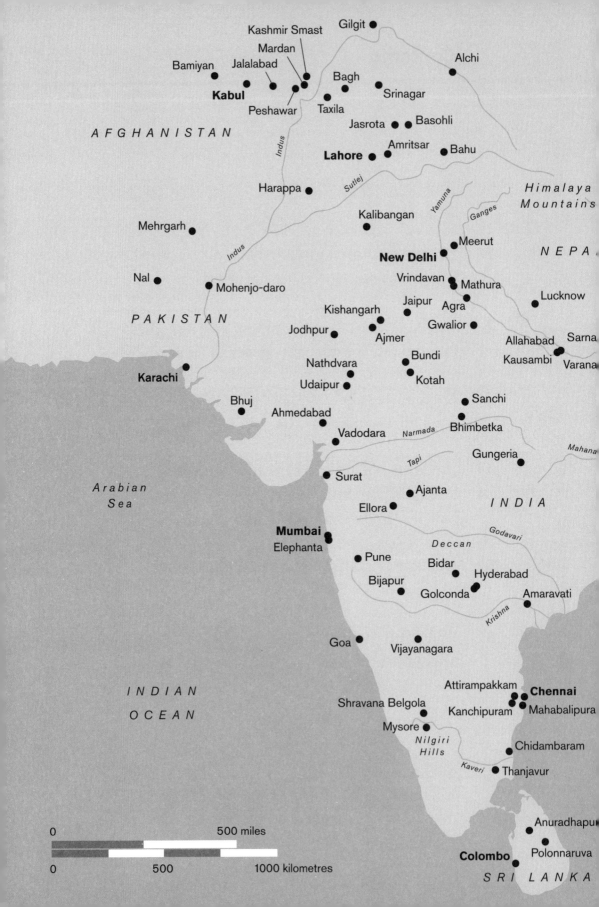

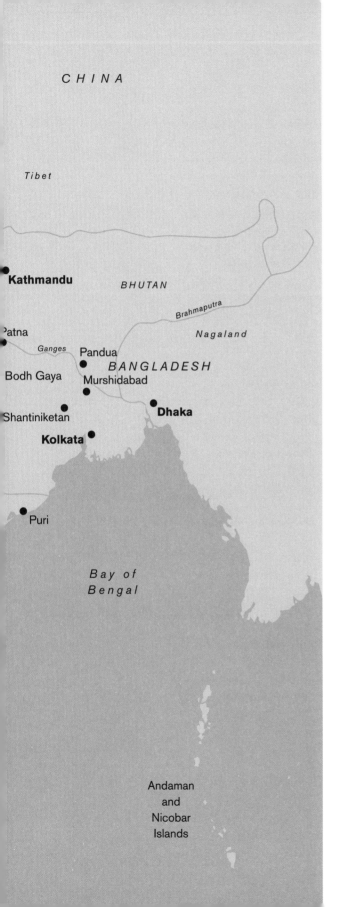

India and neighbouring regions

In this book, the word India is used in its historical sense, meaning South Asia, not – for the most part – the modern country known as India. Thus, the history and cultures of present-day Pakistan, India, Nepal, Bangladesh and Sri Lanka are all discussed.

Some of the place names in modern South Asia have changed in recent decades, and further changes continue. When referring to historical locations, the older names are used in this book, but when considering modern places, the modern names are given; for example, Bombay for the past city and Mumbai for the present city.

Introduction

This book examines the cultural history of South Asia, a zone made up today of the following countries: Pakistan, India, Nepal, Bangladesh and Sri Lanka. In today's South Asia, India has the largest population of any country in the world, only with the exception of China. This statistic, however, is soon likely to change, making India the country with the highest population; it currently stands at close to 1.4 billion. This huge number hints at another feature of the subcontinent – its immense cultural range. In this book a selection of cultural subjects will be presented and illustrated; but this selection can only be partial as the variety is so large. The topics have been placed within a broad chronological frame, though some, for instance, the use of ivory, the long-standing tradition of storytelling, or the epics such as the Ramayana, cut across chronological boundaries. The earliest items discussed come from the Palaeolithic period, reaching back some 1.5 million years; the latest is an artwork produced in 2016.

The variety of South Asia is remarkable in terms of language, script, ethnicity, religion and architecture. Merely taking the first, profusion is immediately apparent. Amongst the hundreds of languages spoken in South Asia, there are four whole language families represented – Indo-European, Dravidian, Austronesian and Tibeto-Burman. And today in India alone, there are more than twenty official languages and a large number of scripts. All of this makes for great regional difference and separate development. Many of the scripts of South Asia descend from the ancient Brahmi script, which itself probably came about through contact with Aramaic, the script used in the ancient Persian empire, part of which was in today's Pakistan. Later scripts, such as Arabic used for Persian and Urdu, and Roman script used for English, reflect more recent history.

In the 20th century language has been an area of controversy, frequently being used to define states (Pakistan – Urdu; Bangladesh – Bengali) as well as regional units in modern India (Andhra Pradesh – Telugu; Tamil Nadu – Tamil; Kerala – Malayalam). Discussion of this topic is fraught with possible misunderstanding. However, for the most part, the languages of the northern part of the subcontinent, including Urdu, Punjabi, Hindi, Nepali, Bengali and others, all belong to the Indo-European group. This does not mean that the people who speak these languages are all of the same origin; ethnic grouping and language are not the same thing. Indeed, what is clear is that the peoples of South Asia are of great variety, and reflect a history of contact, travel, trade and military engagement. Given this situation, multilingualism is common, impressive and necessary.

The land

The South Asian subcontinent is a landmass which geologically is made up of two basic elements, southern and northern. The southern part, which on the map appears as a pendant triangle with the Arabian Sea (to the west)

1. The Virupaksha temple at Vijayanagara (modern Hampi, Karnataka)
The exposed stone surfaces in the foreground and the tumbled rocky landscape beyond are typical of the southern Deccan, where rock surfaces of great antiquity are exposed. The post-and-beam technique of ancient Indian architecture (foreground) is seen throughout the Deccan, with the result that roofs are flat or made up of accumulated though increasingly smaller elements, as in these two temple towers, *gopura*, beyond.

and the Bay of Bengal (to the east), is mostly made up of the central Deccan plateau sloping west to east with, at the southern tip, the plains of the modern state of Tamil Nadu. Yet further south is Sri Lanka which, though today an island, is geologically connected with Tamil Nadu. The upland Deccan plateau is of immense antiquity. Some of the very oldest exposed rock surfaces in the world are to be seen there, dating to the period before the mechanics of continental drift brought the region into contact with the Eurasian plate to the north. Masonry structures are common in this area due to the ubiquity of stone (**1**).

The northern region, beyond the Deccan plateau, is marked to the north by the Himalaya mountains (**2**). These were formed in recent geological time by the collision of the ancient Deccan landmass up against the Eurasian plate, a process that continues to this day. As the southern plate is forced beneath the northern one, the mountains are pushed upwards. The many rivers running out of the Himalayas – the most important being the Indus, Yamuna, Ganges and Brahmaputra – have deposited vast quantities of silt in their river valleys over the millennia, ensuring that the northern Indian plains are fertile, and in ancient times densely forested. Once cleared of forest, however, the fertility of these areas has been dependent upon the monsoon, the annual period of rainfall which in the north comes from June onwards (in the southeast the rains start in October). These river valleys have become rich in alluvium but are not rich in stone. This means that this has mostly been a region of brick architecture. In historic times, only the palaces, forts and places of worship

of the wealthy were built in stone, frequently brought from quarries far off (the main exceptions are the southwestern regions of Sindh, Gujarat and Rajasthan, where building stone is found). The valleys that run out of the mountains to the northwest have provided routes for traders in both directions, as well as for armies entering South Asia.

The geographical diversity of South Asia produces a vegetation ranging from mountain pines through to sub-tropical hardwood forest – and with everything in between. This has meant that much of the history of the subcontinent has been a story of peripheries, rather than of centres. There have been times when a great central power has dominated, but these have been the exception. The different peripheries, frequently based on geographical zones, have often coincided with the differing linguistic zones mentioned above.

Religions

South Asia has been a land of great religious variety. Four of the world's major religions have originated here – Buddhism, Hinduism, Jainism and Sikhism. Other religions from outside the subcontinent, such as Zoroastrianism, Islam and Christianity, have also been prominent. Buddhism, Hinduism and Jainism have all left evidence of buildings and sculpture spanning the last two thousand years; the shorter tally of Christianity is also relevant. Sikhism and Islam have been less concerned with image-making, but they have been prominent in the construction of places of worship – *gurudwara* and mosques.

2. The Langtang range in the Nepal Himalayas
The Himalayas run through northern Pakistan, India, Nepal and Bhutan, and contain the highest mountain in the world, Everest (Chomolungma), located on the Nepal–Tibet frontier, as well as K2 in Pakistan, and Kanchenjunga on the India–Nepal frontier (the second and third highest). To most inhabitants of the subcontinent, the far-away mountains have always seemed highly desirable: lusciously cool, the location of spiritual austerity and achievement, and the home of the gods.

Imagining deities in human form has been a feature of Indian culture and is very evident in Buddhism and Hinduism; this is most clear in the way in which the decoration of temple exteriors is articulated by sculpture in human form. South Asian culture is one where the human form is frequently used also to present ideas: speech is venerated as the goddess Vach, physical features such as the Himalayas or rivers like the Ganges are known as male or female, and philosophical concepts enshrined in texts are anthropomorphized – for instance, the Buddhist deity, Prajnaparamita, whose name means 'the perfection of Wisdom'.

All the religions practised in South Asia have responded to the idea of pilgrimage: the landmass is criss-crossed with routes used by pilgrims, and sacred souvenirs gathered by devotees have been carried from one end to the other. Tied to this has been the idea of the sacred nature of the land, and of its elements – rivers, mountains and holy islands. Such features are very well-attested in Hindu and Buddhist pilgrimage, but pilgrimage is known in all the religions of South Asia (**3**).

There has been a wide variety of different materials used in sculpture production. Stone and bronze are the dominant materials in elite contexts, such as the temples from which much of our understanding of South Asian culture comes. Wood was only used in mountainous areas such as the foothills of the Himalayas or the mountains of the Ghats, south of Bombay. However, terracotta was and still is the most common material for sculpture. The appearance of clay sculpture in the 6th millennium BCE,

3. The tomb-shrine or *dargah* of the saint Nizamuddin Auliya
One of the most famous members of the *sufi* Chishti order, Nizamuddin Auliya (1238– 1325) settled in Delhi and was eventually buried there. His tomb draws pilgrims from all over the subcontinent, especially at the time of the annual *urs* (death anniversary). Both Muslims and Hindus honour the saint and attend the performances of *qawwali*, the emotional *sufi* singing at the shrine. In the complex are also the tombs of others, including the poet Amir Khusrau (1253–1325).

4. Terracotta horses offered to the god Aiyyanar at Viralimalai, near Tiruchirappalli
Distinctive of Tamil Nadu, these brightly painted horses are offered to the god of the village boundaries, Aiyyanar. This rural deity, who looks after the safety of the village, receives horses from devotees so that he can keep watch during the hours of darkness. The individual parts of these horse figures – legs, body, head – are made separately on the wheel and then joined together with wet clay, with details then sculpted and the whole painted. Gifts to local deities of terracotta horses, and also sometimes elephants and tigers, are seen in outdoor shrines throughout the Indian countryside.

a tradition that continues right up to contemporary work from both village workshops and city studios, reminds us of the sacred power in South Asia of Mother Earth (**4**).

From the middle of the 1st millennium CE, the landscape of South Asia has been dominated not by the residences of princes, but by the houses of the gods – temples, mosques, shrines and tombs. For instance, we know almost nothing of the palace architecture of the Chola kings of south India (it was doubtless of wood and has not survived). However, the temples of the same period, such as the Brihadishvara temple at Thanjavur, survive in majestic form. The construction of sacred structures was the standard way in which status, wealth and power was demonstrated in South Asia. Only in early modern times, from the arrival of Islam in the subcontinent, and above all during the rule of the Mughals, their successors and finally the British, has secular architecture become as important. Here, we may think of the fort at Agra built by the Mughal emperor Shah Jahan, the Mehrangarh fortress at Jodhpur or the palace built in British New Delhi as the Viceroy's House and now the residence of the President of India. Here is secular architecture that can compare in grandeur with the Brihadishvara temple, constructed seven or eight hundred years earlier.

Textiles and colour

Colour is one of the most obvious, insistent and frankly delightful elements of South Asian culture (**5**). The Indian world has been and continues to be conceived in technicolour, whether it be the painted figures sculpted over the exterior of south Indian temple gateways, or the popular prints for sale in the bazaar. Artists and craftsmen have for generations been skilful

5. The *theyyam* trance-drama of Malabar

Annually in temple compounds in northern Kerala, *theyyam*'s ritual performers become invested by deities. Here (at the Ukkummal Chamundi shrine at Cherukunnu, Kannur District, northern Kerala), Gulikan, a form of the god Shiva, wears a carved and painted wooden mask and a costume made from cut tender coconut leaves. He brandishes a trident and his body is covered in rice-paste. The reverse of the scarlet headdress of the *theyyam* goddess Chamundi forms a dramatic backdrop for the Gulikan figure. Ancient elements of South Asian culture are evident – the presentation of the divine world through dramatic narrative, intense colour, masked ritualists, trance – along with an understanding of the easy possibility of the divine presence in the human world.

exponents of colour combination. Indian painting makes this clear and the theories that connect different colours with different states of mind ensure that viewing paintings is an exciting experience. This understanding of the power of colour, allied with an early mastery of cotton and silk technology (both already by the 3rd millennium BCE), has meant that the world has been dazzled by coloured Indian textiles for at least two millennia, whether in ancient Rome, medieval Southeast Asia, China and Japan, or more recently in Europe and in Africa – or in the 21st century in the couture houses of Milan.

Final words

It is the aim of this book to make links between works of art and historical change. This has been done using the collections of the British Museum. These collections have been accumulated over more than 250 years and they are of great variety, reflecting the cultures of the subcontinent. Many of the works of art in this book justify themselves purely on aesthetic grounds. However, in our globalized world, there is a further purpose. It is clear that without understanding cultures other than one's own, we are reduced. With South Asians – both in Asia and today dispersed on every other continent – making up a fifth of the worlds' population, it is essential to undertake this task. This book is a modest attempt to do that.

Timeline

c. 1.5 million years ago	Earliest man-made tools in South Asia, at Attirampakkam, Tamil Nadu
45,000–10,000 BC	Microlithic cultures in South Asia
c. 7000 BC	Earliest urbanism in Balochistan
c. 2500–1800 BC	Indus Civilization
c. 2450–2220 BC	Earliest evidence of woven cotton and spun silk in South Asia
c. 2000–1000 BC	Copper Hoard Culture in Central India
c. 1500 BC	The oral compilation of the Vedas
Late 2nd mill. BC–*c.* 100 BC	South Indian Iron Age
c. 8th century BC	Urbanization in the Ganges valley
c. 700 BC	The earliest of the Upanishads are orally gathered together
5th century BC	Ministry of the Buddha
5th century BC	Ministry of Mahavira
c. 400 BC	The first coinage
c. 4th century BC or earlier	The grammarian Panini
Early 4th century BC	Fortification of Anuradhapura, Sri Lanka
269/8–232 BC	The reign of Ashoka; also in Ashoka's rock-cut inscriptions, the first examples of Indian script, in Brahmi

1 Prehistory and early history

1.5 million years ago– 3rd century BCE

1. The excavation trench at Attirampakkam
The investigations at Attirampakkam in northern Tamil Nadu have provided a long sequence for Acheulian stone tool technology in southern India. From the earliest levels have come tools which have now been dated to 1.5 million years ago. New research, such as this carried out by the Sharma Centre for Heritage Education in Chennai, is rewriting the story of early humans in South Asia.

The early cultural history of South Asia is fragmentary, though it is clear that human presence there is of long duration. From sites like Attirampakkam in Tamil Nadu, stone tools used for hunting and skinning wild animals and for digging up roots have been discovered (1). The very earliest can be dated to around 1.5 million years ago. From these tools we get an inkling of how such communities engaged with the world, even what was aesthetically pleasing. Palaeolithic cultures in southern India had a long duration, but by 45,000 BCE stone-chipping technology had developed sufficiently for fine microliths to be produced. At this time also, caves began to be used for shelter. This is the beginning of a long tradition of cave-dwelling in the region that later has resonances in Buddhist and Jain architecture, and in epics like the Ramayana. From such caves also come some of the earliest paintings (2).

These widely spread cultures gave way to Neolithic ones with evidence of ceramic production and the domestication of both wheat and sheep and goats, from the 7th millennium BCE – but far from south India. Excavations at Mehrgarh in Balochistan have revolutionized the understanding of early South Asia. The discovery of the Indus Civilization in the 20th century was equally revelatory; sites dating to *c.* 2500–1800 BCE have been found in the present-day countries of Pakistan, India and Afghanistan. Urban centres such as Mohenjo-daro (3) and Harappa (Pakistan) and Kalibangan and Dholavira (India) indicate the sophistication of these settlements.

2. Cave shelter at Bhimbetka
The wall-paintings at Bhimbetka in Madhya Pradesh – there are several hundred in total – range in date from the Upper Palaeolithic to the medieval period. Subject-wise, animals dominate, indicating the extent to which then, as amongst the local tribal groups until recently, the animal–human relationship was paramount.

3. Cubical weights from Mohenjo-daro
Weights such as these were produced with great precision so that each has a specific weight relationship to the next. They are a striking feature of the uniformity seen in the material culture of Indus sites. This commonality suggests control of the system by a single authority. It also suggests highly developed stoneworking skills. Most that survive are small and suggest the measurement of items of high value but small volume, such as precious metal or stone. Trade and perhaps also taxation are implicit in their existence.

Banded chert, cut and polished
c. 2,500–2,000 BCE
Width 4 cm (right)
Mohenjo-daro, Sindh, Pakistan
Exchanged with the Director-General of Archaeology, India,
1939,0619.239, 236, 231

The causes of the Indus decline are unclear, with no single cataclysmic event visible in the archaeological record. We learn from orally transmitted texts, the Vedas (written down centuries later, though probably reflecting a time around 1500 BCE), of people speaking early Sanskrit, a language of the Indo-European family. The Vedas, the earliest surviving literature from South Asia, are divided into four parts, the first being the *Rig Veda*. This records life amongst the five rivers – the Punjab – while later parts record territory beyond the Indus–Ganges divide. The implication is that movement of these people was west to east, and most scholars today assume an arrival of Indo-European speakers who intermarried with existing Indus populations. The Vedas tell not of urban settlements but of a nomadic cattle-herding people, and for the most part speak about sacrifice and the correct way to do it, along with how to invoke the gods for protection; they are not histories.

No archaeological sites or artifacts can be identified with these people. However, later and by the 8th century BCE, urbanism returns at sites along the rivers of northern India (**4**). These city-states also provided space for philosophical speculation, much of which questioned the formulaic sacrifices laid out in the Vedas; also questioned was the caste hierarchy, which stipulated that brahmins were the only class in society who could access the divine and that they were superior to warriors (*kshatriya*), merchants (*vaishya*) and agricultural

4. The riverside ramparts at Kausambi
Located on the banks of the Yamuna just upstream from modern Allahabad, the extensive ruinfields of Kausambi provide an inkling of the vibrant culture of the early cities of the Ganges valley: perimeter walls, bastions, moats, tanks, wells and monastic establishments are still evident. The earliest levels may be of 8th century BCE date, but the major urban activity is probably three centuries later when large populations were organized to produce the substantial civic works such as the ramparts (see p. 38).

workers (*shudra*). Members of other groups, especially the forest populations of India (probably the oldest inhabitants of the subcontinent), were considered outcaste. Although with many complicated occupational sub-divisions, this is the basis of the historic caste system. From such urban questioning of old certainties came important texts like the Upanishads, which have continued within the fold of Hinduism, though they are full of intellectual doubt. Into this period of philosophical turmoil were born two leaders whose legacy is still clear: Mahavira (the leader of the Jains) and the Buddha (5).

It is difficult to imagine a more important event in the history of Asia than the birth of the Buddha (literally the Awoken One; his birth name was Siddhartha). But despite his importance, we are short of facts concerning his life. Today we cannot even be certain of his dates, though he probably died an old man in the 5th century BCE (earlier scholars thought about 480, but around 400 now seems more likely). He conducted his ministry in what is now Bihar and eastern Uttar Pradesh. It is likely that the teacher Mahavira, who formulated the religious system known today as Jainism, was a near contemporary of the Buddha; there are references in the Buddhist texts to his existence. Both the Buddha and Mahavira belonged to this same period of debate which questioned the Vedic sacrifice and which took place within the newly established cities where there was sufficient wealth to support such uneconomic activity. Our understanding of the cities is greatly aided by

5. The standing Buddha

This bronze image is amongst the earliest of the Buddha to survive. It was cast using the lost-wax method which, along with the theological change that encouraged figural and individualistic representations of the Buddha, made the production of such images possible in the northwestern part of the subcontinent.

Bronze
4th–5th century
Height 41.6 cm, width 16.5 cm
Gandhara, possibly from the Manikyala stupa in present-day Pakistan
Donated by P. T. Brooke Sewell, 1958,0714.1

texts recording the teachings of Mahavira and the Buddha, even though they were written down long after the event.

Towards the end of this period comes the first appearance of a script that is legible today: Brahmi. This is associated with the Mauryan emperor Ashoka, whose adoption of ideas close to or actually Buddhist were promulgated in his realm by inscriptions, mostly on columns or exposed rock faces. He exhorted his subjects to peaceful coexistence and opposed schism. How effective these injunctions were is unclear, though since the time that Brahmi was first deciphered (1837), Ashoka's stock as an idealistic and 'modern' ruler has been high.

1 | 1 The earliest communities

South of Chennai in Tamil Nadu is the site of Pallavaram. Here stone tools of the Palaeolithic period were discovered in 1863 by the geologist Bruce Foote (1834–1912). Foote was a pioneering recorder of Stone Age tools in India and his collection today is primarily held in the Government Museum in Chennai, though a small group is in the British Museum (**1, 2**).

Foote also visited Attirampakkam, a site northwest of Chennai where stone tools offering the earliest evidence of human occupation in South Asia have been found (see p. 16). Here, modern excavators using palaeomagnetic dating techniques have dated the site to c. 1.5 million years ago, comparatively close to the date when hominins are believed to have left Africa. Sadly, no skeletal fossils have been found at these sites, so precise identification of the makers of the tools is not yet possible (**1**).

Later in the Palaeolithic period, much smaller blades known as microliths were produced, chipped from quartzite, obsidian or agate; control of this crystalline material indicates great dexterity (**3**). When set in a wooden haft such bladelets can make tools with useful cutting edges, and they have been found in peninsular India and Sri Lanka.

Probably dating from this time are the paintings found in the rockshelters of Bhimbetka in central India (see p. 17), though the occupation levels probably go back even earlier. The paintings from the Middle Stone Age period (the Mesolithic), are mostly of animals and hunting and were produced using earth colours. Here, we are in the presence of the work of the first artists of South Asia. Later at Bhimbetka, we can also understand how hunter-gatherer communities could coexist with more distant urban societies. Over the centuries such groups have provided a cultural reservoir from which the settled communities, right up to the present day, have drawn upon.

1. Two stone cleavers
The largest of these two cleavers comes from the site of Attirampakkam, where recent excavations have pushed back the date for the presence of hominins in the subcontinent to about 1.5 million years ago. Such tools were used to clean wild animal carcasses and prepare skins.

Quartzite
About 1 million BCE
Left:
Attirampakkam, Tamil Nadu
Length 16 cm, width 9.8 cm
Donated by the Institute of Archaeology, University College London, 1989,0104.1907
Right:
Mirzapur, Uttar Pradesh
Length 12.1 cm, width 8.2 cm
Donated by J. Cockburn, 1894,1227.2

2. Hand-axe

Axes such as this, chipped from quartzite pebbles, provide evidence of both technological knowledge and aesthetic sensibility amongst the early inhabitants of South Asia. This example, excavated by Bruce Foote, was later part of the huge collection of stone tools from all over the world assembled by Dr William Sturge.

Quartzite
About 1 million BCE
Length 21.3 cm, width 10.6 cm
Kadapa (previously Cuddapah),
Andhra Pradesh
Bequeathed by Dr William
Allen Sturge, Sturge.973.a

3. Group of microliths

The miniature form of these blades, and the coloured stone from which they were chipped, present a further advance in the discovery, exploitation and control of useful but very hard materials.

All except (c) from Bundelkhand, Central India, of Mesolithic date, and donated by A. C. Carlyle.
Top row (l–r):
(a) Backed bladelet of flint. Length 2.6 cm. CAR.14.6
(b) Trapeze blade of chert. Length 2.3 cm. CAR.14.95
(c) Scalene triangular blade of rock crystal, Upper Palaeolithic period, Length 1.43 cm. Bandarawela, Sri Lanka. Donated by C. Hartley, 1915,1106.24
Bottom row (l–r):
(d) Lunate blade of chert. Length 1.7 cm. CAR.14.82
(e) Trapeze blade of flint. Length 1.8 cm. CAR.14.108
(f) Scalene triangular blade of chalcedony. Length 1.9 cm. CAR.14.41

1 | 2 Early settlements: Mehrgarh and Nal

The earliest evidence of urbanism in South Asia comes from the edge of the Indus plain, at Mehrgarh. Here an aceramic urban culture developed in the 7th millennium BCE, though by the 6th millennium ceramics were being produced along with the first female terracotta figurines, perhaps indicative of a fertility cult. Evidence of long-distance trade – shell from the coast, and lapis lazuli from northeastern Afghanistan – is present from early times.

Elsewhere, in Balochistan, in the borderlands between the Iranian and South Asian culture zones, early Neolithic sites have been documented. Here in the 4th–3rd millennia BCE agriculture continued to develop along with an increasingly wide range of ceramic assemblages. Many of the ceramics are notable on account of their painted decoration, with designs including geometric, floral and animal motifs. One of the most attractive of these groups of ceramics comes from the site of Nal, where distinctive types have been recorded in a series of burials (**1, 2**). At these locations, and then later in Sindh, at sites such as Amri and Kot Diji, the foundations for the Indus Civilization were laid.

The renowned explorer Sir Aurel Stein (1862–1943) was an early investigator in these borderlands. However, more detailed work was undertaken by Beatrice de Cardi (1914–2016). Stationed in India during World War II, she undertook pioneering excavation and survey work in Balochistan (she had earlier been a student of archaeologist Sir Mortimer Wheeler). She continued archaeological work in peacetime, though eventually her focus shifted westwards, where she recorded evidence for prehistoric contact between the Gulf and the Indus system. The field collection of ceramics that she assembled from her surveys in Balochistan provides an important resource for studying these early cultures (**3**).

1. Ceramic bowl with painted decoration
This bowl comes from the cemetery at Nal in the Las Bela region of Pakistan. Nal and related sites in southern Balochistan were located on trade routes linking Makran (the coastal strip) to the interior. This bowl, with its decoration of bovine heads set between geometric patterning, is typical of the Nal style. Considering the later importance of bovines in the visual language of the subcontinent – on the Indus seals (p. 28) and later, as the vehicle of the god Shiva (p. 93) – the use of such imagery in a cemetery context is intriguing.

Thrown, painted and fired clay
c. 3000 BCE
Height 10 cm
Nal, Balochistan, Pakistan
Donated by Lt-Col. R. A. E. Benn, 1913,0308.3

2. Ceramic canister with painted decoration

The strikingly modern shape of this vessel with its everted rim, is another indicator of the stylistic achievement of the potters of Nal. This visual interest is further accentuated by the use of colours, red and yellow. Like the vessel in Figure 1, this example, also from a cemetery context, has an engaging animal design along with a flanking geometric 'maze' feature.

Thrown, painted and fired clay
c. 3000 BCE
Height 9.5 cm
Nal, Balochistan, Pakistan
Lt-Col. R. A. E. Benn,
1913,0308.1

3. Sherds from the Beatrice de Cardi Collection

These sherds come from the survey undertaken by Beatrice de Cardi and her Pakistani colleagues in Balochistan in 1948. The variety of fabrics as well as the array of designs, even in the fragmentary state they are in today, gives an inkling of ancient aesthetics.

Thrown, painted and fired clay
3500–2500 BCE
Length 9.1 cm (largest sherd)
Balochistan, Pakistan – some from the site of Saiyed Maurez Damb, in Kalat District
1986,1018.1208, 1213, 1217, 1224, 1226, 1245, 1246, 1248, 1249, 1257

1 | 3 Terracotta sculpture

While stone and bronze have been the best-known and most elite materials for sculpture in South Asia, terracotta has always been the most prolifically used over the millennia. In prehistoric societies, the number of terracotta figurines that were produced was enormous, and some of this quantity survives in the archaeological record. The earliest examples come from the western edge of the Indus valley and date to the 7th millennium BCE (**1**).

From many of the Indus sites have come terracotta representations of animals. Some of these miniature sculptures depict beasts that are no longer known in the wild in this part of the subcontinent, such as the elephant and the rhinoceros. Others depict bulls, suggesting the power and importance of these beasts to the Indus people (**2**). Yet other figurines depict female humans which, it is speculated, may actually be images of deities (see p. 26). With all these small depictions – human and animal – the difference between what was a toy, what was an offering to a deity or what was a depiction of a deity, is today difficult to determine. Other pre- and proto-historic sites have also yielded large numbers of small clay sculptures.

In historic times, a striking indication of the link between the fruitfulness of the earth and the divine force is the figure of the goddess Lajja Gauri. In this form, the goddess is depicted as a squatting female, about to give birth; she also sports a blossoming lotus flower instead of a human head. A small terracotta image of her forcefully makes this link between the earth and the fruitful goddess (**3**). In the countryside still to this day, terracotta offerings of animals are frequently deposited in forest shrines (**4**).

This page
1. Female figurine
Clay figurines of this type stand at the very beginning of a lineage which, even in the 21st century, is continuing to diversify. Terracotta images are still being made and offered in shrines in many parts of the subcontinent, though any religious purpose in prehistory is unclear.

Terracotta
Probably 6th millennium BCE
Height 7.1 cm, width 4.5 cm
Balochistan
Bequeathed by Professor
W. G. Lambert, 2013,6001.3537

Opposite, above left
2. Figurine of a bull
Bovines appear frequently amongst figurines found at Indus sites, as they do on the Indus seals (see p. 29). The presence also of model carts in terracotta at these sites, indicates the use to which bulls were put in the Indus economy. Other than boats, they provided the main form of transport for goods.

Terracotta
2500–2000 BCE
Height 7.5 cm, width 5.8 cm
Harappa, Punjab, Pakistan
1986,1018.2009

3. Representation of Lajja Gauri

Here, the link between the earth and the fertile goddess Lajja Gauri is emphasized as she is shown with legs apart and as if giving birth. The cult of this goddess has a long history in the Deccan.

Terracotta
2nd–3rd century CE
Height 5.5 cm, width 6.4 cm
Ter, Maharashtra
Donated by Douglas Barrett, 1958,1017.2

4. Terracotta tiger

Terracotta animals made by Hindu potters are purchased by members of the Bhil community of eastern Gujarat to offer at forest shrines. Animals offered include horses, elephants and tigers to be ridden by the deities; dome-like residences are also offered.

Terracotta, made and fired by Shankarbhai Mangalbhai Prajapati
1985
Height 44 cm, length 47 cm
Chhota Udaipur, Panch Pahals, Gujarat
As1985,15.3

Above
1. The 'Great Bath' at Mohenjo-daro
This brick-built structure has never been fully understood, though early investigators suggested a link with the later ritual water tanks known at Indian temples; today, though, this argument is less accepted. Elsewhere, drains to take foul water away from houses are well attested.

Left
2. Female figurine
The precise function of the terracotta figurines found at Indus sites is unknown; some may depict a Mother Goddess, given the frequent exaggeration of hips and breasts. They were handmade, with features such as eyes and breasts added as pellets of clay.

Terracotta
2,500–2,000 BCE
Height 8.2 cm
Mohenjo-daro, Sindh, Pakistan
Exchanged with the Director-General of Archaeology, India, 1939,0619.205

3. Pillar base
Architecture at Indus sites, as seen in the archaeological record, was almost entirely of brick. This rare example of stone used as a building material was part of a pillar made up of a sequence of these circular elements, all held in place by a central wooden upright.

Sandstone
2,500–2,000 BCE
Diameter 47 cm, height 27 cm
Mohenjo-daro, Sindh, Pakistan
Exchanged with the Director-General of Archaeology, India, 1939,0619.383

The Indus Civilization

Although 'Indus Civilization' is now a misnomer since many sites, all broadly related, have been found outside the Indus valley, the two urban settlements that have defined our view of this ancient culture are both located there. Harappa is on the banks of the Ravi, a tributary of the Indus, while Mohenjo-daro, further south, is on the main channel itself. Sites beyond the Indus/Ganges watershed, such as Kalibangan and – in Gujarat – Lothal and Dholavira, have demonstrated the Indus Civilization's wide geographical range.

The Indus culture, and specifically Mohenjo-daro, was unknown until members of the Archaeological Survey of India – initially R. D. Banerji, and later Sir John Marshall – excavated there, from the mid-1920s. The accepted dates for Mohenjo-daro are c. 2500–1900 BCE. Its demise – date and mechanics – is still a matter of debate.

Strikingly, the street layout at Mohenjo-daro was organized on a grid pattern; similar layouts are seen at other Indus sites. Another remarkable element of the layout at Mohenjo-daro was the installation of drains and wells (1). There is almost no evidence of religion, unless we regard the many terracotta figurines (2) as votive offerings, or depictions of deities. Only at Kalibangan is there some evidence: a row of pits containing ash has been interpreted as fire altars. There is also no evidence of a palace or other centre of control – society seems to have been remarkably egalitarian – and we find a striking degree of cultural uniformity, including in the common system of weights (see p. 17).

The Mohenjo-daro excavations have produced evidence of wheel-thrown ceramics, including fine red wares with painted black designs. Motifs on these wares include leaf patterns identified as pipal leaves, suggestive of the later importance of this tree in South Asian culture.

From Mohenjo-daro, and other Indus sites, come long tubular carnelian beads that have been drilled to be threaded as jewelry. Considering the time needed to make such items – and the technology of both baking the agate to redden it, and then to pierce it with a bow-drill – it is clear that they had a high status. This is substantiated by their export to Mesopotamia (see pp. 32–3), and by the terracotta examples found at Indus sites which imitate carnelian. Other jewelry included cut conch-shell bangles (p. 33). Further technological expertise is demonstrated by finely made blades, chipped from banded chert found in the Rohri Hills of Sindh.

From an early period at Harappa comes evidence of silk. Use of two species of wild silk moth has been recorded, dating to c. 2450–2220 BCE. Further evidence comes from Chanhu-daro with a similar date. The chronology suggests a separate first exploitation of silk to that known from China. This evidence of sericulture taken along with finds recorded by Marshall at Mohenjo-daro of woven and madder-dyed cotton, points to one of the most important cultural activities of South Asia from remote prehistory up to the present day: the weaving and decorating of both silk and cotton.

Agriculture at Mohenjo-daro included domesticated animals – cattle, sheep and goats – as well as wheat, perhaps stored in buildings identified as granaries. The horse was not known. Some of the animals depicted on the distinctive Indus seals (see p. 29), such as elephants and rhinoceroses, indicate that the river valleys were more verdant than today. It has been suggested that the firing of vast quantities of bricks for the construction of the cities may have caused deforestation and subsequent landscape change. This may partly explain the eventual decline of Indus settlements, though there were doubtless many other contributing factors.

1 | 4 Indus seals and the Indus language

Seals and seal-impressions have been found at many Indus sites; the use of these seals is presumed to be for marking traded goods. While not all Indus seals are the same type (a few are circular or prismatic), the majority are remarkably uniform in design, being rectangular and made of steatite. On one side they have a pierced knob for suspension (**1**) and on the other an engraved design. This design is often of an animal (frequently a bovine) standing before a manger, or perhaps a standard; above is a sequence of signs (**2**). Rarer are seals with depictions of humans, which may or may not be cultic, and may or may not be linked to later Hindu deities.

Of the signs on the seals, nowhere do more than a dozen appear together making decipherment very difficult (no bi- nor tri-lingual inscription is known). The language used is also unknown. And this is based on the assumption that the signs record a language and are not just marks used by merchants, listing goods. If these rows of signs are indeed writing, scholars have suggested that the language might be Dravidian, belonging to the language group found in historic times in southern India; there is, however, no certainty and others have suggested a link with the Austro-Asiatic group. Some seals and impressions have been found in dated excavation levels in southern Iraq, thus providing an independent chronological framework – as well as documenting the trade between the two zones (see pp. 32–3).

It remains highly problematic to make an assessment about ancient language – especially when linked to later texts or beliefs – without any texts for guidance; this is equally true when discussing ethnicity. For this ancient period, other than the seals and related items, there are no texts and all attempts to decipher the seal inscriptions have failed, though a corpus of the material, which now numbers some 3,500 examples, has now been published so that computer analysis is possible.

This page
1. Seal (reverse)
The knob on the reverse of this seal shows how these objects were suspended on a thread, and probably kept close to the body, an indication of their importance.

Steatite
2500–2000 BCE
Height 3 cm, width 3.1 cm, depth 2 cm
Mohenjo-daro, Sindh, Pakistan
Donated by the Director-General of Archaeology in India, 1947,0416.3

Opposite
2. Three seals from Mohenjo-daro, with impressions
These three seals (left) with impressions (right) are typical of the range. The bull, or some variety of bovine, appears frequently (top and middle); the presence of a 'standard' before which the animal stands (middle) and rows of signs across the top of the seal in the undeciphered Indus Script (all) are also common. The bottom seal, depicting a rhinoceros, is a dramatic indicator of the change in environment in the Indus region; the nearest such animals today are in the Nepal Terai.

Steatite
2500–2000 BCE
Height 3.7 cm, width 3.7 cm (top); height 3 cm, width 3.1 cm (middle); height 3.3 cm, width 3.3 cm (bottom)
Mohenjo-daro, Sindh, Pakistan
Donated by the Director-General of Archaeology in India, 1947,0416.1, 3 and 4

1 | 5 Dice and the lure of chance

The use of dice in South Asia has an ancient history and many examples have been found at Indus Civilization sites. These dice, some 4,000 years old, include examples of the two standard types found in India throughout its history: cubic and stick varieties. The dice are made from ivory or terracotta and from Mohenjo-daro comes an ivory example of the stick form, with the numbers on each face indicated by dots within inscribed circles (**2**). A very large number of these dice have been recovered from excavations and they stand at the beginning of a long line of dice use that continues to this day (**1**).

There are several famous examples of dice play in Indian tradition, notably the game in which Yudhishthira, the eldest of the Pandava brothers, the heroes of the great epic the Mahabharata (p. 71), games away their joint wife, Draupadi (**3**). His addiction to the throw of the dice marks the beginning of the extensive narrative that eventually ends in the great battle at Kurukshetra. Another famous dice game is the one played by the deity Shiva and his consort Parvati. This episode is memorably recorded in a sculpted panel at Elephanta, the 6th-century rock-cut cave temple dedicated to Shiva on an island in Mumbai harbour.

Other popular games that originate in South Asia include *pachisi* (the precursor of the game ludo), chess and the game we know as snakes and ladders (**4**).

1. Three different dice
Three examples of dice made of different materials: the distinctive south Indian bronze die, a painted wooden cubic die from the Himalayas with Tibetan syllables rather than numbers on the faces, and a painted ivory stick example.

Bronze, wood and ivory
Probably all 19th century
Length 7.8 cm (ivory stick die)
Tamil Nadu, Himalayas and north India
Wooden example donated by Johannes Nikolaus Schmitt and Mareta Meade, 2004,0605.1, 1992,1214.8, 2004,0524.1

2. Ivory stick die
The engraved faces of this damaged die from Mohenjo-daro would have been numbered one to four (one is displayed here).

Ivory
2500–2000 BCE
Length 4 cm
Mohenjo-daro, Sindh, Pakistan
Exchanged with the Director-General of the Archaeology, India, 1939,0619.336

Printed at the Chore Bagan Art Studio. द्रौपदीव वस्त्रहरणा. 24 Bhoobun Banerjee's Lane, Calcutta. 18
Droupadi

3. The Rape of Draupadi
Draupadi's prayer is answered and her never-ending sari saves her from rape. The gaming board in the foreground is the immediate source of her predicament.

Lithograph on paper
c. 1895
Height 41 cm, width 30.5 cm
Chore Bagan Art Studio, Calcutta
Brooke Sewell Permanent Fund,
2003,1022,0.18

4. Snakes and ladders board
By throwing dice, the players hope, through moral excellence, to ride up the ladders, eventually to the abode of the gods – and to avoid the snakes that lead to perdition.

Paint on paper
19th century
Height 57 cm, width 56.5 cm
Punjab Hills
British Museum Friends,
1999,0809,0.1

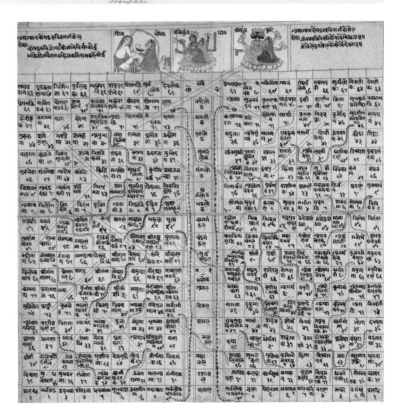

1 | 6 Trade networks

Long-distance trade outside ancient South Asia was already well established in the Indus period.

At Shortughai, on the banks of the Oxus river in northern Afghanistan, there is evidence for an Indus-type settlement. Its location is perhaps to be explained by its proximity to lapis lazuli mines; lapis beads have been found at Indus sites, as also have imitation examples made of faience, indicating the value given to the real thing. However, the presence of gold dust, which in historic times was panned from the Kokcha river close to Shortughai, may be an equally powerful explanation for the location of this Indus outpost.

Equally impressive is the evidence of trade between the ancient Indus and Mesopotamia. Amongst the grave goods in the Royal Tomb at Ur (in present-day Iraq) were tubular carnelian beads (**1**). These are distinctive products of the Indus area, being baked agate which has subsequently been drilled; the industry at Harappa has been well studied. Not only have these colourful stone beads been found in early Mesopotamia but also one example bears an inscription in cuneiform recording its dedication in a city shrine, indicative of its value and significance (**2**). References in cuneiform texts to 'Meluhha' are today believed to refer to the ancient Indus region (**3**).

There were also well-established trade networks within the Indus region. This is substantiated by the existence across large areas of similar items of material culture, and of widespread cultural uniformity (for seals, see p. 28). The example of conch-shell bangles, which are features of many Indus sites, is telling, as the shells are marine items. Consequently, their appearance far inland indicates the existence of long-distance networks (**4**).

1. String of beads from Ur
Spectacular beads of both carnelian from the Indus regions and lapis lazuli from Afghanistan were found in the Royal Tombs of Ur, in southern Iraq, providing clear evidence of the trade between the Indus and Mesopotamia; whether the lapis came the same way, or was traded separately from northern Afghanistan, is less clear. The tombs, which are firmly dated, provide a useful *terminus post quem* for the beads.

Carnelian, lapis lazuli, gold foil
2500–2000 BCE
Length 42.8 cm (string), width 2.8 cm
Ur, southern Iraq
1928,1009.84

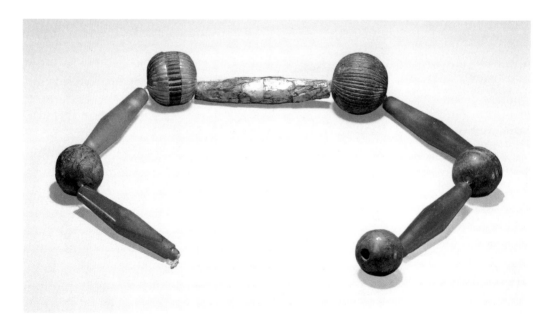

Above

2. Tubular carnelian bead with cuneiform inscription

The inscription on this tubular carnelian bead records its dedication at the shrine of the goddess Nunlil by Shulgi, who describes himself as king of Ur, Sumer and Akkad. Such beads were clearly highly valued.

Carnelian
c. 2000 BCE
Length 7 cm
Indus valley (bead made);
Ur, southern Iraq (inscription)
Part funded by the Art Fund
(as NACF), 1945,1013.37

Left

3. Clay tablet

In the cuneiform text impressed on to this clay tablet there is mention, in the Sumerian language, of a location close to the city of Ur where people named 'Meluhha' lived. It is now believed that these people were merchants from the Indus region.

Clay
Third Dynasty of Ur, c. 2200–2000 BCE
Length 12.3 cm, width 75 cm
Ur, southern Iraq
1894,1015.11

Below

4. Conch-shell bangles

These three shell elements show the stages of production of conch bangles: at left, the spine after the outer parts are cut away; in the centre, a section cut through the spine; and at right the completed bangle (here broken) after further cutting and smoothing. This method of production is still practised in South Asia.

Conch shell
2500–2000 BCE
Length 13 cm (spine at left)
Mohenjo-daro, Sindh, Pakistan
Exchanged with Director-General of Archaeology, India, 1939,0619.363

1 | 7 Bronze Age copper hoards

In the aftermath of the Indus Civilization, attention moves eastwards to the region between the Ganges and the Yamuna, the Doab, and southwards, in central India. In both areas, hoards of heavy bronze blades, harpoons and enigmatic 'anthropomorphs' (bronze objects of approximate human form) have been discovered. In one case only, Gungeria in northern Madhya Pradesh, silver plates were also deposited along with the bronze items. By 2002, some 197 copper hoard deposits had been recorded.

The Gungeria Hoard (**1**, **2**), found in 1870, is perhaps the most remarkable of these hoards on account of its great size. In the original discovery (now dispersed; forty-two items are in the British Museum, others are in the Nagpur Museum), there were 424 copper objects, weighing an astonishing 376 kg. Also remarkable in this hoard is the inclusion of silver plates, both circular and in the shape of bulls' heads with down-turned horns (**1**). The function of this deposited material, all of which must have been of considerable value, is unknown. However, the thinness of the silver and the bluntness of the copper blades suggest that these items were not for everyday use. Votive deposit seems a more likely explanation, though one cannot be sure. Unfortunately, very few of the many hoards that are now known have come from an archaeological context. Consequently, the chronology of this material is difficult and dates between 2000 and 1000 BCE have been posited. However, at the site of Ganeshwar in Rajasthan, a very large hoard has been recorded along with Ochre-Coloured Ware, establishing a date range of 1750–1250 BCE for the hoard.

This page
1. Silver plates from the Gungeria Hoard
These silver plates are representative of the two types from the Gungeria Hoard: circular with depressed centre (above and right) and bovine with downturned horns (left). Their function is unknown, though the large quantity and their thinness make a votive function the most likely answer.

Silver
Late 3rd to end of 2nd millennium BCE
Diameter 12–14 cm (circular), 12–13 cm (bovine)
Gungeria, south of Jabalpur, Madhya Pradesh
1894,0727.53 (top, circular), 1894,0727.55 (bovine), donated by Augustus Wollaston Franks; 1873,1103.32 (bottom, circular), given by Major A. Bloomfield

Opposite
2. Copper blades from the Gungeria Hoard
These copper items are distinctive of the range of blades found in the hoards: axes (top), tanged axes (middle) and bar celts (bottom). All are heavy and difficult to use; a votive and display function seems likely. The wealth of these hoards implies a society with easy access to copper ore.

Copper
Probably late 3rd to end of 2nd millennium BCE
Gungeria, south of Jabalpur, Madhya Pradesh
Fourth bar celt from left: length 56.2 cm, width 10.2 cm
1873 group donated by Major A. Bloomfield, 1873,1103.1, 2, 3, 5, 6, 8, 10, 12, 13, 15, 17, 26, 27, 28, 29, 30; 1880.82, 83

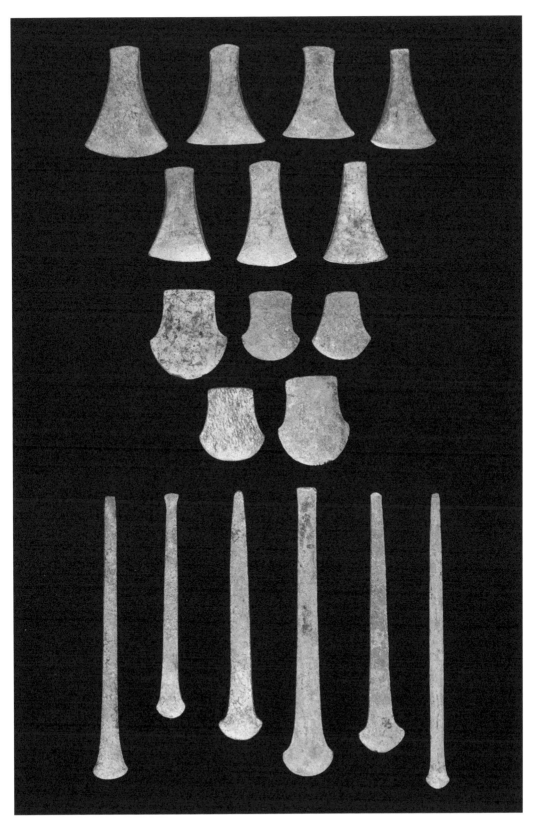

1 | 8 The Iron Age in southern India

The earliest evidence of iron technology in southern India (from Hyderabad in the north to Tirunelveli in the south) comes from graves that are often referred to as being of 'megalithic' type. This term includes burials in pits lined by slabs of stone and then covered with a stone slab; burials set within stone circles; and burials in unmarked pits. Indeed, the variety of grave type is bewilderingly large and even includes some interments associated with alignments of standing stones. However, while the graves are wide-ranging in type, the material culture deposited in them has a striking uniformity, including iron agricultural implements such as hoes, and bladed weapons (1). Adichanallur in the far south is renowned for the large number of iron objects found there in graves, as well as the complexity of some of the items produced. Also found in most of these graves are burnished Black and Red Ware ceramics (2). Later in the sequence and from the Coimbatore region of western Tamil Nadu, vessels of so-called Russett-Dressed Ware are recorded. They depend for their considerable aesthetic appeal on the application of a red slip that is then combed to make a wave-like pattern, revealing the lighter-coloured body of the vessel beneath (3). These 'megalithic' burial practices may have begun towards the end of the 2nd millennium BCE and then continued for at least a thousand years.

The long history of iron-working in the Deccan is now clear from recent survey work in the Karimnagar District of Telangana. Remarkably, it seems that the first production of steel (later known as wootz) took place in this region and that knowledge of how to produce it may date back some 2,000 years, long before it was known in Europe.

1. Iron adze and socketted hoe
These tools, suggestive of forest clearance and plant agriculture, are part of the widely recorded repertoire of iron tools recovered from megalithic tombs in southern India; these examples are from the far south.

Iron
Probably late centuries BCE
Length 19 cm, width 5.4 cm (adze); length 25.1 cm, width 10.5 cm (hoe)
Thought to be from Adichanallur, Tamil Nadu
1880.1250, 1880.1229

2. Black and Red Ware vessel with lid

Bichrome wares such as this are known throughout the southern Deccan and the Tamil country and are associated with the first appearance of iron, and also with megalithic burials. At the end of its chronological sequence, this lidded form is found in Buddhist contexts used as a reliquary.

Burnished fired clay
c. 1600–200 BCE
Height (with lid) 18 cm
Probably the southern Deccan
UCL, Institute of Archaeology
73/107

3. Russett-Dressed Ware vessel

Vessels such as this example, shown on its side to emphasize the decorative scheme, are known from the southern part of the Deccan and from Tamil Nadu. They are connected with the 'megalithic' tombs, though where dated they are from the end of the sequence.

Slipped, combed and fired clay
Late centuries BCE
Diameter 31.8 cm
Perhaps from Coimbatore District, Tamil Nadu
1880.1140

1 | 9 Cities in the Ganges valley: the second urbanization

Urban settlements like those known from Indus Civilization sites are not a feature of the Indian landscape for much of the 2nd millennium BCE and do not feature in the Vedas, the earliest South Asian texts. Nor are they important in the Mahabharata or the Ramayana, the epic narratives respectively of the Pandava brothers, and of king Rama and his adventures rescuing his wife Sita from Ravana (see pp. 86–9).

However, by the time of the first Buddhist texts (orally transmitted in the 5th century BCE), cities are visible once more, especially in the Ganges valley. Today we find the riverside remains of such fortified urban settlements. Kausambi, located on the Yamuna and mentioned in early Buddhist texts, is typical, featuring brick fortification walls with gates, bastions and a moat (**1**); many sherds of sophisticated Northern Black Polished Ware (**2**) have been found at the site. Other cities include, in the northwest, Pushkalavati (present-day Charsadda, near Peshawar) and Taxila, near Rawalpindi, both close to tributaries of the Indus river and linked to trade routes to Central Asia. In the Ganges valley, along with Kausambi, are Mathura (see p. 74), Ahichchatra (p. 77), Varanasi and Rajagriha. From many of them have come early coinage, the so-called punch-marked coins (p. 40). Several of these early cities are associated with the life of the Buddha (Varanasi and Rajagriha) or with the early history of Buddhism (Taxila, Kausambi and Mathura). Jainism also grew out of this early urban society.

Overland trade was an increasing feature of the period, while agriculture included rice cultivation and craft specialization such as metallurgy was established. From the northwest all the way down the Ganges valley, carved circular stone objects, known as ring-stones (**3**), have been found. Sharing a similar imagery are terracotta figurines which are known throughout this zone and which presumably had a votive purpose (**4**).

1. Kausambi ramparts
The extensive ruinfield at Kausambi is delimited by massive fortification walls. They were constructed of brick faced with stone and a moat ran around three sides while the fourth was protected by the river. Northern Black Polished Ware and punch-marked coins have been found at the site.

4. Female figurine

Terracotta figurines of frontally facing nude females, often with elaborate appliqué coiffures, are common from sites in the northwest of the subcontinent. Their precise function is unknown, though some sort of cultic use is presumed; the stick-like base is suggestive of them being placed in the ground, perhaps in shrines.

Terracotta
Late centuries BCE/early
centuries CE
Height 15.9 cm
Spina Warai, Peshawar, Pakistan
1951,1210.29

Above
2. Northern Black Polished Ware

Found throughout the subcontinent, and widely imitated, the best of this tableware is connected with the high degree of craft specialization found in the cities of the Ganges valley. Northern Black Polished Ware has a body of finely levigated clay and a slip with added potassium and iron. When fired at a high temperature and burnished, this results in a distinctively lustrous surface.

Slipped, burnished and fired clay
400–250 BCE
Kausambi, Uttar Pradesh
Length 9.5 cm (top)
UCL, Institute of Archaeology
63/154

Below
3. Ring-stone fragment

Ring-stones are miniature sculptures of great skill. This example is damaged but this enables a close view of the carved inner surface of the once enclosed ring. The function of these items remains unknown, but most are carved with displaying female figures and sprays of honeysuckle.

Stone
3rd century BCE
Width 8.9 cm, depth 1.9 cm
Northwest Frontier Province, perhaps near Dera Ismail Khan, Pakistan
Donated by Angela Kidner and Stephen Dobell in memory of C. H. Dobell
1995,0124.1

1 | 10 Punch-marked coins

Punch-marked coins are mostly associated with the Ganges–Yamuna Doab and with the Punjab as far north as the city of Taxila, but they have been found scattered throughout South Asia. While there is some uncertainty, they probably first appeared in around 400 BCE and continued in use (though not production) into the post-Mauryan period in the late centuries BCE. Also uncertain is the extent to which Achaemenid punch-marked bars – the origin of which is probably to be found in Greek coinage – were the prototypes of the Indian coins (the Achaemenids ruled ancient Gandhara from the late 6th century BCE until the fall of the Persian Empire), or whether these eastern Achaemenid types were influenced by the Indian examples. There is a chronological connection between these distinctive coins and the rise of the cities of the second urbanization (see p. 38), such as Kausambi, Varanasi and Pataliputra (present-day Patna). These were all associated with the group described in the texts as the *mahajanapada*, the territories of the most important tribal groups. These are the city-states in the Ganges valley from which later a single state under the Mauryan kings developed (see p. 48).

The earliest punch-marked coins appear to be those of the 'bent bar' type (**1**); these are characterized by fewer punch marks and upturned ends. Later, increasing numbers of marks appear, including hill, tree-shrine, wheel, svastika, elephant, humped-bull and srivatsa, along with others now difficult to identify (**2**). Some of these signs – tree-shrine, svastika and srivatsa – have a recognized meaning still to this day. The coins bear no inscriptions, though it seems likely that certain designs were used by specific cities. Most examples are rectangular and appear to have been cut from small bars of silver or copper. The use and symbolism of the punched designs was continued by the Mauryan kings, the successors of the *mahajanapada* states (**3**).

1. Bent bar coin (side and front)
This example is typical of the earliest type of punch-marked coins. Its provenance, Afghanistan, is some indication of the possible Persian origin of this form of coinage. The design of crescents with a central line, stamped twice, is of uncertain meaning though it may have a cosmological implication.

Silver
4th century BCE
Height 2.6 cm, width 1.2 cm
Found and possibly minted in Afghanistan
1922,0424.3524

2. Circular punch-marked coin

In contrast to the early bent bar forms, circular punch-marked coins carried many designs. On this example, there are four original punched designs, along with some later ones that were probably used to revalidate the coin during circulation.

Silver
Immediately pre-Mauryan
Diameter 3 cm (max)
From the Varanasi region
1996,0610.22

3. Mauryan punch-marked coin

Coins of the Mauryan rulers based in Pataliputra (present-day Patna) continued the punch-marked form of their predecessors, the *mahajanapada* city-states. However, the distribution of these coins is very wide, from Sri Lanka to Afghanistan, especially in the period immediately after this issue. The stamped designs, including bull, elephant and sun (visible here) are difficult to interpret, but probably had a religious connotation.

Silver
3rd century BCE
Diameter 2.2 cm (max)
Probably Ganges valley, north India
Donated by William Theobald, OR.7296

1. The Dream of Queen Maya

The haloed elephant is shown about to enter the side of the sleeping queen. The curved nature of the slab indicates it came from a stupa. It also shows how narrative episodes were used for didactic purposes.

Schist
2nd–3rd century CE
Height 19.3 cm, width 32.4 cm
Takht-i Bahi, Mardan District,
Pakistan
1932,0709.1

2. The Birth of the Buddha

Queen Maya, clutching the branches of a tree, gives birth from her right side. The child figure is not shown, but his presence is indicated by footprints on the swaddling bands carried by the four figures to her right.

Limestone
2nd–3rd century CE
Height 82.5 cm
Amaravati, Andhra Pradesh
1880,0709.23

3. The Great Departure

The three main sections here show (r–l) Prince Siddhartha leaving the bedchamber, on horseback departing from the palace, and seated in the forest cutting his hair prior to a life of austerity.

Limestone
3rd century CE
Height 37.5 cm, width 140 cm
Amaravati, Andhra Pradesh
Donated by the Government
of Madras, 1880,0709.112

The life of the Buddha and the Jataka stories

The life of the historical Buddha is impossible to delineate today with certainty. Early information was orally transmitted and quickly became elaborated. Fact and legend were eventually gathered together in texts, early examples being the *Mahavastu* and the *Lalitavistara*. Both are compilations of earlier material, with the latter probably in the form we know it today by the 3rd century CE. From such texts we learn that the Buddha-to-be was born as Siddhartha into the royal family of the city of Kapilavastu on today's India–Nepal border. His birth was heralded in a dream in which a white elephant entered the side of Queen Maya (**1**). The birth took place in the Lumbini Garden and was miraculous: the child issued from her right side (the right is the male and auspicious side in South Asian tradition) (**2**). The child's early years were spent in luxury, but one day, disturbed by the sight of a sick man, a corpse and finally a wandering ascetic, he resolved to leave his royal life, including his wife and son, to find a better way to understand human existence. He left the palace in the dead of night, entered the forest and there cut off his hair, symbolic of the change from a secular life to one of austerity (**3**).

In the forest, he followed the teachings of various gurus, and practised strict self-denial. Eventually, realizing that asceticism was not beneficial in his search, he sat in meditation beneath a pipal tree at Bodh Gaya, hereafter known as the *bodhi* tree. Here, he was set upon by the demon Mara, who both tempted and assaulted him. He rebuffed these distractions and called on the earth goddess to witness that through merit accumulated in his previous lives he was no longer affected by any negative *karma*, which would result in a new birth (**4**). He then became Enlightened, a state which would lead to complete liberation or *nirvana*, something he never defined (the word is analogous to the extinguishing of a flame).

Leaving Bodh Gaya (see p. 126) he travelled to Sarnath, and in the Deer Park preached the First Sermon; he set in motion the Wheel of the Law (**5**). He enunciated the knowledge he had gained that would lead to escape from the endless round of rebirths. This teaching was the Four Noble Truths and the Eightfold Path. The Noble Truths are that life is suffering; that suffering is caused by desire; that ceasing to desire leads to release from suffering; and that the way to cease to desire is right conduct. Right conduct he then listed in the Eightfold Path.

For the remainder of his life, the Buddha conducted his ministry in eastern India. Bodh Gaya and Sarnath became and continue to be pilgrimage centres. Following his death, his ashes were divided into eight parts. These were deposited within burial tumuli, becoming the first stupas, the quintessential form of Buddhist architecture.

Following his death, the idea of the Jataka stories – previous life stories – developed. These tell the lives of the Buddha before his final, historical life. They all acknowledge the idea that the Buddha taught of rebirth according to one's *karma* – that is, the fruits of one's actions, moving either up or down the ladder of existence. We are all somewhere on that journey, eventually leading to the snuffing out of the need to be reborn, as all the negative fruits of previous lives become exhausted. As the Buddha achieved this and entered *nirvana*, it must be assumed that he previously experienced many lives, in each one accruing the necessary good *karma* to enable him in his last and human life (some of the earlier ones were animal) to reach liberation. The Jataka stories draw on an ancient reservoir of folk literature and are illustrated in the earliest surviving Buddhist sculpture (**6**). A somewhat unforgiving morality governs the stories, determined by the impersonal law of cause and effect, but compassion is prominent from the beginning.

Below
**5. The First Sermon
at Sarnath**
The Buddha is seated with his
hands in the teaching posture,
while in the pedestal two deer on
either side of a wheel are visual
shorthand for the Deer Park
at Sarnath and the 'setting in
motion of the Wheel of the Law'.
On the reverse, a stupa and the
Buddhist creed are inscribed.

Schist
Bihar
Height 43 cm, width 19.5 cm
Late 7th century
1854,0214.1

Above
**4. The Assault of Mara,
and the Calling of the
Earth to Witness**
The Buddha is depicted beneath
the *bodhi* tree, being tempted
by demonic and erotic figures.
However, he touches the
earth to act as his witness
to Enlightenment.

Sandstone
6th–17th century
Height 50.8 cm
Eastern India, perhaps Sarnath
1880.11

6. The Shibi Jataka

King Shibi, the Buddha-to-be
in a previous life, demonstrates
extraordinary compassion by
offering his own flesh to ransom
the life of a pigeon. The king's
flesh, cut from his leg, is weighed
in the scales, while the pigeon
shelters beneath the throne.
The god Indra, with tubular
headdress and carrying his
thunderbolt weapon, supervises
the transaction.

Schist
2nd–3rd century CE
Height 23.3 cm, width 32.4 cm
Gandhara
1912,1221.1

1 | 11 Mahavira and early Jainism

Mahavira, or 'great hero' (**2**), is believed by the Jains to be the last in a sequence of twenty-four teachers, the *tirthankara*, literally 'the ford-crossers' (**3**). This title refers to the idea that their teachings enable devotees to cross from the world of illusion to an existence from which there is no return to the cycle of rebirth. The *tirthankara* are also known as *jina* or conquerors and this term has given the belief-system its name. The *tirthankara* immediately previous to Mahavira is believed to be Parshvanatha (**4**). Mahavira and the Buddha were probably near contemporaries in the 5th century BCE.

Jain philosophy imagines the existence of a soul, but one weighed down with accumulated attachment to the material world. As in Buddhism and Hinduism, belief in reincarnation is fundamental, as is the desire to escape from the continuing rounds of rebirth. Jains believe that *karma*, the connections to this world caused by both good and bad deeds, can be severed only through asceticism, and primarily through renunciation and the path of monasticism. Both monks and nuns exist and are given high status on account of the extremely austere nature of their lives. Most worldly comforts are removed, wandering is encouraged and strict vegetarianism is followed. Such restrictions on diet are a major element for all Jains, monastic as well as lay. Another fundamental and connected issue is non-violence. The need to avoid even accidentally taking life has precluded laymen from being farmers, let alone soldiers. Traditionally, Jains have been merchants, bankers and professionals.

As in other Indian religions, pilgrimage and image veneration are a part of Jainism. Sites associated with Parshvanatha in Bihar, and with the Jain saint Bahubali at Shravana Belgola, near Mysore in Karnataka (see pp. 138–9), are still important for Jain pilgrims (**1**).

This page
1. Shrine
This unusual stone shrine in the form of a hinged box opens to reveal the standing figure of Bahubali, the saint remembered today at Shravana Belgola. The top of the lid to the box bears images of three of the *tirthankara*.

Soapstone
Perhaps 16th century
Height 11.5 cm, width 8.3 cm
Donated by Sir Augustus
Wollaston Franks, 1888,0515.5

Opposite, above left
2. Head of a *tirthankara*, perhaps Mahavira
Mathura, south of Delhi, was an early centre of Jain activity and the distinctive mottled red sandstone of the region was used extensively in the production of sculpture and architectural carving. Buddhism was also active at Mathura and clearly drew on the same reservoir of depicting the divine, as imaging became a feature of both systems in the early centuries CE.

Sandstone
c. 4th century CE
Height 26 cm, width 21.5 cm
Mathura, Uttar Pradesh
Donated by the Secretary of State for India in Council, 1901,1224.6

Above right
3. The *tirthankara*
Today this sculpted slab of
the twenty-four *tirthankara* is
damaged. Nevertheless, it is
clear how the arrangement of
the figures would have originally
appeared around the single
central standing image. The two
crowned figures at the base are
protective nature spirits, *yaksha*
(male, left as viewed) and *yakshi*
(female, right).

Soapstone
Hoysala period, 13th century
Height 27 cm, width 17 cm
Southern Karnataka
Donated by Henry Oppenheimer,
through the Art Fund (as NACF),
1914,0218.1

Right
4. Parshvanatha
The twenty-third *tirthankara* is
Parshvanatha. He is recognizable
on account of the rearing seven-
headed serpent which protects
him as he stands in motionless
meditation. Although there
is little historical data on the
earlier *tirthankara*, there is some
suggestion of Parshvanatha
in the sources.

Bronze
14th–15th century
Height 35 cm, width 13 cm
Southern Deccan
Donated by Henry Oppenheimer,
through the Art Fund (as NACF),
1914,0218.4

1 | 12 The emperor Ashoka

The most ancient writing from India that can be read is a series of inscriptions cut into rock faces and inscribed on free-standing pillars (**2, 3**). These are associated with the greatest ruler of the Mauryan dynasty, Ashoka, who reigned from 269/8–232 BCE from Pataliputra (present-day Patna). They have been found in many parts of India (though not farther south than Karnataka) and also in Nepal, Pakistan and Afghanistan.

The inscriptions are mostly written in Brahmi script and are in varying Prakrit languages; the different Prakrits, descended from Sanskrit, were the everyday speech of northern India in Ashoka's time. Of the inscriptions not in Brahmi some are in Kharoshthi script, widely used in the northwest at this period; again, the language is one of the Prakrits. One inscription from Taxila (present-day Pakistan) uses Aramaic script and language, as also do some in Afghanistan. A rock-cut and bilingual inscription in Greek and Aramaic is located at Kandahar, in southern Afghanistan. The presence of these two scripts and languages is due to their use in the Achaemenid and Hellenistic kingdoms of the eastern Persian world.

The Ashoka inscriptions indicate the geographical influence of Mauryan rule, though actual control outside the Ganges valley is unclear. They also provided a moral code for the emperor's subjects and have a strikingly modern tone. Ashoka demands his subjects avoid conflict, be tolerant of the religious views of others and avoid taking human and animal life. These ideas ally Ashoka with Buddhism as does his concern for concord in the *sangha* (the monkhood). These unusual but powerfully presented views were – we learn from the inscriptions – caused by remorse at the death of thousands during his conquest of Kalinga (present-day Orissa). Ashoka's endorsement of these views had a profound effect on the trajectory of Buddhism within, and eventually outside, India.

1. Modern banknote
The use of Ashoka imagery by the newly independent state of India deliberately avoided either Hindu or Islamic imagery. It also harked back to a time of unity throughout much of the subcontinent and to a doctrine of collaboration and peace. Its use continues today, along with the motto '*satyameva jayate*', 'Truth shall triumph'.

Paper
1978
Length 14.6 cm, width 7.4 cm
Issued by the Reserve Bank of India
Donated by T. Richard Blurton, 2006,0829.1

2. Pillar from Amaravati

This detail shows one face of an eight-faced column from the Buddhist stupa at Amaravati. A column similar to Ashoka columns is depicted, with a lion seated on an elaborate capital as the terminal. On another face is a pillar surmounted with a wheel, again suggestive of the earlier columns associated with Ashoka.

Limestone from Palnad
1st century BCE
Height 255.5 cm (entire pillar), diameter 38.8 cm
Amaravati, Andhra Pradesh
1880,0709.109

3. Fragment of Major Pillar Edict VI

This section of the pillar inscription tells how Ashoka honoured all religious sects. It is from the pillar once located at Meerut, much later transferred to Delhi, then damaged in the 18th century when this fragment was recovered and sent to the India Museum (disbanded 1879).

Polished sandstone
Mid-3rd century BCE
Height 12.2 cm, width 32.6 cm
Pillar erected at Meerut, Uttar Pradesh
1880.21

Timeline

Late 3rd century BCE	Traditional date for arrival of Buddhism in Sri Lanka
3rd century BCE	Construction of the earliest stupa at Sanchi
2nd century BCE	Patanjali, author of the *Mahabhashya*, mentions the use of scroll-paintings by storytellers
2nd century BCE	Construction of the earliest stupa at Amaravati
2nd century BCE	Earliest rock-cut caves at Ajanta
2nd century BCE– early 1st century CE	Indo-Greek kingdoms flourish in eastern Afghanistan and the Punjab
1st century BCE	The excavation of the first Buddhist cave shrines, such as Bhaja
c. 1st century BCE/CE	The *linga* at Gudimallam
From *c.* 1st century CE	Trade in Indian textiles to Central Asia and Red Sea coast
1st–3rd centuries	The rule of the Kushans in north India; Kanishka rules *c.* 127–150
From 1st century	Substantial Indo-Roman trade
From 1st century	The spread of Buddhism and Indian culture to Central Asia
2nd century	Jainism prominent in Mathura, south of Delhi
4th century	Christianity recorded in Kerala
4th–5th centuries	Near-final form of the Mahabharata and the Ramayana
4th–5th centuries	The rule of the Gupta dynasty
5th century	The first surviving built temples
5th century	Second period of rock-cut caves at Ajanta; fine painting in caves
5th century	Kalidasa writes his dramas
c. 5th century	The first of the *Puranas* are compiled (continues for many centuries)
5th–6th centuries	The finalization of the *Devi Mahatmya*, the text narrating the triumph of the goddess Durga
5th century	Sarnath becomes a centre of Buddhist iconography

2 Early empires and developing religions

Late 3rd century BCE–8th century CE

1. Stupa 1 at Sanchi
Although not the oldest stupa at Sanchi, in Madhya Pradesh, Stupa 1 or the Great Stupa is the most elaborate, with two levels of enclosed walkways and gateways, *torana*, at the cardinal points. These are covered with relief sculpture of Jataka stories and scenes from the life of the Buddha. The building dates from the 1st century CE, although an earlier structure is enclosed within. Badly damaged in the early 19th century, conservation began in the 1880s under Henry Cole; the whole site was only fully conserved in the early 20th century under Sir John Marshall.

The historical canvas of the late centuries BCE/early centuries CE is dominated by the spread of Buddhism and Jainism. What we understand today as Hinduism is also present though less apparent earlier in the sequence. Hindu temple structures survive though from the mid-5th century CE and rock-cut caves with sculpted panels of deities are known from the same period at Udayagiri (central India) and from 7th-century Mahabalipuram (southern India) (see p. 120).

The teachings of the Buddha quickly spread from northeastern India. In central India, the first stupa at Sanchi were probably built in the 3rd century BCE, though repeated rebuilding and redecoration occurred over several centuries (1) (see p. 56). The stupa at Bharhut is also at the beginning of this sequence, along with, further south, the earliest part of the stupa at Amaravati. Jainism also spread at this time, though its diffusion has always been less than that of Buddhism. Trade within India was instrumental in the spread of both teachings and this is especially apparent as Buddhism advanced into Afghanistan, Central Asia and China.

In the post-Mauryan period the political situation is not clear, but kings from a dynasty known as Shunga may have been responsible for the Bharhut stupa. Their remit ran mostly in northern India. Soon afterwards, in the last century BCE, the first rock-cut Buddhist caves were excavated in the Western Ghats, as at Bhaja (2) where the wooden

2. Cave 12 at Bhaja
The 1st-century BCE cave-shrines at Bhaja in Maharashtra are man-made, excavated from the cliff-face, and are amongst the earliest in the long sequence of mostly Buddhist shrines in the Western Ghats. The imitation in cut stone of wooden elements, such as the ribs of the ceiling, indicate the origins of such architecture, though no wooden exemplars survive. At the apsidal end of the columned hall of Cave 12 is a monolithic stupa.

prototypes of such buildings are evident in their design. Slightly later, also in the Deccan were the Satavahana rulers who are connected with the continuing excavation of Buddhist caves in the Ghats, as at Nasik. Then, further southeastwards, the Satavahanas continued the work of earlier Sada kings in construction of the free-standing stupa at Amaravati. Merchants from this region and nearby sites appear to have been active in trade to Sri Lanka, Southeast Asia and westwards towards the Mediterranean.

Following his conquest of the Achaemenid empire, Alexander the Great rampaged through Punjab and Sindh in 327–26 BCE; his brief visit, however, went unnoticed in India. More importantly, Alexander's Greek successors set up kingdoms, in Bactria in the 3rd century BCE and later, an Indo-Greek kingdom in the Punjab. This was then superseded by the rule of invaders from Central Asia, the Kushans. From the mid-1st century CE their empire stretched from Bactria to Mathura. The presence in Gandhara sculpture of the corporeal depiction of the Buddha, rather than symbolic representations, may perhaps be due to contact with the Roman world with its interest in realism, though one cannot be certain. Lost-wax casting with the possibility of figural sculpture did, however, enter India at this time (**3**).

In south India, the first evidence of literature comes from the collection of mostly secular poetry known as the Sangam. This was composed in Tamil, a non-Indo-European language

3. The standing Buddha
One of a small number of early bronze images of the Buddha to survive from Gandhara; it was made using the lost wax process (see pp. 112–13). This example stands at the point when Gupta influence is becoming more prominent. The depiction of the drapery harks back to Gandhara styles, but the visibility of parts of the body through the garment, along with both halo (around the head) and mandorla (around the body), look forward to later developments.

Bronze
5th century
Height 31 cm, width 10 cm
Sahri-i Bahlol, near Peshawar, Pakistan
Brooke Sewell Permanent Fund, 1981,0610.1

of the Dravidian group. The dating of this corpus is debated but most authorities would now agree to a date of around the 3rd century CE. Both Buddhists and Jains were active in the south, but the poetry mostly tells of non-Brahmin communities – kings, warlords, cattle-raiders – and is an important source of information on everyday life. Not least amongst these subjects, though, was romance.

> Ever anew aches my heart!
> Again and again I brush off the burning tears,
> My love, once peaceful at my side, grows restless,
> My heart aches!

The importance of Buddhism declined in the mid-1st millennium CE. The powerful north Indian kings of the Gupta dynasty drove this change. Although influential sculpture of the Buddha was still produced, the cults of recognizably Hindu deities – for instance, Vishnu as boar-headed Varaha (**4**), and Shiva as the *linga*, the phallic column – became increasingly popular. Also, in this period, the texts known as *Purana* began to be produced (continuing over many centuries). These texts list the cosmic activities of the gods and their many forms. In the devotion to Vishnu, the idea of the incarnations, the *avatara*, also developed at this time (see pp. 98–101).

The Gupta period is associated not only with powerful rule but also with cultural brilliance, as illustrated by their coinage (**5**), the strikingly realistic paintings of the Ajanta caves and the flowering of literary Sanskrit. This is the period of the playwright and poet Kalidasa (late 4th–early 5th century), the author – amongst other works – of the drama *Abhijnanashakuntala* (the 'Recognition of Shakuntala') and the poem *Meghaduta* (the 'Cloud Messenger'). He is considered the most important of all the literary figures of ancient India.

In this period, two of the most important texts of South Asia came into approximately their final form. The epics the Ramayana and the Mahabharata were, like so many Indian texts, originally transmitted orally and there are a number of different versions. These texts have provided inspiration for artists, sculptors, playwrights and poets from that time until today. In the poetic outpourings of the south Indian saints, the *nayanmar* and the *alvar* (from around the 7th century; see p. 124) we see the beginning of the *bhakti* movement, which was later to be so influential throughout India (see pp. 162–3).

Increasingly apparent from the early 1st millennium CE is the international trade in textiles. It is difficult to over-emphasize this element of social and economic activity, though the evidence has to be gleaned from outside the subcontinent.

2 | 1 Sanchi

Located in the modern state of Madhya Pradesh in central India, the hilltop site of Sanchi is one of the most important surviving locations for understanding early Buddhism. Three stupas have survived along with various later temple structures. The whole site was extensively exposed and restored between the late 19th and early 20th centuries.

The origins of Sanchi go back to the Mauryan period; an Ashoka pillar was erected there during the 3rd century BCE. The pillar is inscribed with a warning against schism in the *sangha* (the monkhood) and was once crowned with the famous addorsed lion capital that has since become the emblem of independent India (for Ashoka, see p. 48). The presence of this edict indicates the early importance of the site, but Sanchi continued to grow throughout the early centuries of the present era, and fine sculpture of post-Gupta date was still being commissioned in the second half of the 1st millennium CE.

Stupa 1, known as the Great Stupa, has four elaborately carved gateways or *torana* dating from the Satavahana period (1st century BCE–1st century CE). They stand at the four cardinal points and allow access to the walkway around the structure. Each of the four gates was constructed of uprights and then a series of horizontal beams, each ending in scrolled volutes. In the angle between the upright and the beam, female bracket figures were located; these are *yakshis* (see also p. 46) (**1, 2**). As the beneficent *yakshi* kicks the trunk of the tree, it bursts into bloom (**3**).

The condition of the stupa and its sculpture, prior to its full restoration, can be understood from early photographs of the site (**4**).

Aastern Gateway. Great Tope.

Opposite, above left
2. *Yakshi* bracket (front)
The female nature spirit or *yakshi*, clinging to the tree, acts both as a support in the structure of the gateway, and as an indication of auspiciousness. She is depicted as beautiful, voluptuous and encouraging of all that is positive. Such figures are known as *shalabhanjika*.

Opposite, above right
3. *Yakshi* bracket (back)
The survival of fine detail on the reverse of the bracket shows the elaborate headdress worn by the *yakshi*. The flowering and fruiting of the tree is thought to come about when she kicks the trunk of the tree. The detail still visible here suggests the sculpture may have been found with this reverse side buried and the more abraded top face exposed.

Sandstone
1st century CE
Height 65 cm, width 47 cm, depth 18 cm
Sanchi, Raisen District, Madhya Pradesh
Donated by Mrs Tucker, 1842,1210.1

1. *Torana* with a *yakshi* bracket still in place
This image comes from an album of forty-five photographs of Sanchi and environs, perhaps taken during the restoration project by the Archaeological Survey of India under Henry Cole, which began in 1881. Some of the fallen *torana* were re-erected at this time.

Albumen print
Early 1880s or earlier
Height 24.3 cm, width 17.2 cm
(photo only)
1994,0520,0.2

4. Sculptures from Stupa 1
Visible among a group of sculptures gathered together during the 1880s investigation of the site are the addorsed lion sculptures from the top of the Ashoka pillar (3rd century BCE; lying horizontal in the foreground) and a 9th-century sculpture known as the Sanchi Torso, which since 1886 has been in the Victoria and Albert Museum in London. A damaged lion figure at back right may be the terminal of the column in the background.

Albumen print
Early 1880s or earlier
Height 18 cm, width 23.1 cm
1994,0520,0.28

Group of fragments &c.

2 | 2 The early stupa at Amaravati

The discovery near Amaravati, in the Krishna valley, of a fragmentary inscription in Brahmi characters has encouraged some scholars to think of a 3rd-century BCE date for the construction of the earliest stupa at Amaravati. While this is still unproven, the handful of surviving early sculptures recovered from the site clearly have links with the earliest known stone sculptures in India, such as those from Sanchi in Madhya Pradesh (see p. 57). There was much later rebuilding, leading to most of the early sculptures from the first stupa being either discarded, used as packing material in the expanded structure, or occasionally reused.

One early panel was reused in the 3rd century CE and depicts the stupa at that later time (see p. 60, Figure 2). However, on the reverse, something different is still visible (2). Here, devotees with the 'archaic smile' of the earliest Indian sculpture suggest a date in the 2nd century BCE. Furthermore, this is the early, aniconic phase of Buddhist art – the presence of the Buddha is only suggested, not physically shown. It is not known why there was an early interdict on showing the Buddha in corporeal form, but it is distinctive of early Buddhism and may reflect an understanding that if the Buddha had entered *nirvana* he could not be depicted, as *nirvana* was beyond description. At Amaravati such ideas seem to have given way in the 2nd/3rd centuries CE to bodily depictions of the Buddha.

Other early fragments include a coping stone carved with a winged bull and a winged lion (both have Mesopotamian antecedents) (1) and sculpted panels of stupas with unelaborated dome decoration (3 – compare with p. 60, Figure 2).

1. Coping stone from a railing

This fragment from the early railing or *vedika* at Amaravati shows a winged lion, a creature more associated with the ancient cultures of Mesopotamia than with India. Above, the exquisite lotus scroll inhabited by ducks, is carved in shallow relief suggestive of woodworking, indicating perhaps that the earliest *vedika* at Amaravati was of wood.

Limestone from Palnad
1st century BCE
Height 58.8 cm, length 98.1 cm, depth 13 cm
Amaravati, Guntur District, Andhra Pradesh
1880,0709.102

2. Panel from the early stupa at Amaravati

Devotees venerate the Buddha, their hands held in the honorific greeting of *anjalimudra*. The sacred presence is indicated symbolically – the signs of his feet, *Buddhapada*, with distinctive wheel, *chakra*, on the soles; the empty throne on which he meditated; the parasols above; the *bodhi* tree at whose base he sat; and celestial figures who honour him. On the left is part of a column of Mauryan inspiration. The reverse of this slab is illustrated on p. 60.

Limestone from Palnad
2nd century BCE
Height 124.4 cm, width 86.3 cm, depth 12.5 cm
Amaravati, Guntur District, Andhra Pradesh
1880,0709.79

3. Panel depicting an early stupa

Visual contrast is brilliantly articulated in this design, balancing the simple dome decoration and the unelaborated railing on one hand with, on the other, the impressive five-headed *naga* guarding the entrance to the walkway around the stupa, and the protective parasols that issue explosively from the structure which crowns the stupa, the *harmika*.

Limestone from Palnad
1st/2nd century CE
Height 145 cm, width 77.5 cm, depth 10 cm
Amaravati, Guntur District, Andhra Pradesh
1880,0709.39

1. Railing pillar (inner face)
This scene, filled with narrative action, is the Great Departure. The Buddha-to-be leaves his father's palace for the forest. Celestial dwarves hold up his horse's hoofs so that no one hears him leave; other divine figures applaud the prince's decision to search for enlightenment.

Limestone from Palnad
3rd century CE
Height 270 cm, width 83.3 cm, depth 29 cm
Amaravati, Guntur District, Andhra Pradesh
1880,0709.7

2. Drum slab depicting the stupa
This relief 'portrait' gives an idea of what the stupa looked like in the 3rd century CE. In the centre is a gateway guarded by lion figures, and the walkway dominated by a figure of the standing Buddha. Above is the densely decorated dome, little of which survives. The reverse of this slab is illustrated on p. 59.

Limestone from Palnad
3rd century CE
Height 124.4 cm, width 86.3 cm, depth 12.5 cm
Amaravati, Guntur District, Andhra Pradesh
1880,0709.79

3. Drawing of a sculpted slab by Genden Chopel
The dome of the stupa containing a relic is guarded by five-headed *nagas* (compare with Figure 3 on p. 59).

Graphite and colour on paper
c. 1940
Latse Library, Trace Foundation

Amaravati

The stupa at Amaravati was located on the banks of the Krishna river, upstream from the delta. It is not known when this site and the adjacent city of Dharanikota was founded, but it may have been as early as the 3rd century BCE (see p. 58). Sculpture was still being commissioned in the 8th century CE, indicating a period of use of over a thousand years. A single inscription in Sri Lanka lists gifts made to Amaravati in the 14th century, but it is unclear whether this refers to the stupa or a nearby temple dedicated to Shiva. Later, Amaravati was resonant for Tibetans, as its location is believed to be where the Buddha delivered the *Kalachakratantra*. This explains why in 2006 the Dalai Lama preached there, as well as the presence in the mid-20th century of the Tibetan scholar Gendun Chopel, who drew some of the surviving sculptures (3). Amaravati was also influential in the spread of Buddhism to Southeast Asia, where the name is still venerated.

The major monument at Amaravati was a stupa. It was enlarged on several occasions, with some rebuilding accommodating doctrinal change, though the fundamentals always remained the same. At the centre was a solid domed structure within which relics were deposited (these don't survive). The dome of the stupa was set on a masonry drum which was faced with carved reliefs (2). Around the drum was a walkway that enabled devotees to honour the enshrined relic by walking around it in a clockwise direction, leaving it always on the auspicious right side. On the outer side of the walkway was a railing that separated mundane space from sacred space. Both the inner and outer faces of this railing were decorated. Punctuating the railing at the four cardinal points were gates.

During its heyday, the carved decoration on the exterior of the railing was made up of lotus bosses with dancing dwarf figures playing musical instruments. Passing through one of the gates, with its guardian lions, the pilgrim entered the walkway. On the left was the inner face of the railing. Unlike the outer face, this was decorated with very lively figured scenes drawn from the life of the Buddha (1) as well as from the Jataka stories (see p. 43). These sculptures functioned as visual presentations of the narratives, for most people in antiquity could not read. Guiding pilgrims must have been one of the tasks of monks at Amaravati, though the existence of the latter there is only speculative as monastic quarters have not been located.

On the right side as the pilgrim circumambulated the stupa was the drum on which the dome was set. This was mostly decorated with narratives, such as the Birth of the Buddha, or depictions of the stupa itself; the latter are 'portraits' of the great structure and have been instrumental in enabling scholars to envisage the building's appearance (2). Above this rose the dome, finishing in a square cap, *harmika*, from which pennants and an umbrella issued. Little from this upper element has survived.

Amaravati only appears in more recent history when Colin Mackenzie of the East India Company briefly visited in 1798 (he was later Surveyor-General of India). The ruins of the Amaravati stupa were then being used by a local landowner as a source for building stone and for producing lime. Mackenzie returned in 1816 and drawings made at that time survive in the British Library. Some show a tank that had been constructed in the top of the mound; it is for this reason that little information about the upper part of the monument survives. Later investigations caused yet further collapse.

One of these later investigators, in 1845, was Sir Walter Elliot, a British administrator. The sculptures that he excavated make up most of the Amaravati collection at the British Museum. A larger group of sculptures from excavations after Elliot's time are in Chennai.

2 | 3 Greeks in India and trade with the West

Alexander campaigned in northwestern India in the mid-320s BCE. More significant in India, though, was the establishment following his death of a Greek kingdom in Bactria and then later, an Indo-Greek kingdom in the Punjab. Both states were later overthrown by invaders from Central Asia, the Kushans (p. 65).

The presence of these kingdoms in northwestern India meant that elements of Hellenistic culture entered South Asia, including coinage using the image and name of the king (2) and probably the lost-wax technique of bronze casting. Later, in Gandhara, Corinthian columns and other Hellenistic features are encountered in architecture. The Indo-Greek rulers were open to Indian religious beliefs and we know of one Indo-Greek king, Menander, who engaged with Buddhism, and a later Greek, Heliodorus, who was a devotee of Vishnu.

This contact encouraged sea-borne trade with the Roman Empire from Red Sea ports such as Berenike. Through mastery of the monsoon winds, sailors were able to reach ports on the western coast of India such as Bharuch (Barygaza of the Greek texts) and, further south, Pattanam (similarly, perhaps Muziris), and yet others on the southeastern coast such as Arikamedu (1) and Alagankulam. Middlemen in the Gulf, southern Arabia and the Horn of Africa were also parts of this trade nexus. Some commerce also went overland (3).

Items traded to India – as amphorae found at ports indicate – included wine. Gold, as today, was greatly valued in India, a fact emphasized by the complaint of the author Pliny who speaks of quantities leaving Rome in return for fine textiles. This is substantiated by Roman coin hoards found in southern India. Finally, spices were a major export as evidence found even in remote areas of the Roman Empire demonstrates (4).

This page
1. Three sherds of Italian sigillata
These apparently insignificant sherds of pottery are of great interest, having been excavated at the south Indian coastal site of Arikamedu; they were made in Roman Italy. Other excavated examples have stamp marks on the base indicating the workshop in which they were made. The appearance of these ceramics on the south Indian coast is an indicator of Indo-Roman trade in the early centuries CE.

Red-slipped Italian sigillata
1st century CE
Length 9 cm (largest sherd)
Arikamedu, Puducherry (previously Pondicherry), south India
Bequeathed by Sir Mortimer Wheeler, 1976,1103.4.g, h, i

Opposite, above left
2. Silver coin of Antialkidas (r. c. 115–95 BCE)
The Indo-Greek kings ruled in eastern Afghanistan and western Punjab. They produced a striking sequence of coins, often inscribed in Greek and also in a local script and language. This example bears a portrait of Antialkidas and was part of the collection of Charles Masson, the British explorer and archaeologist who was in the Kabul area in the 1830s.

Silver
2nd century BCE
Diameter 1.6 cm
Minted in Afghanistan
Donated by the India Office, IOC.57

Above right
3. Cameo
Small but expensive luxury items
such as this cameo of Hercules
could easily be carried by
merchants engaged in the trade
between Rome and India. It was
found at the habitation mound
of Akra, at the point where trade
routes from Afghanistan entered
the Indus river basin.

Agate
1st–2nd century CE
Height 6 cm, width 4.7 cm
Akra mound, Bannu District,
Khyber Pakhtunkhwa, Pakistan
1893,0502.1

Right
4. Silver-gilt pepperpot lid
There is much evidence for the
use of pepper in Roman Britain,
including this pepperpot lid in
the form of a reclining ibex. It is
part of the Hoxne Hoard of Late
Roman gold and silver, found
in Suffolk.

Silver, gold
3rd century CE
Height 6.2 cm, length 6.2 cm
From the Hoxne Hoard, Suffolk
Acquired with a contribution
from the Art Fund (as NACF),
National Heritage Memorial Fund
and British Museum Friends
(as British Museum Society),
1994,0408.35

1. Head of the Buddha

In the later Gandhara period sculpture was often made of clay rather than stone. It was covered with a thin layer of stucco, ideal for painted decoration. This tradition continued in Afghanistan, demonstrating the expansion of Indian culture.

Stucco
4th–5th century CE
Height 17.5 cm, width 11.1 cm
Gandhara region, Pakistan
Donated by the Trustees
of Surgeon Henry Atkins,
1962,0421.1

2. The monastery of Takht-i Bahi

Shrines were located around the courtyard in the foreground while monastic cells are visible beyond.

3. The standing Buddha

The idea of a Buddha image, standing or seated, became established in Gandhara. He is shown here as a human being, his robe worn like a Roman costume, with ridged folds. His spiritual status is indicated by the halo, the *ushnisha* or topknot of hair, and the mark between the eye-brows, *urna*; these attributes become standard. The right hand was probably held in *abhayamudra*, hand held up and the palm outwards, the gesture of fearlessness.

Schist
2nd–3rd century CE
Height 103 cm, width 32 cm,
depth 22.5 cm
Takht-i Bahi, Yusufzai, Khyber
Pakhtunkhwa, Pakistan
1899,0715.1

Gandhara

The region known in ancient times as Gandhara is today divided between Pakistan and Afghanistan and centred on Peshawar, the Swat valley and the valley of the Kabul river; the city of Taxila to the east was also considered part of this territory. The Kushans, rulers of Gandhara in the early centuries CE, were nomadic people from Central Asia. They entered the subcontinent from Afghanistan and encountered Buddhism as it spread to the northwest, away from its original home in the Ganges plains and into what is now northwestern Pakistan and eastern Afghanistan. As seen elsewhere in South Asia, Buddhism was here connected with trade, with the result that the ancient trade routes connecting India, the western world and China – the Silk Road – became the route also for Buddhism to travel from India into Central Asia, and eventually to China and beyond. The narratives of this spread are lost to us, but the archaeological evidence is unequivocal.

Buddhist architecture flourished, mostly built of local schist (2). The sculpture with which these structures were embellished is intriguing, on account of the influence it had outside the region. This is noted along the trade route through Afghanistan and then along the Silk Road into metropolitan China. Uniquely this sculpture, which was Buddhist in subject matter, was stylistically closer to the Hellenistic west than to the Indian world. So in the 2nd–4th centuries CE a sculptural programme is found that comes from India but is in a style that can almost be characterized as provincial Roman. The use of Roman drapery forms, the appearance of classical characters but with new identities (Hercules becomes Vajrapani, the companion of the Buddha, for example) or classical narratives recast with Buddhist identities all point to the Roman world, as does the frequent use of Hellenistic architectural elements. It seems to have been in Gandhara – and also in Mathura, the Kushan capital in the plains – that the figure of the Buddha was first conceived in corporeal form. This event was to have a profound influence not only in South Asia, but also in Central Asia, China and then Korea and Japan. The surviving sculptural and architectural evidence reflects doctrinal changes as Buddhist teachings developed, changes that were recorded in texts which have almost completely disappeared. An exception is a cache of manuscripts now in the British Library that probably came originally from eastern Afghanistan. They are of birchbark and are dated to the early 1st century CE, probably just before the arrival of the Kushans. They are today thought to be the very earliest surviving Buddhist manuscripts.

This is the cultural background to Gandhara, but what were the religious sites where these important changes were taking place? These were primarily monastic and centred on stupas and their veneration. There needed to be domestic quarters for monks, courts in which the stupas were sited and where devotees could circumambulate the shrine, and chapels where the new cult of the bodhisattvas (see p. 68) could be accommodated. While the monastic living quarters seem not to have been decorated, the stupas and their approaches, and the chapels, provided opportunities for sculpture, in stone (3), and later also in stucco (1). Frequently, relics were housed within the stupas. Bronze items from Gandhara include the earliest figures of the Buddha made using the lost-wax process (see p. 112).

Later, Chinese pilgrims, eager to visit the land of the Buddha, entered South Asia via Central Asia and Afghanistan. The most famous, Xuanzang, describes Gandhara in the 7th century, its monasteries now abandoned, but with stories still vivid about the Buddhist past, providing a further view of this once vibrant centre of Buddhist activity.

2 | 4 Reliquaries

The presence of a reliquary within a stupa sanctified the structure, making it worthy of veneration. Most contained the relics of teachers, renowned monks, or – later – text and images. The earliest are from the region of Sanchi (p. 56) and include some examples made of precious materials such as hardstone or crystal (4). Some bear Prakrit language inscriptions in Brahmi script, mentioning the names of teachers.

Later, in Gandhara (p. 65) to the northwest, a large number of reliquaries have been found. Many contained coins and beads and are made in the form of small stupas, some in bronze or ground stone (2) and some in gold (3). Such items were easily carried to Central Asia as Buddhism spread from the subcontinent, influencing the way reliquaries were made there.

One of the most renowned of the Gandhara reliquaries is the casket from Stupa 2 at Bimaran, near Jalalabad in eastern Afghanistan (1). It is made of sheet gold set with garnets and turquoise and was found by Charles Masson, who investigated many stupa sites in the 1830s. Inside were small gold items, turquoise inlays, beads and coins. The reliquary was itself placed in a steatite container, inscribed in Kharoshthi, the script used in ancient Gandhara. The gold walls are decorated with repoussé figures in an arcade. Each arch contains a standing male figure; there are eight in total. Two figures are of the standing Buddha, and based on the date of the coins in the casket (between the 1st and mid-2nd centuries CE), this depiction is among the earliest showing the Buddha in corporeal rather than symbolic form. The date range for the reliquary is between the 1st century to mid-2nd century CE. The other figures are probably the gods Indra and Brahma and a *bodhisattva* (p. 68); all are depicted twice. On the base is a lotus.

This page
1. The Bimaran Reliquary
The standing Buddha (centre) is one of the very earliest recorded. The haloed figure has a topknot or *ushnisha* and wears Hellenistic-type drapery. The right hand is shown in the fearlessness gesture, *abhayamudra*. The figure of Brahma (to the left as viewed) is identified by the water pot in his left hand. Indra with his royal turban stands on the right, saluting the Buddha figure.

Gold, garnets and turquoise
1st century CE
Height 6.7 cm, diameter at base 6.6 cm
From Stupa 2 at Bimaran, near Jalalabad, eastern Afghanistan
1900,0209.1

Opposite, above left
2. Steatite reliquary in the form of a stupa
This reliquary held a small crystal container and coins (illustrated). The coins are of two rulers of the 1st century CE, thus providing a date after which the deposit was made.

Steatite, crystal, bronze
1st century CE
Height 21.9 cm, diameter 11.8 cm (reliquary)
From Sonala Pind, Manikyala, Punjab, Pakistan
Donated by Maj-Gen Sir Alexander Cunningham,
1887,0717.34 (reliquary),
1887,0717.35 (crystal reliquary),
1887,0717.36, 37, 38 and 39 (coins)

3. Gold reliquary in the form of a stupa
This relic container finely illustrates all the elements of the stupa structure: drum, dome with three-tiered *harmika*, and three protective parasols.

Gold
1st century CE
Height 5 cm, width 3.8 cm
Probably from the region between Jalalabad and Kabul, Afghanistan
Brooke Sewell Permanent Fund,

with contributions from the British Museum Friends and Dr Achinto Sen-Gupta, 2004,0331.1

4. Three reliquaries
The skills needed to produce these vessels, found in stupas near Sanchi, suggest the preciousness of the relics within; two are inscribed.

Steatite
2nd century BCE
Raisen District, Madhya Pradesh

Donated by Maj-Gen.
Sir Alexander Cunningham
(l–r):
From Stupa 2, Andher
Height 14.6 cm, diameter 15.5 cm
1887,0717.18
From Stupa 9, Bhojpur
Height 14 cm
1887,0717.15.a
From Stupa 8, Satdhara
Height 14 cm, width 13.1 cm
1887,0717.9.a

2 | 5 *Bodhisattva*

The doctrines of Buddhism, like those of most religions, changed over time and this is reflected in Buddhist sculpture. One of the most important of these changes is the development and increasing prominence of figures known as *bodhisattva* (meaning an individual with the essence of Buddha-hood). The cults dedicated to these figures first appear in the early centuries CE and are probably to be seen as a move away from a solely monastic system and towards a religion that was important also to the laity, who desired some form of contact with the divine.

The idea behind the *bodhisattva* is, simply speaking, a development of the Buddha's own teaching about reincarnation and the potentiality of all humans to become enlightened. Thus, as one slowly moved up the ladder of existence, over many rebirths, *nirvana* was finally approached. It was argued that those about to reach this state, being filled with good *karma* (almost nothing negative any longer being attached to them), were willing – due to their immense compassion – to forego *nirvana* and instead aid suffering mankind. These are the *bodhisattvas*. They could thus become the focus for intercession and, while less than the Buddha, could be approached for aid on the road to final liberation; they were still of the world, while the Buddha had gone beyond into *nirvana* – and thus was unapproachable. From these ideas the doctrines of the later schools of Buddhism, broadly described under the inclusive term of the Mahayana, developed.

The earliest depictions of *bodhisattvas* are found in the sculpture of Gandhara, where we begin to see groupings around the Buddha: Vajrapani ('the bearer of the thunderbolt') is one of these (**1**), as also is Padmapani ('the bearer of the lotus') (**2**) who later becomes Avalokiteshvara (**3**). One of the inevitable corollaries of these arguments is that there is a Buddha- to-be, currently a *bodhisattva*. He is Maitreya (**4**).

1. Vajrapani
Although apparently depicting Hercules – he wears the skin of the Nemean Lion – this is Vajrapani, 'the bearer of the thunderbolt', the faceted object in his right hand. The depiction of the Buddha flanked by a *bodhisattva* on either side – as was surely once the case here – was an idea that seems to have originated in Gandhara.

Schist
2nd/3rd century CE
Height 54 cm, width 24.1 cm
Gandhara, present-day Pakistan
1970,0718.1

2. Padmapani
Padmapani, 'the bearer of the lotus', is one of the earliest *bodhisattvas* and is often shown wearing a turban and fine jewelry. The small kneeling monks at the base are appropriate for the intercessionary nature of the cult.

Schist
2nd–3rd century CE
Height 54 cm, width 31.4 cm
Takht-i Bahi, Yusufzai, Khyber Pakhtunkhwa, Pakistan
1950,0726.1

3. Avalokiteshvara
The cult of this *bodhisattva* apparently developed from that of Padmapani. Both are seated on lotus bases, carry lotus blossoms and are decked with royal jewelry.

Bronze, inscribed with the donor's name, Singhunaduka
8th or 9th century
Height 9.5 cm, width 6.5 cm
Cast in eastern India; found in Sri Lanka
1898,0702.134

4. Maitreya
The *bodhisattva* who will be the next Buddha is Maitreya. Depicted as a prince, he carries a water pot and holds his right hand in *abhayamudra*, the gesture of fearlessness. His cult is first recorded in sculpture in Gandhara.

Schist
2nd–3rd century
From the Buner-Yusufzai border, Khyber Pakhtunkhwa, Pakistan
Height 91.5 cm, width 40.6 cm
Donated by Sir Harold Arthur Deane, 1889,0703.6

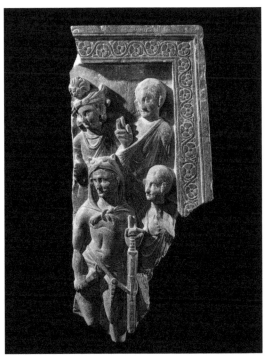

1. King Harishchandra
The king is shown bathing
in the Ganges with his family.
Vishvamitra (left) tempts the hero,
reminding him of his outstanding
debt, which will eventually result
in the sale of his wife and son.

'Paithan' painting
Late 19th/early 20th century
Andhra Pradesh/Karnataka
Height 33 cm, width 44.5 cm
Donated by Professor Dr Anna
Dallapiccola, 2007,3014.36

**2. The death of Bhishma
on a bed of arrows**
The hero Bhishma fought
with the Kauravas against
the Pandava brothers. Fatally
wounded, he delayed his death
until Krishna (blue-skinned) and
the Pandavas could be present
to hear his final discourses.

By the painter Ramdas
Dated 1598
Height 24.4 cm, width 14.4 cm
(whole painting)
Mughal north India
1930,0716,0.1

The Mahabharata

The great epic of the Mahabharata, at some 110,000 couplets, is even longer than the other great Indian epic the Ramayana (see p. 87). Its sweep is immense, encapsulating topics as diverse as mythology, romantic dramas, genealogy, ethics, the dangers of gambling, the nature of the gods and, indeed, the nature of the universe. Like the Ramayana, the Mahabharata was probably originally a series of separate, orally transmitted narratives assembled over many centuries. It probably began to coalesce into a single unit in the 4th century BCE, reaching completion a millennium later. It is filled with digressions and elaborations, some of which are complete narratives in their own right. Some appear in regional variants, with particular differences found in southern versions. The Mahabharata has come down to us in Sanskrit verse and is divided into eighteen individual books, or parva.

Unlike the story of Rama, which primarily deals with the triumph of good over evil (there is some uncertainty at the end, but the basic tenet of the work is positive), the Mahabharata is darker, the end coming only when almost all the participants lie dead on the battlefield. The hopelessness of the human condition is highlighted. There is much less of the theistic element which – in its final version – is so obvious in the Ramayana. Few, if any, of the heroes of the Mahabharata are the recipients of a cult, unlike in the Ramayana.

Much of the action of the Mahabharata develops from an initial encounter between the five Pandava brothers along with their common wife Draupadi, and their cousins the Kauravas. The throw of the dice (see p. 30) proves irresistible to Yudhishthira, the eldest of the Pandava brothers. Gambling against the Kauravas, he loses all his possessions, even eventually his wife Draupadi (wife also to all his brothers). Quick-witted Draupadi's call upon the gods is all that saves her from rape. The Pandava brothers and Draupadi are then forced into a long period of exile, culminating in a final attempt to regain their rightful throne. This results in the climactic battle in which many of the heroes on both sides die.

Despite its less optimistic view of life, the Mahabharata does contain many famous individual narrative texts dealing with rectitude, such as the story of king Harishchandra, who is tested by the gods, and prevails (1). Undoubtedly the most famous separate text within the Mahabharata is the *Bhagavad Gita*. This also deals with ethics and takes place as the battle of Kurukshetra is about to begin. It is cast as an exchange between the hero Arjuna and his charioteer, who is Krishna in disguise. They speak about human duty, *dharma*. What is the correct behaviour, for instance, when Arjuna is preparing himself to kill his adversaries who are also his relatives? Krishna emphasizes the need for each person to practise devotion and to follow his own *dharma*, that is, that which has been laid out for them by society and their family position. It is a statement of traditional values and has been influential up to the present day – for instance, Mahatma Gandhi spoke of its importance to him.

The Mahabharata was one of the texts that, in the 16th century, the Mughal emperor Akbar (r. 1556–1605) had abridged and translated into Persian, the language of his court, as the *Razmnama* (the 'Book of Wars'). This exercise was part of the emperor's policy to provide – both for himself and his court – a better way of understanding the majority of the population over whom he reigned and for whom the Mahabharata was a defining text. The original translation was beautifully illustrated in the atelier of the emperor Akbar, while in the royal centres of various Mughal courtiers a sub-Imperial style flourished, including *Razmnama* paintings in their repertoire (2).

2 | 6 Textiles: early exports

Archaeological excavations record that cotton was woven at Mehrgarh in Balochistan and then later, in the cities of the Indus Civilization. The early cultivation of cotton, and knowledge of how to dye and decorate it, was hugely important in the development of South Asian culture. We don't know when dyed and block-printed cottons were first exported from India, but plain cotton used for sail-cloth is recorded from excavations at the Red Sea ports of Myos Hormos and Berenike, in Early Roman levels. Here, extremely dry conditions have preserved them. Fragments of resist-dyed cotton have also come from the Late Roman horizons at Berenike, these perhaps the earliest surviving examples of this technique. Later examples have been found at Fustat (Old Cairo) in Egypt; the earliest of these are dated to the 8th century and confidently use block-printing and a variety of dyeing techniques. Later examples have been found in Nubia (**1**). These textiles were probably produced in Gujarat, in western India. Meanwhile, from the site of Niya in Central Asia, and again in conditions of extreme dryness, textile fragments of woven wool – perhaps a rug or a shawl – have been recovered (**2**). These fragments, and those from Berenike, are the oldest surviving Indian textiles that we know of today.

From the medieval period, but still before direct European interest in textiles from the subcontinent, we know of exports to Southeast Asia. The best-known examples come from Indonesia, where large quantities were traded and have survived. One of the main centres of production was again Gujarat and a type clearly popular in northern Sulawesi in the 15th and 16th centuries was of cotton decorated with a procession of women, each playing a *vina* (a musical instrument) and with a parrot on their upraised fingers (**3**).

Below left
1. Cotton fragment from Qasr Ibrim
This fragment – perhaps part of a curtain – is of cotton, dyed with iron and an unidentified red colouring material. When it was traded in the medieval period, Indian cloth had already been exported to Egypt for a thousand years.

Cotton
13th–14th century
Length 65 cm, width 46 cm
Woven and dyed in Gujarat; found at the excavations at Qasr Ibrim in Lower Nubia, Egypt
Donated by the Egypt Exploration Society,
1990,0127.457

Opposite, below right

2. Textile fragment from Niya

This fragment of woven wool,
perhaps from a shawl or rug,
is amongst the earliest surviving
examples of Indian cloth. The
weave and the design remind
us that in the early centuries CE
Indian culture was dominant in
the southern oasis settlements
of the Taklamakan desert.

Wool
1st–3rd century CE
Northern India, perhaps Kashmir;
found in Niya, Xinjiang, western
China
Length 48.5 cm, width 34 cm
1907,1111.105

Right

**3. Export textile for the
Indonesian market**

Twelve walking women, two of
whom are shown here, decorate
this cloth. Each one plucks a *vina*
that rests on her shoulder, while
in their right hands they hold a
parrot, the symbol of the god
of love. The colour scheme
alternates between red and
blue. The dating of this and
related textiles is based on
comparisons with western Indian
painting, especially the use of
'the projecting eye' (see p. 136,
Figure 1).

Cotton cloth decorated using
block-printing, resist- and
mordant-dyeing, and painting
16th century
Total length of cloth 502 cm,
width 96 cm
Gujarat; found in Mondongo,
northern Sulawesi, Indonesia
Donated by F. A. Killik,
As1944,08.4

2 | 7 Early Jain sculpture at Mathura

Jainism has proved popular throughout South Asia over a long period. Unlike Buddhism (the Buddha and Mahavira were near contemporaries; see pp. 18, 46–7), it has remained active in India, the country of its birth. But also unlike Buddhism, it has only spread more widely in recent times, on account of the late 19th- and early 20th-century Gujarati diaspora to East Africa and subsequently to Europe and the USA.

In the Kushan period (early centuries CE – see p. 65) stupas were constructed by Jain devotees at Mathura (stupas were a feature of Jain activity in this period). Like Buddhist examples, Jain stupas at Mathura were separated from mundane space by a railing made of uprights and beams. Some of these upright pillars were sculpted with *yakshi*, female figures whose position at the base of the structure was considered auspicious and supportive (**2**). Another feature of these Jain shrines in Mathura were the *ayagapata* reliefs. The exact function of these rectangular panels with their sequence of positive and celebratory images is unclear, but they were perhaps surfaces on which offerings were placed (**1**). The majority of the early sculptures of Jain teachers, *tirthankara* (see pp. 46–7), come from Mathura. Already by this date the iconography of such figures is becoming established (**3**). At Mathura, *tirthankara* were also depicted with haloes, sometimes highly decorated, though this feature is frequently replaced with honorific parasols in later images.

Jainism doesn't survive today in Mathura, but it does elsewhere in India, with concentrations in western and southern India (see pp. 136–9).

1. *Ayagapata* **relief fragment**
A Jain *tirthankara* seated beneath a parasol, a pot-bellied figure with a garland (outer register) and a vase of plenty, *purnaghata* (inner), are all appropriately auspicious images.

Flecked red sandstone
2nd century CE
Height 38.5 cm, width 39.8 cm
Kankali Tila, Mathura, Uttar Pradesh
Donated by the Secretary of State for India, 1901,1224.10

Left
**2. Jain *yakshi* from
a stupa railing**
As at Buddhist sites, protective
railings at Jain stupas were
decorated with auspicious and
supportive figures. The idea that
the depiction of a voluptuous
young woman is appropriate at a
sacred structure continues here,
several centuries after it is first
recorded at Sanchi (see p. 57).

Flecked red sandstone
2nd century CE
Height 59.5 cm
Mathura, Uttar Pradesh
Brooke Sewell Permanent Fund,
1975,1027.1

Above
3. Sculpture of a *tirthankara*
The established iconography
of the twenty-four Jain teachers
included broad shoulders, snail-
shell curls, elongated earlobes,
and an auspicious symbol on the
chest, the *shrivatsa*. Here, the
figure is also depicted with a halo
decorated with lotus petals and
a scalloped outer edge.

Red sandstone
3rd century CE
Height 34 cm
Mathura, Uttar Pradesh
Donated by the Secretary of State
for India, 1901,1224.5

2 | 8 The first temple structures

For almost two millennia South Asia has been a region where the divine has been imagined in a structure – at least as far as settled, urban society is concerned. Temple-building is so innately part of the Indian experience that, wherever South Asians are settled, this is one of the distinctive indicators of their presence. However, it was not always thus, and the South Asians of the Vedic period had no use of buildings in which to worship. Temple-building is intimately connected with worship of the divine through the medium of an image housed in a building; there are no images from the Vedic period. Worship in India has in historic times been carried out through the performance of *puja*, an act of devotion but also in essence contractual as gifts are offered in exchange for protection returned. Therefore, once the divine was imaged and an intercessor (usually a brahmin) was needed to mediate the prayers of the faithful, temples became a necessity.

Rock-cut shrines are known in the Western Ghats from the late centuries BCE and onwards for a thousand years (see p. 80). The earliest of these were clearly based on wooden structures, as indicated by the beam construction seen replicated in the rock-cut architecture, but none of these wooden structures survives today (see p. 53). Shrine-like buildings are known from Mathura in the early centuries CE, and from at least the 4th century at Nagarjunakonda in southern India, but we only know of these from the archaeological record. The earliest surviving temples come from Gupta-period northern India. At sites such as Bhitargaon, brick temples with external decoration in the form of terracotta plaques still survive; examples may be figural (**2, 3**), floral or geometric. Central India in the 6th century is witness to the earliest surviving temples in stone. Examples include the Dashavatara temple at Deogarh with its reliefs from the mythology of Vishnu. These temples frequently have exquisitely decorated doorjambs (**1**).

1. Fragment of a doorjamb
The gambolling and auspicious dwarves with luxuriant ringlets sculpted on the left side, along with the dense and swirling tendrils of scrollwork on the right, are typical of early Hindu temple decoration, especially at the doorways where devotees moved from mundane to sacred space. The concern not to leave any blank space evident in this fragment is a feature that continues throughout the medieval period.

Sandstone
c. 550 CE
Central India
Height 62.5 cm
Donated by Douglas Barrett in memory of Madhuri Desai, 1976,0621.1

2. Terracotta plaque and architectural element

Perhaps intended as an auspicious dwarf, the youthful character on the left-hand plaque holds a hand-bell, perhaps for accompanying *bhajan* (devotional songs). As Shiva is often attended by mischievous dwarfs, *gana*, this relief sculpture from Ahichchatra may have once adorned a Shiva shrine at the site. The figural decoration on the shrines at Ahichchatra were framed by architectural elements such as that shown on the right. The central element is probably the capital to a pilaster while cusped arch arcades are suggested on either side.

Terracotta
5th century CE
Height 15.4 cm, width 16.5 cm
(left); height 17.5 cm, width
19.2 cm (right)
Ahichchatra, Bareilly District,
Uttar Pradesh
1901,1224.30, 1901,1224.14

3. Terracotta plaque

This plaque depicts a hunter carrying his prey. Although damaged, the flowing ringlets – distinctive of Gupta-period sculpture – can be made out. The confident modelling of the clay reminds us of the long history of the use of this material in South Asia.

Terracotta
5th century
Height 48.3 cm, width 30.5 cm
Probably from the southern
part of the Ganges valley
1976,0205.1

2 | 9 Sarnath and Buddhism in the Gupta period

Buddhism continued to flourish in the Gupta period (4th–5th centuries CE) (1). However, the religious emphasis of the royal house shifted from Buddhism towards the deities of early Hinduism – Varaha and other forms of Vishnu.

Nevertheless, Sarnath, near Varanasi, remained an important Buddhist centre. It was here in the Deer Park that – according to tradition – the Buddha delivered his First Sermon – to use the Buddhist terminology, he 'set in motion the Wheel of the Law' (2). We do not know when Sarnath became a major pilgrimage centre, but it was already renowned by the time of Ashoka (see pp. 48–9) as he set up an inscribed pillar there. The site has remained important to Buddhist pilgrims to this day.

In addition to its role in pilgrimage is the important position Sarnath developed as the centre for imagining anew how the Buddha figure was to be presented. Early sculpture depicted him either as a superhuman hero (Mathura) or as an individual human being (Gandhara). The new Sarnath imagery, however, saw him as a figure in touch with the divine – perhaps even being divine. He is shown not engaged with the world but withdrawn from it, deep in meditation. The eyes are downcast or closed and the body, whether standing (3) or, more usually, seated, is enveloped in a robe; the musculature and skeletal structure of the body are no longer apparent. The Buddha is becoming less human, and more divine (1). This vision of the Buddha was to spread and profoundly change how he was depicted throughout the rest of South Asia and, indeed, eventually across all of Asia.

1. The teaching Buddha
Few metal representations of the Buddha survive from this period, but this powerful example shows him with his hands held in the *dharmachakramudra*, the gesture indicating teaching. His heavy-lidded eyes look downwards in concentration and this suggestion of withdrawal, from this time onwards, becomes increasingly influential. There is a dedicatory inscription on the plinth.

Gilded bronze
Gupta period, 5th–early 6th century
From a hoard at Danesar Khera, Banda District, Uttar Pradesh
Height 35 cm, width 22 cm
Brooke Sewell Bequest, 1969,0725.1

2. The seated Buddha

The haloed Buddha is here
shown not only enthroned but
also, unusually, with his feet firmly
placed on the ground; his hands
are held in the teaching position,
dharmachakramudra. The throne,
with distinctive flanking mythical
animals, is the prototype for
many future Buddha images,
in stone and in bronze.

Sandstone
5th century
Eastern India, in Sarnath style
Height 118 cm
1880.7

3. The standing Buddha

Withdrawn and heroically serene,
the haloed Buddha displays
with his right hand the gesture
of fearlessness, *abhayamudra*.
The nearly transparent and
clinging garment, articulating
but not hiding the body beneath,
becomes the standard in future
depictions. The beauty of the
Sarnath style, especially in
the depiction of the face, has
long meant that it has been
considered the epitome of
Indian sculpture.

Sandstone
5th century
Height 144 cm
Eastern India, in Sarnath style
1880.6.a-b

2 | 10 Rock-cut architecture

The tradition of Buddhist architecture cut from the living rock begins in the Western Ghats – the mountainous country inland from Mumbai. The earliest of these shrines is dated to the late centuries BCE. Broadly speaking, the rock-cut monuments can be divided into either shrines of columned halls leading to stupas or domestic quarters for monks during the monsoon retreat. The tradition of rock-cut shrines is one that travels out of India along with Buddhism and is brilliantly reworked in Afghanistan, at Bamiyan (2), and then in China, for example, at Dunhuang.

The finest sequence of Buddhist rock-cut architecture in India was excavated at Ajanta, in present-day Madhya Pradesh. Here in the cliff-face above the Waghur river, shrines and monks' accommodation were cut in two phases, during the 2nd century BCE and then later in the 5th century CE. Equally important at Ajanta, however, are the mural paintings, substantial fragments of which still survive. These are the earliest of any paintings in South Asia that have come down to us and date from both periods of activity at the site. The subject matter includes Jataka stories, the life of the Buddha and various of the *bodhisattvas* (see p. 68). Varied Buddhist traditions – for example, the presence or absence of *bodhisattvas* or of multiple Buddha images – are evident at the site (3).

It is not known when the Ajanta shrines fell out of use, but they were unknown and overgrown in 1819 when they were rediscovered. Since then there have been a number of attempts to record the paintings, both in painted copies and also in photographs. The paintings at Bagh, a rock-cut shrine northeast of Ajanta were copied in the 1920s by the Bengali artist Mukul Chandra Dey (1895–1989) (see also p. 288) (1).

1. An elephant procession: a copy of a mural at Bagh
The Bagh cave complex in Madhya Pradesh is much smaller than that at Ajanta. The copying of the murals in the 20th century at both sites, as in this example by Mukul Chandra Dey, was influential in establishing the presence of an indigenous Indian painting style.

Watercolour on paper
1920s
Height 147.8 cm, width 315.8 cm
Copy of murals at Bagh caves, Dhar District, Madhya Pradesh
1926,0411,0.44.a

2. Rock-cut image of the standing Buddha

At Bamiyan in central Afghanistan, in the mid-1st millennium CE, two massive figures of the standing Buddha were cut into the cliff-face – one is shown here. The Chinese pilgrim, Xuanzang, mentioned them in 630 CE. Mural paintings drawing on Indian painting styles, decorated the soffit of the vault in which the Buddha figure stood. Both figures were destroyed by the Taliban in 2001.

Sandstone sculpture with details in clay
Complete by 630 CE
Height 53 m
Bamiyan valley, Hazarajat, Afghanistan

3. Wall-painting of the *bodhisattva* Padmapani from Cave 1 at Ajanta

The still very striking paintings at Ajanta are indicators of the highly developed aesthetic of the 5th century; little anywhere else in the subcontinent compares with them. They are also rich in information about that remote time, providing us with knowledge of architecture, textiles, and many features of everyday life, including religious practice. Padmapani ('the holder of the lotus'), an early form of the *bodhisattva* Avalokiteshvara, is a key personality in the Mahayana; his presence here, crowned and serene, is a sure statement of the religious affiliation of the monks who used this rock-cut shrine.

Painting
Late 5th century CE
Ajanta, Madhya Pradesh

2 | 11 Buddhism in Kashmir

Situated to the northeast of Gandhara, fertile Kashmir and its surrounding valleys inherited many cultural traits from its neighbour. Buddhism was important for at least a thousand years and, if the tradition that claims Ashoka (see p. 48) was responsible for the evangelization of the region can be relied on, its history is even longer. Also, it is believed that the most important of the Kushan rulers, Kanishka, convened the Fourth Buddhist Council here. There is no doubt, though, that in the second half of the 1st millennium CE Kashmir was a renowned centre of Buddhist learning, especially in the study of the later schools, Mahayana and Vajrayana (the way of the thunderbolt, *vajra*, concerned with methods of realization of spiritual power through intense mental practice, often guided by a master). The commissioning and endowment of stupas and temples is recorded, not least by Chinese pilgrim visitors, such as Xuanzang in 631–33 CE. Today, no structures survive, the nearest indication being the remains of a stupa excavated at Harwan.

Buddhist sculpture in terracotta (**1**) and stone is known from at least the 7th century and bronze sculpture from only slightly later. Later still, metal sculpture, influenced by both Gupta (see p. 54, Figure 3) and post-Gupta styles in northern India, was of increasing sophistication (**4**). Wood (often painted) and ivory are also distinctive of this period (**3**).

Meanwhile, the spread of Buddhism eastwards from Kashmir into western Tibet, which took place in several phases in the latter part of the 1st millennium CE, meant that easily portable bronze images from Kashmir found a welcome in western Tibet, remaining there until the 1960s. Areas to the east of Kashmir, such as Ladakh and Lahul, also produced bronze images in the medieval period which were later influential in Tibet (**2**).

Below left
1. Female head
Terracotta as a medium for sculpture continues the late Gandhara tradition (see pp. 64–5), though stylistically production in Kashmir owes much to the Gupta style where a beautiful and idealized personality is projected through the sculpture.

Terracotta
Probably 6th century
Height 15 cm, width 14.5 cm
Akhnur, Jammu District, Jammu and Kashmir
Donated by P. T. Brooke Sewell, 1953,0512.1

Opposite, below right
**2. Inlaid sculpture
of Vajrasattva**
The Buddhist diety Vajrasattva,
'He whose essence is
adamantine', is identified by the
thunderbolt, *vajra*, that he holds
vertically in his right hand. The
vajra symbolism is taken up in
the halo with its chased imagery,
a regional feature within
Kashmiri Buddhism, typical
of Lahul or Spiti in Himachal
Pradesh, an important zone
in the spread of Buddhism
to Tibet.

Bronze, inlaid
with copper and silver
Mid-11th century
Height 10.5 cm
Lahul or Spiti, western Himalayas
Brooke Sewell Permanent Fund,
2015,3010.1

Above right
3. Portable shrine
This fragment from a portable
shrine was designed as a
miniature temple – note the
gabled and arched elements
typical of medieval temples in
Kashmir. In the ivory centrepiece,
a crowned *bodhisattva* is seated
surrounded by celestial figures,
while the now-empty niches
probably once held attendant
figures, also of ivory.

Ivory, painted wood
8th century
Height 14.5 cm
Kashmir
Brooke Sewell Permanent Fund,
1968,0521.1

Right
**4. Inlaid sculpture of the
bodhisattva Avalokiteshvara**
The inlay of coloured metals
into bronze forms, cast using
the lost-wax process, was a
technique practised in Kashmir;
from here it later spread to Tibet.
The cult of Padmapani (see
p. 68) developed into that of
Avalokiteshvara in later Indian
Buddhism and then spread
throughout Asia.

Bronze, inlaid with brass,
silver and copper, and gilded
c. 1000 CE
Height 24 cm
Kashmir
Brooke Sewell Permanent Fund,
1969,1103.1

2 | 12 Hindu deities in Kashmir

The religion known today as Hinduism became more established from the Gupta period onwards. Devotion to deities such as Shiva and Vishnu (both male) and a goddess who is given distinguishing names according to her remit, became common. Temple worship of images was an important element. Early sculpture of Hindu deities in Kashmir indicates a debt to the sculpture of Gandhara, with imagery of both Karttikeya and Lakshmi revealing the influence of the cosmopolitan Gandhara style (**2**). Later, however, the stylistic links lessen, and the distinctive features of a Kashmiri style in stone and bronze sculpture, both Buddhist (p. 82) and Hindu, become established.

Devotion to Shiva was significant throughout the medieval period and later. Even today, pilgrims make their way to the Amarnath cave-shrine near Pahalgam, where Shiva is venerated in the form of an ice *linga*. In the late 1st millennium CE, distinctive forms of Shiva both in bodily, sometimes three-headed, forms (**3**, **4**) and as a *linga* (**5**) were popular Kashmir (the *linga* is the standing phallic pillar form of Shiva, see p. 96). Ganesha was also popular and his cult continued in the northwest long after the arrival of Islam. The *Vishnudarmottara-purana*, a text of iconographic descriptions from the mid-1st millennium CE, is useful in understanding this body of sculpture associated with Shiva (adj. Shaiva) and Vishnu (Vaishnava). A typical feature of Vishnu images from Kashmir is the way the god is shown with his attributes of a staff and a wheel at his side (**1**). Other depictions of Vishnu were also popular: four-headed Vaikuntha, and also the boar-headed incarnation, Varaha.

Left
1. Vishnu
The god's weapons are personified as small figures at his feet – Gadadevi (the club) on his right and Chakrapurusha (the disc) on his left. Garuda, the hawk mount of Vishnu, appears between the god's feet, looking up in adoration.

Copper alloy, silver
9th–10th century
Kashmir
Height 23.7 cm, width 13.5 cm
Brooke Sewell Permanent Fund, 1966,0616.1

Opposite, above left
2. Lakshmi
In this image of Lakshmi, goddess of abundance, the Gandhara past is evident in the folds of the drapery and the cornucopia she holds. She is cooled by water poured from above, coins are thrown at her feet and she holds a lotus in her right hand.

Chlorite
Second half of the 6th century
Height 36.5 cm
Kashmir
Donated by the Simon Digby Memorial Charity, 2016,3059.1

Opposite, above right
3. Shiva and Parvati
The gods with their offspring – elephant-headed Ganesha (at the right of Shiva's feet) and Karttikeya (between the two figures). Behind is Nandi, bull mount of Shiva (see p. 93), the latter shown in a distinctive Kashmiri three-headed form.

Green chlorite
c. 800 CE
Height 27 cm, width 19.5 cm
Kashmir
Brooke Sewell Permanent Fund and the Simon Digby Memorial Charity, 2017,3050.1

Opposite, below left
4. Shiva
The crown of three-headed Shiva is made up of Iranian-style crescent elements, while that of fearsome Bhairava (left) is formed of skulls and severed arms. Shiva's consort Parvati is also depicted (right).

Green chlorite
Kashmir
9th century
Height 41 cm
1988,0312.1

Opposite, below right
5. Shiva-*linga*
Shiva was venerated both in bodily form and as a standing pillar or *linga* (see p. 96). The face of the deity appears in the shaft of this example. Such images were made for domestic use.

Chlorite
7th–8th century
Height 8.9 cm
Kashmir
Donated by Maj-Gen W. Scott Cole, 1959,1013.1

1. Rama and Sita leave the palace

Rama departs from the palace of his father Dasharatha (visible with one of his wives on the left). Rama (identified by his lotus-crown and blue skin) is accompanied by Sita and his faithful brother Lakshmana.

Gouache on paper
c. 1700–10
Height 21.6 cm, width 31,2 cm
Kulu, Himachal Pradesh
Brooke Sewell Permanent Fund, 1966,0212,0.2

2. Rama, Sita and Lakshmana in the forest

The three exiles are shown wearing garments made of leaves. The blue border punctuated with small flowers is typical of later paintings from the Kangra region in Himachal Pradesh.

Gouache on paper
c. 1820
Kangra, Himachal Pradesh
Height 30.4 cm, width 25.9 cm
1925,0406,0.4

The Ramayana

Along with the Mahabharata (see p. 71), the story of Rama, the Ramayana, has been the most influential – and loved – epic of South Asian history. Rama is today considered an *avatara* or form (see p. 99) of Vishnu, and the epitome of kingship. The sage Valmiki is believed to be the author of the epic, though probably only a very small part goes back to any specific individual. The text probably existed first in orally transmitted form before it was committed to writing. The earliest part may date to the middle of the 1st millennium BCE where the heroic element of the story is more pronounced; later Rama's *avatara* nature becomes established and incorporated into the text (he is thenceforth considered the seventh incarnation of Vishnu). The epic seems to have been substantially complete by the 5th century CE.

With some exceptions, such as the Ramachandra temple at Vijayanagara, temples dedicated to Rama the hero are rare. However, he has been celebrated in painting (1–3), dance and literature. Perhaps the version of the Ramayana written in the vernacular by Tulsi Das in the 16th century has been the most influential. Tulsi Das wrote his verse form of the story in Benares in the local speech (Awadhi, a form of Hindi), rather than in Sanskrit, thus enabling easy access for all. Southern versions are also known, especially renowned being that in Tamil by Kamban from the 12th century or earlier. In this version as in others from southern India, the moral emphasis is somewhat different, especially as regards the nature of Ravana, who is not unequivocally evil.

The narrative is filled with many diversions, but broadly speaking the story can be summed up as follows. Rama is one of four brothers all fathered by king Dasharatha, with different mothers. One of the mothers, Kaikeyi, secures a boon from elderly Dasharatha and forces him to anoint her son Bharata as the next ruler, rather than rightful Rama.

Rama, his new young wife Sita and Rama's loyal brother Lakshmana are forced into exile in the forest (1, 2). They live far from palace life for many years and during this period develop their heroic characters, slaying demons and protecting hermits and wise men. Sita is presented as the ideal wife, though actually she turns out to have a fascinating story of independence, the outlines of which have still not yet been completely erased by patriarchy. One of the demons they encounter, Shurpanakha, is the sister of the king of Lanka, ten-headed Ravana (3). After altercations with both Rama and Lakshmana, she returns to Lanka and encourages her brother to act against Rama.

Ravana tricks both Rama and Lakshmana to leave Sita alone in the forest. Again, through deceit, Ravana snatches Sita and carries her away to Lanka. There she is incarcerated, though she refuses Ravana's advances. The rest of the epic is taken up with the rescue by Rama and his brother of Sita and their eventual return in triumph to his rightful throne.

Rama is aided by one of the story's most loveable and entertaining characters, his loyal monkey lieutenant Hanuman (4). This simian accomplice finds the imprisoned Sita, builds a bridge to Lanka (see p. 89), and flies through the air setting the city alight using his long tail as a torch. It is not for nothing that Hanuman is the patron saint of wrestlers.

Ideal for orally transmitted declamation, with episodes elaborated or excluded at will, the Ramayana has provided many opportunities for artists for at least 1,500 years. Not surprisingly, Rama also features in Buddhist lore, where one of the Jataka stories is based on his tale, and his story is well known throughout Southeast Asia, memorably in the shadow play of Indonesia, Malaysia and Thailand.

3. Rama meets Ravana in battle

Colour, drama, excitement and great design – the hallmarks of a fine Indian painting – are all evident here. Ten-headed and twenty-armed Ravana faces the hero Rama, mounted on Hanuman, at the climactic moment in the epic. The outcome – not in doubt – is mirrored at their feet by the contest between a monkey member of Hanuman's army and one of Ravana's demonic followers. Typical of south Indian paintings is the lavish use of gold, highlighting jewelry and crowns.

Gouache on paper
1810–20
Height 29.5 cm, width 20.3 cm
Either Thanjavur of
Tiruchchirapalli, Tamil Nadu
1974,0617,0.14.2

4. Processional image of Hanuman

The heroic monkey Hanuman is depicted carrying herbs from the Himalayas that will heal Lakshmana, grievously wounded on the field of battle. Large bronze images such as this were produced in south India to be carried through the streets during temple festivals (see p. 146).

Bronze
18th century
Height 63 cm, width 43.6 cm
South India, probably Tamil Nadu
Donated by H. S. Sim,
1922,1020.4

2 | 13 *Nagas*

Nagas, semi-divine serpent deities, have been a feature of South Asian culture for at least 2,000 years. Traditionally, they are believed to live below the ground and to be the guardians of great treasures. In early Buddhism they are positive and protective forces who figure in the Jataka stories and appear in sculpture at the entranceway to shrines (see p. 60). From then on, the idea of multi-headed beasts – usually with five or seven heads – became established. The way in which a cobra puffs out its rearing head when angered is doubtless behind the ancient conception of multiple heads.

In Jainism, Parshvanatha, the twenty-third of the *tirthankara* (see p. 138) is also protected beneath the hoods of a seven-headed serpent. And in early Hinduism, Balarama, one of the deities sometimes included in the list of Vishnu's *avatara* (illustrated on p. 100), is shown in a similar way in early sculpture. In later Vaishnava schemes, Vishnu is seated on the great *naga*-king Shesha (also known as Ananta) (**3**) and Krishna, often considered an incarnation of Vishnu, subdues the *naga*-king of the river Yamuna and converts him and his queens to be his devotees. The latter event is remembered today at the Nagapanchami festival, during which prints and paintings are nailed to doors to protect the inhabitants from snakebites in the year ahead.

There is also a long tradition of the veneration of snake deities at anthills or at the foot of trees, in the form of *naga*-stones (**1**). Impressive sculptures, both ancient (**2**) and recent, are features of this cult.

1. *Naga*-stones under worship
This wayside shrine is on the pilgrim route from Tirupati to the Venkateshvara temple at Tirumala, northwest of Chennai. The *naga*-stones have been covered with turmeric powder (yellow) and sindhur (scarlet), and offered hibiscus flowers and *bilva* leaves.

Tirumala Hills, Chittoor District, Andhra Pradesh
Late 20th century

2. *Naga*-stone
Two intertwined *nagas*, one seven-headed and one five-headed, rear up in a protective, but also threatening way.

Sandstone
8th century
Height 89 cm, width 60 cm
Orissa
Donated by the Bridge family, 1872,0701.108

3. Vishnu seated on the seven-headed *naga*-king, Shesha

The usually dangerous serpent here lovingly provides a throne and canopy for the deity. Vishnu is accompanied by his wives, Shri (on his right) and

Sarasvati playing a *vina* (left). The asymmetric design along with the vibrant colour scheme is typical of traditional Indian aesthetics.

Thickened watercolour on cotton, on a wooden support, perhaps from a shrine

18th century
Height 18 cm, width 11.6 cm
Andhra Pradesh or coastal Orissa
Donated by Hernu, Peron and Stockwell Ltd, 1971,0920,0.7

2 | 14 *Vahanas*

It is not clear when deities in South Asia were first connected with specific animal vehicles, known as *vahanas*. At Besnagar in northern Central India, an inscribed pillar dedicated to Vasudeva (a name for the deity later known as Vishnu) was erected in about 110 BCE. It was raised by Heliodorus, a visiting ambassador from Taxila, and was probably once topped by a sculpture of the hawk Garuda as an inscription on the pillar describes it as a 'Garuda standard of Vasudeva'; the sculpture does not survive. So, already by this time, Garuda is associated with the deity Vasudeva-Vishnu. Later, in the Gupta period, Garuda on a standard appears on coinage as a royal device, while later still, this part-bird, part-human being carries the god through the heavens (**2**).

The bull who accompanies Shiva, Nandi (**3**), is perhaps prefigured in the deity, accompanied by a bull, that appears on the coinage of the Kushans. Nandi is not only a vehicle for the god, but also becomes his foremost devotee. From an early period other deities are connected with specific animals – Lakshmi with lustrating elephants, Karttikeya with a peacock (see p. 172) and Durga with a lion (**4**); comically, the animal on which Ganesha rides is the rat (**1**). This association between animal vehicles and deities is most pronounced in Hinduism, but in Buddhism the presence of animals is also suggestive – for instance, two deer facing each other with a wheel between them indicate the Deer Park at Sarnath where the Buddha preached his First Sermon (see p. 43), and two lions holding up a throne remind the viewer that the Buddha is 'the Lion of the Shakya clan'. In Jainism, too, animals placed in the lower part of a throne identify the *tirthankara* (see p. 46).

1. The rat *vahana* of Ganesha
The rat vehicle of Ganesha is the focus of flower offerings at the entrance to a shrine to the elephant-headed deity in the Umananda temple. This temple, dedicated to Shiva, is on an island in the Brahmaputra river at Guwahati, in Assam.

2. Garuda, the mythical bird mount of Vishnu
The *vahana* of the god Vishnu appears in *anjalimudra*, the gesture of adoration and greeting. A flower garland is pressed between his hands, an offering to the deity. In this depiction, other than his wings (one now lost) and his pointed beak-like nose, he is almost entirely human in form.

Schist
13th century
Height 62.5 cm, width 31 cm
Orissa
Donated by the Bridge family,
1872,0701.67

3. Nandi, the bull mount of Shiva
Images of Nandi are usually placed in the direct sight-line of the enshrined Shiva-*linga*, especially in south India. Nandi is thus not only the mount of Shiva but also, in the temple compound, the first of those who receive his *darshana*, or auspicious eye-contact. He wears a chaplet of bells, a chain necklace, and decorations over his ears, forehead and back.

Granite
16th century
Height 86 cm, width 96 cm
Southern Karnataka
1923,0306.1

4. The goddess Durga riding her lion vehicle
In Bengal, the goddess Durga has a distinctive story celebrated each year in October at her annual festival, Durga Puja. The Puja begins when she arrives at her father's house. Here, he is shown welcoming her, a gesture reciprocated by elephant-headed Ganesha who rides with his mother on her lion *vahana*.

Oil on canvas
Late 19th/early 20th century
Height 79.5 cm, width 60 cm
Bengal
1990,1031,0.1

2 | 15 Indian culture in Central Asia

It is clear from archaeological evidence that the cultural baggage which accompanied the spread of Buddhism from India along the Silk Road to Central Asia, and ultimately to China, was significant. From the early centuries CE, Indian coinage, sculpture in human form, script, painting styles and the ritual material of Buddhism are found in the excavated remains of the now-abandoned settlements of the Silk Road; some aspects, however, such as Indian coinage and script, did not ultimately survive there. The way the figures of the Buddhist pantheon were depicted relied heavily on Indian prototypes, as did much of the notion of sculpture in human form, less known in China before the arrival of Buddhism in the first centuries CE.

One activity in which this South Asian origin is clear is painting. Examples include items that were imported into Central Asia, or were painted there by craftsmen trained in the Indian tradition. Several found at Dunhuang in northwestern China are in a style that must be close to that of 8th-century Kashmir. This is especially important as no medieval paintings from Kashmir survive. A painting of Vajrapani from Dunhuang offers an example (**3**). Today, we are able to compare this richly dressed deity with the precious survival in the Sumtsek temple at Alchi in Ladakh (**1**) of painted sculpture (**2**); the two are clearly related. Elements in the painting from Dunhuang also seen in Kashmiri Buddhist sculpture (see p. 83) include the three-leafed crown, the triangular shape of the face, the double-lotus on which he stands and the sacred thread, *yajnopavita*, over the left shoulder. This painting, and a small group of others from Central Asia, are important indicators of a lost Indian painting tradition, as well as reminders of the reach into East Asia in the 1st millennium CE of these styles from the holy land of Buddhism.

1. The Sumtsek at Alchi
This photograph of the exterior of the early 13th-century temple was taken in 1945. It records parts of the upper structure no longer extant. The carved wooden entranceway draws on Kashmiri styles as does the interior, which is dramatically laid out on three storeys and is a jewel of sculpted and painted decoration (see Figure 2).

Photograph by Col. Reginald Schomberg
c. 1945
The Sumtsek, Alchi,
Leh District, Ladakh
Ladakh.168

2. Free-standing painted clay sculpture of the *bodhisattva* Avalokiteshvara

The sculpture in the Sumtsek of the *bodhisattva* is striking on account of its size (around 4 m high) and because of the lively depictions of architecture on the dhoti (the lower garment) that he wears. As in the painting from Dunhuang (Figure 3), the dhoti clings to the thigh of the figure and has brightly coloured bands of textile at the garment edges; both figures also wear jewel-studded belts and are depicted bare-chested.

3. The *bodhisattva* Vajrapani

The *bodhisattva* looks directly at the viewer ready to receive prayers of intercession. He holds the *vajra*, or thunderbolt, vertically in his right hand while his left holds the stalk of a lotus which blooms at his shoulder. The jewelry and colourfully striped dhoti knotted on his right hip all point to the Indian aesthetic of this painted image.

Painting on silk
Height 55 cm, width 14.5 cm
1st half of the 9th century
Cave 17, Dunhuang, Gansu, China
1919,0101,0.103

2 | 16 The powerful Shiva-*linga*

The Hindu deity Shiva is sometimes depicted in bodily form – as the great cosmic dancer (see pp. 142–5), the saviour of the universe (p. 146), a deity triumphant over all others (p. 148) or as the loving husband of Parvati (p. 157). However, the most frequently encountered form of this powerful god is not in human form, but as the *linga* (literally 'sign' or 'symbol'). As a standing phallic pillar, this way of imagining the god has an ancient history from at least the 2nd century BCE, and has been popular ever since. In this *linga* imagery, the god is most often depicted set within a pedestal, or *yoni*. These terms – *linga* and *yoni* – are multivalent, but both, in part, draw on sexual imagery. The *linga* is a phallic image (some *linga*, such as at Gudimallam in Andhra Pradesh, make this equation clear). Meanwhile, the *yoni* is in plan circular with a spout and approximates to the female vulva. The *linga*, however, rises out of the *yoni*, rather than enters into it. The two together are understood as a symbol of creative power; this is about potentiality and not – despite the imagery – about sexual activity. Indeed, most devotees would be horrified at the suggestion. The *linga* is the form in which the god is venerated in the inner chamber of a Shiva temple, his human image being reserved for the outer areas, or for processional activities.

Most *linga* from temple sanctuaries are of stone (**1**, **2**), but a *linga* can be made of anything – legends speak of sand, earth or crystal *linga*. Some are also considered *svayambhu*, that is, self-manifest. Examples of these include rolled pebbles from the Narmada river or the ice *linga* in the cave at Amarnath, in Kashmir (see p. 84). A further variant has the standing *linga* set with four faces, indicative of the varied nature of the deity (**2**). The *linga* can be the focus of intense personal devotion, irrespective of the caste of the devotee (**3**).

1. *Linga* and *yoni*
This *linga* with a protective snake, is of the type found in the sanctum of a Shiva temple. It is set within a circular element, the *yoni*. The latter ends in a spout to drain offerings poured over the *linga*.

Polished sandstone
18th century or earlier
Eastern India
Height 35 cm, width 59 cm
Donated by the Bridge family,
1872,0701.119

2. Four-faced *linga*
Some *linga* are shown with multiple heads to indicate different aspects of Shiva's personality. Here, there are four: ascetic, terrifying, tender and demonic.

Schist
8th century
Height 37.5 cm
Eastern India
1880.24

శ్రీ మెన్సనాశుని, శ్శక్కను శం రం రక్కు, సం కాం

3. Kannappa offering his eyes to the *linga*

Kannappa, a low caste hunter, was one of the *nayanmar* (see p. 124). During his devotion to Shiva, when the eye of the image starts to bleed he offers first one and then the other of his eyes to the god. As his second offering will blind him, he puts his foot on the place for the offering, to guide him. Just as he is about to pluck out his second eye, the hand of Shiva comes out of the garlanded *linga* and stops him.

Album painting in watercolour, on European watermarked paper and captioned in Telugu
c. 1830

Height 22.6 cm, width 17.6 cm
Thanjavur, Tamil Nadu
Bequeathed through Francis Egerton, 8th Earl of Bridgewater, with a contribution from Charles Long, Lord Farnborough,
1962,1231,0.13.72

1. Matsya, the fish incarnation of Vishnu

The texts record that during a primordial flood, Vishnu took the form of a fish, Matsya. In this form he was able to save the Vedas from destruction, along with other elements such as the shrine he bears on his back.

Sandstone
9th–10th century
Height 135 cm, width 81.2 cm
Central India
Donated by the Bridge family,
1872,0701.50

2. Varaha, the boar incarnation of Vishnu

In this narrative, the boar incarnation is remembered for rescuing the earth goddess Bhu from imprisonment at the bottom of the ocean. She is seen here on Varaha's shoulder as they surface from the deep.

Schist sculpture
9th century
Height 49.5 cm
Kashmir
Brooke Sewell Permanent Fund,
1973,1031.1

Avatara

One of the distinctive features of ancient Indian religion is its characteristic of defining the abundance and variety of the Divine by imagining it in different forms, often including opposites. As Buddhism developed in the 1st millennium, this feature became increasingly visible. However, it is most evident in Hinduism. For instance, Shiva is visualized as an ascetic, as a devoted husband, as a deranged mendicant, as a cosmic dancer, as the saviour of the world – or even in aniconic form as the standing phallic pillar, the *linga* (see p. 96). This listing of differing aspects may also represent the coming together – either by force or good fortune – of different cults, which have coalesced over time.

In the worship of the other great male deity of Hinduism, Vishnu, this feature is so pronounced that the idea of *avatara* (literally 'descent') developed. A product of the early centuries CE, and probably first in the region around Mathura, this idea was based on the belief that, in times of dire cosmic trouble, the godhead would manifest itself on earth, thus saving mankind and re-establishing rightful conduct, *dharma*. In the canonical list of these *avatara*, which developed over some centuries,

there are ten 'descents', the *dashavatara*, whose actual names may change depending on the region and the period. A further feature is that those at the beginning of the list today are mostly concerned with cosmology and creation, and those that appear later are generally salvific and the objects of personal devotion. The tenth *avatara* is Kalki, a riderless horse, and is still to come. The notion of *avatara* enabled all the immense variety of the divine to be acknowledged. Some *avatara* are concerned with cosmic danger, or the sustaining of the fixed order, while others have more emotional contexts. Today, the usual list of the *dashavatara* of Vishnu is as follows: Matsya (**1**), Kurma, Varaha (**2**), Narasimha (**3**), Vamana, Parashurama, Rama (**4**), Krishna (**6**), the Buddha and Kalki. In some listings, Parashurama is replaced by Balarama (**5**), and is placed after, rather than before Rama.

It is clear that certain *avatara* were more popular or important at different times and this reflects the continuously changing nature of the list. Thus, in recent centuries, Krishna and Rama have been the most popular. However, in the Gupta period, Varaha, symbol of powerful rescue from violence and rape, was more important.

3. Narasimha, the lion incarnation of Vishnu
The fourth *avatara* of Vishnu is half-man, half-lion. Narasimha is remembered for gorily killing the demon Hiranyakshipu by tricking him into thinking he is invincible. Beside the disembowelling of the demon by Narasimha stands the Vishnu devotee Prahlada.

Watercolour on paper
Early 19th century
Height 28.9 cm, width 23.6 cm
Bihar, probably Patna
1880,0.2063

4. Rama, the royal incarnation of Vishnu

Rama, the central figure of the epic Ramayana (see p. 87), is accompanied by his faithful brother Lakshmana and is shown crowned and wearing elaborate jewelry as befits a king. This plaque was once perhaps a panel forming part of a domestic shrine.

Ivory, carved, painted and partly gilded
Nayaka period, 16th–17th century
Height 14.5 cm, width 9.2 cm
South India, perhaps from court workshops in Thanjavur
Brooke Sewell Permanent Fund, with the assistance of Dr Henry Ginsburg, 1995,1006.1

5. Balarama, the plough-carrying incarnation of Vishnu

In ancient times, Balarama was depicted as lord of the snake kingdom, as well as being associated with agriculture (hence the plough). In other traditions Balarama is the brother of Krishna, and in this form is celebrated at the temple in Puri, Orissa. The image in the temple there depicts him and Krishna along with their sister, Subhadra (see p. 164).

Dyed cotton canopy (for further examples of this technique, see pp. 244–5)
Early 20th century
Length 107 cm, width 107 cm (whole canopy)
South India, probably Shrikalahasti, Chittoor District, Andhra Pradesh
Brooke Sewell Permanent Fund, 2005,0604,0.1

6. Krishna, the heroic incarnation of Vishnu

While Krishna is the centre of a cult saturated with emotion, in this painting his heroic characteristic is to the fore. He is depicted killing his evil uncle Kamsa who had tried to murder him as a child; this is narrated in the *Bhagavata Purana*, the fundamental text of the Krishna cult (see p. 163).

Gouache on paper
c. 1710
Height 28.6 cm, width 20.6 cm (including border)
Mankot, Himachal Pradesh
Brooke Sewell Permanent Fund, 1966,0725,0.2

1. Durga Mahishasuramardini

The *Devi Mahatmya* describes the moment when, under intense cosmic pressure, all the energies of the gods had to be combined in Durga to defeat the demon Mahishasura, who had taken the form of a buffalo. She kills him and his spirit is seen leaving the body of the beast.

Schist
13th century
Height 106.8 cm, width 48.3 cm
Coastal Orissa, perhaps from Konarak
Donated by the Bridge family, 1872,0701.78

2. Chamunda

Chamunda, shown as a skeletal old woman, is terrifying. Living in the cremation ground, she contemplates the impermanence of life and the illusory nature of opposites; her followers can access her powers through meditation on these same non-dualities.

Sandstone
9th century
Height 94 cm, width 72.4 cm
Orissa
Donated by the Bridge family, 1872,0701.83

3. Sculpture from a set of *yogini*

This unknown goddess is depicted with unloosed hair (a sign of dangerous power), a staff topped with a skull, a skull-cup in her lower left hand, and in her ears a severed hand (on the right) and a serpent (left) – all symbols of her ability to reconcile opposites. Her lower right hand (now broken) probably once held food to her mouth.

Granite
Early 10th century
Height 108 cm, width 63.4 cm
Kanchipuram, Tamil Nadu
Donated by P. T. Brooke Sewell, 1955,1018.2

Goddesses: strong, fierce, prosperous and peaceful

The earliest images of the goddess Durga killing the buffalo demon Mahishasura are from Mathura in the early centuries CE. However, although doubtless transmitted orally long beforehand, the writing in the 5th–6th century CE of the *Devi Mahatmya* – which glorifies Durga – ensured that the worship of this goddess became fully incorporated into Hindu practice. Remarkably, by the 7th century there is sculpture of her killing the buffalo demon at Mahabalipuram in Tamil Nadu, and only a century later, a sculpture of her at Tapa Sardar in eastern Afghanistan, a truly extraordinary range.

Durga is perhaps the most renowned Hindu goddess, and she is often depicted in sculpture in the form of Durga Mahishasuramardini ('Slayer of Mahishasura') (**1**). During her annual festival in Calcutta, every neighbourhood competes to produce temporary images of the goddess destroying the demon; this festival has become increasingly popular from the 18th century onwards. Also popular in Bengal is Kali, who accepts blood sacrifices but is also known, paradoxically, as Mother. The goddess Kamakhya receives blood sacrifices also at her temple in Guwahati in Assam. The *yoni* of the goddess is honoured there but there is no image, only a crack in the rock. A final alarming goddess is the skeletal Chamunda, who is linked with cremation grounds (**2**).

Of equal importance to the fierce goddesses are those who operate peacefully and eschew blood offerings. Of these, Lakshmi – goddess of plenty – is perhaps the most important. Today she is connected with financial plenty and everyone wants to meet her, but imagery from at least the 1st century BCE onwards, in which she appears on a lotus and lustrated by elephants, suggests that agricultural prosperity was her original purview. This image, with its connotations of water and human fertility, appears on early coins throughout the subcontinent. Although originally separate, the goddess Shri ('auspiciousness') is now, with Lakshmi, often spoken of as a single unit, Shri-Lakshmi.

Rivers are considered life-providing goddesses (only the Brahmaputra is male). These include the Kaveri (south India), the Narmada (central India) and, especially, the Ganges (or Ganga; north India). The Ganges also has an important position in the mythology of Shiva and his city, Varanasi, is located on its banks. The water is considered sacred and pilgrims bathe in it for the cleansing of sin, and then bring it home for use in domestic ritual (**4**). Both Ganga and Yamuna (the goddesses of the rivers Ganges and Yamuna) often appear in sculptures at the base of temple entrance-ways (**5**). Another ancient but benign goddess is Sarasvati, identified with music and literature, and honoured by both Hindus and Jains (**6**).

Sometimes goddesses were grouped together: with children; as groups of seven 'Mothers'; or, as the sixty-four *yogini*, as at the temple of Hirpur in Orissa; or in other numbered configurations (**3**). Shrines to village goddesses are common throughout India. Here, the goddess is often imagined in aniconic form, as a rock or tree, and is often concerned with fertility or the control of epidemics.

Left
4. *Chambu*
Metal vessels known as
chambu, made in Varanasi,
are traditionally filled with holy
Ganges water and carried by
pilgrims returning home from
the city sacred to Shiva. The
sides of this vessel are engraved
with a range of scenes using a
technique in which both copper
(upper section) and brass (lower)
are combined; this is known as
Ganga-Yamuna technique after
the colours of the two sacred
rivers. An inscription around the
neck reads 'Shri Ram, Jay Ram',
'Honour to God, victory to God'.

Cast and engraved brass
and copper
19th century or earlier
Height 19 cm, diameter 18 cm
Varanasi, Uttar Pradesh
Donated by Simon Digby,
1991,0814.2

Opposite, below

5. Ganga

The goddess Ganga, with her
auspicious, sensuous and fruitful
qualities, is often depicted at
the base of doorways into Hindu
temples. Here, she carries a
full-bellied vessel from which
the river flows and she stands
on the tail of a water-monster
or *makara*.

Sandstone
10th century, under the
Gujara-Pratihara kings
Height 41.9 cm
Central India
Brooke Sewell Permanent Fund,
1967,0215.1

Above

6. Sarasvati

This painting is the second
in a sequence of sixty that tells
the story of Harishchandra (see
pp. 70–71); they were used as
visual aids by itinerant bards
narrating the story. Sarasvati
is involved at the beginning of
the performance as she is the
goddess of literature and music
(she holds a manuscript and
a musical instrument, the *vina*).
Her avian *vahana* appears
by her side.

Painting on paper
Late 19th/early 20th century
'Paithan' style, but probably from
the Karnataka/Andhra border
Height 29 cm, width 40.5 cm
Donated by Professor Dr Anna
Dallapiccola, 2007,3014.2

2 | 17 Early wooden architecture

Although the majority of temple architecture in ancient South Asia was built of brick (in the north) or stone (in the west and south), wood was also used wherever it was available. The foothills of the Himalayas, all the way from the Hindu Kush in the west to the mountains of northern Burma in the east, is one such region and sacred architecture in wood has been plentiful.

A remarkable survival has been recorded at the cave shrine of Kashmir Smast, near Mardan in present-day Pakistan (despite the name, the location is not in Kashmir). In the late 19th century the cave (**1**) was investigated and, from the ruined shrine within, a number of wooden items were recovered (**2, 3**). Since that time, both legal and illegal excavations have been carried out in the cave and also on the cliff face around it. From these investigations it is clear that the cave shrine was dedicated to the goddess Bhumidevi (in a copperplate inscription found at the site the cave mouth is described as the *yoni* of the deity). Further supporting this connection are the many sealings recovered from the site on which are depicted the Lajja Gauri form of the goddess – legs apart as if giving birth and with a lotus in place of a head. The shrines scattered over the nearby cliff face were clearly dedicated to Shiva and *linga* have been found there.

The wooden remains from the cave shrine are remarkable – the column with its Corinthian capital and the beam ends with their dentils are clearly inheritors of the Gandhara tradition. However, the subject matter and the style of carving of the Shaiva figures is unequivocally Indian and completely un-Western (**3**).

This page
1. Kashmir Smast
In the 1st millennium CE this huge cave in the cliff face at Kashmir Smast, near Mardan, was considered by devotees to be the *yoni* of the local mountain goddess, Bhumidevi. It became the centre of a substantial pilgrimage.

Opposite, left and top right
2. Column and lotus boss from Kashmir Smast
The wooden column from the shrine inside the cave is a remarkable survival, not least on account of its Corinthian-style capital, still in use several centuries after the end of the Gandhara period. The lotus boss draws on the South Asian link between beneficent goddesses and these glorious blossoms of the Indian flora.

Carved wood, probably coniferous
9th–10th century
Column: height 133 cm, width 17 cm; boss: diameter 24 cm
From Kashmir Smast cave, Mardan District, Khyber Pakhtunkhwa, Pakistan
Donated by Sir Harold Arthur Deane, 1889,0703.8 (column), 1889,0703.7 (boss)

Above right
**3. Decorated beam end
from Kashmir Smast**
This dancing male figure
accompanied by four musicians
brings to mind the story of
Shiva as the cosmic dancer
(see pp. 142–5). On another
surviving beam end (not shown),

a mendicant is depicted –
an additional connection with
narratives in the myth of Shiva.
Both reinforce the Bhumidevi–
Shiva link at this important site,
connecting Kashmir Smast
with other cave shrines in the
Himalayas, such as Amarnath
(see p. 96).

Carved wood, probably coniferous
9th–10th century
Height 31.7 cm, width 54.3 cm
From Kashmir Smast cave,
Mardan District, Khyber
Pakhtunkhwa, Pakistan
Donated by Sir Harold Arthur
Deane, 1889,0703.9

2 | 18 Buddhism in south India

Evidence for Buddhism in southern India is well attested in the early centuries of the present era. Amaravati (see pp. 58–61) and a cluster of nearby sites in the Krishna delta (1), and later Nagarjunakonda, provide clear evidence for this. However, further south in the region of the modern state of Tamil Nadu, the evidence is less clear, and there is also less clarity as to how long organized Buddhism survived.

Early Buddhism in the far south is known from surviving sculptures as well as a small number of texts in Tamil, perhaps the most famous being the *Manimekalai* of around the 6th century. Buddhism is also referred to in the literature of the Tamil saints from about the same date (see p. 124), but invariably from a negative point of view. Otherwise, there is mostly silence on Buddhism other than occasional but remarkable evidences of continuation. At Buddhapad, near Amaravati, bronze images of the Buddha have been found (2). One of these is remarkably similar to images found in Java (3), recalling the links between southern India and Indonesia (dyed textiles produced on this same Andhra coast were a further export to the Indonesian archipelago; see p. 72).

Evidence from texts tells us that Kanchipuram, now a bastion of Hinduism, was an important centre of Buddhist activity in the 1st millennium, as was Nagapattinam. At the latter centre, in the delta of the Kaveri river and ideally suited for international trade, Buddha images have been found (4). These are close to examples from Sri Lanka, indicating contact between the two regions. At the other end of the chronology is a record of a Buddhist structure at Nagapattinam that survived, though ruined, into the 19th century.

2. Three sculptures of the standing Buddha
The Buddha wears the monastic robe in the 'southern' style, with one shoulder bare. These images emphasize the large right hand, suggesting the qualities of the Buddha: boon-fulfilling (*varadamudra*), left and centre, and fearlessness (*abhayamudra*), right.

Bronze
(l–r): 7th–8th century;
6th century; 5th–6th century
Height (l–r) 38 cm, 31.7 cm, 31.2 cm
Buddhapad, Andhra Pradesh
Donated by the Secretary for State for India, 1905,1218.1-3

3. The standing Buddha
While probably cast in Java, the south Indian ancestry of images such as this is clear. Like the images from Buddhapad, the robe only covers the Buddha's left shoulder and descends in folds on his left side.

Bronze
9th–10th century
Height 19 cm
Java, Indonesia
Donated by Revd William Charles Raffles Flint, 1859,1228.98

4. The seated Buddha
Here the Buddha is imagined as a divine rather than a human figure; the hand position, the *mudra*, suggests meditation. The flame-like *ushnisha* (protuberance from the head of the Buddha), links south Indian Buddhism with that of Sri Lanka (see p. 110, Figure 1), though the double-lotus base is an eastern Indian feature.

Bronze
13th century
Height 17 cm, width 11.9 cm
Nagapattinam, Tamil Nadu
1928,1016.13

1. Railing pillar fragment
This beneficent female figure would have faced a devotee approaching the stupa at Goli. She holds auspicious lotus blossoms in her right hand and has an elaborate coiffure filled with arrows, a feature seen throughout South Asia amongst images of divine female figures in the early centuries CE.

Limestone, perhaps from Palnad
1st or 2nd century
Height 99 cm, width 63.7 cm
Probably Goli, near Amaravati, Andhra Pradesh
Donated by P. T. Brooke Sewell, 1955,1017.1

2 | 19 Buddhism in Sri Lanka

When and how Buddhism arrived in Sri Lanka is uncertain. Legend speaks of the son of the emperor Ashoka, Mahinda, arriving on the island along with his sister and making the first conversions in the 3rd century BCE. According to the same story, they also brought with them a cutting of the *bodhi* tree from Bodh Gaya and a descendant of this tree is still venerated at Anuradhapura (**1**). Such a narrative emphasizes the connectedness of Buddhism in Sri Lanka with northeastern India, the region above all associated with the historical Buddha. This explanation does not, however, take account of the substantial early presence of Buddhism in coastal Andhra, a location much closer to Sri Lanka than eastern India. Elements typical of Andhra Buddhism also appear in Sri Lanka. A small sculpture apparently in the Palnad limestone of Andhra but found in Sri Lanka (**2**) suggests that items were brought from centres such as Amaravati to the island. The connection is also reflected in architectural similarities in stupa design in both places.

The royal city of Anuradhapura in Sri Lanka was already in existence in the 3rd century BCE. It was the foremost centre of Buddhism until the 10th century when it was destroyed in the Chola invasion of the northern and central parts of the island. (Polonnaruva further south was capital to both Chola and later Sinhalese rulers.) During the later Anuradhapura period, both the Theravada and Mahayana schools of Buddhism were prominent, at the Mahavihara and Abhayagiri monasteries, respectively. Evidence of both is apparent in the surviving sculpture (**3**); one of the very finest bronze images known from ancient Sri Lanka is from the Mahayana school (**4**).

1. The *bodhi* tree at Anuradhapura

The tree enshrined at Anuradhapura is believed to be a descendant of a cutting brought from north India in the 3rd century BCE. This 19th-century watercolour depicts the shrine, along with a leaf from the tree – a sacred souvenir.

Watercolour on paper, by Lt.-Col. Harry H. St George (1845–1897)
Painted and leaf gathered
3 February 1889
Anuradhapura, Sri Lanka
Donated by Ione Moncrieff St George Brett, 1996,0330,0.4

2. Slab of limestone carved with a *naga*-king

This carved slab appears to be of Palnad limestone, from Andhra Pradesh in southern India. A *naga*-king rears up protectively. On the left are two other *nagas*, while a royal parasol is just visible above the central *naga*.

Limestone, probably from Palnad in Andhra Pradesh
c. 4th century
Height 20.3 cm, width 15 cm
Probably Andhra Pradesh
1898,0702.195

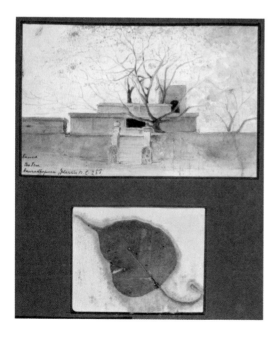

3. The seated Buddha

This small Buddha image is
typical of the influential style
developed at Anuradhapura.
The Buddha is seated with the
hands in the meditation gesture,
dhyanamudra, and with flame-
like *ushnisha*. This sculpture and
the slab in Figure 2 are part of
the large collection assembled
by Hugh Nevill (1847–1897),
a British officer stationed
in Sri Lanka.

Gilded bronze with inset red stone
9th century
Height 13 cm
Sri Lanka
1898,0702.29

4. The goddess Tara

This almost life-size figure of
Tara, consort of Avalokiteshvara,
shows the importance of the
Mahayana school of Buddhism
in Sri Lanka in the late 1st
millennium. The sculpture was
made using the lost-wax process
(see p. 112) and, unusually, was
cast solid and then gilded. The
tall chignon, with its probably
once bejeweled niche, is in stark
contrast to the unadorned body.

Solid cast and gilded bronze
c. 8th century
Height 143 cm, width 44 cm
Found between Trincomalee and
Batticaloa, eastern Sri Lanka
Donated by Sir Robert Brownrigg,
1830,0612.4

2 | 20 Lost-wax bronze casting

While there are a handful of metal sculptures from remote antiquity known in South Asia, such as the Dancing Girl from Mohenjo-daro and the hoard from Daimabad in Maharashtra, bronze casting in the round using the lost-wax process has only been practised in South Asia from the early centuries CE. This technique probably entered the subcontinent from Afghanistan and Iran, with the result that the earliest surviving examples in the round come from the northwest (see p. 19; items made from one-piece moulds are known from about this time in the Deccan (1), but this is a different tradition which didn't produce three-dimensional sculpture).

In the lost wax process, the image to be produced is first sculpted in wax, sometimes on a clay core, sometimes in solid wax. The sculpted outer face of the wax is then covered in wet clay and allowed to dry. Then the combined clay and wax are heated and the wax runs out, leaving an accurate mould. This can then be filled with molten bronze (an alloy of copper and tin) and left to cool. Once cold, the outer clay is broken away, revealing the finished bronze sculpture, which is then chased and polished before it is used. The presence of a clay core in some of these bronzes allows direct dating using the thermoluminescence technique.

Lost-wax casting was mastered successfully in the 1st millennium in the service of Buddhism (2), Jainism (3) and Hinduism (4). The finest examples are surely those produced in south India during the Chola period, in the 9th–13th centuries. Bronze sculpture production using this method continues to this day in the south, most famously at Swamimallai in Tamil Nadu.

1. Standing goddess
This small sculpture was cast using a single flat mould. The frontal stance, heavy beaded girdle, full youthful breasts and necklace falling between them recall early historic imagery at sites such as Sanchi (see p. 56).

Brassy copper alloy
c. 1st century CE
Height 16 cm, width 6.4 cm
The Deccan
Brooke Sewell Permanent Fund, 1963,0215.1

2 The standing Buddha
Already by the time this sculpture was produced, the technique of lost-wax casting had been perfected and sublime images such as this could be made. Although cast in India, the presence of blue azurite in the hair indicates it was, at some point, taken to and then used in Tibet.

Cast bronze, gilded and with traces of azurite
Early 7th century
Height 35.5 cm
Bihar
Heritage Lottery Fund, the Art Fund, Brooke Sewell Permanent Fund, Victoria and Albert Museum and Friends of the V&A; this sculpture was acquired jointly by the British Museum, 2004,0401.1, and the Victoria and Albert Museum, IS 3-2004

3. *Yaksha* and *Yakshi*
This bronze image of a *yaksha* and *yakshi*, with a *tirthankara* above, was made using the lost-wax process. Such figures have played an important role in Jain devotion. Their origin is probably to be found in nature spirits who were co-opted into Jainism and Buddhism as the two faiths developed.

Bronze
9th–10th century
Height 14.1 cm, width 10 cm
The Deccan
Acquired through the Art Fund (as NACF), 1914,0218.13

4. Shiva as a hunter
The narrative of Shiva as a forest hunter is told in the Mahabharata (see p. 71). The god is imagined as a beautiful young man with, in his right hand, the *pashupata* weapon. Cast using the lost-wax process, this is an outstanding example of the bronze-worker's skill, with its many angled forms into which the molten metal must penetrate.

Bronze
Early 10th century
The Deccan
Height 24.5 cm, width 12.5 cm
Brooke Sewell Permanent Fund, 1967,0727.1

2 | 21 The presentation of narrative

One of the distinctive features of the subcontinent from the late centuries BCE until today has been an interest in the pictorial presentation of narrative. We know from texts of the existence already in the late centuries BCE of itinerant storytellers who amplified their message through the use of painted scrolls. Patanjali, the 2nd-century BCE author of the *Mahabhashya*, refers to such people when discussing Panini, a 4th-century BCE grammarian. While there are no surviving painted scrolls from these times, their use is known throughout the subcontinent, from Tibet in the north to Sri Lanka in the south, and from Bengal in the east to Gujarat in the west.

Some indication of the development of the tradition can be seen not in painting but in sculpture. At early Buddhist sites, such as Amaravati (see p. 58), the narrative elements of the life of the Buddha are shown in sequence, as if in a painted scroll (**1**). Indeed, the spread of Buddhism out of India – to Central Asia, Tibet and Southeast Asia – must have been accompanied by monk-storytellers illustrating the narratives of the new religion. And, considering the quantity of narrative (the life of the Buddha, along with all the Jataka stories) and the lack of common language between Buddhist teachers and new communities, the necessity of painted scrolls becomes obvious. Again, actual scrolls from antiquity do not survive, though mentions of them in texts do, as do later examples (**2**).

In more recent times in Tamil parts of Sri Lanka, storytellers have used dyed depictions on cloth of the Ramayana to amplify its oral presentation (**3**), while in Bengal a vibrant tradition of telling stories with scrolls has survived up to the present day (see p. 237).

1. Narrative frieze from the main stupa at Amaravati
This narrative from the life of the Buddha runs from right to left, just as a pilgrim to the stupa would experience it while walking round in a propitious clockwise fashion. Following a small panel showing an auspicious couple, *mithuna*, Prince Siddhartha is represented stepping down from his bed and leaving his sleeping womenfolk, then on his horse leaving the palace surrounded by celestial figures, and finally seated in the forest, sending away his groom and his horse.

Limestone from Palnad
3rd century
Height 37.5 cm, width 140 cm
From the stupa at Amaravati, Guntur District, Andhra Pradesh
Donated by the Government of Madras, 1880,0709.112

2. Banner painting from Dunhuang

This painting on silk from a cave at Dunhuang in China illustrates three scenes from the early life of the Buddha. At the top, the kneeling horse and the groom take their leave of the young prince; in the middle, Siddhartha's head is shaved; below, the Buddha-to-be is shown in full meditation, his concentration so intense that birds have built a nest on his head.

Painting on silk
8th or 9th century
Height 58.5 cm, width 18.5 cm
(painted image)
Cave 17, Mogao, Dunhuang,
Gansu, China
1919,0101,0.97

3. Scenes from the *Aranya-kanda*, the Forest Book of the Ramayana

Cloths such as this one were used in Tamil areas to accompany recitations of the Ramayana. This detail shows, among other episodes: (bottom row) Bharata and Shatrughna (brothers of Rama) crossing the Ganges; (middle row) Rama, Sita and Lakshmana meet a group of ascetics; (top row) the demoness Shurpanakha, approaching her ten-headed brother Ravana in his palace.

Cotton with stencilled outlines, dyed colours and inked captions
Early 19th century
Tamil Nadu, or northern Sri Lanka
Height 110 cm, length 762 cm
(entire cloth)
Brooke Sewell Permanent Fund,
1993,0724,0.2

2 | 22 *Rishi, sadhu* and *sannyasi*

Already in the Vedas, reflecting a time of about 1,500 BCE, spiritual seers or *rishis* are recorded. Later, in the Upanishads (early to mid-1st millennium BCE), we encounter men who have abandoned everyday life and taken refuge in the forest to further their spiritual understanding; they also are *rishi*. Only slightly later, the retreat to the forest of the Buddha-to-be fits into this archetype (see pp. 42–3, 114). Such retreat from everyday life is based on the ideas that want of distraction is conducive to spiritual thought; simplicity of life aids spiritual advance; responses can be enhanced through concentration and exercise, *yoga*; and success in self-denial indicates spiritual advance (**1**). Such people may also be known as *sadhu*, with many acknowledging the teachings of a *guru*, a spiritual preceptor, sometimes gathering around him in an *ashrama* and rejecting all the ties that bind – family, language, caste (**2**). Being a *sadhu* has also functioned as an escape route for those not fitting into caste-bound society.

Some *sadhu* wander, some are stationary, many have abandoned all attachment to this world and seek food by soliciting alms (**3**). They feature throughout South Asian literature and are looked on with awe and admiration – and sometimes fear at the powers that they are believed to exercise. Contrarily, there is also a vein of mockery directed towards bogus *sadhu* who beguile the innocent. A variant of the *sadhu* is the *sannyasi*, a traditional Hindu householder who, having fulfilled his family duties, can leave his house to seek his own salvation. Meanwhile, his wife – now in effect a widow – remains to eke out her days on the margins of society.

Renunciants are known in all parts of Jain, Hindu and Muslim society. The latter are often members of *sufi* orders (see p. 163) and congregate at the tomb-shrines of saints.

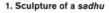

1. Sculpture of a *sadhu*
The abandonment of everyday life by this mendicant is indicated by his near nudity, the rosary or *akshamala* in his right hand along with the beads around his neck and upper arm, and his unkempt beard and piled-up ropes of matted hair, *jata*, across the top of his head. These features are all ones connected with Shiva, who is regarded as the quintessential renouncer.

Marble
Late 10th century
Height 81 cm, width 20 cm
Rajasthan
Brooke Sewell Permanent Fund,
1964,0413.2

Above
2. The sage Medhas and his disciple
The teacher sits on an animal skin outside his modest hut in the forest, far from human contact. In his hands he holds the text, the *Devi Mahatmya*, which tells of the triumph of the goddess (see p. 103). Two devotees, Surath and Samadhi (left), have come to hear his discourse on the power of Durga.

Gouache on paper
c. 1780
Height 14.6 cm, width 23.4 cm
Kangra, Himachal Pradesh
Bequeathed by P. C. Manuk and Miss G. M. Coles through the Art Fund (as NACF), 1948,1009,0.140

Left
3. Vaishnava *sadhu*
This renunciant, Bajrang Das, wears a *tilak* (religious marking) with an enlarged vermillion *bindu*. His matted hair, coated with ash, is arranged into a single mass at the back of his head. He belongs to a famous lineage of ascetics, the Ramanandi, who venerate Rama, the *avatara* of Vishnu (see p. 86). Bajrang Das is a *khareshvari*, a *sadhu* who has vowed to stand only on one foot, never lying down. When this photograph was taken, he had maintained this austerity for six years.

Photograph by Dolf Hartsuiker
1970s
From the Hartsuiker Archive at the British Museum

Timeline

6th century	The construction of Elephanta, probably by the Kalachuri kings
6th–7th centuries	Distinctive sculptural style seen in Nepal
7th–9th centuries	Pallava rule in Tamil Nadu
7th century	Rock-cut shrines at Mahabalipuram
c. 630–645	Chinese pilgrim and translator Xuanzang in India
7th–10th centuries	The *nayanmars* and the *alvars* flourish in southern India
8th century	Excavation of the Kailashanatha temple at Ellora
8th–12th centuries	Pala rule in eastern India
9th–13th centuries	The rule of the Chola dynasty
c. 10th century	The *Bhagavata Purana* composed, probably in southern India
948	The monolithic sculpture of Bahubali at Shravana Belgola, Karnataka
c. 985–1012	Rajaraja I, Chola king ruled in south India
1000–27	Afghan raids into northern India
c. 1010	Consecration of the Brihadishvara temple, Thanjavur, by Rajaraja I
9th–11th centuries	Chandella dynasty rule in central India: the temples at Khajuraho are built
1055–1110	Reign of Vijayabahu of Sri Lanka and end of Chola rule
1160	First mosque dated by inscription in South Asia built at Badreshvar in Kutch
12th century	The poet Jayadeva composes the *Gitagovinda*
Late 13th century	The work of Newari metalworkers from the Kathmandu valley renowned as far away as China
12th–mid-14th centuries	Hoysala rule in southwest India
Late 11th–14th centuries	Eastern Ganga rulers in Orissa

3

Dynasties
and the rise
of devotion
6th–14th centuries

1. Mahishasuramardini temple at Mahabalipuram
The rock-cut shrines at Mahabalipuram, south of Chennai, include some with impressively large panels of relief sculpture. This mid-7th-century example depicts the goddess Durga, riding on her lion *vahana* and confronting the retreating buffalo demon Mahishasura; it exhibits a fine sense of movement and drama as well as a mastery of sculptural technique.

There was no single, pan-Indian dynasty during the medieval period (6th–13th centuries), but instead many powerful regional kingdoms.

In the south, following the Satavahana and Ikshvaku rulers, the Pallava and Pandya kings dominated. The Pallavas ruled from Kanchipuram, where temples to Shiva and Vishnu were constructed during the 8th century and also where Buddhism remained important. From their port of Mahabalipuram, they traded extensively from the 7th century. The importance of the port is indicated by rock-cut shrines dedicated to Hindu deities: Vishnu (in various forms), Shiva and Durga, the goddess who defeated Mahishasura (1). The Pandyas, further south around Madurai, also practised rock-cut architecture, as at Kalugumalai. This period saw the beginning of devotional cults centred on Shiva and Vishnu, which were also manifested in the poetry of the itinerant saints, the *nayanmar* and the *alvar* (see p. 124). This personal worship, *bhakti*, was later immensely influential throughout the subcontinent, especially in the worship of Krishna (for *bhakti*, see pp. 162–3). In the Deccan, the Early Chalukya dynasty is remembered for rock-cut shrines at Badami (6th century onwards) (2), and for built temples at Aihole (similar dates) and Pattadakal (mostly 8th century).

Still in the south, the single successor of these dynasties, the Cholas, are of major significance; they ruled from the fertile

2. Cave 3 at Badami
This towering image of the lion incarnation of Vishnu, Narasimha, dated by inscription to 578 CE, is located at one end of the verandah of the rock-cut Cave 3 at Badami (ancient Vatapi), the royal centre of the early Chalukya kings. This man-made cave was excavated into the cliff face above a water tank, which was also man-made, an indication of the importance of the control of the water supply.

delta of the Kaveri river from the 9th to the 13th centuries and were builders of temples on a scale larger than anything previously seen – examples include the Brihadishvara temple in Thanjavur built by Rajarajeshvara in 1010 and the Gangaikondacholapuram temple constructed by his son Rajendra. Inscriptions, in temples and on copperplates recording land grants, are numerous and allow a more chronological history. This was not only a period of temple construction and decoration in stone, but also a time when bronze casting reached its apogee in South Asia. Funds necessary for work on this scale were assembled through trade as well as conquest (parts of the Deccan as well as most of Sri Lanka were brought under Chola rule, while parts of Southeast Asia acknowledged their authority). The decline of this dynasty brought the Hoysala rulers to prominence around Mysore; they are remembered today primarily for temples based on circular or stellate plans with deeply cut-away sculpture.

In northern India, following the decline of the Gupta dynasty in the 5th century, various regional powers grew up, including the Kalachuris (the 6th-century shrine of Elephanta is associated with them) **(3)**, king Harsha at Kanauj (recorded in the 7th century by the Chinese Buddhist pilgrim Xuanzang), and the Rashtrakutas (8th-century patrons of the

3. Three-headed sculpture of Shiva, Maheshamurti (literally 'image of the great lord')
A striking and powerful sculpture, this huge 6th-century image of Shiva – it is 7 m in height – is located on the back wall of the rock-cut temple on the island of Elephanta. The three visible heads illustrate different characteristics of the god: Bhairava, terrifying (Shiva's right); Parvati, graceful (left); and Lord Shiva as withdrawn and serene, yet full of potential (centre). This excavation, with its eight other large sculpted panels illustrating the mythology of Shiva, is an impressive aesthetic and religious evocation.

Kailashanatha temple at Ellora) in the Deccan (**4**); from the 10th century in central India the Chandellas (the builders of the temples at Khajuraho) were prominent. Slightly later and in eastern India was the Pala dynasty, followed by the Senas. The Pala's international trajectory – not through conquest, but through their 'cultural offer' – makes them, along with the Cholas in southern India, the most important dynasty of the medieval period. Originating in Bengal, their power grew due to control of the sacred sites of Buddhism. Pilgrims came from throughout Asia to visit the shrines, especially Bodh Gaya, and carry back with them examples of portable sculpture in clay, stone and especially bronze. Consequently, the Pala style was exported to China, Tibet, Burma, Thailand and Indonesia. Bronze casting – for example, at Kurkihar – was of the highest quality. Along with sculpture and devotion went Sanskrit, palm-leaf manuscripts and ideas about sacred space, such as *mandala* (see p. 160). The Pala Buddhist package was highly influential, but while Buddhism was important in eastern India, Hindu cults were also patronized by the Palas, and their successors, the Senas.

To the north of the Pala domains lies Nepal, which has been closely connected culturally with the plains of northern India for many centuries. Both Buddhism and Hinduism have flourished there, especially in the Kathmandu valley,

4. Kailashanatha temple at Ellora
Excavated out of the solid cliff face in the 8th century, this temple dedicated to Shiva as Lord of Kailash (his home, high in the Himalayas), is one of the great achievements of ancient Indian engineering. It is free-standing, but not built – with both the architecture and sculpture only cut from above. Copperplate grants from elsewhere indicate that the Rashtrakuta king Krishnaraja I (r. 756–73) was the main patron, though it was probably only completed after his reign.

the cultural hub of the region, perhaps even from the time of Ashoka. In Nepal, syncretism is noted in both Hinduism and Buddhism.

Meanwhile, Jainism had also developed since its foundation in eastern India and spread widely, including to the Tamil country where it was well known in the Pallava period, though it later suffered at the hands of the *bhakti* movement. Meanwhile, in central India, Jain rock-cut shrines are known, for instance at Gwalior and Ellora. However, the strongholds that we know of in the medieval period and which are still important today were in western India (Rajasthan and Gujarat) and in Karnataka.

Perhaps the most impressive change in the Indian landscape during this period, was the appearance of large-scale temples. Rulers were patrons of built structures in which the object of devotion – whether it was the Buddha, a Jain teacher or the gods of Hinduism – was enshrined. The tradition of rock-cut shrines continued to be excavated, culminating in the astonishing bravura of the Kailashanatha temple at Ellora (**4**). However, increasingly the built structure is important, rather than the excavated one. Architectural principles of pillar and beam construction, along with corbelling for vaults, were established. Gigantism, as seen in the temples of the Chola kings presented a southern paradigm which was to continue in succeeding periods.

3 | 1 The *nayanmar* and the *alvar*

These two terms refer to the early medieval Hindu poet-saints of south India who sang the praises of Shiva (*nayanmar*) and Vishnu (*alvar*). Their dates are not known for certain, but from the internal evidence of their poetry, it seems likely that they lived in the mid- to late 1st millennium CE, with perhaps the Shaiva saint Appar being first in the sequence, in the 7th century (**1**).

At this time, southern India had a very different religious landscape to the one we know today, with both Buddhism and Jainism prominent and patronized by royalty. By the turn of the millennium, however, this had changed: Buddhism was far less evident and Jainism remained a minority religion from then onwards, though it has survived to the present day (see p. 138). These changes were mostly due to the work of the saints who, in contrast to the cults of Buddhism and Jainism, developed a religious life of emotion and unencumbered engagement with the deity. This can, perhaps, be seen as the beginning of what is later known as *bhakti* (see p. 162).

There are sixty-three *nayanmar*, although little is known about some of them. Appar, Sambandar (**3**) and Sunderar are the most famous and their poetry is gathered together in a collection known as the *Tevaram*. There are twelve *alvar* including one woman, Andal. Like that of the *nayanmar*, the poetry of the *alvar* speaks of surrender and unconditional love towards the deity. It was sometimes transgressive verse that was addressed to the deity by devotees who were often socially ostracized. Kannappa, who offered Shiva his eye, was a hunter (see p. 97) and the *alvar* Tirumangai was a bandit (**2**). In this view of reality, the constraints of caste, wealth and position are unimportant; what matters is complete devotion to the deity.

1. The *nayanmar* Appar
Recognizable as Appar on account of the spade he carries on his shoulder, this bronze sculpture by Mohan Sthapati is part of a group of images, all of the *nayanmar*, commissioned in the late 1980s. It is both a record of the iconographic variety of the saints and an indicator of the quality of bronze casting still practised in southern India.

Bronze
1991
Height 38 cm
Cast at Ramapuram, on the outskirts of Chennai, Tamil Nadu
1992,0727.3

2. The *alvar* Tirumangai
In this processional image Tirumangai carries an unsheathed sword and a shield, suggestive of his early life of violent banditry. This came to an end after a sudden encounter with divine Vishnu; Tirumangai's outpouring of devotional poetry began thereafter.

Bronze
18th–19th century
Height 46.5 cm, width 25 cm
Tamil Nadu
Donated by H. S. Sim,
1922,1020.6

3. The *nayanmar* Sambandar
The child poet-saint Sambandar, devoted to Shiva, is shown here, dancing and pointing upwards to the deity. Such sculptures would have been lashed to a wooden platform using the rings visible at the base, and processed by devotees during temple festivals (see p. 144, Figure 2).

Bronze
12th century
Height 43.3 cm
Tamil Nadu; probably the Thanjavur region
Bequeathed by Professor Samuel Eilenberg, 2001,1126.2

3 | 2 Bodh Gaya

The Enlightenment of the Buddha took place at Bodh Gaya, in Bihar. Here, meditating beneath a pipal tree, he came to understand the nature of existence. He was tempted but didn't succumb (see p. 44). Instead, he called on the earth goddess to witness his freedom from attachment gathered over many rebirths, and thus his readiness to become Enlightened; the earth shook in acknowledgment. Henceforth, he taught his understanding of attachment and the way to escape from it. His First Sermon was delivered at Sarnath (see p. 78). Thus, Bodh Gaya (the Enlightenment) and Sarnath (the First Sermon) are closely linked.

Since the 1st century BCE, Bodh Gaya has been honoured by Buddhists and the tree beneath which the Buddha sat has been an important element of this, becoming an acknowledged symbol of the Enlightenment; leaves from the tree became popular souvenirs. It was during the Pala period (see p. 130) that the Mahabodhi temple became the focus for pilgrims from all over the Buddhist world. By the 19th century, though, Buddhism was no longer known at Bodh Gaya and the structure was in disrepair. Restoration – and perhaps re-creation – of the structure began (1) and excavations within revealed jewelry offerings (2).

In the medieval period terracotta souvenirs were produced depicting the *bodhi* tree and the temple (3). Such plaques were carried all over the Buddhist world and provided visual aids for building replicas of the holy site; such replicas survive in Burma (at Pagan), Thailand (Chiang-mai) and Tibet (Golok). Also, small stone images of the shrine survive: one was excavated at the site and another was found many hundreds of miles away in Tibet, where it had been carried by a pilgrim (4).

1. The Mahabodhi temple at Bodh Gaya during restoration
The temple at Bodh Gaya appears to have had a towering brick superstructure from early in its history. It was often repaired, notably by the Burmese in the late 11th century and, more recently, by the Archaeological Survey of India (ASI) in the 1880s, by which time the building was in danger of collapse. The overseer of the work of the ASI was Joseph David Beglar, who may also have produced this image.

Photograph on paper
1880–81
Height 24.2 cm, width 19.4 cm
Bequeathed by
Sir Augustus Wollaston Franks,
1897,0528,0.117.a

2. Jewelry offerings from Bodh Gaya

These items, all assumed to be offerings, were discovered at the temple in the 1880s. The beads are strikingly similar to those found in reliquary deposits within stupas (see p. 66). The gold flowers are set with sapphires and strung together with gold beads in the form of conch shells; other beads are in the form of similarly auspicious symbols.

Gold, precious and
semi-precious stones
Early centuries CE
Shorter string of coloured beads
c. 11 cm in length
Eastern India, found at Bodh
Gaya, Bihar
Donated by Maj-Gen Sir Alexander
Cunningham, 1892,1103.13, 14,
16–20, 22–24, 38, 39

3. Terracotta plaque

This plaque, a pilgrim souvenir, depicts the temple at Bodh Gaya and shows the Buddha in the earth-touching *mudra* at the moment of his Enlightenment. The Buddha is shown within a niche, surmounted by the tower of the temple; visible beyond are the branches of the *bodhi* tree. These easily carried plaques – in shape imitating a leaf from the *bodhi* tree – were influential in spreading ideas as to the design of this important shrine, thus enabling its replication.

Terracotta
c. 9th century
Height 15.3 cm, width 11 cm
Excavated at Bodh Gaya, Bihar
Donated by Maj-Gen Sir Alexander
Cunningham, 1887,0717.81

4. Model of the Mahabodhi temple at Bodh Gaya

This sacred souvenir from Bodh Gaya was brought back to Tibet by a 12th-century pilgrim who had made the hazardous journey over the Himalayas and down into the plains of India. Carved on the base, but at a later date, are crossed thunderbolts, symbols of great power.

Mica schist
12th century
Height 10.8 cm
Eastern India
1922,1215.7

3 | 3 Early painting in South Asia

Leaving aside the rock paintings at Bhimbetka (see p. 17) and the cave paintings at Ajanta (see pp. 80–81), the earliest paintings to survive from South Asia are illustrated palm-leaf manuscripts and the wooden book covers used to hold them together (**1**). Such palm-leaf manuscripts survive from the 11th–15th centuries, though the later examples are rare (**2**).

The earliest known today are of such quality that we have to assume the tradition was established well before this time. The surviving examples are Buddhist, many of the influential Mahayana text, the *Prajnaparamitasutra* (**3**). These illustrations could only be of limited size on account of the long and thin format of the palm-leaf. Also, holes at the side of each manuscript leaf which enabled a cord to pass through to keep the leaves in the correct order, further limited available space. The paintings frequently show seated deities of the Mahayana pantheon. Colours are red (from vermillion), white (chalk), blue (indigo), yellow (orpiment) and green (yellow and blue mixed). The painting position was either in the centre or at the two sides of the leaf.

The tradition of making and illustrating palm-leaf manuscripts is one that survived in other Pala-influenced states, such as Nepal (where most of the surviving eastern Indian manuscripts have been found).

The wall paintings of eastern India have been lost and the only hint we have of the dazzling effect of these is from such small manuscript paintings, along with wall paintings from temples outside India where Pala influence was strong, such as at Pagan in Burma. There, especially in the Myinkaba Gubyaukgi shrine where the wall paintings have now been conserved, we get an inkling of what the great pilgrimage temples of eastern India must have looked like.

Opposite, above
1. Painted wooden book covers
These book covers were produced in eastern India or possibly Nepal. In the centre of both are seated Buddha figures. The upper image of the Buddha is crowned and in earth-touching posture and set in front of a towered temple structure, while the lower one is shown in the gesture of teaching and is set against a Nepalese-style backplate (see p. 159, Figure 4). At each end, *bodhisattvas* sit against exquisitely drawn rinceaux.

Painted wooden boards
Late 12th century
Height of each cover 6.2 cm, length 42 cm
Eastern India, or Kathmandu valley, Nepal
1977,0124.1.a-b

Above

2. Book cover painted with scenes from the Jataka stories

This book cover (one of two) was produced to enclose a manuscript of the *Kalachakratantra*, a late Indian *tantra*, and is dated to 1446. This is long after the monastic centres of Buddhism in eastern India had been destroyed, indicating the extent to which, at some level, Buddhism continued after the abandonment of the monasteries in the 12th century.

Painted wooden board
1446
Height 6 cm, length 33.5 cm
Bihar
Cambridge University Library,
MS Add. 1364

Below

3. Painted manuscript leaf

The Buddhist goddess Mahapratisara is depicted in this manuscript of the *Prajnaparamitasutra* with, on either side, lines from the text. The earliest tenets of Buddhism were memorized, only later being committed to writing. Birchbark and later palm-leaf was used – the latter prepared from the talipot palm (*Corypha umbraculifera*) both for writing and illustration.

Palm-leaf, paint
Late 11th century
Height 6.2 cm, width 39 cm
Nepal, or eastern India; later taken to Nepal
Donated by Douglas Barrett, 1972,0410,0.2

3 | 4 Stone sculpture: the Pala dynasty

Rulers of the Pala dynasty were committed patrons of religious art, both in bronze (see p. 132) and stone. They were major supporters of Buddhism, but sculpture of both the Hindu and Buddhist traditions was produced in a period of prosperity, due not least to the international links maintained by the Pala kings. These links were greatly enhanced by the presence in the Pala domain of the holy sites of Buddhism, above all Bodh Gaya (see p. 126), to which many pilgrims flocked from Southeast and East Asia. Pala styles in both stone and bronze sculpture, as well as in painting, were spread throughout Asia as a result of this pilgrimage activity, influencing Buddhist imagery in China, Indonesia, Burma, Nepal and Tibet (Hindu imagery, so closely linked to the land of India, spread less, but is evident in parts of Southeast Asia).

Although Pala architecture only survives in a very fragmentary state – as at the monastery of Nalanda and Paharpur – it is clear that the many stone sculptures that survive came from Buddhist monasteries or shrines (1), or Hindu temples. By far the majority are large stele of dark schist, carved on one side with a central subject surrounded by celestial figures, donors or musicians; these were slotted into niches all over the brick temple structures (brick was the favoured building material in this region). Frequently, the central figure, the Buddha (3) or a Hindu deity (2), is placed (seated or standing) on a double-lotus base. Rich decoration of the backplate is another feature as are, amongst the Buddhist images, inscriptions of the creed or depictions of donors. Workshops were extraordinarily productive and many hundreds of images survive.

1. The Death of the Buddha
The entry into *nirvana* of the Buddha is depicted in this stone panel. He is shown larger than his disciples below, indicating his importance. His last disciple (centre) sits in meditation as instructed by his Teacher. He is unmoved by the death, while other disciples show signs of emotion. Above the recumbent Buddha is a stupa (suggestive of his death), and – at the very top – celestial musicians play a double-ended drum and cymbals.

Basalt
10th century
Height 58.4 cm
Eastern India
1880.1

2. Standing Vishnu
Vishnu is shown here crowned, as befits the ideal king, and four-armed (the two front arms are damaged). He wears fine jewelry and, hanging to his knees, his *vanamala*, the garland of forest flowers. He is also attended by his two consorts, Sri and Bhu. The intense and luxuriating lotus scrolls, especially around the feet, are typical of Pala sculpture.

Schist, later blackened
11th century
Height 164 cm, width 78 cm
Eastern India
Donated by the Bridge family,
1872,0701.32

3. The crowned Buddha

This majestic image of the standing, crowned and bejeweled Buddha is surrounded by other images reflecting episodes from his life. At his right shoulder is an inscription – the so-called Buddhist creed, a condensed version of the teaching of the Buddha on suffering and its cessation. At bottom left is the prostrate figure of the donor with, below the double-lotus pedestal, a further inscription.

Schist
11th–12th century
Height 195 cm
Bodh Gaya, Bihar
Donated by the Bridge family,
1872,0701.30

3 | 5 Eastern Indian bronzes

From the 9th to the 12th centuries, eastern India (the present-day states of Bihar and Bengal) and today's Bangladesh witnessed a remarkable flowering of bronze image production. Here, in the service of both Buddhism and Hinduism, and during the reigns of the Pala and Sena kings, lost-wax bronze-casters were responsible for producing many outstanding images.

While the historical Buddha appears repeatedly – this is, after all, the land where he conducted his ministry – the majority of sculptures produced were of deities of the Mahayana and Vajrayana pantheons (**1**, **2**). Many of the surviving examples have been preserved because they were small enough to be carried to other centres of Buddhism, such as Nepal, Tibet and then onwards to China, by pilgrims who had visited holy sites such as Bodh Gaya (see p. 126). Thus, far away from their place of production, they were influential in the development of local sculptural styles. Figures are either standing or seated on temple-derived plinths and are imbued with the Gupta idiom along with a svelte beauty often accentuated by the use of inlaid silver (eyes and jewelry) and copper (details of dress).

While Buddhist bronze images predominate, those with Vaishnava subject-matter are also present (**3**, **4**). Some of these were taken to Tibet where they were used in ritual, as is clear from the azure or red powder found in the hair (depending on whether the deity was considered pacific or fearful) and the cold gold found added to the faces. The mere fact that these bronze images came from the land of the Buddha's birth seems sufficient for them to have been cherished and worthy of worship, irrespective of whether they were strictly Buddhist in original affiliation.

1. Avalokiteshvara

The deity depicted in this sculpture is a form of the ever-popular *bodhisattva* of compassion, Avalokiteshvara. He is shown within an architectural frame. The stepped base and the plinth on which the deity sits are mirrored in the outline of the shrine. The presence of blue powder in the hair indicates a post-Indian use, in Tibet.

Gilded bronze with silver inlay
Early 12th century
Height 18 cm, width 9.2 cm
Eastern India
1985,0511.1

2. *Mandala* in lotus form

Inscribed on the base with the name of the layman Dantanaga, this is a three-dimensional form of a sacred diagram, *mandala*. At its centre is the Buddha Akshobhya who, in *mandala* theory, is one of the Buddhas believed to sit in the cardinal directions; he is the Buddha of the East. In Mahayana thought there must be Buddhas prior to the historical Buddha (including these directional Buddhas) just as there will be others in the future. In this fine example of bronze casting the lotus opens and closes and is supported by *naga* figures in the scrollwork below.

Bronze, partially gilded, with silver and copper inlay
12th century
Height 14 cm
Eastern India
1982,0804.1

3. Four-armed Vishnu

The god is presented haloed and standing against a throne-back. The extensive wear from touching demonstrates devotional use over many centuries. The sculpture also indicates the extent of Vaishnava presence east of the Ganges delta, with a distinctive local way of presenting the deity's attributes, the *chakra* (wheel) in his lower right hand and *gada* (staff) in his lower left.

Bronze
9th century
Height 19.5 cm, width 10 cm
Southeastern Bangladesh, perhaps Chittagong
Bequeathed by Dr Alan Taylor, 2014,3025.1

4. Balarama with Ganesha and Lakshmi

This highly elaborate image is built up of five different elements that slot together to make the complete ensemble. Balarama, identified by the plough held at his right shoulder, is usually a less important member of the Vaishnava panoply; here he is at the centre, flanked by major auspicious deities. At some point this sculpture was carried to Tibet, where it had a second life in a Buddhist monastery.

Bronze with silver inlay
12th century
Height 28.5 cm, width 15 cm
Eastern India
1985,0719.1

3 | 6 Medieval Jain goddesses

While the veneration of the Jain *tirthankara* (see p. 46) approaches worship, the fundamental tenets of Jainism eschew such activity – there are, after all, no ultimate deities in this world view. However, early in the history of the religion, a subset of female deities became apparent in the Jain cosmos, recognizably Jain on account of the *tirthankara* figure that is frequently depicted at the top of each sculpture.

These female deities are usually referred to as *yakshi*, an ancient term that indicates their origin in the cult of fertility deities whose appearance in early Buddhism is equally well known. They are associated with fertility, children and prosperity, as well as knowledge. They mostly had a following amongst the laity and are clearly connected with their Hindu namesakes; examples include Ambika (fertility) (**1**) and Sarasvati (wisdom) (**2**). In the medieval period, images of these goddesses in bronze and stone were common. The bronze images were, for the most part, for domestic shrine use (they are small in scale). The stone depictions come from the exterior of Jain temples or from the part-open halls, *mandapa*, that connect the exterior to the recess of the temple where the image of the *tirthankara* was enshrined.

Jainism has flourished in the past in many parts of South Asia, including in central India. Evidence of this comes from Jain rock-cut shrines at Ellora (see p. 123), and also from structural temples at sites such as Khajuraho. A sequence of central Indian sculpted panels depict goddesses, some of whom are still known today (**3**), while others are now unknown (**4**).

1. Ambika

Holding one child in the crook of her left arm and giving a bunch of mangoes, a fruit associated with her, to another, the goddess Ambika embodies maternal and peaceful characteristics. The scroll that forms a frame around her is filled with small figures, while above her, clearly indicating the Jain milieu of this image, is the *tirthankara* Neminatha.

Schist
11th century
Height 47 cm, width 22.9 cm
Orissa
Donated by the Bridge family,
1872,0701.94

2. Sarasvati

As a goddess of wisdom, Sarasvati appropriately holds a palm-leaf manuscript (in her left hand). Jains are renowned for their commitment to learning and images of the Indian goddess of knowledge are frequently found in Jain contexts. Here, the Jain affiliation is made obvious by the presence, above the goddess, of a *tirthankara* seated beneath tiered parasols.

Bronze
10th century
Height 33 cm, width 15 cm
Deccan, probably Karnataka
Donated by P. T. Brooke Sewell,
1957,1021.1

3. Sulochana

Panels of figural sculpture were traditionally placed on the exterior walls of temples, often in series. This example depicts an eight-armed goddess, Sulochana, whose name is inscribed on the base. A *tirthankara* above indicates the Jain affiliation of the figure.

Sandstone
850–900
Height 76.2 cm, width 47 cm
Probably from Gyaraspur, Madhya Pradesh
Donated by the Bridge family, 1872,0701.65

4. Unidentified Jain goddess

With one of her twelve arms this goddess places a *tilak* (religious marking) on her forehead. The triangular mark at the top of the stele probably indicates the former position of a seated *tirthankara*.

Sandstone sculpture
10th century
Height 106.5 cm, width 74 cm
Northern Madhya Pradesh
Donated by the Bridge family, 1872,0701.81

3 | 7 Jainism in western India

The presence of Jains in western India can be documented through bronze and stone sculpture (**3**, **4**), as well as the production of illustrated manuscripts (**1**) and paintings (**2**). Medieval temples survive in Gujarat and Rajasthan, many constructed of white marble, the most renowned being at Mount Abu (11th century and onwards) and Ranakpur (15th century). Images venerated at these temples are often of the same white marble (**4**) and are sometimes today honoured with textile backdrops.

Bronze casting using the lost-wax process became well-developed in western India, along with the inlaying of bronze images with silver and copper (**3**). Since merit was gained through the donation of images, many Jain sculptures bear inscriptions recording the date of the gift and the name of the donor (**4**).

Among Jains, the production of texts has been a religious obligation. This has meant that library stores of manuscripts, *bhandara*, have built up accumulations of illustrated texts. Rare examples from the 12th century survive and are on fragile palm-leaf, the usual material for the earliest Indian manuscripts (see pp. 128–9). More common are those on paper, mostly dating from the 14th century and onwards. Figures are frequently set against a red background; the use of gold and especially blue (from lapis lazuli) being a later feature (**1**). Although paper allowed greater space for text and illumination, Jain manuscripts on paper still followed the long rectangular layout of the palm-leaf examples; sacred precedent was paramount.

Paintings were also made on cloth, some depicting the Jain universe (**2**), while others illustrate pilgrimage, an important aspect of Jain life. A more racey type illustrates the punishments awaiting the sinful in hell.

1. The *Kalpasutra*
This text tells the life story of Mahavira, the last of the *tirthankara*. Typical of Jain paintings of this period is the use of gold and blue, the latter made with lapis lazuli from northeastern Afghanistan. The eye farthest away from the viewer is shown projecting beyond the outline of the face – a distinctive western Indian painting convention (see p. 73).

Painted paper
c. 1500
Height 22.4 cm, width 15.5 cm
Western India, probably Gujarat
Bequeathed by Percy Manuk and Miss G. Coles, through the Art Fund (as NACF), 1948,1009,0.159

2. The mortal realm in *mandala* form
This is the world of humans, as imagined by Jain teachings. Jambudhvipa, 'the island of the rose-apple tree', on which the Indian subcontinent is located, is the middle section, with Mount Meru at the centre. Further out, the yellow circular elements are outer continents separated by a great cosmic sea, containing auspicious symbols and animals.

Painting on cotton
17th or 18th century
Height 104 cm, width 105 cm
Gujarat or Rajasthan
Donated by the Luigi and Laura Dallapiccola Foundation and the Brooke Sewell Permanent Fund, 2002,1019,0.1

3. The *tirthankara* Parshvanatha
Parshvanatha, the penultimate of the twenty-four Jain *tirthankara*, is protected by the hoods of a seven-headed *naga*. Seated below left and right are the *yaksha* Dharanendra and *yakshi* Padmavati; in front are small disembodied heads representing the Nine Planets, *navagraha*, that inform human destiny.

Bronze with silver and copper inlay
Mid-11th century
Height 34 cm
Western India, probably Gujarat
Brooke Sewell Permanent Fund, 1974,0411.1

4. A *tirthankara*
The figure is seated in the lotus position with a prominent *shrivatsa* on his chest. A donor's inscription is incised on the cushion.

White marble
Mid- to late 12th century
Height 68.5 cm
Gujarat
Donated by Sir Alfred Lyall, 1915,0515.1

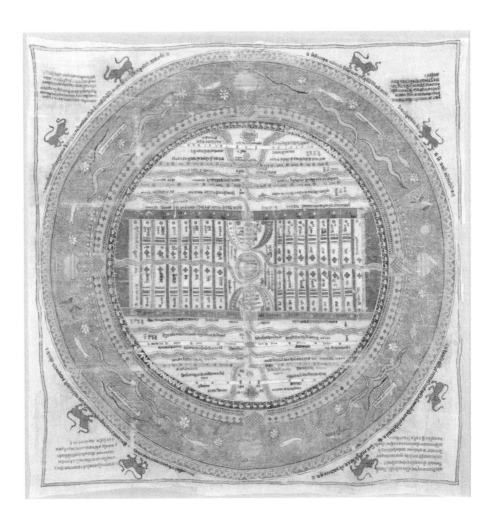

3 | 8 Jainism in southern India

Other than in western India, the main stronghold of Jainism in South Asia has been in the south.

Early legend speaks of a group in the Mauryan period leaving the original Jain heartland of Bihar and moving southwards to avoid famine. Later, in historic times, Jain presence is clear in the physical record. At the 7th-century rock-cut shrine of Sittanavasal in Tamil Nadu, now fragmentary though once extensive wall paintings survive along with sculpture of the *tirthankara*. Also from about this time is evidence from the still-functioning Jain temple in Kanchipuram, which may have been founded in the Pandyan period. Providing a different but contemporary perspective of Jains are the negative views of them found in the poetry of the Tamil Shaiva and Vaishnava saints in the 7th century and onwards (see p. 124).

Today, southern Karnataka is the main Jain stronghold, with its most famous centre of pilgrimage being the monolithic 17.7-m standing figure of the saint Bahubali (sometimes also known as Gommateshvara). Dating from the 10th century, it stands crowning the top of the hill at Shravana Belgola. Every twelve years pilgrims gather in huge numbers and the monolith is ceremoniously lustrated with purifying substances such as milk, saffron and yoghurt (**1**). Jain ascetics, some naked, having shed all attachments (followers of the *digambara* sect), and also clothed monks and nuns (these are the *shvetambara*), come to Shravana Belgola at the time of the great festivals. Another important centre is on the nearby coast at Mudabidri.

Parshvanatha, the twenty-third of the twenty-four *tirthankara*, has been popular in this region and sculptures of him in bronze (**2**) and stone are frequently recorded. Metal diagrams covered with invocations or *yantra* are also used at Jain shrines.

1. Lustration of the figure of Bahubali
The image of Bahubali at Shravana Belgola in Karnataka is venerated at a twelve-yearly festival. As a part of their devotion, pilgrims pour precious substances over it (here, milk). This is the *Mahamastakabhisheka*, and merit is accrued to those who provide for it. In the Jain tradition, Bahubali is the great exemplar of ascetic attachment – he stood still in meditation for so long that vegetation grew around his legs.

2. The *tirthankara* Parshvanatha
Parshvanatha is enthroned beneath his identifying serpent canopy and set against a luxuriant backplate, the arch of which springs from the mouths of *makara*, mythical water monsters. On either side of him are royal fly-whisk holders; below are the *yaksha* Dharanendra (left) and *yakshi* Padmavati (see p. 136).

Bronze
11th century
Height 35.1 cm
Southern Deccan
Donated by Mrs Kenneth Kay,
1936,1219.1

3|9 The Cholas: bronze sculpture

Bronze sculptures from Chola-period south India (9th–13th centuries) are internationally renowned. Drawing on metalworking traditions in the previous Pallava period, but benefitting from the devout and wealthy patronage of the Chola rulers, the metalsmiths of the Thanjavur region of Tamil Nadu brought the production of cast metal sculpture to its finest realization (for bronze casting, see p. 112).

Chola bronze sculptures of deities were mostly not worshipped within the temple sanctum. Dressed and garlanded, they were primarily for parading, either on palanquins or on the top of great chariots dragged through the streets at annual festivals (see p. 146). On such conveyances the god and also their attributes could be viewed; the god was also sometimes accompanied by a consort and children (**1**), or by saints (**3**). In this processional worship, devotees were able to make eye contact with the gods, *darshan*, as well as present their offerings. Through touching and lustration, the surface of the bronzes, which may be brassy or closer to green depending on the history of the image, has often become smoothed (**2**). Some sculptures were buried for safety, the most famous being those found at Tiruvengadu: this hoard contained bronze images now universally acclaimed as the most moving of all sculptures of the Chola period.

Dating these images is based on a few inscriptions, along with a handful of sculptures linked to historical figures. There is, however, a definite chronological connection between Chola bronze and stone images, as well as an assumption that the more austere, undecorated examples are closer to the sculpture of the Pallavas. Recently, the realization that stylistic difference is not only a chronological indicator, but also a feature of regional variation, has become accepted (**4**).

This page
1. Somaskanda group
The term Somaskanda denotes Shiva, his consort Parvati (also known as Uma) and Skanda, her son. The concept of the three deities together in this form is distinctive of the period.

Bronze
c. 1100
Height 48 cm, length 60.5 cm
Thanjavur, Tamil Nadu
Brooke Sewell Permanent Fund, 1984,0403.1

Opposite, left
2. The trident of Shiva
The figure of Shiva leaning against Nandi has been smoothed over centuries of devotional touching. Shiva's trident weapon is believed to cut through the bonds of ignorance.

Bronze (with modern wood)
c. 950
Height 85 cm, width 33.5 cm
Tamil Nadu
Bequeathed by Professor Samuel Eilenberg, 2001,1126.1

Right
3. Chandesha
The saint Chandesha is one
of the *nayanmar* (see p. 124)
and is remembered as a
devout worshipper of Shiva.
His adoration is accentuated by
his hands, which are held in the
anjalimudra gesture (palms
held together).

Bronze
c. 970
Height 48 cm, width 17 cm
Thanjavur region, Tamil Nadu
Donated by Eton College,
1988,0425.1

Below
4. Vishnu with his attributes
Stylistically different from the
bronze images of the Thanjavur
region (compare with Figure 1),
this sculpture is thought to
come from western Tamil Nadu.
The tangs at the side once held
a bronze halo (*prabha*).

Bronze
c. 950
Height 35 cm, width 27.4 cm
Kongu-nadu, western Tamil Nadu
Brooke Sewell Permanent Fund,
1967,1215.1

1. Shiva Nataraja
Shiva, the cosmic dancer,
is surrounded by a flaming
aureole. The goddess Ganga,
the river Ganges, is caught in
his unbound locks on his right
side with her hands together
in adoration.

Bronze
c. 1100
Height 89.5 cm
Tamil Nadu, probably
the Thanjavur area
Brooke Sewell Permanent Fund,
1987,0314.1

2. Shiva Nataraja (detail)
The drum whose sound
produces creation in the
right hand of Shiva.

3. Shiva Nataraja (detail)
The fire of destruction held
in the left hand of Shiva.

Shiva Nataraja

The image of the god Shiva dancing blissfully within a ring of fire is probably the most well-known encapsulation of ideas about Hindu India (**1**). All around the world, sculptures of Shiva Nataraja, 'Lord of the Dance', can be found. The concentration on this icon of the deity is, in part, a legacy of Ananda Coomaraswamy (1887–1947), writer, thinker and artist, born to an English mother and a Sri Lankan Tamil father. His writings, along with those of others such as the French sculptor Auguste Rodin, have ensured the continuing popularity of the form, though it is now clear that Coomaraswamy's is but one of a number of possible interpretations.

Part of the myth behind the image is of cosmic activity. In Indian traditional thought, time is conceived as cyclical, not linear. The image of Shiva Nataraja is imagined as standing at both the end and the beginning of time; he 'dances out' one cycle and 'dances in' the next. Typically for Shiva, he appears at the extremities of time, not in the middle. The destructive and creative elements of this narrative are symbolized by the attributes he holds: fire for destruction in his upper left hand at the end of one cycle (**3**), and the hourglass-shaped drum for creation in his upper right (the sound of which causes creation to commence) (**2**).

This depiction of Shiva was popular in the Chola period (9th–13th centuries) and is associated especially with the temple at Chidambaram in the Chola heartland of the Kaveri delta. The Chidambaram temple greatly benefitted from Chola patronage. At such temples, the verses of the *bhakti* saints (see p. 124), such as the 7th-century poet Appar, are remembered and recited (see p. 145).

The origin of the image of dancing Shiva is unclear. At Elephanta (see p. 122), the island cave shrine in Mumbai harbour, there is a relief panel of this subject dating from the 8th century. However, it seems clear that the concept of Shiva Nataraja in the pose of *anandatandava*, four-armed and with one foot raised across the body, and dancing within an aureole, is a Tamil notion. When it was first produced in bronze is not known, but one example has a good chance to be amongst the earliest (**5**). Metallurgical analysis suggests that this object has much in common with those few bronze sculptures we can associate with the Pallava kings, the rulers who preceded the Cholas. Also, from an iconographic point of view, the sculpture suggests an early date given: the oval rather than circular aureole; the sash at the god's left side, which hangs down rather than flies out to connect with the ring of fire; and the way in which the hair is still contained around the head rather than, again, flying out to connect with the aureole. In addition, the dwarf figure representing ignorance on which the god tramples, is depicted at right angles to the figure rather than in the same plane, as with later images.

The large bronze images of Shiva Nataraja were made for processional use. Later drawings and paintings of Nataraja carried through the streets were made by Indian artists for British visitors. These provided mementoes for those unfamiliar with the tradition in the years before photography (**4**). The large painting illustrated overleaf perhaps shows Shiva Nataraja at Chidambaram itself (**6**).

4. Shiva Nataraja and his devotees in procession

This drawing by an Indian artist for a European client (see p. 146) shows Shiva Nataraja accompanied by his consort Shivakami on a palanquin in the form of a miniature shrine. They are attended by priests with flares, banners, fly-whisks and parasols.

Ink and wash on laid European paper
c. 1820
Height 35.5 cm, width 22 cm
Tamil Nadu, probably Shrirangam
1990,1029,0.4

5. Shiva Nataraja

The depiction of erect feathers in the headdress is an early feature and one also that appears in the hymn praises of early Tamil devotional poetry.

Bronze
800 or a little later
Height 33.5 cm, width 21.5 cm
Tamil Nadu
Brooke Sewell Permanent Fund,
1969,1216.1

**6. Shiva Nataraja
and Shivakami**

In this painting, Nataraja and his
consort Shivakami are depicted
within a shrine, perhaps the
one at Chidambaram; on either
side are priests offering *bilva*
leaves sacred to Shiva (right),
and lamp-offerings of light (left).
This sumptuous realization was
produced with relief decoration,
inlaid coloured glass and gold.

Gouache on cloth, relief-work
and with coloured glass inlay
c. 1800
Height 48.7 cm, width 47.5 cm
Thanjavur, Tamil Nadu
Donated by Mrs J. H. Drake,
1939,0311,0.1

If you could see
the arch of his brow,
the budding smile
on lips as red as the *kovvai* fruit,
cool matted hair,
the milk-white ash on coral skin,
and the sweet golden foot
raised up in dance,
then even human birth on this wide earth
would become a thing worth having.

Appar, 7th century (trans. Indira Peterson)

3 | 10 Shiva as saviour of the universe

This sculpture is one of the finest Chola-period bronzes to survive (**2**).
From a stylistic point of view it is thought to date to about 970 CE. This
would place it in the period in which Chola power was expanding out of
the original heartland around Thanjavur in the delta region of the Kaveri
river; the Cholas were becoming a major political power in the south.

The cosmic narrative behind the sculpture invokes pastoral imagery:
the churning of milk to make butter. The story tells how the gods and the
demons – one at each end – took the cosmic serpent Vasuki and, wrapping
it around Mount Mandara, churned the cosmic ocean. From this churning
came both good and evil elements, the first being a poison that threatened
the very future of the universe. Shiva, acting as saviour of the world, heroically
swallowed it. What we believe is depicted in the bronze image is the very
moment after his ingestion of the noxious liquid. The power of the god
overcomes the evil of the poison, but the taut and drawn-in quality of
Shiva's body gives some idea of the intensity of the struggle.

The plinth on which the god sits and the tangs at the side (these are for
holding in place a now-lost aureole around the sculpture) tell us that this is
an image made specifically to be processed through the streets at festival
time (**1**). The back of the sculpture is almost as beautiful as the front, with
a fan-like array of the god's ringlets across his shoulders and a glorious
wheel ornament, the *siraschakra*, that covers the knot of the headband (**2**).

**1. Shiva and his family
in procession**
Drawings such as this indicate
how bronze images of the gods,
such as Shiva, were paraded
through the streets in the early
19th century. Shiva is depicted
with his consort, Parvati, and
preceding them, their children,
Ganesha (the remover of
obstacles, who should always
go first) and Subrahmanya
(accompanied by his two wives).
For another drawing from the
same sequence, see Figure 4
on p. 144.

Ink and wash on laid
European paper
c. 1820
Height 37.4 cm, width 23.2 cm
Tamil Nadu, probably Shrirangam
1990,1029,0.5

Above and left

2. Shiva Vishapaharana, or 'Shiva who swallows the poison'

This sculpture depicts the god Shiva at the moment of cosmic victory. On the auspicious right side, his lower hand gives the gesture of fearlessness, *abhayamudra* – his devotees are assured and the future of the cosmos is certain. The skill of the metalsmiths in producing an image of this beauty, which includes many backward curving elements into which the molten alloy had to be poured before any of it solidified, is remarkable. The attention that the sculptor has lavished on the reverse (see detail, left), not usually seen in procession, is a token of the devotional quality inherent in its creation. The cascade of ringlets across the shoulders is dramatic and the details of the piled up matted hair, *jata*, are also beautifully articulated.

Bronze
c. 970
Height 58 cm, width 41 cm
Tamil Nadu, probably Thanjavur
Brooke Sewell Permanent Fund,
1970,0921.1

3 | 11 The Cholas: stone sculpture

Temple buildings are one of the most prominent ways in which the Chola kings are still apparent in the south Indian landscape. The size and grandeur of their imperial shrines mark them out when compared with their predecessors. The temple in Thanjavur dedicated to Shiva – the Brihadishvara – was built by Rajaraja I and consecrated in 1010 CE (1). Thanjavur was the Chola capital and is situated in the fertile lands of the Kaveri delta, the heartland of the Chola kingdom. The region boasts many other temples built by the kings of the Chola dynasty, all embellished with stone sculpture of great sophistication. These include the Gangaikondacholapuram temple, which records Chola prowess on the banks of the Ganges, the Airavateshvara temple at Darasuram and parts of the Nataraja temple at Chidambaram (see p. 145); they are all dedicated to Shiva.

The exterior of Chola temples, especially the part which wrapped around the central zone where the deity is enshrined, was the most important space in which the sculptor in stone could display his skills. Here, there are usually two storeys of the building articulated with niches in which sculpture was placed. The sculptural programme displayed the narrative and iconographic variety of the enshrined deity. One of the prominent Shaiva narratives is of the god as *lingodbhavamurti*, demonstrating his superiority over other deities (3). Another important image of Shiva frequently found on the exterior wall of Chola temples is Shiva as teacher, *dakshinamurti* (2).

While the Chola kings were great followers of Shiva, devotion to Vishnu is also evident. Temples decorated with the image of Vishnu, or his *avatara*, are well known.

1. The Brihadishvara temple at Thanjavur
The pyramidal tower of this famous temple rises above the enshrined *linga* within. The niches on the exterior of the first two storeys hold sculptures such as those in Figures 2 and 3.

2. Shiva as a teacher, *dakshinamurti*
Shiva is shown here as a sweet-faced young man teaching his followers, with his lower right hand held out in *abhayamudra*, the gesture of fearlessness. As with depictions of Shiva Nataraja (see p. 142), he rests his foot on a dwarf representing ignorance.

Granite
Mid-10th century
Height 109.2 cm
Central Tamil Nadu
Brooke Sewell Permanent Fund, 1961,0410.1

3. The *lingodbhava* form of Shiva
In this form of the deity, Shiva demonstrates his superiority over both Brahma and Vishnu, emerging from within a *linga* of infinite height and depth. The other two deities had tried to delimit the *linga*, Brahma as a gander, trying to fly to its summit, Vishnu as a boar, trying to reach its base. Both were unsuccessful and had to acknowledge the supremacy of Shiva. Such sculptures, which are both narrative and demonstrations of the god's power, are often seen on the outer face of the shrine of Chola temples dedicated to Shiva.

Granite
c. 900
Height 138 cm, width 42 cm
Tamil Nadu
Donated by P. T. Brooke Sewell, 1955,1018.1

3 | 12 Temple vessels

In both Hindu and Jain temples where images are enshrined, bronze vessels of various types are found; these are used in conducting worship, or *puja*, and are mostly concerned with the provision of gifts to be offered to the god – fragrance (censers), taste (trays to hold fruit), water (bronze vessels) and cool air (fans). Although examples from recent times are well known, those from the medieval period are very rare since they have frequently been melted down and recast – or perhaps plundered (a few survive in hoards of ritual equipment hidden ahead of war).

A censer of 9th–10th century date from Kashmir is known (**2**). It has, perhaps, survived on account of having been buried; this would account for the loss of its (wooden?) handle and also much of the backward-pointing leg of the flying four-armed figure. A later Deccani censer is in the form of a prancing feline (**3**), apparently drawing on the lion imagery used heraldically by the Hoysala dynasty of the southern Deccan in the 12th–13th centuries. A still later and more flamboyant group of peacock censers is associated with the Sultanate states of the Deccan in the 15th–16th centuries (**4**).

Spouted water vessels from the medieval Deccan are satisfying examples of the metalsmith's craft and would have stood on tripods at the entrance to the inner shrine of the temple. The globular and wonderfully tactile quality of the gadrooning on the example shown below make it one of the masterpieces of medieval vessel-making in metal (**1**). The decoration on the tripod is rich in the same leonine imagery seen in the censer described above, and is of an approximately similar date.

This page
1. Ritual ewer and tripod
These temple accoutrements – a spouted water vessel on a tripod – have been variously dated between 1000 CE and about 1325; they were used during image worship in a shrine. The voluptuous but plain gadrooning contrasts with the busy lion imagery of the feet.

Bronze
14th century or earlier
Height 15.3 cm (ewer), 10.9 cm (tripod)
Bijapur region, Karnataka
Donated by Mrs Kenneth Kay, 1936,1219.3 and 4

Opposite, above left
2. Censer in the form of a flying celestial figure
This four-armed bronze figure holds a hinged bowl. Burning incense provided sweet-smelling smoke from a hole in the top of the vessel. The celestial figure has been identified as Pushpadanta, a presenter of floral garlands to Shiva.

Bronze
Late 9th–10th century
Height 19.2 cm
Kashmir
Brooke Sewell Permanent Fund and the Art Fund, 2011,3041.1

Opposite, above right
3. Censer in feline form
Playing with scale was typical of Deccani art – note the elephant under the feline's paw. Previously assumed to be a lion, the beast has tiger stripes across its body, suggesting the metalsmith was uncertain what a lion actually looked like (they are unknown in the wild in the Deccan).

Bronze
11th century
Height 15.9 cm
Southeastern Deccan
Donated by Dr Walter Leo Hildburgh, 1953,0713.15

Right
4. Censer in the form of a peacock

The notion of a peacock grappling with elephants is well known in Deccan visual culture. Here, the body of the bird holds the incense and is pierced to allow smoke to escape. Incense sticks could be added to the upswept tail and the trunk of the left-hand elephant, while the handle at the back enables the priest to offer sweet scent to an enshrined image.

Bronze
16th century
Height 29 cm (max)
Deccan
Donated by Dr Chen Kang Shuen, 1993,1223.1

3 | 13 The Hoysala kings

Major temples associated with the Hoysala kings of southwestern India are located at Belur (amongst these is the Chenna-Keshava temple, completed in 1117) and Halebid (the Hoysaleshvara, begun in 1121). Another impressive temple of the same period is situated further south, at Somnathpur (completed in 1268) (**1**). Stellate plans are common in Hoysala architecture, a feature that produces dazzling architectural complexity.

Remarkable at all three temple sites is the quality of the figural sculpture that decorated their exterior walls (**2**). Gods and goddesses are sculpted almost completely in the round, and clothing, jewelry and crowns are carved with baroque extravagance. This stylistic exuberance is also dramatically pronounced in the trees and creepers, which provide niches for the figures. All these elements are epitomized by the female bracket figures that were placed, at an angle, between the horizontal line of the eaves and the vertical line of the temple wall (**2**). Exceptionally, many sculptures at Hoysala temple sites bear the signatures of individual artists.

The dynasty's royal badge was a lion with one paw raised in defiance (see p. 151, Figure 3), a decorative device that continues in the Deccan for some centuries after the collapse of the Hoysala kings and the emergence of their successors, the Sangama dynasty based further north at Vijayanagara (modern Hampi), on the Tungabhadra river.

1. Somnathpur
Situated in its own courtyard, the temple at Somnathpur is made up of three distinct but joined shrines. It is the latest and perhaps most dramatic of the Vaishnava temples of the Hoysala era. It is renowned for the reliefs on its exterior illustrating scenes from the epics, and the corbelled domes of its interior. The stellate plan is a feature that continues from the temple platform right to the highest element of the buildings.

2. Three female bracket figures

These sculptures are essays in sensuous movement: dance and music are strikingly evoked. One figure plays a drum, while of the other two dancers, one gazes languidly into a mirror. It was from sculptures such as these, along with the study of texts, that dance enthusiasts in the early 20th century came to formalize Indian dance. The Marquess of Dalhousie, Governor-General of India from 1848 to 1856, was probably given these sculptures as gifts; they were acquired by the British Museum from his descendants.

Schist
12th century
Southwestern Karnataka
Height 83.8 cm (above right);
90.4 cm (right and above left)
Brooke Sewell Permanent Fund,
1962,0721.1–3

3 | 14 The Nilgiri hills

The cultural history of the Nilgiri hills in the Western Ghats, today mostly in northwestern Tamil Nadu, provides a fascinating opportunity to study how a remote upland area maintained relations with the settled cultures of the plains. Densely forested, the Nilgiris were peopled by non-caste groups, including the peoples known as the Toda. These groups seem to have gathered forest products such as spices, cane, medicinal plants, gems, honey and hardwoods, trading them with the inhabitants of the plains. An inscription of the 12th-century Hoysala ruler Vishnuvardhana confirms that contacts existed between the plains and the hills and that the former tried to control the latter. From this we can speculate as to whether a theoretical system can be suggested for similar areas where so-called tribal groups came into contact with more settled, urban cultures.

The Nilgiris are also renowned for their hilltop tombs, often set within stone circles; some of these were excavated during the British period, importantly by the scholar/administrator Sir Walter Elliot. They were assumed to be prehistoric but are now thought to date to the 1st millennium CE, not least on account of the range of grave-goods found in them. These include high-tin bronze bowls with central knobs (1), gold jewelry (2) and a bronze mirror of unknown provenance along with unusually shaped iron swords. Along with these elite items – presumably imports – were ceramics of a distinctive kind. The fabric is rough and the shapes include many examples of tiered bowls with lids topped by animals or, on occasions, humans (3). While not technically sophisticated, these sculptures are lively and attractive; the vessels were apparently cinerary urns.

1. Bronze bowl

On account of their sophisticated production, bowls such as this one are considered imports when found in the tombs of the Nilgiri hills; however, it is unclear where they were made. Knobbed vessels of the 1st century CE are known from Taxila, far to the northwest, but few other comparisons exist.

Cast bronze
Mid-1st millennium CE
Nilgiri hills, Tamil Nadu
Height 4.7 cm, diameter 14.1 cm
Bequeathed by James Breeks, 1879,1201.3

2. Gold jewelry

These three items all come from burials excavated and published by Sir Walter Elliot. Like the knobbed bronze bowls (Figure 1), they are assumed to be greatly valued imports into the highland area of the Nilgiri hills, traded in return for forest products.

Gold and (circular item) also coloured stone
Probably first half of 1st millennium CE
Nilgiri hills, Tamil Nadu
Height 3.5 cm (left), 3 cm (right); diameter 2.5 cm (centre)
Donated by Sir Walter Elliot, 1886,0515.3, 10, 6

3. Cinerary urns

Many of the tiered vessels used for burial of funerary ashes in the Nilgiri hills have animal or human figures as terminals. The example on the left here has a buffalo terminal, which may be linked to the later cult importance of the animal in Toda society. The lid on the right features a human figure.

Earthenware
Mid-1st millennium CE
Height 39.5 cm (left), 22.8 cm (right)
Nilgiri hills, Tamil Nadu
Donated by James Wilkinson Breeks, 1879,1201.9; 1880.459

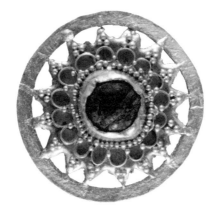

3 | 15 Temple sculpture of Orissa

The kings of the Eastern Ganga dynasty in the 12th and 13th centuries patronized a remarkable temple-building programme in coastal Orissa. A feature of these temples is the towering *shikhara* (the superstructure above the shrine), as can still be seen at Bhuvaneshvar (the Lingaraja temple) and Puri (the Jagannatha temple, p. 164). A massive example can now only be imagined at Konarak, where the lower structure survives but the *shikhara* has collapsed.

The sculptors of Orissa developed a style mostly devoted to depicting Hindu deities (in northern Orissa, Buddhism continued at sites such as Ratnagiri, but this was exceptional). Orissa sculpture is remarkable for its deeply cut imagery and dense figuration usually arranged around larger, central – and thus most important – figures. In the example illustrated here (**3**), the god Shiva is accompanied by his consort Parvati while at the base are the vehicles, *vahana*, of the two deities: the bull of Shiva, Nandi, and the lion of Parvati (more usually seen as the support for Parvati's fierce form, Durga). Also visible are items needed in temple worship: a tripod, a censer and a conch-shell trumpet as well as a diminutive depiction of the son of Parvati, Ganesha. The elephant-headed god was also depicted in Orissa in the medieval period, including in a five-headed form (**1**). Where many such sculptures were placed on temples is not always clear. However, we know that auspicious sequences depicting the planets (**2**) were placed over temple door lintels.

1. Ganesha
This rare depiction of five-headed Ganesha, along with his consort, suggests that it came from a context in which tantric practices were prevalent. His pose, with one leg stepping down, implies his ability to respond in the world of his devotees.

Schist
13th century
Height 101.6 cm, width 54.6 cm
Coastal Orissa, perhaps Konarak
Donated by the Bridge family,
1872,0701.60

2. Rahu, the eclipse
This depiction comes from a sequence of the Nine Planets, or *navagraha*. Here Rahu – considered a planetary body – is represented.

Schist
13th century
Height 99 cm
Orissa
Donated by the Church
Missionary Society, 1951,0720.2

3. Shiva and Parvati
The heavenly couple are seated within a trilobed arch. A host of divine musicians above play flutes, cymbals and drums; garland-bearers and fly-whisk holders are also part of this royal setting. At the base of the double-lotus throne, donors feature on both sides, while at the bottom left are eight lines of text still just visible; an inscription was begun but never completed.

Schist
12th–13th century
Height 184.2 cm, width 119.4 cm
Coastal Orissa
Donated by the Bridge family,
1872,0701.70

3 | 16 Nepal

The state of Nepal lies to the north of the plains of India and includes the foothills of the Himalayas and also some of the highest mountains in the world. Historically, the most important zone of the country was the Kathmandu valley. Here, a vibrant culture based on both Buddhism and Hinduism has flourished from the late centuries BCE, based on its location on the route between India and Tibet. The valley has been an important zone for the survival of Indian art styles, sometimes long after they have been superseded in India. A case in point is the continuation there of Buddhist manuscript production in the 12th-century eastern Indian style (on palm-leaf and within wooden coverboards; see pp. 128–9).

Stupas and tiered wooden temples are the most obvious architectural components of the Kathmandu valley, the most famous of the former still surviving today being the Svayambhunath and Bodhnath stupas. Bodhnath has been a market as well as a place of pilgrimage, being especially popular with visitors from Tibet. Stone sculpture from both Buddhist and Hindu structures is well known from around the 7th century onwards (**1**). While sculptures in stone, ivory and wood were produced in the valley, it is really bronze casting – of figured sculpture, religious equipment and vessels – in which the original inhabitants of Kathmandu, the Newaris, excelled. Their skills have been in demand all over the Himalayas and into Tibet. Buddhist sculptures from the 10th century onwards (**3**) demonstrate Newar craftsmanship as do repoussé backplates (**4**) and spouted ewers used in *puja*. Painting on cloth, *paubha* (**2**), and on wooden book covers has a long history in Nepal in the service of both Hinduism and Buddhism.

1. The standing Buddha
The serene beauty of this image of the Buddha, with its large, downward gazing eyes and oversized right hand making the gesture of boon-granting, recalls the earlier Gupta style from sites such as Sarnath (see p. 78). At the base, below a donor figure, is an inscription in which the merit gained from commissioning the sculpture is dedicated to several beneficiaries.

Schist
7th–8th century
Height 62 cm
Nepal
Brooke Sewell Permanent Fund,
1966,0217.2

2. *Mandala*
The popular goddess Vasudhara is able to convey wealth, both monetary and agriculturally (in one hand she holds a head of ripe rice). In the *mandala* (see p. 160) she appears at the centre surrounded by her entourage. At each cardinal point

is a guarded gateway into her realm. The sinuous scrollwork seen between the two square elements of the inner part of the *mandala* are features of late Indian Buddhist painting that spread to Tibet from Nepal.

Painting on cloth
1504 (dated by inscription)
Height 115 cm, width 86 cm
(whole textile)
Kathmandu valley, Nepal
Donated by Sir Herbert
Thompson, 1933,0722,0.1

3. Vajrasattva, 'he whose being is unbreakable'

Whether as the primordial figure at the centre of a *mandala*, or depicted singly as a *bodhisattva*, Vajrasattva carries the thunderbolt, *vajra*, in his right hand and the bell, *ghanta*, in his left. The regal stature of this Newari sculpture is completed by the three-leafed crown with fluttering terminals.

Gilded bronze
15th century
Height 44.5 cm
Kathmandu valley, Nepal
Donated by Mrs Griffith,
1932,0211.4

4. Backplate

This backplate is missing the image for which it was made, but shows the high relief repoussé for which the Newari metalsmiths of the Kathmandu valley were renowned. The Garuda figure at the apex of the plate and the florid mythical water monster, *makara*, are typical of later Nepalese work.

Bronze, gilded and painted; worked in the repoussé technique
Previously dated to the 19th century, but perhaps as early as 1500
Height 52.8 cm, width 44.8 cm
Newari craftsmanship, but acquired in Tibet
1905,0519.96

3 | 17 *Yantra, mantra* and *mandala*

The terms *yantra*, *mantra* and *mandala* are found in all three ancient religions of South Asia. *Yantra* and *mandala* are conceived two-dimensionally, while *mantra* is imagined in space – it is sound, and specifically sacred sound. In ancient speculation, it is often sound that causes creation, as in the sounding of Shiva's drum which brings each new cycle into being (see p. 143). Correctly articulated sound is believed to have inherently creative and protective power. Thus, in Hinduism, Jainism and Buddhism, enunciations of specific sounds, *mantras*, are connected with individual deities and are believed to be beneficial, even if, as is usually the case, they have no obvious meaning; they are sound alone. The most well-known of these *mantras* is 'Om', frequently found at the beginning of invocations.

Yantras are designs in which sound is encapsulated through writing (**1, 2**). They are, however, more specifically designs that are used in *puja* to invoke the deity to be present. They are often realized as metal plates, usually circular or triangular, with *mantras* engraved on them specific to an individual deity. The triangular *yantra* are usually part of the ritual for a goddess, the shape being an approximation of female genitalia.

Mandalas are two-dimensional and thought of as the habitation of deities into which the divine force can be encouraged to enter. The most frequently seen *mandalas* are painted (**3**). They were especially prominent in late Indian and then Tibetan Buddhism, as aids for meditation. However, in Cave 12 at Ellora a three-dimensional *mandala*, with a central Buddha figure surrounded by *bodhisattvas* in a rectangular grid, was carved in the 8th century.

1. *Yantra*
The lotus-petal imagery and the central triangle in the design of this *yantra* indicates its use in rituals to invoke a goddess. The different surfaces are covered in short texts, *mantra*, used in the invocation. Equidistant along each side of the square in which the design is set are the gateways into the palace realm of the goddess (see Figure 3 for similar).

Bronze
19th century or earlier
Height 19.4 cm, width 19.3 cm
Nepal
Donated by Sir Augustus
Wollaston Franks, 1894,0520.14

2. Jain *yantra*

At the centre of this large circular *yantra* is a powerful sequence of syllables written as a single unit. They are the *mantra* 'hrim'. In meditation, such *mantras* are considered efficacious when concentrating on the *tirthankara*. Triangles, circles and lotus petals filled with inscribed *mantra*, here make up a potent scheme.

Inscribed copper
Western India
Diameter of complete
object 41 cm
1631, dated by inscription
1880.4057

3. *Mandala* of the Buddhist deity Samvara

Paintings on cloth in the Tibetan tradition are generically known as *thang-ka*; this example, more specifically, is a *mandala*. At the centre is the deity Samvara, a form of the Buddha Akshobhya, who, in the cosmic *mandala*, sits in the East. Samvara is shown embracing his wisdom-partner. In the repeating circles of the central element are members of the deity's entourage, all set within the gated walls of the divine palace.

Painting on cloth
1861, dated by inscription
Width *c*. 44 cm (area shown)
Nepal
Donated by Louis Clarke,
1961,1014,0.7

1. Page from an illustrated manuscript of the *Bhagavata Purana*

Krishna, shown blue-skinned, appears in both registers speaking to the cow-herders of Vrindavan, the area on the banks of the Yamuna where he performed his youthful exploits. The text appears on the reverse (see also p. 215, Figure 2).

Opaque watercolour on paper
c. 1525
Height 18.1 cm, width 23.9 cm
Uncertain, but probably around Mathura, or further south
Brooke Sewell Permanent Fund, 1958,1011,0.4

2. Hanuman

The simian features of the fierce hero Hanuman are in contrast to the hands held in the posture of adoration, *anjalimudra*. This is the position of *bhakti*, in which the devotee surrenders everything in the presence of the divine.

Granite
17th century
Height 145 cm, width 45 cm
South India
1880.298

3. The Chishti shrine at Ajmer

This popular print depicts the tomb-shrine of the famous Sunni teacher and mystic, Moinuddin Chishti (1143–1236) in Ajmer, Rajasthan; it is an important centre of devotional pilgrimage to all comers.

Chromolithograph
20th century
Height 35.1 cm, width 49.3 cm
Printed in Delhi
Gift of Claudio Moscatelli in memory of Nicholas Owston, 2016,3051.1

Bhakti

A feature of South Asian religious activity over the last thousand years – especially present in Hinduism but also noticeable in Sikhism, Islam and Christianity – is the notion of *bhakti*, a Sanskrit word suggesting absolute love for, and total devotion to, the deity. In the Hindu imagination, Hanuman, the ally and companion of Rama (see pp. 86–9), is the quintessence of this selfless devotion (**2**). His union of heroic strength and compassionate love is characteristic of the *bhakti* saints. These features – strength and love – are demonstrated in the story in the Ramayana of how he brings the mountain of healing herbs from the Himalayas to wounded Lakshmana.

The origins of *bhakti* are doubtless to be found in south India amongst the Tamil saints (see p. 124). Sometimes this poetry suggests that the devotee is the lover of the deity and the outpouring of devotion is filled with a mixture of chiding, separation and yet-to-be delivered fulfilment. The cults of the Hindu deities, especially Shiva and Vishnu, triumphed in the south at the expense of Buddhism and Jainism, previously both influential, but both lacking the abandonment to the deity that is found in *bhakti*.

An important text in the development of *bhakti* was the *Bhagavata Purana*, probably composed in southern India in the 10th century, and under the influence of the earlier cults of the saints. It tells of the beautiful young god Krishna (see p. 165, Figure 3), whose cult in the 2nd millennium has been of such importance throughout South Asia, and beyond (**1**). The deeds of Krishna and the intense longing for communion with him has inspired many poets in the *bhakti* tradition, such as Chaitanya, Mirabai and Shankaradeva.

Bhakti is also seen in the worship of other deities, such as: Shiva (venerated by the Kannada poet Basava, who founded the *Lingayat* sect in the 12th century); Vishnu (sung of by the 17th-century saint

Tukaram, a devotee of the god in his form as Vithoba, at Pandhapur); and Kali (adored and written about in verse by the 18th century Bengali ecstatic, Ramprasad Sen).

Running through the songs of the *bhakti* poets is the idea that access to God, however the divine is imagined, is available to all. There is an implicit – sometimes explicit – denial of the need for a brahmin intermediary in the search for a personal relationship with God. In addition, there is a negation of caste structure – some *bhakti* saints were from low-caste families, and they invariably placed the love of God above caste position. A final element is the use of the vernacular, whether it was Kannada (the language of Karnataka) in the verses of Basava, Marathi (in Maharashtra) in the case of Tukaram, or Bengali in the case of Ramprasad Sen. For each of these poets, the immediacy of their own vernacular, as opposed to the rule-bound nature of Sanskrit, allowed beneficial contact with their audience.

Although *bhakti* is primarily a manifestation of Hinduism, the implicit equality of man before God highlighted in Islam was attractive to Hindu devotees moving away from ritualized, temple-based activity towards a closer personal devotion. This allowed a devotional cross-over, especially at the popular level, between the cults of Hindu and Muslim saints, demonstrated in Mughal paintings where ascetics of all religious types are depicted receiving veneration from devotees. The Muslim saints, especially those belonging to *sufi* orders such as the Sunni Chishti or the Shi'a Qalandari, still receive devotion from all comers at their *dargahs*, or tomb-shrines, whether the pilgrims are Muslim or Hindu. Perhaps the most famous are the two Chishti shrines at Ajmer in Rajasthan (**3**) and Nizamuddin Auliya in Delhi (see p. 11).

3 | 18 Krishna as Lord of the World

The origins of the Jagannatha temple at Puri on the coastal belt of Orissa are unknown. What is certain, though, is that the imagery of Krishna, accompanied by his brother Balabhadra and his sister Subhadra, is unusual (**1**). Also clear is that, by the 12th century, the temple had become not only a local shrine but also a dynastic centre for the rulers of the Eastern Ganga dynasty.

At Puri, Krishna is worshipped as Jagannatha, the Lord of the World. Perhaps indicating a forest and tribal origin of the cult, the images of the three gods are renewed periodically, with expeditions made to the interior to choose carefully assessed wood from which new images are made. Throughout central India, forest deities are often represented as standing wooden pillars with few human characteristics. The so-called Puri Triad may thus have been such a deity, devotion to which has been slowly assimilated into orthodox temple practice and imagined in increasingly human form.

Puri is also important as a pilgrimage centre, since it is one of the four imagined points that mark out the limits of sacred India, the *dhama*. Puri is the eastern point amongst these; the others are Dwarka (west), Badrinath (north) and Rameshvaram (south). Consequently, images of the Puri temple are known throughout India (**2**).

Pilgrims also come to Puri because, according to tradition, it was here that the 12th-century poet Jayadeva wrote his *Gitagovinda* ('the Love Song of the Dark Lord') (**3**). Verses from this passionate evocation of the love between Radha and Krishna are still sung daily at the Jagannatha temple in Puri. This connection with Jayadeva is also why the Bengali saint Chaitanya (*c.* 1486–1533) settled here in the later part of his life, close to Krishna and to his devotees. His legacy, both in India and internationally, is still very apparent in the worldwide cult of Krishna devotion.

1. The Puri Triad
Krishna (black-bodied) and Balabhadra stand with Subhadra between them. They have been replicated in many different media, including stone, wood, bronze and clay; there are also printed and painted depictions. Most are small and easy for pilgrims to carry away and are consequently found throughout India. The example here is part of a group of clay figures, probably made for an international exhibition in London in the late 19th century.

Painted clay, on a straw armature
19th century
Height 44 cm, width 56 cm
West Bengal, probably from Krishnanagar
1894,0216.7

2. The temple at Puri

In its colouration, small scale and subject, this painting is typical of the Puri style. Carried away by a pilgrim, it can provide *darshana* ('beneficial view') far from the temple. It shows the building in plan (the square outline), in section (the gods are visible in the centre), in profile (the tower of the temple rises above the gods) – and mythically (the temple is believed to be located 'within the conch-shell of Vishnu', the red line that runs around the temple).

Varnished paint on cotton
19th century or earlier
Height 37 cm, width 71.3 cm
Puri, Orissa
1880,0.301

3. Page from an illustrated manuscript of the *Gitagovinda*

The blue-skinned god, handsome young Krishna, plays the flute amongst the flowering trees of the forest. On either side are two *gopi*, female devotees, swooning at their proximity to him. Below are flowering trees filled with bees, while at the top is the Sanskrit verse from the *Gitagovinda* that is illustrated.

Paint on paper
18th century
Height 24.5 cm, width 15.2 cm
Coastal Orissa
1947,0412,0.2

3 | 19 Krishna textiles from Assam

In South Asia the making of beautiful textiles for religious use – for veneration or in ritual – has a long history. One of the most remarkable types to survive is the so-called Vrindavani Vastra, from Assam; the name means 'the cloth of Vrindavan' (the forest country where Krishna is believed to have spent his youth). A number of these woven silk textiles have survived (**2**). It seems that their survival is due, almost without exception, to the cold climate of Tibet where many of them were traded, perhaps in the 18th century.

The complex technique used to weave these cloth, known as *lampas*, enables two warps and two wefts to be woven at once, allowing a foreground (usually a figure, or text) and a background to be woven at the same time (**3**). The scenes from the life of Krishna depicted on these woven cloths include his vanquishing of the serpent-demon Kaliya, the hiding of the clothes of his female devotees, the *gopis*, and his defeat of the crane-demon Bakashura. Demonstrating extraordinary skill, captions were woven into the cloth as well as, on one cloth, eleven lines of text from the religious drama *Kali-daman*, which tells the story of Krishna's defeat of the demon Kaliya (see top register of **2**). This drama – amongst many others – was written by the great Assamese teacher of Krishna devotion, Shankaradeva (d. 1568). It is still performed, some of it with masked actors, in the monasteries on Majuli, an island in the Brahmaputra river (**1**). Each strip of woven cloth may have been used to wrap a manuscript, in the case of the one with the quotation, perhaps the drama *Kali-daman* itself.

1. Mask of Bakashura
In the Krishna-centred drama of Assam, *bhaona*, great effort is lavished on the masks worn by the demons. Here the crane-demon Bakashura has articulated jaws which enable the monk-actor to play the fool, trying to grab other members of the cast with his long beak.

Painted cotton cloth on substrate of woven split bamboo
2015
Height 25.2 cm, width 21 cm
Made in the workshop of Hemchandra Goswami at Samaguri monastery, Majuli, Assam
Luigi and Laura Dallapiccola Foundation, 2015,3041.5

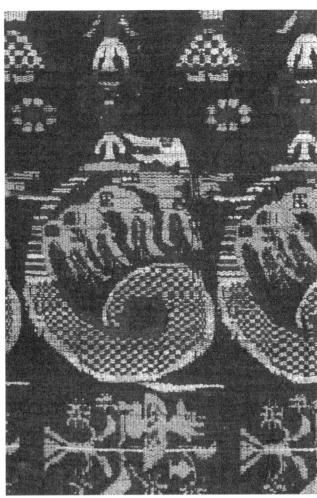

2. Vrindavani Vastra textile

Strips of textile such as this were woven with scenes from the life of Krishna, or the *avatara* of Vishnu. Some were sold or taken to Tibet; in this case they were stitched together as wall-hangings, with Chinese silk brocade added at the top. The section of Vrindavani Vastra illustrated here depicts: a panel of text from the drama, the *Kali-daman* (top register), Garuda, Krishna and the *gopi*, and Krishna's defeat of the serpent- and crane-demons (Kaliya and Bakashura).

Lampas woven silk
17th century
Width of area shown *c.* 80 cm
Lower Assam
Donated by Perceval Landon,
As 1905,0118.4

3. Krishna defeating Kaliya, the serpent-demon

In this close-up of another strip of the British Museum Vrindavani Vastra textile, the *lampas* technique is demonstrated – the brown background is woven with one set of warp and weft, while the figure of Krishna dancing on the head of defeated Kaliya is woven with another one.

3 | 20 Christianity in South Asia

Christianity in the subcontinent has a long history, probably from the mid-4th century. Indeed, tradition associates the Apostle Thomas with first bringing the Gospel to the Kerala coast, where Christians still claim him as their own. The liturgy in use in southern India is the Syriac one and contact is still close between the various Christian groups of Kerala and other churches of the East. Indications of the early presence of these Christian groups is clear from inscriptions in churches in Pahlavi script and the distinctive floriated crosses which are part of the early tradition (**1**).

The arrival of the Portuguese on this southern coast from 1498 eventually changed Christian practice. Conversion of both Hindus and indeed local Christians to Catholicism meant that Christianity flourished in its Roman guise wherever the Portuguese settled, above all in Goa and on the coast around Bombay. Images of Christ (**2**) and of the saints, especially those associated with the evangelization of the East, such as St Francis Xaxier, have become popular (he is buried in Goa, see p. 226). Ivory was often used in the production of Christian imagery, with one of the distinctive image-types being the Good Shepherd. In the example illustrated here (**3**), sculptors used the elongated shape of the elephant tusk to fashion a highly individual image.

As Europeans moved to the court of the Mughal rulers in Delhi, lured there by trade, imagery of a Christian nature travelled with them. The interest expressed in Christianity at Akbar's court – witnessed by paintings from the Mughal atelier (**4**) – led some Europeans to look for conversions. However, this was due to a mistaken understanding of the intellectual curiosity evident at the court, where members of royalty were equally intrigued by other religious systems.

This page
1. The church of the Holy Virgin Mary, Kottayam Valiyappally
Crosses with inscriptions in the Pahlavi script of pre-Islamic Iran substantiate Christian presence on the Kerala coast from at least the 6th century.

Opposite, above left
2. Ivory plaque
The Christ Child is shown in the Ship of Salvation, imagined as a European vessel. Goa was well-known for ivory carving, and the portability of such items explains their wide distribution.

Ivory
Early 17th century
Height 13 cm, width 9.8 cm
Goa
Brooke Sewell Permanent Fund, 1959,0721.1

Opposite, right
3. Christ the Good Shepherd
Christ is depicted as a young man surrounded by his flock. At the base is the recumbent Mary Magdalene.

Ivory
Early to mid-17th century
Height 23.1 cm
Goa
1856,0623.161

Opposite, below left
4. The Crucifixion
Jesuit priests brought European prints to the courts of the early Mughal emperors. Artists copied the subject matter and used European techniques to show volume and distance, but in an entirely Mughal manner.

Ink, gouache and gold on paper
c. 1590
Height 29.3 cm, width 17.7 cm
Perhaps by the painter Keshu Das
Brooke Sewell Permanent Fund, 1983,1015,0.1

1. Gazi *pir* riding a tiger

The saint, or *pir*, who carries
a string of beads in his right
hand, rides fearlessly, his power
emphasized by the deadly cobra
he holds as a sceptre in his left
hand. This saint clearly controls
the most dangerous elements of
the natural world. With its bold
colouring and complex design,
this register, one of 53 from a
Bengal storytelling scroll, is one
of the finest examples of its type
(see also p. 237, Figure 2).

Paint on paper (now mounted
on cloth)
c. 1800
Height 38 cm, width 36.5 cm
(entire scroll is 13 m long)
Bengal, probably the Sunderbans
The Art Fund (as NACF),
1955,1008,0.95

Animals of the forest: tiger, elephant and peacock

Tigers are still found in South Asia, but only in small numbers. They are limited to the Ganges delta region, and to a handful of reserves in India, Bhutan and Nepal. The figures are low and habitat loss everywhere is a major concern, as is poaching fuelled by the mistaken view in Chinese medicine that the animal's powdered bones can cure ailments.

However, the tiger has an important cultural history in the subcontinent. This ferocious feline has always been viewed as near-impossible to tame, so it is only exceptional individuals, such as the Muslim saint of eastern Bengal, Gazi, who can ride a tiger (1). It was through his control of wild animals that the settlement of the dense forests of the Sunderbans – the delta region of the Ganges-Brahmaputra – was possible. In Hindu tradition, it is the goddess Ambika who rides on a tiger, reflecting her power over the natural world.

It is this power that is again invoked in the use of the tiger's skin as a seat for ascetics. And combining all the tiger elements in a politically astute way was the Tiger of Mysore, Tipu Sultan (see p. 238).

The Indian elephant has had a long history of interaction with humans. The power of the wild animal has ensured its appearance in literature, art and religion; over all, the symbolism is positive, regal and, on occasion, erotic. Elephants appear early in the record (see pp. 24, 40) and elephant tusks have been used to make ivory items since prehistory, when elephants roamed the forests of the Indus Valley (see p. 27). In early history, the link with royalty begins (4).

Ganesha, the elephant-headed deity, is the Lord of Beginnings, as well as the Placer and – if appeased – the Remover of Obstacles. In temples, elephants attend on the god and in Sri Lanka an elephant still carries the Tooth Relic of the Buddha in the annual Perahera Procession.

In literature, the clouds of the monsoon are likened in their size and colouring to the behemoths of the forest. This equivalence is seen further in the elephants who purify the goddess Lakshmi with revivifying water (5). Elephants are also traditionally the means by which royalty show themselves to their subjects. This ancient tradition linking the king of the jungle and the king in his palace was still understood when the Viceroy of India, Lord Curzon, processed on elephant-back at the 1901 Delhi Durbar, using the old Mughal court ceremonial, or *darbar*, to present himself to the people. The elephant is the quintessence of royalty: strong, huge and irresistible.

The flashy plumage of the male peacock, displayed as he attempts to win the attention of the peahen, has become linked especially with two of the gods of Hinduism. These are Krishna, who jauntily wears a peacock feather in his headband, and Karttikeya the son of Shiva who was mothered by the Pleiades, the Krittika (hence his name). The mount that ever-youthful Karttikeya rides is a peacock (2, 3) whose colourful display is typical of the impetuous god. The coinage of the 5th-century Gupta king, Kumaragupta I, bore the image of the displaying peacock, which is a play on the king's name, as Kumara is a synonym of Karttikeya. Similarly ostentatious is the way the young Krishna wears a feather of the strutting peacock in his headband during his erotic escapades in the forests of Vrindavan.

The famously bejeweled throne of the Mughals – the Peacock Throne – ended its days in Tehran after the Sack of Delhi by Nadir Shah in 1739. More mundanely, fans from all parts of the subcontinent have been made from peacock feathers.

2. Karttikeya on his peacock mount

Around the youthful martial god's neck is a chain set with tiger claws, denoting bravery.

Basalt
7th–8th century
Height 58 cm, width 40.5 cm
Eastern India, perhaps eastern Uttar Pradesh
Donated by the Bridge family, 1872,0701.66

3. Karttikeya on his peacock mount

This small carving (shown front and back) of the son of Shiva on his beautiful peacock vehicle was discovered in Khotan (present-day China), offering evidence of commerce between Indian merchants and their Central Asian counterparts on the far side of the Karakoram mountains.

Carved and gilded agalmatolite (a type of soapstone)
8th century
Height 6.4 cm
Northwestern India, perhaps Kashmir
Donated by Sir Clarmont Skrine, 1925,0619.40

4. Two silver roundels

The lively depiction of these silver elephant plaques marks them out as the products of accomplished metalsmithing using the repoussé technique. Their probable source in the northwest of the subcontinent suggests the habitat of elephants was much further north and west than it is today.

Silver
2nd century BCE
Diameter 7.5 cm (left),
7.1 cm (right)
Northwestern India
Donated by M. Longworth
Dames, 1937,0319.6, 5

5. Lakshmi lustrated by elephants

Lakshmi, the goddess of good fortune sits on an open lotus blossom and is bathed by elephants, all symbolic of prosperity to come.

Gouache on paper
1700–15
Height 22.9 cm,
width 27.7 cm
Bundi, Rajasthan
1956,0714,0.32

Timeline

1192–1193	The Ghorid (Afghan) conquest of north India and the capture of Delhi
1197	The Quwwat ul-Islam mosque constructed in Delhi
1206	The construction of the Qutb Minar begun
1336	The foundation of the Vijayanagara empire in southern India
1338	Foundation of the sultanate of Bengal
1469	Guru Nanak, religious teacher, born
1478	Birth of Vallabhacharya, religious teacher
Early 16th century	Chaitanya, Bengali Krishna devotee flourishes
1450–1526	The Lodi dynasty, the last of the sultans of Delhi
1489–1512	The Deccan Sultans are established as the Bahmani Sultanate collapsed
1526–1530	Babur, the first Mughal emperor, rules
1556–1605	Reign of Mughal emperor Akbar
1565	The battle of Talikota and sack of Vijayanagara
1568	Death of Shankaradeva, religious teacher in Assam
1590–1624	The painter Mansur flourishes
1601	The East India Company is founded in London
1605–1627	Reign of Mughal emperor Jahangir
1627	Shivaji, leader of the Marathas, born; d. 1680
1627–1658	Reign of Mughal emperor Shah Jahan
1632–1643	Construction of the Taj Mahal by Shah Jahan
1658–1707	Reign of Aurangzeb, last major Mughal ruler
1666	Birth of Guru Gobind Singh, 10th Sikh guru

4 Deccan sultans, Mughal emperors and Rajput kings

Late 12th–18th centuries

Islam arrived in South Asia early in its history, with excavated evidence from Banbhore in Sindh (in present-day Pakistan) for the foundations of a mosque dated by inscription to 728. Gujarat and Kerala, regions connected with the western sea-borne trade, were also early locations of Islamic presence, with Bhadreshvar in Kutch (western Gujarat) being the site of the earliest still-surviving mosque in South Asia, dated by inscription to 1160. This small mosque was built with a corbelled dome and lotus decoration in local Jain style.

In the early 11th century, Islam had made itself known in a more forceful way when the Afghan ruler, Mahmud of Ghazni, entered the plains of India from eastern Afghanistan, seeking booty rather than trade. It was, however, almost two centuries later before groups – mostly Afghans and Turks – succeeded in defeating Rajput rulers. They established a state centred on Delhi, and controlled much of northern India. Over the next 200 years, mosques, tombs and fortifications were built. In Delhi the sultans constructed their first mosque, the Quwwat ul-Islam (1197), using columns and other features from dismantled Hindu and Jain temples. Nearby, but slightly later in date, they built a great tower of victory, the Qutb Minar, the decoration of which set a new precedent, employing not only well-understood Indian motifs (pearled bands, open lotus blossoms and vegetal scrolls) but also Arabic calligraphy. The combination of natural forms and calligraphy proved to be a rich decorative vein in India in the succeeding centuries.

The Turkic and Afghan sultans of Delhi, although argumentative amongst themselves (there were four dynasties of rulers from 1206, ending with the Lodi kings in 1526), nevertheless maintained their rule in northern India; there were other, separate sultanates including those established in Bengal to the east and in Gujarat to the west. The latter two states had their capitals at Gaur/Pandua in northern Bengal, and at Ahmedabad. At the former, many ruined brick buildings with basalt stone facings and glazed tile decoration still give an idea of the original grandeur (see p. 182), while in Ahmedabad (and nearby Champaner), fine mosques built in a distinctive style give a clear indication of the wealth of the

rulers (1). In the Deccan, the upland region to the south of the Vindhya mountains, following what were initially booty raids by the Delhi sultans, other Muslim rulers – the Bahmani sultans – established themselves from the mid-14th to the early 16th centuries. They controlled much of this region, but following war with the Vijayanagara kingdom to the south, the Bahmani state collapsed and a series of smaller sultanates were established. The Vijayanagara kings went on to control most of southern India (2), but it was the sultanate rulers to the north who, in 1565 at the battle of Talikota, caused the fall of their kingdom.

While the Mughal emperors are the most well known of the Muslim rulers of India – the most famous Indian building, the Taj Mahal, was built by a Mughal emperor (3) – they did not appear in the subcontinent until the 16th century. The first Mughal ruler, Babur (1483–1530), who hailed from

the Ferghana valley in modern Uzbekistan, entered India
from Afghanistan and after a series of campaigns defeated the
last of the Delhi sultans of the Lodi dynasty in 1526. Babur
seems to have been an engaging individual whose memoir,
the *Baburnama*, includes responses to his new life in India;
he wrote in Chughtai Turkish, recalling his Central Asian
rather than Persian ancestry, though Persian later become the
language of the Mughal court. Following the death of Babur,
the new dynasty suffered a setback and Humayun, Babur's
son, was forced into exile in 1540 by the Afghan Sher Shah
Sur, spending long years in Iran and Afghanistan and only
returning to Delhi in 1555. Within a year, though, Humayun
died and was succeeded by the greatest of the Mughals,
Akbar (r. 1556–1605). While not the apogee of Mughal power,
this was a period when the best qualities of the dynasty were
demonstrated. Akbar was an exceptional individual, open
to discussion and debate, especially on matters religious,
and today he is often spoken of in the same breath as Ashoka.
Akbar may have been dyslexic, but nevertheless demonstrated
great enthusiasm for manuscripts and their illustration. The
empire continued to expand under his successors, his son
Jahangir (r. 1605–27) and grandson Shah Jahan (r. 1628–58).
The latter is remembered as the constructor of the Taj Mahal,
but all the Mughals were great builders – Akbar built an
entirely new city at Fatehpur Sikri. During the reigns of

3. The Taj Mahal, Agra
This famous monument was built by the Mughal emperor Shah Jahan as a tomb for his wife Mumtaz Mahal; he was later buried next to her. The structure is built on a platform and is set within a paradisiacal garden on the banks of the river Yamuna. White marble, inlaid with semi-precious stone, is set dramatically against the red sandstone of the other buildings in the complex, which includes a mosque and gateways.

Akbar, Jahangir and Shah Jahan, imperial painting studios were established, producing imagery appropriate to the ruler of the day; subjects included epics, natural history and portraits. In addition, all of the emperors recorded the history of their own reigns, following the example of their forebear, Babur.

The last of the great Mughal rulers was Aurangzeb (r. 1658–1707) who, unlike his predecessors, was austere in character. Strictly Sunni by religious profession he was not given to the arts of music or painting. During his reign, the Mughal empire was at its greatest extent, with all the Deccan finally brought under Mughal authority. However, although successful, the conquest of the Deccan was hugely demanding and the Mughal empire never recovered its financial stability or acceptance of plurality. The successors of Aurangzeb lacked the stature of their predecessors and the fifty years following Aurangzeb's death saw the empire reduced and new players upon the stage. Amongst these were the Maratha rulers in the Western Ghats, as well as European merchants and increasingly the English East India Company.

In western India, the old-established Rajput courts, such as Jaipur, Jodhpur and Udaipur, released from the Mughal hold, re-established themselves as separate states, demonstrating this through independent artistic patronage in architecture, painting and devotional arts.

4 | 1 Sultanate north India

The architecture of the sultans of north India includes the famous Qutb Minar (**1**). This is a victory pillar built by the founder of the Delhi Sultanate, Qutbuddin Aibek (r. 1206–10). He was the viceroy of the Ghorid rulers of Afghanistan. Built mostly of red sandstone, the Qutb Minar is constructed of rounded and then angled elements that run up the height of the tower. It is magnificently carved with scrolling and carved inscriptions including from the Qur'an.

The fortress of the later Tughlaq dynasty, Tughluqabad, as well as the citadel of Firuz Shah Kotla, can still be seen in Delhi, along with the domed tombs of the last dynasty, the Lodis (**4**; **2**). The buildings of these rulers are their greatest legacy, not only in Delhi but also in Jaunpur to the east (the centre of the Sharqi Sultanate) and Ahmedabad in Gujarat (also the seat of an independent sultanate, remembered today for its fine architecture, especially the Mosque of Sidi Sayyid with its exquisite window tracery). At the court of the Delhi sultans, painters flourished, although surviving examples of their work, such as illustrations to texts in Persian like the *Khamsa* of Amir Khusrau (**3**), are rare.

Fissiparous and argumentative, the dynasties fought amongst themselves but held sway over much of the north, from Bengal in the east to Punjab in the west, until the arrival of the Mughals in 1526. The foray deep into southern India by Malik Kafur, general of the Delhi Sultan Ala ud-Din Khilji, in 1309, was devastating but did not result in permanent rule. The governors appointed by the Delhi sultans in the Deccan eventually broke away, establishing the sultanate of the Bahmanis (see p. 186). Further south, the Vijayanagara kingdom developed in the power vacuum left as the Muslim armies retreated.

1. The Qutb Minar
This great tower, now swallowed up in the sprawl of modern Delhi, was often painted by Indian artists for European visitors. This page from an album of views clearly shows the use of both red sandstone (lower part) and white marble (upper).

Paint on paper, from an album
Early 19th century
Height 29 cm, width 21.7 cm
Delhi, north India
Bequeathed by Francis Edward
Paget, 1945,1013,0.9.8

2. Censer
The hexagonal plan of this elegant censer reflects the use of geometric shapes in the Islamic architecture of Sultanate India (see Figure 4).

Cast and pierced brass
16th century
Height 15 cm, width 16 cm
North India, perhaps Delhi
Brooke Sewell Permanent Fund,
1992,0715.1

**3. The *Khamsa* of
Amir Khusrau**
The poet Amir Khusrau
(1253–1325) wrote his *Khamsa*
or quintet of idyllic narratives,
at the court of the Delhi sultans.
In this detail of a manuscript
page from the *Khamsa*, the
priestess of Kandahar is shown
venerating an image. The intense
red background is a feature from
local Indian painting traditions.

Opaque watercolour on paper
Mid-15th century
Height 33.9 cm, width 29.2 cm
(entire painting)
Probably Delhi
1996,1005,0.5

**4. The tomb of Muhammad
Shah Sayyid**
Surviving in Delhi in the
landscaped Lodi Gardens, this
tomb was built for one of the last
sultans of the Sayyid dynasty,
whose reign ended in 1443.
The central octagonal chamber
is domed; around it is an arched
and open gallery surmounted
with miniature domed pavilions,
all features typical of the Islamic
architecture of the subcontinent.

4 | 2 The Sultanate of Bengal

At Gaur, capital of the Bengal sultans, extensive ruinfields can still be seen, as also at nearby Pandua where the Adina mosque (completed in 1375) was, at the time, the largest in the whole subcontinent. Although now ruined, the central space is still impressive with its remnants of a huge barrel vault, a type of vaulting otherwise little known in Indian Islamic structures, the dome being more usual. This mosque, like many others of the period in Bengal, was built of brick with basalt facings (**2**), especially along the wall in which is set the *mihrab*, the niche that indicates the direction of Mecca for prayer. These carved stone facings suggest the way in which local craftsmen were used in its construction, since motifs such as full-blown lotus blossoms and vegetal scrolls, typical of pre-Islamic eastern India, were combined with more obviously Islamic decorative features such as the *mihrab* and hanging lamp; this was a happy synthesis (**3**). Many buildings in the city were decorated on the exterior with coloured glazed tiles, though few of these tiles survive.

Marking their independence from Delhi, the sultans issued their own coinage. They were also responsible for a series of remarkable inscriptions on their buildings. These were executed in black basalt in an elegant form of Arabic script, *tughra'i*, which has highly extended vertical elements that produce a dramatic visual effect; an impressive example is the five-slab panel believed to be the foundation stone from the Tantipara mosque in Gaur, with an inscription recording the installation of the slab in 1480 during the reign of Yusuf Shah (1474–81) (**1**).

1. Inscription
On this black basalt slab from the entrance to the Tantipara mosque at Gaur, the newly introduced Arabic script names the ruling sultan, Yusuf Shah.

Basalt
Inscribed 26 March 1480
Height 49.5 cm, width 265.5 cm
Gaur, north Bengal
Donated by Col. William Franklin, 1826,0708.2.a–e

2. Column
The lustrous quality of the basalt and the rich visual vocabulary of the carving are typical of the stone facings to the brick architecture of Bengal.

Basalt
15th century
Probably from the Adina mosque, Pandua, north Bengal
Height 112 cm
1880.352

3. Slab carved with a *mihrab*
The vegetal scrolls and lotus blossoms draw on pre-Islamic decorative schemes.

Basalt
15th century
Height 84.1 cm
Probably from Gaur, north Bengal
1880.145

184   Deccan sultans, Mughal emperors and Rajput kings

The Deccan sultans

By the middle of the 14th century, a substantial Muslim state had been established by the Bahmani sultans, based in Bidar in northern Karnataka. There is little surviving from the court of these rulers, other than their remarkable architecture, an augury of what was to come. The Bahmani state fell apart in the late 15th century, leading to the establishment of five separate states – Bidar, Berar, Ahmadnagar, Golconda and Bijapur. The rulers of these realms dominated the political, religious and cultural life of the region until the last was finally snuffed out by a combination of relentless attack by the last great Mughal emperor, Aurangzeb (r. 1658–1707), and the emergence of a new power in the Deccan, the Marathas. Strong Persian and Central Asian influence in these Deccan states – a counterpoint to Mughal presence to the north – meant that rulers espoused Shi'a as well as Sunni Islam. In most of their realms, however, they were always part of a religious and aesthetic elite, as most of their subjects were Hindu.

Painting flourished at the courts of the Deccan sultans, especially at Golconda and Bijapur, the two largest and longest-surviving sultanates. Examples are full of daring colour combinations and the use of gold. Imagery often uses unreal, but engaging, changes in scale. Mysterious night-scenes were popular – one can almost smell the heady scent of jasmine (1). And at both Golconda and Bijapur, music, dance and poetry were important subjects as also were scenes of courtly life (2). We get some understanding of the characters of the rulers from these paintings, Ibrahim Adil Shah II of Bijapur being especially resonant (1). He is remembered for his love of music and literature and his mystical inclinations. He was clearly not only interested in his Indo-Persian legacy, but also the beauty and importance of the culture of the majority of his subjects. Paintings from these courts are sometimes accentuated by beautiful mounts, water-marbled papers and fine calligraphy.

Very little worked ivory survives from this period but a small number of spectacular musical instruments, *sarinda*, are known. These can give us some idea of skills in this area (4). Further south, worked ivory panels were used in the decoration of small Hindu shrines (see p. 83) and in Goa ivory sculptures with Christian subject matter were produced (see p. 169), including for the export market.

The making of brightly coloured tiles for the decoration of the exterior of buildings was also a craft that was realized with great skill in the Deccan. Their use across the area is known from still *in situ* arrays of decoration. A few examples are found in museum collections (3) as also are fragments – and occasionally whole – examples of imported Chinese blue and white wares of the Ming period (5). These were highly valued and also appear in paintings of court scenes.

1. Ibrahim Adil Shah II of Bijapur
Famed for his interest in music, the sultan (r. 1579–1627) is depicted at night holding castanets. He is robed in diaphanous garments and wrapped in a shawl of golden thread.

Opaque watercolour and gold on paper
c. 1615
Height 17 cm, width 10.2 cm
Bijapur, Karnataka; attributed to the painter Ali Riza
1937,0410,0.2

2. The court of Muhammad Qutb Shah of Golconda

The youthful ruler Muhammad (r. 1612–26) here receives courtiers, one of whom, kneeling, may be Shaikh Muhammad ibn-i Khatun, appointed ambassador to Iran in 1616. This painting may portray his departure on that assignment, with horses and grooms waiting wide-eyed below.

Opaque watercolour on paper
c. 1612–20
Golconda, Telangana
Height 25 cm, width 15.5 cm
1937,0410,0.1

3. Two hexagonal tiles

Tilework to decorate buildings, often the exterior of mosques, entered the subcontinent from Iran and Central Asia. These examples use a palette of three colours – white, turquoise and blue on a reddish fabric.

Underglaze-painted earthenware
17th century
Height 15.5 cm
Bijapur, Karnataka
Donated by Sir Augustus Wollaston Franks,
1895,0603.152, 153

4. Sarinda

While this type of stringed instrument is an import from the Iranian world, the decoration includes local Deccan elements such as the terminal mythical animal spewing out of its mouth an elephant while grasping another one in its claws.

Ivory
c. 1700
Height 59.7 cm, width 16.1 cm
Hyderabad region of the Deccan
Donated by W. Tyndale; collected by Col. Shuldham, 1829,1114.1

5. Porcelain bottle

Archaeological excavations have uncovered sherds of Chinese ceramics at the Deccan courts. This bottle of double-gourd shape, decorated in the export style, known in Europe as 'kraak', is a rare intact survival.

Porcelain with underglaze blue and white decoration
1600–20
Height 15.5 cm
Jingdezhen, southern China; found in Bijapur, Karnataka
Donated by Mrs B. C. Kennedy, 1927,0519.1

4 | 3 Deccan metalwork

Traditions of metalworking in bronze, iron and steel are of great antiquity in the Deccan, as slag heaps found in Karimnagar District, Telangana, demonstrate. Steel was probably being produced in the early 1st millennium CE, long before it was in Europe. This depth of experience, combined with the refined aesthetic of the Deccan courts, produced outstanding examples of metalsmithing in the 16th and 17th centuries. Vessels for both secular and religious use were made, with earlier as well as imported Persianate designs being incorporated. Amongst the secular items are containers of many types (for *bidri*, see p. 212), especially for the enjoyment of *pan* (see p. 210). Perhaps for keeping jewelry safe are a small number of rectangular boxes with hammered designs of animals; they are of 17th century date, though very few survive (**2**). Similarly surviving in only very few numbers and of the same date are heavily cast bowls, using lotus petal designs with flamboyance (**4**).

Religious metalwork is seen in censers, some drawing on geometric and pan-Islamic design and octagonal in shape. Others are in animal form, such as lions or peacocks (see p. 151), drawing on long-established traditions of animal depiction. The lion with upraised paw is well known as the badge of the Hoysala dynasty (see p. 151). Meanwhile the peacock, or a mythical version, is seen in many media standing on, clutching, consuming or battling with elephants. We see this same imagery in ivory inlay in Indo-Portuguese furniture, in storytelling scrolls from Telangana (see pp. 236–7) (**3**) and in the coinage of the Vijayanagara kings, rulers of the southern Deccan until 1565 (**1**). This is an enduring image in the Deccan, wonderfully reworked in the Sultanate period.

1. Gold coin of King Achyutadevaraya
Issued at the height of the Vijayanagara empire, based at Hampi, this gold coin uses for its obverse design the double-headed eagle grasping elephants, *gandabherunda*, a symbol of magical strength.

Gold
1530–42 (regnal dates of Achyutadevaraya)
Diameter 10 mm
Minted at Vijayanagara (modern Hampi), Karnataka
Donated by Sir Walter Elliot, 1886,0505.44

2. Casket
Indian animals – elephants, fish and a variety of birds including peacocks – decorate the exterior of this casket; on the other side, two royal figures feature. The knob to open the casket is in the form of a lotus in full bloom.

Hammered brass
Second half of 17th century
Height 15.2 cm, width 22.1 cm
Northern Deccan
1939,0117.1

3. Register from a storytelling scroll

The traditional *gandabherunda* motif of a two-headed bird grasping elephants in its beaks and claws appears in this scroll illustrating the epic of Bhavana Rishi. He is considered the forebear of the weaver sub-caste of Telangana, the *padmasali*. This scroll, more than 9 m in length, tells the heroic origin of this group of weavers. The narration, usually at night, and using song and the images of the scroll to tell the story, would take many hours and is a sort of cinema-before-cinema – one colourful register after another, telling of enchanted mythical events at great length.

Paint on sized cotton
Late 18th century
Length 930 cm, width 85.5 cm
(entire scroll)
Telangana
Brooke Sewell Permanent Fund,
1996,0615,0.1

4. Lotiform basin

Water features such as fountains and pools in geometric or lotus shape are known from elite buildings of the Deccan, such as the Lal Bagh in Bidar and the Bibi ka Maqbara in Aurangabad. In this basin, the same idea is used to produce an aesthetically pleasing as well as functional object.

Cast and engraved brass
17th century
Diameter 22.5 cm
Deccan
Brooke Sewell Permanent Fund,
1963,1017.1

4 | 4 The Princes of the House of Timur

Much has been written about this famous Mughal painting since it was acquired by the British Museum in 1913. It depicts a group of princely descendants of Timur seated around and within a garden pavilion, in the centre of which sits the second Mughal emperor, Humayun (r. 1530–40 and 1555–56; identified by his specific turban); they are attended by servants (**1**). The original style of the painting is Persian, but there were two separate occasions when additions were made in the Mughal period. However, its Persian origins, along with the identity of the central figure, have enabled scholars to attribute its beginnings to one of two Persian artists who joined Humayun in Kabul in 1545, Abd al-Samad and Mir Sayyid Ali. Although damaged (approximately a quarter of the total is missing), it is nevertheless revealed as an important and beautiful document of early Mughal painting.

The painting's original purpose is uncertain, but later parts were extensively reworked in a Mughal style and various figures were inserted (with captions), particularly descendants of Humayan, thus 'bringing it up to date' (**2**). This was probably done in the first years of the reign of Jahangir (r. 1605–27) and again early in the reign of Shah Jahan (r. 1628–58). Some figures were completely changed, while the scale of others was altered. Though never finished, the painting must have been envisaged as a dynastic record emphasizing the link between the Mughal rulers and Timur, their Central Asian forebear; such ancestral linkages were important to the Mughal emperors.

1. The Princes of the House of Timur
Even with sections missing, the grandeur of the original painting can still be gauged. Instructive is the prominently Persian quality of the earlier elements – the garden pavilion, the plane trees, the golden sky and the rocky hill-scape – all of which are offset by the later Mughal attendees within the pavilion.

Opaque watercolour on cloth
c. 1550–55 (first element);
c. 1605 and 1628 (second and third elements)
Height 109 cm, width 108 cm
Perhaps begun in Kabul, Afghanistan; added to in north India
The Art Fund (as NACF), 1913,0208,0.1

**2. The Princes of the
House of Timur**
The centre of the painting
depicts the main players in the
narrative: Humayun with pointed
turban sits to the right as viewed,
with Akbar, Jahangir and Shah
Jahan facing him. Mughal princes
look into the pavilion from left
and right.

4 | 5 Painting during the reign of Akbar

Early in his long reign, Akbar (r. 1556–1605) became familiar with the work of the Persian painters Abd al-Samad and Mir Sayyid Ali; they had been brought to Delhi by his father, Humayun, and provided a Safavid template for early Mughal painting (see p. 190). The great achievement of Akbar's reign was the melding of this tradition with local Indian practices – and then the addition of some of the new notions for depicting volume and distance that were being learnt from viewing European prints, brought to the Mughal court by Jesuit priests, and traders.

One of the first undertakings of Akbar's imperial atelier was the illustration, in an astonishing 1,400 paintings, of the *Hamzanama*, a text in which the legendary activities of the hero Hamza are described (**3**). We know Akbar was fond of this collection of adventure stories and enjoyed hearing the text read to him. In the paintings the Indian feeling for colour and for the natural world make for a sequence of visually exciting scenes. The project took fifteen years to complete, though today only a small number of the paintings survive.

Akbar was also keen for his Persian-speaking and Muslim courtiers to understand the great epics of their mostly Hindu subjects (see also p. 71). Consequently, he had both the Ramayana and the Mahabharata translated from Sanskrit into Persian. Both were illustrated by court artists (**2**). Other major undertakings of the atelier included illustrating Persian literature, as well as the text of Babur's memoirs, the *Baburnama*, and the history of Akbar's own reign, the *Akbarnama*. Portraiture was also encouraged and the format that later became the Mughal standard – standing male figure in profile on a coloured surface with no background – was established. One of the greatest painters of Akbar's later court was Mansur (**1**).

1. A *vina*-player, probably Naubat Khan Kalawant; ascribed to the painter Mansur (fl. 1590–1624)
Mansur is mostly remembered for his paintings of the natural world during the reign of Akbar's son Jahangir. Here, though, the musician dominates the painting; birds and flowering plants are also present, an intimation of what was to come.

Opaque watercolour and gold on paper, inscribed and sealed
c. 1590–95
Height 11.2 cm, width 9 cm (image only)
Mughal India
Brooke Sewell Permanent Fund, 1989,0818,0.1

2. Yudhishthira wrestles with Karna
The *Razmnama* is a Persian precis and translation of the Mahabharata. In this detached page from a now-dispersed *Razmnama* manuscript, the senior brother of the Pandavas, Yudhishthira, wrestles with his half-brother Karna. The relationship between these two figures is typical of the character of this huge epic, in which closely related individuals are remorselessly pitted one against the other.

Opaque watercolour on paper
1598
Height 20.3 cm, width 11.1 cm (image only)
Mughal India
1921,1115,0.13

**3. Page from the
Hamzanama**
The Prophet Elias rescues
Prince Nuruddahr from drowning.
Although this painting dates
from early in Akbar's reign,
the marriage of Persian

and Central Asian subject matter
with Indian feeling for the natural
world is clearly demonstrated;
the forest is alive with sound
and beauty.

Opaque watercolour on cotton,
attributed to the painter Basavana
c. 1567–72
Height 67.4 cm, width 51.3 cm
Mughal India
Donated by the Revd. Stratton
Campbell, 1925,0929,0.1

4 | 6 Embroidered counterpanes for export

The Portuguese were the first Europeans to trade with India in the modern period. Although their first settlements were on the west coast, especially at Goa, they also traded in eastern India from the town of Satgaon in the Ganges/Brahmaputra delta, above all in textiles. Popular in Portugal from this source were quilted and embroidered counterpanes, largely dating to the early 17th century. Most were made of cotton while the stitching was usually executed in *tussar*, undyed golden-yellow silk (a few examples survive with rose-pink embroidery). Some were commissioned for specific noble families in Portugal, with coats of arms prominently displayed in the embroidery.

Of special interest is the mixed imagery found in these textiles – partly local and partly European. Of the European imagery, we see Portuguese soldiers engaged in the hunt (**1**). The figure of Justice with her scales appears at the centre of another counterpane, which also has scenes in its four quadrants copied from European prints (these copperplate prints were produced in Antwerp and exported in large numbers) (**2**). The Bengali embroiderers, faced with scenes of classical or biblical origin, did not always understand the references and today it is difficult to identify everything that is represented. Two depictions, however, are clear: the Death of Actaeon and the story of Pyramus and Thisbe from Ovid's *Metamorphoses*.

The tradition of fine embroidery continued after these exotic export items were produced and surfaces several centuries later in the smaller and more domestic *kantha* found throughout Bengal (see pp. 278–9).

1. Embroidered counterpane
Densely embroidered and quilted textiles such as this one were popular in Portugal in the 17th century. They rely for their appeal on the subtle contrast between the white cotton ground and the golden-coloured *tussar* silk. Portuguese soldiers frequently appear on these quilts, often in hunting scenes. This detail shows them in distinctive dress, including headgear, riding on horseback and brandishing swords.

Cotton, silk
Early 17th century
Bengal, probably from Satgaon
Collection of Lanto Synge, Esq.

2. Embroidered counterpane

The roundel in the centre of this embroidered cotton counterpane depicts Justice with her scales; she is surrounded by a band of mermaids, one of whom (immediately below Justice) plays a guitar, a European instrument. The detail shown at right shows the Death of Actaeon, copied from a European print (probably produced in Antwerp). The unfortunate hero appears in the lower part having been transformed into a deer by the goddess Diana, while above he is torn apart by his own hounds.

Cotton, silk
Early 17th century
Length 272 cm, width 236 cm
Bengal, probably from Satgaon
Brooke Sewell Permanent Fund,
2000,1213,0.1

4 | 7 Chintz textiles

The astonishing variety of Indian textiles caught the attention of early European traders. Textiles that dazzled with colour and variety, produced through a mastery of dyeing techniques, made southwestern India – from Machilipatnam to the Kaveri delta, or the Coromandel coast to Europeans – a place of great interest. Such dyed textiles were known, in England, as chintz.

When Europeans first arrived in India at the end of the 15th century, there was already a well-established trade in Indian textiles to Southeast Asia (see pp. 72–3), and soon Europe became part of this trade. The textiles rarely survive but we can get an idea of them from slightly later examples (3). Hunting imagery is typical of textile production at the princely courts of the Deccan and is seen in more complete form, for instance, in floor-spreads from Golconda, dated to the mid-17th century.

Later exports from this region, probably via the port of Machilipatnam, include the famous chintz *palampore* (coverlets or wall-hangings). The international character of this trade is demonstrated in the huge cloth illustrated here (2), where design elements copied from Chinese screens en route for Europe can be seen, as well as themes from Japanese printed books and also prints from the Netherlands and England. Providing an intriguing comment on this huge textile is a fragment of an apparently identical chintz, now in the Tapi Collection in Surat, which was found in Sulawesi. A final indicator of the international nature of the chintz textile trade comes from a bag (1). It was made from two fragments of larger cloths, saved and reused in Sri Lanka, but originally produced on the Coromandel coast.

2. Large chintz *palampore*
This expansive dyed and painted textile is remarkable for the range of Asian and European sources visible in the imagery. Perhaps most remarkable though, on the reverse, is a customs stamp in Cyrillic letters indicating its presence in St Petersburg in 1772, thus providing a *terminus ante quem* for its production.

Dyed and painted cotton
Mid-18th century, before 1772
Height *c.* 500 cm, width
c. 500 cm
Coromandel coast, probably Machilipatnam
Brooke Sewell Permanent Fund, 1998,0505,0.1

3. Fragment of a floor-spread
Textiles decorated with hunting and animal imagery were used for floor-spreads at the Deccan courts. The Portuguese called them *pintado* and this word appears in lists of export items. Although the name implies the act of painting, the designs were all produced through the use of different resist and mordant dyeing processes which produce different colours.

Resist-dyed cotton
c. 1630
Height 45.5. cm, width 205 cm
Coromandel coast
Brooke Sewell Permanent Fund, 1964,0208,0.1

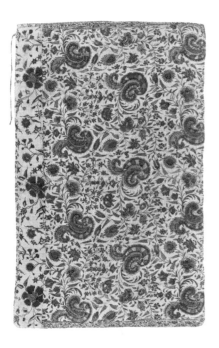

1. Bag
Two unequally sized fragments of dyed cotton cloth – probably originally hip-wrappers – have been stitched together to make a bag. Given its shape, this bag was perhaps made to carry palm-leaf manuscripts.

Dyed cotton
18th century
Length 105 cm, width 64.5 cm
Coromandel coast; exported to and found in Sri Lanka
Brooke Sewell Permanent Fund, 2002,0408,0.4

4 | 8 Mughal jade

Under the Indo-Islamic rulers of India, especially the Mughals, jade from Khotan in what is now far western China was greatly prized. Vessels as well as single individual objects of Khotan jade were made in workshops at the Mughal court. The proximity of Khotan to Kashmir (beloved of the Mughal rulers and ruled by them), provided a comparatively short trade route and one well-established by this period, despite the height of the Karakoram mountains over which the route passed. Once in the Mughal cities, the vessels and other jade items were carved and also often inscribed. The predilection for jade, with its contrasting qualities of extreme hardness and delicate translucence, was a taste that the Mughal rulers probably inherited from their Timurid ancestors, who were also renowned as patrons of jade production. Jahangir is recorded as owning jade items that had been made for his Timurid predecessors and some of the inscriptions on his vessels imply this close connection (**1**).

Cups and dishes (**1, 2**) are the most commonly found vessels and some of the finest are those that make use of the inherent quality of the stone to best effect. Later examples were sometimes inlaid with different coloured jade and also with precious stones such as lapis lazuli and rubies. One of the most striking of this later type is a pair of *huqqa*-bases (**3**). These are impressive examples of Mughal jade craftsmanship, complete with veining carved in each iris flower of inlaid lapis lazuli and in every leaf of dark green jade. They are believed to have once belonged to the eccentric English collector William Beckford (1760–1844).

1. Cup

The beauty of this remarkable jade cup, in the form of a cut gourd, is enhanced by the inscription it bears below the rim, which indicates it belonged to the Mughal emperor Shah Jahan. In this inscription he refers to himself as 'the Second Lord of the Conjunction', a reference to his ancestor Timur who bore a similar title, 'the First Lord of the Conjunction'.

Jade
1647–48 (given in the inscription) or earlier
Height 6 cm, length 17.8 cm
Mughal India
Bequeathed by Oscar Raphael, 1945,1017.259

2. Dish

Later Mughal jade items tended to be more highly decorated with inlaid gemstones and precious metal. This elegant dish with its floral shape picks up the same imagery in the floral sprigs of gold inlay in the decoration of the interior.

Jade, inlaid with gold, ruby and pearl
18th century
Diameter 24.2 cm
Mughal India
Donated by P. T. Brooke Sewell, 1938,1011.1

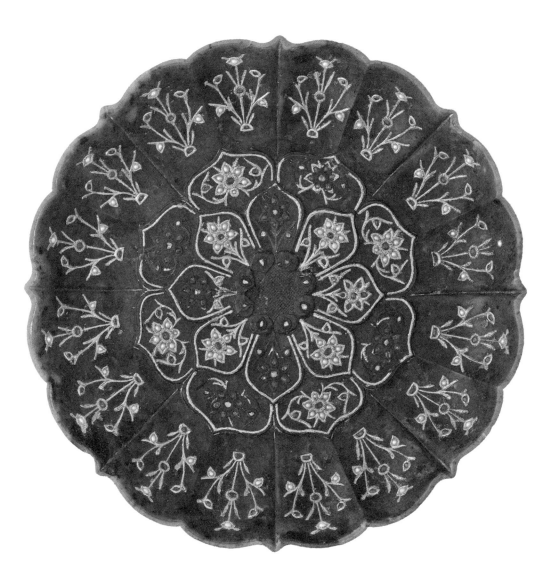

3. *Huqqa*-bases

A taste for the sumptuous is demonstrated in these magnificent inlaid jade water-pipe bowls, *huqqa* (see p. 211). Both vessels are decorated with floral designs using inlaid dark green jade, lapis lazuli and rubies all set in gold. Later, when brought to Europe, they were placed on gilded metal mounts set on marble stands.

Jade, gold, lapis lazuli and rubies
c. 1700
Height 19.4 cm
Mughal India
Donated by P. T. Brooke Sewell,
1956,0724.1, 2

Later Mughal painting

In Jahangir's reign (1605–27), courtly interest in illustrating epics and historical narratives ceased and attention turned to recording the natural world. This was intensified through Jahangir's exposure to Kashmir, which he visited repeatedly and described elegiacally in his memoirs, the *Tuzuk-i Jahangiri*. Among his artists, Mansur was one of the best at depicting the natural world, especially floral and animal subjects.

Topics related to the ruling house were also popular under Jahangir. One famous painting records the repurposing of the ancient Indian custom of weighing a ruler (in this case, Jahangir's son) against gold (1); this event is recorded in Jahangir's memoirs. Christianity continued to be a curiosity at Jahangir's court and a drawing of the Annunciation (2) may date from his reign. The iconography must have been copied from a Western print, though the execution is entirely Indian, as is the glorious floral border.

Jahangir was succeeded by his son Shah Jahan (r. 1628–58), whose great painting project was the illustration of his official history, the *Padshahnama*. Portraits were popular and streaked golden skies and rows of flowering plants at the base of paintings became widespread, along with elaborate turbans and weapons (see p. 209, Figure 3).

Aurangzeb's reign (1658–1707), however, was quite different. He adopted an austere Sunni ideology, frowning on the pleasures of earlier Mughal courts, including the compilation of dynastic narratives. For the most part, painting flourished only away from the court, a precursor of what was to come following Aurangzeb's death when the disintegration of the Mughal empire began. Temporary stability appeared in the person of Muhammad Shah (r. 1719–48), though the sack of Delhi by the Persian king Nadir Shah in 1739 was the final death-knell. Painters began to find patrons elsewhere, especially in Lucknow and Bengal (p. 226).

1. The weighing of Prince Khurram

Jahangir – in diaphanous *jama* (cotton outer garment) – faces his son, the future emperor Shah Jahan, who sits cross-legged in the scales. Attendants load the balance with bags of money later distributed to the poor. In the foreground are trays of rich cloth and jeweled weapons. In the far background Chinese ceramics can be seen on shelves.

Opaque watercolour and gold on paper
About 1615
Height 30 cm, width 19.6 cm
(image only)
Mughal India
Bequeathed by P. C. Manuk and Miss G. M. Coles through the Art Fund (as NACF), 1948,1009,0.69

2. The Annunciation

Demonstrating the interest at the Mughal court of the imagery of Christianity, this tinted drawing was doubtless based on a European print. Certain Indian features have crept in, however, such as the angel performing a full-length prostration.

Drawing with colour, on paper
17th century
Mughal India
Height 16.3 cm, width 9.3 cm
(image only)
1920,0917,0.13.21

3. Sayyid Abdullah Khan holding court

In the immediate aftermath of the death of Aurangzeb, several rulers came to power in swift succession, aided in part by the two Sayyid brothers Abdullah Khan and Husain Ali Khan who acted as ruthless king-makers. They came from a family long-established at the Mughal court and were used to its political methods. Here, Abdullah Khan is depicted holding court, attended by advisors and entertained by musicians.

Paint on paper
Early 18th century
Height 21.4 cm, width 34.5 cm
Mughal India
1921,1011,0.4

4 | 9 The later art of Kashmir

By the late 16th century, the Kashmir valley had been annexed by the Mughal emperor, Akbar. However, in the centuries immediately prior to this, Islam had become the dominant religion of Kashmir, with the first Muslim ruler being a local convert ruling from around 1320. It seems that Iran and Central Asia were probably more prominent in the evangelization of Kashmir than were the plains of India.

In the 17th century, we learn a good deal about Kashmir as the Mughal rulers found both the temperature and beauty of the valley irresistible. Jahangir was an especially keen visitor and, along with his wife Nurjahan, built gardens in the environs of Srinagar that are, even today in their reduced condition, still exquisite with their pools, fountains and lush planting of both flowers and trees. Most famous of these are the Shalimar Gardens (**2**), connected to Dal lake and memorialized in literature, from early 17th-century travelogues up to English songs of Edwardian times. Jahangir was also responsible for the recording of the natural history of the region.

At this time tombs and mosques were both built and restored. Amongst the latter is the tomb of Sayyid al-Madani, the gateway of which was decorated with brightly coloured tiles (**1**). The metalworking skills of Kashmiri craftsmen in the medieval period have already been noted (see p. 150), but in the Mughal and later periods these skills were channelled into the production of vessels, many of which used both arabesque and calligraphic decoration to considerable effect (**3**).

1. Floral tile
Mughal-period coloured tiles frequently used the palette seen here, with reddish-brown being prominent. Decoration, applied using the *cuerda seca* ('dry cord') technique to stop the colours running into each other, was limited almost entirely to flower and leaf designs.

Glazed earthenware
c. 1655
Height 19.5 cm, width 17.2 cm
Made in Lahore and taken to Kashmir, or made in Srinagar
Ashmolean Museum, University of Oxford, EA1994.77

2. The Shalimar Gardens
The Mughal rulers laid out a series of gardens around Dal lake at Srinagar. The Shalimar Gardens were constructed in 1616 during Jahangir's reign and, like others such as the Nishat Bagh, are made up of terraces descending to the lake, divided by a series of cascades and fountains. A description of Shalimar was given by the European traveller François Bernier in the 1660s.

3. Inscribed bowl
Vessels such as this have previously been described as Persian but there is evidence for assuming this example was made in Kashmir, as it was acquired there while the donor was working on the construction of New Delhi. The inscription around the rim is from the Persian poet Hafez (1325–1390) and suggests it may have been used for drinking wine.

Cast and engraved copper
1600–30
Diameter 25 cm (max)
Kashmir
Donated by H. A. N. Medd, 1969,0212.1

4 | 10 The Taj Mahal

This building, probably the most famous symbol of India, is, ironically, a structure of mixed heritage. It owes much to Persian and Central Asian royal tomb structures, though elements of the extensive vegetal, floral and architectural decoration equally mark it out as Indian. It was built between 1632 and 1643 on the banks of the Yamuna at Agra, downstream from the Mughal fort (**2**). Shah Jahan, the fifth Mughal emperor, commissioned it as a mausoleum for his favourite wife Mumtaz Mahal (d. 1631). Her tomb, accompanied later by that of Shah Jahan himself (d. 1666), is located in the basement.

The Taj Mahal was laid out at the end of a formal garden featuring water channels suggestive of Paradise. The mausoleum itself is built on two large platforms – the lower massive one faced with red sandstone, still visible on the river front, and the upper one faced with white marble. The glorious domed tomb in the centre of the upper platform is also sheathed in white marble, much of it with floral inlay of semi-precious stone (**3**). Marking the edges of the square upper platform are four minarets, while beyond them to the west and east are a mosque and an assembly hall. Whatever your belief, or your views on Shah Jahan, this is unquestionably one of the great buildings of human civilization, a 'teardrop on the cheek of eternity',[1] and – not surprisingly – it has been drawn and photographed repeatedly (**1**).

1. Rabindranath Tagore, quoted in *Rabindranath Tagore: The Myriad-Minded Man* by Krishna Dutta & Andrew Robinson, 1995, p. 191.

1. The Taj Mahal
This long view of the Taj Mahal in its gardens stands near the beginning of a long and continuing sequence of photographic depictions of this great monument.

Albumen silver print from a glass negative; photographer unknown
1860–70
Height 22 cm, width 28 cm
Agra, Uttar Pradesh
Gift of Matthew Dontzin,
The Metropolitan Museum of Art, New York, 1985.1168.26

2. Bird's eye view of the Taj Mahal
This unusual perspective, with the landscape flattened out to show as much detail as possible, including Agra Fort (top left), may have been produced as a souvenir for a European visitor.

Opaque watercolour on paper (unfinished)
c. 1800
Height 18.6 cm, width 26.6 cm
Agra, Uttar Pradesh
Donated through the Hon. Anne MacDonnell, 1940,1012,0.1

3. Album painting of a screen in the Taj Mahal
The combination of cut white marble, inlaid with coloured semi-precious stone, makes for an exquisite arrangement for the octagonal screen around the cenotaphs of Mumtaz Mahal and Shah Jahan, whose tombs are located beneath, in the basement.

Watercolour on paper
c. 1820
Height 21.7 cm, width 29 cm
Agra, Uttar Pradesh
Donated by Francis Paget, Esq.,
1945,1013,0.9.5

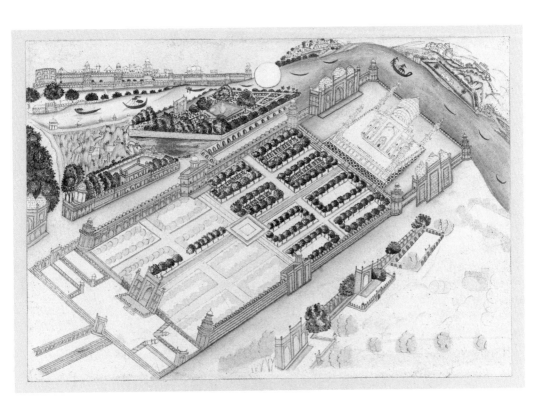

1. Railing pillar roundel

In the roundel from the stupa at Amaravati (see pp. 60–61), a female dancer faces the viewer, while around her are a variety of musicians: drummer, harpist, flautist and – with her back to the viewer – lute-player (the instrument's neck to left, belly to right).

Limestone from Palnad
3rd century CE
Height 225 cm, width 60 cm
(total dimensions of pillar)
Amaravati, Guntur District, Andhra Pradesh
1880,0709.17

2. A ruler with dancers

Court musicians accompany two dancers whose performance has just reached its climax. They appear with legs akimbo and with hands held aloft towards their admiring prince.

Opaque watercolour on paper
Mid-18th century
Height 22.6 cm, width 19.8 cm
Rajasthan, probably Jaipur
1920,0917,0.155

Dance

In ancient India, sculpture and dance were closely linked, both in aesthetic theory, *rasa*, and in practice. The importance of the figure in temple decoration substantiates this link; Indian sculpture is filled with scenes of dance and music-making (**1**), and dance in antiquity was a feature of both temple and courtly life. Dance was a means of entertainment for god and king, an offering of homage, important in both earthly and spiritual realms. The link between divine activity and dance is further seen in the image of Shiva Nataraja (see pp. 142–3).

There has always been regional variety in South Asian dance, but there are today basic differences in the northern and southern traditions. For more than 500 years, elite dance forms in the north have been primarily court activities, as dance does not feature in orthodox Muslim practice. Dance and music were, however, important aspects of the Muslim courts of the Deccan sultans (see p. 187) and later of the Mughals (p. 192) and their successors (**2**). The dance form we know today as *kathak* is the descendant of that tradition, based on energetic footwork with virtuosic spinning and stamping to heighten emotion.

In southern India, dance connected to temple life continued in areas beyond Muslim cultural influence, though in the later 19th century there was a reaction to it based on British moral indignation; local temple dance almost completely died out. One of the revivers/reinventors of the south Indian dance style, *bharatanatyam*, was Rukmini Devi Arundale (1904–1986). Slightly later, and involved in Indian dancing both in the subcontinent and also in the West, was Ram Gopal (**3**), who danced with ballet stars such as Alicia Markova. Somewhat earlier than both was Uday Shankar (brother of Ravi Shankar, pp. 294–5) who also re-created Indian dance with, amongst others, Anna Pavlova. For his choreography of Indian dance, he is recorded as having studied Indian sculpture in the British Museum.

3. The dancer Ram Gopal
Half-Burmese and half-Indian, Ram Gopal (1912–2003) took London by storm in the years before World War II with his recreations of Indian dance. Polish artist Feliks Topolski repeatedly sketched him, here as Krishna.

Gopal dancing No. 3
Feliks Topolski (1907–1989)
Ink on paper
1939
Height 18 cm, width 13.5 cm
London
Brooke Sewell Permanent Fund, 2006,0116,0.9

4 | 11 Arms and armour

From the first appearance of metal in South Asia, swords and other weapons were produced. Examples have been found in prehistoric deposits, an indication of the long period in which iron and steel have been forged, particularly in southern India. This expertise in the south continued throughout the historic period with watered steel blades of the armoury of Thanjavur in Tamil Nadu being especially renowned. Arms are also known from sculpture in the medieval period.

However, it is not until the Mughal and later periods that large numbers of swords, shields, axes, daggers and armour (both human and animal) survive. These can be elaborately decorated using techniques of gold- and silver-inlaying, enamelling and carving, and with blades frequently of watered steel; they were made for both ceremonial and actual use.

There was much courtly display and surviving examples of daggers with jade and other hard-stone hilts are well known (**2**); such items were often presented by Mughal rulers as gifts to vassals. Large numbers of swords survive from western India, whose rulers were generals in the Mughal armies. These include *talwar*, a common type of Indian sabre, often with inlaid decoration on the pommel as well as shields of steel or buffalo skin, usually marked with four bosses on the outer surface (**3**). Other frequently seen weapons include the punch-dagger, or *katar*, which is found throughout India though little known outside the subcontinent; it is prominently seen in portraits of nobles at the Mughal court (**3**), and often bears fine decoration (**4**). Elephant goads (**1**) and axes have similarly been exquisitely decorated.

1. *Ankusha*
The use of an elephant goad, or *ankusha*, to control elephants can be documented from at least the 2nd century BCE (see p. 173, Figure 4). This example is elaborately decorated with gold inlay and jingles in the handle (the sound of which surely 'encouraged' the elephant).

Steel, gold
17th century
Length 56.5 cm
Mughal India
Donated by Lady Bradford,
1948,0415.2

2. Dagger
The jade hilt to this dagger is inlaid with rubies, emeralds and diamonds, in gold settings. Such blades made handsome presents at the Mughal court and the gifting of beautiful objects, whether weapons or fine cloth, was an established way of ensuring loyalty.

Jade, steel, rubies, emeralds, diamonds, gold; velvet, wood
17th century
Length 43.5 cm, width 7.5 cm
Mughal India
Anonymous gift, 2001,0521.41

3. Portrait of Faqir Khan
In this portrait of a nobleman at the court of Shah Jahan, we can see three of the important elements of the Mughal armoury: *katar*, or punch-dagger, visible in the richly woven waistband; *talwar*, or sabre, with gilded decoration to the hilt and crimson velvet scabbard; and *dhal*, or shield, usually made of buffalo hide and with painted decoration.

Opaque watercolour on paper
1640–50
Height 21.9 cm, width 12.2 cm
(painted image)
Mughal India
1920,0917,0.13.11

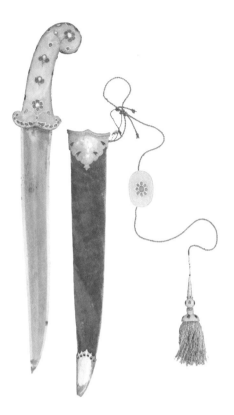

4. *Katar* and scabbard

A common weapon in the
Mughal period, the punch-
dagger or *katar* is frequently
seen in portraits (see Figure 3).
This one, like many others, is a
masterly combination of aesthetic
refinement and deadly purpose.

Gilded and chased steel, inlaid
paste, imitating ruby and emerald;
wood, velvet
18th century
Length 48 cm, width 10.5 cm
(max)
Mughal India
Lt-Gen Augustus W. H. Meyrick,
1878,1101.472

4 | 12 Inlaid metal vessels

The inlaid metalwares made in Bidar in the Deccan, and consequently known as *bidri* ware, were probably produced from at least the 17th century. The striking decoration is made by contrasting silver or sometimes silver and brass (**2**) inlay on a black surface. Items produced were mainly vessels, many connected with the preparation or consumption of *pan* (see p. 212) (**1**) or tobacco (**3**). Other shapes included bottles, ewers and basins.

Objects were cast using an alloy partly of zinc. The method for condensing zinc during the smelting process was understood in India prior to it being known in Europe (from at least the 14th century). Mines at Zawar in Rajasthan produced ore that was smelted on site and then exported.

The vessels for which Bidar was renowned were special on account of the silver wire or sheet that was let into a design that had already been etched on to the surface of the vessel. At the end of the inlay process, the surface was covered in a mud paste which included ammonium chloride; when the paste was removed and the surface polished, the metal became highly lustrous, thus enhancing the contrast between the vessel body and the inlay.

The earliest examples, of 17th-century date and now rare, have highly sophisticated surface decoration made up of sheet silver almost completely covering the surface of the object; this is the *aftabi* technique. Later examples have less inlay and more blackened surface; many, especially *huqqa*-bases, appear in paintings (**4**). The *bidri* style was popular in the 18th and 19th centuries, and in Hyderabad production continues to this day. Early 19th-century items made for European use in India are sometimes decorated with classical designs. Later items were made in Purnea, in Bihar, and Lucknow, where the technique was introduced in the British period (**1**).

1. *Pandan*
This small box is of a type frequently seen in the repertoire of craftsmen working in the *bidri* technique. Known as a *pandan*, it is a container for the ingredients to make a *pan* quid (see p. 212). The interior has a tray with compartments for holding various ingredients, while the section beneath the tray is for keeping betel leaves.

Zinc alloy inlaid with silver
Late 18th or early 19th century
Height 9.5 cm, length 12 cm
Purnea, Bihar; or Lucknow,
Uttar Pradesh
Donated by the Simon Digby
Memorial Charity, 2017,3038.23

2. Bottle with stopper
This fine vessel has beautiful floral decoration, using inlay in both silver and brass for a dramatic effect. The bottle shape is an import from Iran, another indication of the close links between the Deccan and the lands to the west.

Zinc alloy inlaid with silver
and brass
17th or early 18th century
Height 30 cm, width 17 cm
Bidar, the Deccan
Bequeathed by John Henderson,
1878,1230.758

3. *Huqqa*-base
Vessels used for smoking tobacco through scented water were made in large quantities in Bidar using the *bidri* technique. Those of globular shape are usually thought to be earlier than bell-shaped examples (see p. 212, Figure 2).

Zinc alloy inlaid with silver
c. 1740
Height 16.5 cm, width 14.5 cm
Bidar, the Deccan
Donated by Alfred Mitchell-Innes,
1934,0514.6

4. Muhammad Shah

Indian portraits of rulers in the 17th and 18th centuries frequently show them smoking. Often, the *huqqa*, as here, appears almost as a royal accoutrement, along with the sword lying beside the emperor Muhammad Shah (r. 1719–48), and the hawk perched on his gloved right hand. This *huqqa*, apparently of *bidri* ware, is placed on its own circular mat on the floor and is of the later, bell-shaped variety, typical of the 18th century.

Paint on paper
Mid-18th century
Height 44 cm, width 25 cm
North India
1974,0617,0.17.20

4 | 13 Tobacco and the culture of the *pan* quid

Along with other plants now considered completely Indian – chilli, tomato and potato – tobacco comes from the New World. It was introduced to India by the Portuguese and quickly became popular, despite the displeasure of Jahangir. Tobacco was usually smoked using a *huqqa* or water-pipe. In this method, the smoke is passed through scented water before it is inhaled. There is thus the need to have a container for the water; this has varied from the very mundane, the receptacle made of clay or coconut, to the most refined with vessels of inlaid jade (see p. 199), coloured glass, or imported porcelain (**1**). Many were made of metal (see p. 211) (**2**), as frequently depicted in portraits from the 17th century onwards. Smoking a *huqqa* was a habit that Europeans in India also became happy to adopt.

Chewing *pan* is another pleasure of South Asian society. The *pan* quid (an edible leaf 'envelope' containing spices) is made from the leaf of the betel vine (**3**). On each leaf, slaked lime is pasted and then spices, sugar, slivers of the mildly psychoactive nut of the areca palm and frequently tobacco are added – the contents can be varied according to taste. The whole quid is chewed, often after a meal as a *digestif* with a spittoon placed nearby as chewing *pan* produces a lot of red spittle.

Containers or *pandan* to hold the impedimenta for preparing *pan* were common (**4**). These have a flat cool part where the betel leaves are kept (usually in the base) and then somewhere for the different ingredients to be stored. The areca nut is cut with special nut-cutters, many examples of which have been the focus of decorative ingenuity (as too have separate portable boxes for holding the slaked lime).

1. Globular *huqqa*-base
This deluxe porcelain item, made in China probably for the late Mughal court, demonstrates the wide range of materials used in the pursuit of smoking tobacco, as well as the established trade route between the two great Asian empires, Mughal India and Qing China.

Underglazed porcelain with overglaze enamels
Kangxi reign, 1662–1722
Diameter 14 cm, height 18 cm
Jingdzhen, southern China
Donated by R. Soame Jenyns, 1956,1017.2

2. Bell-shaped *huqqa*-base
More quotidian than the porcelain example in Figure 1, but still handsome, is this later *huqqa*-base, made and decorated in the *bidri* technique (see p. 210). The use of poppy blossoms as a decorative motif is a hallmark of later *bidri* production.

Zinc alloy with silver inlay
Early 19th century
Height 19 cm, diameter 17.5 cm (base)
The Deccan, probably from Bidar
1880.229

3. Betel vine

Identified with both botanical and local Indian names, this painting of a betel vine from the Pearson Album shows the individual leaves, each one of which would be used to prepare a betel quid. Many of the paintings in this album by an unknown artist illustrate the flora – useful as well as decorative – of the subcontinent (see also p. 229).

Opaque watercolour on laid paper
c. 1820
Height 49 cm, width 37 cm
Probably painted at the Sibpur Botanic Garden, Calcutta
Bequeathed by Major J. P. S. Pearson, 1999,0203,0.2

Piper Betle, of Linnæus.   *Diandria Trigynia.*   *Paun Leaves.*

4. Octagonal *pandan*

Boxes such as this were made to hold the ingredients for the *pan* quid – leaves in the cool, lower part and spices in trays above. The engraved decoration of carnations – a favourite of Mughal artists – was originally filled with a black paste to highlight the design (fragments remain visible on the lid).

Beaten and engraved brass, inlaid with paste
Late 17th century
Height 10.2 cm, width 14.6 cm
North India
Donated by P. T. Brooke Sewell, 1956,0726.18.a-b

4 | 14 Rajput paintings: early schools

Some of the most beautiful and vibrant paintings produced in South Asia were commissioned from the courts of western Indian states, now mostly within the modern political unit of Rajasthan. These were ruled by families who called themselves Rajput or 'Sons of Kings', and were associated with warrior lifestyles both under the Mughal and the British rulers of India. Their origin is obscure though they are probably a mixture of local and incoming groups in the 1st millennium CE. Some princely states outside western India, such as in the Punjab Hills, or even in Nepal, considered themselves Rajput. Major centres of painting were located at the courts of Jodhpur, Jaipur, Bikaner and Kishangarh as well as at smaller courts, including some today in adjoining political units. Paintings produced at some of these different courts are illustrated in the next four sections (see pp. 216–23).

Some rare examples can be placed chronologically in the period prior to or coeval with the arrival of the Mughals in the subcontinent (**1, 2**), but the majority were produced during the period of the presence in Delhi (or Agra or Lahore) of the Mughal emperors. Some ateliers continued to produce fine paintings into the British period.

While their distinctive colour schemes and large expanses of unmediated colour link Rajput paintings with age-old traditions, they also include elements linked to the paintings of the Mughal court. Broadly speaking, the paintings from Rajput court workshops – and almost everything is from the court, with the exception of temple paintings – combine aspects from both sources; they can be cosmopolitan, originally owing something to Persian traditions, as well as local, bardic, colourfully vibrant, heroic and emotionally stirring.

Most Rajput paintings were produced on paper (cloth was only used in temples) and were intended to be viewed individually, passed from hand to hand as part of a (male) entertainment; they were never produced to be viewed on a wall surface. Individual viewing in the hands also meant that the painted surface could be moved to catch the light on metallic surfaces, or to illuminate other elements of the painters' art.

1. Page from the Bhagavata Purana
The many paintings from this dispersed manuscript are amongst the earliest of surviving Rajput paintings – vibrant and intriguing despite their invariably damaged state. The *Bhagavata Purana* includes the narratives of the early life of Krishna (identified by his blue skin). In the upper register he receives gifts in a domed pavilion with his wife; also depicted is a suggestively waiting but unused bedchamber, and a scene where they eat together. In the bottom register he rides away in a chariot. The text appears on the reverse (see also p. 162, Figure 1).

Opaque watercolour on paper
c. 1525
Height 17.3 cm, width 23.2 cm
Uncertain, but probably around Mathura, or further south
Brooke Sewell Permanent Fund, 1958,1011,0.2

2. Page from the Chandayana of Da'ud

The epic story of the lovers Laurik and Chanda first became popular in the Sultanate period. The text was probably assembled from an older bardic tradition, but its author injected a *sufi* element into the narrative. Typical of these paintings are the flat-coloured backgrounds enhanced by gold flecks upon which the figures are placed, all visible here despite the painting's damaged state. Produced outside the Rajput region (strictly defined), stylistic elements in this sequence of paintings were influential in later Rajput painting – for example, the solid single colour background and the way the transparent garments are painted.

Opaque watercolour on paper
c. 1530
Delhi–Agra region
Height 24.9 cm, width 19.4 cm
(including border)
Brooke Sewell Permanent Fund,
1968,0722,0.2

4 | 15 Jaipur and Jodhpur

Jaipur is today the most famous of the cities of Rajasthan and, being situated closest to Delhi, was the most influenced by the Mughals. The 16th- and 17th-century rulers of Jaipur maintained close matrimonial and political ties with the Mughal state, and during this period there is a royal style that combines both Mughal and Rajput aesthetic ideas. The city as we know it today is a comparatively late construction (1728) and the earliest paintings therefore come from the period when the Amber Fort – located in the hills above Jaipur – was the capital. As Mughal influence declined, following the death of Aurangzeb in 1707, religious subjects became popular and many examples are known (**1**). By the 19th century, painters were demonstrating a mastery of European perspective.

The rulers of Jodhpur, farther out into the desert than Jaipur, were the Rathore family; they controlled the region of Marwar. They, too, were close to the Mughals in the early 17th century and campaigned for them. We have some indication of early painting through a *ragamala* (see p. 222) (**2**) which – though damaged – gives an idea of the aesthetic that gave way to the Mughal one (**3**). As Mughal power declined in the 18th century, Jodhpur experienced a dramatic flowering of painting that emphasized colour, design, hierarchy and portraiture, all at the expense of Mughal naturalism (**4**).

This page
1. Shiva
Seated on the flayed skin of a slain elephant demon, the quintessential *yogi* is depicted using a striking colour scheme of three different shades of grey – the elephant skin, the hill on which the god sits and the Ganges flowing from his hair – all offset by a scarlet border.

Opaque watercolour on paper
c. 1750
Jaipur, Rajasthan
Height 30.2 cm, width 23.5 cm
(including border)
Donated by Mrs. A. G. Moor,
1940,0713,0.45

Opposite, above
2. *Sorathi Ragini*
This painting is from a series devoted to music, imagery and emotion; such paintings are known as *ragamala* (see p. 222). Each example represents a melody and the emotion connected with it. These can be *raga* (male) or *ragini* (female). This early series from Jodhpur has distinctive dark and high horizons.

Opaque watercolour
c. 1630
Marwar, perhaps Jodhpur,
Rajasthan
Height 21.9 cm, width 15.2 cm
The Art Fund (as NACF),
1955,1008,0.37

Below left
3. Gaj Singh I of Jodhpur
Gaj Singh (r. 1619–38) appears here as a high noble of the Mughal court, replete with jeweled weapons, sash of cloth of gold and pearled turban. Following the established standard for court portraiture, he is set against a green background with a high horizon. A marriage alliance made him a cousin of Shah Jahan.

Opaque watercolour on paper
c. 1630–38
Height 36 cm, width 24 cm
(central image only)
Mughal India
1920,0917,0.13.14

Below right
4. Hari Singh of Chandawal
Colour, design and enticement are the guiding principles in this painting of a Marwar noble. Note the fine *huqqa*-base and the *pan* equipment laid out along the base of the page.

Opaque watercolour on paper
c. 1760
Height 27.2 cm, width 23 cm
Marwar, Rajasthan
1947,0412,0.3

4 | 16 Udaipur and Devgarh in Mewar

The earliest paintings associated with Mewar, the last of the Rajput kingdoms to hold out against the Mughals, are dated to 1605. These were produced at Chawand during a period of exile from the stronghold of Udaipur. The paintings come from a *ragamala* sequence (see pp. 222–3) and are in a style that is still uninfluenced by Mughal sensibility (**1**). Following submission to the Mughals in 1615, court painting at Udaipur became increasingly exposed to Mughal styles, and portraits influenced by the imperial ateliers were being produced by the end of the century. From a decade or so later, comes a fascinating group of paintings drawing on the appearance in 1711 in Udaipur of a Dutch embassy to the Mughal court (**2**). A couple of decades later again, in the reign of Sangram Singh (1710–34), painters were producing illustrations to the epics in large horizontal format and in his and following reigns, a tradition of depictions of great public spectacles as well as a distinctive style of portraiture developed at Udaipur (**3**).

As power at Udaipur declined in the 18th century, some of the court painters found patrons in more profitable centres. One such painter was Bakhta, along with his son Chokha, both of whom found patronage at the court of Devgarh, to the northwest of Udaipur. Here they espoused a somewhat wild but highly attractive style, using colour combinations to great effect. Portraits of the Devgarh rulers are common, with those on horseback especially successful (**4**).

1. A depiction of the musical composition, *Sorathi Ragini*
Figures with their distinctively rectangular heads placed against blocks of vibrant colour and within domed architecture are features of the early Mewar style. In this painting from the Chawand Ragamala, the lady passes a *pan* quid to her lover, a prelude to the greater intimacy to come.

Opaque watercolour on paper, by the painter Nasiruddin
c. 1605
Height 27.8 cm, width 22.5 cm
Chawand, Mewar, Rajasthan
Brooke Sewell Permanent Fund, 1978,0417,0.3

2. Two lovers in European dress
Whether this is a portrait of specific individuals is unclear. What does seem certain, though is the European print template for the painting – note the stippling imitating the mezzotint technique and the random lines at the edges, suggestive of letterpress.

Painting on paper
c. 1720
Udaipur, Mewar, Rajasthan
Height 18.6 cm, width 11.4 cm
1956,0714,0.27

3. Maharana Ari Singh of Udaipur
The period of Ari Singh's rule (1761–73) is remembered for the decline of the Mewar state, but he is nevertheless shown here decked with pearl strings and carrying heavily jeweled weapons. His garments are of the finest cloth. The large golden and fringed halo is a feature seen repeatedly in the royal portraiture of Mewar.

Opaque watercolour on paper
1764
Height 20.7 cm, width 17.2 cm
Udaipur, Mewar
1956,0714,0.23

Left
4. Gokul Das, the Rawat (ruler) of Devgarh, and Kunvar Devi Singh
Two members of the Devgarh ruling family are depicted in this large format painting at the completion of the hunt, along with their fancifully plump and prancing horses. The smaller state of Devgarh was a vassal, or *thikana*, of the rulers of Udaipur.

Opaque watercolour on paper, attributed to the painter Bakhta
Mid-1780s
Height 43.8 cm, width 33.6 cm
Devgarh, Rajasthan
Donated by P. T. Brooke Sewell, 1958,1011,0.11

4 | 17 Other Rajput centres

At both Bundi and Kotah in southern Rajasthan, palace murals as well as paintings on paper have survived. At Bundi, paintings are noted by the 17th century for the depiction of verdant vegetation, dramatic weather effects and the evoking of the *sringara rasa*, the erotically charged atmosphere (**1**). Later, in nearby Kotah, paintings of the royal hunt were a speciality (**2**).

Kishangarh further north also had its own specific style which is associated with the reign of Raja Raj Singh (**3**). The heavy-lidded and large-eyed beauties of this style are distinctive.

In Nathdvara, also in southern Rajasthan, sanctuary was granted to a group of religious refugees in the late 17th century. They were followers of the Krishna teachings of Vallabhacharya (1478–1530). Originally located in Vrindavan, redolent with the life of Krishna, the new cult existed there until, under threat of death in the late Mughal period, devotees fled, carrying with them the image of the god. They settled eventually at Nathdvara, which from the 1670s until today has been the site of their main temple.

One of the features of the cult is its rich calendar of festivals, and paintings frequently depict them (**4**). Often the image of Krishna is shown centrally in his distinctive form holding up Mount Govardhan, using merely a single finger to provide an umbrella beneath which his followers can shelter; in this form he is known as Srinathji.

1. Painting from a *barahmasa* sequence, depicting the month of Vaisakh
The text at the top of this page is from the poetry of Keshavdas (1555–1617) and describes the plight of lovers in early summer. The god of love, Kama, takes aim from the jungle; his arrow of bees launched from a bow of jasmine is directed at Radha and Krishna on the terrace.

Opaque watercolour on paper
1680–1700
Height 30.2 cm, width 22 cm
(whole page)
Bundi, Rajasthan
Anonymous donor,
1999,1202,0.5.7

2. A royal hunt at Kotah
The 18th-century paintings from Kotah, many of which depict hunting scenes, are striking for the highly volumetric style that they often adopt – trees and animals especially show an almost tubular quality, which strikes a chord in a 21st-century post-surrealist aesthetic.

Opaque watercolour on paper
c. 1780
Height 31.8 cm, width 53.6 cm
Kotah, Rajasthan
1953,0411,0.10

3. Raja Raj Singh on horseback
The gaze of longing exchanged by the two figures in this painting (by or in the style of Bhavanidas), along with the abundance of fruit in the mango tree, emphasize the erotic charge in this depiction of the Raja visiting his lover. The unusual feature of him riding through water may reflect local architecture at Kishangarh.

Opaque watercolour
and gold on paper
c. 1725
Height 21.8 cm, width 15.4 cm
Kishangarh, Rajasthan
1959,0411,0.1

Below right
4. Krishna as Srinathji
The mounded food in the foreground indicates that this is the autumn festival of Annakuta. This painting,

probably new when acquired, is from the collection of Major Edward Moor (1771–1848), one of the first writers in English to systematically describe Hinduism.

Opaque watercolour and silver on paper
c. 1785
Height 31.5 cm, width 21.1 cm
Nathdvara, Rajasthan
Donated by Mrs A. G. Moor,
1940,0713,0.67

4 | 18 *Ragamala*: 'the garland of melodies'

The word *ragamala*, literally 'a garland of *raga*, or musical melodies', is a multivalent word. Primarily, it is concerned with aesthetic response and is most commonly encountered in the appreciation of a type of Indian painting (**1**, **2**). Inherent in its use is the idea that there is an emotional connection between on the one hand, poetry and a painted depiction of the emotion of the poetry, and on the other the response to a melody. Certain melodies, *raga*, are also specific to particular times of day and also the seasons (**3**). Thus, poetry, painting and music are all gathered together in a system that is linked to time. The Indian love of categorizing has produced a system connecting all these elements together: this is *ragamala*. In this system, there is a male *raga* who has a series of wives, *ragini*, and sometimes they have sons, *ragaputra*; they all have specific characteristics that may be invoked in poetry and also in music.

Frequently, the separation of lovers, *viraha*, is the sentiment behind the paintings, and it is usually the heroine (in the Krishna paintings, this is understood to be his consort Radha) who is depicted as longing for the presence of her lover – often the empty bed, waiting for his return, appears in the corner of the painting (**4**). For any viewer of such paintings in the 17th and 18th centuries, this would have immediately brought to mind a yet further element, the *bhakti* poetry of devotees who understood the separation of lovers as a metaphor for the longing of the human soul for union with the divine (for *bhakti*, see pp. 162–3).

1. *Vilaval ragini*

The heroine prepares herself for her lover, combing her hair before a mirror held by her attendant. The emotion of *viraha*, separation, is engendered by the image. She sits within a pavilion of pre-Mughal type, harking back to earlier imagery. The paintings of this *ragamala* sequence are distinguished by dark skies and stylized trees.

Opaque watercolour on paper
Mid-17th century
Height 19.7 cm, width 14.5 cm
Malwa, central India
Donated by Calouste Gulbenkian, 1924,1228,0.3

Right
2. *Asavari ragini*
This musical expression is imagined as a tribal woman, complete with peacock-feather skirt, charming the snakes out of the trees with her singing; here she accompanies herself on the *vina*. The scene is imagined on a rocky island, surrounded by flowering water lilies.

Opaque watercolour on paper
c. 1740
Height 31.9 cm, width 21.6 cm
Deccan
Marjorie Coldwell Fund,
1964,0411,0.2

Below left
3. *Vasanta ragini*
The *Vasanta*, or springtime, *ragini* is imagined here as the heroine dancing with her beau, depicted as Krishna, in a lush garden. They are accompanied by musicians while, in the background, the bed awaits.

Opaque watercolour on paper
c. 1650
Height 38.4, width 24.9 cm
Malwa, central India
Donated by Dr Ananda
Coomaraswamy, 1927,0223,0.1

Below right
4. Probably *Dipak raga*
Similar emotions of longing are suggested here as in Figure 1. The distraught heroine awaits her lover, holding a lamp with a guttering flame. Meanwhile, the empty bed awaits and the moon shines above in a starlit night.

Opaque watercolour on paper
c. 1660
Height 27.7 cm, width 18 cm
(including border)
Bundi, Rajasthan
Brooke Sewell Permanent Fund,
1958,1011,0.7

Timeline

1510	The Portuguese establish a trading post at Goa
c. 1605	The painter Nasiruddin flourishes
1615	Udaipur, the last of the Rajput kingdoms, falls to the Mughals
1660s	The *Rasamanjari* is illustrated with vibrant paintings from the court of Nurpur
c. 1660s onwards	Chintz popular in Europe; Samuel Pepys mentions the craze in his diaries
c. 1680–1695	The 'Shangri Ramayana' painted
1690	Job Charnock founds European settlement at Calcutta
Late 17th century onwards	Embroidered counterpanes exported to Europe from Gujarat
1719–1748	Muhammad Shah, Mughal emperor, rules in Delhi
1728	Construction of the city of Jaipur
c. 1730–1775	The painter Nainsukh flourishes in Himachal Pradesh
1739	Sack of Mughal Delhi by Nadir Shah of Persia
1754–1775	Shuja al-Daula rules in Lucknow (succeeded by his son, Asaf al-Daula, 1775–1797)
1757	Battle of Plassey won by Robert Clive; Bengal falls to the British
1761–1782	Reign of Haider Ali in Mysore
1774–1785	Warren Hastings, first Governor-General of India
1777–1783	Sir Elijah and Lady Impey commission natural history paintings in Calcutta from Shaikh Zain ud-Din; early 'Company Paintings'
1782–1799	Reign of Tipu Sultan in Mysore
1784	Founding of the Asiatick Society of Bengal
1787	Botanic Garden at Sibpur founded by Robert Kydd; William Roxburgh appointed Superintendent in 1793
1792–1839	Reign of Ranjit Singh in the Punjab
c. 1800	Production of the oldest surviving Bengal storytelling scrolls
1815	Kingdom of Kandy ends; British rule begins
1857	Mutiny in Meerut develops into uprisings throughout north India
1858	End of East India Company rule; establishment of direct British government rule through a Viceroy
1858	Linnaeus Tripe, photographer, in south India
c. 1860 onwards	Oomersee Mawjee, silversmith, active in Bhuj

5

Europeans and the British in India

1510–1900

European traders were increasingly active on the political stage in India in the later Mughal period: initially the Portuguese, whose settlement at Goa was founded in 1510 (1), and then the Dutch, prominent in Surat in western India and in Sri Lanka, followed by the French and the English. It was eventually the latter who were sufficiently able to take advantage both of the chaos of the collapsing Mughal empire and the engagement with successor states. They moved from being merely traders in highly lucrative commodities into being politically controlling, especially in the gathering of tax revenues. This process was gradual and piecemeal but continuous. In the 17th century the fort at Madras (now Chennai) on the southeast coast was important as it was from here that trade with the all-important spice mart in what is now Malaysia and Indonesia was carried on; interest in Sri Lanka, the only part of South Asia other than the Himalayas where Buddhism still flourished, also came early. Later, and especially following the career of Robert Clive (1725–1774) and his victory at the battle of Plassey (1757), the focus moved to Bengal, already hugely wealthy on account of the extensive textile trade. Here, the seat of power was in Calcutta (now Kolkata) and great fortunes were made both by British and Bengali bankers and merchants, some of whom – such as members of the Tagore family – went on to have a great impact in later generations. Trade was not only in textiles such as muslin (especially from Dacca, now Dhaka), but also in indigo, opium and, in the 19th century, tea.

1. The Basilica of Bom Jesus in Old Goa
Constructed in 1594–1605 and one of the most important of the Portuguese churches in Goa, the Bom Jesus is also famous as the location of the tomb of St Francis Xavier. The saint is renowned not only as one of the founders of the Jesuit order, but also as an evangelizer of Roman Catholicism in India, and then also in Japan and China. Churches in this distinctive baroque style were constructed in many of the Portuguese trading settlements along the western coast of India.

2. Varaha, the boar incarnation of Vishnu, rescues the earth goddess from a sea-demon

The violence of this narrative of the rape of the earth goddess by the demon is impressively suggested in this painting, a page from a sequence of the *dashavatara*, the ten incarnations of Vishnu (Varaha is the third). The bold juxtaposition of colours and the drama of the narrative are typical of the early ateliers of the Punjab Hills – at Basohli, Nurpur and, as here, Mankot. These characteristics make them still greatly admired today.

Gouache on paper
c. 1710
Height 29.6 cm, width 19.7 cm
The court atelier of Mankot (in present-day Himachal Pradesh)
Brooke Sewell Permanent Fund, 1966,0725,0.1

As the Mughal empire collapsed in the 18th century following the death of Aurangzeb in 1707, smaller states emerged in the subcontinent, set up by erstwhile governors or generals who proclaimed their independence; they all to a greater or lesser extent engaged with the European traders. Three powerful examples were the courts of Lucknow, on the Gomti river (a tributary of the Ganges) and to the east of Delhi; Murshidabad on the Hugli river in Bengal, to the north of Calcutta; and Hyderabad in the Deccan. In each of these courts, Iranian-influenced Shi'a Islam was prominent, a feature that provided their architecture, painting activities and decorative arts with a distinctive characteristic. The vast majority of their subjects were, however, always Hindu.

In the Punjab, to the north of Rajasthan, the Sikhs, who had been troublesome to the later Mughal authority, failed to coalesce around any specific individual until the reign of the impressive Ranjit Singh (r. 1792–1839). Through sheer force

Narasinghavatara or 8th avatar vishnu relieving on the serpent Amonta (eternity) Contemplating the creation of the world.

3. Vishnu enshrined at Shrirangam, Tamil Nadu
This painting with its gorgeous colours comes from a portfolio where almost all of the works show individual Hindu deities, some in specific temples, as here. Rich colouring and the depiction of the fine textiles, for which the region was famous, are features of this group of south Indian 'Company paintings'. They illustrate aspects of local religious life which were, for the British, new, exciting and important to record. The deity, being the most important feature, is shown much larger than in reality, but elements of the temple layout are also included such as the circular tank at top right, the Chandra Pushkarini, and nearby a sacred tree and Krishna shrine.

Gouache on European laid and watermarked paper
c. 1820 (watermarks include the date '1816')
Height 29.2 cm, width 22.9 cm
Probably Tamil Nadu
Brooke Sewell Permanent Fund, 2007,3005.39

of personality he forged the region into a single kingdom. While the teachings of the Sikh gurus were the most honoured, this kingdom was equally home to Hindus – and, indeed, to a small number of European mercenaries.

Also considered Rajput, though ruling from the foothills of the Himalayas, were a group of princelings whose political insignificance was completely out of scale to their cultural importance. It was here that some of the most intense and thrilling paintings ever produced in India were made in the late 17th century (2). Approximately a century later, this same region produced painters of a different quality – the so-called Pahari painters.

One general feature of the post-Mughal cultural world was that the huge centralized patronage associated with the court was dispersed. The artistic flowering at regional centres such as Lahore and in the courts of Rajasthan was also seen among the craftsmen and artists who found new patrons amongst the Europeans. Magnificent furniture made from luxurious woods such as ebony, rosewood and sandalwood, and inlaid with

**4. A plant of the
Clerodendrum genus,
from the Pearson Album**

This painting is from a fine album
of fifty-eight illustrations by an
unknown artist, the history of
which before 1999 is unknown.
They provide faithful botanical
representations while also being
aesthetically fine examples of
the work of the artists engaged
by the East India Company
in Calcutta.

Opaque watercolour on laid paper
c. 1800
Height 50.8 cm, width 37.2 cm
Probably painted at the Sibpur
Botanic Garden, Calcutta
Bequeathed by Major J. P. S.
Pearson, 1999,0203,0.32

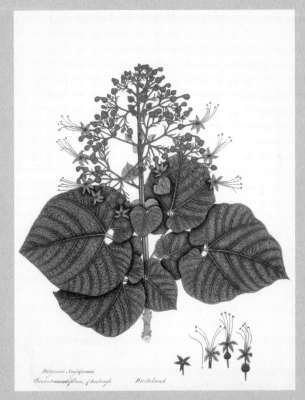

mother-of-pearl, ivory or bone, became popular in Europe.
Painters also found new outlets in the booming cities associated
with European trade. They learnt different techniques, in part
from studying prints that came in large numbers from England.
Their works for European clients were less about formal court
scenes or illustrations to the epics (as in the past), but more
about recording scenes that for many European and above all
British residents in India were new, fascinating and exceptional.
Thus were produced the works which go under the general
name of 'Company paintings'. From Thanjavur in the south (**3**)
to Delhi in the north, these have little stylistic connection. What
they do share, however, is a clientele, a 19th-century date and a
concern with record (**4**). The finest often had a higher purpose
than merely acting as aides-memoires following the return to
Europe of those who had had them produced. At the other end
of the scale were sets of paintings made on small sheets of mica
which listed the different castes, occupations or festivals of the
population, all of which were new to the British in South Asia.

1. A royal encampment, from the Polier Album

Antoine Polier (1741–1795) was a Swiss-born military officer who lived in Faizabad and then Lucknow. He patronized Indian artists, many of whom enjoyed demonstrating their mastery of European techniques such as single-point perspective, as here.

Opaque watercolour on paper
1780–85
Height 54 cm, width 76 cm
Lucknow, Uttar Pradesh
1974,0617,0.5.1

2. Silver bowl

Amongst the several centres producing silver vessels for British and Anglophile Indian households in the 19th and early 20th centuries, Lucknow specialized in a design filled with palm trees, inhabited with wildlife.

Repoussé and chased silver
2nd half of 19th century
Diameter (top) 24 cm, height 15 cm
Lucknow, Uttar Pradesh
Bequeathed by Oppi Untracht, 2011,3014.72

Successor states

Throughout the 18th century, as the control of the Mughal empire declined, separate and increasingly independent states emerged. These included Lucknow in the middle Ganges plain, Murshidabad in Bengal and Hyderabad in the Deccan. They all developed their own cultural styles and all engaged with Europeans culturally and militarily.

Situated on the Gomti, a northern tributary of the Ganges, Lucknow was the centre of the Mughal province of Awadh before it became the capital of an independent dynasty, the most important of whom were the father and son Shuja al-Daula (r. 1754–75) and Asaf al-Daula (r. 1775–97); later, Ghazi al-Din Haidar (r. 1814–27), although politically unremarkable, was culturally important. These rulers (known as nawabs) are today remembered for their building activities. Palaces, mosques, tombs and *imambara* (for marking the Shi'a festival of Muharram, see p. 234) were constructed in an exciting style, drawing on Mughal as well as European elements. They are also known for their patronage of European artists in the late 18th century, including Tilly Kettle and Johann Zoffany, as well as for the presence of European soldiers of fortune, not least Claude Martin, a French soldier but also a man of acute intellectual curiosity. Indian painters, many refugees from the court of Delhi (sacked by the Persian Nadir Shah in 1739), developed styles of painting that excelled in architectural vistas, often using both a bird's eye view and a single vanishing point (**1**), and also flights of fantasy, this associated especially with the painter Mir Kalan Khan.

Lucknow became entangled in the 1857 Indian Uprising and in its aftermath many of the nawabi buildings were destroyed or damaged. Contemporary photographs nevertheless give some idea of the brilliance of their style. The city, however, remained a centre of creativity, not least in the production of silverware (**2**).

Located further down the Ganges river system, Murshidabad was the capital city of eastern India under the Mughals. In the 18th century it became increasingly independent under the nawabs of Bengal, descendants of Murshid Quli Khan after whom the city is named. A sophisticated late Mughal style of painting developed under the patronage of the nawabs (**3**) and the city quickly became a centre for finance and trade. A number of magnificent nawabi palaces were built (**4**), as were mansions for wealthy merchants, especially Jain bankers who had settled in the city. However, its proximity to the English settlement at Calcutta inevitably brought it into conflict with that expanding power, especially following Clive's victory at Plassey in 1757, when the right to gather revenues in the region passed to the British. Murshidabad was also renowned as a centre for silk weaving and ivory carving.

The great city of Hyderabad in the Deccan was ruled by the Asaf Jah family from the period of the break-up of Mughal power in the mid-18th century until the state of Hyderabad accessed to the Union of India in 1948. The Hyderabad rulers were descendants of the Mughal noble Nizam al-Mulk (**5**), who was originally based at the court of the Mughal ruler, Muhammad Shah (r. 1719–48). He broke away, establishing Jah rule in this part of India. The links between Shi'a Iran and this dynasty were strong, and the memory of Persian *sufi* presence significant. But, although the city was predominantly Muslim, and Shi'a, it was always surrounded by a much larger Hindu population.

A group of painters from the city focused on court portraits using a bright and colourful palette (**5**). The immensely wealthy Nizams, as the Hyderabad rulers were known, were great builders in the 19th century and their palaces, such as the Chowmahalla and the Falaknuma (**6**), were constructed in a variety of styles (the latter in neoclassical form).

3. A nawab in a garden setting

The nawab is shown seated, bejeweled and smoking a *huqqa*. Behind him is a servant with a peacock standard, *morchal*, while on the floral floor-spread are both *pandan* (holder of *pan* quids) and *pikdan* (spittoon), both necessary items of hospitality.

Opaque watercolour on paper
c. 1760
Height 24.4 cm, width 35.8 cm
Probably Murshidabad, West Bengal
1920,0917,0.239

4. The palace of the nawab of Murshidabad

This painting by an otherwise unknown Mrs Pattle shows the nawab's palace before the building of the neoclassical Hazarduari in 1829. The pleasure boats shown on the water include a famous type with peacock figureheads, *murpankhi*.

Watercolour on paper
c. 1813
Height 35.8 cm, width 65.8 cm
Murshidabad, West Bengal
Donated by J. L. Douthwaite, 1958,1118.8

5. Nizam al-Mulk in a garden pavilion

Nizam al-Mulk (1671–1748) was the governor of the Deccan in the post-Aurangzeb era of the Mughal empire. His successors were the Asaf Jah family, rulers of Hyderabad until 1948.

Opaque watercolour on paper
c. 1800
Height 20.5 cm, width 14.2 cm
Painted either in Sholapur or Hyderabad
1856,0712,0.911

6. The Falaknuma Palace, Hyderabad

Originally built by a relative of the sixth Nizam of Hyderabad and designed by the English architect William Ward Marrett, this palace soon passed to the Nizam who used it as guest accommodation; today it is a hotel. It is built in a mixed but mostly neoclassical style and is typical of the adoption of architectural styles by the Indian princes during the 19th century.

5 | 1 The Muharram procession

For Shi'a Muslims the death of Imam Husayn – the grandson of the Prophet – at the battle of Kerbala in 680 CE is remembered every year with re-enactments of the battle in which he was martyred, and with processions. This remembrance is known as the Muharram. In the processions, which are common in South Asia, temporary models of the mausoleum of Husayn – known as *ta'ziya* and made of bamboo and cloth – are carried by men through the streets with much evidence of mourning including breast-beating and self-flagellation (**1**). Also carried in the processions are wooden standards with metal terminals, many of which are in the form of a hand with outstretched fingers, *'alam* (**2**, **3**).

Muharram processions take place throughout India, especially memorable being those at Murshidabad in Bengal, at Lucknow in Uttar Pradesh and in many of the cities of the Deccan, pre-eminently Hyderabad. In the Deccan, Shi'a cultural and political influence from Iran was particularly marked during the 16th–19th centuries – and this included the Muharram processions. For most of the year, the *'alam*, impressive examples of the metalsmith's work, are stored, only to come out for the processions, during which they are also often covered in cloth and honoured with garlands of jasmine. Some *'alam* are believed to have healing powers and are approached by devotees for relief from sickness. Many have engraved decoration which frequently includes calligraphy with Qur'anic and specifically Shi'a texts (**2**).

1. Album painting of the Muharram procession
The domed structure carried in the procession is a model of the mausoleum of Husayn, while between it and the elephant a man carries an *'alam* decked with a floral garland. Immediately in front of him two figures each carry further models of the sacred tomb.

Opaque watercolour and gold on paper
1820–30
Height 30.8 cm, width 44 cm
Tamil Nadu, probably Tiruchirappalli
Brooke Sewell Permanent Fund, 2005,0716,0.1.7

Mahommedan Procession during the Moharrum Feast

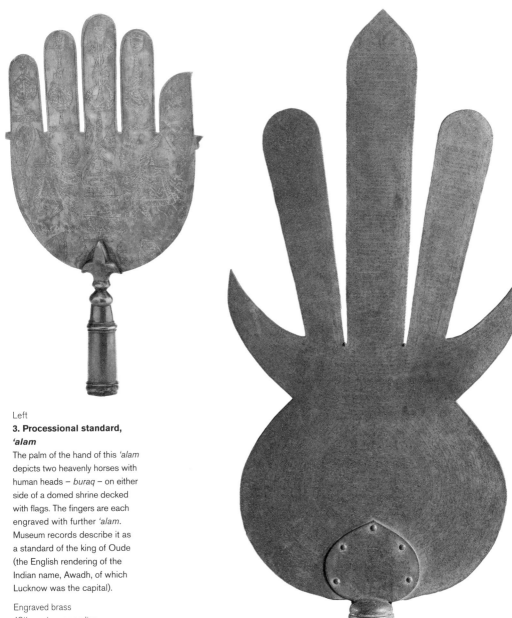

Left

3. Processional standard, *'alam*

The palm of the hand of this *'alam* depicts two heavenly horses with human heads – *buraq* – on either side of a domed shrine decked with flags. The fingers are each engraved with further *'alam*. Museum records describe it as a standard of the king of Oude (the English rendering of the Indian name, Awadh, of which Lucknow was the capital).

Engraved brass
18th century or earlier
(in the British Museum by 1860)
Lucknow, Uttar Pradesh
Height 41 cm
As1863,1101.1

Right

2. Processional standard, *'alam*

These standards, shaped as open hands, commemorate the battle of Karbala in which Husayn, the grandson of the Prophet, and his family were killed. This example, to be carried in Muharram processions, is of a huge size and is inscribed on every surface, including a panel listing the names of the Twelve Imams.

Engraved brass
Perhaps 18th century
The Deccan
Height 214.5 cm, width 78.3 cm
Donated by Mrs Hallinan,
1920,0707.1

5|2 Storytelling scrolls

There is a long-standing tradition in India of itinerant storytellers using painted scrolls to accompany their tales (see p. 114). The examples illustrated here – from Bengal, Telangana and Rajasthan – share an ancient Indian aesthetic which is unconcerned with photo-reality but interested in colour, hierarchy, emotional response and pattern. The size of these items, the division into frames, the colour and the action in the stories, makes them the equivalent of cinema, long before its invention.

In Bengal, painted scrolls on paper survive from the last couple of centuries though they were certainly used much earlier. The constant rolling and unrolling of the scrolls as the bard sings the narrative has meant that few old examples now exist. One tells the stories of Muslim saints, *pir*, associated with the settlement of the delta region of the Ganges–Brahmaputra river (**2**). Another in a very similar style depicts scenes from the Ramayana, indicating that the artists involved could be oblivious to religious difference.

A similar tradition of painted scrolls is known in Telangana, though with a quite different style. Here, the origin narratives of individual castes are depicted. One dramatic story illustrates the origin of the Padma Sale or weavers' caste; they are the descendants of Bhavana Rishi, the hero shown on the register illustrated here (**1**). Appropriately, the first register of these scrolls depicts Ganesha, who is honoured before the recitation of the legend.

The final example comes from Rajasthan and was used, at night, to tell the legends of the hero Pabuji (**3**). The narrative is painted on a large cotton cloth or *par*, not a scroll. The storyteller's wife carried a lamp to illuminate the scenes while the narrator moved in front of the cloth as he sang the story.

1. Storytelling scroll from Telangana
Bhavana Rishi, the hero of the narrative of this scroll and the ancestor of the weavers of Telangana, is depicted riding a tiger and battling with a *rakshasa*, a demon – he can control both the natural and the supernatural worlds.

Paint on sized cotton
Late 18th century
Entire scroll 9.3 m, register shown 85.5 cm
Telangana
Brooke Sewell Permanent Fund, 1996,0615,0.1

Above left and right
2. Storytelling scroll from Bengal
In the central register of this 13-m long scroll (see also p. 170), at left, Manik *pir* is shown miraculously causing a cow to lactate and bringing other cattle to life that had died in a fire. The scarlet ground against which the animals and the saint are placed is typical of the ancient Indian style, full of drama but uninterested in landscape or realism. Throughout this scroll, the depiction of animals is especially fine, no more so than in the register shown at right. In South Asia the elephant is associated especially with royalty, as here where a Muslim royal figure is seen in a howdah with a figure behind him holding a fly-whisk (another indicator of high status).

Paint on paper (now mounted on cloth)
c. 1800
Height of Manik *pir* register 34 cm (entire scroll is 13 m long)
Bengal, probably the Sunderbans
The Art Fund (as NACF), 1955,1008,0.95

Right
3. Cloth painting of the Pabuji *par*
The legend of the Rajasthan hero Pabuji is full of escapades of cattle-rustling, romance and brigandage. In this detail the hero sits in his castle, armed but also, like a Mughal emperor, with a sweet-smelling blossom pressed to his nose.

Paint on cotton
Early 20th century
Length 540 cm, width 132 cm (entire cloth)
Rajasthan, probably Marwar
1994,0523,0.1

5 | 3 Tipu Sultan, 'the Tiger of Mysore'

Haider Ali (r. 1761–82) (**1**) and his son, Tipu Sultan (r. 1782–99) (**3**), played pivotal roles in the story of British expansion in southwestern India at the end of the 18th century. Muslim rulers in a mostly Hindu region, Mysore, they founded a kingdom which waxed and waned as it was first successful but then collapsed, unable to withstand spreading British power. In the complex web of alliances that operated in southern India following the breakup of Mughal power, Tipu was – in the British imagination – considered especially malign, holding British prisoners captive and allying himself with the French; he was too independent, resisting inclusion in British sovereignty.

Despite the four Anglo-Mysore wars in which he and his father were involved, Tipu Sultan maintained a sophisticated court at which Persian as well as the Kannada and Telugu languages were current; Mysore was also the centre of important trade networks. Most of the items produced at Tipu Sultan's court were marked with his distinctive tiger imagery – either the beast itself (**4**) or tiger-stripes, *babri*.

The rule of Tipu came to an end following the battle of Seringapatam in 1799 (the name is an anglicized version of his capital Shrirangapatnam). After the battle, the palace was ransacked and many items removed, most famous of which were the parts of Tipu's dismantled gold throne. A medal commemorating the British victory was struck and distributed to soldiers who had taken part (**2**). The memory of Tipu as a figure who stood up to British power has meant that he remains a talismanic figure in southern India. In this context one of India's foremost modern playwrights, Girish Karnad, has written a play in which Tipu – and his dreams – are the foremost characters.

1. Haider Ali

Haider Ali, the father of Tipu Sultan, usurped the throne of the Wodeyar rulers of Mysore and later fought two campaigns against the British. In the late 19th century, the Chitrashala Steam Press, one of the earliest to produce cheap popular prints, made a speciality of local heroes of the Deccan.

Print from the Chitrashala Steam Press
1878–1900
Height 50 cm, width 33.7 cm
Pune, Maharashtra
1990,0707,0.15

2. The Seringapatam medal

The imagery on this gold medal is clear – the British lion is conquering the Indian tiger; it is dated 1799, the year of the battle in which Tipu was killed, and on the reverse is a scene of the battlefield. With Tipu's death, the kingdom, under British suzerainty, was returned to the Wodeyar family, who had been dethroned by Haider Ali fifty years earlier.

Gold
1799
Diameter 4.8 cm
Produced in Birmingham
Donated by HM George IV,
G3,EM.57

3. Tipu Sultan

Tipu was of enormous interest to the British public, and in the aftermath of his death, paintings and then prints were produced. Many of these were fanciful but this portrait has some chance of being close to a portrait.

Mezzotint print by S. W. Reynolds, from an original drawing
Published in May 1800
London
Height 27.1 cm, width 18.8 cm
Donated by Campbell Dodgson, 1917,0809.27

Engraved by S.W. Reynolds.

TIPPOO SULTAUN.
From an original Drawing in the Possession of the Marquis Wellesley.

4. Sword from the armoury of Tipu Sultan

Distinctively marked with a prowling tiger, and with a tiger-stripe just below the hilt, this weapon is clearly linked to Tipu Sultan. The Persian inscription in the tiger stripe specifically mentions his name. Many weapons from Tipu's armoury bore similar decorative schemes and, following his defeat, were taken to Europe as trophies.

Forged blade with cast hilt and gold inlay
Late 18th century
Length 97.5 cm, width 9.5 cm
Mysore region, southwestern Deccan
Donated by Lt-Gen Augustus W. H. Meyrick, 1878,1101.450

5 | 4 The Sikhs: devotion and defence

Sikhism traces its origins to the teacher Guru Nanak (1469–1539) (**1**). He was one of a number of spiritual teachers who became prominent in the turbulent years before the establishment of the Mughal state in northern India. Guru Nanak operated primarily in the Punjab region, famously teaching that being a Hindu or a Muslim was unimportant; what was crucial to him was man's love for God, and that religious labels (and thus antagonisms) were distractions. His teachings, along with those of other saints, were later gathered together in a great volume, the *Guru Granth Sahib*. In a Sikh shrine, this is the main object of reverence; there are no images.

After the death of Guru Nanak came a sequence of nine further gurus who guided the disciples of the original teacher. Several of these later gurus suffered at the hands of the Mughal emperors: the fifth, Arjun, was executed during the reign of Jahangir, while the ninth, Tegh Bahadur, was executed on the orders of Aurangzeb. The last of the Ten Gurus was Guru Gobind Singh (1666–1708) (**2**) who, under the pressure of persecution, turned his followers into a martial community, keen to defend their beliefs even if it meant suffering martyrdom. This emphasis on martial life later resulted in the development of the Akali, itinerant warriors recognizable by their distinctive tall blue turbans filled with weapons (**3**).

Sikh temples, or *gurudwara*, are found throughout South Asia, though the Punjab is their stronghold. The most renowned example is the Harmandir, popularly known as the Golden Temple, which is located in Amritsar (**4**).

1. Guru Nanak
Created long after his death, this painting of Guru Nanak includes a rebab-player (at left); this is Mardana, a Muslim musician who travelled with the saint, singing the hymns that he composed.

Opaque watercolour on paper
c. 1820
Height 13.8 cm, width 18.5 cm
Kangra, Himachal Pradesh
1922,1214,0.2

2. The formation of the *khalsa*
The last of the Sikh gurus, Guru Gobind Singh, is shown here enthroned and administering the *amrit* to his followers – this was a drink of water and sugar, but all who drank it were then bound as a community to defend their beliefs; they became the *khalsa*. This event took place at Anandpur at the spring festival of Vaisakhi, an event recorded in the inscription in Gurmukhi script above the figures.

Hand-coloured print
c. 1890
Height 26.3 cm, width 40.4 cm
The Punjab, probably Lahore
1994,1216,0.5

3. Akali turban
The towering blue turbans of the Akali frequently hold weapons, especially quoits. Symbolic items and insignia are also often wrapped in; here they include a badge of the 45th Rattray's Sikhs, a regiment of the British Indian Army famous for their military deeds.

Blue-dyed cotton (modern); steel ornaments and insignia
Second half of 19th century
Height 72.5 cm, diameter 28.5 cm (max)
Given to the Banqueting House Museum in 1894 by Lt-Col. H. A. Sawyer, Commander of the 45th Rattray's Sikhs; later transferred to the British Museum, 2005,0727.1.a-p

Below

4. The Harmandir, Amritsar
This famous temple in Amritsar in the Punjab, also known colloquially as the Golden Temple, is the most sacred for all Sikhs. It is built of white marble, the upper part sheathed in gilded bronze plates and the lower part inlaid with coloured stone in floral patterns. The building is located in a man-made pool and approached across a stone causeway (at right).

Paint and gold on paper
Mid- to late 19th century
Height 18.7 cm, width 23 cm
The Punjab, probably Lahore
Brooke Sewell Permanent Fund,
1984,0124,0.1.17

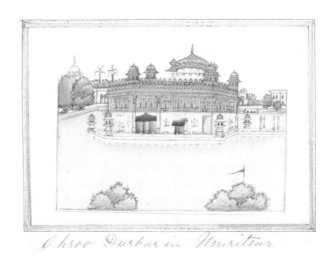

5 | 5 Ranjit Singh

As the Mughal empire collapsed in the 18th century, the peripheral parts asserted their independence. The Punjab and surrounding territories were fought over by Persians, Afghans and Marathas, with Sikh warriors also involved. The last of the Sikh gurus (see p. 240), Guru Gobind Singh, had been assassinated in 1708 and it was only under the leadership of Ranjit Singh (r. 1792–1839) that unification of the various Sikh groups was affected. During his reign a single and increasingly powerful Sikh presence became established in the Punjab.

Although small of stature and scarred by smallpox in his youth (this resulted in the loss of sight in one eye), Ranjit Singh was clearly a ruler of exceptional character (**2**). He managed to bind together the warring Sikh factions and, through force of arms (**1**), extend his rule as far as Kabul in Afghanistan, Multan in Sindh and the hill states north of the Punjab; he also controlled Jammu and Kashmir. Based in the old Mughal city of Lahore, he was successful too in diplomacy and during his reign there was peace between the British in Delhi and the Sikh kingdom.

While alive, he held the various Sikh groups together, but following Ranjit Singh's death, five family members – three sons and one grandson – followed him in quick and bloody succession. The British intervened in this chaos on their frontier in the two Anglo-Sikh Wars. After the first, at the Treaty of Bhairowal, they set up the surviving young son of Ranjit Singh, Dalip Singh, as a puppet king (**3**). The Second Anglo-Sikh War, three years later, resulted in Dalip Singh being deposed and sent into exile in England. Peace returned to the Punjab, but under British rule (**4**).

1. Quoit
Although this highly decorated example was probably made only for display, the quoit was a weapon used by the Sikhs to deadly effect. As in the example illustrated on p. 241, quoits were often carried in a warrior's turban.

Blackened steel with gold inlay
18th century
Diameter 19.7 cm
The Punjab
Bequeathed by John Henderson, 1878,1230.945

2. Ranjit Singh and the Maratha ruler Jaswant Rao Holkar
At this meeting Holkar unsuccessfully tried to garner support for his campaign against expanding British power. Ranjit Singh (in red) more astutely maintained peace with the British.

Opaque watercolour on paper
1805–10
Height 17.1 cm, width 24.2 cm
The Punjab
1936,0411,0.1

3. The Treaty of Bhairowal, 26 December 1846

The young Dalip Singh appears amongst members of the Sikh court, facing Lord Hardinge, Governor-General of India, and other British officers.

Opaque watercolour on paper
c. 1847
Height 39.5 cm, width 53.9 cm
The Punjab
Bequeathed by P. C. Manuk and Miss G. M. Coles, through the Art Fund (as the NACF), 1948,1009,0.109

4. Sikh women riding in a covered cart

The use of European perspective and shading to indicate volume is seen in the later 19th century as in this painting by Kapur Singh. The bullocks are finely caparisoned, as if the travellers are en route to a wedding.

Opaque watercolour and gold on paper
1874
Height 36.9 cm, width 49.8 cm (painting)
Lahore, the Punjab
Brooke Sewell Permanent Fund, 1997,0616,0.1

5 | 6 *Kalamkari* cloth from south India

Renowned as coming from southern India, but especially from the town of Kalahasti in southern Andhra, is a type of narrative painting on cloth: *kalamkari*. These were mostly made for temple use. Other centres further south in Tamil Nadu are less well known. These large textiles use the range of dyeing techniques for which the region is famous. *Kalamkari* are, in technical terms, the local equivalent of the chintz wares that were so greatly admired in Europe in the 17th and 18th centuries (see pp. 196–7). In the past, these large cloths have had Hindu subject matter, though in recent decades Christian subjects have also been treated. Frequently, a large central panel shows the main deity or event, with all around in comic-strip format, further elements of the story of the figure shown in the centre (**2**). Captions in the local script, Telugu, are also often added.

 Kalamkari cloths were probably mostly shown behind images of the deity in temples, or hung in columned halls, *mandapa*, in temple compounds. In the latter location, they were displayed to allow devotees to understand the narratives of the deity concerned. This was especially useful in the past when literacy was low and, in this respect, such paintings belong to the same category as storytelling scroll paintings (see pp. 236–7). Other examples show scenes from the epics, such as the Ramayana (**1**), or depict individual deities (**3**).

 Kalamkari were prepared on sized cotton. The production process is lengthy but it begins with the painting of the outlines of the individual figures using a bamboo pen, or *kalam*, though repeated outlines were sometimes block-printed. The colour is provided by the repeated immersion of the cloths in dye baths with certain areas reserved using a resist (for blue), or the application of a mordant (for the distinctive red). Some painting was also carried out by hand, so the finished cloth is an amalgam of different techniques.

1. *Kalamkari* textile depicting scenes from the Ramayana
This detail, in comic-strip form around the main image of crowned Rama, depicts the building of the bridge to Lanka. This is one of the exploits engineered by Hanuman and his monkey army. Fishes, crabs and other denizens of the sea are shown below the monkey army building the bridge.

Cotton, pen-drawn, block-printed and dyed, using both a reserve and a mordant
20th century
Length 358 cm, width 175 cm (entire cloth)
Andhra Pradesh, probably Kalahasti
As 1966,01.496

2. *Kalamkari* textile

The roundel at the centre of this large cloth depicts Vishnu lying on the cosmic serpent, Ananta. This image is the one venerated at the Ranganatha temple on the island of Shrirangam, near Tiruchirappalli in Tamil Nadu, here indicated by the blue circle filled with fish. Beyond this central zone are registers in which episodes from the Mahabharata are illustrated.

Cotton, pen-drawn, block-printed and dyed, using both a reserve and a mordant
19th/early 20th century
Height 335 cm, width 390 cm (entire cloth)
Andhra Pradesh, probably Kalahasti
Brooke Sewell Permanent Fund, 1991,0327,0.1

3. *Kalamkari* textile of the goddess Durga

The twelve-armed goddess rides on her *vahana*, the lion. Durga's fierce nature is indicated by her weapons, her flaming hair and the chequered sari she wears, the latter distinctive of other fierce goddesses in Andhra Pradesh.

Cotton, pen-drawn, block-printed and dyed, using both a reserve and a mordant
c. 1920
Height 254 cm, width 248.5 cm
Andhra Pradesh, probably Kalahasti
Brooke Sewell Permanent Fund, 1995,1109,0.1

5 | 7 Embroidery

In the array of textile techniques dazzlingly practised by the craftsmen of South Asia, that of embroidery has a long history, with a wide range of stitches, threads and grounds being used. Northwestern and northeastern India have been the main regions of production. Amongst early examples are those made for the export market in Portugal (see pp. 194–5). However, embroidered floor-spreads and counterpanes made in Gujarat – arguably the most important centre in India for embroidery – and again for the European market, are known from the late 17th century onwards. These are of great quality and worked in chain stitch by professional craftsmen (**1**).

From more recent times are shawls used at marriages in the Punjab and known as *phulkari* ('flower-covered') and *bagh* ('garden'). Other embroidered textiles were made for religious use, such as *picchvai* from Rajasthan, which were used in Krishna shrines (**2**). Meanwhile the *rumal* of the Punjab Hills – also embroidered with scenes from the life of Krishna – were used to cover trays of offerings to the deity. Lastly amongst the religious embroideries are banners worked with metal thread and produced for Shi'a ceremonial (**3**).

Not surprisingly, embroidered cloth is also found in costume. A few spectacular Mughal items survive but more common are items of clothing from rural communities, especially in western India. Head-coverings, *odhni*, worn by women in western Gujarat and Sindh, are embroidered with designs, often of floral or circular patterning (**4**). Also from rural western India is a custom of heavily embroidering clothing, especially for children.

Amongst other well-known traditions are those associated with Lucknow (white-on-white embroidery, *chikan*), Bengal (*kantha*; see pp. 278–9) and from the semi-nomadic communities of the Deccan, the Banjara (see pp. 264–5).

1. Embroidered floor-spread
The vivid and fixed colours, and the mix of exotic and fantastical imagery stitched on export items such as this one made them greatly sought after in Europe. The visual vocabulary here is drawn from courtly Mughal as well as local Gujarati sources.

Coloured silk on cotton
c. 1700
Length 320 cm, width 274 cm (entire spread)
Gujarat
Collection of Lanto Synge

2. Embroidered *picchvai*
Doubtless made for a shrine of the Pushtimarg (see p. 220), this *picchvai* shows Krishna playing the flute and flanked by *gopis* (adoring female cowherders). He stands nonchalantly beneath the flowering tree, the *kadamba* with which he is associated. Beneath and around are images related to his youth spent in the pastoral idyll of Vrindavan.

Silk embroidery in chain stitch on satin
Late 19th or early 20th century
Height 211 cm, width 134 cm
Kutch, Gujarat
Brooke Sewell Permanent Fund, 1992,0131,0.1

3. Embroidered banner
One of a pair, this banner was probably used in the annual Muhurram procession (see p. 234), especially as the names of the Shi'a imams are embroidered on it. The use of gold-wrapped thread resulting in high relief embroidery is typical of Muslim styles of needlework.

Cotton, satin, silk, velvet, sequins, glass spangles and gold thread
Late 19th or early 20th century
Height 164 cm, width 46.5 cm
North India
Brooke Sewell Permanent Fund, 2003,0718,0.1

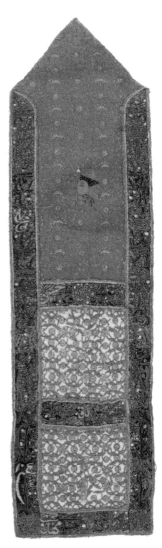

4. Embroidered *odhni*

Decorated overall in chain stitch embroidery, this shawl (of which a detail of the central design is shown here) makes a striking aesthetic statement with its black ground with maroon and yellow stitching, set with shining mirrorwork. Such items are typical of the southern Thar Desert, near the current border of India and Pakistan.

Silk shawl with embroidery and glass mirrorwork
Late 19th or early
20th century
Length 195 cm, width 170 cm
(entire shawl)
Kutch, Gujarat
Brooke Sewell Permanent
Fund, 2012,3020.1

5 | 8 Paintings from the Punjab Hills

Some of the most visually exciting paintings – in subject matter and colour combination – were produced in the small courts of the Punjab Hills at the turn of the 17th–18th century. Today, the brilliance of the colours and the violence of the imagery has meant that these are greatly sought after. The svelte character of Mughal painting, or the sweetness of later Pahari painting is absent; violence, often for cultic or martial reasons, is frequently apparent and the pre-Islamic inheritance of Indian painting is still clear. We know, or can infer, the names of a number of the artists involved.

Amongst the earliest paintings, from around 1660–70 and probably by Kripal (the head of a family of artists from Nurpur), are dramatic works illustrating the *Rasamanjari*, a text by the poet Bhanudatta in which the archetypes of hero, *nayaka*, and heroine, *nayika*, are described and depicted. The use of iridescent green beetle carapaces inset into the page surface is a distinctive feature of the paintings in this *Rasamanjari* sequence (**2**). Somewhat later, from about 1715 and probably by the painter Golu, the grandson of Kripal, is another sequence of paintings illustrating the *Rasamanjari* (**3**). Here, the male archetype is no longer Krishna but a courtly figure, perhaps the painter's patron, Raja Daya Dhata of Nurpur.

From nearby Bahu comes a painting from a *ragamala* series (see pp. 222–3). Clashing colours are again prominent, with a narrative that is only slightly less alarming (**1**). Also probably from Bahu, is a Ramayana sequence known as the 'Shangri Ramayana'; paintings from this group are dated to about 1680–95. Amongst another of the memorable court styles is that from Mankot – illustrations to the *Bhagavata Purana* (see pp. 162–3) are justifiably renowned, with bold single colour backgrounds, a high horizon and an accomplished use of colours (see p. 101).

1. Painting related to the musical composition, *Ahiri Ragini*
Spectacular colour combinations along with the subject matter that includes close proximity to a deadly snake make for an arresting image. The music suggested is described in texts as similar to the sound of a slithering snake.

Opaque watercolour on paper
c. 1720
Height 19.1 cm, width 17.9 cm
Bahu, Himachal Pradesh
Bequeathed by P. C. Manuk and Miss G. M. Coles, through the Art Fund (as NACF), 1948,1009,0.108

2. Painting from a *Rasamanjari* series, perhaps by Kripal
In this listing of heroic types, the hero is imagined as Krishna, blue-skinned and wearing his signature yellow dhoti. Meanwhile, this heroine in poet Bhanudatta's text is the one who is clever in speech, and she is shown here insouciantly suggesting that the heat of the day is oppressive while the shade of the bedchamber is cool. The dramatic colour scheme only emphasizes the not too subtle message.

Opaque watercolour and gold, with inlaid iridescent beetle carapaces
1660–70
Height 23.4 cm, width 33 cm
Basohli, Himachal Pradesh
Bequeathed by P. C. Manuk and Miss G. M. Coles, through the Art Fund (as NACF), 1948,1009,0.107

3. Painting from a *Rasamanjari* series, by Golu
A slightly later series of paintings but of the same type as Figure 1 depicts two lovers in separate chambers with a female go-between. Agonizing separation, *viraha*, is the emotion suggested by this image, which is emphasized by the way the heroine's back is arched upwards, pushed up by her left foot pressed down firmly on the gorgeous floor-spread.

Opaque watercolour on paper
c. 1710
Height 17.2 cm, width 27.6 cm
Nurpur, Himachal Pradesh
Brooke Sewell Permanent Fund, 1961,0211,0.2

5 | 9 The painter Nainsukh and his family

Nainsukh was one of the greatest painters of the later Punjab Hills, or Pahari, school. He was born around 1710 into the family of an established painter, Pandit Seu, in the hill state of Guler (in present-day Himachal Pradesh). He flourished mostly in the middle years of the 18th century in the employ of the ruler of a nearby state, Jasrota, probably dying in 1778.

Although he worked at other courts both before and afterwards, he is, above all remembered for the paintings he produced at the court of Jasrota, especially those depicting the ruler, Balwant Singh (r. 1724–63), with whom he seems, unusually, to have had a close personal bond (2). The empathy between the painter and his subject is clear to see in the finished works. His patron seems to have been a connoisseur of music as performances frequently appear in Nainsukh's paintings, though subjects also include the quotidian, an unusual feature in Indian painting.

Whether Nainsukh and his family trained in the Mughal court ateliers is still debated. Paintings depicting the Mughal ruler Muhammad Shah and attributed to Nainsukh (1) may have been produced by him in Delhi, or by him in the hills but with knowledge of painting in the plains. Other members of Nainsukh's family included a brother, Manaku, who was probably responsible for a dramatic painting sequence, in large folios, illustrating the Ramayana (3). Sons and nephews of Nainsukh and those they influenced, continued the Pahari style into the 19th century.

1. Painting of the Mughal emperor Muhammad Shah, attributed to Nainsukh
Muhammad Shah was painted extensively by artists in his Delhi atelier. Compared to other paintings from the late Mughal court, the young Nainsukh's rather spare production was probably painted before he had developed the style that is recognized in his mature works.

Opaque watercolour on paper
1735–40
Height 25.4 cm, width 35.6 cm
Guler, Himachal Pradesh
Bequeathed by P. C. Manuk and Miss G. M. Coles through the Art Fund (as NACF),
1948,1009,0.148

ॸ३ॺॖॺॺॺ॑ॺॷॻ॑ॷॵॼ । ॸ३ॺ॒ॷक़ॎॗक़ॱॷॣॻॖॺॱॷॻ   ॷॺॴॻॱॺॺॱॷॻॱ

2. Painting of Raja Balwant Singh listening to music, by Nainsukh

Intense concentration, both on behalf of the ruler and of the musicians he is listening to, is clear in this evocation of small courtly life. Such qualities seem to have endeared the work of Nainsukh to early collectors of Indian painting such as the Armenian Percival Chater Manuk and his English companion, Miss Coles, who bequeathed part of their huge collection to the British Museum.

Opaque watercolour on paper
1745–50
Height 19.2 cm, width 32.5 cm
Jasrota, Himachal Pradesh
Bequeathed by P. C. Manuk and Miss G. M. Coles through the Art Fund (as NACF), 1948,1009,0.130

3. Unfinished page from the 'Siege of Lanka' series, perhaps by Manaku

Ferocious demons pour out of the gates of Lanka to do battle with Rama's army of bears and monkeys. Rama, his wife Sita and brother Lakshmana are shown seated on the top of the hill, along with Jambavan and Sugriva, kings respectively of the bears and monkeys.

Opaque watercolour on paper
1725–1730
Height 59 cm, width 79.8 cm
Guler, Himachal Pradesh
The Art Fund (as NACF), 1955,1008,0.78

5 | 10 Divine mobility

A conspicuous feature of religion in many parts of South Asia is the temporary movement of images of the gods through the landscape (for the processing of *ta'ziya*, see p. 234). At festival time, these images of the temple deities are processed through the streets to enable devotees to see them and to have beneficial eye contact, *darshan*. In the past, many temples barred low-caste groups from entry and thus exposure of the deity to all who could cram into the processional space, even if the image was covered entirely in garlands, was a popular event. These images taken through the streets, either on their own *vahana*, in turn held aloft on the shoulders of worshippers (see p. 146), or carried in specially prepared chariots, are usually not the images of the gods enshrined inside the temple, but specially produced festival versions cast in bronze, *utsavamurti*.

Examples of these temporary visits for the gods outside their temples are seen all over India, from Tamil Nadu in the south (**1**) to Orissa in the east, where the famous temple chariots are dedicated to Krishna as Jagannatha (see p. 164), and to Nepal in the north, where Shiva as Bhairava is paraded in the form of a fearsome mask. The chariots in which the gods are carried vary, but one of the most striking is the example from Shrirangam near Tiruchirappalli in Tamil Nadu, a scale model of which was made in the late 18th century and given to the British Museum in 1793 (**3**). Chariots like this are made up of two parts, a lower permanent part made of wood which is decorated with individual panels carved with imagery appropriate to the deity whose image is carried above (**2**), and a temporary upper part of bamboo and cloth which is rebuilt every year.

1. A temple chariot, perhaps at Shrirangam
Around the outer walls of the temple the chariot, with its enshrined and garlanded image visible within, is dragged by devotees, keen to have the honour of proximity to the god. The banner of Hanuman, flying from the caparisoned elephant, suggests that the processed image is of Rama.

Opaque watercolour on paper
c. 1820
Height 20.5 cm, width 29.4 cm
Tamil Nadu, probably Tiruchirappalli
1974,0617,0.14.5

2. Sculpted chariot panel
This panel, complete with a tenon at the top for fixing to the structure, once decorated the lower section of a chariot. Warriors on rearing horses were part of the repertoire of artists at Shrirangam, famously seen at the Shesha Mandapa, a columned hall on the east side of the main temple there.

Wood
19th century or earlier
Height 43.5 cm, width 29 cm
Tamil Nadu, perhaps Shrirangam
Brooke Sewell Permanent Fund,
1997,0127.2

3. Scale model of a temple chariot
Intrigued by the possibility that living religious traditions might explain discoveries at Pompeii, 18th-century savants looked to India for clues. Enquirers such as Charles Marsh acquired Indian objects from David Simpson's 1792 sale in London. Simpson, who was a surgeon, had been based at Shrirangam for the East India Company in the 1780s. Simpson saw at first hand the ceremonial at the Shrirangam temple and had something of it recorded in this model.

Wood, textile, paint
1780s
Height 220 cm, width 90 cm
Tamil Nadu, probably Shrirangam
Donated by Charles Marsh,
1793,0511.1

5 | 11 Masks on the move

In Himachal Pradesh in the western foothills of the Himalayas, the processional form of the god frequently takes the form of a metal mask or *mohra* (1), rather than a three-dimensional image. Such an arrangement is also known in the Kathmandu valley where, during the Matsyendranath festival, a mask of Bhairava (a fierce form of Shiva), rather than the more usual image, is processed in a chariot.

In Himachal, in the area to the north of Shimla, at festival time the *mohra* are brought out of the temple (in the hills these shrines are usually built of wood, or a combination of stone and wood) and placed in wooden palanquins, which are then decorated with flower-offerings and carried in procession by male devotees (2). The movement of the image through the landscape allows all to view the divinity, a beneficial and auspicious experience. It also enables the limits of the god's physical remit to be confirmed and he or she can also visit divine brothers and sisters in nearby villages, re-establishing previous relationships. The garlanded palanquin is accompanied by a crowd, some of whom play distinctive open-mouthed trumpets (3, 4) or serpentine instruments similar to those used in the Middle Ages in Europe. The tradition of producing masks such as these survives today.

1. *Mohra*, perhaps of the god Shiva

The *mohra* acts as a repository of the divine essence during processional tours through the countryside at festival time. This image with its third eye and the snake across the chest indicates a connection with the god Shiva.

Cast bronze
Perhaps 18th century
Height 15.7 cm, width 10 cm
Kullu valley, Himachal Pradesh
Donated by the Simon Digby
Memorial Charity, 2017,3038.57

2. Photograph of a decorated palanquin

The palanquin, *ratha*, contains the masks of the deities; it is covered in garlands. Wooden poles enable the *ratha* to be carried in procession so that devotees can see the faces of the deities.

Colour photograph by Christina Noble
1970s
Manali, Himachal Pradesh
Brooke Sewell Permanent Fund

3. Painting by Nainsukh

Nainsukh (see p. 250) lived
in Himachal Pradesh, a region
where musicians playing these
distinctive open-mouthed
trumpets traditionally accompany
the *mohra* processions. This
painting once belonged to the
British artist Winifred Nicholson
(1893–1981), who recorded
how her experience of India
influenced her own work.

Opaque watercolour on paper
c. 1740
Height 16.3 cm, width 23.7 cm
Jasrota, Himachal Pradesh
Brooke Sewell Permanent Fund
and the Art Fund, 2019,3004.1

4. Photograph of trumpeters

These trumpeters accompanying
a *mohra* procession in the Manali
region in the 1970s are of the
same type as those depicted in
the 18th century by Nainsukh in
the painting above.

Colour photograph by Christina
Noble
1970s
Manali, Himachal Pradesh
Brooke Sewell Permanent Fund

5 | 12 Sri Lanka

Buddhism in Sri Lanka during the later medieval and modern periods has been based on Theravada rather than Mahayana teachings. This is despite the presence in the physical record in earlier history of images associated with Mahayana doctrine, such as *bodhisattvas* (see pp. 68–9). Following the decline in the 13th century of Polonnaruva, the capital city of the island under both Tamil and then later Sinhalese rulers, the centre of power moved increasingly to the southeast of the island. Large-scale sculpture is seen less, while wood, ivory and small bronze sculptures become the norm. Ivory work is especially noteworthy; caskets are known from the 16th century, some used as diplomatic gifts to Europe (**1**). Other examples of ivory carving include fan-handles, furniture inlays and combs. Metal sculpture continued but almost entirely of images of the Buddha – seated or standing. All of these are typical products of the last independent capital of Sri Lanka, Kandy.

Religious syncretism is noted, with the Mahayana deity Avalokiteshvara, morphing into a local deity, Lokeshvara Natha, and devotion to the Hindu deity Skanda (Karttikeya) becoming established at shrines such as Kataragama. This shrine is remarkable in that all members of Sri Lankan society are drawn to it, irrespective of religious or economic background. At other shrines exorcism rituals involved specifically produced textiles (**2**) and masks (**3**).

1. Chest decorated with ivory plaques
Chests such as this, as well as smaller caskets made entirely of ivory, were amongst the earliest objects from Sri Lanka to be seen in Europe, being sent as diplomatic gifts, following the first exchanges between the rulers of Sri Lanka and the Portuguese in the 16th century. Although today missing some of its decoration, the overall grandeur of the scheme of dancing figures and mythical and auspicious animals is clear.

Wood with applied ivory plaques
c. 1600
Height 32.4 cm, width 51.9 cm
Donated by Sir Augustus Wollaston Franks, 1892,0216.25

2. Shawl (detail)
At the centre of this cloth, which may have been used in an exorcism ritual, a female, presumably a goddess, appears to have just eaten the head of a figure she holds in her right hand. In her left hand is a trident, perhaps suggesting a link to Shiva, whose weapon this is.

Resist-dyed cotton
Probably 19th century
Length 204 cm, width 108 cm
(entire shawl)
Sri Lanka
As 1910,-.486

3. Exorcism mask

Exorcism rituals involving masked dance are well established in Sri Lanka. Mental disturbance is thought to be especially amenable to this type of treatment, which may include violent episodes in which the demonic possession of the patient is ended.

Painted wood
Probably 19th century
Height c. 30 cm
Sri Lanka
As 1972,Q.1188

5 | 13 Company painting

The term 'Company painting' is an all-embracing term used for the work of Indian artists commissioned by Europeans in the late 18th and early 19th centuries (the word 'Company' refers to the East India Company). Many of these paintings are captioned in English, or another European language. They were produced throughout the subcontinent, with significant centres at Calcutta (**1**), Delhi (**2**), Patna (**3**) and Thanjavur; they have no over-arching stylistic similarity, other than their use of some European techniques and their frequent concern with record. In many respects they acted as photographs were to do later; they could have both aesthetic as well as documentary functions, with the latter especially noted where elements of Indian life that were new and unusual to Europeans were being painted.

Artists were thus frequently called on to illustrate the varieties of everyday life, rather than the exquisite nature of courtly existence, as had been more common in earlier traditions of painting in the subcontinent. Company paintings also demonstrate the extraordinary ability of Indian painters to produce pictures in whatever style they were called upon to use. Many were trained in a late Mughal idiom and had perhaps early in their lives been attached to one of the royal courts, but without difficulty they later produced work for their new patrons that called on a knowledge of European perspective, depiction of volume through the use of shading, and a different medium of expression (watercolour rather than gouache). Quality ranges considerably, but some examples are amongst the finest Indian paintings as well as being sensitive records.

This page
1. *Senna occidentalis*, from the Impey Album
This botanical painting was produced by Shaikh Zain ud-Din, one of three artists who worked for Sir Elijah and Lady Impey during their stay in Calcutta in 1777–83. The Impeys commissioned paintings of birds and animals, as well as plants; well over three hundred are recorded.

Opaque watercolour on European paper
c. 1780
Height 63.6 cm, width 93.7 cm
Calcutta, West Bengal
Brooke Sewell Permanent Fund, 1992,0130,0.1

Opposite, above
2. A party of Sikhs
Named on an accompanying paper, the Sikhs depicted here are similar to those in the paintings of the so-called Fraser Album, commissioned in and around Delhi in the early 19th century by William Fraser, an officer of the East India Company involved in the recording of landholding for the correct collection of tax; he also became deeply embedded in the culture of north India. The recruitment of soldiers, as here, and the recording of new territory were the two engines of this artistic endeavour.

Watercolour on paper
c. 1820
Height 24.4 cm, width 38 cm
Delhi or environs
1966,1010,0.9

Below
**3. A seller of clay images,
perhaps by Shiva Dayal Lal**
In Patna, the painters Shiva
Dayal Lal and his cousin Shiva
Lal produced images of everyday
life to satisfy the European
demand for descriptive
paintings. Here, a seller of
devotional images and the
potter producing them are
depicted. At least two other
paintings of similar everyday
subjects by the same artists
are known – a milk-seller
and a fruit-seller.

Opaque watercolour on paper
c. 1850
Height 26.5 cm, width 39.8 cm
Patna, Bihar
Bequeathed by P. C. Manuk
and Miss G. M. Coles, through
the Art Fund (as NACF),
1948,1009,0.156

5 | 14 Plants and animals – and gods

The Indian flora and fauna were intriguing to Europeans and were consequently painted by Indian artists for their British clientele. In the late 18th century, north Indian artists, drawn to new patrons, settled in Calcutta where their clients included the Impey family and Lord Wellesley (Governor-General, 1798–1805), for whom they produced natural history paintings of carefully observed detail (**2**). These painters also worked for the East India Company, particularly for its surgeon-botanists who documented Indian natural history for scientific and economic reasons.

The Company's Botanic Garden in Calcutta, at Sibpur, was a centre of plant painting and is associated with William Roxburgh, Francis Buchanan and Nathaniel Wallich, all of whom travelled extensively and commissioned artists to record plants. Many paintings in the Pearson Album (see pp. 213, 229) were produced at Sibpur.

South Indian painters were mostly anonymous, rare exceptions being Rungiah, Govindoo (plants) and Yellapah (caste types). A survival of the southern school, using mica as a support and a vibrant palette, is evident in an album depicting orchids (**3**).

Many Company paintings (see pp. 258–9), of landscape, architecture and people, were bound in albums and sent to England. In northern India, the Mughal monuments at Agra, especially the Taj Mahal (see pp. 204–5), were painted, as were people in all their variety. Religion also provided a rich vein – sequences from Patna (**1**) and Tamil Nadu (**4**) are noteworthy.

This page
1 Virabhadra
Striking religious imagery such as this painting of multi-armed Virabhadra, a terrifying form of the god Shiva, was easily misunderstood when viewed by Europeans new to India. This work belongs to a large group of loose paintings in the British Museum illustrating deities and heroes of Hinduism and apparently from the same studio.

Watercolour on paper
c. 1820
Height 27.2 cm, width 22.4 cm
Bihar, probably Patna
1880,0.2022

Opposite, above left
2. Vulture
The note in English on this painting of a young vulture speculates about the similarity between this bird and one known in the 18th century in east Africa, reinforcing the fact that such beautiful images were also part of a scientific exercise of categorization.

Watercolour on paper
c. 1800
Height 53.9 cm, width 40.8 cm
West Bengal, probably Calcutta
Donated by Stuart Cary Welch,
1956,0211,0.2

Above
3. Orchid
This painting, of the orchid *Laelia purpurata*, is from an album by an anonymous artist. The album is unusual for three reasons: it only contains paintings of orchids; the paintings are on large sheets of mica, notoriously poor as a support for paint; and the images are copied from a book published in London in 1875 on orchid-growing.

Opaque watercolour on mica
After 1875
Height 28.5 cm, width 21.5 cm
Tiruchirappalli, Tamil Nadu
Brooke Sewell Permanent Fund,
2003,0222,0.10

Right
4. Shiva and Parvati
Here the gods are imagined on Mount Kailash, their heavenly home in the Himalayas. They wear sumptuous textiles and much expensive gold paint has been used on their jewelry. This is part of a portfolio of sixty-three paintings produced for sale to British military or commercial personnel keen to secure a memento of their life in southern India.

Opaque watercolour and gold on European paper (one sheet watermarked 1816)
c. 1820
Height 18.3 cm, width 19 cm (image)
Southern Andhra Pradesh/ northern Tamil Nadu
Brooke Sewell Permanent Fund,
2007,3005.17

5 | 15 Folk bronzes

The all-inclusive term 'folk bronze' is used for an immense variety of mostly small sculptures found throughout the subcontinent. As a group, these items are only united by the non-urban and frequently forceful style of their production: cult affiliation, size, and technique and standard of production vary widely. Such non-elite traditions have also acted as reservoirs from which later, more refined sculptural styles have developed.

A large group of sculptures from inland Maharashtra depict the herdsmen's god, Khandoba, accompanied by his consort (**1**). He shares many iconographic features with Shiva, while his consort who rides beside him is imagined also as Parvati: their narratives, however, remain local (**2**). Other folk bronzes are connected with tribal groups in areas of central India such as the Satpura hills (**3**) and western Orissa, where metal images are offered in open-air shrines.

Yet further imagery was for use in domestic shrines (**4**), while the dictates of individual cults, such as of Virabhadra with his shield, produce specific bronze images (**5**). Female deities worshipped in non-temple, countryside shrines are frequently connected with the earth, with fertility and with wealth – and may be propitiated with animal sacrifice.

This page
1. Palanquin of Khandoba
At the annual Mallanna festival at Mailara in central Karnataka, images of Khandoba are carried in palanquins through the streets by devotees. Here, the images of god and consort are garlanded and ready for the procession; auspicious turmeric powder has been sprinkled over them.

Opposite, above left
2. Khandoba and his consort
This sculpture of Khandoba, protector of the herds, is typically vibrant. On the god's right side is his dog, facing a small *linga*. The connection with Shiva is also made clear by the trident Khandoba holds.

Cast bronze
Perhaps 18th century (already in the UK by 1853)
Height 11.5 cm, width 5.6 cm
Probably Maharashtra
Donated by the Earl of Mountnorris, 1853,0108.4

Opposite, above right
3. Shiva
The unsophisticated but impressive modelling seen in this image is typical of the genre. The reduction in realistic depiction and the emphasis on important elements such as eyes, ears and the trident he holds, are typical of the tribal aesthetic.

Cast bronze
19th century or earlier
Height 6.2 cm
Satpura, Madhya Pradesh
Donated by Mrs Cynthia Hazen Polsky, 1998,0616.4

Opposite, below left
4. Shiva *linga*
A *linga*, probably from a domestic shrine, is depicted with a protective five-headed serpent; a *yoni* functions as a drain for offerings. Nandi, the bull mount of Shiva, looks on in adoration; to his right are a pile of offerings.

Cast bronze
Collected by or made for Major Edward Moor
c. 1790
Height 5.3 cm, width 5 cm
Perhaps Pune, Maharashtra
Donated by Mrs A. G. Moor, 1940,0716.96

Opposite, below right
5. Virabhadra
This plaque (and *linga* in Figure 4) belonged to Major Edward Moor. He was stationed in Pune in the 1790s; his 1810 publication *The Hindu Pantheon* was an early study in English of Indian religion. His very large collection of small bronzes and paintings, now in the British Museum, informed that study.

Cast bronze
Collected by, or made for Major Edward Moor
c. 1790
Height 34.5 cm, width 27 cm
Maharashtra
Donated by Mrs A. G. Moor, 1940,0716.29

5 | 16 Banjara textiles

The term Banjara (or sometimes Lombarni) is used for a group of itinerant workers of probably western Indian origin who are today found in many other areas, especially in Karnataka and Andhra Pradesh. Their origin is uncertain but they may have left western India when, as dealers in salt and grain, they followed the Mughal armies southwards into the Deccan in the 17th century, providing them with these commodities. Since then they have remained in this part of India and today often earn a living as casual labourers. Their comparatively humble method of living belies their vibrant aesthetic sense, which is mostly expressed through the decoration of women's clothing.

Embroidery (**1**) and appliqué are the main techniques used, sometimes on cloth that has already been decorated by tie-dye or block-printing. True to their Rajasthan-Gujarat ancestry, the women wear a flounced skirt rather than a sari, along with a backless blouse, the two sides being secured with ties. This assemblage is completed with a head-covering of a piece of cotton cloth, also usually decorated with appliqué and embroidery (sometimes with added coins) (**3**).

When working, women also often wear a cloth on their heads to ease the carrying of pots, either of water or of earth if working on a construction site. This is made up of a flat cloth for the top of the head to which is attached a thick ring of goats' hair, providing support for a pot, and with a further flap of cloth hanging down the neck. These three elements are usually the focus of extensive and elaborate embroidery as well as decoration using cowrie shells (**2**). Reminiscent also of their western Indian background is the use of inset mirror elements within the embroidery, producing a colourful and dazzling design (**3**).

1. Embroidered purse
This bag or purse with its brightly coloured embroidery and added cowrie shells is typical of the Banjara aesthetic.

Cotton, cowrie shells
Early 20th century
Length 30 cm, width 26 cm
(incl. tassels)
Northern Deccan
Collected by Rai Bahadur
Hira Lal, c. 1914; donated by
Sir Hyde Clarendon Gowan,
As 1933,0715.319

2. Decorated pot-carrier
Everyday objects such as this pot-carrier were, for special occasions, the focus of lavish attention – here including embroidery in a variety of stitches, the addition of cowrie shells and appliqué cloth. This example was part of a bride's costume.

Cotton, cowrie shells, wool, metal
Late 19th century (acquired
by donor in c. 1900)
Length 49 cm, width 25 cm
Shimoga District, Karnataka
Donated by Mrs E. M. Slater,
As 1953,02.6

3. Banjara woman's costume

This ensemble is made up of a skirt, blouse and head-covering, all parts of which are covered in colourful embroidery and mirror-work. The blouse is open at the back and fastened solely with ties. The skirt has similar decoration including appliqué work, brass buttons and tassels.

Cotton, mirror-work, metal tassels
Late 19th century (acquired 1895–1910)
Blouse: length 56 cm, width 75 cm; skirt: length 102 cm, width 48 cm (at waist); head-covering: length 197 cm, width 129 cm (incl. forehead piece)
Probably Karnataka
Donated by Miss R. Hudson (collected by her parents),
As1974,23.29–31

Timeline

1877	Proclamation of Queen Victoria as Empress of India
1878	Raja Lala Deen Dayal begins his photographic career by documenting the monuments of Sanchi
1885	Indian National Congress founded
1906	Foundation of the All-India Muslim League
1911	Delhi Durbar; capital moves from Calcutta to New Delhi
1913	Rabindranath Tagore wins the Nobel Prize for Literature
1930	M. K. Gandhi organizes the Salt March
c. 1940	Tibetan pilgrim Gendun Chopel visits Amaravati and records its sculpture
Early 1940s	Jamini Roy patronized by middle class Bengalis and by Allied servicemen
1943	The 43 Group founded in Sri Lanka; one of the founders, pioneering photographer Lionel Wendt, dies the following year
1943	The Bengal Famine; artists such as Zainul Abedin respond
1947	Independence of India and Pakistan (East and West) from Britain
1947	Formation of the Progressive Artists Group in Bombay
1948	Independence of Ceylon (later Sri Lanka)
1948	M. K. Gandhi assassinated
1948	Muhammad Ali Jinnah, political leader, dies
1949	F. N. Souza leaves India for London; S. H. Raza leaves for Paris the next year
From 1950	Film-maker Satyajit Ray produces sequence of internationally acclaimed films
1950–1976	Print-maker Krishna Reddy works at Atelier 17 in Paris; later moves to New York
1956	B. R. Ambedkar, the framer of the Indian constitution, embraces Buddhism with many followers; dies later same year
1956	The States Reorganisation Act begins process of dividing Indian states on linguistic lines
1957	Nomination of *Mother India* at Oscars
1962	China invades Northeast Frontier Agency and Assam, and then withdraws
1964	Death of Jawaharlal Nehru, first Prime Minister of independent India
1965	War between India and Pakistan over Kashmir
From 1965	Ravi Shankar makes Indian classical music known internationally
1971	Creation of Bangladesh and independence from Pakistan
Early 1980s	Jangarh Singh Shyam moves to Bhopal, to paint at Bharat Bhavan
1984	Assassination of Indira Gandhi
1989	Foundation of the Drik Photo Agency, Dhaka, Bangladesh
1991	Satyajit Ray receives an Academy Award just prior to his death
1992	Babri Masjid in Ayodhya destroyed
1995	Bhupen Khakhar paints portrait of Salman Rushdie, now in National Portrait Gallery, London
2008	Nepal ceases to be a monarchy and becomes a republic

6 Colonial India, independence and modernity

Late 19th century–the present

1. Jonathan Duncan (1756–1811), Governor of Bombay
This is an informal portrayal of a senior East India Company man. Spread on his table is a rough map, perhaps of India. The furniture of local hardwood is typical of the local craftsmen who, early on in the period of European contact, copied designs and produced European-style tables, beds, chairs and other items for those who, like Jonathan Duncan, spent their lives in India. This painting once belonged to Edward Moor (see p. 262).

Gouache on paper, by an unknown Indian artist
c. 1800
Height 17 cm, width 21 cm
Bombay
Brooke Sewell Permanent Fund, 2019,3010.1

In north India, the British expansion from Calcutta (founded as an East India Company commercial station in 1690) was initially up the Ganges to Patna, Allahabad and eventually Delhi. It then continued northwards through the Punjab (British by 1843) and Sindh, to the borders of Afghanistan (secured by 1858). In central India, the later Mughals had been undermined by the Maratha chief, Shivaji (1627–1680), and his successors were thus able to expand out of their homeland. Later, they came up against the British as the latter advanced towards the Maratha centre at Poona (present-day Pune). Neutralizing Maratha power ensured that Bombay (1) (today known as Mumbai), to the west of Poona, had a hinterland in the hands of the British. The islands, which were later linked together to became the city of Bombay, had come under British control when they were included in the dowry of the Portuguese bride of Charles II, Catherine of Braganza. From the late 18th and throughout the 19th century, Calcutta (now Kolkata) was the capital of British India and the seat of the Governor-General, and later of the Viceroy (2). An early Governor-General was Warren Hastings (in office 1774–85), a controversial but accomplished administrator and an enthusiast for Indian culture.

Much of the British expansion through South Asia was predicated on trade, especially in the early period when the

2. St John's Church, Calcutta

Thomas and William Daniell, a duo of uncle and nephew artists, travelled extensively in India in the late 18th century. Here, they provide an idea of the architecture of expanding Calcutta. St. John's Church is shown at the time of its consecration in 1787; with only minor changes it survives today, along with an altar painting of the Last Supper by the German artist Johan Zoffany. In the distance, at right, is the octagonal tomb of Job Charnock, the founder of the British settlement at Calcutta.

Hand-coloured print with aquatint, no 12 in a series of views
1788
Height 40.2 cm, width 52.5 cm
Calcutta
1870,0514.1486

London shareholders of the Company were the final authority. The 1857 rebellion, which began in Meerut as a mutiny, was a turning point for the Company. This event resulted in the death of both British military and civilians, as the disturbance spread across northern and central India. Its titular head was Bahadur Shah (1775–1862), descendant of the last Mughal emperor. The outbreak was eventually controlled, but the British response was brutal and out of proportion. From this time onwards, the mercantile interests of the Company were replaced by British government authority, which had been shocked by the events of 1857; it also meant that the notion of a Mughal restitution was dead. This new understanding was finally substantiated in the proclamation of Queen Victoria as Empress of India in 1877. From this point onwards and until 1947, India was ruled as a department of the British state, under the authority in India of a Viceroy. By the early decades of the 20th century, the subcontinent, from Kanyakumari in the south to Gilgit in the north, was a mosaic of regions ruled directly by the British, or indirectly, by treaty, through Residents at the various princely courts (Sri Lanka was ruled separately from the Colonial Office). Calcutta remained the most important city until in 1911, at the Delhi Durbar, the King-Emperor George V announced that the capital would move to Delhi and that a new city would be built on the outskirts of the old one. The architects for this enterprise were Edwin Lutyens and Herbert Baker.

The 20th century became increasingly dominated by demands for political freedom. These were initially modest but became far-reaching. Latterly, the two main groups involved were the National Congress and the All-India Muslim League. Major figures included M. K. Gandhi (1869–1948), known as the Mahatma or 'Great Soul' and an advocate of non-violent resistance, Jawaharlal Nehru (1889–1964), the first Prime Minister of independent India, and Muhammad Ali Jinnah (1875–1948), the founder of Pakistan – all three were British-trained lawyers. Also of impressive moral stature, and again a lawyer, was B. R. Ambedkar (1891–1956). He framed the constitution of newly independent India, and was the standard-bearer of the untouchables (those outside the caste system), of which he was one (3). These men, and many others involved in the struggle for independence, are imaged in popular culture and each has a recognizable iconography; Gandhi famously abandoned Western clothing, returning to hand-spun, hand-woven – and indigenous – cotton cloth, *khadi*. Ambedkar, meanwhile, did not share Gandhi's romantic view of Indian village life and is always depicted in a Western suit and tie, symbols of his desire to break away from caste-bound traditional India.

Tragically, the speed with which the British departed from India following the exhausting events of World War II, and the difficulty of accommodating the demands of both Hindu and Muslim populations, meant that Partition of the South Asian landmass along religious grounds became inevitable. When it came in August 1947, Partition resulted in huge movements of people: Hindus moved into India from newly created Pakistan, and Muslims moved into Pakistan from India. There were many deaths, certainly over a million, and probably considerably more though exact figures will never be known. Thus were created West and East Pakistan (the latter became Bangladesh in 1971), and India. Sri Lanka became independent in 1948. Nepal and Bhutan maintained their status as separate states; Sikkim, initially separate, became a state of the Union of India in 1975.

3. Dr B. R. Ambedkar
One of the remarkable personalities of the independence movement, Ambedkar came from an untouchable family in Maharashtra. Through great perseverance, he trained as a lawyer in India and abroad, and was fundamental in the drafting of the constitution of independent India. In 1956, he and his followers embraced Buddhism, outside caste Hinduism. Some today consider him a *bodhisattva*, though his main message always remained 'educate and organize'.

Print on paper
Late 20th century
Height 42.5 cm, width 29.8 cm
North India
British Museum Friends (Townley Group), 2003,0714,0.14

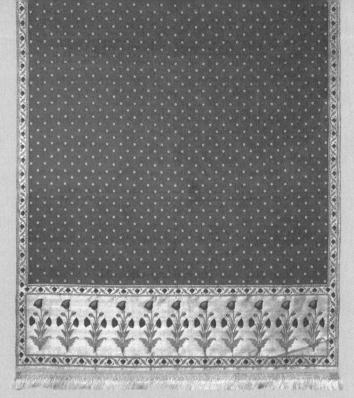

4. Shawl

This striking shawl was produced in 1996 at the ASHA workshop in Delhi, set up by the textile historian Rahul Jain. Following his study of both Mughal-period weaving technology and the floral imagery of the Shah Jahan period (r. 1628–58), Jain's workshop has produced items of great weaving complexity as well as impressive beauty.

Handwoven silk,
and silver-gilt thread
1996
Length 242 cm, width 90 cm
Delhi (drawing on the weaving traditions of Varanasi)
Donated by the Textile Art Society, New Delhi, 2001,0602,0.1

The political narrative in South Asia since independence has been varied, but has included a series of wars between India and Pakistan over Kashmir, the war of independence in Bangladesh in 1971 and then civil war in Sri Lanka between the Tamil minority and the Sinhalese. Economic and social progress has varied, but is especially noted in India, Bangladesh and Sri Lanka. In the cultural realm, film, popular prints and literature have all flourished, mostly but not always without censorship. In many parts of South Asia, artists, often marrying their own visions with skills and ideas gained through international exposure, have found outlets for their work, both at home and abroad (the diaspora as well as increased ease of communication have encouraged this). One of the most ancient cultural traditions of the subcontinent – the making of handmade textiles – has been brought back from the edge of extinction by supporters, both in the area of *khadi* and also haute couture, where Indian craftsmanship is in demand internationally (**4**). It is worth remembering that already at the time of the Indus Civilization in the 3rd millennium BCE, both silk and cotton were used; the wheel has come full circle.

6 | 1 Kalighat painting

The Kali temple in Calcutta has been popular since at least the early 19th century. It is located at the *ghat*s, the steps leading down to the river where devotees bathe. In the past, local and visiting pilgrims who wished to take away some sacred souvenir from the temple patronized painters of images who congregated there. These swiftly executed but engaging and colourful items are known, from the temple location, as Kalighat paintings.

The painters of these mementoes were probably drawn from the same group as had previously been the itinerant painters and storytellers of the Bengal countryside (see pp. 236–7). Indeed, there are some moral stories that appear both in the scroll imagery and in Kalighat paintings. Taking advantage of their new urban situation, the artists used unthickened watercolour and machine-made paper. The subject matter of the Kalighat paintings was mostly religious and particularly involved the goddesses Kali and Durga (**1**) and the god Shiva (**2**). Also popular were paintings of Krishna and his consort Radha, figures especially connected with the Bengali mystic Chaitanya (**3**). A few secular subjects of the day – a famous court case, a Bengali proverb, or the antics of fashionable dandies and their courtesans – were also illustrated.

The Kalighat painters were active for only a short period, perhaps forty or fifty years. As hand-coloured lithography, quickly followed by chromolithography (see pp. 284–5) appeared at the end of the 19th century, these hand-produced paintings were replaced by cheap mass-produced images. Ironically, some paintings from the Kalighat temple were acquired by English missionaries to demonstrate the perceived depravity of Indian devotees. Some of these have survived (**4**) as they were used in fundraising exhibitions for the missions.

1. Durga
The beautiful and bejeweled goddess, hair unloosed and standing on the back of her lion vehicle, is depicted here at the moment of her final battle with the buffalo demon Mahishasura.

Watercolour on machine-made paper
c. 1860
Height 46 cm, width 27.5 cm
Kalighat temple, Calcutta
1949,0409,0.76

2. Five-headed Shiva
As the consort of Durga, Shiva is consequently often seen in Kalighat imagery. In his right hands he carries a *vina* (below) and his distinctive double-headed drum (above), the sound of which generates life in the cosmos. Ascetics, of which he is the greatest, are often shown with tiger skins, either sitting on one or – as here – worn around the loins. One of Shiva's many names is Pashupati, the Lord of Animals, a name suggested by this control of the fiercest jungle beast, the tiger.

Watercolour on machine-made paper
c. 1860
Height 46.2 cm, width 27.5 cm
Kalighat temple environs, Calcutta
1949,0409,0.84

3. Composite form of Rama, Krishna and Chaitanya

This Bengali form of divinity combines three perceived *avatara* of Vishnu: green-armed Rama with his bow held aloft; blue-armed Krishna playing his flute (both of these belong in the standard listings of *avatara*); and also Chaitanya, the Bengali saint, with the bag and staff of the ascetic. His epithet is Gauranga, literally 'golden limbs', that is not dark-skinned like Krishna and thus his complement – as shown here.

Watercolour on machine-made paper
c. 1890
Height 46 cm, width 28 cm
Kalighat temple environs, Calcutta
Donated by Dr Francesca
Fremantle, 1993,0810,0.4

4. Ganesha and his rat vehicle

A suggested explanation for the unusually large format of this Kalighat painting (it is about four times the size of most examples) is the remains on the reverse of a label indicating its use in a missionary exhibition. The existence of such exhibitions is recorded in mission literature, with displays used to indicate the unseemly nature of Indian religion.

Watercolour on paper
c. 1870
Height 129 cm, width 100 cm
Kalighat temple environs, Calcutta
Brooke Sewell Permanent Fund,
1995,0404,0.1

6 | 2 Photography in India

Photography was already established in India by the early 1850s. Initially, it was a hobby enthusiastically followed by British residents and soon afterwards by Indians; later it was an instrument of government recording. One of the earliest of the British photographers of note was Linnaeus Tripe (1822–1902), whose documentation of temple architecture in southern India (**1**), the excavations at Amaravati and the architecture of Burma (he was part of the embassy to the Burmese court in 1855) is renowned to this day. His images, along with those of others working at the same time, such as Biggs and Pigou, have left us with a visual resource of great documentary value. In the late 19th century amateurs, as well as official bodies such as the Archaeological Survey of India, produced a rich record of India's historic past.

The leading Indian photographer of the later 19th century was Raja Lala Deen Dayal (1844–1905), whose company ran a number of successful studios. Photography was also used by government agencies to record ethnographic subjects (**2**), and topics such as the rulers of India, as well as great public moments of display, including the 1911 Durbar of the King-Emperor George V. In the 20th century photography became universal and documentary work was widespread throughout the subcontinent; it has since become a recognized form of artistic expression amongst artists such as Dayanita Singh (b. 1961, India) and Bani Abidi (b. 1971, Pakistan) (**3**).

1. 'Jewels of the Pagoda' from *Photographs of Seringham* by Captain L. Tripe, government photographer

Linnaeus Tripe was in the Tiruchirappalli region in January 1858. His record of the Shriranganatha temple on the island of Shrirangam includes this striking image of jewelry, vessels and other temple equipment. Amongst the latter are vehicles, *vahana*, in the form of Hanuman (left) and Garuda. These are for carrying processional images of Rama and Vishnu through the streets at festival time.

Photograph
1858
Height 25 cm, width 35.5 cm
Shrirangam, Tamil Nadu
1862,0308,0.232

Right
2. Unnamed Andamanese islander, by Maurice Portman

This image is from an archive assembled by Maurice Portman, who was 'officer in charge' of the Andaman Islands between 1879 and 1900. It depicts an islander who is described as wearing human bones and medicinal leaves around his chest to counter respiratory disease. Portman also used photography to measure differing body elements of islanders in ways that today emphasize uncomfortably the difference between the ruler and the ruled.

Photograph
1890s
Height 20.1 cm, width 15.1 cm
Andaman Islands
Donated by Maurice Vidal
Portman, As,Portman,B27.69

Below
3. 'Chandra Acharya, 7:50pm, 30 August, 2008, Ramadan, Karachi', from Karachi Series I by Bani Abidi

In each of the six photographs from this series, Bani Abidi shows a quotidian activity. Here, a woman in a sari sits at her dressing table. Her clothes immediately mark her out as Hindu, as does her name. All six images in the series are timed and dated, indicating that this is Ramadan, when most inhabitants of Karachi are indoors breaking their fast. Only minorities – Christians, Hindus and Parsis – are on the streets.

Photograph
2008
Height 50.8 cm, width 80 cm
Karachi, Pakistan
Brooke Sewell Permanent Fund,
2011,3001,1.3

1. The stupa at Gorsam, by Sonam Tsering

This painting depicts the large stupa located on the route from northwestern Arunachal into Tibet, approximately 20 km from the frontier. The episodes of the foundation narrative of the stupa are shown, from bottom left in a clockwise direction, with one panel featuring the Dalai Lama passing the stupa on his first day in exile (bottom row, second from right).

Paint on canvas; silk, metal and wood
2007
Length 139 cm, width 91 cm
Tawang, Arunachal Pradesh
Brooke Sewell Permanent Fund, 2008,3017.1

2. Neck ornament

Typical of Naga material culture, this boar tusk neck ornament draws on both the animal and plant kingdoms of the remote hill country in which the Naga peoples lived. Woven rattan, often coloured, as here, is a common feature.

Boar tusk, ivory, carnelian and coloured rattan
19th century or earlier (acquired 1874)
Diameter 13 cm, height 2 cm
Naga Hills, northeast India
As1972,Q.2079

3. Cap or helmet

Head-coverings of woven and coloured basketry, decorated with dyed horsehair, were frequently seen amongst the highly militarized Nagas before the arrival of Christian missions in the late 19th century. Weapons such as spears were also frequently elaborated with dyed horsehair.

Woven and coloured rattan, horsehair
Naga Hills, northeast India
19th century or earlier (acquired 1871)
Height 20 cm, width 24 cm
Donated by Sir Augustus Wollaston Franks, As.7343

Nagaland and Arunachal Pradesh

These two states in modern northeast India represent a different cultural story to much of the rest of South Asia. Although today increasingly Indianized, they remain linguistically, ethnically and culturally distinct. Historically, both states had cultural contacts over today's international borders and both have been characterized by oral rather than written literature. In recent times they have also been the focus of Christian missionary activity. Traditional religion was animistic and included animal sacrifice, though Tibetan-style Buddhism was practised along the Tibet frontier while Theravada Buddhism is known close to the Burma frontier.

Arunachal Pradesh boasts some thirty different tribal groups, with Apatani, Monpa and Nyishi among the most prominent. In Nagaland there is a similar number of groups, among them the Angami and Konyak Naga. Almost all these peoples speak Tibeto-Burman languages. The ancient past of this region is little known, though finds of Neolithic stone tools have been recorded.

In both states, cotton cloth woven on backstrap looms is important aesthetically and as a status symbol. Ornaments of split and woven bamboo are well known and beads amongst many of these groups have both a mystique and a value; shell, often brought from far away, is prized. The jewelry of the Nagas is distinctive, using coral, ivory and boar tusks (**2**), and the tradition of local warfare has resulted in the production of woven rattan armour (**3**). Amongst the Monpa on the Bhutan/India/Tibet frontier, Tibetan-style painting is still practised (**1**). Utilitarian but beautiful basketry is also a feature of these societies, and given the intense rainfall of the region much ingenuity has gone into the making of rain-shields of rattan and palm fibre (**4**).

4. Apatani rain-shield (inside view)
The foothills of the eastern Himalayas are intensely wet. Many of the groups of central Arunachal make rain-shields of palm fibre attached to bamboo frames. Elaborate examples have knapsacks of woven rattan between the frame and the back of the wearer, as in this one made by Apatani craftsmen.

Palm fibre, rattan
Early 20th century
Height 76 cm, width 54 cm
Apatani valley, central Arunachal Pradesh
As 1957,11.9

6 | 3 *Kantha*

A distinctive feature of rural society throughout Bengal was the production of embroidered quilts or *kantha* (**1–3**). As well as being useful as bed- or cot-covers, they provided an avenue for domestic creativity for women. They frequently have exuberant and engaging designs, drawing on local religious and social themes. The oldest examples were apparently made from old garments – especially saris – whose unpicked threads could then be reused in both the quilting of the background as well as the embroidery of the designs. This background quilting not only produced a pleasing pattern but also held together the ground for the embroidery.

The repertoire of imagery used by women embroiderers was extensive but also specific, depending on location, the local landscape, and their religious or even sectarian connections. Some designs must have been copied from popular prints or Kalighat paintings brought back from the cities, above all Calcutta. Animals are a frequent subject, especially fish, a staple of the Bengali diet. Other animals, such as peacocks, are both attractive as well as being connected with Lord Krishna (he wears a peacock feather in his headband) and elephants also have a symbolic meaning linked to royalty (**3**). Some *kantha* are more adventurous, and include steam trains, soldiers, processional temple chariots (**1**) and well-known proverbs. Inscriptions sometimes appear demonstrating simple literacy as well as providing us with names of both embroiderers and locations.

These unpremeditated 'paintings in cloth' offer an insight into the rapidly changing social panorama in the Bengal countryside during the 19th and 20th centuries, where otherwise little else is available.

This page
1. Kantha
In this detail from a densely embroidered *kantha*, a temple chariot is shown being dragged through the streets at festival time.

Cotton
c. 1870
Length 177 cm, width 121 cm (entire textile)
Bengal
Brooke Sewell Permanent Fund, 2003,1025,0.1

Opposite, above
2. Kantha
The central lotus medallion here is a common *kantha* motif. More unusual are the four tableaux on each side (from bottom, clockwise): the goddess Devi riding on her lion; Rama enthroned with prostrate Hanuman; the Five Pandava Brothers; and an unknown scene.

Cotton, embroidered by Srimati Sundari Dasya
Late 19th or early 20th century
Height 86 cm, width 85 cm
Bangladesh, perhaps from Faridpur
Polsky Fund for Indian Folk Art, 2002,0520,0.6

Opposite, below
3. Kantha
Kantha are filled not only with human life but with every animal of the forest, fish of the river and insect and bird of the air. In this detail, elephants and peacocks are depicted.

Cotton
Late 19th or early 20th century
Height 86.5 cm, width 83 cm (detail shown *c.* 54 cm wide)
Bangladesh, perhaps from Faridpur
Polsky Fund for Indian Folk Art, 2002,0520,0.1

6 | 4 19th-century neckwear

Here, two very different items of British-period neckwear are contrasted. One is the collar of the Order of the Star of India, the other is also a collar, but one worn by prisoners, mostly political, incarcerated by the British authorities on the Andaman Islands.

The collar and badge of the chivalric order instituted by Queen Victoria in 1861, officially known as the Most Exalted Order of the Star of India (**2**), was bestowed on Indian and British recipients – the former mostly members of the princely houses of India, the latter mostly senior members of the British administration. It was considered to be more exclusive than the other chivalric order of British India – the Order of the Indian Empire – and had fewer members; the sovereign was the head of the Order. The admission of new members ceased in 1948 following Indian independence and the last surviving member of the Order has died.

The neck-ring with a wooden tablet attached is of the type used in the Cellular Jail at Port Blair on the Andaman Islands (**1**). Each convict was forced to wear an iron ring around their neck with identification numbers stamped on the wooden tag. Built in the 1890s, this jail became notorious for the political prisoners held there by the British administration; its physical location, on an island in the middle of the Bay of Bengal, made it an ideal jail. Its connection with now famous leaders has meant that the building is today a museum devoted to the nationalist struggle.

Both of these items can be read as means of controlling those involved in the grand project of empire, though at opposite ends of the comfort zone!

This page
**1. Neck-ring worn
by a convict**
Identification tags such as this one were worn under duress by prisoners, many of whom were incarcerated in the Andaman islands on account of their political activities. These included the brother of the revolutionary and later spiritual leader Sri Aurobindo.

Iron, wood
Late 19th or early 20th century
Height 27.1 cm, width 15.5 cm
Andaman Islands, Bay of Bengal
Donated by Mrs W. H. Burt,
As 1933,0603.3

Opposite
**2. Collar and star of a Knight
Grand Commander of the
Order of the Star of India**
The sovereign was the head of the Order of the Star of India. With its motto 'Heaven's Light our Guide', this chivalric order with its own ritual, and order of precedence, maintained an aura of exclusivity. The Viceroy was the Grand Master.

Brass, enamel, diamonds
(star only)
Late 19th or early 20th century
Diameter 9 cm
London, England
Donated by HM the Queen,
1958,0901.2

6 | 5 Indian silver for a British clientele

Unlike in Europe, silver was not traditionally used in South Asia for vessels; bronze was more common. However, in the 19th century, no doubt under the influence of the British, silver became more widely used. A few British silversmiths set up in the big cities in the 18th century providing tableware, some in a restrained neoclassical style. Later, local silversmiths started to participate and handsome commemorative items were produced; fortunately, many of these bear inscriptions and dates (**2**).

By the late 19th century there was a flourishing market for domestic wares aimed at those stationed in India, and for Anglophile Indians. The work of Indian silversmiths from Lucknow, Calcutta (Kolkata), Poona (Pune) and Karachi became popular and their work can still be recognized. The most widely patronized of these Indian silversmiths was based in Bhuj, in Kutch. This was Oomersee Mawjee, now widely known simply as 'OM' from the identifying stamp on his wares. His workshop produced tableware, boxes, salvers, desk furniture, cruet sets and card cases amongst much else (**1, 3**). Craftsmen at the Bhuj workshop, and later at Baroda where Oomersee Mawjee's son moved in the 1920s, prepared fine drawings for clients, offering different options as to design, size, metal, weight – and therefore cost (**4**).

Such workshops invoked a late 19th-century aesthetic still familiar in England before World War I. Indeed, the London store Liberty & Co. placed orders for wares directly with OM for sale in their Regent Street emporium. In the 1920s, however, this style fell out of fashion as modernist ideas became popular.

This page
1. Teapot with elephant spout
The drinking of tea amongst both British and Indian populations became hugely popular in the 19th century. This teapot has two disks of ivory in the handle which act as heat-breakers, ensuring the handle can be grasped safely. The dense mixture of animal and vegetal patterning is a hallmark of the 'OM' style.

Silver, ivory
c. 1900
Height 15 cm, diameter at base 7.5 cm
Stamped and from the workshop of Oomersee Mawjee in Bhuj, Kutch
Bequeathed by Oppi Untracht, 2011,3014.58

Opposite, above left
2. Commemorative presentation cup
An inscription gives the name of the receiver of this fine vessel: Lt-Col. Thomas Ruddiman Steuart, 'Collector and Magistrate in Upper Sind'; also the date of the presentation, 1 January 1861. The Steuart family crest – a unicorn head on a shield – appears on the exterior, which is otherwise a mass of repoussé decoration, featuring hunting and vegetal motifs.

Silver and silver-gilt
1860
Height 43.7 cm, diameter of mouth 20.5 cm
Poona (present-day Pune), Maharashtra
Brooke Sewell Permanent Fund, 2006,0404.1

Above right
3. Cruet set
In its original case, this cruet set – not indigenous types of vessel – is made up of four salt cellars (circular, at the back), four pepper shakers and two napkin rings. All items are marked as coming from the workshop of Oomersee Mawjee.

Silver in satin and velvet presentation case
c. 1900
Napkin ring: height 3 cm, diameter 5 cm
Stamped and from the workshop of Oomersee Mawjee in Bhuj, Kutch
Bequeathed by Oppi Untracht, 2011,3014.7

Right
4. Design drawing
Annotated drawings from the OM workshop provide varied information, including – as here – the amount of metal to be used for specific designs (100 *tola* of silver). Also provided is the cost of an optional extra: an ebonized wooden base for the urn, at 6 rupees.

Pencil on paper
Late 19th or early 20th century
Height 38 cm, width 27.3 cm
Stamped and from the workshop of Oomersee Mawjee in Bhuj, Kutch
Bequeathed by Oppi Untracht, 2011,3014.138

6 | 6 Popular imagery

From the late 18th century, South Asia experienced an explosion of popular visual imagery, beginning with reverse glass painting, which was commonly used to depict both deities and rulers (**2**).

Later, in Bengal, printed popular imagery in colour was first produced at the Calcutta Art Studio and then the Chore Bagan Art Studio (**3**). The founders of these companies had studied lithography at the Calcutta School of Art. Another centre of print production was Poona (Pune), where the Chitrashala Steam Press produced images of local heroes and deities (see p. 238). Most influential was printmaking associated with the painter Raja Ravi Varma (1848–1906) who, at the end of his career, set up a printing press outside Bombay where popular prints based on his paintings were produced.

In the 20th century prints were made for every public activity: politics, cinema, pedagogy and religion. The political print gained universal prominence with calligraphic, symbolic and figural imagery all employed (**1**). And throughout South Asia, schools use printed charts to spread public health and educational messages. Religious imagery, however, has been the most prolific with some prints becoming widely known, others being localized, associated with the tomb-shrine or *dargah* of a Muslim saint, or the shrine of a Hindu deity (**4**). Prints describing pilgrimage are frequently carried home and placed in domestic shrines – the range of Hindu iconography has ensured that these are common, but Muslim, Jain and Christian shrines have also been the source of such prints.

1. Political poster

Peasants break their chains and brandish weapons, while world leaders run away: (l–r) Alexei Kosygin with a gun, Bhutto holding dollar bills, an unknown figure – perhaps a landlord – and Richard Nixon.

Print on paper
1974
Height 47 cm, width 76 cm
Pakistan
Donated by Judy Greenway,
2018,3023.2

Above left
**2. Reverse glass painting
of Nana Phadnavis**
Nana Phadnavis (1742–1800)
was chief minister of the
Peshwas, de facto rulers
of Poona in the 18th century.

Paint on glass
Early 19th century
Height 57.5 cm, width 42.4 cm
Maharashtra
1989,0412,0.1

Above right
**3. Pramoda Sundari,
'the Passionate Beauty'**
With revealing sari and loose
hair, this image addressed
a market for titillating prints.

Printing ink on paper
Chore Bagan Art Studio, Calcutta
Height 40.5 cm, width 30.5 cm
1880s
1989,0204,0.59

Right
4. Saptashrungi
This goddess, a local form
of Durga, is venerated
in a renowned temple in
the mountains near Nasik,
Maharashtra.

Chromolithograph
Early 1980s
Height 49.5 cm, width 34.3 cm
Printed in Surat
1988,0209,0.45.35

**1. 'The Buddha-to-be bids
farewell to his horse'
by Abanindranath Tagore**
The painter takes an episode
from the ancient Buddhist history
of India – the final renunciation of
Prince Siddhartha – and imbues
it with an immediacy and emotion
quite different from the academic
European style against which
he was reacting.

Watercolour on paper
Early 20th century
Height 17.5 cm, width 12.8 cm
Probably Calcutta
Donated by Louis Clarke,
1925,0304,0.1

The Bengal School

A recurring question for artists in 20th-century South Asia was how to be a modern international artist as well as a committed representative of South Asian society. Was inspiration to be found in traditional Indian sources, or from the West – or neither? For many in the last years of the 19th century, brought up in the art schools of the British Indian government, the answer to this question was the production of paintings and sculpture that fitted into Western aesthetic ideals based on the study of the antique and the pursuit of naturalism. One such painter was Jamini Prakash Gangooly (1876–1953), who is remembered for his fine landscape paintings. A relative of the Tagore family (for Rabindranath Tagore, see pp. 290–91), he grew up with Abanindranath Tagore (1871–1951).

Unlike Gangooly, Abanindranath Tagore (1) was not prepared to accept the old art school certainties and was encouraged in his search for a new idiom by E. B. Havell, the Principal of the Government College of Art in Calcutta (1896–1906). Havell was keen that Indian artists should move away from purely academic copying, and find an inspiration that was specifically Indian. An appreciation of Mughal monuments and paintings was productive for Abanindranath in defining his new style. This was, for the most part, based on watercolour and the use of colour washes and the depiction of specifically Indian subjects. These images from Indian cultural history were often imbued with nostalgic emotion (1).

Later, the pan-Asianist ideas of the Japanese theoretician Kakuzo Okakura Tenshin (1862–1913) were also important in furthering Abanindranath's style. Okakura's linking of all Asian art, in which Indian culture – especially that of Buddhism – was seen to be fundamentally connected with the cultures of China and Japan, led many artists following Abanindranath to adopt a quasi-oriental painting style, with subdued colouring and the use of watercolour washes, as well as local subject matter (2–4).

The impact of this break from Western classicism and new interest in Asian techniques and Indian subject matter coincided with the beginnings of nationalism in Calcutta and ensured the long survival of Abanindranath's style, known as the Bengal School. Of his students probably the most important was Nandalal Bose (1882–1966), whose exposure to Japanese art (he visited the Far East with Rabindranath Tagore in 1924) was important early in his career, as were later visits to view the murals of Ajanta (he had a significant career later in life as a muralist). One of Bose's greatest students was Benode Behari Mukherjee (1904–1980), who worked both as a painter (4) and a muralist – and also as a teacher at Shantiniketan.

Most of Abanindranath Tagore's pupils were Bengali. An indirect exception was the painter Abdur Rahman Chughtai (1897–1975), who trained at the Mayo School of Art in Lahore under Samarendranath Gupta (1887–1964), himself a pupil of Abanindranath Tagore. Chughtai's paintings (3) still use the wash technique of Abanindranath, but notch up the eroticism inherent in his teacher's gentler view of the past.

The importance of the artists of the Bengal School lay in their stand against Western classicism, and in the establishment of the certainty that Indian subjects and 'eastern' techniques could produce artwork of quality which was internationally admired and was undoubtedly Indian. These ideas were also very evident in the work of another student of Abanindranath, Jamini Roy (1887–1972). His distinctive vision was inspired by Bengali folk art, a thoroughly Indian understanding of colour and a realization that design and immediacy were just as important as realism (5).

Above left
2. 'Flower girl', by Mukul Chandra Dey
Dey (1895–1989) was an artist who skilfully worked in a number of different media, not least in drypoint etching. In this painting, though, he demonstrates the influence of the visit he made, along with Rabindranath Tagore, to Japan in 1916; significantly, this painting is mounted in silk, mirroring the Japanese style.

Paint on paper, silk mount
Early 20th century (before 1920)
Height 20.7 cm, width 13.5 cm
Probably Calcutta
1920,1216,0.3

3. Painting by Abdur Rahman Chughtai

This painting, with its use of colour washes and drawing for its subject on an emotional view of the past, is typical of Chughtai's style. Here, at night and by lamplight, a young woman visits a heavily inscribed tomb. Two years before he produced this painting, Chughtai (1897–1975) visited Calcutta and met Abanindranath Tagore, whose influence can perhaps be seen here.

Watercolour on paper, signed and dated
1918
Height 52.7 cm, width 35.6 cm
Lahore
Probably donated by Abdallah Chughtai, the brother of the artist, 1998,0722,0.1

Opposite, below
4. 'A Flowering Jasmine Tree', by Benode Behari Mukherjee

Influenced both by indigenous Indian as well as Far Eastern painting traditions, Mukherjee (1904–1980) evolved a distinctive personal style. One of his favoured subjects was flowers, as here. He spent much of his life teaching at Shantiniketan, where his students included the sculptor Somnath Hore (see p. 308) and the filmmaker Satyajit Ray (see p. 304).

Thickened paint on paper
c. 1940
Height 52.5 cm, width 27 cm
Probably painted at Shantiniketan
Brooke Sewell Permanent Fund, 2015,3040.1

5. 'Three Women', by Jamini Roy

In the paintings of his mature style, Roy (1887–1972) used forms pared down to their essentials and with little or no background. Here, that means that the effect of the painting depends entirely on design and vibrant colour.

Gouache on cotton
1950s
Height 77.1 cm, width 40 cm
Calcutta, Bengal
Brooke Sewell Permanent Fund, 2012,3026.1

6 | 7 Rabindranath Tagore

Rabindranath Tagore (1861–1941) was the most subtle and brilliant thinker of the intellectual movement of cultural renewal in the late 19th and early 20th century known as the Bengal Renaissance (**1**). Born into privilege and wealth, he became a world-renowned poet – he was the first Asian to win a Nobel Prize, for literature, in 1913. However, he was much more than a poet, being an educationist, novelist, dramatist, columnist and painter.

His success with volumes such as *Gitanjali*, the collection of poems for which he won the Nobel Prize, endeared him to early 20th-century society in Europe (famously, Wilfred Owen was carrying a poem from *Gitanjali* in his wallet when he was killed). However, Tagore's later life is equally worthy of renown: he was the founder of the university at Shantiniketan and of the rural institute Shriniketan, both located in the countryside north of Calcutta. Strikingly, in a world that was becoming increasingly polarized, he saw his life as a testament to internationalism and variety. His national and international stature allowed room for cosmopolitanism and in this he was different to Gandhi. His poetry forms the national anthem not only of India but also of Bangladesh, and many composers around the world have set his words to music.

In the last ten years of his life, Tagore expressed himself increasingly in painting, working in a style drawing on his own interior world (**2**). His was a genius of exceptional and unexpected type and he never explained any of his work; he had no predecessors nor any comparable successors (**3**, **4**). The passage of years has only increased the status of his painting, just as his poetry – much of it in new translations – is today undergoing reassessment.

1. Rabindranath Tagore by Sir William Rothenstein
Rothenstein met Tagore in Calcutta in 1911, where this drawing – one of a triptych – was probably produced. The following year Tagore was in London when the English translation of *Gitanjali* was published. This then led to him winning the Nobel Prize for literature in 1913.

Pencil on yellow paper
1911
Calcutta, probably at Jorasanko
Height 19.1 cm, width 9.2 cm
The Chatterjee Foundation, John Morrish and Dr Achinto Sen-Gupta, 1999,0329,0.8

2. Fantasy animal
There is no indication of what inspired this painting; it is without title. The non-representational quality of the image, which makes its impact through the force of line and through colour combination, is typical of Tagore's style. The origin of his visual language in doodling on the manuscript page is clear.

Coloured inks on handmade paper, signed
1930s
Height 26.5 cm, width 38.5 cm
Perhaps Shantiniketan
Brooke Sewell Permanent Fund, 2005,0107,0.1

3. Two birds

This small jewel-like image is part of a group all of which have animal subjects, united by a scary, sometimes demonic quality. This underscores the nightmarish nature of many of Tagore's paintings. Despite the nationalist adoration that Tagore enjoys today, it is clear that much of his personal narrative was troubled.

Paint on paper
1930s
Height 16.6 cm, width 13.4 cm
Probably Shantiniketan
Brooke Sewell Permanent Fund,
2004,0422,0.8

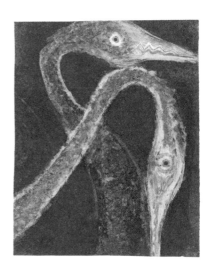

4. A female face

A woman's staring face is frequently seen in Tagore's paintings, a fact that has fuelled discussion as to who she is. One possible explanation is that this is Kadambari, the wife of his brother, Jyotirindranath. Rabindranath is known to have been very close to her and we also know that four months after Rabindranath's own marriage, she committed suicide. The sudden commencement by Tagore of painting, many years later, seems to have brought this painful episode to the surface, once more.

Coloured inks and paint on paper
1928–30
Height 29 cm, width 20 cm
Perhaps Shantiniketan
Brooke Sewell Permanent Fund,
1999,0329,0.2

6 | 8 Bengal and Bangladesh

Bengal was the heartland of British India in the 18th and 19th centuries. In the 20th century, however, it suffered a series of crises: temporary division between 1905 and 1911; the removal of the capital of imperial India from Calcutta to New Delhi in 1911; and then division again at independence in 1947 into West Bengal within the Union of India, and East Pakistan, part of the separate country of Pakistan. In 1971, after a brutal war, East Pakistan became the sovereign state of Bangladesh, 'the country of the Bangla-speakers'.

Another crisis hit Bengal in 1943 – a devastating famine. The usual supplies from Burma were cut off due to the invading Japanese. There was consequent hoarding and inflation, Indian refugees poured in from Burma, transport was compromised, administration was inept and disease was rife. Grain from elsewhere in India was also diverted from famine relief to military use. Numbers cannot now be determined with certainty, but it is estimated that between two and three million died in Bengal from starvation and disease, especially amongst the rural poor. Not surprisingly, the artistic response is still resonant today. Amongst artists, Chittaprasad (1915–1978) and Zainul Abedin (1914–1976) responded to the horrifying scenes of famine in an intense and personal way (**2**).

The eventual establishment of the state of Bangladesh saw only a certain amount of stability return. The role of artists continued to be important as commentators on social, economic and political justice. Photography has been an important component and the agency Drik, established by Shahidul Alam (b. 1955), has been at the forefront (**3**). Naeem Mohaieman (b. 1969), meanwhile, uses film, cultural history and photography to comment on social conditions and the complexities – and absurdities – of nationalism (**1**).

This page
1. 'Kazi in Noman's Land', by Naeem Mohaiemen
This installation, which as well as stacks of postage stamps also includes printed images and texts, reflects on the way in which the Bengali poet Nazrul Islam (1899–1976) was claimed by three different countries, and thus the folly of possessive nationalism. Through the issue of commemorative stamps, he was honoured by India (his country of birth), by Pakistan (initially the country of Muslim Bengalis, though Nazrul remained in India) and by Bangladesh (the country that claimed him as their national poet, and to which he was moved towards the end of his life). Poignantly, Nazrul wrote intensely about the brotherhood of different religious groupings and opposed Partition.

Postage stamps
2008
Length 4.5 cm, width 3.8 cm
(Bangladesh stamp)
New York, USA
Brooke Sewell Permanent Fund, 2012,3050.1.1

Opposite, above
2. Drawing by Zainul Abedin
Abedin's drawings of famine victims are renowned for their stark realism. This is perhaps an early sketch for the drawing that appears as the frontispiece of the book *Darkening Days* by Ela Sen, published in Calcutta in 1944. This volume of short stories unflinchingly chronicled the horror of the famine. After independence, Abedin moved to East Pakistan and later became one of the foremost artists of independent Bangladesh.

Ink on paper
1943
Height 45 cm, width 29 cm
Pre-Partition Bengal
2012,3027.1

Below
3. Photograph by
Shahidul Alam
This evocative image by the founder of the Drik agency was shot at a time of great emotion. Alam, renowned internationally as a photographer and a human rights activist, had just been released from jail and, driving back to Dhaka, he saw a woman in the jute fields, colourful in her red sari set against the green crop. This reminded him of the colours in the Bangladesh flag – red and green – and the role of the heroic migrant labourers and farmers of his country.

Photograph
November 2018
Photograph from the Drik Agency, Dhaka

6 | 9 Indian music in the modern world

A remarkable feature of Indian culture in the 20th century has been its internationalization, partly due to the diaspora of South Asian peoples all over the world, but mostly because of the genius of a committed band of artists. This is especially evident in the fields of dance and music, with the name of Pandit Ravi Shankar (1920–2012) particularly associated with the latter.

Although from a Bengali family, Ravi Shankar was born in Benares (Varanasi today). While still an adolescent he joined his brother, the dancer Uday Shankar, performing in Europe. However, on returning to India in the late 1930s he moved from dance to music, studying intensively under a guru.

He went on to perform widely in India, and his playing has always remained popular there; he also played for films – the score for *The Apu Trilogy* by Satyajit Ray (see pp. 304–5) is by Shankar. From the mid-1950s onwards he performed in Europe and the USA, and through the 1960s and 1970s he became increasingly renowned worldwide, not only on account of his own playing of Indian music, but also because of his ability to work with musicians from other traditions – famously with Yehudi Menuhin (**1**), and then George Harrison of the Beatles. This ability to experiment was based on his absolute grounding in his own tradition and the mastery of his instrument (**2**).

His legacy lies in his presentation (along with other Indian musicians) of the riches of Indian music to an international audience, through concerts, his compositions and his many recordings. His legacy is also seen in his pupils, including his daughter Anoushka Shankar who continues to plough her own distinctive furrow in the world of music (**3**).

1. Yehudi Menuhin and Pandit Ravi Shankar

These two great artists were masters of their own instruments and internationally famous at the time this photo was taken in the studios at Abbey Road in 1966. Their album *West meets East*, being recorded here, was perhaps the most famous collaboration between musicians from such totally different traditions and marked the way for other global fusion-type music encounters.

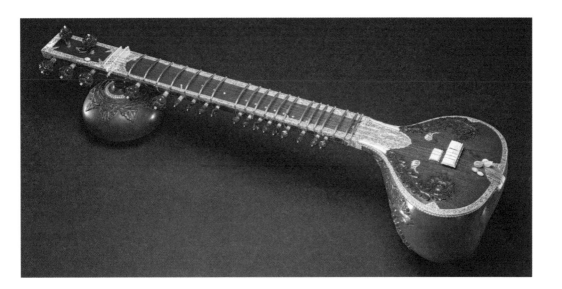

2. Sitar of Pandit Ravi Shankar

This sitar is one of four made by the Calcutta-based instrument-maker Nodu Mallick for Pandit Ravi Shankar. Mallick frequently travelled with Shankar to look after his instruments and to play the tambura, the drone instrument in the Indian ensemble.

Teak, gourds (the two resonators), and inlaid and carved bone
1961
Length 126 cm, width 36 cm (max)
Calcutta
Donated by Sukanya Shankar, Anoushka Shankar and the Ravi Shankar Foundation, 2017,3039.1

3. Anoushka Shankar playing the sitar

The daughter of Ravi Shankar is now renowned as a sitar player in her own right. Here she plays her father's sitar (seen in Figure 2) in the British Museum prior to its entry into the museum collection, where it speaks eloquently as to the international quality of Indian music.

1. Warli painting from Maharashtra

Paintings based on the forest environment and in which animals rather than humans predominate, are typical of Warli paintings. Here, a narrative that includes a forest shrine (centre left) along with diminutive humans amidst great arboreal variety, makes for an intriguing image.

Paint on dung-washed paper
1980s
Height 58 cm, width 90.5 cm
Maharashtra, inland from Thane
1988,0209,0.2

2. Print by Jangarh Singh Shyam

Although humanity appears in this vision of the forest (bottom centre), it is animal life in all its variety that dominates the Gond world-view. There is surely some narrative here in which crabs, cobras, a tiger and swarming bees participate, amongst much else – but at present it remains unknown.

Photogravure on paper
1980s
Height 69 cm, width 39.5 cm
Probably Bhopal
1988,0209,0.9

Rural cultures

It is clear that in many areas of cultural life – music, religion, painting and sculpture – there has been, over many centuries, a continuing reinvigoration of urban culture by currents from the countryside and the forests (the latter much more extensive in the past than today). Although now rapidly changing, the population of South Asia is still predominantly rural. In the past, this was even more the case and rural culture has acted as a reservoir providing new impetus and ideas for urban elites.

In modern times, one of the most striking ways in which this has happened is the discovery of rural and tribal non-representational art by urban artists and cultural promoters. This has been especially striking in the mid-20th century, a time when Indian artists were still being trained to look to European art and its dependence on realism. Just as artists in Europe were beginning to understand the power and beauty of abstraction, pattern-making and design, artists in India were finding its existence on their very doorsteps. The result has been a much greater appreciation of the work of tribal and rural artists. Many of these non-urban artists have adapted painting traditions that are rooted in the prophylactic power of painted spaces in village environments. Thus, narratives and designs used in the past to protect domestic space by rural communities, such as the Saora (Orissa) and the Warli (Maharashtra) (1), have been transferred to paper. Perhaps the most impressive of these transfers, from remote rural and village life to international art galleries, is the work of the Mithila (or Madhubani) artists of north Bihar, first championed in the 1930s by the British administrator and later art historian, W. G. Archer (1907–1979). The most famous of the later Madhubani artists was Ganga Devi (1928–1991), whose visualizations of Washington DC, for instance, are of striking originality. Other artists from the same background include Lakshmi Devi, working in the 1970s (3).

Another artist drawing on similar traditions, again with impressive originality, was Jangarh Singh Shyam (1962–2001). A Gond from Maharashtra, he found early renown working at Bharat Bhavan with the studio artist Swaminathan. He later went on to have an international career, drawing extensively on his forest and tribal background (2). Other artists have since followed in his pioneering footsteps.

3. Painting by Lakshmi Devi
Some of the protective and encouraging designs found on the wattle and daub walls of houses in the Mithila District of Bihar were in marriage chambers. While not overtly sexual, the imagery includes depictions of the generative organs, along with auspicious symbols suggestive of the happiness brought by children, especially sons.

Poster paint and ink on handmade paper, in Madhubani style
Late 1960s
Height 56.2 cm, width 76 cm
Mithila District, Bihar
Donated by Dr Achinto Sen-Gupta, 2000,1012,0.13

6 | 10 Sri Lanka: the 43 Group

Modernism arrived in Sri Lanka in the form of a group of artists who gathered around the larger-than-life character Lionel Wendt (1900–1944). Born into a wealthy family of Dutch and Sri Lankan ancestry (such families are known as burgher families), Wendt studied music and law in London but later, back in Sri Lanka, produced haunting photographs of the island. While talented in a wide range of artistic fields, he is remembered above all today for these images, the range of which included landscapes, wistful portraits of young men (**2**) and latterly, experimental images of surrealist type. Sadly, he died only a year after the foundation of the 43 Group, so one of its most brilliant stars was lost very early on. However, the painters Ivan Peries and Harry Pieris continued to organize the group.

Other artists who formed the initial group included the painters George Claessen, Justin Daraniyagala and George Keyt. Keyt (1901–1993) – again from a burgher family – produced paintings and drawings, distinctly his own but also referencing Western styles. Sri Lankan Buddhist texts also influenced his work and the drawing illustrated here (**1**) typically draws on a narrative from the chronicle, the *Mahavamsa*. Keyt exhibited in London, an event recorded by his entry in the guest book of the Institute of Contemporary Arts, which is today housed in the British Museum.

Another figure who played an important early role was an English civil servant in the Department of Education, Charles Freegrove Winzer (1886–1940); he was also an accomplished draughtsman inspired by the cultural history of Sri Lanka (**3**).

1. 'Sre Sanghabodhe gives away his head', by George Keyt

The subject of this drawing, like much of Keyt's output, comes from his knowledge of traditional Sri Lankan sources. Here he depicts a scene from the chronicle, the *Mahavamsa*, in which a hermit (though a one-time king) gives away his head as he has nothing else to give; a supreme example of charity, the most important Buddhist virtue.

Graphite on paper, signed and dated
1953
Height 50 cm, width 52.5 cm
Sri Lanka, probably Colombo
Donated by Robert Knox,
1994,0704,0.1

2. Unknown boy, by Lionel Wendt

Some of Wendt's photographs were published in book form during his life, but the actual prints have only come to light in recent years (all his negatives were apparently destroyed). His interest in playing with technical aspects of photography places him amongst the most innovative artists of 20th-century South Asia.

Photograph
Probably late 1930s
Height 25.6 cm, width 20 cm
Sri Lanka, probably Colombo
Funded by Jeff Soref, in honour of Richard Blurton, 2003,0811,0.1

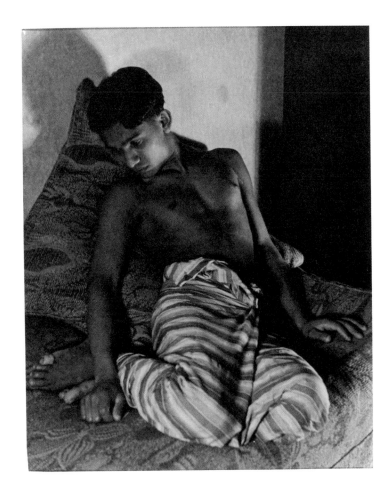

3. 'The Rock of Sigiria, Ceylon', by Charles Freegrove Winzer

Winzer proved to be an important catalyst in the development of the 43 Group, establishing the Ceylon Art Club in 1928. In this print, Winzer highlights the female figures carrying flower offerings that form part of the still-surviving mural on the rock-face as one climbs to the top of the Rock of Sigiriya. This famous rock-top citadel in central Sri Lanka was an important royal centre in the mid-1st millennium and also includes extensive water gardens surrounding the base of the rock.

Lithograph, signed and dated; numbered 5 of 15
1920–30
Height 28 cm, width 37.5 cm
Sri Lanka
Donated by the artist, 1932,0706.5

6 | 11 The Progressive Artists Group

The Progressives were a group of Indian artists keen to break away from cultural dependence on existing models, especially the stifling embrace of colonial art-school teaching. They came together in Bombay in 1947, eager to be part of international artistic activity. Two of this group, Sayed Haider Raza (1922–2016) and Francis Newton Souza (1924–2002) spent most of their careers outside India (Paris and the UK/USA, respectively), while a third, M. F. Husain (1915–2011) was greatly honoured for much of his life in India but was, for his last years, forced into exile by right-wing politics. Others in the group included K. H. Ara, and later V. Gaitonde and Tyeb Mehta.

Eager to demonstrate they were not tied to Indian traditions, they embraced modernist ideas such as cubism and abstraction. However, some eventually found the lure of Indian aesthetics too difficult to resist. Raza is prominent in this respect, working on canvases in oil and acrylic – neither traditional Indian materials – but inspired by Hindu notions of sacred geometry and space (1). Souza's paintings often reference violence and/or sexually explicit imagery. His best works include these themes along with others from his Catholic upbringing, demonstrating the tensions between creativity, sex and religion (2). Husain came to painting in a different way, initially painting billboards for a living, only later becoming a professional artist. He is remembered particularly for his paintings of horses, scenes from the Indian epics (3), and images of Mother Teresa.

As is the way with such artistic groupings, these artists eventually developed their own different languages. What they had in common, though, was a determined concern to be 'not merely' Indian but to be part of an international, cosmopolitan world response. In this respect they succeeded.

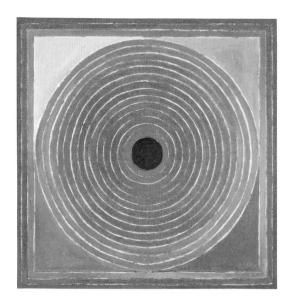

1. 'Aarakta Shyam', by Sayed Haider Raza
In his later work, Raza concentrated on the notion of *bindu*, the central point of power. In this painting the *bindu* is set within rings of solar colour and energy. Although a Muslim by birth, Raza repeatedly drew inspiration from Hindu metaphysics, his exposure to which was most years re-energized by visits to India from Paris, where he spent the majority of his adult life.

Acrylic paint on canvas
2012
Height 100 cm, width 100 cm
Delhi
Donated by the artist and the Grosvenor Vadehra Gallery, London, 2012,3052.1

2. Untitled painting by Francis Newton Souza

Perhaps depicting a church hierarch, or anyway drawing upon his Goan background, this work was painted in London, the year after Souza's departure from India. It is typical of his style with its intense and stylized imagery, prominent facial features, thick impasto and his own signature distinctively placed in the picture.

Oil paint on board
1950
Height 76.3 cm, width 60.7 cm
Brooke Sewell Permanent Fund, 1993,1015,0.1

3. Print from the Hanuman series by M. F. Husain

Husain famously prepared a print series detailing the rollicking adventures of Hanuman, the monkey-general of the Ramayana. Here, he wittily uses a wrestler's mace (Hanuman is the guardian deity of wrestlers) as the head of the monkey hero. This image records the moment when Hanuman sets on fire the city of Lanka with his tail.

Lithograph, on paper, signed and dated; numbered 61 of 350
1982
Height 61 cm, width 45.7 cm
Probably printed in Bombay
Donated by Chester and Davida Herwitz, 1997,0503,0.30

6 | 12 Printmakers in the 20th century

The production of artists' prints, as opposed to popular chromolithographs (see pp. 284–5), is a mostly 20th-century activity, though British printmakers such as Charles D'Oyly were active in India from the mid-19th century. Early Indian print artists include Mukul Chandra Dey (see p. 288, Figure 2), who trained in both Japan and London (for his work at Bagh, see p. 80). Haren Das (1921–1993), a fellow Bengali of the next generation, worked almost exclusively in the print medium, producing imagery of the Bengal countryside (**1**) as well as prints that were critical of social mores.

Dey was a teacher at Kala Bhavan, part of Tagore's university at Shantiniketan, and a pupil there in the 1940s was the Andhra-born artist Krishna Reddy (1925–2018) who later studied in London, and then worked with the British artist Stanley Hayter, in Paris. Here, he learnt the technique of viscosity printing, with which he went on to produce a range of prints, demonstrating an impressive understanding of colour combination (**2**). He later settled in New York. Another exceptional print-artist, also from Andhra, is Laxma Goud (b. 1940), who has revitalized the linkage between eroticism and the forest, so well known from earlier centuries (**3**).

Other print artists include Rini Dhumal, Jyoti Bhatt and Jaidev Thakore (Baroda); Sultan Ali and Palaniappan (Tamil Nadu); and Kanchan Chander (Delhi). Prints by these artists are all held in the British Museum.

1. 'Going to the Fair', by Haren Das
The lyrical and mostly rural images produced by Das doubtless hark back to his youthful experience growing up in the Bengal countryside around Dinajpur (now in Bangladesh). His use of the woodblock technique is a reflection of the interest in Japanese art techniques, which were so admired in mid-20th-century Bengal.

Woodblock print, on paper
1960s
Height 15 cm, width 11 cm
Probably Calcutta
1988,0209,0.17

2. 'Plants', by Krishna Reddy

Reddy's understanding of colour, perhaps uniquely Indian, meant that his long sequence of print production, over at least fifty years, is characterized by great subtlety. Examples from the 1950s until 2003 are in the British Museum collection.

Viscosity print
1966
Height 44 cm, width 34.5 cm
Probably Paris, while at
Atelier 17
Brooke Sewell Permanent Fund,
1997,1209,0.1

3. 'Nizampur IV', by Laxma Goud

Primarily a print artist, Goud is also known for his startling drawings. In this print, named for his birthplace in the south Indian state of Andhra Pradesh, he depicts naked male and female characters in a dream forest landscape. The towers of the palace in the background and the trees to the right have a phallic presence that add to the erotic charge of the image.

Etching on paper
1975
Height 40 cm, width 55 cm
Probably Hyderabad, Andhra
Pradesh
Donated by Dr Achinto
Sen-Gupta, 2003,1002,0.14

1. Academy award citation for *Mother India* (left)
This famous film was directed by Mehboob Khan and was the first Indian film to be nominated for an Oscar (it missed by one vote).

Ink on laminated wood
1957
Height 34.5 cm, width 30 cm
Los Angeles, USA
Donated by Shaukat Khan,
2017,3047.1

Filmfare award (right)
Awarded to Bimal Roy as Best Director for his Hindi-language film *Parakh*.

Brass (once black-lacquered); inscribed around base
1960
Height 40.5 cm, width (widest point) 8 cm
Probably Bombay
Donated by the Bimal Roy family,
2017,3051.1

Film and cinema

The production and consumption of film has been highly important in the life of modern South Asia. Many hundreds of films are produced in India each year, and some two billion annual cinema visits are made. Film production in Hindi is based for the most part in Bombay/Mumbai (hence the sobriquet, Bollywood), but regional industries also flourish reflecting the different languages of South Asia. Indian films have been popular not only in India and throughout South Asia, but also in the Gulf, the rest of the Middle East, in Russia and in Central Asia – and wherever people from South Asia have settled in the 20th-century diaspora.

Dadasaheb Phalke was the director of the first film ever produced in India, *Raja Harishchandra* (1913); it was, of course, silent. From this modest beginning, the film industry developed, initially in black and white, though with sound from the 1930s and then with the first colour from the late 1950s. With the coming of sound, music – especially singing – became an integral feature of Indian popular cinema. The 'stars' have nearly always been the dominant attraction and are featured prominently in the visual culture of Indian cinema (although since the 1940s they don't sing the songs, which are pre-recorded by playback artists). In the 1950s, actor/director Raj Kapoor and actress Nargis were the first internationally known figures of Hindi film; she famously starred in *Mother India* (1). This popular couple went on to win thousands of fans in the Middle East, Russia and China.

Like film culture in many parts of the world, the cinema of South Asia offers its vast audiences both art films that have important social themes, as well as popular cinema with an emphasis on escapist and romantic storylines, peppered with song and dance routines. There is some fluidity across these divisions: a notable example is *Parakh*, which is both romantic and realistic, and with singing by the renowned Lata Mangeshkar. The film's director, Bimal Roy, was the winner of the 1960 Filmfare award (1).

Advertising for films has over the years produced a rich array of visual material. Prior to the digital age, publicity material included booklets, hoardings, posters, postcards and handbills. The style of the imagery has changed over the decades but immediacy of recognition of the lead cast has remained constant. The use of text and the variety of script in the publicity material has been telling – in 1940s Bombay, text in English, Hindi, Urdu and Gujarati was used; the last two are now rarely seen, reflecting changes in population.

The most famous exponent of art cinema was the Bengali filmmaker and polymath Satyajit Ray (1921–1992), whose films such as *Devi*, *Charulata* and *The Apu Trilogy* brought him enormous international attention. His most famous works were made in black and white, and only latterly did he use colour (2). Rooted in Bengali culture, Ray's films are nevertheless regarded as classics of world cinema.

2. Title-card by Satyajit Ray
This is one of twelve cards drawn by Satyajit Ray for the credit sequence in his film *Kanchenjungha* (1962), his first essay in colour film.

Watercolour and ink on paper
c. 1960
Height 29 cm, width 39 cm
Probably Calcutta
Donated by Sandip Ray,
2017,3045.1

6 | 13 Painters and symbols

Partly reflecting a nationalist need for an aesthetic based on Indian, non-Western ideas, a group of artists developed in the mid-20th century who deliberately turned away from Western-style figuration and took inspiration from the non-representational traditions of the subcontinent; they have been loosely grouped together as the Neo-tantrics, though all have their own specific ideas and are not tantric adepts in the historic sense. They drew on the patterning seen in *yantras* and other forms of sacred geometry such as *mandalas* (for both, see pp. 160–61); along with mental and physical exercise, *yoga*, and the enunciation of powerful syllables, *mantras*, these elements are collectively part of *tantra* – a potent reservoir for 20th-century artists. Some, such as K. C. S. Paniker (1911–1977) and Dipak Banerjee (b. 1936) (**2**), have used words often in powerful combination, as well as abstract designs such as circles, squares, triangles, all of which are full of meaning in the tantric imagination. Others, such as Biren De (1926–2011), depended on pulsating symbolic visual language (**3**). Sexual imagery, again drawing on ideas associated with *tantra*, has sometimes been included, as in the work of Ghulam Rasool Santosh (1929–1997) (**1**).

Inherent in the work of many of the Neo-tantrics are ideas concerning integration of positive and negative, the resolution of opposites, the power of colour, and the way in which elements such as the *bindu*, a single dot, can represent the entire cosmos (**4**). The work of these artists is often powerful and thought-provoking, but it is unconnected with the mundane, the political or the socially active; these are images of the mind.

1. Untitled painting by Ghulam Rasool Santosh
Although never realistically sexual, the imagery that Santosh developed in his paintings clearly invokes tantric ideas, especially those of his native Kashmir. These include the idea that spiritual insight can be accessed through the combination – either through meditation or in actuality – of male and female powers, thus resolving opposites and eliminating duality.

Acrylic paint on canvas
1974
Height 44 cm, width 34 cm
Probably Delhi
Donated by Dr Achinto
Sen-Gupta, 1997,0121,0.4

2. 'Yantra', by Dipak Banerjee
Although tantric imagery is known throughout the subcontinent, interest in it has been particularly noteworthy in Bengal, where Banerjee and also De (Figure 3) were born. Single-syllable *mantras* are used here both within and around the superimposed triangles, as well as in the central circle in the form of the powerful *mantra*, Om.

Viscosity print
Probably 1960s
Height 49 cm, width 29.5 cm
Calcutta
2005,0801,0.2

3. Oil painting by Biren De
Biren De used dense but also contrasting colour to seduce the viewer into looking closely at his images. He drew on Indian concepts of *tantra*, but was also aware of the work of Abstract Expressionist artists in the USA, where he worked in the 1960s.

Oil paint on canvas, signed and dated
1974
Height 96.8 cm, width 66 cm
Calcutta
Donated by Dr Achinto Sen-Gupta, 2004,0408,0.2

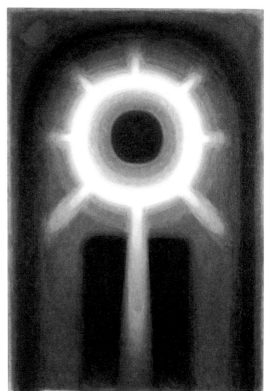

4. 'Neela', by Prafulla Mohanti

The aesthetic vision of Prafulla Mohanti (b. 1936) can be seen as a product of his birth and early years in rural Orissa, combined with his cosmopolitan life based in London for the last fifty years. The wellspring of his inspiration is frequently recharged by return travel to his home village of Nurpur, a source about which he has repeatedly written.

Watercolour on paper
1989
Height 65 cm, width 50 cm
London
Brooke Sewell Permanent Fund,
1993,1014,0.1

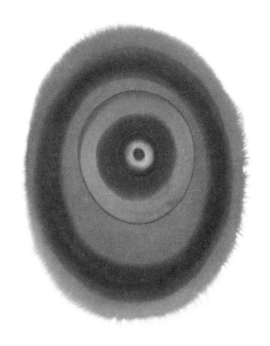

6 | 14 20th-century sculpture in India

In the art schools founded during the British period, sculpture of an academic, European type was taught to students. This encouraged a derivative style and in the early 20th century it took several decades to move beyond such prototypes. By the mid-20th century, however, several figures were developing a style of sculpture that was distinctively modern and yet also unequivocally Indian. These sculptors included three individuals closely associated with the university at Shantiniketan: Ramkinkar Baij, Somnath Hore and Mrinalini Mukherjee, the latter being the youngest of the three, and a woman.

Both Baij (1906–1980) and Hore (1921–2006) were politically committed and their work is famous for its social involvement. Baij worked mostly in concrete and plaster, but was also an engaging draughtsman (**1**). Hore's work based on the Bengal Famine of 1943 is especially renowned (**2**), with its evident and deeply resonant response to the tragedy. Meanwhile, Mukherjee (1949–2015) was different from the other two in that, although closely connected to Shantiniketan (her father was the artist Benode Behari Mukherjee, see p. 289), she initially studied in Baroda in western India, lived most of her life in Delhi and also studied in the UK on a British Council scholarship. She was further unusual in the media that she chose for her sculpture: primarily hemp fibre, dyed and knotted, but also bronze and latterly clay (**3**). In her late group of monumental sculptures, produced when Mukherjee could take advantage of large kilns available to her while on a scholarship in the Netherlands, she skilfully reassessed the South Asian obsession with figuration and returned to the most fundamental medium for sculpture production in India – clay.

1. Watercolour sketch by Ramkinkar Baij
Like many of his contemporary Bengali artists, Baij found inspiration in the countryside around Shantiniketan where he studied. He is mostly remembered today for his sculpture, especially in concrete which allowed him to work with fluidity and immediacy, characteristics also visible in his painted sketches.

Watercolour on paper, signed
1940s
Height 20.2 cm, width 28.5 cm
Shantiniketan
Brooke Sewell Permanent Fund,
2010,3002.1

2. Sculpture by Somnath Hore

Forty years after the Bengal Famine, Hore was still haunted by the experience; here the arms and legs are reduced to sticks and the face is sunken and withdrawn. Born in Chittagong (now in Bangladesh), Hore experienced political upheaval and its appalling consequences throughout his life. These he chronicled from his base at Tagore's university, Shantiniketan, in rural West Bengal.

Cast bronze
1988
Height 49 cm, width 19 cm
Shantiniketan
Brooke Sewell Permanent Fund, 2013,3008.1

3. 'Night Bloom II', by Mrinalini Mukherjee

In the different media Mukherjee used for her sculpture, the engagement with natural forms both vegetal and human is very pronounced. This draped, perhaps veiled figure is part of a group of large clay sculptures which are highly fluid, suggesting – but not defining – human experience.

Fired ceramic, partly glazed
1999/2000
Height 110.5 cm
European Ceramic Work Centre, 's-Hertogenbosch, the Netherlands
Brooke Sewell Permanent Fund and the Art Fund (with a contribution from the Wolfson Foundation), 2017,3019.1

6 | 15 Reinvention in Lahore

Lahore, capital of the province of the Punjab in Pakistan, has maintained its position as a major cultural centre not least because of the presence there of the National College of Art (previously the Mayo College of Art; Lockwood Kipling, father of Rudyard Kipling, was the first Principal).

Anwar Jalal Shemza (1928–1985) studied at Mayo College, though the latter part of his life was spent in Britain (1). In the 1980s one of the students at the National College of Art who also went on to study in London (at the Royal College of Art), but returned to teach, was Quddus Mirza (b. 1961) (2). Artists at the college are encouraged to study the Mughal tradition of miniature painting and many have used this knowledge to inform their own work. This influence is in no sense a slavish reproduction of earlier work, but a route through which new and exciting possibilities have been found. These contemporary paintings present something modern, thoughtful and completely individual. The artists (mostly painters) live in a society that has seen political oppression and economic deprivation. However, unlike in neighbouring India where miniatures are reduced to uninspired copies, they have re-energized the tradition.

Artists who have contributed to this new Pakistan vision include Ali Kazim (b. 1979) (3), Rashid Rana, Imran Qureshi and Waseem Ahmed. Another is Khadim Ali (b. 1978), a displaced member of the Hazara community. In the past, the Hazaras lived in central Afghanistan, including the Bamiyan valley, and the presence there of the majestic rock-cut images of the standing Buddha (see p. 80) and their destruction by the Taliban in 2001 has informed an entire sequence of Ali's work (4).

1. 'City Walls', by Anwar Jalal Shemza
Shemza developed a distinctive style in painting and printmaking in which forms drawn from Urdu calligraphy and Mughal architecture are fused in an abstract vision of striking colour.

Gouache on board
1961
Height 25 cm, width 39 cm
Stafford, England
Brooke Sewell Permanent Fund, 2012,3030.1

2. 'Portrait of my Village XIV', by Quddus Mirza
Today Mirza is known as a painter of narrative scenes depicted in planes of flat colour, but also as an educator and a writer on art for the print media.

Acrylic paint on paper
1992
Height 42 cm, width 58.5 cm
London
1992,1006,0.1

3. Untitled self-portrait by Ali Kazim
Despite being a nude, this image is completely devoid of lubricity, an effect caused by the isolation of the figure and its pose, leaning forward and not engaging with the viewer.

Watercolour on *wasli* paper (a handmade organic paper used for miniature painting)
2012
Height 153.3 cm, width 75.3 cm
London
Brooke Sewell Permanent Fund, 2012,3048.1

4. 'The heart that has no love, pain and generosity, is not a heart', by Khadim Ali
In this painting, the cannon in front of one of the Bamiyan Buddhas, along with apparently religious text which drains down into a lotus and a pool of blood, conjures up emotions of terrible loss in the name of religion.

Watercolour on *wasli* paper
2010
Height 28 cm, width 23 cm
Kabul, Afghanistan
Brooke Sewell Permanent Fund, 2012,3031.1

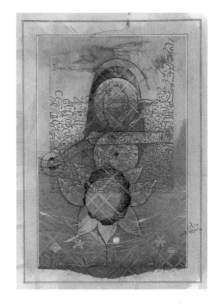

6 | 16 Modernity in South Asia

Today one is almost overwhelmed by the explosion of artistic activity in South Asia. There is no corner of this vast region in which inspiring new work is not being produced, all in different ways reflecting rapidly changing societies. Artistic variety and the greater availability of gallery space are fostered by international gatherings such as the Dhaka Art Summit (Bangladesh), and Biennale meetings in Colombo (Sri Lanka), Kochi (India) and Karachi (Pakistan). As the middle classes expand, both the producers and consumers of art have increased; this is a market that is cognizant of international practice, a situation that is increased by auction houses that promote artists to diaspora as well as to local collectors.

Film, photography and mechanical reproduction are important elements (1), as also are the theoretical arguments of conceptual artists (2). Artists from throughout South Asia have now become known internationally, and some of these have explored challenging subjects such as sexuality (3) and the position of women in a paternalistic society. Artists at Baroda in India – both teachers and pupils – have been at the forefront of political engagement, especially in the late 20th century, and this has been mirrored artistically in productive experimentation under teachers such as K. G. Subramanyan and Gulammohammed Sheikh. Today, artists throughout South Asia argue through their work against negative elements in contemporary society such as the racism of the caste system, economic disadvantage and the marginalization of religious groups. Techniques have also expanded to include digital manipulation and electronic artworks. Everywhere in South Asia, artists remain at the forefront of new ways of seeing and understanding the society in which they live.

Above
1. 'Dreamings and Defilings', concertina-album by Nalini Malani
In this painted book, the artist Nalani Malani (b. 1946) uses xerox images, transparent film and paint to tell her narrative. Women's stories, violent and otherwise, have frequently figured in Malani's work.

Paper and cardboard, signed and dated
1991
Height 21 cm, width 30.5 cm
Probably Bombay
2003,0723,0.4

Left
2. 'The Intermediaries', by Bharti Kher
Kher (b. 1969) has here altered a group of modern devotional images to encourage the viewer to question the position of the traditional in the life of the subcontinent.

Fired and glazed clay
2016
Heights 10–35 cm
Delhi
Brooke Sewell Permanent Fund,
2017,3062.1-10

Right

**3. 'In the river Jamuna',
print by Bhupen Khakhar**

Bhupen Khakhar (1934–2003)
was a figurative painter of
distinctive immediacy as well
as a printmaker. Courageously,
from the late 1980s onwards
he included images both of
himself and of his male lover in
his work (as here), making his
sexual orientation unequivocal.
His artistic as well as social
influence in India, especially
in Baroda where he lived,
has been considerable.

Print on paper
1993
Height 63 cm, width 63.5 cm
Probably Baroda, Gujarat
1995,0406,0.3

Selected bibliography

General

Ahuja, Naman. *The Body in Indian Art and Thought*. Brussels. 2013.

Basham, A. L. *The Wonder that was India. A Survey of the Culture of the Indian Sub-continent before the Coming of the Muslims*. London. 1954.

Blurton, T. Richard. *Hindu Art*. London. 1992

Brockington, J. L. *The Sacred Thread. A Short History of Hinduism*. New Delhi. 1981.

Crill, Rosemary (ed.) *The Fabric of India*. London. 2015.

Dallapiccola, Anna. *Dictionary of Hindu Lore and Legend*. London. 2002.

Dehejia, Vidya. *Indian Art*. London. 1997.

Elliot, Mark. *Another India. Explorations & Expressions of Indigenous South Asia*. Cambridge. 2018.

Guy, John and Deborah Swallow (eds.) *Arts of India: 1550–1900*. London. 1990.

Khilnani, Sunil. *Incarnations. India in 50 Lives*. London. 2016.

Kosambi, D. D. *Myth and Reality*. Bombay. 1962.

Kramrisch, Stella. *The Art of India. Traditions of Indian Sculpture, Painting and Architecture*. London. 1954.

Kramrisch, Stella. *Exploring India's Sacred Art*. Selected Writings edited by Barbara Stoler Miller. Philadelphia. 1983.

Singh, Upinder. *A History of Ancient and Early Medieval India from the Stone Age to the 12th Century*. Noida. 2009.

Zwalf, Wladimir (ed). *Buddhism. Art and Faith*. London. 1982.

Introduction and Chapter 1: Prehistory and early history

Ahuja, Naman. *Art and Archaeology of Ancient India. Earliest Times to the Sixth Century*. Oxford. 2018.

Allchin, Bridget and Raymond Allchin. *The Rise of Civilization in India and Pakistan*. Cambridge. 1982.

Allchin, F. R. and K. R. Norman. 'Guide to the Aśokan inscriptions' in *South Asian Studies* 1. 1985.

Chakrabarti, Dilip K. *The Archaeology of Ancient Indian Cities*. Oxford. 1995.

Coningham, Robin and Ruth Young. *The Archaeology of South Asia. From the Indus to Asoka, c. 6500 BCE–200 CE*. New York. 2015.

Cook, Jill and Hazel E. Martingell. *The Carlyle Collection of Stone Age Artefacts from Central India*. British Museum Occasional Paper 95. London. 1994.

Cribb, Joe. 'The Origins of the Indian Coinage Tradition' in *South Asian Studies* 19. 2003.

Durrans, Brian and T. Richard Blurton (eds.). *The Cultural Heritage of the Indian Village*. British Museum Occasional Paper 47. London. 1991.

Finkel, Irving. '*Dice in India and Beyond*' in Mackenzie, Colin and Irving Finkel (eds.). *Asian Games: The Art of Contest*. New York. 2004.

Gupta, P. L. and T. R. Hardaker. *Punchmarked Coinage of the Indian Subcontinent: Magadha-Mauryan Series*. Revised edition. Mumbai. 2014.

Kenoyer, Jonathan Mark. *Ancient Cities of the Indus Valley Civilization*. Oxford. 1998.

Parpola, Asko. *Deciphering the Indus Script*. Cambridge. 2009.

Possehl, Gregory L. *The Indus Civilization. A Contemporary Perspective*. Lanham, Maryland. 2002.

Poster, Amy G. *From Indian Earth. 4,000 Years of Terracotta Art*. New York. 1986.

Ratnagar, Shereen. *Other Indians. Essays on Pastoralists and Prehistoric Tribal People*. Gurgaon. 2004.

Shah, Haku. *Votive Terracottas of Gujarat*. New York. 1985.

Sharma, G. R. *The Excavations at Kausambi 1957–59*. Allahabad. 1960.

Thapar, Romila. 'Aśoka: A Retrospective' in Olivelle, Patrick, Janice Leoshko and Himanshu Prabha Ray (eds.). *Reimagining Ashoka. Memory and History*. New Delhi. 2012.

Topsfield, Andrew (ed.). *The Art of Play. Board and Card Games of India*. Mumbai. 2006.

Witzel, M. 'The Languages of Harappa (Early linguistic data and the Indus civilisation)' in Kenoyer, J. (ed.). *Proceedings of the Conference on the Indus Civilisation*. Madison. 1998 [online and forthcoming].

Chapter 2: Early empires and developing religions

Barnes, Ruth. 'Indian Textiles for Island Taste: the Trade to Eastern Indonesia' in Rosemary Crill (ed.). *Textiles from India. The Global Trade*. Calcutta. 2006.

Barnes, Ruth, Steven Cohen and Rosemary Crill. *Trade, Temple and Court: Indian Textiles from the Tapi Collection*. Mumbai. 2002.

Begley et al. *The Ancient Port of Arikamedu. New Excavations and Researches 1989–1992*. Vol. I Pondichéry, 1996; Vol. II Paris, 2004.

Boisselier, Jean. *Ceylon*. Geneva. 1979.

Brockington, J. L. *Righteous Rama: the Evolution of an Epic*. Delhi. 1984.

Dehejia, Vidya. *Devi. The Great Goddess. Female Divinity in South Asian Art*. Washington DC. 1999.

Errington, Elizabeth. *Charles Masson and the Buddhist Sites of Afghanistan: Explorations, Excavations, Collections 1832–1835*. British Museum Research Publication 215. London. 2017.

Errington, Elizabeth and Vesta Curtis. *From Persepolis to the Punjab. Exploring ancient Iran, Afghanistan and Pakistan*. London. 2007.

Gittinger, Mattiebelle. *Master Dyers to the World: technique and trade in early Indian dyed cotton textiles*. Washington DC. 1982.

Goepper, Roger, Christian Luczanits, et al. *Alchi*. New edition, forthcoming.

Hartsuiker, Dolf. *Sadhus. Holy Men of India*. London. 1993.

Jain, Jyotindra (ed.). *Picture Showmen. Insights into the Narrative Tradition in Indian Art*. Mumbai. 1998.

Khan, Nasim. 'Lajjā Gaurī Seals and Related Antiquities from Kashmir Smast, Gandhāra' in *South Asian Studies* 18. 2002.

Knox, Robert. *Amaravati. Buddhist Sculpture from the Great Stupa*. London. 1992.

Kramrisch, Stella. *Manifestations of Shiva*. Philadelphia. 1981.

Lopez, Donald S. Jnr. *Gendun Chopel. Tibet's first modern artist*. New York and Chicago. 2013.

Marshall, John, M. B. Garde, J. P. Vogel, E. B. Havell, J. H. Cousins and L. Binyon. *The Bagh Caves in Gwalior State*. London. 1927.

McGill, Forrest (ed.). *The Rama Epic. Hero, Heroine, Ally, Foe*. San Francisco. 2016.

Monius, Anne E. *Imagining a place for Buddhism. Literary Culture and Religious Community in Tamil-Speaking South India*. Oxford. 2001.

Padma, Sree and A. W. Barber (eds.). *Buddhism in the Krishna Valley of Andhra*. Albany. 2008.

Pal, Pratapaditya et al. *The Peaceful Liberators. Jain Art from India*. London and Los Angeles. 1994.

Pal, Pratapaditya et al. *The Arts of Kashmir*. New York. 2007.

Raghavan, V. (ed.). *The Ramayana Tradition in Asia*. New Delhi. 1981.

Ray, Himanshu. *The Winds of Change. Buddhism and the Maritime Links of South Asia*. Oxford. 1994.

Salomon, Richard. *Ancient Buddhist Scrolls from Gandhara*. London. 1999.

Schopen, Gregory. *Bones, Stones and Buddhist Monks. Collected Papers on the Archaeology, Epigraphy and Texts of Monastic Buddhism in India.* 1996.

von Schroeder, U. *The Golden Age of Sculpture in Sri Lanka.* Hong Kong. 1992.

Shaw, Julia. *Buddhist landscapes in Central India.* London. 2007.

Shimada, Akira. *Early Buddhist Architecture in Context. The Great Stupa at Amaravati (ca. 300 BCE–300 CE).* Leiden. 2013.

Shimada, Akira and Michael Willis (eds.). *Amaravati: the Art of an Early Buddhist Monument in Context.* British Museum Research Publication 207. London. 2016.

Siudmak, John. *The Hindu-Buddhist Sculpture of Ancient Kashmir and its Influences.* Leiden. 2013.

Snellgrove, David. *Indo-Tibetan Buddhism. Indian Buddhists and their Tibetan Successors.* London. 1987.

Stargardt, Janice and Michael Willis (eds.). *Relics and Relic Worship in Early Buddhism: India, Afghanistan, Sri Lanka and Burma.* British Museum Research Publication 218. London. 2018.

Tomber, Roberta. *Indo-Roman Trade. From pots to pepper.* London. 2008.

UNESCO. *The Cultural Triangle of Sri Lanka.* Colombo. 2006.

Williams, Joanna G. *The Art of Gupta India. Empire and Province.* Princeton. 1982.

Willis, Michael. *Buddhist Reliquaries from Ancient India.* London. 2000.

Willis, Michael. *The Archaeology of Hindu Ritual. Temples and the Establishment of the Gods.* Cambridge. 2009.

Zwalf, Wladimir. *A Catalogue of the Gandhara Sculpture in the British Museum.* Vols. I and II. London. 1996.

Chapter 3: Dynasties and the rise of devotion

Beltz, Johannes (ed.). *Shiva Nataraja. Der kosmisches Tänzer.* Zürich. 2008.

Blurton, T. Richard. *Krishna in the Garden of Assam.* London. 2016.

Dehejia, Vidya et al. *The Sensuous and the Sacred. Chola Bronzes from South India.* Seattle. 2002.

Dehejia, Vidya et al. *Chola. Sacred Bronzes of Southern India.* London. 2006.

Digby, Simon. 'Flower-Teeth and the Bickford Censer: the Identification of a Ninth-Century Kashmir Bronze' in *South Asian Studies* 7. 1991.

Donaldson, T. E. *Hindu Temple Art of Orissa.* Vol. I (1985), II (1986), III (1987). Leiden.

Eschmann, A., Hermann Kulke and Gaya Charan Tripathi. *The Cult of Jagannath and the Regional Tradition of Orissa.* New Delhi. 1978.

Frykenberg, Robert. *Christianity in India. From the Beginnings to the Present.* Oxford. 2008.

Guy, John. *Indian Temple Sculpture.* London. 2007.

Huntington, Susan L. and John C. Huntington. *Leaves from the Bodhi Tree. The Art of Pala India (8th–12th centuries) and its International Legacy.* Washington. 1989.

Leoshko, Janice. *Sacred Traces. British Explorations of Buddhism in South Asia.* Aldershot. 2003.

Losty, Jeremiah P. *The Art of the Book in India.* 1982.

Michell, George. *Elephanta.* London. 2012.

Michell, George. *Temples of Deccan India. Hindu and Jain 7th–13th Centuries.* Woodbridge. 2021.

Michell, George and Gethin Rees. *Buddhist Rock-cut Monasteries of the Western Ghats.* Mumbai. 2017.

Miller, Barbara Stoler (ed. and trans.). *Love Song of the Dark Lord. Jayadeva's Gitagovinda.* New York. 1977

Pal, Pratapaditya. *Art of Nepal.* Los Angeles. 1985.

Peterson, Indira Viswanathan. *Poems to Siva. The Hymns of the Tamil Saints.* Delhi. 1991.

Ramos, Imma. *Tantra. Enlightenment to Revolution.* London. 2020.

von Schaik, S, Daniela De Simone, Gergely Hidas and Michael Willis (eds). *Precious Treasures from the Diamond Throne.* British Museum Research Publication 228. London. 2021.

von Schroeder, U. *Indo-Tibetan Bronzes.* Hong Kong. 1981.

De Simone, Daniela. 'Grave Goods from Megalithic Burials in the Upland Forests of the Nilgiri Mountains, South India: Analysis and Chronology' in *Asian Perspectives* 60(2). 2021.

Smith, David. *The Dance of Siva: Religion, Art and Poetry in South India.* Cambridge. 1996.

Srinivasan, Sharada. 'Dating the Nataraja Dance Icon: Technical Insights' in *Marg* 52(4). 2001.

Chapter 4: Deccan sultans, Mughal emperors and Rajput kings

Ahluwalia, Roda. *Rajput Painting. Romantic, Divine and Courtly Art from India.* London. 2008.

Akbarnia, L. et al. *The Islamic World. A History in Objects.* London. 2018.

Asher, Catherine B. *Architecture of Mughal India.* Cambridge. 1995.

Brigitte, Nicholas and Jacqueline Jacqué. *Féerie indienne. Des rivages de l'Inde au Royaume de France.* Mulhouse. 2008.

Brownrigg, Henry. *Betel Cutters from the Samuel Eilenberg Collection.* London. 1991.

Canby, Sheila (ed.). *Humayun's Garden Party. Princes of the House of Timur and Early Mughal Painting.* Bombay. 1994.

Crill, Rosemary. *Marwar Painting. A History of the Jodhpur Style.* Mumbai. 1999.

Diamond, Debra (ed.) *Garden and Cosmos. The Royal Paintings of Jodhpur.* London. 2009.

Dimock, Edward C. *The Place of the Hidden Moon. Erotic Mysticism in the Vaisnava-Sahajiya Cult of Bengal.* Chicago. 1966.

Elgood, Robert. *Hindu Arms and Ritual: Arms and Armour from India 1400–1865.* Ahmedabad. 2004.

Glynn, Catherine, Robert Skelton and Anna L. Dallapiccola. *Ragamala. Paintings from India from the Claudio Moscatelli Collection.* London. 2011.

Gopal, Ram and Serozh Dadachanji. *Indian Dancing.* London. 1951.

Haidar, Navina Najat, Marika Sardar, et al. *Sultans of Deccan India, 1500–1700. Opulence and Fantasy.* New York. 2015

Koch, Ebba. *The Complete Taj Mahal and the Riverfront Gardens of Agra.* London. 2012.

Losty, J. P. and Malini Roy. *Mughal India. Art, Culture and Empire.* London. 2012.

MacGregor, Arthur. *Company Curiosities. Nature, Culture and the East India Company, 1600–1874.* London. 2018

Michell, George (ed.). *The Islamic Heritage of Bengal.* Paris. 1984

Michell, George. *Architecture and Art of Southern India: Vijayanagara and the Successor States 1350–1750.* Cambridge. 1995.

Michell, George and Mark Zebrowski. *Architecture and Art of the Deccan Sultanates.* Cambridge. 1999.

Mittal, Jagdish. *Deccani Scroll Paintings in the Jagdish and Kamla Mittal Museum of Indian Art.* Hyderabad. 2014.

Porter, Venetia. *Islamic Tiles.* London. 1995.

Shokoohy, Mehrdad. *Muslim Architecture of South India.* London and New York. 2003.

Skelton, Robert (ed.). *The Indian Heritage. Court Life and Arts under Mughal Rule.* London. 1982.

Stronge, Susan. *Bidri Ware. Inlaid Metalwork from India.* London. 1985.

Topsfield, Andrew. *Paintings from Rajasthan in the National Gallery of Victoria.* Melbourne. 1980.

Zebrowski, Mark. *Deccani Painting.* London. 1983.

Zebrowski, Mark. *Gold, Silver and Bronze from Mughal India.* London. 1997.

Chapter 5: Europeans and the British in India

Archer, Mildred. *Company paintings. Indian Paintings of the British Period.* London. 1992.

Bayly, C. A. (ed.). *The Raj. India and the British 1600–1947.* London. 1990.

Coomaraswamy, Ananda K. *Medieval Sinhalese Art* (2nd ed.). New York. 1956

Crill, Rosemary. *Indian Embroidery.* London. 1991.

Dallapiccola, Anna L. *South Indian Paintings. A catalogue of the British Museum Collection.* London. 2010.

Dallapiccola, Anna L. *Kalamkari Temple Hangings.* Ahmedabad and London. 2015.

Dalrymple, W. (ed.). *Forgotten Masters. Indian Painting for the East India Company.* London. 2019.

Goswamy, B. N. *Nainsukh of Guler, a Great Painter from a Small Hill State.* Zürich. 1997.

Kwon, Charlotte and Tim McLaughlin. *Textiles of the Banjara: Cloth and Culture of a Wandering Tribe.* London. 2016.

Llewellyn-Jones, Rosie (ed.). *Lucknow. Then and Now.* Mumbai. 2003.

Mallebrein, Cornelia. *Die Anderen Götter. Volks- und Stammesbronzen aus Indien.* Köln. 1993.

Mallebrein, Cornelia and Heinrich von Stietencron. *The Divine Play on Earth. Religious Aesthetics and Ritual in Orissa, India.* Heidelberg. 2008.

Markel, Stephen with Tushara Bindu Gude. *India's Fabled City. The Art of Courtly Lucknow.* Los Angeles. 2010.

Noble, Christina. *At Home in the Himalayas.* London. 1991.

Noltie, H. J. *Botanical Art from India. The Royal Botanic Garden Edinburgh Collection.* Edinburgh. 2017.

Noltie, H. J. 'Moochies, Gudigars and other Chitrakars: Their Contribution to 19th-Century Botanical Art and Science' in *The Weight of a Petal: Ars Botanica.* Mumbai. 2018.

Noltie, H. J. 'Indian Export Art? The botanical drawings' in Dalrymple, W. (ed.). London. 2019.

Skelton, Robert and Mark Francis (eds.). *Arts of Bengal. The Heritage of Bangladesh and Eastern India.* London. 1979.

Stewart, Tony K. *Witness to Marvels. Sufism and Literary Imagination.* Oakland. 2019.

Stronge, Susan (ed.). *The Arts of the Sikh Kingdoms.* London. 1999.

Stronge, Susan. *Tipu's Tigers.* London. 2009.

Chapter 6: Colonial India, independence and modernity

Alam, Shahidul. *My Journey as a Witness.* Turin. 2011.

van Banning, Nicky, Shanay Jhaveri, and Stephan Sanders. *Lionel Wendt. Ceylon.* Amsterdam. 2017.

Blackburn, Stuart. *Himalayan Tribal Tales. Oral Tradition and Culture in the Apatani Valley.* Leiden. 2008.

Craske, Oliver. *Indian Sun. The Life and Music of Ravi Shankar.* London. 2020.

Dadi, Iftikhar (ed.). *Anwar Jalal Shemza.* London. 2015.

Dallapiccola, Anna L. *Reverse Glass Painting in India.* New Delhi. 2017.

Dalmia, Yashodhara. *Painted World of the Warlis: Art and Ritual of the Warli Tribes of Maharashtra.* New Delhi. 1988.

Datta, Sona. *Urban Patua. The Art of Jamini Roy.* Mumbai. 2010.

Dehejia, Vidya (ed.). *Delight in Design. Indian Silver for the Raj.* Ahmedabad. 2008.

Dewan, Deepali and Deborah Hutton. *Raja Deen Dayal. Artist-Photographer in 19th-Century India.* New Delhi. 2013.

Dutta, Krishna and Andrew Robinson. *Rabindranath Tagore. The Myriad-minded Man.* London. 1996.

Dwyer, Rachel and Divia Patel. *Cinema India. The Visual Culture of Hindi Film.* London. 2002.

Elwin, Verrier. *The Art of the North-East Frontier of India.* Shillong. 1959.

Falconer, John. 'Photography in Nineteenth-Century India' in Bayly, C. (ed.). London. 1990.

Guha, Ramchandra. *India after Gandhi. The History of the World's Largest Democracy.* London. 2007.

Hyman, Timothy. *Bhupen Khakhar.* Bombay and Ahmedabad. 1998.

Jain, Jyotindra (ed.). *Other Masters. Five Contemporary Folk and Tribal Artists of India.* New Delhi. 1998.

Jain, Jyotindra. *Kalighat Painting. Images from a Changing World.* Ahmedabad. 1999.

Jain, Rahul. *Minakar: Spun Gold and Woven Enamel.* New Delhi. 1997.

Javeri, Shanay. *Mrinalini Mukherjee.* New York. 2019.

Jumabhoy, Zehra and Boon Hui Tan. *The Progressive Revolution: Modern Art for a New India.* London. 2018.

Kapur, Geeta, Sabeena Gadihoke and Christopher Pinney. *Where Three Dreams Cross. 150 Years of Photography from India, Pakistan and Bangladesh.* London. 2010.

Malani, Nalini. *Can You Hear Me?* London. 2021.

Mason, Darielle (ed.). *Kantha. The Embroidered Quilts of Bengal.* Philadelphia. 2010.

Mehra, Mona (compiler). *Foy Nissen. The Quiet Genius.* Mumbai. 2017.

Mitter, Partha. *Art and Nationalism in Colonial India 1850–1922. Occidental orientations.* Cambridge. 1994.

Mitter, Partha. *The Triumph of Modernism. Indian Artists and the Avant-garde.* London. 2007.

Mohanti, Prafulla. *Shunya. Prafulla Mohanti Paintings.* London. 2012.

Neumayer, Erwin and Christine Schelberger. *Popular Indian Art. Raja Ravi Varma and the Printed Gods of India.* Oxford. 2003.

Oppitz, Michael, Thomas Kaiser, Alban von Stockhausen, Rebekka Sutter and Marion Wettstein. *Naga Identities. Changing Local Cultures in the Northeast of India.* Ghent. 2008.

Robinson, Andrew. *The Art of Rabindranath Tagore.* London. 1989.

Robinson, Andrew. *Satyajit Ray. The Inner Eye* (3rd ed.). London. 2021.

Sheikh, Gulammohammed (ed.). *Contemporary Art in Baroda.* New Delhi. 1997.

Sunish, Lina Vincent. *Between the Lines: Identity, Place and Power.* Chicago. 2012.

Taylor, Roger and Crispin Branfoot. *Captain Linnaeus Tripe. Photographer of India and Burma, 1852–1860.* Munich. 2015.

Tonelli, Edith A. and Lee Mullican (eds.). *Neo-tantra. Contemporary Indian Painting Inspired by Tradition.* Los Angeles. 1985.

Weeraratne, Neville. *43 Group. A Chronicle of Fifty Years in the Art of Sri Lanka.* Melbourne. 1993.

Willcox, Timothy (ed.). *Pakistan. Another Vision. Fifty years of painting and sculpture from Pakistan.* London. 2000.

Acknowledgments

This book accompanies new displays on South Asia at the British Museum. These were generously funded by the Sir Joseph Hotung Charitable Settlement, and opened by HM the Queen in November 2017. What appears in the book both reflects those new displays and the author's own particular concerns in the history of South Asia.

The immense chronological and regional range that is covered by the Museum's collections means that many debts have been incurred. Also, production of the manuscript during the Covid pandemic has brought its own challenges. I consequently called on many people, some reading sections of the book, with others generously providing information which I could not otherwise access. Amongst those in the British Museum, I am grateful to Jane Portal (Keeper, Department of Asia); also, my curatorial colleagues, Alexandra Green, Jessica Harrison-Hall, Sushma Jansari, Imma Ramos and Michael Willis. It is a pleasure to acknowledge Sophie Sorrondegui, without whom the images in the book would not have been assembled; I owe her a special debt. Also, Daniela De Simone, erstwhile staff-member (now, University of Ghent), who was extremely helpful in matters archaeological, and much else. Also in the department my thanks go to Simon Prentice and his staff, Paul Chirnside, Stephanie Richardson, Lucy Romeril, Daryl Tappin, Ben Watts; also, Nathan Harrison. Mica Benjamin-Mannix and Courtney Lovell delivered administrative services with aplomb. Elsewhere in the Museum I acknowledge advice from Philip Attwood, Robert Bracey, Joe Cribb, Vesta Sarkhosh Curtis, Elizabeth Errington, Irving Finkel, Imogen Laing, Venetia Porter, Roberta Tomber, Helen Wang, Sarah Watson, Helen Wolfe and Evan York. In the Photo Studio, my thanks go particularly to Kevin Lovelock and John Williams; also, to David Agar, Stephen Dodd, Joanne Fernandes, Dudley Hubbard, Claudio Mari, Saul Peckham and Mike Row. My thanks also to the Museum's Security Staff. Finally, although retired, Marjorie Caygill

yet remains a remarkable source of information on the history of the Museum, and I am grateful to her.

The publication team within the Museum ensured that the text was finally written and I am in debt to Claudia Bloch, Bethany Holmes and especially Kathleen Bloomfield. At Thames & Hudson, Philip Watson, Susanna Ingram and Susannah Lawson have been invariably supportive. I also wish to record my thanks to Ben Plumridge for his sterling work as copy-editor and to Anjali Bulley who proofread the book; and last – but far from least – my thanks to the designer, Avni Patel.

Those who have kindly given images for the book and generously provided advice include: Thomas Antony, Anna Dallapiccola, Nasim Khan, Cornelia Mallebrein, Shanti Pappu, Anoushka Shankar, Sukanya Shankar, Diccon Pullen, Pepita Seth and Lanto Synge. I am grateful to them all.

I am especially grateful to the film-historian Nasreen Munni Kabir for enabling the inclusion in the Museum's collection of items concerning Indian cinema and music. Also, in the UK, Europe, USA and South Asia, I acknowledge the following: Roda Ahluwalia, Nick Barnard, Stuart Blackburn, Mehreen Chida-Razvi, Oliver Craske, Rosemary Crill, Steven Cohen, Sona Datta, Ann David, Rajan Dowerah, Arthur Duff, the family of Guru Dutt, Robert Frykenberg, Robert Harding, Saiful Islam, the family of Raj Kapoor, the family of Mehboob Khan, Nurool Khan, Rosie Llewellyn-Jones, Donald S. Lopez, Jnr, Christian Luczanits, Arthur MacGregor, Father Pius Malakandathil, George Michell, Vayu Naidu, Christina Noble, Henry Noltie, the late Graham Parlett, Helen Philon, Christopher Pinney, Sandip Ray, Nasreen Rehman, the family of Bimal Roy, Snehal Shah, Mehrdad Shokoohy, N Sivasambhu, Sharada Srinivasan, Tony Stewart, Richard Widdess, Michael Wood and Monika Zin.

All mistakes or inaccuracies that remain are my own.

Credits

The publisher would like to thank the copyright holders for granting permission to reproduce the images illustrated. Every attempt has been made to trace accurate ownership of copyrighted images in this book. Any errors or omissions will be corrected in subsequent editions provided notification is sent to the publisher. All images © 2022 The Trustees of the British Museum, apart from: **Introduction 1** Yeven Lyashko / Alamy Stock Photo; **2** Roger Cracknell 01/classic / Alamy Stock Photo; **3** Roy Johnson / Alamy Stock Photo; **4** Photo courtesy of Anna L. Dallapiccola; **5** Photo courtesy of Pepita Seth; **Chapter 1 Intro 1** Photo courtesy of Professor Shanti Pappu; **2** Subhendu Sarkar / Contributor/ Getty; **4** Dinodia Photos / Alamy Stock Photo; **Indus Civilization 1** Suzuki Kaku / Alamy Stock Photo; **1.8.2** © UCL, Institute of Archaeology; **1.9.1** Photo by the author, August 2013; **1.9.2** © UCL, Institute of Archaeology; **1.12.1** Rights reserved; **Chapter 2 Intro 1** MJ Photography / Alamy Stock Photo; **2** Dinodia Photos / Alamy Stock Photo; **Amaravati 3** Photo courtesy of the Trace Foundation's Latse Library; **Gandhara 2** Xinhua / Alamy Stock Photo; **2.10.1** © The estate of the artist; **2.10.2** Photo by the author, 1976; **2.10.3** yaktai/Shutterstock.com; **2.13.1** Photo by the author; **2.14.1** Photo by Lanto Synge, 2020; **2.15.1** Reproduced by permission of the estate of the artist; **2.15.2** Photo courtesy of Jaroslav Poncar; **2.17.1** Photograph courtesy of Nasim Khan; **2.22.3** Courtesy Dolf Hartsuiker; **Chapter 3 Intro 1** Photo by the author; **2** Paramvir Singh / Alamy Stock Photo; **3, 4** Photo by the author; **3.1.1** Rights reserved; **3.8.1** Photo courtesy Diccon Pullen, 2018; **3.11.1** Robert Harding / Alamy Stock Photo; **3.13.1** Dinodia Photos / Alamy Stock Photo; **3.20.1** Photo courtesy Martin Thomas Antony, from 'Saint Thomas Cross – A Religio-Cultural Symbol of Saint Thomas Christians', NSC network www.nasrani.net; **Chapter 4 Intro 1** Photo by Nurool Khan; **2** Photo by C. Ganesan, courtesy Anna L. Dallapiccola; **3** Lucas Vallecillos / Alamy Stock Photo; **4.1.4** Image Professionals GmbH / Alamy Stock Photo; **4.9.1** © Ashmolean Museum,

University of Oxford; **4.9.2** Aliaksandr Mazurkevich / Alamy Stock Photo; **Dance 3** © The estate of Feliks Topolski; **Chapter 5 Intro 1** Dinodia Photos / Alamy Stock Photo; **Successor states 6** VIREN DESAI / Alamy Stock Photo; **5.7.1** Photo by Lanto Synge; **5.11.2**, **4** Photo courtesy Christina Noble; **5.15.1** Photo courtesy Dr Cornelia Mallebrein, 1995; **Chapter 6 Intro 4** Reproduced by permission of the artist; **6.2.3** Reproduced by permission of the artist; **Bengal school 2** Reproduced by permission of the Mukul Dey Archives; **3** Reproduced by permission of the artist's estate; **4** Reproduced by permission of the Trustees of the Mrinalini Mukherjee Family Estate and Foundation; **5** © The estate of the artist; **6.8.1** Kazi in Nomansland, install view at Green Cardamom, London, 2009. Photo Vipul Sangoi. Courtesy of the artist; **6.8.2** © The estate of the artist; **6.8.3** Photo from the Drik Agency, Dhaka with the help of Mr Saiful Islam; **6.9.1** Photo by David Farrell; **6.9.2** Reproduced by permission of the artist; **6.9.3** Photo by John Williams, 2017; **Rural cultures 2** © The estate of Jangarh Singh Shyam; **3** © Lakshmi Devi, rights reserved; **6.10.1** Rights reserved; **6.11.1** Reproduced by permission of the artist; **6.11.2** © The estate of F. N. Souza. All rights reserved, DACS 2020; **6.11.3** © The estate of the artist; **6.12.1** Reproduced by permission of the estate of Haren Das; **6.12.2** Reproduced by permission of the artist; **6.12.3** Reproduced by permission of the artist; **6.13.1** Reproduced by permission of the artist; **6.13.2** Reproduced by permission of the artist; **6.13.3** Reproduced by permission of Ulla De, in honour of her husband, Biren De; **6.13.4** Reproduced by permission of Prafulla Mohanti; **6.14.2** Reproduced by permission of the artist; **6.14.3** Mrinalini Mukherjee Foundation; **6.15.1** Reproduced by permission of the artist's estate; **6.15.2** Reproduced by permission of the artist; **6.15.3** Reproduced by permission of the artist; **6.15.4** Reproduced by permission of the artist; **6.16.1** © Nalini Malani; **6.16.2** Reproduced by permission of the artist; **6.16.3** Reproduced by permission of the artist's estate. Text credits (by page): **54** Poem trans. J. R. Marr, quoted in Basham 1954; **145** Peterson 1989, p. 118.

Index

First published in the United Kingdom in 2022 by
Thames & Hudson Ltd, 181A High Holborn, London WC1V 7QX

First published in the United States of America in 2022 by
Thames & Hudson Inc., 500 Fifth Avenue, New York, New York 10110

India: A History in Objects © 2022 The Trustees of the
British Museum/Thames & Hudson Ltd, London

Text © 2022 The Trustees of the British Museum

Images © 2022 The Trustees of the British Museum,
unless otherwise stated on p. 317

Design concept by Peter Dawson gradedesign.com

British Library Cataloguing-in-Publication Data
A catalogue record for this book is available from the British Library

Library of Congress Control Number 2021943301

ISBN 978-0-500-48064-9

Printed and bound in Slovenia by DZS

Be the first to know about our new releases,
exclusive content and author events by visiting
thamesandhudson.com
thamesandhudsonusa.com
thamesandhudson.com.au

This book is dedicated to the memory
of Martin U. L. Williams (1944–2014)
and is a gift for Lanto M. Synge

PRAISE FOR THOM JONES'S
NIGHT TRAIN

"*Night Train* is a most welcome chance to celebrate Jones's legacy…All of Jones's obsessions — Vietnam, drugs, boxing, fractured families, manual labor, dogs, death — are gathered under one roof in a glorious cacophony, elbowing each other and demanding to be heard."

— Jeff Baker, *Seattle Times*

"The stories in this collection are sometimes profane, sometimes hilarious, and always brilliant. Thom Jones was an extraordinary writer."

— Kevin Powers, author of *The Yellow Birds*

"What keeps drawing me into Jones's stories is the precision of his language…These stories put you off, draw you in, show you states of mind that you may never have experienced. They are intensely lively and down to earth; adventurous, often harsh but subtly self-effacing; both a generational portrait and a self-portrait of one of the strangest writers of our times."

— Jane Smiley, *The Guardian*

"There's a feeling of magic at work, as though Jones was an oracle channeling the voices of his crazed, raucously funny, deeply damaged gallery of characters. Jones was himself a temporal-lobe epileptic, and his stories were most at home in sites of devastating trauma: the boxing ring, the battlefields of Vietnam, and the minds of the wounded and disturbed…It's impossible not to marvel at the urgency of these stories. Reviewers like to say that good writing feels alive, but living things are subject to the laws of decay…Immortality is too much to demand of anyone's work, of course, and yet there are moments in Jones's stories where the writing seems capable of transcending the forces of destruction it so unforgettably evokes."

— Sam Sacks, *Wall Street Journal*

"Thom Jones is a one-of-a-kind, real-deal genius. I would scream it from a skyscraper if it would help, I'd sell his books door to door just to let people know, and if I had enough copies I'd break into every motel and hotel I come across and leave a copy. He's one of America's great masters."
— Willy Vlautin, author of *Don't Skip Out On Me*

"Jones has a distinctive voice that comes through often in raw, direct, almost driven language, as if he felt short of time. His mostly blue-collar characters were often fiercely alive, whether he was writing about soldiers, boxers, victims, or miscreants... Jones offers a poignant, compelling view of the human condition."
— *Kirkus Reviews* (starred review)

"Jones was a master of the short story, a master of the same brand of incandescent, hallucinatory creation of voices that made his contemporary Denis Johnson famous. It is a great gift for all of us to have the best of his work, new and old, here in one place. *Night Train* will be an amazing discovery for anyone who cares about literature."
— Philipp Meyer, author of *The Son*

"Jones's style is characterized by compassion, surprising humor, and his characters and their determination to survive. This superb volume, richly introduced by Amy Bloom, will renew appreciation of Jones's literary power."
— *Booklist* (starred review)

"Thom Jones wrote like his hands were on fire. The stories collected in *Night Train* are radioactive with soul, bleak humor, and savage truth. This book affirms Jones's standing as one of short fiction's timeless masters."
— Wells Tower, author of *Everything Ravaged, Everything Burned*

NIGHT TRAIN

NIGHT TRAIN

New *and* Selected Stories

THOM JONES

BACK BAY BOOKS
Little, Brown and Company
New York Boston London

For my grandmother, Mag

———————

Compilation copyright © 2018 by Sally L. Jones
Introduction © 2018 by Amy Bloom

Hachette Book Group supports the right to free expression and the value of copyright. The purpose of copyright is to encourage writers and artists to produce the creative works that enrich our culture.

The scanning, uploading, and distribution of this book without permission is a theft of the author's intellectual property. If you would like permission to use material from the book (other than for review purposes), please contact permissions@hbgusa.com. Thank you for your support of the author's rights.

Back Bay Books / Little, Brown and Company
Hachette Book Group
1290 Avenue of the Americas, New York, NY 10104
littlebrown.com

Originally published in October 2018
First Back Bay paperback edition, October 2019

Back Bay Books is an imprint of Little, Brown and Company, a division of Hachette Book Group, Inc. The Back Bay Books name and logo are trademarks of Hachette Book Group, Inc.

The publisher is not responsible for websites (or their content) that are not owned by the publisher.

ISBN 978-0-316-44934-2 (hc) / 978-0-316-44936-6 (pb)
LCCN 2018933124

10 9 8 7 6 5 4 3 2 1

LSC-C

Printed in the United States of America

Contents

NEW STORIES

The Truth of Thom Jones

- *The two enemies of human happiness are pain and boredom.*
- *Just remember, once you're over the hill you begin to pick up speed.*

— from Thom's favorite guy: Schopenhauer

Thom Jones's lies — his sentences and stories — were more persuasive, more important, and more deeply felt than most men's truths. "I would work hard to free the truth that's within me and make it art," he said in one interview. No lie there.

Thom and I met the night before the 1993 National Book Awards, when all the finalists got to read for five minutes (firm time limit, firm looks) from their nominated books. Thom and I were newly published writers — as we both said, "Yeah, new, not young" — and we clung to each other that night like sibling wallflowers: smart-ass, awkward, and wise enough to be surprised. When people were kind to us (tap or sparkling?), we looked at them like dogs brought home from the pound might, and when Annie Proulx swept by us the next night to claim the National Book Award ("Thank you, I deserved it," she said), we just pulled our coats and our clunky shoes in a bit more, so as not to get in her way.

But the night before, Thom slayed. He read the first five minutes of "I Want to Live!" from *The Pugilist at Rest*, a story that would later be selected by John Updike for his *Best American Short Stories of the Century* anthology. It's a monologue by an older woman, dying of cancer. She loves her painkillers and cartoons, and there is true love between her and her concerned, hapless son-in-law, checking in on her. I actually saw people in the audience laugh and then cry and then shake their heads at their roller-coaster feelings and at the drama of human beings and our ridiculous, indomitable will to live. Whenever I reread that story, to remind myself how to build character, how to wield voice, I see Thom reading and I see the damp faces before him.

My own other, most personal favorite is "Cold Snap," the title story of Thom's second collection. Before I was a writer, I'd had some other jobs, not as a janitor or a copywriter, like Thom had, but mostly as a bartender and social worker. My sympathy for the burned-out helper cannot be exaggerated. Richard, our hero in "Cold Snap," is a hot mess, as is often the case for the Jones protagonist. Thom avoided the "worried well" and the complacent as suitable subjects almost as assiduously as he avoided the lucky and the measured optimist. Richard has a quintessentially Jonesian terrible outlook. "I can fuck up a wet dream with my attitude," the man says and no reader would argue. He has gotten himself sent home from Africa, with malaria and minus his medical license, because he's one inch shy of being a junkie and people have noticed. (In Jones's fiction, not only are characters free to make bad choices, but they also suffer the consequences. There's no room for bravado and not much for freewheeling self-deception.) Richard, being a mess, has cut his thumb and it's giving him no end of trouble, and he has to — *he has to* — get some pain pills, as so many of Jones's characters do. His sister, Susan, is a schizophrenic, which is not as central to this story as the self-inflicted lobotomy she endured when she tried to kill herself.

Richard shows off for us by playing Russian roulette. He claims that not dying has made him euphoric, like Van Gogh, minus the slicing of the ear. He doesn't die. But he doesn't fool Thom Jones, and therefore he doesn't fool us. The man is wild with grief and the only help on the horizon, the unlikely and lovely and damaged cavalry to the rescue, is his sister. Susan tells Richard that she dreams of a happy life for them, driving a '67 Dodge around heaven, and after the telling of the dream, in their real life together, they have an elaborate lunch ("the best little lunch of a lifetime") in Richard's car. They listen to "This Is Dedicated to the One I Love" on the radio. "What can be better," Richard says, "than a cool, breezy, fragrant day, rain-splatter diamonds on the wrap-around windshield of a Ninety-eight Olds with a view of cherry trees blooming in the light spring rain?" I love this story more than I can say. It is peace and trouble, love and grief, doom and the tiny flicker of hope, if one can bear to have it.

There are plenty of critics who have raved about Thom's Vietnam stories, exceptional feats of imagination from a man who, while a Marine himself, wasn't actually there, having been prevented from deploying after suffering temporal-lobe epilepsy when he was soundly beaten in a boxing match. (Boxing, like that war, is a preoccupation throughout his fiction.) Each time his collections came out, the reviews were pyrotechnic: for Thom's irresistible voice, his bravery, his audacity and grit, and his knack for unnerving cheer in the face of catastrophe. In short, for his "amazing blend of knowledge, skill, terror, and release," according to Robert Stone, who seems to me to have been a fair judge of these things.

Thom's sentences have crack and clarity. His paragraphs build to stories and places that you hadn't thought to go, with people you hadn't known you could recognize, and even love. "Give Baker a compass and a topographical map," says the soldier narrator of "Pot Shack," "and one could bear witness to — indeed, become a part of — the elusive, semi-mystical Tao of military science. Such were Baker's leadership skills that his every thought, word, and action could propel a lesser personality into selfless, right actions in the service of the Big Green Machine."

You will see all this, Thom Jones's whole wide, deep, rambunctious, grief-stricken, and melancholy range of gifts, in the twenty-six stories gathered in these pages. Thom Jones is, as a character describes his man Schopenhauer, an "august seeker of truth." He was a friend to the friendless, a strong voice for the maimed, funny as hell, and from the first to the last, a great American writer.

— *Amy Bloom*

SELECTED STORIES

The Pugilist at Rest

H EY BABY GOT caught writing a letter to his girl when he was supposed
to be taking notes on the specs of the M-14 rifle. We were sitting in a stifling hot Quonset hut during the first weeks of boot camp, August 1966,
at the Marine Corps Recruit Depot in San Diego. Sergeant Wright
snatched the letter out of Hey Baby's hand, and later that night in the
squad bay he read the letter to the Marine recruits of Platoon 263, his
voice laden with sarcasm. *"Hey, Baby!"* he began, and then as he went
into the body of the letter he worked himself into a state of outrage
and disgust. It was a letter to *Rosie Rottencrotch*, he said at the end, and
what really mattered, what was really at issue and what was of utter importance was not *Rosie Rottencrotch* and her steaming-hot panties but
rather the muzzle velocity of the M-14 rifle.

Hey Baby paid for the letter by doing a hundred squat thrusts on the
concrete floor of the squad bay, but the main prize he won that night
was that he became forever known as Hey Baby to the recruits of Platoon 263 — in addition to being a shitbird, a faggot, a turd, a maggot,
and other such standard appellations. To top it all off, shortly after the
incident, Hey Baby got a Dear John from his girl back in Chicago, of
whom Sergeant Wright, myself, and seventy-eight other Marine recruits
had come to know just a little.

Hey Baby was not in the Marine Corps for very long. The reason
for this was that he started in on my buddy, Jorgeson. Jorgeson was my
main man, and Hey Baby started calling him Jorgepussy and began
harassing him and pushing him around. He was down on Jorgeson

because whenever we were taught some sort of combat maneuver or tactic, Jorgeson would say, under his breath, "You could get *killed* if you try that." Or, "Your ass is *had*, if you do that." You got the feeling that Jorgeson didn't think loving the American flag and defending democratic ideals in Southeast Asia were all that important. He told me that what he really wanted to do was have an artist's loft in the SoHo district of New York City, wear a beret, eat liver-sausage sandwiches made with stale baguettes, drink Tokay wine, smoke dope, paint pictures, and listen to the wailing, sorrowful songs of that French singer Edith Piaf, otherwise known as "The Little Sparrow."

After the first half hour of boot camp most of the other recruits wanted to get out, too, but they nourished dreams of surfboards, Corvettes, and blond babes. Jorgeson wanted to be a beatnik and hang out with Jack Kerouac and Neal Cassady, slam down burning shots of amber whiskey, and hear Charles Mingus play real cool jazz on the bass fiddle. He wanted to practice Zen Buddhism, throw the I Ching, eat couscous, and study astrology charts. All of this was foreign territory to me. I had grown up in Aurora, Illinois, and had never heard of such things. Jorgeson had a sharp tongue and was so supercilious in his remarks that I didn't know quite how seriously I should take this talk, but I enjoyed his humor and I did believe he had the sensibilities of an artist. It was not some vague yearning. I believed very much that he could become a painter of pictures. At that point he wasn't putting his heart and soul into becoming a Marine. He wasn't a true believer like me.

Some weeks after Hey Baby began hassling Jorgeson, Sergeant Wright gave us his best speech: "You men are going off to war, and it's not a pretty thing," etc. & etc., "and if Luke the Gook knocks down one of your buddies, a fellow Marine, you are going to risk your life and go in and get that Marine and you are going to bring him out. Not because I said so. No! You are going after that Marine because *you* are a Marine, a member of the most elite fighting force in the world, and that man out there who's gone down is a Marine, and he's your *buddy*. He is your brother! Once you are a Marine, you are *always* a Marine and you will never let another Marine down." Etc. & etc. "You can take a Marine out of the Corps but you can't take the Corps out of a Marine." Etc. & etc. At the time it seemed to me a very good speech, and it stirred me deeply.

Sergeant Wright was no candy ass. He was one squared-away dude, and he could call cadence. Man, it puts a lump in my throat when I remember how that man could sing cadence. Apart from Jorgeson, I think all of the recruits in Platoon 263 were proud of Sergeant Wright. He was the real thing, the genuine article. He was a crackerjack Marine.

In the course of training, lots of the recruits dropped out of the original platoon. Some couldn't pass the physical fitness tests and had to go to a special camp for pussies. This was a particularly shameful shortcoming, the most humiliating apart from bed-wetting. Other recruits would get pneumonia, strep throat, infected foot blisters, or whatever, and lose time that way. Some didn't qualify at the rifle range. One would break a leg. Another would have a nervous breakdown (and this was also deplorable). People dropped out right and left. When the recruit corrected whatever deficiency he had, or when he got better, he would be picked up by another platoon that was in the stage of basic training that he had been in when his training was interrupted. Platoon 263 picked up dozens of recruits in this fashion. If everything went well, however, you got through with the whole business in twelve weeks. That's not a long time, but it seemed like a long time. You did not see a female in all that time. You did not see a newspaper or a television set. You did not eat a candy bar. Another thing was the fact that you had someone on top of you, watching every move you made. When it was time to "shit, shower, and shave," you were given just ten minutes, and had to confront lines and so on to complete the entire affair. Head calls were so infrequent that I spent a lot of time that might otherwise have been neutral or painless in the eye-watering anxiety that I was going to piss my pants. We *ran* to chow, where we were faced with enormous steam vents that spewed out a sickening smell of rancid, superheated grease. Still, we entered the mess hall with ravenous appetites, ate a huge tray of food in just a few minutes, and then *ran* back to our company area in formation, choking back the burning bile of a meal too big to be eaten so fast. God forbid that you would lose control and vomit.

If all had gone well in the preceding hours, Sergeant Wright would permit us to smoke one cigarette after each meal. Jorgeson had shown me the wisdom of switching from Camels to Pall Malls — they were much longer, packed a pretty good jolt, and when we snapped open our brushed-chrome Zippos, torched up, and inhaled the first few drags, we shared the overmastering pleasure that tobacco can bring if you use it seldom and judiciously. These were always the best moments of the day — brief respites from the tyrannical repression of recruit training. As we got close to the end of it all Jorgeson liked to play a little game. He used to say to me (with fragrant blue smoke curling out of his nostrils), "If someone said, 'I'll give you ten thousand dollars to do all of this again,' what would you say?" "No way, Jack!" He would keep on upping it until he had John Beresford Tipton, the guy from *The Millionaire*, offering me a check for a million bucks. "Not for any money," I'd say.

While they were all smoldering under various pressures, the recruits were also getting pretty "salty" — they were beginning to believe. They were beginning to think of themselves as Marines. If you could make it through this, the reasoning went, you wouldn't crack in combat. So I remember that I had tears in my eyes when Sergeant Wright gave us the spiel about how a Marine would charge a machine-gun nest to save his buddies, dive on a hand grenade, do whatever it takes — and yet I was ashamed when Jorgeson caught me wiping them away. All of the recruits were teary except Jorgeson. He had these very clear cobalt-blue eyes. They were so remarkable that they caused you to notice Jorgeson in a crowd. There was unusual beauty in those eyes, and there was an extraordinary power in them. Apart from having a pleasant enough face, Jorgeson was small and unassuming except for those eyes. Anyhow, when he caught me getting sentimental he gave me this look that penetrated to the core of my being. It was the icy look of absolute contempt, and it caused me to doubt myself. I said, "Man! Can't you get into it? For Christ's sake!"

"I'm not like you," he said. "But I am into it, more than you could ever know. I never told you this before, but I am Kal-El, born on the planet Krypton and rocketed to Earth as an infant, moments before my world exploded. Disguised as a mild-mannered Marine, I have resolved to use my powers for the good of mankind. Whenever danger appears on the scene, truth and justice will be served as I slip into the green U.S.M.C. utility uniform and become Earth's greatest hero."

I got highly pissed and didn't talk to him for a couple of days after this. Then, about two weeks before boot camp was over, when we were running out to the parade field for drill with our rifles at port arms, all assholes and elbows, I saw Hey Baby give Jorgeson a nasty shove with his M-14. Hey Baby was a large and fairly tough young man who liked to displace his aggressive impulses on Jorgeson, but he wasn't as big or as tough as I.

Jorgeson nearly fell down as the other recruits scrambled out to the parade field, and Hey Baby gave a short, malicious laugh. I ran past Jorgeson and caught up to Hey Baby; he picked me up in his peripheral vision, but by then it was too late. I set my body so that I could put everything into it, and with one deft stroke I hammered him in the temple with the sharp edge of the steel butt plate of my M-14. It was not exactly a premeditated crime, although I had been laying to get him. My idea before this had simply been to lay my hands on him, but now I had blood in my eye. I was a skilled boxer, and I knew the temple was a vulnerable spot; the human skull is otherwise hard and durable, except at its base. There was a sickening crunch, and Hey Baby dropped into the ice plants along the side of the company street.

The entire platoon was out on the parade field when the house mouse screamed at the assistant D.I., who rushed back to the scene of the crime to find Hey Baby crumpled in a fetal position in the ice plants with blood all over the place. There was blood from the scalp wound as well as a froth of blood emitting from his nostrils and his mouth. Blood was leaking from his right ear. Did I see skull fragments and brain tissue? It seemed that I did. To tell you the truth, I wouldn't have cared in the least if I had killed him, but like most criminals I was very much afraid of getting caught. It suddenly occurred to me that I could be headed for the brig for a long time. My heart was pounding out of my chest. Yet the larger part of me didn't care. Jorgeson was my buddy, and I wasn't going to stand still and let someone fuck him over.

The platoon waited at parade rest while Sergeant Wright came out of the duty hut and took command of the situation. An ambulance was called, and it came almost immediately. A number of corpsmen squatted down alongside the fallen man for what seemed an eternity. Eventually they took Hey Baby off with a fractured skull. It would be the last we ever saw of him. Three evenings later, in the squad bay, the assistant D.I. told us rather ominously that Hey Baby had recovered consciousness. That's all he said. What did *that* mean? I was worried, because Hey Baby had seen me make my move, but, as it turned out, when he came to he had forgotten the incident and all events of the preceding two weeks. Retrograde amnesia. Lucky for me. I also knew that at least three other recruits had seen what I did, but none of them reported me. Every member of the platoon was called in and grilled by a team of hard-ass captains and a light colonel from the Criminal Investigation Detachment. It took a certain amount of balls to lie to them, yet none of my fellow-jarheads reported me. I was well liked and Hey Baby was not. Indeed, many felt that he got exactly what was coming to him.

The other day — Memorial Day, as it happened — I was cleaning some stuff out of the attic when I came upon my old dress-blue uniform. It's a beautiful uniform, easily the most handsome worn by any of the U.S. Armed Forces. The rich color recalled Jorgeson's eyes for me — not that the color matched, but in the sense that the color of each was so startling. The tunic does not have lapels, of course, but a high collar with red piping and the traditional golden eagle, globe, and anchor insignia on either side of the neck clasp. The tunic buttons are not brassy — although they are in fact made of brass — but are a delicate gold in color, like Florentine gold. On the sleeves of the tunic my staff sergeant's chevrons are gold on red. High on the left breast is a rainbow display of fruit salad representing my various combat citations. Just below these are my marksmanship badges; I shot Expert in rifle as well as pistol.

I opened a sandalwood box and took my various medals out of the large plastic bag I had packed them in to prevent them from tarnishing. The Navy Cross and the two Silver Stars are the best; they are such pretty things they dazzle you. I found a couple of Thai sticks in the sandalwood box as well. I took a whiff of the box and smelled the smells of Saigon — the whores, the dope, the saffron, cloves, jasmine, and patchouli oil. I put the Thai sticks back, recalling the three-day hangover that particular batch of dope had given me more than twenty-three years before. Again I looked at my dress-blue tunic. My most distinctive badge, the crowning glory, and the one of which I am most proud, is the set of Airborne wings. I remember how it was, walking around Oceanside, California — the Airborne wings and the high-and-tight haircut were recognized by all the Marines; they meant you were the crème de la crème, you were a recon Marine.

Recon was all Jorgeson's idea. We had lost touch with each other after boot camp. I was sent to com school in San Diego, where I had to sit in a hot Class A wool uniform all day and learn the Morse code. I deliberately flunked out, and when I was given the perfunctory option for a second shot, I told the colonel, "Hell no, sir. I want to go 003 — infantry. I want to be a ground-pounder. I didn't join the service to sit at a desk all day."

I was on a bus to Camp Pendleton three days later, and when I got there I ran into Jorgeson. I had been thinking of him a lot. He was a clerk in headquarters company. Much to my astonishment, he was fifteen pounds heavier, and had grown two inches, and he told me he was hitting the weight pile every night after running seven miles up and down the foothills of Pendleton in combat boots, carrying a rifle and a full field pack. After the usual what's-been-happening? b.s., he got down to business and said, "They need people in Force Recon, what do you think? Headquarters is one boring motherfucker."

I said, "Recon? Paratrooper? You got to be shittin' me! When did you get so gung-ho, man?"

He said, "Hey, you were the one who *bought* the program. Don't fade on me now, goddamn it! Look, we pass the physical fitness test and then they send us to jump school at Benning. If we pass that, we're in. And we'll pass. Those doggies ain't got jack. Semper fi, motherfucker! Let's do it."

There was no more talk of Neal Cassady, Edith Piaf, or the artist's loft in SoHo. I said, "If Sergeant Wright could only see you now!"

We were just three days in country when we got dropped in somewhere up north near the DMZ. It was a routine reconnaissance patrol. It was not supposed to be any kind of big deal at all — just acclimation. The morning after our drop we approached a clear field. I recall that it gave me a funny feeling, but I was too new to fully trust my instincts. *Everything* was spooky; I was fresh meat, F.N.G. — a Fucking New Guy.

Before moving into the field, our team leader sent Hanes — a lance corporal, a short-timer, with only twelve days left before his rotation was over — across the field as a point man. This was a bad omen and everyone knew it. Hanes had two Purple Hearts. He followed the order with no hesitation and crossed the field without drawing fire. The team leader signaled for us to fan out and told me to circumvent the field and hump through the jungle to investigate a small mound of loose red dirt that I had missed completely but that he had picked up with his trained eye. I remember I kept saying, "Where?" He pointed to a heap of earth about thirty yards along the tree line and about ten feet back in the bushes. Most likely it was an anthill, but you never knew — it could have been an NVA tunnel. "Over there," he hissed. "Goddamn it, do I have to draw pictures for you?"

I moved smartly in the direction of the mound while the rest of the team reconverged to discuss something. As I approached the mound I saw that it was in fact an anthill, and I looked back at the team and saw they were already halfway across the field, moving very fast.

Suddenly there were several loud hollow pops and the cry "Incoming!" Seconds later the first of a half-dozen mortar rounds landed in the loose earth surrounding the anthill. For a millisecond, everything went black. I was blown back and lifted up on a cushion of warm air. At first it was like the thrill of a carnival ride, but it was quickly followed by that stunned, jangly, electric feeling you get when you hit your crazy bone. Like that, but not confined to a small area like the elbow. I felt it shoot through my spine and into all four limbs. A thick plaster of sand and red clay plugged up my nostrils and ears. Grit was blown in between my teeth. If I hadn't been wearing a pair of Ray-Ban aviator shades, I would certainly have been blinded permanently — as it was, my eyes were loaded with grit. (I later discovered that fine red earth was somehow blown in behind the crystal of my pressure-tested Rolex Submariner, underneath my fingernails and toenails, and deep into the pores of my skin.) When I was able to, I pulled out a canteen filled with lemon-lime Kool-Aid and tried to flood my eyes clean. This helped a little, but my eyes still felt like they were on fire. I rinsed them again and blinked furiously.

I rolled over on my stomach in the prone position and leveled my field-issue M-16. A company of screaming NVA soldiers ran into the field, firing as they came — I saw their green tracer rounds blanket the position where the team had quickly congregated to lay out a perimeter, but none of our own red tracers were going out. Several of the Marines had been killed outright by the mortar rounds. Jorgeson was all right, and I saw him cast a nervous glance in my direction. Then he turned to the enemy and began to fire his M-16. I clicked my rifle on to automatic and pulled the trigger, but the gun was loaded with dirt and it wouldn't fire.

Apart from Jorgeson, the only other American putting out any fire was Second Lieutenant Milton, also a fairly new guy, a "cherry," who was down on one knee firing his .45, an exercise in almost complete futility. I assumed that Milton's 16 had jammed, like mine, and watched as AK-47 rounds, having penetrated his flak jacket and then his chest, ripped through the back of his field pack and buzzed into the jungle beyond like a deadly swarm of bees. A few seconds later, I heard the swoosh of an RPG rocket, a dud round that dinged the lieutenant's left shoulder before it flew off in the bush behind him. It took off his whole arm, and for an instant I could see the white bone and ligaments of his shoulder, and then red flesh of muscle tissue, looking very much like fresh prime beef, well marbled and encased in a thin layer of yellowish-white adipose tissue that quickly became saturated with dark-red blood. What a lot of blood there was. Still, Milton continued to fire his .45. When he emptied his clip, I watched him remove a fresh one from his web gear and attempt to load the pistol with one hand. He seemed to fumble with the fresh clip for a long time, until at last he dropped it, along with his .45. The lieutenant's head slowly sagged forward, but he stayed up on one knee with his remaining arm extended out to the enemy, palm upward in the soulful, heartrending gesture of Al Jolson doing a rendition of "Mammy."

A hail of green tracer rounds buzzed past Jorgeson, but he coolly returned fire in short, controlled bursts. The light, tinny pops from his M-16 did not sound very reassuring, but I saw several NVA go down. AK-47 fire kicked up red dust all around Jorgeson's feet. He was basically out in the open, and if ever a man was totally alone it was Jorgeson. He was dead meat and he had to know it. It was very strange that he wasn't hit immediately.

Jorgeson zigged his way over to the body of a large black Marine who carried an M-60 machine gun. Most of the recon Marines carried grease guns or Swedish Ks; an M-60 was too heavy for traveling light and fast, but this Marine had been big and he had been paranoid. I had known him least of anyone in the squad. In three days he had said nothing to me, I suppose because I was F.N.G. and had spooked him. Indeed, now he was dead. That august seeker of truth, Schopenhauer, was correct: *We are like lambs in a field, disporting themselves under the eye of the butcher, who chooses out first one and then another for his prey. So it is that in our good days we are all unconscious of the evil Fate may have presently in store for us — sickness, poverty, mutilation, loss of sight or reason.*

It was difficult to judge how quickly time was moving. Although my senses had been stunned by the concussion of the mortar rounds, they were, however paradoxical this may seem, more acute than ever before. I watched Jorgeson pick up the machine gun and begin to spread an impressive field of fire back at the enemy. *Thuk thuk thuk, thuk thuk thuk, thuk thuk thuk!* I saw several more bodies fall, and began to think that things might turn out all right after all. The NVA dropped for cover, and many of them turned back and headed for the tree line. Jorgeson fired off a couple of bandoliers, and after he stopped to load another, he turned back and looked at me with those blue eyes and a smile like "How am I doing?" Then I heard the steel-cork pop of an M-79 launcher and saw a rocket grenade explode through Jorgeson's upper abdomen, causing him to do something like a back flip. His M-60 machine gun flew straight up into the air. The barrel was glowing red like a hot poker, and continued to fire in a "cook off" until the entire bandolier had run through.

In the meantime I had pulled a cleaning rod out of my pack and worked it through the barrel of my M-16. When I next tried to shoot, the Tonka-toy son of a bitch remained jammed, and at last I frantically broke it down to find the source of the problem. I had a dirty bolt. Fucking dirt everywhere. With numbed fingers I removed the firing pin and worked it over with a toothbrush, dropping it in the red dirt, picking it up, cleaning it, and dropping it again. My fingers felt like Novocain, and while I could see far away, I was unable to see up close. I poured some more Kool-Aid over my eyes. It was impossible for me to get my weapon clean. Lucky for me, ultimately. Suddenly NVA soldiers were running through the field shoving bayonets into the bodies of the downed Marines. It was not until an NVA trooper kicked Lieutenant Milton out of his tripod position that he finally fell to the ground. Then the soldiers started going through the dead Marines' gear. I was still frantically struggling with my weapon when it began to dawn on me that the enemy had forgotten me in the excitement of the firefight. I wondered what had happened to Hanes and if he had gotten clear. I doubted it, and hopped on my survival radio to call in an air strike when finally a canny NVA trooper did remember me and headed in my direction most ricky-tick.

With a tight grip on the spoon, I pulled the pin on a fragmentation grenade and then unsheathed my K-bar. About this time Jorgeson let off a horrendous shriek — a gut shot is worse than anything. Or did Jorgeson scream to save my life? The NVA moving in my direction turned back to him, studied him for a moment, and then thrust a bayonet into his heart. As badly as my own eyes hurt, I was able to see Jorgeson's eyes — a final flash of glorious azure before they faded into the unfocused and glazed gray of death. I repinned the grenade, got up on my knees, and scrambled away until finally I was on my feet with a useless and incomplete handful of M-16 parts, and I was running as fast and as hard as I have ever run in my life. A pair of Phantom F-4s came in very low with delayed-action high-explosive rounds and napalm. I could feel the almost unbearable heat waves of the latter, volley after volley. I can still feel it and smell it to this day.

Concerning Lance Corporal Hanes: they found him later, fried to a crisp by the napalm, but it was nonetheless ascertained that he had been mutilated while alive. He was like the rest of us — eighteen, nineteen, twenty years old. What did we know of life? Before Vietnam, Hanes didn't think he would ever die. I mean, yes, he knew that in theory he would die, but he *felt* like he was going to live forever. I know that I felt that way. Hanes was down to twelve days and a wake-up. When other Marines saw a short-timer get greased, it devastated their morale. However, when I saw them zip up the body bag on Hanes I became incensed. Why hadn't Milton sent him back to the rear to burn shit or something when he got so short? Twelve days to go and then mutilated. Fucking Milton! Fucking second lieutenant!

Theogenes was the greatest of gladiators. He was a boxer who served under the patronage of a cruel nobleman, a prince who took great delight in bloody spectacles. Although this was several hundred years before the times of those most enlightened of men Socrates, Plato, and Aristotle, and well after the Minoans of Crete, it still remains a high point in the history of Western civilization and culture. It was the approximate time of Homer, the greatest poet who ever lived. Then, as now, violence, suffering, and the cheapness of life were the rule.

The sort of boxing Theogenes practiced was not like modern-day boxing with those kindergarten Queensberry Rules. The two contestants were not permitted the freedom of a ring. Instead, they were strapped to flat stones, facing each other nose-to-nose. When the signal was given, they would begin hammering each other with fists encased in heavy leather thongs. It was a fight to the death. Fourteen hundred and twenty-five times Theogenes was strapped to the stone and fourteen hundred and twenty-five times he emerged a victor.

Perhaps it is Theogenes who is depicted in the famous Roman statue (based on the earlier Greek original) of "The Pugilist at Rest." I keep a grainy black-and-white photograph of it in my room. The statue depicts a muscular athlete approaching his middle age. He has a thick beard and a full head of curly hair. In addition to the telltale broken nose and cauliflower ears of a boxer, the pugilist has the slanted, drooping brows that bespeak torn nerves. Also, the forehead is piled with scar tissue. As may be expected, the pugilist has the musculature of a fighter. His neck and trapezius muscles are well developed. His shoulders are enormous; his chest is thick and flat, without the bulging pectorals of the bodybuilder. His back, oblique, and abdominal muscles are highly pronounced, and he has that greatest asset of the modern boxer — sturdy legs. The arms are large, particularly the forearms, which are reinforced with the leather wrappings of the cestus. It is the body of a small heavyweight — lithe rather than bulky, but by no means lacking in power: a Jack Johnson or a Dempsey, say. If you see the authentic statue at the Terme Museum, in Rome, you will see that the seated boxer is really not much more than a light-heavyweight. People were small in those days. The important thing was that he was perfectly proportioned.

The pugilist is sitting on a rock with his forearms balanced on his thighs. That he is seated and not pacing implies that he has been through all this many times before. It appears that he is conserving his strength. His head is turned as if he were looking over his shoulder — as if someone had just whispered something to him. It is in this that the "art" of the sculpture is conveyed to the viewer. Could it be that someone has just summoned him to the arena? There is a slight look of befuddlement on his face, but there is no trace of fear. There is an air about him that suggests that he is eager to proceed and does not wish to cause anyone any trouble or to create a delay, even though his life will soon be on the line. Besides the deformities on his noble face, there is also the suggestion of weariness and philosophical resignation. *All the world's a stage, and all the men and women merely players.* Exactly! He knew this more than two thousand years before Shakespeare penned the line. How did he come to be at this place in space and time? Would he rather be safely removed to the countryside — an obscure, stinking peasant shoving a plow behind a mule? Would that be better? Or does he revel in his role? Perhaps he once did, but surely not now. Is this the great Theogenes or merely a journeyman fighter, a former slave or criminal bought by one of the many contractors who for months trained the condemned for their brief moment in the arena? I wonder if Marcus Aurelius loved the "Pugilist" as I do, and came to study it and to meditate before it.

I cut and ran from that field in Southeast Asia. I've read that Davy Crockett, hero of the American frontier, was cowering under a bed when Santa Anna and his soldiers stormed into the Alamo. What is the truth? Jack Dempsey used to get so scared before his fights that he sometimes wet his pants. But look what he did to Willard and to Luis Firpo, the Wild Bull of the Pampas! It was something close to homicide. What is courage? What is cowardice? The magnificent Roberto Duran gave us "*No más,*" but who had a greater fighting heart than Duran?

I got over that first scare and saw that I was something quite other than that which I had known myself to be. Hey Baby proved only my warm-up act. There was a reservoir of malice, poison, and vicious sadism in my soul, and it poured forth freely in the jungles and rice paddies of Vietnam. I pulled three tours. I wanted some payback for Jorgeson. I grieved for Lance Corporal Hanes. I grieved for myself and what I had lost. I committed unspeakable crimes and got medals for it.

It was only fair that I got a head injury myself. I never got a scratch in Vietnam, but I got tagged in a boxing smoker at Pendleton. Fought a bad-ass light-heavyweight from artillery. Nobody would fight this guy. He could box. He had all the moves. But mainly he was a puncher — it was said that he could punch with either hand. It was said that his hand speed was superb. I had finished off at least a half rack of Hamm's before I went in with him and started getting hit with head shots I didn't even see coming. They were right. His hand speed *was* superb.

I was twenty-seven years old, smoked two packs a day, was a borderline alcoholic. I shouldn't have fought him — I knew that — but he had been making noise. A very long time before, I had been the middleweight champion of the 1st Marine Division. I had been a so-called war hero. I had been a recon Marine. But now I was a garrison Marine and in no kind of shape.

He put me down almost immediately, and when I got up I was terribly afraid. I was tight and I could not breathe. It felt like he was hitting me in the face with a ball-peen hammer. It felt like he was busting light bulbs in my face. Rather than one opponent, I saw three. I was convinced his gloves were loaded, and a wave of self-pity ran through me.

I began to move. He made a mistake by expending a lot of energy trying to put me away quickly. I had no intention of going down again, and I knew I wouldn't. My buddies were watching, and I had to give them a good show. While I was afraid, I was also exhilarated; I had not felt this alive since Vietnam. I began to score with my left jab, and because of this I was able to withstand his bull charges and divert them. I thought he would throw his bolt, but in the beginning he was tireless. I must have hit him with four hundred left jabs. It got so that I could score at will, with either hand, but he would counter, trap me on the ropes, and pound. He was the better puncher and was truly hurting me, but I was scoring, and as the fight went on the momentum shifted and I took over. I staggered him again and again. The Marines at ringside were screaming for me to put him away, but however much I tried, I could not. Although I could barely stand by the end, I was sorry that the fight was over. Who had won? The referee raised my arm in victory, but I think it was pretty much a draw. Judging a prizefight is a very subjective thing.

About an hour after the bout, when the adrenaline had subsided, I realized I had a terrible headache. It kept getting worse, and I rushed out of the NCO Club, where I had gone with my buddies to get loaded.

I stumbled outside, struggling to breathe, and I headed away from the company area toward Sheepshit Hill, one of the many low brown foothills in the vicinity. Like a dog who wants to die alone, so it was with me. Everything got swirly, and I dropped in the bushes.

I was unconscious for nearly an hour, and for the next two weeks I walked around like I was drunk, with double vision. I had constant headaches and seemed to have grown old overnight. My health was gone.

I became a very timid individual. I became introspective. I wondered what had made me act the way I had acted. Why had I killed my fellow-men in war, without any feeling, remorse, or regret? And when the war was over, why did I continue to drink and swagger around and get into fistfights? Why did I like to dish out pain, and why did I take positive delight in the suffering of others? Was I insane? Was it too much testosterone? Women don't do things like that. The rapacious Will to Power lost its hold on me. Suddenly I began to feel sympathetic to the cares and sufferings of all living creatures. You lose your health and you start thinking this way.

Has man become any better since the times of Theogenes? The world is replete with badness. I'm not talking about that old routine where you drag out the Spanish Inquisition, the Holocaust, Joseph Stalin, the Khmer Rouge, etc. It happens in our own backyard. Twentieth-century America is one of the most materially prosperous nations in history. But take a walk through an American prison, a nursing home, the slums where the homeless live in cardboard boxes, a cancer ward. Go to a Vietnam vets' meeting, or an A.A. meeting, or an Overeaters Anonymous meeting. *How hollow and unreal a thing is life, how deceitful are its pleasures, what horrible aspects it possesses.* Is the

world not rather like a hell, as Schopenhauer, that clearheaded seer —
who has helped me transform my suffering into an object of understanding — was so quick to point out? They called him a pessimist and
dismissed him with a word, but it is peace and self-renewal that I have
found in his pages.

About a year after my fight with the guy from artillery I started having
seizures. I suffered from a form of left-temporal-lobe seizure which is
sometimes called Dostoyevsky's epilepsy. It's so rare as to be almost unknown. Freud, himself a neurologist, speculated that Dostoyevsky was a
hysterical epileptic, and that his fits were unrelated to brain damage —
psychogenic in origin. Dostoyevsky did not have his first attack until the
age of twenty-five, when he was imprisoned in Siberia and received fifty
lashes after complaining about the food. Freud figured that after Dostoyevsky's mock execution, the four years' imprisonment in Siberia, the
tormented childhood, the murder of his tyrannical father, etc. & etc. —
he had all the earmarks of hysteria, of grave psychological trauma. And
Dostoyevsky had displayed the trademark features of the psychomotor
epileptic long before his first attack. These days physicians insist there is
no such thing as the "epileptic personality." I think they say this because
they do not want to add to the burden of the epileptic's suffering with
an extra stigma. Privately they do believe in these traits. Dostoyevsky
was nervous and depressed, a tormented hypochondriac, a compulsive
writer obsessed with religious and philosophic themes. He was hyper-
loquacious, raving, etc. & etc. His gambling addiction is well known. By
most accounts he was a sick soul.

   The peculiar and most distinctive thing about his epilepsy was that
in the split second before his fit — in the aura, which is in fact officially
a part of the attack — Dostoyevsky experienced a sense of felicity, of
ecstatic well-being unlike anything an ordinary mortal could hope to
imagine. It was the experience of satori. Not the nickel-and-dime satori
of Abraham Maslow, but the Supreme. He said that he wouldn't trade
ten years of life for this feeling, and I, who have had it, too, would have
to agree. I can't explain it, I don't understand it — it becomes slippery
and elusive when it gets any distance on you — but I have felt this down
to the core of my being. Yes, God exists! But then it slides away and I

lose it. I become a doubter. Even Dostoyevsky, the fervent Christian, makes an almost airtight case against the possibility of the existence of God in the Grand Inquisitor digression in *The Brothers Karamazov*. It is probably the greatest passage in all of world literature, and it tilts you to the court of the atheist. This is what happens when you approach Him with the intellect.

It is thought that St. Paul had a temporal-lobe fit on the road to Damascus. Paul warns us in First Corinthians that God will confound the intellectuals. It is known that Muhammad composed the Koran after attacks of epilepsy. Black Elk experienced fits before his grand "buffalo" vision. Joan of Arc is thought to have been a left-temporal-lobe epileptic. Each of these in a terrible flash of brain lightning was able to pierce the murky veil of illusion which is spread over all things. Just so did the scales fall from my eyes. It is called the "sacred disease."

But what a price. I rarely leave the house anymore. To avoid falling injuries, I always wear my old boxer's headgear, and I always carry my mouthpiece. Rather more often than the aura where "every common bush is afire with God," I have the typical epileptic aura, which is that of terror and impending doom. If I can keep my head and think of it, and if there is time, I slip the mouthpiece in and thus avoid biting my tongue. I bit it in half once, and when they sewed it back together it swelled enormously, like a huge red-and-black sausage. I was unable to close my mouth for more than two weeks.

The fits are coming more and more. I'm loaded on Depakene, phenobarbital, Tegretol, Dilantin — the whole shitload. A nurse from the V.A. bought a pair of Staffordshire terriers for me and trained them to watch me as I sleep, in case I have a fit and smother facedown in my bedding. What delightful companions these dogs are! One of them, Gloria, is especially intrepid and clever. Inevitably, when I come to I find that the dogs have dragged me into the kitchen, away from blankets and pillows, rugs, and objects that might suffocate me; and that they have turned me on my back. There's Gloria, barking in my face. Isn't this incredible?

My sister brought a neurosurgeon over to my place around Christmas — not some V.A. butcher but a guy from the university hospital. He was a slick dude in a nine-hundred-dollar suit. He came down on me hard, like a used-car salesman. He wants to cauterize a small spot in a nerve bundle in my brain. "It's not a lobotomy, it's a *cingulotomy*," he said.

Reckless, desperate, last-ditch psychosurgery is still pretty much unthinkable in the conservative medical establishment. That's why he made a personal visit to my place. A house call. Drumming up some action to make himself a name. "See that bottle of Thorazine?" he said. "You can throw that poison away," he said. "All that amitriptyline. That's garbage, you can toss that, too." He said, "Tell me something. How can you take all of that shit and still walk?" He said, "You take enough drugs to drop an elephant."

He wants to cut me. He said that the feelings of guilt and worthlessness, and the heaviness of a heart blackened by sin, will go away. "It is *not* a lobotomy," he said.

I don't like the guy. I don't trust him. I'm not convinced, but I can't go on like this. If I am not having a panic attack I am engulfed in tedious, unrelenting depression. I am overcome with a deadening sense of languor; I can't *do* anything. I wanted to give my buddies a good show! What a goddamn fool. I am a goddamn fool!

It has taken me six months to put my thoughts in order, but I wanted to do it in case I am a vegetable after the operation. I know that my buddy Jorgeson was a real American hero. I wish that he had lived to be something else, if not a painter of pictures then even some kind of fuckup with a factory job and four divorces, bankruptcy petitions, in and out of jail. I wish he had been that. I wish he had been *anything* rather than a real American hero. So, then, if I am to feel somewhat *indifferent* to life after the operation, all the better. If not, not.

If I had a more conventional sense of morality I would shit-can those dress blues, and I'd send that Navy Cross to Jorgeson's brother. Jorgeson was the one who won it, who pulled the John Wayne number up there near Khe Sanh and saved my life, although I lied and took the credit for all of those dead NVA. He had created a stunning body count — nothing like Theogenes, but Jorgeson only had something like twelve minutes total in the theater of war.

The high command almost awarded me the Medal of Honor, but of course there were no witnesses to what I claimed I had done, and I had saved no one's life. When I think back on it, my tale probably did not sound as credible as I thought it had at the time. I was only nineteen years old and not all that practiced a liar. I figure if they *had* given me the Medal of Honor, I would have stood in the ring up at Camp Las Pulgas in Pendleton and let that light-heavyweight from artillery fucking kill me.

Now I'm thinking I might call Hey Baby and ask how he's doing. No shit, a couple of neuropsychs — we probably have a lot in common. I could apologize to him. But I learned from my fits that you don't have to do that. Good and evil are only illusions. Still, I cannot help but wonder sometimes if my vision of the Supreme Reality was any more real than the demons visited upon schizophrenics and madmen. Has it all been just a stupid neurochemical event? Is there no God at all? The human heart rebels against this.

If they fuck up the operation, I hope I get to keep my dogs somehow — maybe stay at my sister's place. If they send me to the nuthouse I lose the dogs for sure.

The Black Lights

COMMANDER ANDY HAWKINS, chief psychiatrist of the neuropsych ward at Camp Pendleton, received the inevitable nickname Eaglebeak, or Eagle, early in his first tour in Vietnam when a crazy Marine attacked him out of the clear blue and bit off his nose. It became a serious medical event when Commander Hawkins developed a resistant staph infection in his sinuses, which quickly spread to his brain — a danger that is always present with face wounds. To complicate matters, Hawkins was allergic to the first antibiotics administered to him and went into anaphylactic shock. When that was finally controlled, his kidneys shut down, and he had to be placed on dialysis, as the infection continued to run rampant through his system. Hawkins developed a raging fever and had to be wrapped in ice blankets for two days, and weeks later, after his kidneys and immune system kicked in again, he came down with hepatitis B and nearly died from that. He resigned his commission, quit doctoring altogether for a time, and went to the Menninger Foundation in Kansas, where he did some work — work on himself. He wanted to regain some compassion for his fellowman before trying to go back into private practice, but his dreams of a successful civilian career were destroyed by the fact that he had no nose. He wore a tin nose, complete with a head strap, crafted by a Vietnamese peasant, and it made him an object of ridicule, led to a divorce from his wife, and prompted him to rejoin the Navy, where it didn't really matter that much what you looked like if you had enough rank. It mattered socially — at the Officers' Club and so on — but not on the job.

Commander Hawkins started out with a plastic prosthetic nose, but it was easily detectable, so he decided to make the best of a bad situation by wearing the tin nose and being up front about it. He was always quick to point out that he, more than anyone, realized how absurd his condition was, and in doing so he attenuated in part the sniggering he was subjected to for wearing a tin nose. What bothered him more was what he imagined people said about it in private. He became a virtual paranoid in this regard.

I was sent to Pendleton's neuropsych facility — that bleak, austere nuthouse — some weeks after defending my title as the 1st Marine Division Middleweight Champ in a boxing smoker at Camp Las Pulgas. I lost on a K.O. My injuries resulted in a shocking loss of weight, headaches, double vision, and strange, otherworldly spells. EEG readings taken at the hospital indicated that I had a lesion on my left temporal lobe from a punch to the temple that had put me out cold for over an hour. I was a boxer with over a hundred and fifty fights, and I had taken a lot of shots, but this last punch was the hardest I had ever received and the first punch ever to put me down. I had seen stars before from big punches; I had seen pinwheels; but after that shot to the temple I saw the worst thing you ever see in boxing — I saw the black lights.

There I sat in a corner of the dayroom on the kelly-green floor tiles, dressed in a uniform of pajamas and bathrobe, next to a small, tightly coiled catatonic named Joe, who wore a towel on his shoulder. Here in this corner — the most out-of-the-way place in the ward — was one of the few windows. Occasionally a Marine would freak out and bolt for the window, jump up on the sill, shake the security screen, and scream "I want to die!" or "I can't take it anymore, let me out of this motherfucker!" At these times Joe would actually move a little. By that I mean he would tilt to the left to give the screamer a little space. Except for me and one of the corpsmen, Joe would not let anyone touch him or feed him or change him.

As I said, Joe wore a towel on his shoulder. He drooled constantly, and he would grunt in gratitude when I dabbed his mouth dry. Joe gave off a smell. Schizophrenics give off a smell, and you get used to it. Sometimes, however, it would get so bad that I could swear I saw colors coming off Joe — shades of blue, red, and violet — and to get away from it I would get up and walk over to the wall-mounted cigarette lighter, a spiral electrical device much like the cigarette lighters in cars. The staff didn't trust us with open flames or razor blades.

Sitting next to Joe, I would chain-smoke Camels until the Thorazine and phenobarbital that Eagle had prescribed to contain my agitated restlessness got to be too much and I fell into heavy, unpleasant dreams, or I had a fit and woke up on the tile with piss and shit in my pants — alone, neglected, a pariah. The same corpsman who changed Joe would change me. The others would let you lie in your filth until the occasional doctor or nurse came in and demanded that they take action.

I was having ten to twenty spells a day during my first month, and I was so depressed that I refused to talk to anyone, especially when some of the fits marched into full-blown grand mal seizures, which caused me much shame and confusion. I refused to see the buddies from my outfit who came by to visit me, and I did not answer my mail or take calls from my family. But as I got used to the Thorazine I began to snap out of my fits quicker. I began to shave and brush my teeth, and mingle with the rest of the neuropsych population. With Eagle as my living example, I had decided I would make the best of a bad situation; I would adjust to it and get on with my life.

As a rule, there were about thirty men in our ward — the Security Ward, where they kept the craziest, most volatile Marines in all of Pendleton. Eagle seemed to regard me as super-volatile, although I was anything but at the time. He always kept me at arm's length, but he would get right in and mix with really dangerous, really spooky whacked-out freaks. I figured he was afraid of me because of my history as a recon Marine with three tours in Nam, or because I had been a boxer. But he was a doctor, and his professional fear made me wonder about myself.

One day a great big black man named Gothia came into the ward. I had been there about two months, and this was the first new admission I had witnessed. He was extra-big, extra-black, extra-muscular, and extra-crazy. Gothia was into a manic episode and talking fast: there was a Buick waiting outside with a general in it, and he and Gothia were going to fly off to the Vatican, where the pope urgently awaited Gothia's expertise concerning the impending apocalypse. He kept repeating, "It's going to come like a thief in the night — a thief in the night!" until he had everyone half believing that the end of the world was at hand. I immediately liked Gothia. He made things interesting in the ward. As my hair got long, Gothia arranged with the other brothers to give me a hair treatment, a kind of pompadour. It looked like shit, but I was flattered to be admitted into the company of the brothers, which was difficult, my being white and a sergeant and a lifer and all.

A few weeks after he arrived, Gothia bolted unseen up the fence in the exercise yard, did the Fosbury Flop over the barbed wire that topped it, and returned with a six-pack of cold malt liquor. I drank three as fast as possible on an empty stomach and had my first cheap satori — though whether it was epilepsy or the blast from the alcohol is difficult to say. As I finished a fourth can of the malt liquor, sitting against the fence in the warmth of the golden sun, I realized that everything was for the best. Years later, I read a passage from Nietzsche that articulated what I felt in that fifteen-second realization: "Becoming is justified...war is a means to achieve balance....Is the world full of guilt, injustice, contradiction and suffering? Yes, cries Heraclitus, but only for the limited man who does not see the total design; not for the contuitive God; for him all contradiction is harmonized."

Weird. Sleeping in the neuropsych ward at night, I sensed the presence of a very large rabbit under my bunk. A seven-foot rabbit with brown fur and skin sores, who took long, raking breaths. I didn't want to do it, but I had to keep getting out of bed to look. Gothia, who never slept, finally came over and asked me what was the matter, and when I told him about the rabbit he chuckled sympathetically. "Hey, man, there's no *rabbit*. Just take it easy and get some rest, baby. Can you dig it? Rabbit. Shit." But by and by my compulsive rabbit checks got on his nerves, until one night he came over to my bed and said, "I told you there was no rabbit under the bed. If you don't stop this shit, I am going to pinch you." He said it louder than he meant to, and the corpsman on watch came over with his flashlight and told Gothia that if he didn't get to bed he was going to write him up. I lay in the darkness and waited and listened to the rabbit breathe like an asthmatic until I had to check again, whereupon Gothia popped up in his bed and pointed his finger at me and shouted, "There ain't no goddamn rabbit, goddamn it! Knock that shit off!"

I shouted back at him. "It's that rabbit on the Br'er Rabbit molasses jar. That rabbit with buckles on his shoes! Bow tie. Yaller teeth! Yaller! Yaller!" For causing such a commotion we were both shot up, and put in isolation rooms. It was my first experience with a straitjacket, and I nearly lost it. I forced myself to lie still, and it seemed that my brain was filled with sawdust and that centipedes, roaches, and other insects were crawling through it. I could taste brown rabbit fur in my teeth. I had a horror that the rabbit would come in the room, lie on my face, and suffocate me.

After my day of isolation, a brig rat, a white Marine named Rouse, came up to me and said, "Hey — you can tell me — you're faking this shit so you can get out of the service, aren't you?" Rouse, an S-1 clerk-typist, a "Remington raider" who had picked up a heroin habit in Saigon, had violet slash marks on his arms, and liked to show me a razor-blade half he had in his wallet. He offered to let me use it and often suggested that we use it together. Rouse had a lot of back pay saved up and ordered candy and cigarettes from the commissary, and innumerable plastic airplanes to assemble. He always claimed to have nasal congestion and ordered Vicks Inhalers, which at that time contained Benzedrine. Rouse would break them open and swallow the cottons and then pour airplane glue on a washcloth and roll it into a tube and suck on it. I got high with Rouse once by doing this, but the Benzedrine made me so restless that I begged Thorazine from the guys who used to cheek it and then spit it out after meds were issued.

Actually, Rouse was wrong about me: I didn't have anything to hide, and I wasn't faking anything. At the time, I didn't want out. I intended to make the Marine Corps my home. At group-therapy sessions I reasonably insisted that mine was a straightforward case of epilepsy, and for this I was ridiculed by inmate enemies and the medical staff alike. When I saw I was getting nowhere, I refused to speak at the group-therapy sessions at all, and I spent a month sitting sullenly, listening to everyone argue over an old record player one of the residents had brought in to spice up the dayroom. The blacks liked Smokey Robinson and the

Miracles; the war vets were big on the Doors, the Rolling Stones, and C.C.R. I started getting fat from inactivity — fat, although the food was cold and tasted lousy, and in spite of the fact that I fasted on Fridays, because Thursday's dinner was always rabbit. The thought of eating rabbit after a night of sensing the molasses rabbit under my bed gasping for air, and hearing the air whistle between his yellow teeth as he sucked desperately to live — the sight of fried rabbit put me off food for a solid day.

When I had been on the ward about six months and my fits were under better control, a patient named Chandler was admitted. Chandler was a college graduate. His degree was in French. He had joined the Marine Corps to become a fighter pilot but quickly flunked out of flight school and was left with a six-year enlistment as a grunt, which was unbearable to him. I wasn't sure if he was going out of his way to camp things up so he could get a Section Eight discharge, or if he always acted like a fairy. No one held it against him. In fact, a number of the borderline patients quickly became devotees of his and were swishing around with limp wrists, putting on skits and whatnot, and smoking Chandler's cigarette of choice — Salem. Rouse was the first to join in with Chandler by wearing scarves, kerchiefs, and improvised makeup. Rouse even changed his name to Tallulah.

But Chandler wasn't just some stupid fairy. He was erudite, well read, and well mannered. He had been to Europe. Chandler turned me on to Kafka and Paul Valéry. He knew how to work the library system, and soon I found that as long as I had a good book I did not mind the ward half as much.

Under Chandler's influence, Gothia somehow became convinced that he was Little Richard. After about the five hundredth time I heard Gothia howl, "It's Saturday night and I just got paid," and Chandler respond, "That's better, but try and put a little more pizzazz in your delivery!" I was glad to see Gothia go. They transferred him to a long-term-care psychiatric facility in North Carolina. In truth, Gothia was pretty good as Little Richard. He was better at it than Chandler was at Bette Davis or Marlene Dietrich — although at that time I had never seen Marlene Dietrich and had no basis for comparison.

Overwhelmed by boredom one afternoon in the dayroom, as we

watched Chandler execute yet another "grand entrance" (a little pivot with a serious lip pout and a low and sultry "Hello, darlings"), I confided to Rouse that I suspected Eagle of being a "closet" faggot, and shortly afterward I was called into the Eagle's den for a rare appointment. Obviously Rouse had snitched on me. I told Eagle that I thought he was a homosexual because he had surfing posters in his office, and I watched him scribble three pages of notes about this. Eagle's desk was cramped, and his office was hot in spite of a pair of twelve-inch portable fans beating like they could use a couple of shots of lightweight motor oil, and I began to perspire heavily as I watched Eagle write. He was a spectacle — a tall man, cadaverously thin, with his long, angular legs crossed tightly at the knees, his ass perched on the front edge of his chair as he chain-smoked with one hand, flicking ashes into a well-filled ashtray on his desk while he scribbled at the notepad on his lap with his other hand; turning pages, lighting fresh cigarettes off the butts of old ones, scribbling, flipping the pad, seemingly oblivious of me until he looked up and confronted me with that incredible tin nose. "Do you realize that you are sweating?"

"It's hot."

"It's hot," he repeated. He looked down at his notepad and proceeded to write a volume.

By now I was drenched with sweat, having something very much like a panic attack. Without looking up, Eagle said, "You're hyperventilating."

Everything was getting swirly. Eagle dashed out his cigarette and reached into a drawer, withdrawing a stained paper sack from McDonald's. "Here," he said. "Breathe into this."

I took the bag and started breathing into it. "It isn't working," I said between breaths.

"Just give it a minute. Have you ever done this before? Hyperventilated?"

"Oh, God, no." I felt like I was dying.

Eagle pushed himself back in his chair and placed his hands on his knees. "There's more at work here than just a seizure disorder," he said. "I'm seeing some psychopathology."

"It's that fucking nose," I said, gasping. "I'm freaking out."

"You don't like the nose?" Eagle said. "Well, how do you think I feel about the nose? What am I supposed to do, go off on some island like Robinson Crusoe and hide?"

"I didn't mean that," I said. "It's just — "

"It's just too fucking weird, isn't it, Sergeant?"

"Yes, sir," I said. "Not normally, I mean, but I'm on all this medicine. You've got to cut back my dosage. I can't handle it."

"I'll make you a deal. I'm going to cut you back if you do something for me."

The paper bag finally started to work, and everything began to settle down. "What?"

Eagle removed a notepad and pencil from his desk. "Take this. I want you to jot down your feelings every day. This is just between you and me. I mean, it can be anything. If you were a kind of breakfast cereal, for instance, what would you be? Would you be — oatmeal? Would you be — mush? Would you be — FrankenBerries? Would you be — Count Chocula?" Eagle reclined in his chair, extracted a Lucky Strike, and lit it — with the same effeminate gestures, I noted, that Chandler used to light his Salems. Eagle had very broad shoulders for such a thin man. The sleeves of his tropical uniform were rolled up past his elbows. He brushed what few strands of hair he had back across his shiny pate. It was impossible to ignore his nose. He looked like an enormous carrion bird, and although I knew I could break him in pieces, he terrified me. He took a deep drag and exhaled through his tin nose. "Would you be — a Wheatie?"

"Don't try to fuck with my head!" I protested, crushing the McDonald's sack. I got up and stalked out of Eagle's office, but that night, when I went to bed, I found the notepad and pencil on top of my footlocker.

To disprove Eagle's theory that I was borderline psycho, I began to write what I thought were mundane and ordinary things in the diary, things which I thought proved my mental health, e.g., "A good day. Read. Played volleyball and had a good time smoking with the brothers. Picked up a lot of insight in group. Favorite breakfast: Shit on a Shingle. Two hundred push-ups. Happy, happy, happy!" I found such a release in writing that I started a diary of my own — a real one, a secret one, which I recently glanced through, noting that the quality of my penmanship was very shaky.

JANUARY 11, 1975: Sick.

JANUARY 13, 1975: Sick. Managed to read from Schopenhauer.

JANUARY 15, 1975: Borrowed some reading glasses and read Cioran. Sickness unto death. Better in the evening. Constipated. Food here is awful. There are bugs crawling on the wall and through the sawdust that is my brain. My personality is breaking down? I am having a nervous breakdown? Curiously I don't have the "stink" of schizophrenia.

MARCH 14, 1975: Vertigo. Double vision. Sick. Can't eat.

MARCH 18, 1975: There is a smell. A mousy smell.

APRIL 34, 2007: *I am a boxer dog of championship lineage dating back to the late nineteenth century, when the breed was brought to a high point of development in Germany. I have a short, clean brindle coat involving a pattern of black stripes over a base coat of golden fawn. At seventy-five pounds, I am considered large for a female. My muzzle is broad and gracefully carried, giving balance and symmetry to my head. In repose or when I am deep in thought my face is the very picture of dignified nobility.*

APRIL 40: *My under jaw is somewhat longer than the upper jaw and is turned up at the end, as it should be. The jaw projects just enough to afford a maximum of grasping power and holding power (but without the exaggeration and underbite you sometimes see in poorly bred or inbred boxers). Once my jaws are clamped on something it cannot escape.*

My entire muzzle is black. My nose is completely black, the nostrils wide and flaring. My eyes are of a deep brown and are set deeply in the skull. I do not have that liquid, soft expression you see in spaniels, but rather assertive eyes that can create a menacing and baleful effect when I am irritable. This is particularly the case when I fix my piercing stare on its target. I can burn a hole through steel and escape this Mickey Mouse jail anytime I want, and I will as soon as I get my rest. Arf!

APRIL 55: *Before my accident I was a circus performer with the simple-minded animal consciousness of the here-and-now. That I had been a great hero of the circus — the dog shot from cannons, the dog that dove from fifty-foot platforms into shallow barrels of water, the dog that rode galloping stallions bareback — that I was Boris, the Great One, a celebrated hero of Mother Russia, beloved by my countrymen meant... nothing to me.*

Eagle has me back in his little office, and he confronts me not only with my fake diary but with my real one as well. I'm pissed that they've been rummaging through my personal gear.

"Let me get this straight. You say you were this circus dog in Russia, and you got a brain injury when you were *shot from a cannon?*"

"I forgot to wear my safety helmet."

"So a famous neurosurgeon put your brains back together and sent you to a health spa — "

"Only the V.I.P.s went there. Nikita K. was there. I knew him. Dancers from the Bolshoi. Army generals. K.G.B. officials. Chess champions."

"And you... a dog?"

"I wasn't *just* a dog. I was the Rin Tin Tin of Russia."

"You're pretty bright and well informed. How can you know all this kind of thing?"

"Because it's true," I said.

"How would you like it if I sent you to the brig?"

"Fine. The brig would be fine. I'm a howlin' wolf. Put me in a cage or let me go."

Eagle drummed his fingers on his desk, changing pace. "Tell me something. What does this old saying mean to you? 'People who live in glass houses shouldn't throw stones'?" Fingers drumming. "Well?"

"I don't know — "

" 'A rolling stone gathers no moss.' What does that mean?"

"Don't know."

Eagle began to write furiously.

"Why would anyone live in a glass house? It would be hot," I said. "And everyone could see you."

"I hear you like to read Kafka. That's heavy stuff for a young guy. You're pretty bright. Have you ever read any books on abnormal psychology?"

"Hey, man, just let me out of this motherfucker. I'm going down in this place. Put me in a normal ward and let me see a real doctor."

"I'll give it some thought. In the meantime, I'd like you to check this out," Eagle said, clapping me on the shoulder. He handed me a copy of *Love Against Hate*, by Karl Menninger.

STARLOG, JANUFEB, 2010: "Gate is straight/Deep and wide/ Break on through to the other side...."

There was an old piano in the dayroom. When a Marine freaked out and broke the record player, Chandler started playing the piano day and night — driving me crazy. "Canadian Sunset" over and over and over again! One night I rubbed cigarette ashes all over myself for camouflage, crawled into the dayroom recon style, and snapped off the little felt hammers inside the piano. Shoulda seen the look on Chandler's face when he sat down to play. This was not insane behavior. I knew I was not really insane. I was just a garden-variety epileptic temporarily off my game. Thrown a little by the war. I laughed and said to Chandler, "Hey man, what's the sound of one hand clapping?"

After I put the piano out of commission, I noticed Chandler was losing weight. They had him on some new medication. He quit camping around and took a troubled leap into the darkness of his own soul. He grew quiet and started sitting in the corner with catatonic Joe. A black Marine, a rotund and powerful murderer from South Carolina named Bobby Dean Steele, was admitted to the ward for observation, and he began to dominate. Despite the charges pending against him, he was buoyant and cheerful. He walked over to Joe's corner a lot and would say, "Joe-be-doe, what's happening? What's the matter, man? You saw some bad shit in the Nam, didn't you? Well, that's okay. We're going to fix you up — not those doctors, but us, the jarheads. We'll help you. I know you can hear me. Go easy, man."

Bobby Dean Steele gave Joe back rubs and wiped his face and in a matter of a few days was leading him around the ward in a rigid, shuffle-step fashion. The patients began to rally around Joe, and soon everyone was giving him hugs and reassuring him. One of the corpsmen warned me that catatonics often snap out of their rigid stupors to perform sudden acts of extreme violence. It was a catatonic who had bitten off Eagle's nose, he said.

For a brief period during Bobby Dean Steele's tenure, my temporal-lobe visions jumped more and more into grand mal seizures. Just before the fits, instead of having otherworldly spells, I felt only fear and would see the black lights of boxing. I was having very violent fits. In one of these I bit my tongue nearly in half, and for two weeks I sat in Joe's corner with Chandler, overloaded on anticonvulsants. My corpsman came by with a little spray bottle and sprayed my tongue. It had swollen so much that I could not shut my mouth, and it stank. It stank worse than schizophrenia, and even the schizophrenics complained. Bobby Dean Steele and I got into a fistfight over the tongue, and I was amazed at my ability to spring into action, since I felt nearly comatose when he came over to the corner and started jawing at me, kicking at me with his shower shoes. I got up punching and dropped him with a left hook to the jaw. The sound of his huge body hitting the tile was like that of a half-dozen rotten melons dropped on concrete. Bobby Dean Steele had to be helped to the seclusion room, but I was not required to go there, nor was I shot up. I guess it was because my tongue made me look miserable enough.

When Bobby Dean Steele came out of isolation, he was so heavily loaded on Thorazine that his spunk was gone, and without his antics and good cheer there was suddenly no "character" on the ward. Joe, who had seemed to be coming out of his catatonia, reverted back to it, but rather than seeking out his corner, he assumed and maintained impossible positions of waxy flexibility wherever he happened to be. It was like some kind of twisted yoga. I had heard that Joe had been at Khe Sanh during the siege and, like Jake Barnes in The Sun Also Rises, received a groin wound — that he had lost his coconuts. I often wonder why that is considered such a terrible thing. I brought this up and was roundly put down. Better to lose your sight, arms, legs, hearing, said Rouse. Only Chandler, who rarely spoke up anymore, agreed with me. "If there was a hot-fudge sundae on one side of the room and a young Moroccan stud with a cock like a bronze sculpture on the other," he said, "I'd make for the ice cream."

Eagle came to Chandler's rescue, just as he had bailed me out for a while with the diary idea. Eagle appointed Chandler his clerk, and in a few weeks Chandler began to put on weight. As a clerk, he was allowed to leave the ward under the escort of one of the corpsmen. Invariably he went into Oceanside to the bookstores or to restaurants to gorge on big meals. He brought me delicious food in doggie bags, and books: Dostoyevsky, Spinoza, Sartre — the writers he insisted I read — and the lighter stuff I preferred. I was reading a lot and having fewer seizures; I had begun to get better. Chandler was better, too, and up to his old mischief. He constantly mimicked his new boss, and his devastating imitations were so accurate that they actually made me realize how much I respected Eagle, who had the advantages of a good education and presumably had a history of confidence and self-esteem, but now, with his tin nose, had been cut adrift from the human race. The humiliation of epilepsy had unmanned me, and I felt empathy for the doctor. At least I looked like a human being. According to Chandler, Eagle had no friends. Chandler also told me that Eagle would get drunk and remove his tin nose and bellow, "I am the Phantom of the Opera. Ah ha ha ha!"

Patients came and went, and time passed — I had been in the nuthouse for fourteen months. I was becoming one of the senior patients on the ward. We got very good meals on the anniversary of the founding of the Marine Corps, on Thanksgiving, at Christmas. In fact, at Christmas, entertainment was brought in. I remember a set of old geezers who constituted a Dixieland band. They did not play that well, but it made for a welcome break in the routine of med calls, of shower shoes flip-flopping across the kelly-green tiles, of young men freaking out at the security screen near Joe's corner, of people getting high on airplane glue and Vicks Inhalers, of people trying to kill themselves by putting their heads in plastic bags, of the long nights in the ward with the bed springs squealing from incessant masturbation, punctuated by nightmares and night terrors and cries of "Incoming!," of the same cold starchy meals over and over again, of a parched mouth from drug dehydration and too many cigarettes, of a life without hope.

When the band took a rest between sets, two old farts, one white and one black, played a banjo duet of "Shanty Town" that brought tears to my eyes. Then a group of square dancers came in. They were miserable-looking middle-aged types in Western getups, the women with fat legs. You could sense their apprehension, and I realized that I had forgotten how frightening someone like Bobby Dean Steele, who had been copping an attitude of late, wearing an Afro and a pair of black gloves, must have seemed to people like them. Once the music began, however, the misery was erased from their faces and replaced by a hypnotic expression as they mechanically went through their paces. From my folding chair, swooning on phenobarbital, overly warm from all the body heat, I was in agony until I saw — with a rare and refined sense of objectivity — that their sufferings and miseries vanished in their dancing, as they fell into the rhythm of the music and the singsong of the caller's instructions. And for a moment I saw myself as well; I saw myself as if from on high, saw the pattern of my whole life with a kind of geometrical precision, like the pattern the dancers were making, and it seemed there was a perfect rightness to it all.

One day after chow, Bobby Dean Steele was summoned to the meds kiosk by one of the doctors, and a corpsman buzzed a pair of enormous brig chasers through the heavy steel door of the ward. They cuffed Bobby Dean Steele, while the resident on duty shrugged his shoulders and told Steele that he was being transferred back to the brig to stand General Court-Martial for three counts of murder in the second degree. It had been decided, Chandler informed us, that Bobby Dean Steele was not especially crazy — at least not according to observation, the M.M.P.I., and the Rorschach. Chandler told us that Steele would end up doing twenty years hard labor in a federal prison.

My own departure was somewhat different. Eagle called me into his office and said, "I'm sending you home. Don't ask me whether you're cured or not. I don't know. I do know you were an outstanding Marine, and I have processed papers for a full disability pension. Good luck to you, Sergeant."

"Thank you." I was dumbfounded.

"When you get home, find yourself a good neurologist....And keep your ass out of the boxing ring."

"Yes, sir."

As I turned to leave, Eagle saluted me. I returned the salute proudly, and I heard his booming, operatic laugh start up after I pulled his door shut behind me.

* * *

The next morning I collected over nine thousand dollars in back pay and I went out to the bus stop with my seabag on my shoulder. A master sergeant came by, and I asked him what time the bus came. He told me that I could not leave the base until I got a No. 1 haircut and I told him to forget it, that I was a civilian. A moment later a jeep pulled over and a captain with an M.P. band on his sleeve hopped out. I showed him my discharge papers, the jump wings on my set of blues, the Navy Cross and the two Silvers, and he said, "Big fucking deal. You got a General Discharge, Sergeant. A psychiatric discharge, Sergeant. I want you off this base immediately."

"Well, give me a ride and I'll be glad to get off the motherfucker," I said. I was beginning to see cockroaches crawling through the wet sawdust inside my skull, and I kept wiping my nose for fear they would run out and brush across my lips.

"You're a psycho," the master sergeant said. "Go out there and wreak havoc and mayhem on the general population, and good riddance."

"You could cut me some slack," I said. "I was a real Marine, not some rear-echelon blowhard, and by the way, fuck the Corps. Eat the apple, and fuck the Corps. I curse the day I ever joined this green motherfucker."

"I want you off this base and I want you to hump it off this base," the master sergeant said.

"You mean I don't have to get a haircut after all?" I said in my best nellie voice.

"Fucking hit the road, Marine. Haight-Ashbury is that way."

"Well, fuck you," I said.

"And fuck you. Go fuck yourself."

I threw my seabag down and was about to fight when a Marine in a beat-up T-bird pulled over to the bus stop and asked me if I needed a lift. Without another word I tossed my seabag in his back seat and hopped into the car. Before I could say thanks he hit me up for five bucks in gas money. "It's twenty-three miles to Oceanside," he said. "And I'm runnin' on empty. I ain't even got a spare tire, no jack, no nothing." He looked at me and laughed, revealing a mouth filled with black cavities.

He said, "Hey, man, you wouldn't happen to have a cigarette, would you?" I handed him my pack. "Hey, thanks," he said.

"That's all right," I said.

He lit the cigarette and took a deep drag. "You want to hear some strange shit?"

"Why not?" I said.

"I just got six, six, and a kick." The Marine took another pull off the cigarette and said, "Six months in the brig, six months without pay, and a Bad Conduct Discharge."

"What did you do?" I asked. I was trying to stop the vision of bugs.

"AWOL," he said. "Which is what I'm doing now. I ain't going to do no six months in the fucking brig, man. I did two tours in Nam. I don't deserve this kind of treatment. You want to know something?"

"What's that?"

"I stole this fucking car. Hot-wired the motherfucker."

"Far out," I said. "Which way you going?"

"As far as five bucks in gas will take me."

"I got a little money. Drive me to Haight-Ashbury?"

"Groovy. What are you doing, man, picking your nose?"

"Just checking for cockroaches," I said weakly. I was afraid I was going to have a fit, and I began to see the black lights — they were coming on big time, but I fought them off. "What was your M.O.S.?"

"Oh-three-eleven, communications. I packed a radio over in I Corps. Three Purple Hearts and three Bronze Stars with valor. That's why I ain't doing six months in no brig. I just hope the 'P. waves us through at the gate. I don't want no high-speed chases." The Marine lit another of my cigarettes from the butt of the first one. "Hey, man, were you in the war? You look like you got some hard miles on you. Were you in the war? Did you just get out? You're not going AWOL, too — that ain't no regulation haircut. Man, you got a headful of hair. On the run? How about it? Were you in the war? You got that thousand-yard stare, man. Hey, man, stop picking your nose and tell me about it."

Arf!

"Goddammit, are you zoned or what?"

Bow wow!

"I can't believe this shit. That motherfucker 'P. at the gate is pulling me over. Look at that. Can you believe this shit? They never pull you over at this gate, not at this time of day — and I haven't got any identification. Shit! Buckle up your seat belt, nose-pickin' man, we are gonna motate. This fucking Ford has got a blower on the engine and it can boogie. Haight-Ashbury, here we come or we die tryin'. Save us some of that free love! Just hope you get some of that free lovin' — save me some of that *good* pussy!"

The Marine slammed his foot down full on the accelerator. The T-bird surged like a rocket and blew by the guard post, snapping off the wooden crossbar. For a moment I felt like I was back in the jungle again, a savage in greasepaint, or back in the boxing ring, a primal man — kill or be killed. It was the best feeling. It was ecstasy. The bugs vanished. My skull contained gray matter again. I looked back at the M.P. in the guard post making a frantic call on the telephone. But the crazy Marine at the wheel told me not to worry, he knew the back roads.

I Want to Live!

S HE WONDERED HOW many times a week he had to do this. Plenty, no doubt. At least every day. Maybe twice...three times. Maybe, on a big day, five times. It was the ultimate bad news, and he delivered it dryly, like Sergeant Joe Friday. He was a young man, but his was a tough business and he had gone freeze-dried already. Hey, the bad news wasn't really a surprise! She... *knew*. Of course, you always hope for the best. She heard but she didn't hear.

"What?" she offered timidly. She had hoped... for better. Geez! Give me a break! What was he saying? Breast and uterus? Double trouble! She *knew* it would be the uterus. There had been the discharge. The bloating, the cramps. The fatigue. But it was common and easily curable provided you got it at stage one. Eighty percent cure rate. But the breast — that one came out of the blue and that could be really tricky — that was fifty-fifty. Strip out the lymph nodes down your arm and guaranteed chemo. God! Chemo. The worst thing in the world. Goodbye hair — there'd be scarves, wigs, a prosthetic breast, crying your heart out in "support" groups. Et cetera.

"Mrs. Wilson?" The voice seemed to come out of a can. Now the truth was revealed and all was out in the open. Yet how — tell me this — how would it ever be possible to have a life again? The voice from the can had chilled her. To the core.

"Mrs. Wilson, your last CA-125 hit the ceiling," he said. "I suspect that this could be an irregular kind of can...cer."

Some off-the-wall kind of can...cer? A kind of wildfire cancer! Not the easygoing, 80 percent-cure rate, tortoise, as-slow-as-molasses-in-January cancer!

January. She looked past the thin oncologist, wire-rimmed glasses, white coat, inscrutable. Outside, snowflakes tumbled from the sky, kissing the pavement — each unique, wonderful, worth an hour of study, a microcosm of the Whole: awe-inspiring, absolutely fascinating, a gift of divinity gratis. Yet how abhorrent they seemed. They were white, but the whole world had lost its color for her now that she'd heard those words. The shine was gone from the world. Had she been Queen of the Universe for a million years and witnessed glory after glory, what would it have mattered now that she had come to this?

She…came to…went out, came back again…went out. There was this…wonderful show. Cartoons. It was the best show. This wasn't so bad. True, she had cancer but…these wonderful cartoons. Dilaudid. On Dilaudid, well, you live, you die — that's how it is…life in the Big City. It happens to everyone. It's part of the plan. Who was she to question the plan?

The only bad part was her throat. Her throat was on fire. "Intubation." The nurse said she'd phone the doctor and maybe he'd authorize more dope.

"Oh, God, please. Anything."

"Okay, let's just fudge a little bit, no one needs to know," the nurse said, twisting the knob on Tube Control Central. Dilaudid. Cartoons. Oh, God, thank God, Dilaudid! Who invented that drug? Write him a letter. Knight him. Award the Nobel Prize to Dilaudid Man. Where was that knob? A handy thing to know. Whew! Whammo! Swirling, throbbing ecstasy! And who was that nurse? Florence Nightingale, Mother Teresa would be proud…oh, boy! It wasn't just relief from the surgery; she suddenly realized how much psychic pain she had been carrying and now it was gone with one swoop of a magic wand. The cartoons. Bliss…

His voice wasn't in a can, never had been. It was a normal voice, maybe a little high for a man. Not that he was effeminate. The whole problem with him was that he didn't seem real. He wasn't a flesh-and-blood kinda guy. Where was the *empathy*? Why did he get into this field if he couldn't empathize? In this field, empathy should be your stock-in-trade.

"The breast is fine, just a benign lump. We brought a specialist in to get it, and I just reviewed the pathology report. It's nothing to worry about. The other part is not...so good. I'm afraid your abdomen...it's spread throughout your abdomen...it looks like little Grape-Nuts, actually. It's exceedingly rare and it's...it's a rapid form of...can...cer. We couldn't really take any of it out. I spent most of my time in there untangling adhesions. We're going to have to give you cisplatin...if it weren't for the adhesions, we could pump it into your abdomen directly — you wouldn't get so sick that way — but those adhesions are a problem and may cause problems further along." Her room was freezing, but the thin oncologist was beginning to perspire. "It's a shame," he said, looking down at her chart. "You're in such perfect health...otherwise."

She knew this was going to happen yet she heard herself say, "Doctor, do you mean...I've got to take — "

"Chemo? Yeah. But don't worry about that yet. Let's just let you heal up for a while." He slammed her chart shut and...whiz, bang, he was outta there.

Goodbye, see ya.

The guessing game was over and now it was time for the ordeal. She didn't want to hear any more details — he'd said something about a 20 percent five-year survival rate. Might as well bag it. She wasn't a fighter, and she'd seen what chemo had done to her husband, John. This was it. Finis!

She had to laugh. Got giddy. It was like in that song — *Freedom's just another word for nothing left to lose*...When you're totally screwed, nothing can get worse, so what's to worry? Of course she could get lucky...it would be a thousand-to-one, but maybe...

The ovaries and uterus were gone. The root of it all was out. Thank God for that. Those befouled organs were gone. Where? Disposed of. Burned. In a dumpster? Who cares? The source was destroyed. Maybe it wouldn't be so bad. How could it be that bad? After all, the talk about pain from major abdominal surgery was overdone. She was walking with her little cart and tubes by the third day — a daily constitutional through the ward.

Okay, the Dilaudid was permanently off the menu, but morphine sulfate wasn't half bad. No more cartoons but rather a mellow glow. Left, right, left, right. Hup, two, three, four! Even a journey of a thousand miles begins with the first step. On the morphine she was walking a quarter of an inch off the ground and everything was...softer, mercifully so. Maybe she could hack it for a thousand miles.

But those people in the hospital rooms, gray and dying, that was her. Could such a thing be possible? To die? Really? Yes, at some point she guessed you did die. But her? Now? So soon? With so little time to get used to the idea?

No, this was all a bad dream! She'd wake up. She'd wake up back in her little girl room on the farm near Battle Lake, Minnesota. There was a depression, things were a little rough, but big deal. What could beat a sun-kissed morning on Battle Lake and a robin's song? There was an abundance of jays, larks, bluebirds, cardinals, hummingbirds, red-winged blackbirds in those days before acid rain and heavy-metal poisoning, and they came to her yard to eat from the cherry, apple, plum, and pear trees. What they really went for were the mulberries.

Ah, youth! Good looks, a clean complexion, muscle tone, a full head of lustrous hair — her best feature, although her legs were pretty good, too. Strength. Vitality. A happy kid with a bright future. Cheerleader her senior year. Pharmacy scholarship at the college in Fergus Falls. Geez, if her dad hadn't died, she could have been a pharmacist. Her grades were good, but hard-luck stories were the order of the day. It was a Great Depression. She would have to take her chances. Gosh! It had been a great, wide, wonderful world in those days, and no matter what, an adventure lay ahead, something marvelous — a handsome prince and a life happily ever after. Luck was with her. Where had all the time gone? How had all the dreams...fallen away? Now she was in the Valley of the Shadow. The morphine sulfate was like a warm and friendly hearth in Gloom City, her one and only consolation.

He was supposed to be a good doctor, one of the best in the field, but he had absolutely no bedside manner. She really began to hate him when he took away the morphine and put her on Tylenol 3. Then it began to sink in that things might presently go downhill in a hurry.

They worked out a routine. If her brother was busy, her daughter drove her up to the clinic and then back down to the office, and the thin oncologist is...called away, or he's...running behind, or he's...*some-thing*. Couldn't they run a business, get their shit together? Why couldn't they anticipate? It was one thing to wait in line at a bank when you're well, but when you've got cancer and you're this cancer patient and you wait an hour, two hours, or they tell you to come back next week...come back for something that's worse than anything, the very worst thing in the world! Hard to get up for that. You really had to brace yourself. Cisplatin, God! Metal mouth, restlessness, pacing. Flop on the couch, but that's no good; get up and pace, but you can't handle that, so you flop on the couch again. Get up and pace. Is this really happening to me? *I can't believe this is really happening to me!* How can such a thing be possible?

Then there were the episodes of simultaneous diarrhea and vomiting that sprayed the bathroom from floor to ceiling! Dry heaves and then dry heaves with bile and then dry heaves with blood. You could drink a quart of tequila and then a quart of rum and have some sloe gin too and eat pink birthday cakes and five pounds of licorice, Epsom salts, a pint of kerosene, some Southern Comfort — and you're on a Sunday picnic compared to cisplatin. Only an archfiend could devise a dilemma where to maybe *get well* you first had to poison yourself within a whisker of death, and in fact if you didn't die, you wished that you had.

There were visitors in droves. Flowers. Various intrusions at all hours. Go away. Leave me alone...please, God, leave me...alone.

Oh, hi, thanks for coming. Oh, what a lovely — such beautiful flowers...

There were moments when she felt that if she had one more episode of diarrhea, she'd jump out of the window. Five stories. Would that be high enough? Or would you lie there for a time and die slowly? Maybe if you took a header right onto the concrete. Maybe then you wouldn't feel a thing. Cisplatin: she had to pace. But she had to lie down, but she was squirrelly as hell and she couldn't lie down. TV was no good — she had double vision, and it was all just a bunch of stupid shit, anyhow. Soap operas — good grief! What absolute crap. Even her old favorites. You only live once, and to think of all the time she pissed away watching soap operas.

If only she could sleep. God, couldn't they give her Dilaudid? No! Wait! Hold that! Somehow Dilaudid would make it even worse. Ether then. Put her out. Wake me up in five days. Just let me sleep. She *had* to get up to pace. She *had* to lie down. She *had* to vomit. *Oh, hi, thanks for coming. Oh, what a lovely — such beautiful flowers.*

The second treatment made the first treatment seem like a month in the country. The third treatment — oh, damn! The whole scenario had been underplayed. Those movie stars who got it and wrote books about it were stoics, valiant warriors compared to her. She had no idea anything could be so horrible. Starving in Bangladesh? No problem, I'll trade. Here's my MasterCard and the keys to the Buick — I'll pull a rickshaw, anything! Anything but this. HIV-positive? Why, just sign right here on the dotted line and you've got a deal! I'll trade with anybody! Anybody.

The thin oncologist with the Bugs Bunny voice said the CA-125 number was still up in the stratosphere. He said it was up to her if she wanted to go on with this. What was holding her up? She didn't know, and her own voice came from a can now. She heard herself say, "Doctor, what would you do...if you were me?"

He thought it over for a long time. He pulled off his wire rims and pinched his nose, world-weary. "I'd take the next treatment."

It was the worst by far — square root to infinity. Five days: no sleep, pacing, lying down, pacing. Puke and diarrhea. The phone. She wanted to tear it off the wall. After all these years, couldn't they make a quiet bell? — did they have shit for brains or what? *Oh, hi, well...just fine. Just dandy. Coming by on Sunday? With the kids? Well...no, I feel great. No. No. No. I'd love to see you...*

And then one day the thin-timbre voice delivered good news. "Your CA 125 is almost within normal limits. It's working!"

Hallelujah! Oh my God, let it be so! A miracle. Hurrah!

"It is a miracle," he said. He was almost human, Dr. Kildare, Dr. Ben Casey, Marcus Welby, M.D. — take your pick. "Your CA is down to rock bottom. I think we should do one, possibly two more treatments and then go back inside for a look. If we do too few, we may not kill it all but if we do too much — you see, it's toxic to your healthy cells as well. You can get cardiomyopathy in one session of cisplatin and you can die."

"One more is all I can handle."

"Gotcha, Mrs. Wilson. One more and in for a look."

"I hate to tell you this," he said. Was he making the cartoons go away? "I'll be up front about it, Mrs. Wilson, we've still got a problem. The little Grape-Nuts — fewer than in the beginning, but the remaining cells will be resistant to cisplatin, so our options are running thin. We could try a month of an experimental form of hard chemotherapy right here in the hospital — very, very risky stuff. Or we could resume the cisplatin, not so much aiming for a cure but rather as a holding action. Or we could not do anything at all..."

Her voice was flat. She said, "What if I don't do anything?"

"Dead in three months, maybe six."

She said, "Dead how?"

"Lungs, liver, or bowel. Don't worry, Mrs. Wilson, there won't be a lot of pain. I'll see to that."

Bingo! He flipped the chart shut and...whiz, bang, he was outta there!

She realized that when she got right down to it, she wanted to live, more than anything, on almost any terms, so she took more cisplatin. But the oncologist was right, it couldn't touch those resistant rogue cells; they were like roaches that could live through atomic warfare, grow and thrive. Well then, screw it! At least there wouldn't be pain. What more can you do? She shouldn't have let him open her up again. That had been the worst sort of folly. She'd let him steamroll her with Doctor Knows Best. Air had hit it. No wonder it was a wildfire. A conflagration.

Her friends came by. It was an effort to make small talk. How could they know? How could they *know* what it was like? They loved her, they said, with liquor on their breath. They had to get juiced before they could stand to come by! They came with casseroles and cleaned for her, but she had to sweat out her nights alone. Dark nights of the soul on Tylenol 3 and Xanax. A lot of good that was. But then when she was in her loose, giddy *freedom's just another word for nothing left to lose* mood, about ten days after a treatment, she realized her friends weren't so dumb. They knew that they couldn't really *know*. Bugs Bunny told her there was no point in going on with the cisplatin. He told her she was a very brave lady. He said he was sorry.

A month after she was off that poison, cisplatin, there was a little side benefit. She could see the colors of the earth again and taste food and smell flowers — it was a bittersweet pleasure, to be sure. But her friends took her to Hawaii, where they had this great friend ("You gotta meet him!") and he...he made a play for her and brought her flowers every day, expensive roses, et cetera. She had never considered another man since John had died from can...cer ten years before. How wonderful to forget it all for a moment here and there. A moment? Qualify that — make that ten, fifteen seconds. How can you forget it? Ever since she got the news she could...not...forget...it.

Now there were stabbing pains, twinges, flutterings — maybe it was normal everyday stuff amplified by the imagination or maybe it was real. How fast would it move, this wildfire brand? Better not to ask.

Suddenly she was horrible again. Those nights alone — killers. Finally one night she broke down and called her daughter. Hated to do it, throw in the towel, but this was the fifteenth round and she didn't have a prayer.

"Oh, hi. I'm just fine" — *blah blah blah* — "but I was thinking maybe I could come down and stay, just a while. I'd like to see Janey and — "

"We'll drive up in the morning."

At least she was with blood. And her darling granddaughter. What a delight. Playing with the little girl, she could forget. It was even better than Hawaii. After a year of sheer hell, in which all of the good stuff added up to less than an hour and four minutes total, there was a way to forget. She helped with the dishes. A little light cleaning. Watched the game shows, worked the *Times* crossword, but the pains grew worse. Goddamn it, it felt like nasty little yellow-tooth rodents or a horde of translucent termites — thousands of them, chewing her guts out! Tylenol 3 couldn't touch it. The new doctor she had been passed to gave her Dilaudid. She was enormously relieved. But what she got was a vial of little pink tablets and after the first dose she realized it wasn't much good in the pill form; you could squeeze by on it but they'd *promised* — no pain! She was losing steam. Grinding down.

They spent a couple of days on the Oregon coast. The son-in-law — somehow it was easy to be with him. He didn't pretend that things were other than they were. He could be a pain in the bun, like everyone, bitching over trivialities, smoking Kool cigarettes, strong ones — jolters! A pack a day easy, although he was considerate enough to go outside and do it. She wanted to tell him, "Fool! Your health is your greatest fortune!" But she was the one who'd let six months pass after that first discharge.

The Oregon coast was lovely, although the surf was too cold for actual swimming. She sat in the hotel whirlpool and watched her granddaughter swim a whole length of the pool all on her own, a kind of dog-paddle thing but not bad for a kid going on seven. They saw a show of shooting stars one night but it was exhausting to keep up a good front and not to be morbid, losing weight big time. After a shower, standing at the mirror, scars zigzagging all over the joint like the Bride of Frankenstein, it was just awful. She was bald, scrawny, ashen, yet with a bloated belly. She couldn't look. Sometimes she would sink to the floor and just lie there, too sick to even cry, too weak to even get dressed, yet somehow she did get dressed, slapped on that hot, goddamn wig, and showed up for dinner. It was easier to do that if you pretended that it wasn't real, if you pretended it was all on TV.

She felt like a naughty little girl sitting before the table looking at meals her daughter was killing herself to make — old favorites that now tasted like a combination of forty-weight Texaco oil and sawdust. It was a relief to get back to the couch and work crossword puzzles. It was hell imposing on her daughter but she was frightened. Terrified! They were her blood. They *had* to take her. Oh, to come to this!

The son-in-law worked swing shift and he cheered her in the morning when he got up and made coffee. He was full of life. He was real. He was authentic. He even interjected little pockets of hope. Not that he pushed macrobiotics or any of that foolishness, but it was a fact — if you were happy, if you had something to live for, if you loved life, you lived. It had been a mistake for her to hole up there in the mountains after John died. The Will to Live was more important than doctors and medicines. You had to reinvigorate the Will to Live. The granddaughter was good for that. She just couldn't go the meditation-tape route, imagining microscopic, ravenous, good-guy little sharks eating the bad cancer cells, et cetera. At least the son-in-law didn't suggest that or come on strong with a theology trip. She noticed he read the King James Bible, though.

She couldn't eat. There was a milk-shake diet she choked down. Vanilla, chocolate fudge, strawberry — your choice. Would Madame like a bottle of wine with dinner? Ha, ha, ha.

Dilaudid. It wasn't working, there was serious pain, especially in her chest, dagger thrusts — *Et tu, Brute?* She watched the clock like a hawk and had her pills out and ready every four hours — and that last hour was getting to be murder, a morbid sweat began popping out of her in the last fifteen minutes. One morning she caved in and timidly asked the son-in-law, "Can I take three?"

He said, "Hell, take four. It's a safe drug. If you have bad pain, take four." Her eyes were popping out of her head. "Here, drink it with coffee and it will kick in faster."

He was right. He knew more than the doctor. You just can't do everything by the book. Maybe that had been her trouble all along — she was too compliant, one of those "cancer" personalities. She believed in the rules. She was one of those kind who wanted to leave the world a better place than she found it. She had been a good person, had always done the right thing — this just wasn't right. It wasn't fair. She was so...angry!

The next day, over the phone, her son-in-law bullied a prescription of methadone from the cancer doctor. She heard one side of a lengthy heated exchange while the son-in-law made a persuasive case for methadone. He came on like Clarence Darrow or F. Lee Bailey. It was a commanding performance. She'd never heard of anyone giving a doctor hell before. God bless him for not backing down! On methadone tablets a warm orange glow sprang forth and bloomed like a glorious, time-lapse rose in her abdomen and then rolled through her body in orgasmic waves. The sense of relief shattered all fear and doubt though the pain was still there to some extent. It was still there but — so what? And the methadone tablets lasted a very long time — no more of that *every four hours* bullshit.

Purple blotches all over her skin, swollen ankles. Pain in her hips and joints. An ambulance trip to the emergency room. "Oh," they said, "it's nothing...vascular purpura. Take aspirin. Who's next?"

Who's next? Why hadn't she taken John's old .38 revolver the very day she heard that voice in the can? Stuck it in the back of her mouth and pulled the trigger? She had no fear of hellfire. She was a decent, moral person but she did not believe. Neither was she the Hamlet type — what lies on the other side? It was probably the same thing that occurred before you were born — zilch. And zilch wasn't that bad. What was wrong with zilch?

One morning she waited overlong for the son-in-law to get up, almost smashed a candy dish to get him out of bed. Was he going to sleep forever? Actually, he got up at his usual time.

"I can't. Get. My breath," she told him.

"You probably have water in your lungs," the son-in-law said. He knew she didn't want to go to the clinic. "We've got some diuretic. They were Boxer's when she had congestive heart failure — dog medicine, but it's the same thing they give humans. Boxer weighed fifty-five pounds. Let me see . . . take four, no, take three. To be cautious. Do you feel like you have to cough?"

"Yes." *Kaff, kaff, kaff.*

"This might draw the water out of your lungs. It's pretty safe. Try to eat a banana or a potato skin to keep your potassium up. If it doesn't work, we can go over to the clinic."

How would he know something like that? But he was right. It worked like magic. She had to pee like crazy but she could breathe. The panic to end all panics was over. If she could only go . . . number two. Well, the methadone slows you down. "Try some Metamucil," the son-in-law said.

It worked. Kind of, but it sure wasn't anything to write home about.

"I can't breathe. The diuretics aren't working."

The son-in-law said they could tap her lung. It would mean another drive to the clinic, but the procedure was almost painless and provided instantaneous relief. It worked but it was three days of exhaustion after that one. The waiting room. Why so long? Why couldn't they anticipate? You didn't have to be a genius to know which way the wildfire was spreading. Would the methadone keep that internal orange glow going or would they run out of ammo? Was methadone the ultimate or were there bigger guns? Street heroin? She'd have to put on her wig and go out and score China White.

The little girl began to tune out. Gramma wasn't so much fun anymore; she just lay there and gave off this smell. There was no more dressing up; it was just the bathrobe. In fact, she felt the best in her old red-and-black tartan pattern, flannel, ratty-ass bathrobe, not the good one. The crosswords — forget it, too depressing. You could live the life of Cleopatra but if it came down to this, what was the point?

The son-in-law understood. Of all the people to come through. It's bad and it gets worse and so on until the worst of all. "I don't know how you can handle this," he'd say. "What does it feel like? Does it feel like a hangover? Worse than a hangover? Not like a hangover. Then what? Like drinking ten pots of boiled coffee? Like that? Really? Jittery! Oh, God, that must be awful. How can you stand it? Is it just like drinking too much coffee or is there some other aspect? Your fingers are numb? Blurred vision? It takes eight years to watch the second hand sweep from twelve to one? Well, if it's like that, how did you handle *five days*? I couldn't — I'd take a bottle of pills, shoot myself. Something. What about the second week? Drained? Washed out? Oh, brother! I had a three-day hangover once — I'd rather die than do that again. I couldn't ride out that hangover again for money. I know I couldn't handle chemo…"

One afternoon after he left for work, she found a passage circled in his well-worn copy of Schopenhauer: *In early youth, as we contemplate our coming life, we are like children in a theater before the curtain is raised, sitting there in high spirits and eagerly waiting for the play to begin. It is a blessing that we do not know what is really going to happen.* Yeah! She gave up the crosswords and delved into *The World As Will and Idea*. This Schopenhauer was a genius! Why hadn't anyone told her? She was a reader, she had waded through some philosophy in her time — you just couldn't make any sense out of it. The problem was the terminology! She was a crossword ace, but words like *eschatology* — hey! Yet Schopenhauer got right into the heart of all the important things. The things that really mattered. With Schopenhauer she could take long excursions from the grim specter of impending death. In Schopenhauer, particularly in his aphorisms and reflections, she found an absolute satisfaction, for Schopenhauer spoke the truth and the rest of the world was disseminating lies!

Her son-in-law helped her with unfinished business: will, mortgage, insurance, how shall we do this, that, and the other? Cremation, burial plot, et cetera. He told her the stuff that her daughter couldn't tell her. He waited for the right moment and then got it all in — for instance, he told her that her daughter loved her very much but that it was hard for her to say so. She knew she cringed at this revelation, for it was ditto with her, and she knew that he could see it. Why couldn't she say to her own daughter three simple words, "I love you"? She just couldn't. Somehow it wasn't possible. The son-in-law didn't judge her. He had to be under pressure, too. Was she bringing everyone in the house down? Is that why he was reading Schopenhauer? No, Schopenhauer was his favorite. "Someone had to come out and tell it like it is," he would say of the dour old man with muttonchops whose picture he had pasted on the refrigerator. From what she picked up from the son-in-law, Schopenhauer wrote his major work by his twenty-sixth birthday — a philosophy that was ignored almost entirely in his lifetime and even now, in this day and age, it was thought to be more of a work of art than philosophy in the truest sense. A work of art? Why, it seemed irrefutable! According to the son-in-law, Schopenhauer spent the majority of his life in shabby rooms in the old genteel section of Frankfurt, Germany, that he shared with successions of poodles to keep him company while he read, reflected, and wrote about life at his leisure. He had some kind of small inheritance, just enough to get by, take in the concerts, do a little traveling now and then. He was well versed in several languages. He read virtually everything written from the Greeks on, including the Eastern writers, a classical scholar, and had the mind to chew things over and make something of the puzzle of life. The son-in-law, eager to discourse, said Freud called Schopenhauer one of the six greatest men who ever lived. Nietzsche, Thomas Mann, and Richard Wagner all paid tribute to this genius who had been written off with one word — pessimist. The son-in-law lamented that his works were going out of print, becoming increasingly harder to find. He was planning a trip to Frankfurt, where he hoped to find a little bust of his hero. He had written to officials in Germany making inquiries. They had given him the brush-off. He'd have to fly over himself. And she, too, began to worry that the works of this writer would no longer be available…she, who would be worms' meat any day.

Why? Because the *truth* was worthwhile. It was more important than anything, really. She'd had ten years of peaceful retirement, time to think, wonder, contemplate, and had come up with nothing. But new vistas of thought had been opened by the curiously ignored genius with the white mutton-chops, whose books were harder and harder to get and whom the world would consider a mere footnote from the nineteenth century — a crank, a guy with an ax to grind, a hypochondriac, a misogynist, an alarmist who slept with pistols under his pillow, a man with many faults. Well, check anyone out and what do you find?

For God's sake, how were you supposed to make any sense out of this crazy-ass shit called life? If only she could simply push a button and never have been born.

The son-in-law took antidepressants and claimed to be a melancholiac, yet he always seemed upbeat, comical, ready with a laugh. He had a sense of the absurd that she had found annoying back in the old days when she liked to pretend that life was a stroll down Primrose Lane. If she wasn't walking down the "sunny side of the street" at least she was "singin' in the rain." Those were the days.

What a fool!

She encouraged the son-in-law to clown and philosophize, and he flourished when she voiced a small dose of appreciation or barked out a laugh. There was more and more pain and discomfort, but she was laughing more, too. Schopenhauer: *No rose without a thorn. But many a thorn and no rose.* The son-in-law finessed all of the ugly details that were impossible for her. Of all the people to come through!

With her lungs temporarily clear and mineral oil enemas to regulate her, she asked her daughter one last favor. Could they take her home just once more?

They made an occasion of it and drove her up into the mountains for her granddaughter's seventh birthday party. Almost everyone in the picturesque resort town was there, and if they were appalled by her deterioration they did not show it. She couldn't go out on the sun porch, had to semi-recline on the couch, but everyone came in to say hello and all of the bad stuff fell away for…an entire afternoon! She was deeply touched by the warm affection of her friends. There were…so many of them. My God! They loved her, truly they did. She could see it.

You couldn't bullshit her anymore; she could see deep into the human heart; she knew what people were. What wonderful friends. What a perfect afternoon. It was the last...good thing.

When she got back to her daughter's she began to die in earnest. It was in the lungs and the bowel, much as the doctor said it would be. Hell, it was probably in the liver even. She was getting yellow, not just the skin but even the whites of her eyes. There was a week in the hospital, where they tormented her with tests. That wiped out the last of her physical and emotional stamina.

She fouled her bed after a barium lower G.I. practically turned to cement and they had to give her a powerful enema. Diarrhea in the bed. The worst humiliation. "Happens all the time, don't worry," the orderly said.

She was suffocating. She couldn't get the least bit of air. All the main players were in the room. She knew this was it! Just like that. Bingo! There were whispered conferences outside her room. Suddenly the nurses, those heretofore angels of mercy, began acting mechanically. They could look you over and peg you, down to the last five minutes. She could see them give her that *anytime now* look. A minister dropped in. There! That was the tip-off — the fat lady was singing.

When the son-in-law showed up instead of going to work she looked to him with panic. She'd been fighting it back but now...he was there, he would know what to do without being asked, and in a moment he was back with a nurse. They cranked up the morphine sulfate, flipped it on full-bore. Still her back hurt like hell. All that morphine and a backache...just give it a minute...ahhh! Cartoons.

Someone went out to get hamburgers at McDonald's. Her daughter sat next to her holding her hand. She felt sorry for them. They were the ones who were going to have to stay behind and play out their appointed roles. Like Schopenhauer said, the best they would be able to do for themselves was to secure a little room as far away from the fire as possible, for Hell was surely in the here-and-now, not in the hereafter. Or was it?

She began to nod. She was holding onto a carton of milk. It would spill. Like diarrhea-in-the-bed all over again. Another mess. The daughter tried to take the carton of milk away. She...held on defiantly. Forget the Schopenhauer — what a lot of crap that was! She did not want to cross over. She wanted to live! She wanted to live!

The daughter wrenched the milk away. The nurse came back and cranked up the morphine again. They were going for "comfort." Finally the backache...the cartoons...all of that was gone.

(She was back on the farm in Battle Lake, Minnesota. She was nine years old and she could hear her little red rooster, Mr. Barnes, crowing at first light. Then came her brother's heavy work boots clomping downstairs and the vacuum swoosh as he opened up the storm door, and then his boots crunch-crunching through the frozen snow. Yes, she was back on the farm all right. Her brother was making for the outhouse and presently Barnes would go after him, make a dive-bomb attack. You couldn't discourage Mr. Barnes. She heard her brother curse him and the *thwap* of the tin feed pan hitting the bird. Mr. Barnes's frontal assaults were predictable. From the sound of it, Fred walloped him good. As far as Mr. Barnes was concerned, it was his barnyard. In a moment she heard the outhouse door slam shut and another tin *thwap*. That Barnes — he was something. She should have taken a lesson. Puffed out her chest and walked through life — "I want the biggest and the best and the most of whatever you've got!" There were people who pulled it off. You really could do it if you had the attitude.

Her little red rooster was a mean little scoundrel, but he had a soft spot for her in his heart of steel and he looked out for her, cooed for her and her alone. Later, when young men came to see her, they soon arranged to meet her thereafter at the drugstore soda fountain uptown. One confrontation with Barnes, even for experienced farm boys, was one too many. He was some kind of rooster all right, an eccentric. Yeah, she was back on the farm. She...could feel her sister shifting awake in the lower bunk. It was time to get up and milk the cows. Her sister always awoke in good humor. Not her. She was cozy under a feather comforter and milking the cows was the last thing she wanted to do. Downstairs she could hear her mother speaking cheerfully to her brother as he came back inside, cursing the damn rooster, threatening to kill it. Her mother laughed it off; she didn't have a mean bone in her body.

She...could smell bacon in the pan, the coffeepot was percolating, and her grandmother was up heating milk for her Ovaltine. She hated Ovaltine, particularly when her grandmother overheated the milk — burned it — but she pretended to like it, insisted that she needed it for her bones, and forced it down so she could save up enough labels to get a free decoder ring to get special messages from Captain Cody, that intrepid hero of the airwaves. She really wanted to have that ring, but there was a Great Depression and money was very dear, so she never got the decoder or the secret messages or the degree in pharmacology. Had she been more like that little banty rooster, had she been a real go-getter... Well — it was all but over now.)

The main players were assembled in the room. She... was nodding in and out but she could hear. There she was, in this apparent stupor, but she was more aware than anyone could know. She heard someone say somebody at McDonald's put "everything" on her hamburger instead of "cheese and ketchup only." They were making an issue out of it. One day, when they were in her shoes, they would learn to ignore this kind of petty stuff, but you couldn't blame them. That was how things were, that's all. Life. That was it. That was what it was. And here she lay... dying.

Suddenly she realized that the hard part was all over now. All she had to do was... let go. It really wasn't so bad. It wasn't... anything special. It just was. She was trying to bring back Barnes one last time — that little memory of him had been fun, why not go out with a little fun? She tried to remember his coloring — orange would be too bright, rust too drab, scarlet too vivid. His head was a combination of green, yellow, and gold, all blended, and his breast and wings a kind of carmine red? No, not carmine. He was just a little red rooster, overly pugnacious, an ingrate. He could have been a beautiful bird if he hadn't gotten into so many fights. He got his comb ripped off by a raccoon he'd caught stealing eggs in the henhouse, a big bull raccoon that Barnes had fought tooth and nail until Fred ran into the henhouse with his .410 and killed the thieving intruder. Those eggs were precious. They were income. Mr. Barnes was a hero that day. She remembered how he used to strut around the barnyard. He always had his eye on all of the hens; they were his main priority, some thirty to forty of them, depending. They were his harem and he was the sheikh. Boy, was he ever. She remembered jotting down marks on a pad of paper one day when she was home sick with chickenpox. Each mark represented an act of rooster fornication. In less than a day, Mr. Barnes had committed the sexual act forty-seven times that she could see — and she didn't have the whole lay of the land from her window by any means. Why, he often went out roving and carousing with hens on other farms. There were bitter complaints from the neighbors. Barnes really could stir things up. She had to go out on her bicycle and round him up. Mr. Barnes was a legend in the country. Mr. Barnes thought the whole world belonged to him and beyond that — the suns, the stars, and the Milky Way — all of it! Did it feel good or was it torment? It must have been a glorious feeling, she decided. Maybe that was what Arthur Schopenhauer was driving at in his theory about the Will to Live. Mr. Barnes was the very personification of it.

Of course it was hard work being a rooster, but Barnes seemed the happiest creature she had ever known. Probably because when you're doing what you really want to do, it isn't work. No matter how dull things got on the farm, she could watch Barnes by the hour. Barnes could even redeem a hot, dog-day afternoon in August. He wasn't afraid of anything or anybody. Did he ever entertain a doubt? Some kind of rooster worry? Never! She tried to conjure up one last picture of him. He was just a little banty, couldn't have weighed three pounds. Maybe Mr. Barnes would be waiting for her on the other side and would greet her there and be her friend again.

She nodded in and out. In and out. The morphine was getting to be too much. Oh, please God. She hoped she wouldn't puke... So much left unsaid, undone. Well, that was all part of it. If only she could see Barnes strut his stuff one last time. "Come on, Barnes. Strut your stuff for me." Her brother, Fred, sitting there so sad with his hamburger. After a couple of beers, he could do a pretty good imitation of Mr. Barnes. Could he... would he... for old time's sake? Her voice was too weak, she couldn't speak. Nowhere near. Not even close. Was she dead already? Fading to black? It was hard to tell. "Don't feel bad, my darling brother. Don't mourn for me. I'm okay"... and... one last thing — "Sarah, I do love you, darling! Love you! Didn't you know that? Didn't it show? If not, I'm so, so very sorry...." But the words wouldn't come —

couldn't come. She...was so sick. You can only get so sick and then there was all that dope. Love! She should have shown it to her daughter instead of...assuming. She should have been more demonstrative, more forthcoming....That's what it was all about. *Love your brother as yourself* and *love the Lord God almighty with all your heart and mind and soul.* You were sent here to love your brother. Do your best. Be kind to animals, obey the Ten Commandments, stuff like that. Was that it? Huh? Or was that all a lot of horseshit?

She...nodded in and out. Back and forth. In and out. She went back and forth. In and out. Back and forth...in and out. There wasn't any tunnel or white light or any of that. She just...died.

Silhouettes

W INDOW FELL FOR Catherine his senior year in high school when both were given special education assignments in East High School's laundry room. The job didn't pay much but it gave them a little spending money, which Catherine spent buying Marlboro cigarettes, Thunderbird wine, candy bars, blotter acid, and marijuana, and which Window spent on Catherine.

Their boss, Meldrick, immediately saw potential in Window but found Catherine useless and had her transferred to lunch room duty. Meldrick was the custodian in charge of the washer, dryer, and the centrifugal extractor in the laundry room, a comfortable hideaway attached to the boiler room where he could sit and read while his bunch of "special ed" assistants washed and folded the P.E. towels. Meldrick expected little from the students but because there were so many, if they performed even minimally, most of his own work was done. When this was the case he permitted the students to clown around and indulge in a kind of Fagin's Band brand of tomfoolery. Their antics were a welcome reprieve after a forty-five-minute dose of Spinoza or David Hume. Sometimes Meldrick would join in the fun and perform a rendition of "Hambone" by rhythmically slapping his chest and thighs with his palms and fingertips, and then when he was finished, he would imitate Ricky Ricardo from "I Love Lucy" and say, "Eet's so ree-diculous!"

A journeyman custodian, Meldrick owned the most advanced college degrees in the school and was working diligently on his doctorate although he was convinced he would never find a better job. This was especially true when he discovered Window, whose capacity for work amazed him. Window was trustworthy and responsible, so much so that Meldrick found that he could hand Window his keys and turn him loose in the shop area where he would do an A-number-one job without screwing up, so that all Meldrick had to do was a casual inspection afterward to make sure the paper towel dispensers were full, the glass was spotless, the floors properly mopped, and that all the lights were out and the doors were locked. On days when Window was focused and his powers of concentration were high, Meldrick didn't even bother to check.

Meldrick's penchant for investigating the riddle of existence caused the other janitors to avoid him, and Meldrick found little in common with anyone on the faculty, with their state university degrees, who would get a glazed-over look in their eyes when he wanted to expound on some philosopher who obsessed him. Meldrick sometimes thought he was the only person at the school, perhaps the only regular job-holder in the whole country, with the leisure to read philosophy, and thanks to Window he had an abundance of time. Moreover, it was only with Window that he felt completely at ease, with whom he could talk and simply be himself — Window, who didn't have a very high-priced vocabulary but who would patiently watch while Meldrick took him into a classroom and illustrated concepts like "nihilism" or "existentialism" on the chalkboard and explained to Window how they were relevant to his own situation, including those times when Window was lovesick over Catherine and would zone out so badly that Meldrick actually had to clean the shops himself or even dump the filthy cloth bag of his "Pig," a noisy but durable commercial vacuum cleaner. Thus Meldrick attempted to instruct Window on such topics as love between the sexes and other practical matters taking an airy, detached, and theoretical view that made the problems of life seem simple and resolvable. Meldrick could get on a kick and rave for an hour until Window would practically topple over like a chicken that had been hypnotized by having its beak placed on a line scratched in the dirt.

Although Meldrick repeatedly warned Window about Catherine, who was notorious at East High for her temper tantrums and sexual escapades, once she let Window have sex with her, Window was deaf to all advice. Like Odysseus, he had heard the "lovely tones" from the Siren's isle and had lost all sense of reason.

Meldrick became exasperated. "I talk to you until I am blue in the face. You just won't listen. What's the matter with you, huh? Hello dere, is anybody home?"

"I'm home, Meldrick."

"Why, mercy, Window. I thought you were lost in space."

"No, Meldrick. Window's on earth today."

"Then perhaps we can work the conundrum through. Perhaps we can slash the Gordian knot. Let's try something new. Listen closely, Window, this is serious. As I count forward from one to seven, you will become more and more relaxed. I want you to picture yourself walking down a set of stairs, and with each step you will find yourself going deeper and deeper into relaxation. One...two...three...(you are becoming more and more relaxed). Please wipe that shit-eating grin off your face, Window — four...five...six...seven. There! You are now in touch with the Higher Power, that part of you which knows all. What does it say?"

Window began to guffaw. "I know, I know, Meldrick. Leave the bitch alone!"

"You've got it, pal. Keep clear from that woman. Man, she's bad. She's gonna drive you crazy."

"I steer clear."

"You promise?"

"Yes."

"Okay, now as I count back from seven to one, you will emerge from the dank basement of your subconscious mind and step into the glorious sunshine of life unbound from the snarls and tangles of that evil black magic web the nasty spider has ensnared you with. Seven...six... five — stop smiling, Window! Four...three...two...one — bingo. How do you feel, Window?"

"I have pain in my head."

"Ooh, this is so ree-diculous!" Meldrick said. "Take two aspirin and I'll see you tomorrow. You can go."

Meldrick liked to sit in the laundry room with a cup of coffee and a thick book, listening to the comforting sound of the dryer while

Window managed all of his jobs. Window had a bubble butt and short feet, and when he ran back and forth into the laundry room to get supplies with short mincing steps, Meldrick was reminded of Kirby Puckett legging out a triple for the Minnesota Twins and would have to chuckle. He knew Window was hustling so that he would have time to find Catherine and steal a kiss or two from his beloved, the love of his life. Meldrick was aware of these shenanigans but ignored them as long as Window performed.

Catherine did not especially like Window. She was still pining over a guy who knocked her up her junior year and then moved off to Spokane, leaving her and her parents to cope with the abortion. She did not like Window because he was such a square and because he had ambitions of graduating from high school and becoming a full-time custodian. But Catherine's parents liked Window and encouraged his visits to their trailer home out on the Hoquiam Indian Reservation even if he was a blue-eyed, fair-skinned ultra-white boy. Window was so white he was almost translucent — you could almost see through him, thus the nickname. His real name was Albert Thomas. Albert Thomas or Window — it didn't matter to Catherine's parents — he was a "prospect" and they felt he would calm Catherine down. She had a wild streak in her and she needed taming. Maybe, even, Window would be their savior and marry Catherine. For this reason they looked the other way when Catherine took Window into her room, where the two lovers soon had the whole trailer rocking like a small boat on the high seas. It was almost impossible to watch television, especially during the sexual climaxes, but the parents quickly accommodated themselves to these sessions and even laughed about them.

Meldrick and the other custodians at East High continued to dissuade Window from seeing Catherine and told him outright that she was no good. Josie, the matron, who had to break up the catfights the female students got into at lunch or attend to Catherine during her pseudo-epileptic fits, did not warn Window so much as she told Meldrick to use his limited powers over Window to destroy the relationship. It was a shame, she said, because Window was such a good kid and Catherine was nothing but trouble, upside and down, but Meldrick would protest weakly, "It's the metaphysics of the sexes — my hands are tied. Every time the bitch comes around, his eyes turn into two stars."

Packard, a graveyard-shift custodian, confronted Window one morning when, after he went out to turn off the alarms in the greenhouse, he caught Catherine and the school's worst troublemaker screwing shamelessly in the bushes. "You want to know who she was fucking, dipstick? She was fucking Centrick Cline; need I say more? That bitch is insane, Window, and she's taking you for a ride. She's *hustling* you, man!"

When Meldrick came in on swing shift and heard of the incident, he became genuinely angry and harangued Window in the laundry room until Window blushed red. Seeing that he was getting through, Meldrick amplified his argument with the exaggerated body posturing of a courtroom lawyer and threatened to fire Window. It was just play-acting, but Meldrick got so carried away that all Window could do was let his head slump forward and say, "I know. I know. She's no good." Window worked an extra hour on his own time that night and before he left he came up to Meldrick and apologized for letting him down.

"You dope, you say that shit but you don't mean it. You're crazy, man. That bitch is going to bring you down." Meldrick's censure caused Window to writhe in agony. "Dammit, Window, you're breaking my heart with this shit. I go out of my way to help you, I try to be your friend and look what you do to me. Why don't you just drink a bottle of Drano and get it over with? I can't stand watching you go through this bullshit."

"That's right," Josie said. "She's a whore. Keep away from her. Tell him, Meldrick."

"I'm telling him, dammit, but it isn't sinking in. Window, you're completely out of control. We're your friends: listen! What's the matter with you, anyhow? You aren't dumb. Quit giving me dumb. I'm sick of that fucking act. Use your head."

In the ensuing weeks Meldrick browbeat Window into agreeing to stay away from Catherine, and for a time Window avoided her. This was a source of consternation for Catherine since she thought she had Window in her pocket, and when he stopped calling or avoided her at school, a strange kind of emptiness welled up in her and she began to tell her friends that she was in love with Window and was carrying his baby.

Window then came to Meldrick and reported that he "had" to marry Catherine, and rather than scream a diatribe, Meldrick shook his head in resignation and said, "Well, if you really love her, go ahead and do it. My good thing is over. I knew it was too good to be true. I'm going to have to fucking work for a change."

Window asked Meldrick to be his best man after Window's special ed buddy, Paul Palmer, who was slated for this honor, had an epileptic seizure in his bed and suffocated facedown in his pillow. Meldrick refused to be a party to the wedding. In the meantime, Catherine and Window pressed forward and made plans.

In the first part of June, a few weeks before school was out, the librarians went into one of the custodian closets to get a two-wheeled cart and there they found the custodian Mancini, a known alcoholic, passed out on the floor with an alarm clock ticking by his ear and a six-pack of Olympia beer at his side. Mancini, in a full-length beard and filthy flannel shirt, lay on the floor with one shoe missing. He was breathing erratically and the frightened librarians summoned the head custodian, who got the principal. The principal was unable to rouse Mancini, but he had seen enough drunks to know that Mancini would revive and merely wrote a note — "You're fired!" — dated it, signed it, and taped it to the six-pack. Meldrick waited a few days and then made a pitch to the principal that Window, a product of the school's special education program, was a good worker — reliable, cheerful, and an excellent candidate for the job. The principal heard him out and then said that Window was too young. Meldrick said, "He's nineteen. What good is the vocational program if it can't get its graduates jobs?"

This was a telling point, and the principal told Meldrick to have Window submit an application and said that he would consider it. While Window cleaned Meldrick's area that night, Meldrick went into the business area and typed out the application forms including a short essay, written in the style of Window's speech, and after Window read and signed the forms, Meldrick neatly folded them and stuck them in the principal's box.

Window was interviewed a week later and hired to replace Mancini. Catherine's parents were ecstatic over the news and threw an impromptu party for Window out on the reservation. The school district paid well and had an excellent health and retirement program. They encouraged Window even when Catherine lost the baby. That summer when all of the custodians reverted to day shift, Meldrick, Packard, and Josie gang-banged Window, launching a new assault against Catherine, and Catherine, relieved over the miscarriage, lost interest in Window, called him boring, and flung his ring in his face.

Catherine refused to see Window and in a matter of ten days, Window, who apart from his fat ass verged on slender, lost twelve pounds and began to look like a concentration camp victim. At work he seemed distracted, and when the custodians took their frequent breaks, Window dozed off at the table.

Ted Frank Page, the gymnasium custodian, would laugh as Window's mouth fell open. "He's doing an 'O,' " Page would say, or if Window exposed his tongue, however slightly, Page would slap the table and proclaim that Window was doing a "Q." The custodians would roar with laughter and Window, who was painfully shy, would jerk awake and blush like a beet. Sometimes he would bolt away from the table and disappear for hours. Although the janitors were familiar with all of the hiding spots, no one could find Window when he was off somewhere nursing his hurt. There was speculation that he went up on the roof to do this and most of them were too lazy and out of shape to climb the iron-rung ladder that led to the roof. Generally Window would later turn up in Meldrick's area to see if he had been missed, and just as Meldrick could berate Window, at these times he would calm Window by painting pictures of a new and better life — Thunderbirds and motorcycles, a healthier body through a better diet and physical training, sharp clothes, braces to straighten his teeth, Window's very own apartment, and the ultimate prize — a beautiful wife. Soon Window would forget all about Catherine and spin out his fantasies about Whitney Houston or Paula Abdul, singers that Meldrick was barely familiar with. Meldrick cautioned Window to be realistic but he did not entirely discount the possibility. "You're a really neat guy, Window. Who knows. Play your cards right and maybe it will happen, dude. You know the universe is filled with abundance. Sometimes all you got to do is ask."

With his full-time paychecks Window bought the old Citroën behind the autoshop, and the autoshop teacher, who was teaching a summer school course, got it running for him. The janitors kidded Window about the Citroën, which looked like a flying saucer, and Ted Frank Page said, "Well, how else do you expect him to get back and forth from the Planet Fringus except in some sort of a spacecraft?"

The head custodian laughed and said, "I guess you can't drive there in a Ford?" He belly-bumped the table with his big stomach and tossed his head back to laugh. "I can't believe this place."

Late that summer, Window seduced Catherine with presents and protestations of love. Stewing in boredom out on the reservation, Catherine had really begun to hate her parents, especially her father, who drew disability pay because of a bad back and nagged Catherine to wait on him. Catherine often came over to East High with her friend Lutetia, a fat girl who always walked behind her rather than at her side. The janitors were curious about this, but Lutetia was also a product of the special education program and that seemed to explain just about any eccentricity. The purpose of Catherine's visits to the high school was almost always money, and if Window did not have any, Catherine would clutch her fists at her sides, scrunch down in a rage, and scream at Window through clenched teeth. Window would turn red and hang his head submissively and try to appease her. "Please, Catherine, relax or you'll have a seizure."

"If I have a goddamn seizure, it will be your stupid fault, Window. You fucking asshole. You son of a bitch. You motherfucking cocksucker. I hate you!"

These scenes caused Packard and Meldrick to renew their efforts to destroy the relationship, and while Window agreed that Catherine was too wild for him, he also became stubborn. He was stubborn because he had a full-time job and was flush with money (his janitor's pay was a relative fortune for a nineteen-year-old) and Window didn't really care at times what Meldrick thought. Meldrick suspected there was more to it than this and one afternoon up in the library he used his guile to extract a confession from Window that Catherine was pregnant again. Window said that he knew for sure that it was his baby. He told Meldrick that he loved her and once they got their own place and she was away from the firecracker tension of her parents' trailer, where her dad was often drunk, everything would be fine.

In the meantime, the head custodian warned Window that he was sick of Catherine coming over to the school, sick of her rages, and told him to keep his personal life separate from his professional life. After the head man left the custodian's room, Meldrick gave Window an ironic look and said, "He's right, Window. This special ed shit has got to stop. You're a janitor now. Act like a professional."

Shortly after the birth of his son, Joey, Window began to gain weight. Meldrick accused Window of seeking substitute gratification, but Window refused to acknowledge any problems between himself and Catherine. After the swing shift was over, however, rather than rush home to be with his bride, Window liked to play volleyball with the custodians in the gym. Ted Frank Page organized these games and came in early to play before his graveyard shift started. Meldrick and Page hit the weight room after the games and encouraged Window to lift weights and take better care of his body. In the weight room Window finally confessed that Catherine refused absolutely to have sex with him after the birth of their son, that she had run up a shitload of credit-card charges and that he was forced to have his brother, Roy, move into their apartment in order to help pay the bills.

Although Roy was Window's brother, and also a product of East High's special education program, he was tall and good looking. He had better teeth than Window. Ted Frank Page teased Window that while Window was busting his ass on the swing shift, Roy was home dicking Catherine. *That* was the reason she wouldn't sleep with Window. One night at the dinner break after Meldrick and Window dined on Meldrick's "macrobiotic special"—a combination of brown rice, black beans, and raisins—Meldrick went into one of his classrooms and found Window watching television as he ate from a half-gallon carton of Neapolitan ice cream into which he had stirred a pound of M&M's. A six-pack of iced cappuccino was at his side. "Aha, caught you!" Meldrick said as he assumed his district attorney posture. "Have you gone totally insane?"

Window gave Meldrick a startled look and then looked down at his bowl of ice cream and began to guffaw.

"You're completely out of control," Meldrick said, parroting the vice-principal. "Something has got to be done. We're looking at six thousand calories here." Meldrick shook his head and told Window he was going to take a nap in the library workroom. "Make sure I'm awake by ten, okay? I need a nappy-poo. My yin-yang is all out of whack."

"Get your beauty rest, Meldrick, I'll wake you up at ten."

"Come in whistling, so I know it's you. I almost got caught last night. Ray's been sneaking around. I think he's keeping a journal. He thinks he's in the KGB or something."

A few days later, an exotic package arrived from Marseilles, France, addressed to Window. The package aroused the curiosity of the office staff and for a solid day caused much speculation among them. Even the administrators were intrigued by it, until Window showed up at two P.M., opened the mysterious box, and revealed a rebuilt starter for his Citroën, which had sat in the back parking lot with a flat tire all summer. Meldrick and Ted Frank Page installed the starter that evening, but the Citroën was soon abandoned in the back parking lot again when the radiator overheated and blew. Window did not have the money to have it rebuilt.

Meldrick gave Window a lecture about blowing all of his money on junk food, porno flicks, and pornographic magazines. "Are you oversexed or what?" Meldrick said. "I know you're nineteen but you are really driving this into the ground. The librarians found one of your porno magazines in their workroom and it totally grossed them out. Ray told them a student left it and covered your ass, but use your head, dammit. Think."

One evening Window sought out Meldrick and, much alarmed, told him that Catherine had paged him at work and said she was going to have another baby in two weeks. Window asked Meldrick how it could be possible since he hadn't slept with her in over a year. "She says I did once when we got drunk and that I don't remember, but she lies."

Meldrick said, "Page is right, Roy is dicking her. Geez! Your own brother! This *is* ridiculous!"

Meldrick immediately demanded to know how Catherine could be eight and a half months pregnant without Window's knowing it. Window hung his head down and said, "She's so fat, I couldn't tell."

Later, Window showed Meldrick phone bills to Catherine's first love, the old boyfriend in Spokane. Meldrick asked Window if he might be the culprit, but Window was sure it was Roy. He remembered a night back in the fall when he was in the next-door apartment mediating a fight between the couple that lived there. "You see, Johnny hit Karen on the back of the head with a frying pan and they were crashing furniture. I told them fighting wasn't the answer and that they should talk things out. Karen said, 'What I hear you saying, Johnny, is that *Another World* is dumb, that Carl Hutchins is a skinny-ass, short crotch with a greasy ponytail and that I've got a TV crush on him, but I —' "

Meldrick said, "Window, I don't want to hear a fucking soap opera plot!"

"Okay, okay, but listen to this — when they calmed down I went back home and the shade was down and I saw their shadows. Catherine and Roy were on the couch, kissing. He had her bra off. I could see her big hard tits through the shade."

"He saw silhouettes," Meldrick told Ted Frank Page that night at volleyball. "Silhouettes on the shade — " Everyone fell silent at this declaration, and Meldrick's words continued to resonate through the unusual acoustics of the gym.

Finally Ted Frank Page said, "Window, why didn't you go in and kick ass?"

Window began to strut around the basketball court with his fists on his hips and his bubble butt high. "There's this loose rock in the yard. I'm always tripping on it in the night. I'm so mad at Roy and Catherine, I tried to dig up the rock with my fingers until I'm breaking my fingernails and chipped my tooth."

"He was biting the rock," Meldrick said. "It's solid granite. I've seen that rock."

"It kept wobbling in the ground like it would come out easy but I can't get it out until I get the jack handle out of my trunk and dig it up — "

"How big?" Page said. "What did you do?"

"Plenty big," Window said. "A bowling ball, only heavier. I ran up to the window and threw the fucker in — *Boom!*" Window took his janitor keys from his belt and heaved them against the glass blackboard at the far end of the gym. Then he kicked a number of volleyballs so hard they cracked ceiling tiles. The janitors waited for Window to finish with his tantrum.

"Well, what did they do, Window? What did Catherine and Roy do? What the fuck happened?" Page asked.

"He ran and hid in the bushes," Meldrick said.

"You didn't go inside and kick ass?" Page asked. "Jesus, Window."

"I was afraid I would get arrested. Catherine called the cops. I stayed in the bushes until the police officers left. Then I went back to Johnny and Karen's and had beer — "

"Eventually you went home. What did you *say*?" Page said.

"I didn't say anything. Catherine said some crazy person chunked a boulder in the window. A dope fiend or some nut who escaped from Eastern State Hospital."

"And you didn't kick ass?" Page asked.

"I puked up the beer in the toilet," Window said.

"He was upset," Meldrick said. "And he can't argue with this manipulative and domineering woman. She's trying to sell him a story that he knocked her up when he was drunk one night. And half the time she's going around with Roy's hickeys on her neck. Mercy me! I fear this is not the idyllic dream of connubial bliss Window had envisioned."

Ted Frank Page stood in the center of the gym bouncing a volleyball. "Ha, ha, ha, fucking Meldrick! 'Connubial bliss.' Where did you come up with that shit? 'Connubial bliss.' Ah, ha, ha — fuck!"

Meldrick turned serious. "Think, Window. You know for certain that you did not sleep with your wife for at least nine months?"

Window looked up, his eyes wide. "I don't think so," he said. "I'm pretty sure."

"Then get a blood test when the kid is born. Divorce the bitch — "

Window could not sleep or eat and rushed through his area every night so that he could go upstairs and help Meldrick, so that Meldrick, in his gratitude, would offer him psychological consolation. Meldrick was the only custodian who didn't dismiss him with an "I told you so."

"I know it's Roy's baby, it looks just like him," Window said. "It's got his Bugs Bunny nose — "

"Window, think. When was the last time you slept with Catherine? Are you sure there is no possibility?"

"It can't be mine, Meldrick. I just know it. Can we ask the *I Ching*?"

Meldrick took Window into the library and got the *I Ching* from the shelves. The two custodians went into the librarian's office and while Window tossed the coins, Meldrick wrote down the resulting hexagram — Number 29.

"What does it mean?" Window said.

"Bad. It means bad," Meldrick said.

"Meldrick," Window said with some hope, "can you ask it if I'm going to win the lottery?"

"Window. Geez! Are you still pissing your money away on lottery tickets? What's the fucking use? You won't listen. This is futile, pure and simple futile."

Catherine initiated divorce proceedings against Window and got everything except for the useless Citroën. The court ordered Window to pay six hundred dollars a month in child support and after his lawyer's monthly payment, the credit-card charges and room and board at his parents' home, Window was left with a pathetic seventy dollars for pin money. He walked six miles to work and six miles home again. Ted Frank Page liked to take out a pencil and paper at the janitor's table and calculate how much Roy's baby would ultimately cost Window…a figure well over sixty thousand dollars. "You could have gone to that ranch in Las Vegas and got some *good pussy* for that kind of money, Window."

Josie sat down with Window one afternoon and tried to calculate a way to pay off his outstanding bills and save enough money to initiate a blood test to determine the father of Catherine's second baby.

"My dad said the test won't work on two brothers."

"They've got a new test. It will work, believe me," Josie said.

Whenever Window mentioned the possibility of going to a lawyer to get a court order for DNA testing, Catherine clenched her fists, scrunched down, and flew into a rage.

"You see," Meldrick said, "if she wasn't worried, she'd just laugh in your face and call you a fool. She's guilty as hell, and she's scared."

Yet no matter how Josie figured it, there was no way Window could come up with the two thousand dollars for legal and medical fees necessary for the blood test. "Can't your parents loan you the money?" Josie asked.

"They said I'm on my own," Window said. "I think they are — you know — embarrassed — "

"Because of what your brother did. It really is low. They ought to be embarrassed."

"That's fucking special ed for you," Ted Frank Page said.

"We told you not to marry the bitch," Meldrick said, puffing on a cigarillo in the janitor's room.

"Think," Page said, "of all the high-class pussy you could have had for all that bread you're laying out. What an idiot!"

"Window," Josie said, "the next time you want a date, go to church and meet a girl there. A girl with virtue."

Window took to blowing his seventy dollars cash the first day he got it each month. Invariably he spent the money on pornography and junk food. While his mother provided Window with board, she did not supply junk food, so Window used his key to the student store and began to raid the candy supplies until the diversified occupations teacher had the lock changed. Then Window began taking the cook's key to the freezer and started stealing student pizzas. One day, when he went for the key in the top drawer of the cook's desk, he found that it was gone. "They're on to you," Packard said. "Don't admit anything. If you get called in, deny it."

"If I get *called in?*" Window said with real fear in his voice.

"Yeah, if you get called in and they grill you — lie, motherfucker."

"Called in?" Window said. "*Into the office?*"

"I don't know why in the fuck you are worried," Ted Frank Page said. "You are the motherfucker who's busting ass and — hey! who is collecting? I'll tell you, it's that fat-ass ex-wife and your brother, taking your money, welfare, and all the rest of it. If I was you, I'd hop in that Citroën and fly off to Fringus, go back among your own kind. If they fired you they would be doing you a favor."

"He's right, Window," Meldrick said. "You are a noble spirit, an innocent — a pure soul and much too good for this pitiless brutal planet. You deserve a better fate than this."

*   *   *

The vice-principal began to write Window up for tiny infractions. Once Window left his vacuum cleaner in the band room and the band instructor complained to the office. "The next time it happens," the vice-principal said jauntily, displaying his palm with a flourish, "probation."

On another occasion Window forgot there was a senior parents' meeting and took a shortcut to the Coke machine, bursting into the conference room in a T-shirt with his Walkman blasting *Fine Young Cannibals*. The vice-principal wrote him up for not wearing his custodian's shirt and for listening to a headset, a safety hazard. Window finally made probation when another custodian claimed Window used his mop and bucket and left it dirty in the janitor's closet. It was not a major crime, but there had been an accumulation of misdemeanors.

Window put his nose to the grindstone for six months, but two weeks after the probation was officially lifted, he left the vacuum cleaner in the band room again. "If you do this once more," the vice-principal said, "you will be fired."

Window received an unexpected windfall on his income tax return — eleven hundred dollars. Josie immediately made an appointment with Window's attorney only to learn that the cost of the blood test had gone up substantially. Window was so upset he frittered away the money and then he left his vacuum cleaner in the band room for the third time. When the vice-principal read the union contract and learned that he could not fire Window for this offense, he instructed the head custodian to give Window more area to clean and to ride him, but the head custodian only paid lip service to the order. For one thing, Window never gave him any guff and for another, Ted Frank Page, who was bench-pressing over three hundred and fifty pounds, physically threatened the head custodian. It was not entirely for Window's sake. Ted Frank Page learned that the head custodian had been bad-mouthing Page for laziness and like everything that was said at the janitors' table, it worked its way around the grapevine in less than a day.

When a clutch cable for Window's Citroën arrived from the auto supply house in Marseilles, a note went up on the custodians' bulletin board stating that no custodian was to receive personal mail at the school.

Meldrick and Ted Frank Page installed the clutch cable and the auto instructor boiled out the radiator on the Citroën, but scarcely two weeks after it was running, the clutch cable snapped. It had been installed backwards and the Citroën sat in its accustomed home in the back parking lot for three more months until another cable was dispatched from Marseilles, France.

Window learned to consult the *I Ching* on his own and spent hours in the library asking it questions. Ray, the custodian who worked the special education area, asked Meldrick what Window was doing. Mystified, Ray hid by the library door and watched. "He shakes pennies in his hand and then tosses them down on the desk and writes something down and then he looks something up in a book. What is he doing?"

"It's beyond comprehension," Meldrick said. "Don't even attempt an understanding."

Meldrick and Packard installed the second clutch cable on the Citroën in the correct fashion and a week after it was running, Window came into the school clutching a check for five thousand dollars. A car collector spotted the Citroën and had given Window a check on the spot. The head custodian called the buyer a fool while Ted Frank Page insisted that Window could have gotten three times that amount. Before Window could cash the check, Josie called his lawyer and then personally drove him to the bank and then to the law office where the blood test was paid for — in full, in advance.

Catherine came by the school and had a tantrum. She had court papers in her hand directing her to submit to blood tests. She screamed at Window and told him that the welfare lawyer told her Window wasn't going to get to first base since the blood tests were a "cruel invasion" and that she had recently become a Jehovah's Witness and would not, under any circumstances, spill a drop of her own blood.

"Is that how you act," Ted Frank Page said, "when you get religion, cursing and having tantrums?" Catherine stalked out of the building with her friend Lutetia trailing after her.

"Yeah," Window said, puffing up, "you should wash your mouth out with soap."

The blood tests proved conclusively that Window's brother, Roy, was the father of Catherine's second child and Window's lawyer got the double child-support payment lifted from Window's check. Because of the rise in income, welfare immediately seized a larger payment for Window's uncontested son.

The custodian who had Window written up for using his mop bucket sneered, "All that fucking rigmarole to save a hundred bucks a month. That's what you get for listening to that asshole, Meldrick," he said.

For his part, Meldrick consoled Window by telling him that life wasn't fair.

Josie placed a call to Window's attorney and asked if the brother would have to pay the child support retroactively. The attorney said Roy would have to make the retroactive payments but that Window would not receive any of the money. "So you mean welfare is collecting *twice*?"

"Yes, we could appeal, but I would advise against it. It's going to cost a lot of dough."

Window used the balance of his Citroën money to pay off his debts and buy new clothes. Ted Frank Page, always appalled by Window's taste, found the new clothes especially bad. "Fucking special ed. Don't fucking *buy* clothes, Window, unless you take me along. Where did you get that shit?"

"At D&R's. What's the matter with these clothes? My ma says they look snazzy."

"Your mother came from the old country, Window. You look like you just hopped off the boat yourself. The Neon Boat."

"Don't talk to me like that," Window said sharply.

"Well, fuck you," Ted Frank Page said.

"Hey," Meldrick said, "it's his money, his clothes."

"So how much did you save after all of this shit? Anything?" Page asked.

"In the long run, he saves fourteen thousand," Josie said. "Next time you want a date, Window, go to church. Meet a nice girl. A girl with virtues."

"I can't go to the damn church without falling asleep," Window said, "and all the church girls are ugly. Plus, *Ted Frank Page*, I didn't do it for the money! I just wanted to know if the baby was mine. If it was mine,

I pay gladly. Now in my heart I'm satisfied." Window looked at Page squarely and Ted Frank Page returned the look.

"Well good for you, Window. I am sorry I said that. Please accept my humble apology."

"And no more special ed jokes!" Window said.

"I'm going to shut my mouth," Page said.

The head custodian said, "Window has become a man. He's making inroads. Now let's go scrub that lower hall." It was Christmas break and the custodians were all working the day shift. The school was quiet and they had taken an hour-long break, which was now becoming oppressively long.

Window said, "I'm tired of being the mop jockey."

"Window runs the scrubber," Page said. "I'll sling the mops."

The custodial crew set out the yellow caution signs in the lower hallway and without a word, each picked out a task. One laid down the stripper solution. Another took the doodlebug and began edging the sides of the hall. Yet another set up the wet vac while Window plugged in the scrubber, looked to his left and right to see that everyone was in position and then squeezed the power trigger. The black stripping pad was dry, causing the scrubber to lurch violently for a few seconds. Window had to muscle the big machine until it picked up enough water and then began to sing as it glided effortlessly over the scuffed tile. When Ray turned on a country/western station on the radio, Window said, "Turn off that hillbilly shit and play some rock and roll." As the designated operator of the scrubber, Window had that right since at East High, the designated operator of the scrubber was janitor king of the day.

Mosquitoes

I GUESS THE REASON I can't relate to Clendon:...he almost cracked up getting his Ph.D., got weird, and took off to Vermont, bought a Volvo, and married this cool slim blonde with long legs, nine thousand dollars' worth of capped teeth and a heart colder than the dark side of the moon. Victoria. Spoiled single child, rich and indulged. Sarah Lawrence degree in art history. Clothes are DKNY. She drives a BMW and Clendon *worships* her and all the time I was there I saw her make him squirm and humiliate him. I'm thinking he's getting some kind of masochistic thrill out of this. There was something *in that* that has estranged us as brothers and has made us like Cain and Abel. I mean, I can't identify with somebody who won't fight back. I can't work up any sympathy for him.

"The kids," he says. "You have to think of the kids."

Or: "A divorce would leave a psychic scar."

Clendon teaches at Middlebury College in Vermont. Middlebury is really a beautiful place but it's that old bullshit: Greenpeace. You know, I don't want to overgeneralize but it's a style I find hard to take. They really let you have it up there. Throw it right in your face. Self-righteous do-gooders. I mean, I think we ought to save the dolphins, too. Torpedo those Japanese fishing boats if they don't lay off! But spare me the folksingers!

Anyhow, I went out to see Clendon one summer expecting the weather to be cool, praying that it would be cool that summer, and it was atypically hot and there was some kind of mosquito convocation going on there — every mosquito in the world flew into Vermont that summer. Historically mosquitoes are among the deadliest enemies of man. Mosquitoes caused the downfall of ancient civilizations around the Mediterranean Sea — sleeping sickness, elephantiasis, dengue, malaria. Plus you know about all of that yellow-fever jive when we dug the Panama Canal, right?

Well, great big monster mosquitoes from Siberia, the size of sparrows, made the trip to Vermont that summer, and there were little ones that were, in a way, worse because they had no fear of the blazing sun, thrived under it, and would attack at high noon like Mirage fighter jets. *Aedis aegypti* if you want to get technical. *Aedis aegypti* is completely dependent on human blood and will attack in the full light of day, like Dracula with sunglasses. I mean, they wouldn't light on you and make preliminary moves to give you warning before they injected their hypo-dermic proboscis into your skin. They were like flying piranhas; they would practically bite you on the wing.

You couldn't buy, beg, or steal insect repellent. There was a run on it. It was more precious than a rhinoceros horn in an Asian bazaar. Clendon was so preoccupied with his marital problems that he scarcely noticed the mosquitoes, but they were all I could think of. There are nearly two thousand species of them and I think most blew in for the big convocation. Mosquito Woodstock.

I hated to watch my brother grovel, the children irritated me, and so I holed up in the guest bedroom with the air conditioner on full blast and a satchel full of medical journals. Victoria had the gall to insist I con-fine my cigarette smoking to the bedroom. "What kind of doctor has a two-pack-a-day cigarette habit?" she says.

"Smoking is good for you; it makes your heart merry," I say.

"Oh bullshit," she says. "It's such a juvenile habit."

If you were my wife, I thought, *you would be a splat on the wall.*

Clendon had given me a number of literary magazines to read includ-ing stories of his own. I'm a reader, I read them but it was always some boring crap about a forty-five-year-old upper-level executive in boat shoes driving around Cape Cod *in a Volvo*. I mean you actually do finish some of them and admit that "technically" they were pretty good but I'd rather go to back-to-back *operas* than read another story like that. It was with relief that I returned to the medical journals.

Boy, that Victoria was a cool one! Chilly. Even with the kids. I made a few points when obese little Jason fell and lacerated his knee. I numbed the knee with lidocaine, debrided the cut, and did a first-class job of suturing the wound. All jokes. No tears. The kids thought Uncle Bob or *Doctor* Bob was great and loved it when I took them out in the Jag V-12 convertible and drove them on the swervy back roads, cutting swaths through the dark clouds of mosquitoes. Victoria didn't like the Jaguar. It was too ostentatious, too L.A., for her blue-blood sensibilities but, hey! I worked like hell to buy that car. And second gear in a V-12 Jag has got more juice than anything short of an Apollo 10. *Va-rrroom!*

What really put a frost on the visit was the night I took the kids out to see *The Exorcist III* and they came home to vomit hot dogs and ice cream and then Jason woke up the whole house with a screaming nightmare. The "Bonecrusher" had been after him. "There, there, baby, Mommy's here and everything is going to be just fine." Fucking little Jason tells Victoria that Uncle Bob punched the V-12 up to 130 m.p.h. and the telephone poles were looking like a picket fence. Fucking little Jason tells Victoria how we fishtailed onto a gravel road, spun around, knocked over a mailbox, and blew out a rear tire.

I swore the little bastard to secrecy!

In the morning Clendon told me he knew Vickie was having an affair and while he hated her for it, it excited him to think of her making love to another man. Clendon told me he was dicking some of his students and that he couldn't get it up for Victoria. I said, "Leave that nasty bitch. I can't work up any sympathy for you, she's runnin' you, man."

"I don't know what to do. You're right. I'm torn. I feel like Hamlet. Good God, what are you doing?"

"What?"

"Put out that cigarette."

"Are you shittin' me? What the fuck is the matter with you?"

"Passive smoke, little brother. The kids. And Jesus! Don't take them out in that goddamn toy anymore either. A hundred and thirty miles an hour?"

"It's not a toy, big brother, it's pure pussy. You're scared shitless, aren't you?" I flipped him the keys to my Jaguar. "Go take it for a ride, motherfucker. Live a little. Go on, drive it; it's good therapy. Primal Scream Therapy."

Clendon went out into the driveway and turned the engine over. He revved the motor and popped the clutch, spinning rubber out into the street. I spotted his reflection in the rearview mirror frozen in the rictus of fear. Not a good sign, I thought. How Clendon could *not* find satisfaction from the rich *thrrraaaghh!* of the dual exhaust system baffled me. It was that sound that made the car worth every bit of the $80-some thousand. I could have thrown the money into a Keogh account but, hey! it was the sound of pure balls.

In a moment the kitchen door opened and Victoria walked in with a tanned young man in his late twenties; both were wearing tennis clothes. I was caught in the act of lighting another cigarette. Victoria introduced me to the young man, Larry, a tennis pro, and exchanged an intimate look with him before she ran upstairs to change. If they thought they were fooling me, and I think they did, they were both dead wrong.

I offered Larry a cigarette and he declined in that particularly annoying Middlebury fashion so I said, "If you weren't such a goddamn faggot, I'd bet you were screwing that bitch."

He began to puff up and I said, "Don't even think about it, motherfucker."

When Victoria came down five minutes later, showered and in fresh sweats, if she missed Larry or was puzzled by his taking leave, she didn't show it, didn't miss a beat, but remained pleasantly aloof and began to whip together a Caesar salad for supper. I was in the mood to tear her head off. Maybe she knew that.

Dinner was consumed with stiff formality, to my thinking, sea trout on a bed of lentils with a coconut crème caramel for dessert, espresso and brandy. Clendon took the edge off things when he spoke of

Victoria's forthcoming show that he had arranged, using his influence with the college art department. Victoria began to talk of her paintings, which were done in the expressionist style. "I like the realists," I said. "What I really like is that trompe l'oeil style. And I always thought Andy Warhol was totally insane and crazy. Have you ever gotten totally insane and crazy, Jason? When your daddy was little, he used to act that way. Are you ever like that, dude?"

"Yeah," Jason said shyly.

"Warhol," Victoria said pompously, "the early Warhol, before he was shot — "

"Where would America be without Andy Warhol?" I said. "He put his stamp on American culture. Think about it, Vickie. He invented superstars and all of that shit. It didn't quit with the Tomato Soup Can. Andy Warhol was a genius. He — what he had, was this great radio antenna. Picked up on all of the cosmic vibrations. He just did it, I don't think he knew the half of it. He was one of those idiot savants, I'm thinking. Your paintings are too goddamn vague, Vick. I can't get a reading on them."

After dinner, Jason and I went into Victoria's studio and painted cans of Campbell's Mushroom Soup. Made a super mess. Pissed her off royally.

In the morning I sat in on a session of Clendon's creative writing class. It didn't take any real brainpower to figure out who his protégé was — a bright bohemian type in black leotards and a turtleneck. She read from a novel in progress in a confident low and sexy voice. She couldn't write and she wasn't really pretty. What she had going for her was the bloom of youth and a headful of platinum blond hair.

She appeared at Victoria's art showing, which was sparsely attended by the faculty, public, and student body. I stuck it through to the bitter end wondering if Larry, from the tennis club, would make an appearance, and the deeper I got into the white wine, the more I hoped he would. He did not. I met a number of Clendon's colleagues that night and began to understand why he had nearly broken down getting his Ph.D. I remembered people like that from medical school. The English faculty had its med school counterparts — the bunch that went into psychiatric residencies. It was those types, the counterpart of those types that considered surgeons to be assholes, but if I have an assholish aspect

I can only say — you better go out and get whatever you want on this trip, because this is *the* trip, the only trip.

On the second night of the showing I stayed at home and babysat the kids. The next morning Clendon told me there had been a light turnout. Then he asked me quite bluntly if I could wrap up the visit and leave. Victoria considered me an "invader," he said. My presence was provoking migraine headaches. She was up in bed now, wasted with a headache because of me.

"The *invader*. It's your fucking house, man. And you're telling me to go?"

"I don't remember — you never had such a filthy mouth. Is that how they talk in the hospital?"

"Fucking-A. She's got you pussy-whipped. I never figured you for a Ph.D. in English — "

"It's her house. Her parents' money."

"Leave her."

"Right, live in a trailer court. Plastic curtains. Alimony. Child support."

"Well, it will be your trailer. Home sweet home."

"No can do — "

"She looks at you and you wither."

"I can't explain it. I need her."

My blood boiled. I didn't know if I wanted to cock my fist and smash his teeth down his throat or write him a script for some Valium and Elavil.

"Well, fuck it then," I said. "I'm going back to Los Angeles."

I got a little loaded. It was late. The kids were in bed. Clendon was at some sort of university function. I went out into the kitchen to make a sandwich and caught Victoria standing over the sink, her platinum hair pinned up to keep her neck cool. I had startled her and when she turned to me, I realized she wasn't altogether surprised. She was wearing an expensive sheer nightgown and her breasts, just bigger than medium and firm — I mean they were *there* — large erect pinkish-white nipples. They were just absolutely the most beautiful tits in the whole world.

It was a matter of some ambivalence for both of us. Neither of us liked the other. Yet the physical attraction right then and there was incredible. After I kissed her, she led me into the bedroom. She said, "Oh, my God!"

I really gave it to her. I really let her have it.

You take the gorilla...I suppose there are probably only about forty of them left on the planet, if that many. Point of fact: the reason the gorilla has such a large brain is not because he has to figure out where to find food or how to make a little nest in the grass. In Gorilla Country food is plentiful; enemies, apart from man, are nonexistent. To find food, make the nest, and then migrate along to the next spot, the gorilla needs a brain the size of a Rice Krispie.

The *reason* the gorilla has such a large brain and the reason it takes so long for the young to mature and develop is because in a gorilla society, in addition to understanding the various nuances of their vocal utterances, they are masters of reading body language. They are skilled psychologists and, in their roughshod way, they are far more diplomatic than a human can ever think of becoming.

In a gorilla troop there is no violence. Everyone gets along. There's a pecking order, true, but everyone has his place and accepts it. Gorillas are happy. They don't need New Balance tennis shoes, or VCRs or Jaguar V-12 convertibles. They don't need DKNY. They don't need crack cocaine. They don't need to write clever stories about some guy driving around Cape Cod with angst. You give a gorilla a banana and a piece of nookie and you've got a happy gorilla; you've got a gorilla that has no desire to commit rape or Murder One, or to paint the Sistine Chapel, or run for president, win a Nobel Prize — any of that. Gorillas don't war upon one another or torture one another. It never happens.

A friend of mine in the ER told me that the animal consciousness is one of the here-and-now and that the human being can approximate it by drinking five martinis while soaking in a hot tub. A Saturday evening condition, if then. The rest of the time...well, just read the newspapers and you'll know what I mean. Human behavior, ninety-eight percent of it, is an abomination.

❋   ❋   ❋

The morning after I screwed Victoria, everyone at the breakfast table *knew*. Humans can read body language, skin color, flushed cheeks, eye pupil size, heads hung in shame, etc., just as well as any gorilla can.

I finished my platter of buttermilk pancakes topped with pure maple syrup and then packed up my valise, gunned the V-12 Jaguar, and roared out of Clendon's life forever. I couldn't wait to get back to the Emergency Room at Valley General in Los Angeles, California, where I practice as a trauma surgeon and save human lives by the score, although I had to drive the Jaguar very carefully. The wheel alignment had been thrown out when I blew the tire and the frame shuddered behind all of that V-12 power.

I knew that either Clendon would become so pissed that he would leave that nasty-ass bitch or he would weasel under and suffer worse than that alienated hero in the Russian novel *Crime and Punishment*, Clendon's favorite character of all time. I believe the dude's name is Raskolnikov.

How Clendon ever married that pit viper is a mystery to me. In that summer of the mosquitoes, I saw that he had capitulated completely...for a Volvo, two overweight kids with "blah" for personalities, and a neurotic wife who took separate vacations to Florence, Italy, to look at artwork. Victoria was a good fuck but I kept thinking of those awful paintings she signed with her maiden name and how she made Clendon use his influence with the art department so she could have that pathetic show over there at Middlebury College.

Beyond that, I knew she'd make him think it was his fault that she screwed the young guy at the tennis club, among others, me included.

Well, Clendon is not the world's first cuckold, and he won't be the last. When I saw her turn around from the sink in that sheer nightie with those breasts made in Heaven, those long slim legs, etc., I can understand what must have happened to my big brother and can see how he got suckered in. Romantic love. Romeo and Juliet. No-fucking-body can look six months down the road. It just doesn't last. How come they can't see it? Why can't they anticipate?

Thus the two fat kids, both null and void. It was plain to see they aren't Clendon's. But he can't leave now ("the kids, the psychic scar of divorce proceedings, plastic curtains in the trailer court"). Hey! I tried to do him a favor.

I remember once when we were in high school and I went into a clothing store with him to buy a new suit and fell under the salesman's spell and in no time I had six hundred dollars' worth of garish clothes piled on the sales counter — clothes that were the antithesis of me, horrible clothes. Clendon dragged me outside into the sunlight. "Have you lost your mind?" he said. "You're going to look like a pimp in all of that shit!" Laughing, we ran down the street out of that salesman's life for all time.

I hope by screwing Victoria I snapped him out of his trance. If not, then I've only made things worse.

I had to do something. I had to try.

According to Darwin the species wants to go on and on, forever and forever, but we are diluting and degrading the species by letting the weaklings live. I am guilty of this more than anyone. I took the Hippocratic oath and vowed to patch up junkies, prostitutes, and violent criminals and send them back out on the streets to wreak more havoc and mayhem on themselves and on others. I try not to think of that. I like to hope for the best.

I was just reading about the real Robinson Crusoe. He was this troublemaker that got kicked out of his hometown in Scotland and became a sailor in the Royal Navy and then on a trip off the coast of Chile, he started bitching about the ship and the conditions aboard and told the captain he wanted off and so they rowed him ashore with his sea chest, dropped him off, returned to the ship, and when they pulled up the dinghy and got ready to take off, Robinson Crusoe changed his mind and called to the captain, "I didn't mean it. I'm sorry!"

The captain called back, "That's too goddamn bad! Fuck you!"

And off they went. Robinson Crusoe spent three months on the beach trying to stay awake, thinking that it had all been a bad dream and that they would come back for him. He lived on king crabs. Funny he didn't develop gout or blow out his kidneys on that rich and monotonous diet.

When it dawned on Crusoe that they weren't going to come back, he moved inland and made a hut for himself. He became self-sufficient and industrious out of necessity, and learned to take a special pleasure in doing things patiently and well. There were goats on the island, coconuts, pineapples, fish, edible tubers, breadfruit, etc. Also, Crusoe had a splendid view. In a way it was a kind of tropical paradise. By and by Robinson Crusoe captured a number of goats and cut their Achilles' tendons to keep them near his shack. Rats were a problem and often bit his toes to the bone as he slept, but he found some wild cats, stole some kittens, raised them, and trained them to sleep with him and kill the rats. This formerly bitter, angry man was said to have come close to God and learned to love Him. Living on pure foods, breathing fresh air, taking in sunshine and the tranquil sound of the surf, he became more healthy and his sense of hearing and eyesight became remarkably keen.

He became a prime physical specimen. He could run a goat down, pounce on it, and slit its throat with his dirk knife. Once, he jumped on a goat that was feeding on the edge of a thirty-foot precipice obscured by dense brush. They both went over and Crusoe, although he landed on the goat, killing it, was so injured himself that he could not move for three days. When he recovered and went back to his hut, the idea of his old age and inevitable helplessness became an *idée fixe*. Portuguese sailors often stopped at the island for food and water, but to reveal himself to them, he knew, would amount to suicide. If they didn't kill him, they would literally make him a galley slave.

Eventually an English ship laid anchor near his island and he went down to greet them in his beard and goatskins and was rescued. What a tale he had to tell.

The real Robinson Crusoe was quickly disillusioned when he returned to England. After a brief moment of sensational attention, he reverted to his old ways, drinking and making trouble. He lost access to God. Finally, he went off, far off in the country, and lived in a sod hut dreaming of his idyllic days of paradise on his island, where he lived less than six years altogether.

*   *   *

I think human beings are despicable. I am sick of saving their miserable lives. I would like to take a boat and my two German shepherds and go off to a tropical island. If anything happens, I can save my own life, pull my own teeth, perform minor surgery. Before I go, I'd have my appendix removed. I know the medicines I need to take and I can get them. I'm sick of junkies, prostitutes, alcoholic street bums, and killers, but they depress me far less than would, say, a Beverly Hills clientele.

I do love my dogs, however.

I'm scheduled to work the weekend night shift at the Valley General Emergency Room. There's a full moon out. I find that it's kinda hard to find access to God in Valley General's ER, especially on a full-moon weekend.

Dufaye owes me a favor. I'll twist his arm and get him to work my rotation. Tell him I got G.I. pain, fake a fever, and get someone to slice that appendix.

A guy driving around Cape Cod suffering from existential despair! Clendon and his Volvo. Victoria and her tits. Those fat kids and all of that prosperity. It just depressed the hell out of me!

There are lots of uninhabited islands in Fiji. Me and the dogs, we're going to pull a Robinson Crusoe. Cutter's Insect Repellent. I'm going to take a whole case of that shit.

I can't stand mosquitoes.

A White Horse

AD MAGIC HAD one of his epileptic premonitions a split second before the collision, and managed to approximate a tuck-and-roll position just as the truck smashed into the back of the mini tour bus. He was seated in the center of the back row enduring the most horrendous hangover of his life when the crash projected him halfway down the center aisle like a human cannonball. There was a moment of stillness after the accident, and then the bus lurched over to the side of the road. A group of five men and a woman from Bahrain sitting in the center of the bus, themselves somewhat discombobulated but unhurt, got out of their seats to help the peculiar American to his feet.

Ad Magic had a jawbreaker-size horehound lozenge in his cheek when the wreck occurred, and now it was caught at the back of his throat. He attempted to swallow the candy discreetly, lodging it farther into his throat, and when he realized it was too large to swallow he tried to cough it up. He panicked as he began to run out of air, however, and dropped to one knee and choked out a cartoonish series of coughs — "*Kaff, kaff, kaff.*"

He could feel a heat wave beneath his breastbone which radiated up to his face and ears, burning like wildfire as he turned to the Bahrainis with furious gesticulations, indicating that he needed someone to perform the Heimlich maneuver on him. The Bahrainis soon got the gist of his problem and began slapping Ad Magic's back, while he clutched his throat like a man being hanged.

At last one of the Bahrainis socked him mightily on the spine with the side of his fist, and, *ka-zeem!*, the lozenge shot out of Ad Magic's mouth, bounced off the windshield of the bus, and fell into the driver's lap. As Ad Magic began to breathe again, a great laugh exploded among the Bahrainis, who were at once relieved and amused by the absurdity of the entire scene. Ad Magic had spent the better part of a day with these people, and while he was grateful to be breathing, he felt that their laughter was tinged with ridicule and hostility, as had been their whole repertoire of Jerry Lewis hilarity. When they cried mocking insults at the enormous statue of a serene, meditating Buddha in the caves of Elephanta, for instance, they stirred up a thousand and one bats, which came screeching past Ad Magic in such profusion that he was buffeted by their wings and their surprisingly hefty bodies. He slipped in bat guano in an attempt to duck under the flock, falling on his knee and hand. The guano was an inch deep and felt like a cold pudding. Fortunately, one of the Bahrainis had a package of Handi Wipes, and he was able to clean the worst of it off, although the stench persisted, and he could still smell it whenever his hand was in proximity to his face.

The bus, with a blown tire, wheeled onto the shoulder of Marine Drive, one of Bombay's busiest streets. Ad Magic straight-armed the side emergency-exit door and staggered outside. He could breathe well enough, but his throat felt bruised. He shucked off his teal-green cashmere V-neck sweater. It had been madness wearing that. The air outside the bus was humid and suffocating. Ad Magic recognized Chowpatty Beach and realized he was on a peninsula that extended into the Arabian Sea like a finger. He knew that Bombay consisted of a series of islands off the coast of India, and that from this point he was less than a few miles from the Gateway of India, where the tour had originated.

A small boy, about eight or ten — it was hard to tell, partly because he had a shaved head — approached Ad Magic, carrying a rhesus monkey on his shoulder. The monkey, dressed in a dirty red uniform with epaulets, gold piping, and a tiny bellman's cap, began an incomprehensible performance in the art of mime. When it was over, the monkey approached the American and presented its upturned hat to him as a collection cup. Ad Magic began to cough again as he fished in his pockets. He placed a halfdozen rupees in the monkey's cap and tossed his expensive sweater to the boy. "Go ahead," he said. "Take it. It's all yours."

The Bahraini woman had seen the monkey's performance and emitted a shrill, trilling cry. One of the men, who could speak a little English, said facetiously, "Bravo. Excellent monkey."

The tour guide climbed out of the bus and callously questioned the American about his condition. Ad Magic said he was all right, and then she chastised him for giving so much money to the boy. "Not is good," she said with a sneer. Ad Magic walked away from the guide and the Bahrainis, wanting nothing more to do with them. He moved from the road onto the sand of Chowpatty Beach, and when he felt sufficiently separated from them he turned and watched as the guide skillfully led the party of Bahrainis across the whizzing four-lane traffic of Marine Drive and into a decrepit establishment called the New Zealand Café.

There were billboards on either side of the grimy, stuccoed building. One, in English, advertised Gabriel shock absorbers. The other, featuring an apparently famous Indian leading man, who had sort of a Rudolph Valentino look, was in Hindi. It was an advertisement for men's hairdressing. Beyond the café, through the filter of buzzing traffic and the haze of diesel fuel, Ad Magic spotted a cardboard shantytown. The settlement was centered around a crescent-shaped drainage ditch, and people could be seen squatting there, shamelessly relieving themselves, while at the other end of the obscene ditch, women were washing laundry.

Looking into the restaurant, Ad Magic could see one of the Bahrainis clutching his throat and pretending to choke while the rest of the party laughed. Their mouths were opened wide, revealing an abundance of golden inlays. They waved to him and cheered heartily. He wondered why they were so jolly. Why couldn't he be like that?

Out front, the bus driver was quarreling with the driver of the truck that had rear-ended the tour bus. Ad Magic turned away again and walked toward the Arabian Sea, out of the envelope of diesel exhaust into a small, pleasantly pungent pocket of gardenia, and then back into a zone of a truly ghastly odor. The tuna cannery in American Samoa had been bad, but it was nothing compared with these little pockets of smell that were all over Bombay, and what was worse was that you had to be nonchalant about it with your fellow travelers and not complain, for no one else seemed to notice it. Ad Magic was suddenly overcome by a sense of unreality — he wondered if he had been to American Samoa at all, or if it had been a dream, and, indeed, if the Bombay of the here and now was a dream.

He surveyed the long, deserted stretch of beach, and spotted a small white horse standing forlornly in the surf. As he moved closer to the horse he saw that it was old and swaybacked, covered with oozing sores, and so shrunken that its ribs protruded and its teeth seemed overly large. The horse was having a hard time staying on its feet, and Ad Magic watched it reel. There were plenty of scenes of poverty and desolation in India, but this was the most abject and miserable sight he had ever laid eyes on. Clearly, the horse was going to die — possibly within the hour. Had it been meant to die so completely alone — abandoned? It occurred to Ad Magic that it was the suffering of a horse that had finally driven Friedrich Nietzsche into an irretrievable insanity in the month of January 1889.

Good God! He had done it again. He had abandoned his seizure meds, flipped out, and somehow gotten on a plane, this time bound for India. He frantically searched his pockets for a passport. There was none. He had no wallet, either — only an enormously fat roll of American hundred-dollar bills, some loose smaller bills mixed with Indian currency, and a ball of heavy change that caused his pocket to bulge. He didn't even know his own name; he knew only "Ad Magic," but as he sorted out the loose cash he discovered a room key from the Taj Inter-Continental. "Suite 7" was imprinted on the tag, and Ad Magic knew that the secret to his identity would be found there, although he was in no particular hurry to return to the hotel. Somehow he felt that it would be better not to know, at least not yet.

His throat continued to bother him. As he rifled through his pockets, he found a pack of Marlboro cigarettes and a beautiful gold lighter. He extracted a cigarette and lit it. The boy with the monkey appeared at his side and bummed a smoke. Ad Magic lit it for him, and watched the boy pass the cigarette to the monkey, who held it in the fashion of an aristocratic S.S. officer in an old black-and-white Second World War movie. The monkey smoked as though he had a real yen for nicotine, and after this demonstration he presented his little bellman's cap for another tip.

Ad Magic gave him a five-dollar bill and then sat down on a small, rusting Ferris wheel, looking out at the horse again. He took a drag off his cigarette, and on his wrist he noticed a stainless-steel Med-Alert bracelet and a solid-gold Rolex. He examined them both with curiosity, as if he had never seen them before. The little bracelet was inscribed with the word "Epilepsy."

Epilepsy. Ad Magic did not have epilepsy in the classic sense, with full-blown, convulsive seizures. He was a temporal-lobe epileptic. He remembered this now. He had suffered an epileptic fugue. He still wasn't sure what his name was, where he lived, whether he was married, whether he had children, or much else, but he did know himself to be an advertising man. That, and an epileptic. He quite clearly remembered the voice of his doctor, the large, high-ceilinged consulting room trimmed in dark oak, a door with a frosted-glass window, and a hands-clasped-in-prayer statue on the doctor's desk. Ad Magic remembered spending hours from early adolescence into maturity in that room. He remembered majestic oak trees, crisp autumn afternoons, the smell of burning leaves, and the palatial brownstone estates of a Midwestern city, but he could not identify the city, could not picture the doctor or remember his name. He did know the man had been more than a doctor to him — he had been a good friend as well, a man whom Ad Magic loved very much. He suspected that the doctor was now dead, but he distinctly remembered something the doctor had told him about his condition. "These spells you have, where you go gadding about the world — they could be a form of epileptic fugue, or you could be suffering from the classical form of global amnesia, which is so often depicted on television soap operas. They are very common in television melodrama but almost unheard of in real life. But so, too, are psychomotor fugues, which are a kind of status epilepticus of the left temporal lobe."

Ad Magic didn't know who he was or how he had come to India. He only knew that there were times when he became so depressed and irritable and finally so raving mad that he had to throw his medication away, bolt out, and intoxicate himself or in some way extinguish his consciousness. He felt this way now. He felt a loathing for everything on the face of the earth, including himself — but the suffering of this white horse was something he could not abide. It was a relief, suddenly, to have something other than himself and his hangover on which to fix his attention.

He summoned the boy, who was now proudly wearing the cashmere sweater, and took him and the monkey across the road to the New Zealand Café. The air inside was laden with cooking grease and cigarette smoke, but a pair of ceiling fans beat through the haze like inverted helicopters. A waiter in a dingy white jacket was serving tea and a plate of sticky cookies to the Bahrainis. From the kitchen, a radio blared a tinny version of "Limehouse Blues." Ad Magic pulled a chair up next to the tour guide and said, "Ask the boy who that horse on the beach belongs to."

The guide was a good-looking woman in her late thirties, who fluctuated mercurially between obsequiousness and sullen aggression. She wore an orange sari that seemed immaculately clean. Ad Magic wondered how she managed that, after the boat trip to Elephanta and the long Bombay city tour. He watched her interrogate the boy. Then she turned to Ad Magic and said, "Horse belongs to circus man, and cannot work anymore. Wandering horse now. Free to come and go."

Ad Magic asked the guide whether she could make a phone call and summon a veterinarian.

"Veterinarian?" she said, reacting to the word bitterly, as if he had made an indecent request.

"You're right. That's silly, isn't it. There must not be any veterinarians, or, if any, relatively few on call, even in such a sophisticated city as Bombay — and you've been through a long day, and now the bus has been wrecked. Forgive me. I'm not feeling very well today. Let me ask you. Can you tell me at which hotel I am staying?"

"The Taj," she said.

"Right, the Taj. That's what I thought." Ad Magic placed a half-dozen American ten-dollar bills on the table. "Please accept this little gratuity. You've been marvelous. Now, I wonder if you can call a *real* doctor. Tell him I will make it truly worth his while. The boy and I will wait for him across the road, on the beach. I'll get back to the hotel on my own. It is the Taj, isn't it?" The woman nodded.

Ad Magic and the boy, with the monkey on his shoulder, crossed the road again and sat on a pair of broken merry-go-round horses that were detached from an abandoned carousel. Next to the carousel was the small Ferris wheel, contrived to be powered by a horse or mule rather than a motor. Nearby was a ticket kiosk decorated with elephant-men and monkey-men painted in brilliant, bubblegum colors. The carnival was defunct and depressing. Ad Magic remembered bright lights — a carnival of his childhood, before he had picked up on the tawdriness of carnivals and saw only the enchanting splendor of them. He couldn't have been more than four. He was sitting in a red miniature car when he saw one of a different color — yellow — that he liked better. Impulsively, he scrambled for the better car. Just as he unbuckled his seat belt and was halfway out of the red one, the ride began and he fell, catching his arm under the car, wrenching and skinning his elbow, and bashing his face against the little vehicle's fake door. Suddenly he was plucked free by a man in a felt hat and a raincoat, who smelled pleasantly of aftershave. His father? A stranger? He wasn't sure; there was no face, as there had been no face on the doctor.

He searched his pockets for his cigarettes and discovered a small, flat, green-and-black tin of Powell's Headache Tablets. He took two of these, dry-swallowed them, and then lit up another cigarette. He spotted an empty tour bus pulling up alongside the damaged bus he had arrived in, and from his seat on the rusting pony Ad Magic watched his party emerge from the New Zealand Café, board the new bus, and take off. There was no goodbye wave, even from the friendly Bahrainis. Again he tried to recover his name and city of origin, but it was hopeless. At least he had come to Bombay rather than Lusaka, or Lima, or Rangoon, or Zanzibar. He remembered coming into Zanzibar on a steamer, seasick — the odor of the spices was so powerful he could smell it twenty miles offshore. He remembered feeling instantly well when the boat reached the harbor, and how the inhabitants of the city were outside — it was midnight — marveling at the recently installed streetlights. An Australian tourist told him that Zanzibar was the last place in the world to get streetlights and that when the bulbs burned out the streetlights would never glow again unless Swiss workers were imported to come in and change them. "The bloody buggers can't even change a light bulb," the Australian said. "It isn't in their makeup." Ad Magic's recollection of Zanzibar was like an Alice-in-Wonderland hallucination. It seemed that he had remained stranded there for weeks, almost penniless, living on bread and oranges.

A faded, light-green Mercedes with a broken rear spring came bouncing too fast across the beach and skidded, sliding sideways as it stopped near the carousel. An elderly European man wearing a white coat over a dirty tropical suit stepped out of the car and stretched. He had a head of unkempt, wiry white hair in the style of Albert Einstein. He brushed it back with his hand and opened the back door of the car. A magnificent boxer dog hopped out and followed the old man over to Ad Magic and the boy.

"Are you a doctor?"

"I am a doctor, yes. You were in a car accident, jah?"

"I was, but it's nothing. I called about the horse. I wondered if you could do something about the horse. What is wrong with that animal?"

The doctor looked out at the sea, lifting his hands to shield his eyes from the afternoon sun. "Probably he has been drinking saltwater in desperation. He will die, very soon."

Ad Magic said, "I will give you five hundred American dollars if you can save the horse."

The doctor said, "I can send him to seventh heaven with one shot. Haff him dragged away. Fifty dollars for the whole shebang."

"Look, I don't want to wrangle. If you can save the horse, I will pay you a thousand dollars."

The doctor opened the trunk of the Mercedes and removed a piece of rope. He sent the boy down to the edge of the water and had him lead the horse up onto the dry sand while he backed the car another fifty feet down the beach, where the sand became too loose and he had to stop. Then he got out of the car and removed his medical bag from the back, setting it on the hood. He quickly looked the horse over. "Malnutrition, dehydration, fever." He opened the horse's lips. "Ah! He has infected tooth. This is very bad...."

"What about all the sores? Why does he have so many sores?"

"Quick," the doctor said. "In my trunk I have glucose *und* water. We haff to getting in fluids."

Ad Magic carried two pint-size bottles of glucose and sterile-water solution over to the horse and then stood holding them as the doctor ran drip lines into large veins in the horse's neck. Ad Magic watched the bottles slowly begin to drain as the doctor put on a pair of rubber gloves and began to scrub the sores on the horse's body with a stiff brush and a kind of iodine solution, making a rough, sandpaper sound.

"Doesn't that hurt?"

"Animals don't experience pain in the same fashion humans," the doctor said, with some irritation. "Pain for humans is memories, anticipation, imagination — "

"I don't care about that. What you're doing has got to hurt."

The doctor came around from behind the horse. "How much does he weigh? Unless the liver is bad, I will give him morphine. I am not Superman. I haff not got X-ray vision. Maybe the liver is bad. Parasites. Who knows?" The doctor dug in his bag and removed a large hypodermic syringe. He filled it with morphine and injected it into the horse's shoulder. Then he took the same syringe and filled it with antibiotics and injected these into the horse. After this, he picked up the brush and again began working on the large, putrescent sores on the horse's skin. Ad Magic's arms began to hurt from holding the bottles of liquid.

The doctor looked at him. "You are an American? Jah? Who was scratched your face *und* black eye?"

"Huh? Oh, that," Ad Magic said. "I forgot that. Last night, I gave some money to this street person. A woman with eleven kids. I gave her some money as they were laying down a cloth to sleep on the street — "

"Yes?"

"Well, after I gave her the money — these men had seen me pass it to her, and they took it away from her. Slapped her around. I hit one of them, knocked him down, but there were so many of them. I just couldn't fight them all. They tried to steal my watch. I got drunk — or I was drunk. I can't remember exactly." Ad Magic leaned over and looked at his face in the side mirror of the Mercedes. He did have an incredible black eye. No wonder the tour party found him peculiar.

The doctor took the glucose bottles from Ad Magic and propped them on the inside of the rear door, rolling up the window until they were upright and secure. "In my bag is green bottle. Take two *und* lie down in the back seat." As Ad Magic rummaged in the bag, the doctor came up alongside him and grabbed his wrist. He examined the little stainless-steel bracelet.

"Epilepsy," the doctor said. "Mmm." He presented Ad Magic with a little flask of gin. "Swallow this *und* lie down," he said. "Horse will take time."

It was dark when Ad Magic came to. The boxer dog was standing over him, sniffing his face. Ad Magic rolled over and abruptly jerked himself upright. A number of oily torches had been lit, and there were fires in metal barrels as well as driftwood fires burning all up and down the shore, which was now teeming with activity. There were hundreds of people roaming the beach, and a brisk breeze blowing off the water offered a variety of smells: the smell of sewage was replaced by the pleasant aroma of gardenia, followed by the odor of bitter orange, of vanilla, of cooked curry, of charcoal, of diesel, and then again of sewage or saltwater, or of the ancient leather seats of the Mercedes. The boxer, openmouthed, panted in Ad Magic's face, and from her mouth there was no odor at all.

Ad Magic pulled himself out of the car and took in the scene. The sights and smells and noises were uncommonly rich. There were roving bands of musicians, dancers, acrobats, food vendors, boys selling hashish. There were holy people, fakirs, snake charmers, more boys with trained monkeys. Ad Magic's own monkey boy watched him leaning against the Mercedes, his eyes roving back and forth between the Rolex and the doctor.

"I can't believe how wonderful I feel," Ad Magic said. "What was that pill you gave me?"

"Just a little something," the doctor said, crouching in the sand as he looked through his black doctor's bag. Lined up by the horse's feet there were a dozen empty glucose bottles and an enormous black tooth — a molar — in addition to several lesser teeth, long yellow ones.

"Abscess tooth. Very bad," the doctor said. "Pus all over everything when I pull it. Horse falling down, goes into shock. I'm having to give him epinephrine. All better now. Then sand in the sores. Clean them all over twice times."

"Is the horse going to be okay?"

"He is looking much better, don't you think? Almost frisky, don't you think?"

"Yes, much better. Much, much better."

"Maybe he will live. It's touch and go."

The boxer dog presented Ad Magic with a piece of driftwood and began a game of tug-of-war. Soon the two were running around the beach and down to the sea. As the small breakers washed over Ad Magic's feet, he noticed human excrement in the water and quickly backed away. He looked out at the sea and took in the sight of fishing dhows, backlit by the moon and glowing with tiny amber lights of their own. The boats were making their way — where? The dog tugged at his pant leg, ragging him, and soon she and Ad Magic were roughhousing — chasing each other, rolling in the sand, wrestling. Then Ad Magic was on his feet, jogging down the beach with the dog beside him. Faster and faster they ran until he was running as fast as he could for the sheer joy of it; he had never felt so good — he ran without getting tired, and it seemed that he never would get tired. Wait a minute. He was a smoker. Or was he? He was running effortlessly, like a trained runner, until at last he did begin to tire a little and sweat. So he and the dog plunged into the sea; he disregarded the filth of it and began to swim out into the surf, and the dog swam with him until they were very far out in the warm water. Then they let the waves carry them back in. Ad Magic walked easily in the sand back to the car and the horse, and when he got to the horse he embraced it and rubbed his face against its neck. "Oh, God, thank you," he said.

"You are okay now?" the doctor said.

"Yes," Ad Magic said. "I think so."

"What is 'ad magic'? You were saying, 'ad magic.' What is that?"

"Oh, that. I am an ad writer, and sometimes I feel magic. I tap into a kind of magic. It's hard to explain."

Ad Magic reached into his pocket and peeled off ten hundred-dollar bills. The roll was so tight that only the outer bills were wet. He handed the money to the doctor. He felt for his cigarettes and found them ruined. His tin of Powell's Headache Tablets was also contaminated with seawater. Ad Magic studied the container for a moment. He said, "Listen to this — ad magic. 'It was a hot day in tough California traffic when a Los Angeles red light made time stand still and gave me a headache like there was no tomorrow. I took two of Powell's Headache Tablets and just like that — beep, beep, toot toot — I was ready to roll again.' Fifty words. That's my magic. It's not that good right now. I'm just getting a little. Just a little is getting through — "

"I see, advertising writer."

"How's this? 'Second-class passage in a Third World railroad car, hotter than the Black Hole of Calcutta, gave me a first-class headache. I traded my Swiss Army knife for a couple of Powell's Headache Tablets. Home or halfway around the globe, Powell's is my first choice for headache relief.' It's not that hot, but that's how they come, from out of nowhere."

"H'okay; you are a hausfrau shopping at Christmas und very busy und a bik hurry — Powell's Tablets. Fifty words."

" 'The day, Christmas Eve; fifteen minutes to midnight; the place, Fox Valley Shopping Center, Aurora, Illinois; the headache, a procrastination special — on a scale of ten, ten. The solution: Powell's Tablets. The happy ending, gaily wrapped presents under a festive tree, a jolly ho-ho, and a merry Christmas to all.' "

"Ad magic. Making money for this?"

"Yes. Making money. I think so. Will the horse live? You see, if the horse lives, then I have my magic. That is God's promise to me. I can do even better for Powell's Tablets. I can do much better, and if the horse lives I will have my magic. How old is the horse?"

"At first I am thinking he is older. Maybe he is twenty years — "

"How long can this horse live? Given the best care?"

"With good care, a long life. Thirty-five years."

Ad Magic peeled five hundred-dollar bills off his roll. "I want you to send this horse on a vacation. I want him to have the best food. If he wants other horses to play with, get them for him. I want this horse to have a grassy field. Do horses like music? I heard that once. Get a radio that plays music. I want the horse to have good accommodations. I want you to be the doctor for this horse and get the best people to take care of this horse. What were those pills you gave me? *I feel fantastic!* Is there some way we can ship this horse back to the States? I'll look into it. Can you drive me to the Taj? This is so crazy — I don't even know my name, but I've got a room key. Tell the boy to watch the horse until I get back. Do you have a business card? Here's what we'll do. I've got it. I've got it now. You stay with the horse. I'll take your car. I've been here before. I know Bombay. I'll take the car back. I don't want you to leave the horse. I don't want anything to happen to this horse. When I get home, you send me a picture of the horse. Stand next to the horse with a copy of the *International Herald Tribune*. When I see that the horse is okay, that his health is flourishing, and I see that the date on the paper is current, I will send you six hundred dollars every month. Will that be enough? Like if this horse needs an air-conditioned stall, I want him to have it. Whatever — TV, rock videos, a pool, anything his little horsy heart desires."

"It can be done."

"Excellent. Look, where did you get this great dog? Will you sell me this dog?"

"For no money," the doctor said.

"C'mon, doctor, I love this dog."

"Anyhow, you cannot take her to America."

"Okay," Ad Magic said. "It was just a thought. You're looking at me funny. I know what you're thinking. You don't trust me with the car. Send the boy to flag a cab. I've got to get back to the States. You know those harnesses Seeing Eye dogs wear? I could wear sunglasses and take the dog back. A white cane. Just let me borrow the dog for a while."

"Mr. Man. She is my best friend. I'm not selling. Not borrowing."

"Okay, okay then. But take care of the horse. I'll send the money. It's a generous amount." Ad Magic reached into his pocket and withdrew his wad of cash, peeling off a few more bills. "See that this kid gets taken care of, okay? Send him to school. C'mon, doctor, don't look at me like that — it's only advertising money. I don't have to *work* for it. *Now I saw when the Lamb opened one of the seven seals, and I heard one of the four living creatures say, as with a voice of thunder, Come! And I saw and behold, a white horse, and its rider had a bow; and a crown was given to him, and he went out conquering and to conquer.*"

When a black-and-yellow Ambassador taxi honked from Marine Drive, Ad Magic gave the horse a final embrace. "Heigh-o, Silver, and *adios amigos,*" he said as he hopped into the cab, brandishing a handful of cash, telling the driver to step on it.

Ad Magic gave the driver a hundred dollars for an eighty-cent cab ride and rushed through the lobby of the Taj Inter-Continental, up to his grand suite in the old part of the hotel. He showered, and after toweling himself off he saw his wallet and passport on the bureau. He cautiously opened the wallet, assiduously avoiding his driver's license. The wallet was heavy with credit cards and cash. In it he saw a picture of an attractive blond woman and two children. At that moment he knew his name, knew his wife of fifteen years, knew his children, and knew himself. He threw the wallet down, and began scribbling on a yellow legal pad. There was so much to get down and his mind was racing out of control. The magic was getting through. He was developing advertising concepts, enough for a year. He phoned the desk and had a porter send up a bottle of scotch and a plate of rice curry.

The scotch calmed him some and by dawn he had most of it written down. He dialed the switchboard and placed a call to his wife in Los Angeles.

Cold Snap

S ON OF A BITCH, there's a cold snap and I do this number where I leave all the faucets running because my house, and most houses out here on the West Coast, aren't "real" — they don't have windows that go up and down, or basements (which protect the pipes in a way that a crawl space can't), or sidewalks out in the front with a nice pair of towering oak trees or a couple of elms, which a real house will have, one of those good old Midwest houses. Out here the windows go side to side. You get no basement. No sidewalk and no real trees, just evergreens, and when it gets cold and snows, nobody knows what to do. An inch of snow and they cancel school and the community is paralyzed. "Help me, I'm helpless!" Well, it's cold for a change and I guess that's not so bad, because all the fleas and mosquitoes will freeze, and also because any change is *something,* and maybe it will help snap me out of this bleak post-Africa depression — oh, baby, I'm so depressed — but I wake up at three in the morning and think, *Oh, no, a pipe is gonna bust,* so I run the water and let the faucets drip and I go outside and turn on the outdoor faucets, which are the most vulnerable. Sure enough, they were caking up, and I got to them just in the nick of time, which was good, since in my condition there was no way I could possibly cope with a broken water pipe. I just got back from Africa, where I was playing doctor to the natives, got hammered with a nasty case of malaria, and lost thirty pounds, but it was a manic episode I had that caused Global Aid to send me home. It was my worst attack to date, and on lithium I get such a bad case of psoriasis that I look like alligator man. You can take Tegretol for mania but it once wiped out my white count and almost killed me, so what I like to do when I get all revved up is skin-pop some morphine, which I had with me by the gallon over there and which will keep you calm — and, unlike booze, it's something I can keep under control. Although I must confess I lost my medical license in the States for substance abuse and ended up with Global Aid when the dust settled over that one. God's will, really. Fate. Karma. Whatever. Anyhow, hypomania is a good thing in Africa, a real motivator, and you can do anything you want over there as long as you keep your feet on the ground and don't parade naked on the president's lawn in Nairobi and get expelled (which I did and which will get you expelled; okay, I lied, you can't do *anything* — so sue me). On lithium, while you don't crash so bad, you never get high, either, and all you can do is sit around sucking on Primus beer bottles, bitching about how hot it is when there's so much work to do.

While I'm outside checking my faucets, I look my Oldsmobile over and wonder was it last year I changed the antifreeze? Back in bed, it strikes me that it's been three years, so I go out and run the engine and sit in the car with my teeth chattering — it's thirteen below, geez! And pretty soon the warm air is defrosting the car and I drive over to the hardware section at Safeway and get one of those antifreeze testers with the little balls in it. At four in the morning I'm sitting in my kitchen try-ing to get it out of the plastic jacket, and it comes out in two parts, with the bulb upside down. No doubt some know-nothing Central American put it in upside down for twenty cents an hour in some slave factory. I know he's got problems — fact is, I've been there and could elucidate his problems — but how about me and my damn antifreeze? I mean, too bad about you, buddy, how about me? And I'm trying to jury-rig it when I realize there is a high potential for breaking the glass and cut-ting my thumb, and just as that voice that is me, that is always talking to me, my ego, I guess, tells me, "Be careful, Richard, so you don't cut your thumb" — at that instant, I slice my thumb down to the bone. So the next thing you know I'm driving to the hospital with a towel on my thumb thinking, A minute ago everything was just fine, and now I'm driving myself to the emergency room!

Some other guy comes in with this awful burn because a pressure cooker exploded in his face, and he's got this receding hairline, and you can see the way the skin is peeled back — poached-looking. The guy's going to need a hairpiece for sure. A doctor comes out eating a sandwich, and I hear him tell the nurse to set up an I.V. line and start running some Dilaudid for the guy, which he deserves, considering. I would like some for my thumb, but all I get is Novocain, and my doctor says, "You aren't going to get woozy on me, are you?" I tell him no, I'm not like that, but I have another problem, and he says, "What's that?" and I tell him I can't jack off left-handed. Everybody laughs, because it's the graveyard shift, when that kind of joke is appropriate — even in mixed company. Plus, it's true.

After he stitches me up, I'm in no pain, although I say, "I'll bet this is going to hurt tomorrow," and he says no, he'll give me some pain medication, and I'm thinking, What a great doctor. He's giving me *pain medication*. And while he's in a giving mood I hit him up for some prostate antibiotics because my left testicle feels very heavy.

"Your left testicle feels *heavy*?" he says skeptically.

Yeah, every guy gets it, shit; I tell him my left nut feels like an anvil. I mean, I want to cradle it in my hand when I'm out and about, or rest it on a little silk pillow when I'm stationary. It doesn't really hurt, but I'm very much conscious of having a left testicle, whereas I have teeth and a belly button and a right testicle and I don't even know. I tell him I don't want a finger wave, because I've been through this a thousand times. My prostate is backing up into the seminal vesicles, and if you don't jerk off it builds up and gets worse, and the doctor agrees — that does happen, and he doesn't really want to give me a finger wave, especially when I tell him that a urologist checked it out a couple of months back. He puts on a plastic glove and feels my testicle, pronounces it swollen, and writes a script for antibiotics, after which he tells me to quit drinking coffee. I was going to tell him that I don't jerk off because I'm a sex fiend; I have low sex drive, and it's actually not that much fun. I just do it to keep the prostate empty. Or should I tell him I'm a doctor myself, albeit defrocked, that I just got back from Africa and my nut could be infected with elephantiasis? Highly unlikely, but you never know. But he won't know diddle about tropical medicine — that's my department, and I decide I will just shut my mouth, which is a first for me.

The duty nurse is pretty good-looking, and she contradicts the doctor's orders — gives me a cup of coffee anyhow, plus a roll, and we're sitting there quietly, listening to the other doctor and a nurse fixing the guy with the burned forehead. A little human interaction is taking place and my depression is gone as I begin to feel sorry for the guy with the burn, who is explaining that he was up late with insomnia cooking sweet potatoes when the pressure cooker blew. He was going to candy them with brown sugar and eat them at six in the morning and he's laughing, too, because of the Dilaudid drip. After Linda Ronstadt sings "Just One Look" on the radio, the announcer comes on and says that we've set a record for cold — it's thirteen and a half below at the airport — and I notice that the announcer is happy, too; there's a kind of solidarity that occurs when suffering is inflicted on the community by nature.

My own thing is the Vincent van Gogh effect. I read where he "felt like a million" after he cut off his ear. It only lasted for a couple of days. They always show you the series of four self-portraits that he painted at different times in his life as his mental condition went progressively downhill. Van Gogh One is a realistic-looking pic, but as life goes on and his madness gets worse he paints Van Gogh Four and it looks as though he's been doing some kind of bad LSD, which is how the world had been looking to me until I cut my thumb. It gave me a three-day respite from the blues, and clarity came into my life, and I have to re-mind myself by writing this down that all the bad stuff does pass if you can wait it out. You forget when you're in the middle of it, so during that three-day break I slapped this note on the refrigerator door: "Richard, you are a good and loving person, and all the bad stuff does pass, so re-member that the next time you get down and think that you've always been down and always will be down, since that's paranoia and it gets you nowhere. You're just in one of your Fyodor Dostoyevsky moods — do yourself a favor and forget it!"

I felt so good I actually had the nerve to go out and buy a new set of clothes and see a movie, and then, on the last day before the depression came back, I drove out to Western State and checked my baby sister, Susan, out for a day trip. Susan was always a lot worse than me; she heard voices and pulled I don't know how many suicide attempts until she took my squirrel pistol and put a .22 long-rifle slug through the temple — not really the temple, because at the last minute you always flinch, but forward of the temple, and it was the most perfect lobotomy. I remember hearing the gun pop and how she came into my room (I was home from college for the summer) and said, "Richard, I just shot myself, how come I'm not dead?" Her voice was calm instead of the usual fingernails-on-the-chalkboard voice, the when-she-was-crazy (which was almost always) voice, and I realized later that she was instantly cured, the very moment the bullet zipped through her brain. Everyone said it was such a shame because she was so beautiful, but what good are looks if you are in hell? And she let her looks go at the hospital because she really didn't have a care in the world, but she was still probably the most beautiful patient at Western State. I had a fresh occasion to worry about her on this trip when I saw an attendant rough-handling an old man to stop him from whining, which it did. She'd go along with anything, and she had no advocate except me. And then I almost regretted going out there, in spite of my do-good mood, because Susan wanted to go to the Point Defiance Zoo to see Cindy, the elephant that was on the news after they transferred the attendant who took care of her, for defying orders and actually going into the elephant pen on the sly to be her friend.

There are seven hundred elephants in North American zoos, and although Cindy is an Asian elephant and a female and small, she is still considered the most dangerous elephant in America. Last year alone, three people were killed by elephants in the United States, and this is what Susan had seen and heard on the color television in the ward dayroom, and she's like a child — she wants to go out and see an elephant when it's ten below zero. They originally had Cindy clamped up in a pen tighter than the one they've got John Gotti in down in Marion, Illinois, and I don't remember that the catalogue of Cindy's crimes included human murder. She was just a general troublemaker, and they were beating her with a two-by-four when some animal activist reported it and there was a big scandal that ended with Cindy getting shipped down to the San Diego Zoo; I think there was some kind of escape (don't quote me on that) where Cindy was running around on a golf course in between moves, and then a capture involving tranquilizer darts, and when they couldn't control Cindy in San Diego they shipped her back up here to Tacoma and put her in maximum-security confinement. It was pretty awful. I told Susan that over in India Cindy would have a job hauling logs or something, and there would be an elephant boy to scrub her down at night with a big brush while she lay in the river, and the elephant boy would be with her at all times, her constant companion. Actually, the elephant would be more important than the boy, I told her, and that's how you should handle an elephant in America — import an experienced elephant boy for each one, give the kids a green card, pay them a lot of overtime, and have them stay with the elephants around the clock. You know, quality time. How could you blame Cindy for all the shit she pulled? And in the middle of this, Susan has a tear floating off her cheek and I don't know if it's a tear caused by the cold or if she was touched by Cindy's plight. The reason they sent my sister to the nuthouse was that you could light a fire on the floor in front of her and she would just sit there and watch it burn. When our parents died, I took her to my place in Washington state and hired helpers to look after her, but they would always quit — quit while I was over in the Third World, where it's impossible to do anything. It was like, *Meanwhile, back in the jungle/Meanwhile, back in the States*...Apart from her lack of affect, Susan was always logical and made perfect sense. She was kind of like a Mr. Spock who just didn't give a shit anymore except when it came to childish fun and games. All bundled up, with a scarf over her ears, in her innocence she looked like Eva Marie Saint in *On the Waterfront.*

We drove over to Nordstrom's in the University District and I bought Suz some new threads and then took her to a hair salon where she got this chic haircut, and she was looking so good that I almost regretted it, 'cause if those wacked-out freaks at the hospital weren't hitting on her before they would be now. It was starting to get dark and time to head back when Susan spots the Space Needle from I-5 — she's never been there, so I took her to the top and she wandered outside to the observation deck, where the wind was a walking razor blade at five hundred and eighteen feet, but Susan is grooving on the lights of Seattle and with her homemade lobotomy doesn't experience pain in quite the way a normal person does, and I want her to have a little fun, but I'm freezing out there, especially my thumb, which ached. I didn't want to pop back inside in the sheltered part and leave her out there, though, because she might want to pitch herself over the side. I mean, they've got safety nets, but what if she's still got some vestige of a death wish? We had dinner in the revolving dining room, and people were looking at us funny because of Susan's eating habits, which deteriorate when you live in a nuthouse, but we got through that and went back to my place to watch TV, and after that I was glad to go to sleep — but I couldn't sleep because of my thumb. I was thinking I still hadn't cashed in the script for the pain pills when Susan comes into my bedroom naked and sits down on the edge of the bed.

"Ever since I've been shot, I feel like those animals in the zoo. I want to set them free," she says, in a remarkable display of insight, since that scar in her frontal lobes has got more steel bars than all the prisons of the world, and, as a rule, folks with frontal-lobe damage don't have much insight. I get her to put on her pajamas, and I remember what it used to be like when she stayed at home — you always had to have someone watching her — and I wished I had gotten her back to the hospital that very night, because she was up prowling, and suddenly all my good feelings of the past few days were gone. I felt crappy, but I had to stay vigilant while my baby sister was tripping around the house with this bullet-induced, jocular euphoria.

At one point she went outside barefoot. Later I found her eating a cube of butter. Then she took out all the canned foods in my larder and stacked them up — Progresso black beans (*beaucoup*), beef-barley soup, and canned carrot juice — playing supermarket. I tell her, "Mrs. Ma'am, I'll take one of those, and one of those, and have you got any peachy pie?"

She says, "I'm sorry, Richard, we haven't got any peachy pie."

"But, baby, I would sure like a nice big piece of peachy pie, heated up, and some vanilla ice cream with some rum sauce and maybe something along the lines of a maraschino cherry to put on the top for a little garnish. Nutmeg would do. Or are you telling me this is just a soup, beans, and carrot-juice joint? Is that all you got here?"

"Yes, Richard. Just soup and beans. They're very filling, though."

"Ahhm gonna have to call Betty Crocker, 'cause I'm in the mood for some pie, darlin'."

Suzie looks at me sort of worried and says that she thinks Betty Crocker is dead. Fuck. I realized I just had to sit on the couch and watch her, and this goes on and on, and of course I think I hear someone crashing around in the yard, so I get my .357 out from under my pillow and walk around the perimeter of the house, my feet crunching on the frozen snow. There was nobody out there. Back inside I checked on Susan, who was asleep in my bed. When I finally saw the rising of the sun and heard birds chirping to greet the new day, I went to the refrigerator, where I saw my recent affirmation: "Richard, you are a good and loving person," etc. I ripped it off the refrigerator and tore it into a thousand tiny pieces. Only an idiot would write something like that. It was like, I can't hack it in Africa, can't hack it at home — all I can hack is dead. So I took all the bullets out of the .357 except one, spun the chamber, placed the barrel against my right temple, and squeezed the trigger. When I heard the click of the hammer — voilà! I instantly felt better. My thumb quit throbbing. My stomach did not burn. The dread of morning and of sunlight had vanished, and I saw the dawn as something good, the birdsong wonderful. Even the obscure, take-it-for-granted objects in my house — the little knickknacks covered in an inch of dust, a simple wooden chair, my morning coffee cup drying upside down on the drainboard — seemed so relevant, so alive and necessary. I was glad for life and glad to be alive, especially when I looked down at the gun and saw that my bullet had rotated to the firing chamber. The Van Gogh effect again. I was back from Van Gogh Four to Van Gogh One.

They're calling from the hospital, because I kept Susan overnight: "Where is Susan?" "She's watching *Days of Our Lives*," I say as I shove the .357 into a top drawer next to the phone book. "Is she taking her Stelazine?" "Yes," I say. "Absolutely. Thanks for your concern. Now, goodbye!"

Just then the doorbell rings, and what I've got is a pair of Jehovah's Witnesses. I've seen enough of them on the Dark Continent to overcome an instinctive dread, since they seem to be genuinely content, proportionately — like, if you measured a bunch of them against the general population they are very happy people, and so pretty soon we're drinking Sanka and Susan comes out and they are talking about Christ's Kingdom on Earth where the lion lies down with the lamb, and Susan buys every word of it, 'cause it's like that line "Unless they come to me as little children..." Susan is totally guileless and the two Witnesses are without much guile, and I, the king of agnostics, listen and think, How's a lion going to eat straw? It's got a G.I. system designed to consume flesh, bones, and viscera — it's got sharp teeth, claws, and predatory instincts, not twenty-seven stomachs, like some bovine Bossie the Cow or whatever. And while I'm paging through a copy of *Awake!*, I see a little article from the correspondent in Nigeria entitled "The Guinea Worm — Its Final Days." As a doctor of tropical medicine, I probably know more about *Dracunculus medinensis*, the "fiery serpent," or Guinea worm, than anyone in the country. Infection follows ingestion of water containing crustacea (*Cyclops*). The worms penetrate the gut wall and mature in the retroperitoneal space, where they can grow three feet in length, and then generally migrate to the lower legs, where they form a painful blister. What the Africans do is burst the ulcer and extract the adult worm by hooking a stick under it and ever so gently tugging it out, since if you break it off the dead body can become septic and the leg might have to be removed. The pain of the Guinea worm is on a par with the pain of gout, and it can take ten days to nudge one out. The bad part is they usually come not in singles but in multiples. I've seen seven come out of an old man's leg.

If and when Global Aid sends me back to Africa, I will help continue the worm-eradication program, and as the Witnesses delight Susan with tales of a Heaven on Earth I'm thinking of the heat and the bugs in the equatorial zone, and the muddy water that the villagers take from rivers — they pour it in jugs and let the sediment settle for an hour and then dip from the top, where it looks sort of clean; it's hard to get through to them that *Cyclops* crustacea may be floating about invisibly and one swallow could get you seven worms, a swallow you took three years ago. You can talk to the villagers until you're blue in the face and they'll drink it anyhow. So you have to poison the *Cyclops* without over-poisoning the water. I mean, it can be done, but, given the way things work over there, you have to do everything yourself if you want it done right, which is why I hate the idea of going back: you have to come on like a one-man band.

On the other hand, Brother Bogue and the other brothers in the home office of Global Aid don't trust me; they don't like it when I come into the office irrepressibly happy, like Maurice Chevalier in his tuxedo and straw hat — *"Jambo jambo, bwana, jambo bonjour!"* — and give everyone one of those African soft handshakes, and then maybe do a little turn at seventy-eight revolutions per minute: "Oh, *oui oui*, it's delightful for me, walking my baby back home!" or "Hey, ain't it great, after staying out late? Zangk heffen for leetle gorls." Etc. They hate it when I'm high and they hate it when I'm low, and they hate it most if I'm feeling crazy/paranoid and come in and say, "You won't believe what happened to me now!" To face those humorless brothers every day and stay forever in a job as a medical administrator, to wear a suit and tie and drive I-5 morning and night, to climb under the house and tape those pipes with insulation — you get in the crawl space and the dryer-hose vent is busted and there's lint up the ass, a time bomb for spontaneous combustion, funny the house hasn't blown already (and furthermore, no wonder the house is dusty), and, hey, what, carpenter ants, too? When I think of all that: Fair America, I bid you adieu!

But things are basically looking up when I get Suz back to the hospital. As luck has it, I meet an Indian psychiatrist who spent fifteen years in Kampala, Uganda — he was one of the three shrinks in the whole country — and I ask him how Big Daddy Idi Amin is doing. Apparently, he's doing fine, living in Saudi Arabia with paresis or something, and the next thing you know the doc is telling me he's going to review Susan's case file, which means he's going to put her in a better ward and look out for her, and that's a load off my mind. Before I go, Suz and I take a little stroll around the spacious hospital grounds — it's a tranquil place. I can't help thinking that if Brother Bogue fires me — though I'm determined to behave myself after my latest mishap — I could come here and take Haldol and lithium, watch color TV, and drool. Whatever happened to that deal where you just went off to the hospital for a "little rest," with no stigma attached? Maybe all I need is some rest.

Susan still has those Jehovah's Witnesses on her mind. As we sit on a bench, she pulls one of their booklets out of her coat and shows me scenes of cornucopias filled with fruit and bounty, rainbows, and vividly colored vistas of a heaven on earth. Vistas that I've seen in a way, however paradoxically, in these awful Third World places, and I'm thinking, *Let them that have eyes see; and let them that have ears hear* — that's how it is, and I start telling Suz about Africa, maybe someday I can take her there, and she gets excited and asks me what it's like. Can you see lions? And I tell her, "Yeah, baby, you'll see lions, giraffes, zebras, monkeys, and parrots, and the Pygmies." And she really wants to see Pygmies. So I tell her about a Pygmy chief who likes to trade monkey meat for tobacco, T-shirts, candy, and trinkets, and about how one time when I went manic and took to the bush I stayed with this tribe, and went on a hunt with them, and we found a honeycomb in the forest; one of the hunters climbed up the tree to knock it down, oblivious of all the bees that were biting him. There were about five of us in the party and maybe ten pounds of honey and we ate all of it on the spot, didn't save an ounce, because we had the munchies from smoking dope. I don't tell Suz how it feels to take an airplane to New York, wait four hours for a flight to London, spend six hours in a transient lounge, and then hop on a nine-hour flight to Nairobi, clear customs, and ride on the back of a feed truck driven by a kamikaze African over potholes, through thick red dust, mosquitoes, black flies, tsetse flies, or about river blindness, bonebreak fever, bilharziasis, dumdum fever, tropical ulcers, AIDS, leprosy, etc. To go through all that to save somebody's life and maybe have them spit in your eye for the favor — I don't tell her about it, the way you don't tell a little kid that Santa Claus is a fabrication. And anyhow if I had eyes and could see, and ears and could hear — it very well might *be* the Garden of Eden. I mean, I can fuck up a wet dream with my attitude. I don't tell her that lions don't eat straw, never have, and so she's happy. And it's a nice moment for me, too, in a funny-ass way. I'm beginning to feel that with her I might find another little island of stability.

Another hospital visit: winter has given way to spring and the cherry blossoms are out. In two weeks it's gone from ten below to sixty-five, my Elavil and lithium are kicking in, and I'm feeling fine, calm, feeling pretty good. (I'm ready to go back and rumble in the jungle, yeah! *Sha-lah la-la-la-lah.*) Susan tells me she had a prophetic dream. She's unusually focused and articulate. She tells me she dreamed the two of us were driving around Heaven in a blue '67 Dodge.

"A '67 Dodge. Baby, what were we, the losers of Heaven?"

"Maybe, but it didn't really matter because we were there and we were happy."

"What were the other people like? Who was there? Was Arthur Schopenhauer there?"

"You silly! We didn't see other people. Just the houses. We drove up this hill and everything was like in a Walt Disney cartoon and we looked at one another and smiled because we were in Heaven, because we made it, because there wasn't any more shit."

"Now, let me get this straight. We were driving around in a beat-up car — "

"Yes, Richard, but it didn't matter."

"Let me finish. You say people lived in houses. That means people have to build houses. Paint them, clean them, and maintain them. Are you telling me that people in Heaven have jobs?"

"Yes, but they like their jobs."

"Oh, God, does it never end? A *job!* What am I going to do? I'm a doctor. If people don't get sick there, they'll probably make me a coal miner or something."

"Yes, but you'll love it." She grabs my arm with both hands, pitches her forehead against my chest, and laughs. It's the first time I've heard Susan laugh, ever — since we were kids, I mean.

"Richard, it's just like Earth but with none of the bad stuff. You were happy, too. So please don't worry. Is Africa like the Garden of Eden, Richard?"

"It's lush all right, but there's lots and lots of dead time," I say. "It's a good place to read *Anna Karenina*. Do you get to read novels in Heaven, hon? Have they got a library? After I pull my shift in the coal mine, do I get to take a nice little shower, hop in the Dodge, and drive over to the library?"

Susan laughs for the second time. "We will travel from glory to glory, Richard, and you won't be asking existential questions all the time. You won't have to anymore. And Mom and Dad will be there. You and me, all of us in perfect health. No coal mining. No wars, no fighting, no discontent. Satan will be in the Big Pit. He's on the Earth now tormenting us, but these are his last days. Why do you think we are here?"

"I often ask myself that question."

"Just hold on for a little while longer, Richard. Can you do that? Will you do it for me, Richard? What good would Heaven be if you're not there? Please, Richard, tell me you'll come."

I said, "Okay, baby, anything for you. I repent."

"No more Fyodor Dostoyevsky?"

"I'll be non-Dostoyevsky. It's just that, in the meantime, we're just sitting around here — waiting for Godot?"

"No, Richard, don't be a smart-ass. In the meantime we eat lunch. What did you bring?"

I opened up a deli bag and laid out chicken-salad-sandwich halves on homemade bread wrapped in white butcher paper. The sandwiches were stuffed with alfalfa sprouts and grated cheese, impaled with toothpicks with red, blue, and green cellophane ribbons on them, and there were two large, perfect, crunchy garlic pickles on the side. And a couple of cartons of strawberry Yoplait, two tubs of fruit salad with fresh whipped cream and little wooden spoons, and two large cardboard cups of aromatic, steaming, fresh black coffee.

It begins to rain, and we have to haul ass into the front seat of my Olds, where Suz and I finish the best little lunch of a lifetime and suddenly the Shirelles are singing, "This is dedicated to the one I love," and I'm thinking that I'm gonna be all right, and in the meantime what can be better than a cool, breezy, fragrant day, rain-splatter diamonds on the wraparound windshield of a Ninety-eight Olds with a view of cherry trees blooming in the light spring rain?

Superman, My Son

W ILHELM BLAINE PULLED his red Volvo wagon under the lone, stubby fig tree in front of his son Walter's California-beige stucco home. Somebody needed to get off their rear, get out here, and do a little landscaping. But Blaine knew it wasn't so bad behind the large cedar fence. It was a little enclave, really, with the pool, the Jacuzzi, the barbecue setup, and the rattan chairs. You could do a Winston Churchill — sit under lofty palms, sip a little brandy, smoke an expensive cigar, and discuss the weighty matters of the world.

Blaine ran down his electric windows and the hefty scent of gardenia from the backyard hit him in the face. Behind the fence, Walter's wife Zona pruned, watered, and fertilized — but out front, nothing. The fig tree was in need of serious medical attention, and in general the whole neighborhood was taking a precipitous slide. Blaine saw lots of "For Rent" signs. Almost every driveway seemed overloaded. If it wasn't a pickup truck with jacked-up monster wheels, it was a pin-striped van or a Harley low rider amid broken bicycles and rusty automobile transmissions. When the subdivision was new, Walter had paid $240K for his place, but Blaine had just seen a chicken prancing across a sun-torched lawn before he hung the left on Millpine Drive.

Blaine inched a few feet farther as he anticipated the amount of time he would spend inside. The Volvo would be an oven when he came out. Would Walter be laid out in a sluggish, torpid depression — insensible to reason or to the comforting reassurance of a father's voice? Or would he be mad as Saul, spewing poison and virulent accusations? Then there was Freddy, just back from Africa. Freddy could bullshit for hours. Blaine pondered these various intangibles. It would either be a lion's den or a morgue in there. He wanted to park the car so that it would be in at least partial shade. He looked back over his shoulder to the east, calculating, and caught a faceful of the 8:30 A.M. sun.

Poor Walter. He was a manic-depressive, and on this most recent flipout, according to Zona, he had somehow got buck-naked outside one of their supermarkets and dropped into the position of a Greek Olympian about to launch the discus. Zona said he locked up like a coiled spring. There was no discus to hurl but rather the Revised Standard Bible that he carried with him everywhere. And he would not let go. No amount of persuasion did any good. Walter *became* a statue, and they had to pick him up and take him to the emergency room just like that. The paramedics were furniture movers on that run. The incident did not have the feel of Walter's routine flipouts, either. Maybe this was a big one. Too bad Walter hadn't let the book sail. There was such a thing as religious toxicity. It was the worst poison of all. But Blaine wasn't going to go inside and say so. He wasn't going to get heavy-handed or come on too strong. He had done enough of that in the old days. He was just going to listen.

Zona had implied that Walter's ineffectual psychiatrist was some sort of "Christian" therapist. He had talked Walter out of his contortions, given him some Xanax, joined his hands in prayer, and then let Zona and Freddy drive Walter home. Blaine was glad he had missed the whole scene. He was worried about Walter but had troubles of his own. There were many things to do. Deals to be made. You just couldn't retire anymore. God almighty no! You had to work right up until the day you died.

Blaine revved the motor for a second and then switched off the ignition. The Volvo was his only means of transportation now, and he had come to love the car, the way it automatically "found" all his destinations in town. He had sold his Ferrari for interest on taxes due — no principal paid off or anything, just penalties. The next thing to go would be the house. But before he did that he had to pour a small fortune into finishing his courtyard.

One of the workers employed on that project, a cheerful green-card, had stolen his Patek Philippe. The guy had been dumb enough to "admire" the watch prior to the theft. Blaine had him figured but realized there was little he could do. The police certainly wouldn't care. Not about a mere property crime. Okay, the poor bastard needed the money, and Blaine left valuables around. The temptation must have been incredible. In the old days, Blaine would have hardly cared, but the Shoprite Food Value Emporium empire was falling to pieces. It was getting impossible to compete with the bigger stores, and Blaine was literally getting taxed out of business — getting reamed to keep people like the green-card afloat in various social programs of dubious worth. The thanks he got was grand theft — grand theft one day and armed robbery the next. Almost immediately after the green-card incident, Blaine had made hot tracks to his bedroom safe for his coin collection — close to fifty thousand in value — and had driven the wagon to a coin shop in downtown Sacramento and then, oh, man — a chain of events ensued that still had him reeling.

There were four black men inside the store when the proprietor buzzed him in through the security gate. Blaine's pockets were laden with gold, and he could literally smell the trouble — on top of the alcohol there was a toxic smell of adrenaline coming from these thugs, and they were getting right into the proprietor's face. "How much this one? How many Rolexes you got, man? You got some in the back? I don't like these here."

It was a tremendous relief to see them go, but suddenly they were back — one of them claiming to have left a pair of sunglasses behind. The Vietnamese coin dealer, Phat H'at, or the Fat Hat, as he was known, buzzed them back in. You would have thought the old man had developed an instinct for trouble, but he acted like a complete fool. Blaine had his coins out on the counter by then, and the bandits quickly brandished little snub-nosed .38s. Hat went for his nickel-plated .45, but one of the men was over the counter faster than a cat. "Motherfucker! One more move out of you and you dead."

Blaine had been glad that the bandit had some agility. He didn't want any shooting, although once the .45 was out of the way the robbers fired three shots into the security camera, *Ka-Pow! Ka-Pow!* Orange-and-blue flames burst out of the gun barrels. *Ka-Pow!* The harsh sound of the gunfire caused exquisite pain in his ears. One of the robbers scooped Blaine's coins into a bag, then executed a deft pirouette and expertly snatched the Cartier off Blaine's wrist and popped it into a pocket. Another man, wearing a ski mask, grabbed Blaine's wallet and began to rifle through it.

"You are welcome to all of it, gentlemen," Blaine had said, hands up, suddenly giddy. The savoir-faire with which he delivered these words seemed to calm the gunmen a little. It took the tension down a couple of notches. The biggest one pulled most of the green out of Blaine's wallet, but twelve bucks floated to the floor, and Blaine took a small satisfaction in stepping on the money. It was sort of a stupid thing to do, but Blaine felt possessed of a kind of Mel Gibson moviehouse invulnerability. His left foot was on the ten, his right on the two singles, and he felt splendidly frozen in time, as if he were in a white tie and tails doing a kind of lithe Fred Astaire — as if he suddenly knew what life wanted of him.

While the bandits fled the shop, Fat Hat ducked into the back room and emerged with a twelve-gauge. Blaine's happy spell was broken. "Hey, there! Wait a minute! Those hoods will come back in here and shoot us both," he said.

"Why you smiling? Why you smiling?" Hat said. "Taking sixteen Rolexes. Got alla my cold, hard cash. Got all your gold, man!"

The Asian darted out into the parking lot, squatted, and leveled the gun from left to right. His movements resembled some ridiculous, partly forgotten foreign army-training maneuver — an action long ago imprinted in an Alzheimer's-demented brain. The bandits were peeling rubber, fishtailing away in an old diesel-powered Oldsmobile Toronado. One of them leaned out the window and blasted a couple of shots back, causing Fat Hat to drop prone and hug the asphalt. Blaine saw the blue-and-orange muzzle flame a second before he heard the shots. He watched the car swing out onto the freeway until the only sign of it was the lingering, thick white smoke of the tail exhaust. And very soon that was gone. The entire incident had lasted no more than a minute or two.

Fat Hat ran back inside and dialed 911. Then he turned on Blaine. "Them get away. Too fast for me. Getaway driver an' shit. Piss on this whole damn country, anyhow. I'm packing up and could go back to

Mauritius! No gun in your face alla time! Why you smiling? Stop that smiling, vexing me! Damn you, man. Why you smiling?"

"I'm smiling because…I'm alive." Blaine picked up his last twelve dollars. "And because I've got enough money to buy lunch."

In some perverse way, the robbery had been fun. It was an adventure. His gold was gone, but if thieves didn't get it, Walter's ineffectual psychiatrist would. Blaine returned to the thought of Wally frozen in a discus-thrower's position. His track specialty in high school had been the discus throw. Zona had told Blaine that Walter had been convinced the Bible was a tiny spaceship containing a crew of three hundred and fourteen perversely evil, micro-sized men who were extorting pocket change from some street bum Walter had recently met during his manic space walk. Walter was going to uncoil and hurl the little bastards to the farthest reaches of the Milky Way. Or something. He never really let the thing fly. Should have, probably. A normal person might find comfort in the fundamental religions, with their laws, promises, and the so-called covenant with God. But why listen to a bunch of cockamamie? Wasn't it better to pursue your own truths? Very few had the courage or the elasticity to go it alone, though. And to view Christianity through the lens of manic psychosis was dangerous. Blaine had shucked his own Bible in Germany just after the war. Blaine was a full-blooded German himself. He even took heat for it at the time ("You're one of *them*, Blaine, a fuckin' kraut"), but he saw what the Germans had done and he had hated them for it. He knew the tendencies. His personality was marred by them, but at least he knew them. You didn't have to let a bug crawl up your ass and get all hellbent and mean or trample over people to make money. You could treat people right without fearing or trying to please God. You could do it simply because it was human to do it, because love was a more ennobling tendency than hate, and if you were lucky, maybe you could live with yourself and sleep nights.

But Walter didn't have Blaine's German genes. Blaine and his wife, Joanna, had adopted Wally. The boy was just three when they got him. This whole manic-psychosis business had to be genetic. He had been a happy kid back in Appleton, Wisconsin. Blaine had racked his brain trying to think of some way in which he had failed his son. There was nothing major. Blaine recalled the streams of dogs, birds, and rabbits, and Walter's pals and girlfriends. Walter hadn't been a very good student, but he had one stupendous season as an all-state catcher on the baseball team. Blaine could still remember the fastball Wally drove deep into the right-centerfield seats, breaking up a no-hitter in the state championship game. The opposing pitcher was brimming with confidence, and he challenged Walter with a fat one right down the middle. *Boom!* As soon as Wally made contact, everyone knew that ball was gone. It was one of those tape-measure jobs — four hundred and four feet. What a day that had been; probably the kid's best day. The very next week, Walter came within a half inch of setting a state record in the discus throw. The first athlete at Appleton to double-letter in spring sports. Blaine bought Walter a brand-new Corvair a few days later, and in less than a month, Walter was in the hospital; he had experienced his first manic flipout and rolled the car. There were subsequent hospitalizations for psychiatric treatment. Successions of therapists. Years of nothing but pain and trouble, really. Hell, trouble was the one constant in life. Pain and trouble. They pervaded everything.

Blaine stepped under the fig tree and examined its leaves. It had once been lush and productive of fruit, and now it was barren. Did it suffer — actually *suffer* on some level? He studied the tree with wonder, stroking its rough trunk. Love could save this plant. Zona could get her ass out here and save this plant if she *felt* like it. But you couldn't stay on top of everything. Blaine walked away from the fig tree. See you later. He was in up to his neck on several levels, and he realized now why he was stalling. He did not want to go inside.

It was a relief to duck into the vestibule and get out of the blazing sun. Blaine was sweating in his seersucker suit. He pushed the doorbell, swept his fingers through his mane of chestnut brown hair, and then rammed both hands in his pockets as he rocked back and forth on his heels. The right words would be there for him.

Zona Blaine clomped down the stairs wearing a short robe and a pair of her husband's slip-ons. She still had nice legs, and, in spite of her pool-lounging in the hot valley sun, she had nice skin. She was cradling a basket full of laundry and talking to her bird, Boo Boo, who was perched high on her shoulder. She looked into the front room and said good morning to Walter's cousin, Freddy, who was leaning forward on the couch with a cup of coffee so hot he was fanning it with a copy of a bird magazine. Freddy didn't look so good. It had been a real shocker to Zona when she first got a load of him at the airport. He was beyond what one might term "a whiter shade of pale," and he had dropped fifty pounds. He claimed it was malaria.

Zona swung open the garage door and loaded the washer. She was back in a second and said, "This bird is crazy."

"Can it talk?" Freddy said.

"You should hear him. I go out into the garage and he says, 'Whacha doin'?' I say, 'I'm doing the laundry, Boo Boo.' He says, 'Need any help?' "

"No!" Freddy declared.

"I'm not kidding. 'Need any help?' "

"That's wild. What else does he say?" Freddy cranked the footrest of the lounger down and made an assault on the hot cup of coffee. Zona wondered how he could drink it so hot.

"He does a one-way telephone conversation: 'Yeah…uh-huh… yeah?' Then he'll pause, you know. 'Oh, yeah? Uh-huh. That's right.' Pause again. 'Oh, yeah? Ah-ha-ha-ha!' "

Freddy said, "Is it like parakeet chatter? Or is it like human?"

"It's just like human. Parakeets — " Zona screwed up her face and cocked her head to the side. " 'Pretta bird, chich chich chich. Pretta bird.' That's all you get from parakeets."

"Parakeets have got that tinny quality," Freddy said. He picked up a bright blue butane lighter and shook a Kool from his pack. "What about Blaine's parrot? That bird can talk."

"Roberto? 'I ham joost hey line man for zee county.' "

Freddy lit his cigarette and inhaled deeply. "Roberto bit me on the cuticle last time I was out here. Took out a chunk of meat. I still got the scar."

"African grays," Zona said. "They are mean, but they're the best talkers. 'Hey, hey, pretty wooman. Wot harrh you wearing such hey sexy blouse for? You h'rr making me so hot, bébé.' "

"He's a smooth one, all right. He gets you to trust him and then he bites you. Does he bite Blaine?"

"He bites them one and all. Roberto is a real card. He's a character," Zona said.

"Who taught him all that Spanish? He must be a pre-owned bird. It's always a sex trip or that stupid song."

"*Bésame Mucho*," Zona said.

"Yes. I hate that song. It makes me depressed. If I bought a pre-owned bird, I'd get it from a soul brother, not some bean head. It always starts in with that song at six in the morning. And, it's like, loud."

Blaine remained in the porchway with his hands in his pockets, rocking on his heels, wondering if the doorbell had shorted out. But then he heard voices inside. He gave the door a little rap. He was thinking of the stickup, wondering if his insurance would cover it. Well, it would or it wouldn't.

He gave the door a second sharp rap and stepped inside. Blaine liked his entrances to seem like explosions. His voice was a rich baritone, and he liked to ham. "Is somebody in here badmouthing my parrot?"

"Hey, hey, hey!" Freddy said. He got up to shake hands with his uncle, but they ended up in a tight, back-slapping embrace. It had been three years. The family had been dying out fast. Freddy was the last of the Blaine line, and, by the looks of him, Blaine wondered how long Freddy would last. He looked terrible.

Blaine held his nephew at arm's length and studied his face. "My God, Freddy, it's good to see you again. Jesus! How are you feeling?"

"Not too bad. How are you? Lucky to be alive, ain't you? Stick 'em up, dude!"

"Oh, Christ," Blaine said dismissively. "I was just thinking about those cocksuckers. They got away clean. I'm lucky to be alive. Or not so lucky, when you consider the state of the world. A bullet between the eyes might have been a blessing. I'm seventy-two, for Christ's sake. I am probably nourishing monstrous occlusions and tumors of which I'm not yet aware but will be presently. Ha! But what about you? What about this number you pulled on the airplane?"

"I hate to go into that," Freddy said. "I'll just get riled up again."

"No, tell me." Blaine said. He was an expert at drawing people out, and he loved lurid tales. Blaine winked at Zona, who ran upstairs to put on some clothes.

"I haven't done anything like that in years," Freddy said. "I thought I was in control, that those days were over. But sometimes there is a black-and-white situation where anger seems completely justified."

"I want to hear the whole story. Don't shortchange me," Blaine said, as he selected a pipe from Walter's pipe rack and began loading it from a canister of coarse tobacco.

Freddy took a quick hit off his cigarette. "Well, imagine," he said. "From Douala, in Cameroon, to Kinshasa, to Dar, to the Africa House in Zanzibar — party, party for a couple of days — and then on to Paris, customs at L.A., blah blah, and then here. Until the water bed in the guest bedroom last night, the last time I was in between sheets and really slept was at the Hotel Akwa on the Boulevard de la Liberté in fucking Douala — the armpit of Africa. That was just before the latest round with this fucking malaria. None of it was too bad, until I hit that airline strike in Los Angeles. I was supposed to be in business class, but they somehow had me in the last seat in the tail section — one of those seats that don't tilt back. You can take that shit when you're young, but I was having my — you know, my epileptic twitches, and I'm back there going off like a machine gun, rat-a-tat-tat, and in the meantime the steward is dishing shit out to everybody, like we're in prison and he's the yard boss. I got into it with him. I just let him have it, that's all. Zona, is there any more coffee?"

"How many cups have you had already?" Zona said. She had fixed her hair in a ponytail and had thrown on a cotton sundress.

"Just two."

Zona looked to her father-in-law. "All he does is sit there, drink coffee, and smoke strong cigarettes. He won't eat. I didn't think doctors smoked anymore."

"Who said doctors had good sense?" Freddy said. "Doctors can be the craziest sumbitches in the world. Behind the bulwark of authority, self-assurance, and the seemingly judicious intelligence of the white coat, too often unrighteousness, lunacy, and sheer incompetence sit at the helm. Thus it is in medicine as in all walks of life; in medicine, more so. Drug addicts, suicides, desperate people. I mean, I publish in the journals. I have a certain renown. So you see what the world's coming to." Freddy presented Zona with the empty mug. "Please. More. I've got jet lag and a real bad case of the poontang blues."

Zona went into the kitchen, and Blaine leaned forward and whispered, "You get much pussy over there — you know, in Africa?"

"Yeah, sure," Freddy said nervously. "A little. Some one-night stands with the ever-circulating network of aid workers. Some of the hard cases will go to the ground and marry natives. A lot of the Catholics sublimate. I can do that, too. I can sublimate."

"You mean you just don't do it?" Blaine said.

"Well, it's pretty risky. AIDS is everywhere. It used to be bad just in the big cities, but now it's all over. It puts the fear of God into you."

Zona returned with a coffee tray. "Tell Willy how you lost your shoe."

Freddy began to fan his mug as soon as Zona filled it. "I'm sure Uncle Willy would rather hear about Walter."

Blaine wiggled a little bag of NutraSweet, ripped off the top, and dumped the contents into his cup. "Zona filled me in about Walter late last night. You tell me about the flight from hell."

Freddy sipped his coffee. "Am I talking too fast?" He didn't wait for an answer. "I am now and was then all whacked-out on Mefloquine. I was not really lucid, but still it dawned on me that whenever anybody had a request that was within this steward's power to fulfill, he just said, 'Yeah, just a minute,' and didn't *do* anything. We were just sitting dead on the ground like for about an hour and a half, and the steward took that rude L.A. tone, 'Everybody on the plane is a revenue-paying customer. If you want another seat you'll have to trade with somebody once we get into the air.' I just lost it. 'Who in the *hell* do you think you are, jacking everybody around? Motherfucker, I have been out in the damn jungle in Cameroon. I have been on an airplane or in a transient lounge for two and a half days, and you think you got it bad 'cause you're working a double shift. Well, how do you think *I* feel?'

"He came right back. 'Fuck you!' he says, and then, bingo, we started wrestling in the aisle, and two cops grabbed me. 'You're under arrest!' I've been three years in Central Africa and nothing happens to me until I get back to the imperialistic, fascist state!"

Blaine had thought he would come into the house and have words for whatever hit him, but the spectacle of Freddy left him speechless.

Freddy gulped down more coffee, lit another Kool, and, thus freshly armed, leaned forward and continued. "People were still trying to get on the plane, it was a big cluster fuck, and the police were dragging me away; I lost a shoe, and some little Greek lady got up and said, 'Hold it right there! That man did nothing wrong! *That man did nothing wrong.* It was *him,* Mr. Sunny Jim there!' and she's pointing to the steward. 'It was all his fault.' So there is some justice in the universe. The cops stopped, like, 'Oh, yeah?' and the steward said, 'Screw this job, who needs it?' I mean, this is the kind of shit that happens on a cross-country Trailways bus ride when some maniac is stoked on fortified wine. And I never did find my shoe. Off to baggage claim wearing socks." Freddy had a pencil-thin mustache and a short goatee, which he fingered nervously while he patted perspiration from his forehead with a folded linen tea napkin. Blaine stared at him.

"Stop looking at me like that," Freddy said. "I get crazy when I tell that story. I'm better now, really, if I could just — if God would just have mercy on me and let me get a little sleep." He laughed nervously. "So tell us about the robbery. Four of them, with gunfire. Was dey blood? Was dey niggazzh?"

"They were thugs," Blaine said. "They just pumped a few shots into the ceiling, that's all. Why do you denigrate them? You are over in Africa for three years, ostensibly saving African lives, dispensing care — "

Freddy flicked his hand at a fly. Blaine took note of the limp wrist action and the way Freddy crossed his legs. In spite of a lifelong fondness for Freddy, Blaine felt himself disapproving of his nephew's whole demeanor.

"It's just a term of speech, Uncle Willy. You yourself referred to them as 'cocksuckers.' Was this coin dealer insured?"

"I still don't know," Blaine said. "My lawyer's handling it. It's depressing. I am down to selling paintings and coins so I can fix up that courtyard. In the morning, I'm importing a fountain from Italy, before lunch I am robbed, and in the afternoon I'm shopping for a double-wide."

"You're such a kidder," Freddy said. "Zona, did you hear that, babe? He's getting a double-wide."

"I'm serious," Blaine said. "I've got some scrub acreage. I'll plop it down there. *Pow!*" Blaine slapped his hand on the coffee table. "Home, sweet home. I'll sit there and call it good." He relit his pipe. "Where is Walter, for God's sake? How is he?"

Zona gave Blaine a cup of coffee. "He's up in the bedroom."

"Won't come out?" Blaine said.

"No," Zona said. "I've been trying to baby him but...well, you know Walter. He's the biggest and best manic depressive in the Golden State. When he's up, *fa-gam!* The planet Krypton. He can fly there in an hour. But when he's down, he's really down. A major crash."

Blaine's face became a mask of concern. "He's back on the lithium, isn't he?"

"Yes," Zona said, "and I could sue that damn psychiatrist! 'Try the Tegretol a little longer.' 'He doesn't need any damn Tegretol,' I said. 'You sit there real calm and say, "Try the Tegretol a little longer; check back in two weeks," and Walter is running around in a three-piece wool suit and no underwear!' He's got the Samsonite out and he's packing. I say, 'Walter, where are you going?' He says, 'I'm blasting back to Krypton. To be among my own kind.' And — *fa-gam!* — out the door he goes, wearing a damn three-piece wool suit, no underwear, a horrible tie, nine pounds of wing tips and no socks; he's got huge blisters on his heels and doesn't even seem to know. It has to be at least a hundred and twelve out and he's wearing that ugly damn brown suit of his, copping a load of b.o. — when he finally ditched it, I burned the damn thing. When you get b.o. into wool, it never comes out. Pick it up with a pole. He says, 'Where's my brown suit?' 'Walter, that suit is out of style.' 'It's so old it went out of style and came back in,' he says. I said, 'They never quite do, they never quite do, and every fool knows that.'"

"But he's on the lithium now?" Blaine asked. His focus was on Zona now. He was completely concentrating on her.

"Finally," Zona said. "I'm about ready to lose my mind. He packed up that Samsonite and was off. I'm not lying. The Eye of Horus and Rosicrucians. I'm serious."

"Can I go up and see him?" Blaine said.

"I don't think that would be a very good idea," Zona said. "His remarks concerning his father have been kind of volatile lately." She picked up one of Freddy's Kools and lit it. "Damn, three months without a cigarette," she said.

"Well, I guess every son wants to kill his dad at some level," Blaine said. "But I thought the Tegretol was doing him good."

"It was at first. His psoriasis cleared up entirely. He was going to his recovery meetings, to Bible study, to bird meetings. When Walter is straight, he's totally on the ball. But this shrink had him on Prozac, too. Got him horny. Let me tell you. Five times a day! I said, 'Walter, I'm not made out of steel. You may be Superman but I'm a forty-six-year-old woman with a hysterectomy last year. Give me a break.'"

Freddy began to finger his goatee again. "Psoriasis. In terms of diseases, it's a metaphor for rage."

"What's that supposed to mean?" Blaine said.

"You are Walter's father," Freddy said. "You would have the insight. The skin is a very emotive organ. Don't get so touchy."

Blaine leaned forward with his forearms balanced on his knees. He gave a little sigh and turned up his palms. "We adopted Wally when he was three," he said. "Most of the psychic damage had to have been done long before. We were good parents. Who knows? Maybe manic psychosis is genetic. The psoriasis comes from the pills. Of course, what he says may be true. He may indeed come from Smallville. Perhaps he truly is Superman. He went through the windshield of a Corvair without a scratch."

"It's a possibility we should consider," Freddy said. "Superman."

Blaine turned to Zona. "What about Turkey? Can't you go back there for the psoriasis?"

"Turkey?" Freddy said, pinching his chin.

"Yes," Blaine said. "There's this village in Turkey that has a kind of hot springs with these weird little fish in it, and what you do is sit in the springs and the fish come up and nibble your skin. There's something in their saliva, or whatever, that causes the skin to heal over. Two weeks and you're in remission."

"I'm not going back to damn Turkey," Zona said. "They don't have any magic carpets. What they got is buses with bald tires, nonexistent shock absorbers, and all the windows stuck shut! Damn! I'm a California girl. I like air conditioners, clean water, and a certain amount of oxygen in my atmosphere." Zona shot a stream of smoke out of the side of her mouth. "And they've got laws from day one over there. They used to hang you for drinking coffee and smoking."

"Pretty soon they'll be doing it here," Freddy said. "Have you noticed that now you can't offend with the sexist or racial remark, but smokers are open game? I mean every news broadcast, the front page of every paper. A cigarette was just a cigarette twenty years ago, but now the smoker is a pariah."

"That's true," Blaine said. "All that hate has to come out. The world needs scapegoats. No one will embrace the other — the inner dark man."

"And in another ten years coffee drinkers will be on the list," Zona said, taking a measured drag on the cigarette. "Coffee makes people violent or something."

"They should tax it, if you want to know," Blaine said. "I mean, if you get right down to it, how much would you pay for a Kool and a cup of rocket fuel before you had to get dressed and hit the road?"

Freddy fiddled with his lighter. "Getting up in the morning, for coffee and a cigarette? I don't know, considering my present financial circumstances, which are meager, every last dime...seven hundred."

"You see. You aren't the only one, either; there are thousands like you," Blaine said. "We could wipe out the national debt."

Freddy shook a Kool from his pack and lit it. He put an arch in his voice, "Excuse me, do y'all mind if I smoke?"

"I like them too much," Zona said as she mashed hers out. "I better go check on Walter."

Blaine waved his daughter-in-law over to him and spoke quietly. "Was there some kind of precipitating event? What the hell *really* happened?"

"A neighbor — this guy, this asshole hurt his back at work and is collecting disability. If you ask me, it's a bullshit claim. He sits in his garage and drinks beer all day, or you'll see him doing real heavy labor, like he's got the strongest back in the world. Anyhow, he comes over here and says Walter's birds are too loud. Calls the city. They come out and say Walter isn't zoned for an aviary. You know how Walter lives for those birds. Well, not only do we have to get rid of the birds, move them out to the stables, but they want us to tear up the construction. If I were a man I would take that guy out with one punch. One punch! End of conversation. End of problem."

"I can't believe Walter is cowed by some guy with a bad back," Freddy said. "He's a damn Sumo."

Zona said, "Yes, but he's not mean, and he really gets into the Christian lifestyle. So now it takes a half hour to drive out to the stables. It takes an hour to cut up fruit. You have to bleach the tables, the cutting boards, and all the paraphernalia because of salmonella, which can wipe out a flock overnight. Lories eat fruit and nectar; they aren't seed eaters. That's the big downside on lories. You do that twice a day and try to run a business and it will snap you. Of course, the city is right. We aren't zoned for an aviary. So there you are."

"And I've got to sell the stables," Blaine said. "I wish we'd dumped the business ten years ago and bugged out for Mexico. We got an offer for seven million at the time, but we were taking in a hundred and ninety-five thousand a month clear. Now I'm stuck. Our traffic is down by half, the lease payments and payroll are killing us. The next thing, I really will be living in a double-wide. In fact, I don't see any way to avoid it."

"We'll all be living in the double-wide when I pay for this last caper," Zona said. She picked up the laundry basket and headed upstairs.

Blaine looked over at Freddy. "So you really love it over there, in Central Africa?"

"I do," Freddy said. "I feel that my life has meaning there. I can't do any good over here. I'm just not built for here. In Africa, I thrive, although it's very hard. Africa generates and consumes at an accelerated rate. You can feel it buzz. An hour of rain can turn a desert green in a day, the grass will grow three inches in a week, and two more days of sun can turn the green brown. Production, consumption. It's so instant. It's just...super. You can understand the whole 'cradle of civilization' business the minute you take a breath over there. They gave me a medical leave. I just came home to recover. This is a horseshit life back here."

"Joanna and I did Kenya and Tanzania just before she died — what, two summers ago? I guess that's just Disneyland compared to Cameroon, but I think I know what you mean."

At these words, Freddy did an ultra-femme double take, and Blaine's suspicions were confirmed. He thought of AIDS, and found himself cringing inwardly, as if in the presence of a vampire.

"Shit," Freddy said, "I didn't know you guys went to Africa. What about your pathological fear of lions? You told me when I was little that a lion was going to eat you."

"You are right. I thought a lion would get me. As a kid, I saw the picture. My mother said it was a dream. They took me to the doctor, but it wasn't a dream. It was some sort of ESP. I was terrified that Barnum and Bailey would drive by in a convoy, have an accident, and let a lion loose — that it would make its way to my house and eat me. This was my greatest fear."

"But you went to Kenya. Why would you go *there?* To tempt fate?"

Blaine said, "Well, when we rented the cherry farm out, up in Oregon — didn't I tell you this? When we rented the cherry farm to those hippies, the lions almost did get me."

"What lions on the cherry farm?" Freddy said.

"Jesus!" Blaine said. "I drove up to the cherry farm in Salem to check on the property when your dad was in the nuthouse. I knew something was going on, and I was right."

"What?"

"Well, hell, the tenants were five months behind in the rent," Blaine said. "Dope-smoking hippies. I rented them the place because they were Walter's friends. 'Oh, Mr. Blaine, we'll take care of the place just like it was our own.' Shit! Everything was either missing or ruined. They even cut a hole in the front door so their Rottweiler could go in and out. They had opium poppies in the front yard — the little pods were oozing juice from razor slits. I figured that if they're growing opium in the yard, they had to have grow lights in the basement. I told the hippie housewife I was going to go down in the basement to check on the furnace, and she panicked — *no, no, you can't do that*. When a little kid started crying upstairs, I had my chance. Down into the basement, I turn around and there's a fully grown African lion — "

"Jesus Christ!"

Blaine came up from the couch with his palms out as if he were summoning up a vision in a crystal ball. His eyes darted from left to right as he reenacted the scene. "A fully grown lioness crouching down in the seven o'clock position, and from the front comes a male. I knew then that my picture was coming true. The male let out a growl that shook the rafters, almost knocked me down — Christ! Ten seconds later the hippie earth-mother bitch is down the stairs with an umbrella, popping it in the female's face. Those were a long ten seconds." Blaine sat back on the couch and sipped his coffee. "The coin shop was a romp."

"God! Mary Poppins," Freddy said, squealing with delight.

"She says, 'Back, Sheena!' " Blaine extended his left leg, pulled his pant leg loose and laughed.

Freddy rattled off a laugh of his own and dabbed at his face with another of Zona's linen tea napkins. "Jesus! You never told me this."

Blaine scowled as he took a swig of coffee. "Freddy, you've got that too-much-Elavil, no-energy fairy voice again."

"My voice isn't *that* bad," Freddy said. "I'm starving, sleep-deprived, malarial, and if I don't take a leak pretty soon, I'm going to piss my pants! Give me a break, dude."

At this Blaine slapped his thigh and laughed. "It is that bad," he mimicked. Then he was on his feet again, acting out the scene in the basement. He would imitate a lion, then himself, then the hippie housewife, and then a lion again. "*Back, Sheena!*"

Freddy mopped his face. "Zona, he's making me laugh. I'm gonna pee on the rug!" He jumped up, and cupping his genitals, began to dance like a pair of scissors. "Quick: what happened to the lions? A zoo?"

"Euthanized," Blaine said. "But the point is my picture was right in the ballpark. I went to Africa because lions in Africa weren't my problem. It was lions in Oregon."

"My voice isn't *that* bad. It's...normal."

"It's airy-fairy," Blaine said. He held his hand out and let it quaver. "I'm just telling you because you're my nephew, and somebody has to point these things out. It was really bad when you said, 'Excuse me, do you mind if I smoke?' "

Freddy threw his head back and laughed. "That was *intentional!* I was doing the nineteen-thirties movie thing. You're just getting crabby because you need to eat. Did you have anything for breakfast?"

"A doughnut," Blaine said.

"Well, you were sugared up and now you're down. You came in booming with good cheer and now you're Mr. Crab Patch. Maybe we should make some eggs or something?" Freddy said.

Zona came downstairs with a thick red copy of the *Physicians' Desk Reference* and shoved it at Freddy's chest, knocking him back on the couch. "Page 2,257," she said. "Interpret the lingo, buster."

"What's going on up there?" Blaine said.

Zona said, "I put Boo Boo in with Walter. They're talking."

"They're talking? You mean like 'How're ya doin'?'" Freddy said.

Zona stroked her cheek, "'Whacha doin'?' 'Just layin' here, Boo.' 'Are you feeling bad, Captain?' 'I feel pretty rough. I sure do.' 'Give me a kiss.' Talking like that."

"Well, at least he's talking. Last night — last night was *bad*," Freddy said.

"It's tearing me up," Blaine said, reaching through the buttons of his shirt to rub his chest. "This on top of everything else."

Zona rapped the *P.D.R.* with her knuckles. "How long before the pills kick in?"

Freddy's finger ran expertly down a column as he scanned the entry for Eskalith. "'Typical symptoms of mania include pressure of speech, motor hyperactivity, reduced need for sleep, flight of ideas, grandiosity, elation, poor judgment, aggressiveness and possibly hostility. When given to a patient experiencing a manic episode, *Eskalith* may produce a normalization of symptomatology within one to three weeks.' Why, it sounds great. We could all do with some."

There was a large crash and the sound of heavy footfalls upstairs. "Goddamn it! Who's laughing down there?" The voice came down like thunder, with an overlay of fear and paranoia.

"I'll be right back," Zona said. She rushed up the stairs, swung open the bedroom door, stepped inside, and pushed it shut.

"Shit," said Blaine. "I'm going up there."

"Zona can handle it. He finds men threatening. We better wait. He's got the strength of twenty."

"Maybe you're right," Blaine said. "She's really been good for him. An angel. Really."

"Most women couldn't handle the psoriasis, let alone the — "

"She doesn't even see it; it's not a consideration," said Blaine. He sat with both arms extended on the top of the couch and managed to sneak a look at his new Timex Indiglo.

*   *   *

At last, Walter appeared at the top of the stairs. He was a huge man, balding, with a six-week beard. He cinched the tie on his white terry-cloth bathrobe. He held a worn Bible in his hand and looked crazed. Zona followed him as he grabbed the railing and worked his way down the steps.

"Hi, Dad. Hi, Freddy," Walter said meekly. He paused on the third step from the bottom and looked down at the two men.

"Walter wants some breakfast," Zona said. "Or should we have lunch? It's getting late. Would you guys like to eat?"

"We were just talking about that," Freddy said. "Eggs. Protein. Whole-wheat toast. Tomato juice. I'm a nervous fucking wreck. I look like hell. At least Walter *looks* like a human being. I'm just a skeleton in a bag of skin. And I don't have AIDS and I'm not gay, if that's what you're all thinking — so you can quit boiling the silverware."

Walter stared awkwardly at the two men and then raised his left hand like an Indian. "I would like to read something. A prayer."

"Read?" Blaine said.

"Great," Freddy said. "I'm going to piss my pants, but first a prayer."

Walter fumbled through his Bible. At first it seemed that he was okay, and then it appeared that the effort was almost too much for him to bear. He had to grab the banister to steady himself. His lips were dry, and he kept running his tongue over them. Large beads of perspiration began to form on his forehead. The onionskin pages of his Bible were sticking together. He flipped through them, stopping occasionally to study the text. From the look on his face, it seemed that he was trying to decipher an incomprehensible language. The Bible began to wobble in his huge hands like a divining rod. "I'm sorry," he said. "Geez! Are you guys hot? Is it hot down here?"

"It's just hotter than a *motherfucker*," Freddy said. "Africa hot! The Libyan desert at high noon!"

"It's warm," Zona said. "Air conditioner or no. But you're sweating because of the lithium, and Freddy has a fever. Don't indulge yourselves with symptomatic lingo. It just makes everything worse."

"You're right, baby," Walter said. He opened the Bible again and, leaning against the wall, studied the page, while Blaine, Zona, and

Freddy waited expectantly. At last Walter was ready. A gleam came to his eye. He was running with sweat. He pulled the Bible up close to his face, as if he were severely nearsighted. He read at an infuriatingly slow pace, but his audience watched with rapt attention:

He who dwells in the shelter of the Most High,
who abides in the shadow of the Almighty,
will say to the Lord, "My refuge and my fortress;
my God, in whom I trust."
For he will deliver you from the snare of the fowler
and from the deadly pestilence;
he will cover you with his pinions,
and under his wings you will find refuge;
his faithfulness is a shield and buckler.
You will not fear the terror of the night,
nor the arrow that flies by day,
nor the pestilence that stalks in darkness,
nor the destruction that wastes at noon-day.

A thousand may fall at your side,
ten thousand at your right hand;
but it will not come near you.
You will only look with your eyes
and see the recompense of the wicked.
Because you have made the Lord your refuge,
the Most High your habitation,
no evil shall befall you,
no scourge come near your tent.

For he will give his angels charge of you
to guard you in all your ways.
On their hands they will bear you up,
lest you dash your foot against a stone.
You will tread on the lion and the adder,
the young lion and the serpent you
will trample under foot.

"Because he cleaves to me in love, I will deliver him;
I will protect him, because he knows my name.
When he calls to me, I will answer him;
I will be with him in trouble,
I will rescue him and honor him.
With long life I will satisfy him,
and show him my salvation."

By the time Walter finished, his robe was soaked, and the sweat was popping off his face, plopping down on the pages of the Bible. His hands were shaking. He continued to work his tongue over his cracked lips. He closed the book and pressed it to his breast.

"I'm still a little bit messed up," Walter said. "But I think I'm going to be okay. The lithium is starting to work. That's why I'm sweating so bad. I'm dehydrated, too. Honey, can I have some Diet Shasta — black cherry, two cans?"

Zona put her arm around his shoulder. "You're going to be just fine, babe. Just fine. I'll get you the pop and then fix all you boys up with some grub."

Freddy got up and hugged his cousin. "It's cool, Wally. I love you, man. But I gotta hit the water closet. Was it a good trip?"

"It was righteous, cuz. I saw the alpha and the omega, but I'm back now. Go forth and pee," Walter said. "And then *everybody* get back out here so we can do a big circle hug and sing joyous praise for a multitude of blessings."

"Fuck you," Freddy said.

"That's right, Walter, just fuck it, huh?" Zona called from the kitchen. Her tone was light.

When it was his turn, Blaine embraced Walter and at once recalled the joy he felt forty-seven years and some before, when he first held this stranger, the adopted little boy.

The Blaine line would end with Walter and Freddy. Zona was sterile, like Joanna. Unless by some remote stretch Freddy got married, it was over, and Blaine was sure now that Freddy was gay and suffering from the first symptoms of AIDS. Blaine took in all these thoughts in a rush, and through eyes slightly blurring with tears, he glanced outside and saw how the shadow of the withering fig tree had disappeared at noon, leaving his Volvo a victim of the blistering sun. Heat waves shimmered off the faded paint job. Most people at least had the satisfaction of knowing that they would live on in their grandchildren. Even atheists took consolation in that.

Blaine gave Walter a tight hug. His son was soaking wet. "You had me worried there, kiddo. It's good to have you back."

"Thanks, Dad," Walter said. "I'm okay now. It's all right."

Blaine broke loose from Walter and with a croaking voice called to Zona, "Just a minute, beautiful. Let me give you a hand out there." As he stepped away from the living room, Blaine dabbed the tears from his eyes, quickly blew his nose, and fought to regain his composure before he "exploded" around the corner singing, "*Bé-sa-me, Bé-same mucho, como si fuera esta noche la última vez....*"

Way Down Deep in the Jungle

D R. KOESTLER'S BABOON, George Babbitt, liked to sit near the foot of
the table when the physician took his evening meal and eat a paste
the doctor had made consisting of ripe bananas and Canadian Mist
whiskey. Koestler was careful to give him only a little, but one scorching
afternoon when the generators were down and the air conditioners out,
Koestler and Babbitt sat under the gazebo out near the baobab tree that
was the ersatz town square of the Global Aid mission and got blasted. It
was the coolest spot you could find, short of going into the bush. The baboon and the man were waiting for a late supper, since the ovens were
out, too. Cornelius Johnson, the mission cook, was barbecuing chickens out in the side yard — not the typical, scrawny African chickens, but
plump, succulent ones that Johnson made fat with sacks of maize that
the generous donors to Global Aid had intended for the undernourished
peoples of the region.

It had been a grueling day, and Koestler was drinking warm
whiskey on an empty stomach. At first, he was impatient for a meal,
then resigned to waiting, then half smashed and glad to wait, and
he began offering Babbitt straight shots of booze. When he saw the
look of sheer ecstasy that came over Babbitt's Lincolnesque face, he
let the simian drink on, convinced that the animal was undergoing
something holy. And perhaps he was, but after the initial rush of in-
toxication, Babbitt made the inevitable novice drinker's mistake of
trying to amplify heaven. He snatched the whole bottle of Canadian
Mist and scampered off into the bush like a drunken Hunchback of

Notre Dame. Koestler had to laugh; it seemed so comical — the large Anubis baboon was unwilling to share the last of the amber nectar with his master. Well, there was always more where it came from, but suddenly Koestler wondered about the rapidity with which Babbitt had been slamming it down. He was afraid Babbitt would poison himself. Koestler took off into the bush after the animal, and he was instantly worried when he did not find Babbitt in any of his favorite trees. But Babbitt, who was perched higher than usual, announced his presence by launching the empty bottle down at Koestler like a bomb, just missing him. It was a calculated attempt at mayhem, Koestler realized, as Babbitt began to rant and rave at him with an astonishing repertoire of hostile invective that not only puzzled Koestler but wounded him to the core. Koestler had been Babbitt's champion and staunchest defender. Virtually no one on the compound had any use for the large and powerful baboon. As Sister Doris, the chief nurse, liked to say, Babbitt was aggressive, noisy, a biter, a thief, and a horrendous mess-maker with no redeeming quality except the fact that he was one of God's creatures. Father Stuart quickly pointed out that crocodiles were God's creatures, too, but that didn't mean you had to let them move in with you. Almost every day someone would come up to Koestler and besiege him with complaints about the animal. Only Father Stuart had the nerve to confront Babbitt directly, once using a bird gun to shoot Babbitt's red ass with a load of rock salt, an incident that caused the priest and the doctor to cease speaking to each other, except through third parties. Koestler and the priest had become so estranged that Koestler refused to dine with the rest of the staff, and this suited him fine, since he no longer had to sit through the sham of hymns, prayers, and all the folderol that surrounded meals in the lodge.

Koestler was a loner, and preferred his own company to that of anyone else after long, hard days of bonhomie with the junior physicians and the in-your-face contact with patients — patients not only deprived of basic necessities but lacking such amenities as soap, mouthwash, and deodorant. Koestler found that it was useful, and even necessary, to remain remote — to cultivate the image of the chief — since an aspect of tribalism invaded the compound in spite of the artificial structure of the church, which was imposed on it and which never seemed to take very well in the bush. The newfangled wet blanket of civilization was thrown over ancient customs to almost no avail. But there were ways to get things done out here, and Koestler embodied those most notable characteristics of the New Zealander: resourcefulness, individualism, and self-reliance. In fact, Koestler carried self-containment to a high art. He had a lust for the rough-and-tumble, and preferred the hardships of Africa to the pleasant climate and easygoing customs of his homeland. As Koestler was fond of thinking, if Sir Edmund Hillary had a mountain to conquer when he climbed Everest in 1953 and breathed the rarefied air there, Koestler had baboons to tame and tropical diseases to vanquish in the here and now of Zaire. Koestler modestly considered himself New Zealand's gift to equatorial Africa.

Now Babbitt was high up another tree, raising so much hell that the majority of the Africans — workers and convalescents — had assembled to watch. Babbitt scrambled back and forth along a limb with a pencil-size twig in his fingers, mimicking the manner in which Koestler smoked his Dunhill menthols à la Franklin Delano Roosevelt. Babbitt's imitation was so precise that it seemed uncannily human. Then, having established his character, he did something far worse: he imitated the way Koestler sat on the toilet during his bowel movements, which were excruciatingly painful because of Koestler's piles.

This was all much to the delight of the Africans, who roared and fell to the ground and pounded it or simply held their sides and hooted hysterically. Babbitt, who was so often reviled, feared, and despised, now gave the Africans enormous pleasure. They roared anew each time Babbitt bared his teeth and shook his fist like evil incarnate, once nearly toppling from his limb before abruptly grabbing hold of it again. Babbitt's flair for the dramatic had roused the Africans to a fever pitch. Some of the natives began to dance as if invaded by unseen spirits, and this frightened Koestler marginally, as it had during his first days in Africa. Koestler thought that when the Africans were dancing — especially when they got out the drums and palm wine — they were as mesmerized by unreason as the mobs who once clamored to hear the irrational, primitive, but dangerously soul-satisfying ravings of Hitler and other megalomaniacs and Antichrists of his ilk.

The doctor retained his composure throughout the episode and, speaking to his pet in reasonable tones, attempted to persuade him to come down. Koestler knew that baboons did not climb trees as a rule, and while Babbitt was not an ordinary baboon, he was very unsteady up in a tree, even when sober. But the more sweetly Koestler coaxed, the more Babbitt raged at him. Koestler instructed Johnson — the only African who was not holding his sides with laughter — to run back to the compound and obtain a stretcher to use as a safety net in case Babbitt passed out and fell from the tree, but as the doctor was intently giving Johnson these instructions, a wedge of smile cracked the African's face and he fell to howling as well.

"So, Cornelius, this is how it is with you," Koestler said with a certain amount of amusement. "You have betrayed me as well." As the others continued to hoot and wail, Koestler remembered that his friend Jules Hartman, the bush pilot, would be flying a pair of new American docs in later that day, and considered what a marvelous story this would make. He wanted to join in the fun, but as Babbitt began to masturbate, Koestler's impulse to laugh and give in to the moment was quickly vanquished by feelings of shame, anger, and real concern at the possibility of Babbitt's falling. Furthermore, it was his job to see that things didn't get out of control. An inch freely given around here quickly became the proverbial mile. The doctor raised his voice just slightly, insisting that the audience make a pile of leaves underneath the tree to break Babbitt's fall, which seemed all but inevitable. "*Mister* Johnson, see that this is done immediately," Koestler said. "I had better see heel-clicking service, do you hear me?"

Johnson wiped the smile from his face and began abusing the Africans. Soon a formidable pile of leaves had been gathered, but then Koestler, who was plotting the trajectory of the possible fall, was distracted when a small boy charged onto the scene and summoned the doctor to the clinic. A child had been bitten by a snake and was dying, the boy said. Koestler hastened back, the heavily laden pockets of his bush shorts jingling against his legs as he trotted alongside the young messenger, trying to get the boy to identify the type of snake responsible for the bite so he would be able to respond immediately with the appropriate dosage of antivenin, based on the victim's body weight, the bite pattern and location, the amount of edema present, and a number of other factors, including the possibility of shock. His alcohol-benumbed mind was soon clicking like a computer.

The child's father, tall, lean, but regal in a pair of ragged khaki shorts — his ebony skin shiny with oily beads of perspiration and covered with a number of pinkish-white keloid scars — stood impassively outside the clinic with a hoe in one hand and a dead cobra in the other. The man muttered something about how the snake had killed his cow, how quickly the animal had fallen stone dead. In fact, he seemed more concerned about the dead animal than about his child, which, after all, was only a girl.

Inside the surgery, Sister Doris was already at work on the girl, who had been bitten twice on the left leg. Koestler assumed that the snake had deposited most of its neurotoxic venom in the cow; if the girl had not been bitten second she would have been as dead as the cow, since the snake was large and the girl was small and frail.

Koestler cautiously administered a moderate dose of antivenin, antibiotics, and Demerol for pain. Then he auscultated the child's chest. Her lungs sounded fine, but since the natives were enamored by hypodermic needles, he gave her a B12 shot — the magic bullet he used on himself to relieve hangovers. Before long the child's color improved, and only then did Koestler's thoughts return to Babbitt's latest caper. It seemed like an event that had happened in the distant past.

Mopping perspiration from his face, Koestler stepped outside and told the girl's father that his daughter was very strong, that the bite had been one of the worst Koestler had ever seen, and that the daughter was very special to have survived it. Actually, the little girl would probably have survived with no intervention whatever. But to survive a serious snakebite gave the victim unique status among the natives. Koestler hoped the father would now see his child in a new light, and that she would in fact have a better life from here on out. Sister Doris picked up on this and embellished the story until the crowd that had gone to witness Babbitt's debauchery had gathered outside the surgery to examine the dead snake and catch a glimpse of the young girl who would have unspecified powers and privileges for the rest of her life.

*   *   *

Koestler returned to the office in his small brick duplex — a mere hundred square feet cluttered with a large desk, five filing cabinets, books, whiskey bottles, medical paraphernalia, ashtrays, and a tricolored, fully assembled human skeleton. Koestler shook the last Dunhill from his pack and lit it. How long had it been since he had eaten last? He had a full-blown hangover now, and the cigarette, which tasted like Vicks VapoRub and cardboard, practically wasted him. He heard Johnson's feet flip-flopping along in an oversized pair of Clarks which Koestler had handed down to him, and looked out to see Johnson rushing toward the office, anxiously followed by a couple of boys who were carrying Babbitt toward the gazebo on a stretcher.

Koestler was not pleased. In the first place, Johnson had let the chickens burn in all the excitement, and now Koestler's fears about Babbitt were realized as he listened to the story of how the baboon had passed out and dropped from the tree with his arms tucked to his sides. He pictured the monkey falling like a black leaden weight, an oversized version of the Maltese Falcon. He would not tell Hartman of the incident after all, since if he did he would never hear the end of the pilot's ridicule about Koestler's misplaced love for the absurd animal. Absurdity was a very big part of his life, even as he strove to attain a kind of nobility in spite of it. Koestler became completely fed up with Babbitt as Johnson explained that the animal was basically unhurt. Koestler wondered if he should get himself a dog for a pet, since every other creature on the planet seemed inclined to shun him. It must be some vibe he gave off, he thought. Beyond superficial relationships, he was alone. Even Hartman, once you got past the fun and games, did not really care one whit about him. Not really. My God, he felt vile! Koestler suddenly realized how his devotion to the monkey must have seemed to the staff: as inexplicable as he had found Philip Carey's pathetic, masochistic attachment to Mildred, the green-skinned waitress in *Of Human Bondage*, a book he had read many years ago as a kid in Auckland, the very book that had pushed him into medicine and off to faraway tropical climes.

To be this much alone offered a vantage point from which he might look into the pit of his soul, but what good was that? How much truth could you bear to look at? Particularly if it left you a drunken sot. Koestler forked down a can of pink salmon; then, to clear his palate of fish, he chewed on stale twists of fried bread dusted with cinnamon and sugar while from his window he watched Johnson and the boys lift Babbitt onto the veranda of the gazebo, out of the sun. In a moment, Johnson was back in Koestler's office in his floppy pair of Clarks, so large on him they were like clown shoes.

"Him falling hard. Missing the falling nest altogether," Johnson exclaimed.

"Well," Koestler said with satisfaction, "you know how it is — God looks out after drunks and such. Maybe it will teach the bugger a lesson." Koestler fixed a Cuba libre and asked Johnson to salvage some of the over-roasted chicken or run over to the kitchen and rustle up something else, depending on what the staff had been eating. According to Johnson, it had been hartebeest, which Koestler, as a rule, found too stringy. He told Johnson to smother some of it in horseradish and bring it anyway. That was about all you could do. There was a tinned rum cake he had been saving since Christmas. He could have that for dessert.

Koestler looked out his window as the sun flared on the horizon and sank behind a curtain of black clouds, plunging the landscape into darkness just as his generator kicked in and the bright lights in his office came on and his powerful air conditioner began to churn lugubriously. He took a long pull on his drink, found another pack of cigarettes and lit one with a wooden match, and waited for the liquor to do its job. Johnson was slow on the draw. An African glacier. It was just as well. Koestler would have time to eradicate his hangover and establish a pleasant alcoholic glow by the time Johnson returned with the food. In the meantime, he got busy with paperwork — stuff that was so dull it could only be done under the influence. Hartman and the green docs were already overdue, and he knew he would be tied up with them once they got in. In the beginning, new physicians were always more trouble than they were worth, and then, when they finally knew what they were doing, they lost heart and returned to lucrative practices back home. The altruism of most volunteers, Koestler thought, was pretty thin. Those who stayed seemed to do so for reasons that were buried deep in the soul.

* * *

Koestler woke up at dawn feeling very fit, while Babbitt spent the morning in abject misery. He would retreat to the corner of the doctor's office and hold his head in his hands; then he would approach Koestler (who was busy at his desk), pull on the doctor's pant leg, and implore him for help. Koestler cheerfully abused the animal by uttering such clichés as "If you want to dance, Georgie, you have to pay the fiddler. Now stop pestering me," and "You've sold your soul to the Devil, and there's not a thing I can do for you! Are you happy with yourself now?"

When Koestler finished his paperwork, he showed the baboon some Polaroids he had taken of it vomiting in the night. "Look at you," he said. "This is utterly disgraceful. What would your mother think of this? I've got a good mind to send them to her."

Babbitt abruptly left the room to guzzle water from a rain puddle but quickly returned when some Africans outside, who had witnessed the folly of the previous afternoon, began laughing derisively. He fled to his corner and held his head and, to Koestler's amazement, he was still there when the doctor came back to the room for a wash before dinner. The animal presented himself to Koestler like the prodigal son.

"I could fix it all with a shot, Georgie, but then you'll never learn, will you? Zip-A-Dee-Doo-Dah and out drunk again."

Babbitt buried his head in his hand and groaned mournfully.

Koestler finally took pity on him and gave him a B12 injection with five milligrams of amphetamine sulfate. In a half hour, Babbitt seemed as good as new, apart from a sore neck. The doctor took care of this by fixing Babbitt up with a small cervical collar cinched with Velcro. Koestler expected Babbitt to rip it off, but the animal was glad for the relief it provided. Koestler watched as Babbitt retreated to a hammock that hung in the gazebo under the baobab tree. In almost no time, he was sleeping peacefully. At the sight of Babbitt snoring in the absurd cervical collar, Koestler began to laugh, and he forgave his pet for most of the nonsense he had pulled during his drunken spree.

After Johnson served breakfast, Koestler took a stroll around the compound, barking orders at everyone in sight. The Africans ducked their heads submissively in his presence. Good, he had them cowed. He would ride them hard for a few weeks to reestablish his absolute power. If he had given them their inch, he would get a yard back from them. When he stuck his head into the mission school for a minute, Brother Cole, who was demonstrating to the children how to write the letter "e" in cursive, took one look at the doctor and dropped his chalk. Koestler imagined that he saw the man's knees buckle. No doubt Father Stuart, with all his carping, had blown Koestler up into a bogeyman. He rarely showed himself at the school. The children whipped their heads around, and when they caught sight of the "big boss," their heads just as quickly whirled back. Koestler tersely barked, "Good morning, please continue. I'm just checking on things. Don't mind me." Ha! Feared by all.

By the time Koestler completed his Gestapo stroll, the compound was as quiet as a ghost town. He went into the clinic at nine, and with the help of the nurses completed over forty-five procedures by four-thirty. No record by any means, but a good day's work.

Late that afternoon, Koestler took his dinner in the gazebo as usual and got drunk with Hartman and the two new young docs, who had spent the greater part of the day with the mission's administrator. Both Americans were shocked by the heat, the long flight, and, no doubt, by the interminable introductions to the staff and the singsong ramblings of that repetitive bore Father Stuart, who delighted in giving visitors a guided tour of the compound. The doctors seemed happy to be knocking back high-proof alcohol, and when Koestler fixed the usual bowl of banana mash and Canadian Mist before bridge, a number of rhesus monkeys rushed in from the jungle to accept the magical paste and soon were drunk and rushing around the compound fighting and copulating. Babbitt, who had ditched his cervical collar, was having none of the paste. The baboon seemed chastened and wiser. Koestler noted this with satisfaction and felt completely reconciled with his pet.

One of the newbies, a wide-eyed young doctor from Hammond, Indiana, said, "I see that the whole fabric of the social structure breaks down when they drink. It's like some grotesque parody of humans, but with none of the subtleties — just the elementals."

"It doesn't take Jane Goodall to see that," said Hartman. He had flown the Americans in that morning, and had got a head start on the

Canadian Mist that afternoon. To Koestler's eye, the pilot appeared to be on the road to a mean, brooding drunk, rather than the more typical Hartman drunk — that of merriment, cricket talk, vaudeville routines, and bawdy songs. Koestler had recently run some blood work on his friend and knew that Hartman's liver was getting a little funny, but he could only bring himself to give Hartman a perfunctory warning and a bottle of B vitamins, since Koestler liked to match Hartman drink for drink when he made his twice-weekly drops at the mission and, as Koestler told Hartman, chastising him would seem like a ridiculous instance of the pot calling the kettle black. Like himself, Hartman was an old hand in Africa, and while he was not a Kiwi, he was close, having been raised in Launceston, Tasmania. Those pretentious types from mainland Australia looked down their noses on Taz, as they did on New Zealand — the poor sisters.

While Hartman had the typical apple cheeks and large ears that made Tasmanians look almost inbred, he liked to claim that he was Welsh. "May the Welsh rule the world!" he often said, but at other times he admitted that a year in Wales, with forays into much detested England, had been the most boring of his life. Whenever the subject came up, whether he was drunk or sober, the English were "Those bloody Pommy bastards!"

From the moment Babbitt had refused the alcohol mash, the doctor had been in a good mood, and now he began to pontificate. "As a rule, a baboon will only get drunk once, a monkey every day. Incredible animals, really, are baboons. Very smart. Did you know they can see in color? Actually, their visual powers are astounding."

"What happened to its neck?" the young doctor from Hammond, Indiana, asked. "It keeps rubbing its neck."

"It's a long story," Koestler replied. His cheerful countenance turned sour for a moment. "George Babbitt is a long-term experiment. He's come from the heart of darkness to the sunshine of Main Street. My goal is to turn him into a full Cleveland."

"What's a full Cleveland?" Indiana asked.

"A full Cleveland is a polyester leisure suit, white-on-white tie, white belt, white patent-leather shoes, razor burn on all three chins, and membership in the Rotary Club and the Episcopal church."

"You forgot the quadruple bypass," the other newbie, who was from Chicago, said.

"Well, he's got a running start there," said Koestler.

The baboon had stationed himself between Hartman and Koestler. Hartman held the stump of a wet cigar in his hand and seemed poised to relight it. Babbitt was intent on his every move.

"Georgie smokes a half a pack of cigarettes a day," Hartman said.

"*Used* to smoke — "

"Still does," Hartman said. "Whatever he can mooch from the Africans."

"Well, I'll soon put an end to that," said Koestler. "He's getting fat and short-winded. His cholesterol is up there. How long has he been smoking this time, the bloody bugger? He'll end up with emphysema, too. And how come I didn't know about this? I used to know everything that went on around here! I've got to cut back on the juice."

"Dain bramage," said Hartman.

"It's not funny," Koestler said.

"What's the normal cholesterol for a baboon?" Indiana asked. His cherubic face made him seem impossibly young.

"Forty to sixty or thereabouts," Koestler replied. "I couldn't even get a reading on his triglycerides — his blood congeals like cocoa butter."

Indiana began to giggle. "Jeez, I still can't believe that I'm in...Africa."

"Tomorrow you will believe," said Koestler. "You will voice regrets."

"I mean, I *know* I'm in Africa. I knew that when Mr. Hartman landed that DC-3. Talk about a postage-stamp runway — and those soldiers! Are those guns *loaded?*"

"That runway is a piece of cake," Hartman said. "More than adequate. And the guns *are* loaded. The political situation is very uptight these days. Not that we can't handle that; it's just that it's getting impossible to make a decent wage. I've got a mind to sell the plane and head back to Oz. I'm getting too old for this caca."

"You won't last a week in Australia and you know it," Koestler said. "All the oppression of civilization. Sydney's getting almost as bad as Los Angeles. Every other bloody car is a Rolls or Jaguar. Not for you, my friend. You'll have to put on a fucking necktie to take in the morning paper."

"Darwin's not so bad," Hartman said, punching at a large black fly. "In Darwin an eccentric can thrive. Colorful characters. Crocodile Dundee and that sort of thing. I can make milk runs to New Guinea, do something — "

Suddenly Hartman seemed drunk, and he glowered at Indiana. "If you think this runway was crude, sonny boy, you've got a fuckin' long way to go." He sailed the half-empty bowl of banana mash into the wisteria bushes, and a few of the monkeys went after it, scrapping over the paste.

"Well, it wasn't exactly O'Hare International," Indiana said. "And how come the Africans sandbagged the tires?"

"To stop the hyenas from eating them," Koestler said. "It's hell to procure tires in these parts."

"Eating tires?" Indiana said. "You're shitting me!"

"The object of our little get-together is to ease you into your new reality," Koestler said. "If you get hit with everything too fast, it can overwhelm. Tomorrow will be soon enough. The leper colony — a rude awakening."

"What kind of scene is that?" the young doctor from Chicago asked. He was a dark man, with a hawk nose and a thick head of hair as black and shiny as anthracite; he was short, muscular, and had copious body hair. Koestler took him to be about thirty.

"It's a bit smelly. Poor buggers. Pretty much Old Testament, if you know what I mean. Your leper is still the ultimate pariah. In the beginning, there's 'gloves and stockings' anesthesia, and in the end, if we can't interrupt the course of the disease, a great deal of pain. They only believe in needles — they love needles. So use disposables and destroy them. That's the first rule. The second rule is this — if you have a patient who requires one unit of blood, do not give it to him. If he requires two units of blood, do not give it to him. If he requires three units of blood, you will have to give it to him, but remember that that blood will most likely be contaminated with HIV, hepatitis B, and God knows what all, despite the assurances from above."

"AIDS — *Slim*," Hartman said evenly. "The only safe sex is no sex. Do not even accept a hand job."

"I've heard that they take great offense if you don't eat with them,"

Indiana said. "I've heard they'll put the evil eye on you if you don't eat with them."

"It's true," Koestler said.

"So you eat with them?"

"Hell no! I don't get involved with them on a personal level. You cannot let your feelings get in your way. If you do, you will be useless. Move. Triage. Speed is the rule. You'll see the nurses doing things that your trauma docs can't handle back in the States. Hell, you'll see aides doing some very complicated work. It comes down to medical managing. The numbers defeat you."

Johnson came out to the gazebo bearing a tray of chilled coconut puddings. He set a dish next to each of the men and then began to light the Coleman lanterns and mosquito coils as the sun did its orange flare and fast fade into the horizon. As it disappeared, Koestler said, "Thank God. Gadzooks! Sometimes too hot the eye of heaven shines, huh, boys? Especially when you're smack-dab on the equator."

The new men said nothing but watched as, one by one, Johnson picked up the last of the drunken rhesus monkeys by their tails and flung them as far as he could before padding back to the kitchen.

Indiana looked out at the monkeys staggering in circles. "They don't know what to do — come back for more or go into the jungle."

"Those that make for the bush the leopard gets. It's one way to eradicate the bastards," said Koestler darkly.

"I see — method behind the madness," Chicago said.

"Johnson's been using his skin bleach again," Hartman observed. "He's gone from redbone to high yellow in a week. Wearing shoes, yet. The Eagle Flies on Friday Skin Pomade for some Sat'day-night fun."

"It's not only Saturdays," Koestler said. "He goes through two dozen condoms a week. His hut is littered with the wrappers. He's insatiable."

"Well, at least you got that part through to him. Use a rubber."

"Johnson is no dummy, Jules. He knows the score, believe me. He's very germ conscious. That's one thing. A compulsive handwasher. I trust him with my food absolutely."

As Indiana spooned down the pudding, he looked nervously at Hartman, who was a bulky man and was glowering at him. "What's this 'redbone, high yellow' stuff?" Indiana said.

Hartman said nothing and continued to stare at the young doctor. Indiana looked at the other men and then laughed, "Hey! What's with this guy?"

Chicago picked up his pudding and began to eat. "And now for something completely different," he said. "The evil eye."

Hartman's face brightened. He relaxed his shoulders and laughed softly. "I remember a doctor — an American, tropical medic — didn't believe in the superstitions, and in the course of things he humiliated a traditional doctor. The old boy put a curse on this hotshot, and it wasn't more than a week before the American stepped on a snake. I had to fly him to Jo'burg, since he was really messed up, was this chap. A year, fourteen months later he's back, forty pounds lighter, and a rabid animal bites him on the second day in. It took us three weeks to get a rabies vaccine, and it came from a dubious source. He took the full treatment, but came down with the disease anyhow. Bitten on the face. Travels to the brain faster. Funny thing about rabies — makes a bloke restless. Nothing to do for it, either. Dr. Koestler, Johnson and I had to lock him up in one of those chain-link-fenced compartments in the warehouse."

"Excessive scanning," Koestler said. "Hypervigilance. You could see the whites of his eyes — "

"From top to bottom," Hartman said. "Very paranoid, drinking in every sight and sound."

"What made it worse," Koestler said, "was the fact that he knew his prognosis."

"Yeahrr," said Hartman. "The paranoiac isn't necessarily wrong about things — he just sees too much. Take your hare, for instance. Your hare is a very paranoid animal. Your hare has basically been placed on the planet as food. He doesn't have a life. When you are an instant meal, you are always on the lookout. So, paranoid. Well, our friend was a lion, which all doctors are, present company included — they're tin gods from Day One — and, while it may work in America, it doesn't cut any ice down here; he humiliated this old witch doctor, so there wasn't any way out. No need to go around asking for trouble in this life, is there? The hare sees too much, the lion not enough — and there's the difference between happiness and hell, provided you are a real and true lion, not some bloody fool who is misinformed."

Hartman had the fleshy, broken nose of a pug, and as he spoke he kept brushing at it with his thumb. He sneezed three times in rapid succession.

"The curious thing," Koestler said, "is that the stupid bleeder died professing belief in science. He had a little slate and a piece of chalk, and when we finally went in to remove the body, I read his last words: *Amor fati!* 'Love your fate.' A stubborn bloody fool."

"Wow," Indiana said. "What did you do for the guy? Did he just die?"

"Of course he died. 'Slathered like a mad dog' is no mere cliché, let me tell you. I was inexperienced back then and had to play it by ear. All you had to do was say the word 'water' and he had esophageal spasms. You try to anticipate the symptoms and treat them, but we just aren't equipped here. The brain swells, you see, and there's no place for it to go."

Koestler accidentally bumped his pudding onto the floor with his elbow, and Babbitt quickly stepped forward and scooped it up in neat little handfuls.

Indiana picked up his dessert and tasted another spoonful. "This is good."

"Good for a case of the shits. Did you boys bring in any paregoric?"

"Lomotil," Chicago said. "Easier to — "

"Transport," Hartman said, picking up a greasy deck of cards and dealing them out for bridge.

"Mix it with Dilaudid and it will definitely cure diarrhea," Koestler said.

"You got some cholera in these parts?" Chicago said. He was beginning to sound like an old hand already.

"No," Koestler said vacantly. "Just the routine shits." He picked up his cards and fanned through them.

As Indiana finished his pudding, Johnson padded back out to the gazebo with a bowl of ice, another quart of Canadian Mist, and four cans of Coke Classic.

"I had this patient call me up at three in the morning," Indiana said.

"Called the doctor, woke him up," Chicago recited.

Indiana said, "Hypochondriac. Right. She's got lower G.I. pain. Diarrhea. Gas. The thing is — she's switched from Jell-O pudding to Royal pudding."

"*Doctor, what can I take?*" Chicago sang.

"I said, 'Delilah, remember how you — Delilah, I don't think you have a ruptured appendix. Delilah! Remember when you switched from RC Cola to Pepsi?' "

"*Doctor — to relieve this bellyache,*" Chicago sang.

"I said, 'Put the lime in the coconut. Yeah, it does sound kind of *nutty*. That's good. Now, haven't you got a lime? You've got lime juice. One of those little green plastic lime things? Okay, that's good, now listen closely — *You put de lime in de coconut an' shake it all up; put de lime in de coconut and you drink it all down.* Trust me, Delilah, an' call me in de morning.' "

"And she never called back," Hartman said soberly. "Very clever."

"Let me get this straight," Koestler said. "You put de lime in de coconut?"

"Yeahrrr," said Hartman. "Jolly good."

"It's not bad, but that's his only routine," Chicago said. "I've spent seventy-two hours with the man, and that's it. That's his one trick. Plus, he's a fuckin' Cubs fan."

"Hey," Indiana said. "Long live Ernie Banks! Speaking of weird, we brought in three cases of sardines," Indiana said. "What's with all the sardines?"

"They are an essential out in the bush," Koestler said, removing a can of King Oscar sardines from his pocket and shucking the red cellophane wrapping. "Look at that, a peel-back can. No more bloody key. It's about time."

Hartman said, "They've only been canning sardines for ninety years."

Koestler jerked the lid back and helped himself to a half-dozen fish, his fingers dripping with oil. "Why, Jules, don't take personal offense. I'm sure His Majesty has enough on his mind without worrying about zip-open cans." Koestler offered the tin around, and when everyone refused, he gave the rest of the fish to Babbitt. "King Oscar sardines are worth more than Marlboro cigarettes in Africa," he declared.

"King Oscar, the nonpareil sardine," Chicago said.

Indiana filled his bourbon glass with Coke, Canadian Mist, and a handful of ice cubes, which melted almost instantly.

Hartman fixed his hard stare on young Indiana. "What exactly brought you to Africa, sonny boy?"

"I came to serve humanity, and already I'm filled with a sense of the inexplicable. I can't believe I'm in Africa. And fuck you very much."

"Speak up. You sound like a bloody poof — 'I came to serve humanity,'" Hartman said.

"And you sound like a major asshole. Why don't you try a little anger-management training?"

"Bloody poof, I knew it. Nancy girl!"

"Fuck!" Indiana said. "You're drunk. I'm not even talking to you."

"Won't last a week. Mark my words," Hartman said.

"Tomorrow you will believe," Koestler said. "The leper colony."

"Separates the men from the boys," said Hartman.

"Way down deep in the jungle," said Chicago, "we have the leper colony. We have Hansen's disease. That which we call leprosy by any other name would smell just as sweet: indeterminate leprosy, tuberculoid leprosy, lepromatous leprosy, dimorphous leprosy. 'What's in a name?'"

To Koestler's astonishment, Chicago pulled out a fat joint and torched it up. He took a long drag and passed it to the other American.

"I did a rotation at the leprosarium in Carville, Louisiana, when I was in the Navy," Chicago said. "I learned how to understand the prevailing mentality of the patient suffering from Hansen's disease."

"Put yourself in their 'prosthetic' shoes, did you?" Hartman said.

"The kid's right," Chicago said. "You're a hostile person. Shut up and listen. I mean, these patients are in denial until a white coat gives it to them straight. Zombie denial, man. You should see the look on their face. It's not a look like you've got cancer, which is a good one, instant shock. The you've-got-Hansen's look is more like, 'I have of late — but wherefore I know not — lost all my mirth —'"

"I know that look," Koestler said. "I see it every morning whilst I shave. Jules, the man knows Shakespeare."

"I suppose a leper colony in Africa is a hut made out of buffalo shit —"

"In your leper colony over there in the States," Hartman said, "are all the lepers bloody nigs?"

"You really are a racist, aren't you?" Indiana said.

Koestler attempted to deflect this inquiry. "I believe the current phraseology is 'African-American,' Jules, or, if you must, 'black.' "

"Some are black. Some are white. Some are Hispanic," Chicago said.

"That word of yours is not in my vocabulary, and if you say it again — "

"You'll what?"

"Jules, please," said Koestler. "Don't be bloody uncouth."

Hartman pitched his head forward and pretended to sob over his cards. "I'm an uncouth ruffian, I won't deny it." He gulped down some whiskey and said, "When that faggot over there wants to fly home for ballet lessons, it won't be in my plane."

"Aryan Brotherhood," Indiana said.

Koestler raised his hand to silence the doctor while he turned on Chicago. "Where on earth did you score that joint?" he asked. "Did you give it to them, Jules?"

"Actually, it was your man, Johnson," Indiana said. "God, am I ever high. Everything is so…surreal."

"Johnson? That bugger!" Koestler said. "He's got his hand in everything."

Koestler put the wet end of the joint to his lips and took a tentative puff. As he did, Chicago pulled out another and lit it.

"Fuck," Koestler said. He took another hit. A much bigger one.

Chicago handed the new joint to Koestler's baboon, who greedily inhaled the smoke, and for the next few moments the whole curious party sat around the table attempting to suppress coughs.

"I'm so fucking high," Indiana said. "Jesus."

"A minute ago I was drunk; now you can't tie your shoelaces," Hartman said. "Poofter!"

"Let's have a little music," said Koestler. He flipped on the shortwave and fiddled with the dial. "I have got nothing but bloody Radio Ireland recently, half Gaelic, and then an hour of bird calls! Needs a new battery." He slapped at the radio and then, with Dixieland accompaniment, an Irish tenor was singing, "I've flown around the world in a plane — "

Koestler joined in. "I've settled revolutions in Spain — "

He flipped the dial and slapped the set until he hooked into American Armed Forces Radio. After an announcer listed the major-league ball scores, Jimi Hendrix came on blaring "Red House."

The men sat back and listened to the music. Koestler popped up to turn up the volume, his weather-beaten face collapsing inward as he took in another draught of marijuana smoke, closed his eyes, tossed his head back, and got into the song. He was soon snaking about the duckboard floor of the gazebo, playing air guitar to the music.

"Hey, if Father Stuart could only see us now," Hartman said. "Father Stuart *can* see you now!" The priest flipped on an electric torch and stepped out of the darkness up into the gazebo. "This is a hospital, not a fraternity house! Kindly remember that. People are trying to sleep. Can't you think of others for a change?" He turned to the new doctors. "I'm glad to see that you two lads are off to an auspicious beginning."

The priest, dressed in a bathrobe and flip-flops, snatched the shortwave, switched it off, slung it under his arm, and clopped back toward the lodge. The beam of his flashlight, which was tucked between his shoulder and chin, panned the wisteria bushes, the ground, the sky, and the buildings of the compound as he attempted to push down the telescopic antenna on the radio. For a moment, the men sat in stunned silence. This was followed by an explosion of laughter.

Koestler started up as if to go after the priest, but then thought better of it and sat down at the table. He reached into his bush shirt and removed another can of sardines, handing them to Babbitt, who quickly tore off the lid, ate the fish, and then licked the olive oil from the inside of the can. "You might not believe it, but Georgie can open a can of sardines even with a key," Koestler said proudly.

"Fuck, he's got the munchies," Indiana said, as he fell into a paroxysm of laughter.

Chicago studied the red sardine jacket, giggling as he read: "Add variety and zest to hot or cold meatless main dishes....By special royal permission. Finest Norway brisling sardines."

"Brisling?"

"It's that advertising thing," Chicago said. "Brisling is Norwegian for 'sprat,' which means small marine fish. Not each and every small fish you pull in is certifiably a herring; some other small fish get picked up by the school. No false advertising this way."

"Wow," Indiana said sardonically. "Are you Norwegian or something?"

"Lebanese," Chicago said. "I already told you that."

Indiana said, "Who runs that country, anyhow? I was there, and I don't know that much. All I remember is that they won't even give you the time of day."

"No way," Chicago said. "The people are friendly as hell. The government of Norway is a hereditary constitutional monarchy, a parliamentary democracy, and the king is endowed with a certain amount of executive power. In reality, however, the king is limited in the exercise of power."

"He's a Norway freak!" Indiana said.

"More likely he's got a photographic memory," Hartman said.

"Touché, Mr. Hartman," Chicago said.

"I still can't believe I'm in Africa," Indiana said. "Heavy. Fourteen-year-old kids with machine guns — and, my God, look at the stars. There are so many of them."

"Stop acting so fucking incredulous," Hartman said. "You're really getting on my nerves."

"Watch Sister Doris," Koestler said. "She's forgotten more about jungle medicine than I'll ever know."

"Doris? Man, she's unattractive. She's ugly, man," Indiana said.

"She'll be looking pretty good in about five months; that is, if you last that long," Hartman said. "You'll be having some pretty intensive fantasies about that woman. Are you going to last, sonny boy?"

"Fuck off. I got through a residency at Bellevue. I guess I can hack Africa."

"The thing about Doris," Koestler said, slicing the air with the edge of his hand, "is that she's what we call an A-teamer. The A-team takes all of this business seriously. Tight-asses. Father Stuart is A-team beaucoup. There are B-teamers, who take a more casual approach. You will line up with one of these factions. Personally, if the political thing doesn't ease up a bit, I'm going to boogie out of this hellhole. I've no desire to have my throat slit. Stuart and Doris will stay until the last dog is hung."

"Go back to Kiwiland and listen to them harp about All Blacks rugby and that bloody yacht trophy," Hartman said. "Family's gone. Africa's your home, man."

"I've got a few cousins left in Auckland, and I do miss New Zealand beer, rather," Koestler said. "I'm not going to hang around and get my throat cut. I'd rather try a little lawn bowling."

"The natives are restless?" Indiana said.

"Yes, Percy le Poof," Hartman said. "The natives are restless."

"Politics as usual. So far, it hasn't filtered down to the villages," Koestler said. "It's a lot safer here than in Newark, New Jersey, I would imagine."

Suddenly the men fell silent and examined their cards. Swarms of insects buzzed the gazebo in successive waves.

Despite the mosquito coils, the insects attacked ferociously. Hartman was the first to hop up, and he moved with a quickness that startled the others. With no warning, he roughly grabbed Indiana's head in the crook of his muscular forearm and savagely rubbed his knuckles over the top of the young doctor's head. His feet shuffled adroitly, like those of a fat but graceful tap dancer, as he yanked the doctor in various directions, never letting him set himself for balance. Hartman ran his knuckles back and forth over the young man's crew cut, crying, "*Haji Baba!* Hey, hey! *Haji Baba!* Hey, hey!"

"Ouch, goddamn!" Indiana shouted. He was tall, with a basketball-player's build, and he finally wrested himself out of Hartman's powerful grip. He stood his ground, assuming a boxer's pose. Both he and Hartman were suddenly drenched with sweat. "You fucker! Shit!"

Hartman threw his hands in the air, his palms open in a gesture of peace. As soon as Indiana dropped his guard, Hartman waded in throwing roundhouse punches. One of these connected, and a chip of tooth pankled off a can of Coke Classic on the table. Indiana pulled Hartman forward, going with the older man's momentum. At the same time, he kicked Hartman's feet out from under him, and the two men rolled off the gazebo, and Indiana rose astride Hartman's broad back like a cowboy. Indiana had Hartman's arm pulled up in a chicken wing with one hand while he felt for his missing front tooth with the other.

"You son of a bitch!" Indiana said. "Fat bastard." He pounded Hartman's large ears with the meaty side of his fist. "I'll show you who's a faggot. How do you like it?"

He continued to cuff the pilot and cranked the arm up higher until Hartman cried, "Oh God, stop!"

"Had enough? Had enough?"

"God, yes. God, yes. I give!"

Indiana released his grip and got up. He was covered with black dirt. He was studying an abrasion on his knee when Hartman leaped atop him pickaback and began clawing at his face.

Hartman cried, "Son-of-a-bitch, I'll kill you!" Once again the two men began rolling about in the dirt. This time Hartman emerged on top, and his punches rained down on the younger man until Chicago and Koestler each snatched him by one of his arms and dragged him off and flung him back into his chair. He started to get up, but Koestler shoved him back down with both hands and then pointed a finger in his face.

"You're drunk. Knock this shit off immediately!"

Hartman clutched his chest and panted frantically, wheezing. Rivulets of sweat coated with black dust rolled down off his face and dropped on his lap like oily pearls. Koestler poured out a large glass of whiskey and handed it to Hartman and said, "Here, old man. Drink yourself sober."

"Just having a bit of fun is all," Hartman said agreeably. "Didn't mean anything by it." Indiana drew away from Hartman, who managed the entire glass of whiskey in three gulps. "I believe all that marijuana got me going. No offense intended. Apologies all around."

Hartman took a mashed cigar out of his pocket, twisted off the broken end, and lighted it. He puffed rapidly without inhaling and wafted the smoke in front of his face to clear away the mosquitoes. Then he pulled himself up, set his glass on the table, and said, "It's been a long day, and here I am, shitfaced again. Good night, all."

Hartman hastily made his way up the path toward the sleeping quarters beyond the surgery. As he went, he laughed again and repeated the famous Monty Python litany, "And now for something completely different — sawing logs. Ah, zzzzz! Ah, zzzzz! Ah, zzzzz!"

Indiana turned to Koestler. "What is with that guy?"

"Don't mind Jules. He's a jolly good fellow. You'll grow to love him. And he won't remember a thing about tonight. Blackout drunk, this — presumably. I might not remember any of it, either."

From the distance, an elephant blared, a big cat roared, the hyenas began their freakishly human wailing, and the whole cacophony of jungle sounds took over the night.

*   *   *

Was it a minute or an hour later that Babbitt hopped on Hartman's empty chair and seemed to beseech the cardplayers to deal him in? The men had drifted off into their separate thoughts. Babbitt grabbed the bottle of Canadian Mist from the card table and, brandishing sharp canine teeth that shone like ivory in the glow of the Coleman lanterns, caused both the young doctors to duck to the floor before he quickly sprang off into the black jungle. Even Koestler hit the deck, wrenching his knee. When he got up, he brushed himself off and said, "That settles it, I'm getting myself a dog."

"Christ, that's one mean son-of-a-bitch!" said Chicago. "And I thought you said a baboon will only get drunk once. Here I thought he was poised to go for that goat-shit cigar. I mean, so much for your full Cleveland."

"Georgie is not your average baboon," Koestler said with a shrug. "Especially when he's stoned. When you've got a stoned baboon, all bets are off."

Indiana looked at Koestler. "What are we going to do? Are we going after him?"

"Not likely — anyhow, you need to clean up. Put something on those scratches. They can go septic overnight in this climate."

"But the leopard."

"Not to worry. I'll send Johnson and some of the men out with flashlights and shotguns. I'm absolutely fried from that joint. I'm not going out there — although we have to do something about that cat. He's getting altogether too bold, and we have children about. I'm going to have to roust Johnson. Anyhow, welcome to the B-team, gentlemen — Har har! Try to get some sleep. Tomorrow is going to be a rather difficult...a rather gruesome...well, shall I say, it won't be your typical day at the office? Up at dawn and that sort of thing." Koestler tossed back the last of his drink. "Rude awakening, the leper colony. Not for the faint of heart."

The young doctors grimly nodded an affirmation as Koestler made a pretense of cleaning up around the card table. He watched the two men stumble back to their rooms in the dorm, and when they were out of sight, he picked up one of the fat roaches that were left over from their party. He lit it with his Ronson and managed to get three good tokes off it. He heard the leopard out in the bush. Who was it? Stanley? Was it Sir Henry Morton Stanley who had been attacked by a lion, shaken into shock, and who later reported that he had felt a numbness that was a kind of bliss — a natural blessing for those creatures who were eaten alive? Not a bad way to go. Of course, leopards were smaller. Slashers.

Koestler picked up Indiana's drink, which was filled to the brim; it was warm, and the Coke in it had gone flat. It didn't matter. There seemed to be a perfect rightness to everything. That was the marijuana. Well, what difference did it make? It was his current reality. When he finished the whiskey, Koestler got up and clicked on his small chrome-plated penlight and followed its narrow beam into the bush. The beam was just long enough to allow him to put one foot in front of the other. Finding Babbitt would be almost impossible. *Amor fati.* Choose the right time to die. Well, there was no need to overdramatize; he was just taking a little midnight stroll. The leopard, unless it was crazy, would run from his very smell.

As soon as Koestler got under the jungle canopy, the air temperature fell ten degrees. The bush smelled damp and rotten. Yet, for the first time in thirty years, Koestler felt at one with the jungle. A little T-Bone Walker blues beamed in from some remote area of the brain: *They call it Stormy Monday, but Tuesday's just as bad.*

At the sound of Koestler's heavy boots, the nocturnal rustlings of the bush grew still. Koestler could then hear drums from the nearby village. There had been an elephant kill. Somehow his peripheral awareness had picked up on that news at some point during this most incredible day. Elephant kill. House of meat. Cause for celebration. The doctor proceeded into the darkness. The penlight seemed to dim; were the batteries low? Beneath the sound of the drumbeats, Koestler heard a branch snap. He stood stock-still in the middle of it all. He flipped his penlight right and left, and in a low, piping voice, said, "Georgie, Georgie? Where are you, my little pal? Why don't you come on back home? Come back home to Daddykins."

Pickpocket

THESE KIDS THAT slashed the top on the Saab (ain't it a shame, twelve hundred miles on it, a black ragtop, turbocharger, five-disc sound system!), these kids call me Chop-a-Leg, which is what I had done to me. They chop a leg when the foot turns gangrene. I had diabetes twelve years and wouldn't quit smokin'. My podiatrist warned me the day was drawing near, but I didn't listen. I was still out there trying to get my kicks. Now I traded the five-speed in for an automatic since when you been chop-a-legged, your prosthetic foot don't rightly feel the clutch and that can mean smash your ass!

I got a hardtop with a V-6 and these kids calling me Chop-a-Leg raked up the paint job with a blade, so now I don't have to take care parking it or lay in bed and worry about no ragtop. See, I'm new to the neighborhood and they don't know who I am. All that shit — "I got a new car, what if it gets nicked?" — is over. I got the problem defused. Those kids did me a favor. I mean I got friends, okay, who could see to it that I could park that car anywhere in the city and nobody but nobody would get near 'cause I'm a stand-up con with connections, but in my old age I find I really do abhor violence, squalor, and ugliness. And I was a kid once. I did stuff like that. So I let it slide and had a talk with those boys. It was a highly effective conversation. There won't be no more *fuck fuck* with that car.

The doctors gave me the first diabetes lecture more than a decade ago. They fine-tuned the spiel over the years. There were updates. In one ear, out the other. I figured, You're gonna die, no matter. But they were right. I got hit with the shortness of breath, blurred vision, border-line kidney function, a limp dick, and armpits so raw I got to use Tussy Cream Deodorant or go aroun' with B.O. Is that *Tussy* like *fussy* or *Tussy* like *pussy?* Heh heh.

One night after I got proficient with my new foot, I hobbled down to the basement: Peg-leg Pete. I like to go down there at night and listen to *Captain Berg's Stamp Hour* on the shortwave. Comes on at 2:00 A.M. I always know the time, right on the money, bro. Serious. I bought a German clock with a radio transmitter in it that computes with the real atomic clock in Boulder, Colorado, and from that I set my watches. I got a solid gold Rolex President — your Captain of Industry watch. I got a two-tone Sea Dweller with a Neptune green bezel, a platinum Daytona, a Patek Philippe, and so on. They all right on time. Believe it. You might think, "Why is he worried about time? 'Cause he got so little left? What is the man's problem? Like God going to cheat him out of a second or something?" When you are fascinated with clocks, it's because you're an existential person. Some guy wears a plain watch with just a slash at the noon, three, six, and nine o'clock positions, you can put your money on that man. If the watch is plain with Roman numerals, he's also a straight guy. Non-neurotic. Trust that individual. That watch is your "tell"; it's a Rorschach. If you see someone with a railroad face — same deal. Arabic numerals on a railroad face, trust him a little less. A watch with extraneous dials and buttons, don't trust 'em at all, especially if they wearing a jogging watch and they ain't in shape. This is just a general rule of thumb — your man may be wearing a watch that goes against type since his father give it to him. Wealthy people buy forty-thousand-dollar timepieces that look worse than a Timex 'cause they don't want to get taken off. The people they want to know how much their watch cost will know, but no pipehead or take-off artist will know. As they say, if it doesn't tick, it ain't shit. You wanna know if your woman cheats? There's a certain watch style and nine times out of ten, if she's wearing it, she's guilty. I swear.

A good pickpocket is very careful. I did very little time in the joint, relatively speaking, and I made incredible income. Never hurt a soul. Didn't like jail. You know, joint chow is conducive to arterial occlusions. It's all starch and fat. It's garbage and then you lay around eating all that commissary candy. Smoking. I hate dead time in the joint. Idleness truly is the devil's workshop. I was goin' nuts watching fucking *Jeopardy!* up in my living room, no cigarettes, no action — just waiting for my stump to heal. Reading medical books. When doctors Banting and Best was up in Toronto processing insulin in 1922 they give what little they had to a vice president of Eastman Kodak's kid, James Havens, and it brought James around and saved his life. Meanwhile everybody is going to Toronto where they are trying to make bathtub insulin as fast as possible. They can only produce just a couple of units a day and they give it to this one and that one while a thousand diabetics are dying each day. One thousand a day. The treatment then in vogue was a semistarvation diet which might give you a year, a couple of months, a few days. When you are a diabetic out of control and you get hungry, it ain't like ordinary hunger. It's a sick hunger — *polyphagia*. Put such a person in the hospital and they'll eat toothpaste. Birdseed. I mean, I said I got connections and I could have gotten some of that 1922 insulin. After that there would come a phone call one day and somebody would want a favor and I would have to say yes to that favor, no matter what. That's part of the life.

Even now insulin isn't cheap. It ain't no giveaway. Shoot up four times a day. Syringes, test strips. They cost as much as three packs a day! Heh heh. But each day I get is a gift, okay? I should be dead. Before 1922, I am dead. The shortwave is an old fart's pleasure, but then I am sixty-seven years old. Most criminals don't live that long outside or in.

Anyhow, I was down there in the basement when I blew a breaker with all my radio gear going, so I went into the little power shed and snapped on the light and seen a pack of Kool Filter Kings layin' in there that I had forgotten all about. I didn't want to smoke a cigarette. Didn't need to. But you know, human nature is strange, so I fired up. I didn't inhale. Face it, it's scary the first time after you've been off. When you're standing there on an artificial leg thinking about the ambiguity of life. Tomes have been written, I know. I'm just standing there when I spotted a skinny-ass spider hanging in its web. There was dust on the cobwebs. I blew smoke on it and the spider didn't move. Looked like a shell. Dead, I figure. It's the middle of winter. I mashed out the cigarette, snapped the breaker, and went back to the radio. Three nights later, I really get this *craving* for a cigarette. I had forgotten the spider, and I went back into the power shed and smoked a Kool all the way down to the filter. It was the greatest goddamn cigarette I ever smoked in my whole fuckin' life! The one I had two nights later was almost as good. I torched up, took a big drag, and blew it all out, and the spider in the web moved like greased lightning. Jesus fuck! I seen a little red hourglass on its belly and Christ — Jesus fuck! Yow! Whew, man. But what the hell, it's just a fucking spider, black widow or no. Still it gave me a thrill and I could identify with this little motherfucker. Your black widow is your outlaw.

After I run through that pack of Kools I find that I'm still going into the room to check on the spider. It was always in the same spot. What is it eating? I wonder. It's the middle of winter. There isn't another bug in sight. That night in bed I am so worried the spider is going to starve that I get up, strap on my leg, take a little ball of hamburger out of the refrigerator, hobble down to the basement like old man Moses, and squeeze the hamburger around a web tentacle and give the string a little twing, like it was a guitar. The spider don't move. Starved to death. I was too late. One day too late, like with my atomic clock transmissions and everything, I'm late. Chop-a-leg and all that shit. Always a day late and a fucking dollar short.

Actually, the spider was planning her attack. I believe she had the sick hunger. When she smelled that meat, she made her move and then I seen the red hourglass flash on her belly again. Seeing that hourglass was like walking into a bank with a nine-millimeter. What a rush! The spider pounced on that hamburger and gave it a poison injection. I wiggled the web a little, so the spider would think she had a live one, you know. Then I realized that the light was on and conditions weren't right for dinner. She was used to permanent dark. I shut off the light and closed the door. After *Captain Berg's Stamp Hour*, I returned and the ball of hamburger was gone. Not only that, the spider seemed to intuit a message to me. The spider was used to having me come in there and blow smoke on her and I think, Aha! I get it, you got a cigarette jones. Fuckin' A! Maybe you would like a cup of coffee, too, you nasty little cocksucker. Piece of chocolate cake with ice cream and some hot fudge. I would like some too. Heh heh.

I peg-legged it over to a deli and bought a package of cigarettes and when I get back, I'm standing there enjoying the smoke and watching the spider — you know, chop-a-leg can't be that bad when you got eight legs — that's when I get the cold, dead feeling in my good leg, the right one. My chest gets tight. My jaw hurts. My left arm hurts. I stagger upstairs and take an aspirin and two of my peptoglycerine tablets or whatever. Heart pills. Nitropep whatever. Put two under your tongue and they make your asshole tickle. Make it turn inside out.

I laid in my bed consumed with fear. My heart was Cuban Pete and it was rumbling to the Congo beat. It took a long time to calm down. When I was finally calm, I said, "Okay, God, I'm ready. Take me out now. I've had it with this whole no-leg motherfucker."

The next thing you know the sun is up and fuckin' birds are cheepin'. Comin' on happy at six in the morning for Chrissakes. I pursued a life of crime because I hate daylight. It's just about that simple. When you hate daylight, when you hate anything, you will develop a certain ambiguity about life and you get reckless in your habits. You overeat. You take dope. You fall in love with a bad person. You take a job you hate. You declare war against society. You do any number of things that don't cut any ice when you try to explain your motivation in a court of law or to a doctor, to a dentist, or to the kids on your block who hate you for having a new car. God didn't take me out when I was ready. I was ready but the next thing birds are cheepin' and somehow you find that you just have to go on.

I didn't even think I was listening at the time but after chop-a-leg I was at the clinic. I heard this doctor say, yeah, yeah, he knew this intern who had high cholesterol. A young guy with a 344. So what this guy does is eats oatmeal three times a day. He puts some skim milk on it to make a complete protein and in three months his cholesterol drops down to 25. Twenty-five! I didn't think I was listening but it registered later. Come back to me.

I drove to the store and bought a large box of Old Fashioned Quaker Oats. I started eating oatmeal morning, noon, and night. I like looking at the Pilgrim on the box. What a happy guy, huh? I discovered that if you like your oatmeal to taste "beefy," you only need to pour some hot water over it. You don't boil it for five minutes. I mean you can, but nobody is going to come in and arrest you if you don't. For a while I liked it beefy. I also liked it regular. Once I forgot and bought Quick Quaker Oats and discovered I liked them even better. Skim milk and oatmeal. Three times a day. My leg started feeling better. I lost that shortness-of-breath thing. How simple. How easy. On the night before Christmas I sat alone in my apartment and ate my oatmeal with a mashed banana in it. What more could a person want out of life, huh? I felt so good I put on a dark Brooks Brothers suit, a cashmere topcoat, and went to the shopping mall where I lifted three thousand in green. Just wanted to see if I still had the touch. Hah! Back in the saddle again. I even boosted a home cholesterol kit. You stick your finger and put a drop of blood on a strip. Fifteen minutes later I get a reading of 42. Can you believe? I can. I sincerely believe that the regression of arterial plaque is possible even in a brittle diabetic such as myself. When they autopsied Pritikin, his coronary vessels were cleaner than a whistle. Already I have lost thirty pounds over and above the amputated leg. I take righteous dumps twice a day. I sleep like a baby. I'm a happy guy. I'm lifted from my deathbed and restored to acute good health. Sex might even be a possibility. I already tol' you, I'm sixty-seven years old but now I'm feeling horny again for the first time in years.

Every night after *Captain Berg's Stamp Hour* I continued to go into the power shed and feed the spider. She's my pal, see. I stacked all my empty oatmeal cartons in her direction with the Pilgrim smiling at her. It adds a little color to an otherwise drab decor. Heh heh.

I come out of retirement. I go out and boost on a regular basis now. I don't need the bread but I like being active. Ain't you glad to hear of my comeback? I bet you are rightly delighted. I plan on living to be a hundred. For insulin discovery, they gave Dr. Fred Banting the Nobel Prize. To keep guys like me going. Heh heh.

The spider, what it wants more than hamburger is that I should light a cigarette and blow smoke at her so she can suck it in through her spiracles and get some nicotine on her brain. Gets this look like, "*Come on, baby, drive me crazy!*" It's just a tiny spider brain. Say, "Jes' a little puff would do it, mah man."

But I look at the spider and say, "*Suffer, darlin'!* It's for ya own good. Take it from a man who knows."

Pot Shack

S HAKE AND BAKE" was much more than what you might call a gung-ho Marine. Second Lieutenant Baker took it one step further. To another realm altogether. This man could drop down a "junk-on-the-bunk" faster than the legendary Sergeant Chesty Puller ever snapped a four-fingered salute off the brim of his Eisenhower piss-cutter. Lieutenant Baker could put out a "junk-on-the-bunk" faster than Doc Holliday slapped leather in the O.K. Corral and pumped hot lead at a half dozen or so of the Clanton Gang from the nickel-plated barrels of his single-action Colt .44's. Dropped them Clanton boys like sacks of cement. This was how fast and emphatically Baker could lay out his gear. He could strip down his M-14 and reassemble it blindfolded faster than any other man in the company could complete the said feat with benefit of 20/20 vision.

Baker's boots and shoes were spit-shined like glass. The lieutenant could go through a tin of Kiwi dark brown shoe polish and a can of Brasso in a month whereas for most Marines said quantities of the above were quite enough for a four-year tour. Give Baker a compass and a topographical map and one could bear witness to — indeed, become a part of — the elusive, semimystical Tao of military science. Such were Baker's leadership skills that his every thought, word, and action could propel a lesser personality into selfless, right actions in the service of the Big Green Machine. Under Baker's influence a Marine no longer thought about himself and his personal woe or travail, that Marine gladly followed orders for God and country. Even misfit individualists such as myself were mesmerized by Baker.

In garrison Baker always wore a fresh set of starched utilities with a blocked cap. Starched and ironed them himself. His creases were sharper than the standard issue Gillette Super Blue double-edged razor blades. Blake was not impressed with the laundry services available in Oceanside, California. But then when you wanted to be the most squared-away Marine that ever lived, how could you find satisfaction from a commercial laundry service? On a hot day after noon chow, Baker would take his second of three shaves, brush his teeth, shower, douse his armpits with Right Guard and change into a fresh uniform. Moreover, he passed the true test of a lifer in that Lieutenant Baker actually *liked* Marine Corps chow. He ate seconds of the grilled liver on Tuesdays, the fried rabbit that was served on Thursdays, and was the only man in the regiment known to eat the sliced carrot and raisin salad on a regular basis. I came to believe that if Lieutenant Baker had lived in ancient Greece and served the Spartan army in the most minor capacity, the Spartans would have won the Peloponnesian War and changed the subsequent course of Western civilization. A man austere enough to endorse grilled liver, fried rabbit, sliced carrot salad, or the ham and lima bean C-rats is capable of anything.

The lieutenant often took his meals with the enlisted men. He got to know them and care about them. He committed none of the unforgivable sins of the typical second lieutenant. Baker was smart enough to know that when he *didn't know,* he didn't have to pretend otherwise. At these times he would defer to the advice of anyone with a brighter idea, even a common private such as myself. Baker had a broad, wholesome, and charitable worldview, and of course, all of the Marines loved this guy. He was almost everything an officer should be. So it was only natural that when he came up for promotion to first lieutenant, he was passed over. We were slowly gearing up for Vietnam and the Marine Corps, in their infinite wisdom, determined that an officer working in S-1 that couldn't qualify at the rifle range would be better off selling refrigerators at the Sears store in Topeka, Kansas, than, say, maybe doing a shitload of paperwork in Saigon. On the other hand we had a captain who should have been selling refrigerators on the South Pole. Captain McQueen.

McQueen nailed me with thirty days' mess duty after he strolled through the barracks one fine morning and spotted my open wall locker. It was a mess and I got mess duty. Thirty days of mess duty per year was allowable for anyone under E-4, but the pot shack was a special hell reserved for the worst of the shitbirds. Captain McQueen believed I was of this species because I hadn't been using enough Kiwi dark brown and Brasso. I wasn't spending enough of my clothing allowance on starched utilities. Furthermore my rifle was in "disgraceful condition," a special court-martial offense! Captain McQueen was of the opinion that the drill instructor that passed me through boot camp — Parris Island boot camp, mind you — was a moron. Captain McQueen said he must have been one "sorry-ass, piss-poor motherfucker" to let a "fucking shitbird" like me squeak through. What was the Corps coming to? And so forth. Furthermore, I was "the most piss-poor, sorry-ass excuse of a Marine" he had ever seen, and furthermore, if he wasn't in such a good mood, he would court-martial my ass, have my single stripe removed and see if thirty days in the brig would motivate me along the lines of housekeeping matters. I had never heard quite so many *motherfuckers* come out of a gentleman's mouth, delivered with such vituperation and in such a short period of time since boot camp.

McQueen wasn't through, however. Who *was* my D.I.? And what the fuck was I doing laying on my rack reading *Ring* magazine and *Batman* comic books at nine hundred hours?

I stood at attention and barked off a lot of "yessirs" and "no sirs" and hoped that Captain McQueen would get a sore throat from screaming and just go away. I prayed he would not open my footlocker, which sat tantalizingly before him with my Master padlock hanging open on the footlocker's hinge and clasp. McQueen was in an energetic mood and kept on screaming as he upended my footlocker and spilled its contents onto the concrete floor of the barracks. But instead of spotting my lid of grass which spilled into plain view, McQueen reached for my Gillette double-edged safety razor and ordered me to dry-shave. I do believe such an act of torture is against the Geneva Convention Rules, especially when your Super Blues have gone three steps beyond "dull" — I mean, it brought tears to my eyes to have to shave in such a fashion but I complied anyhow, artfully kicking a pair of dirty skivvies over the lid of grass as I finished the job. Then I commenced to explain to Captain McQueen that I was a boxer in special services and that the reason I hadn't shaved was the fact that I had a fight coming up in three days. "A close shave will lead to a cut on my nineteen-year-old baby-pink face! Sir!" I said that the reasons I was reading *Batman* were both literary and psychological — I was about to go into battle, one-on-one with a Navy boxer name of Goliath. I said that Sergeant Wright, my D.I. back at Parris Island, had won the Navy Cross in Korea and never tolerated slackers. I was quite relieved to have the lid of grass concealed and confident that the boxing coach, Sergeant Myers, would take care of this Mickey Mouse hassle since Myers was tight with the colonel who himself happened to be a boxing buff. I was penciled in as the light heavyweight even though I had lost two of my last five fights. I smoked, drank, and had quite a gut going in addition to my grass habit. The team's only possible winners figured to be the Menares brothers, Sammy and Flash — twins from the Philippines, a featherweight and lightweight respectively, and our best bet, the middleweight, Hector Greene, who was fifteen pounds lighter than me and my chief sparring partner. Hector could punch harder than me and he was all but impossible to hit. I hated working with him. I figured my own chances against the Navy fighter as pretty much nil, but as a member of the squad I was free to train and sleep as I pleased and to be relieved of all duties extraneous to boxing. I tried to explain this to McQueen.

The captain understood my explanations to be altogether too much smart-mouthing and after a twenty-second phone call, I was over at the chow hall in white cotton mess clothes with a little fluffy white hat designed to prevent the quarter-inch hairs of my jarhead from falling into the massive pots and pans the cook's assistants kept hauling over to the pot shack by the tens and twenties.

The pot shack was a steam room barely big enough for two bantamweights, a box of Brillo pads, and the steady flow of pots and pans. It smelled of hot rancid grease and on the perimeter of the pot shack, where the heat fell from the 110 degree Fahrenheit core range to the 80s and lower, and where the whitish-yellow grease congealed and was smeared all about the floor, it got into your boots, into the cuffs of your pants, on your white apron, on your hands, hair, and face. Where I worked with the pressure washers, the grease atomized and I breathed so much of it through the course of a day I was seldom hungry. The other Marine in the pot shack with me was a grunt from Oxford, Mississippi, larger than myself, and for the first couple of hours all he said to me was "Watch out, goddamn it, and hurry the fuck up! We runnin' nine mahls behind. Gait the cob oucher ass, boah." Mississippi had three teeth in his head, the most prominent being the lower left canine, tooth #22 as it is known in the trade. Due to severe gum recession and lack of collateral support, Mississippi's #22 tooth drifted to the center of his mouth like a tusk. It was about the size and shape of a Bolivian plantain.

My partner had a constant can of Coke going, which he referred to as "sar'dah"; I believe something in that popular beverage's secret ingredients had stripped the enamel off #22, making it amenable to stains. Mississippi smoked enough straight Camels to color it a kind of Boston Baked Bean brown. To watch Mississippi finger #22 or caress it with this thick tongue was just about enough to put me off the fried rabbit or grilled liver let alone a cold can of ham and limas. He said there was a cavity in it and he liked to keep it wet, like a beached whale, otherwise it hurt like shit. Since he was shy about twenty-five teeth, he wasn't the world's best enunciator, and because of his thick southern accent, I was able to ascertain little else of what he said. Nonetheless it took only about forty-five minutes before I was hating him as much as or more than I hated Captain McQueen.

Just before lunch the breakfast pots and pans were finished and one of the cooks signaled for us to grab some chow — bolt it down in the upright position, actually, since in the few moments we were away a new mountain of stainless-steel, brass, and aluminum cookware filled the pot shack. By midafternoon I was moving back and forth on the pot shack's slippery duckboard at all times very much aware of where my partner was standing and as I began to match his output, he began to hate me just a little less whereas my loathing for this lowlife hillbilly had no bounds.

We took the early supper and then worked until midnight finishing up the dinner pots and pans and the green marmite hot food containers that the mess crew brought in from the field where they had been serving the grunts on night maneuvers.

I staggered back to the barracks and put in a piss call with the night watch, fell asleep in my clothes, and when a Marine with a flashlight tapped me on the shoulder at two A.M., I jumped out of bed and made my way through the dark back to Mess Hall Number Three. A new guy, fresh from San Diego, was standing guard and called out, "Halt, who goes there!"

I was no seasoned Marine but neither was I in the mood for this kind of Mickey Mouse, so I said, "Bugs Bunny, motherfucker!" I heard the private chamber a round and thought a bullet in the back of the head wouldn't be so bad the way things had been going ever since I joined the fucking Crotch. The question "*Why* did you join? Why *did* you join? Etc. *Why did you fucking join?*" came up a lot in my interior monologues. It was my impenetrable Zen koan. I had not been coerced to join by the court; I was not a psychopath and I did not join because I became temporarily insane after a girl two-timed me. The pay was something like eleven cents an hour, so it wasn't for the money. I was not drafted but actually *joined* — of my own free will, sober and in full possession of all my mental faculties — the United States Marine Corps. I was convinced that such a fool as myself had never lived.

Mississippi was already dripping with sweat as I stepped inside the pot shack on my second day and pulled on my rubber gloves, which I later realized were useless and gave up altogether. "Whar th' fuck ya been? We nine mahls b'hind!" Liked to have smashed him in the face for about the ninety-fifth time in the last seventeen hours I had known him, but I reminded myself that the Marine Corps has some very bad places for people who don't get with the program. There was the brig McQueen threatened me with, which was pretty much like hell without the fires. There were the chain-link dog cages behind the brig where they threw you in naked except for your drawers, cotton, and where they cooled you off with a fire hose if you complained about the accommodations. Rations in the dog kennels consisted of three slices of stale bread and two canteens of water supposedly followed by a full meal every third day and then back to bread and water. My recruiting sergeant didn't exactly promise me a rose garden, but I certainly wish he would have told me about those dog kennels and the brig chasers with big biceps and billy clubs, most of whom looked like close relatives of Charles "Sonny" Liston, the then current heavyweight champion of the world. I wondered if my recruiter had any colored glossy brochures entitled "The Brig and Its Environs"; I would have liked to have seen them before I joined. I might have changed my mind and done something more sensible like joining the Foreign Legion.

Mississippi was sweating so bad he had his shirt and apron off. He was a redhead with plenty of freckles. There was no gut on him. He was rangy and muscular from humping the boonies. He had the standard USMC tattoo on his left deltoid and above that, emblazoned on his arm, was the name "Nudey." I took note, grabbed a fresh Brillo pad, and got busy. Just at the very moment the last of the jerricans were done, the cook's assistants bore down on us with sadistic grins and huge pots and kettles from morning chow. Some of these kettles, had they not been scrubbed so fastidiously, day after day, year after year — had they been blackened with soot, they would have put you in mind of kettles out in the dark jungles of Africa or the Amazon in which cannibals could cook two or three missionaries, a dog, and a mess of root vegetables all at once. And there were so many of them. And they kept coming! I tried to emulate Lieutenant Baker and get into the Tao of the pot shack. I tried to become a part of its essence, lose my identity, become a molecule or an atom — detach and just flow with it all, but that second day, all twenty-two hours of it, was just a complete motherfucker, pure and simple. Seventy-nine thousand, two hundred seconds of motherfucker.

I was back to the rack at midnight. After a suitable dose of self-pity, about 4.0 seconds, I fell asleep to the lullaby, earth-shaking sound of 220 artillery fired by grunts running night maneuvers. Dreamed I slid from Southern California all the way down to Patagonia and fell off the bottom of the globe into an abyss of dragons, toothy lizards, Gabon vipers, and black Norway rats crawling with typhus fleas. There were scorpions, Tasmanian jumping spiders with sharp ivory teeth, and various other eight-legged, predaceous arachnids with bad attitudes. Horrible as it was, this dream was preferable to the flashlight in the face at two A.M. I got up, took a quick piss, and then ran through the chill night air to Mess Hall Number Three watching red tracers arc across the skyline. An illumination round lit up the night like a full moon and I spotted the private fresh from San Diego standing guard again. I caught him smoking and told him to fuck off before he even challenged me. He just gave me a sly grin. We were both just a couple of shitbirds and we knew it, so why jack around? There was enough hassle for everybody as it was.

Inside I expected green marmite cans up-the-ass and I was more than right. The ensuing shift in the pot shack was very much the same as the preceding, except that I was even more tired and the color was leached out of my hands as they were filled with dozens of stainless-steel slivers. I began to long for the dull, sluggish, futile, languorous and aimless days of life on the boxing team. The pot shack was nothing but hustle.

That afternoon, Sergeant Myers, the boxing coach, showed up while I'm struggling with a grungy-ass pot caked with mashed potatoes. "Where in the hell have you been?" he says.

I started to explain about my underuse of Kiwi shoe polish, Brasso, and rifle-cleaning gear when Mississippi shot me a look of hatred for my falling output. Myers said he would talk to Captain McQueen and after he left, like a prisoner on Death Row, I began to entertain the slight hope that the governor might be a commie liberal opposed to the ultimate punishment. Or that Joan Baez would sing a sweet song to Lyndon Johnson, have him crying his eyes out and soon dispatching *Air Force One* to pick up such an intelligent, sensitive, and promising young man as myself, and send me to Harvard College on free government scholarship after a two-week vacation at Camp David.

That night as per usual, I went to bed at midnight. Piss call at two. The green marmite cans, followed by aluminum bowls used to whisk scrambled eggs, mix pancake batter, and concoct hamburger and white gravy on toast, i.e., "shit on a shingle." There were frying pans from the officers' mess filled with crusted egg, bacon and sausage grease, empty pans of biscuits 'n' gravy, and an endless supply of hot greasy bakery trays the size of solar satellite panels. There were large ladles, spoons, carving knives, and peculiar little dagger utensils that looked like Pygmy spears. Then came the marmite cans again and the beginning of the lunch mess. If you were lucky and you really hustled you could squeeze in a piss and a cigarette about three in the afternoon. The heavy shit came down after that — the supper mess was worse than both the breakfast and lunch jobs together. Mess Hall Number Three was feeding a couple of thousand men a day. We were doing double duty since the Fifth Regiment was ready to ship out to Vietnam and their chow hall was already secured. Mess Hall Number Three was feeding those troopers as well as our own. Still, the Marines working the scullery could clean up the mess hall exactly two hours after the last Marine was served chow and they could go back to their barracks, smoke cigarettes, and grab an hour of sleep before reporting back. They could take a shower or have a game of volleyball. The action in the pot shack, however, was unending. I began to fantasize on the various ways I would like to murder Captain McQueen.

To the Marines pulling mess duty in the scullery, Mississippi and I became objects of mystery, fascination, and much speculation. We looked like a couple of Haitian zombies, only we moved faster. Even the worst of the shitbirds were never condemned to more than three days in the pot shack. Geneva Convention. Soon I was pushing my second straight week and Mississippi, I don't know how long. There was no salvation from Sergeant Myers and of course, no intervention from that wonderful, talented, and elegant entertainer, Ms. Baez.

I really began to think it would have made more sense to join the French Foreign Legion. They had better uniforms and the thought of a posting in Sidi bel Abbes, Algeria, had a certain romance to it. I mean North Africa, check it out: the Atlas Mountains, desert sands, the pyramids, the Sphinx, Berber nomads, camels, date palms, and a policy of "no questions asked." There was the tradition of General Patton, Field Marshal Rommel, and T. E. Lawrence. Of course all I know of Patton came after the fact, when I saw George C. Scott in the role, slapping some poor soldier across the face for cowardice in an otherwise boring movie. Peter O'Toole's movie *Lawrence of Arabia*, which I saw prior to my enlistment, was a lot better. Lawrence, like Baker, seemed to have discovered the elusive Tao of the military arts. The harder things were, the better he liked them.

I decided the best way to murder Captain McQueen was by sleep deprivation. I heard it took about three months to kill a man in such a fashion. I would force McQueen to stand at attention in a brightly lit cell. Whenever he blinked his eyes more than twice in a week, I would order one of my legionnaires to hoist him up by his heels and whip the

soles of his bare feet with a sackful of centimes. "How long are you going to make me stay awake, mon Commandant?"

"I'm going to make you stay awake until you die."

In 1964, Camp Pendleton was nothing but a hundred square miles
of Quonset huts and lots of scorched foothills with names like "Little
Agony" and "Big Agony" and "Sheepshit Hill." These were hills the
Marines humped and were named accordingly. Big Agony was very bad,
Little Agony could half kill you, and a run up Sheepshit Hill required
rock climber's gear. It was nothing but foothills and Quonset huts and
one shade of green. There were no camels or palm-infested oases choked
with humid vegetation. There were no magnificent sweeps of desert with
buzzards flying high in the arid blue sky. There were no nights when you
could see magnificent soul-inspiring constellations of stars. There was
just the fucking pot shack where every day was a repeat of the day before.

Mississippi kept awake on Coca-Cola. I did so by drinking thirty-plus
cups of coffee. I had my head in so many pots and pans for so many
days, I was beginning to hallucinate. Once when I accidentally knocked
over a full can of Mississippi's sar'dah, he grabbed me by the throat with
his left hand while he dug his thumb in my eye and squeezed my face
with his right. "You ever do that again, I'll kill your fuckin' Yankee ass,
you Yankee cocksucker."

"Yeah! Yeah! Yeah!" I said.

Mississippi was a scary guy. On a prior occasion I tried to get neigh-
borly and he took a swing at me for calling him "Nudey." It was a good
punch and I was tired but because of trained reflexes I was just able to
give him a head slip. He tried to follow up with a left hook but I had
my hands up by then and stepped away from the punch as Mississippi
slipped on the soapy duckboard and knocked himself cold when he
banged his head against the sharp edge of the steam compressor's floor
brace. I let him lie there as I resumed my activities. When he got up
about ten minutes later, he had a goose egg on his forehead and there
was no more fight in him. I told him to get his fucking hillbilly ass in
gear. "Sleeping on the job, why mercy me," I said. "Get up. We're nine
mahls behind. Get the cob outcher ass!"

Mississippi liked to talk to himself. He liked to refer to our beloved
Corps as a "goddamn, green, sumbitch, cocksuckin' motherfucker."

On this matter he got no argument from me. But his negativity was infectious. By the third week I had passed through the anger stage and became a neutral Haitian zombie. While I was used to the marvelous nuance, versatility, and precision of the word "fuck" and lived in a universe where "fuck" was every other word, more or less, all of Mississippi's "cocksucks" and "motherfucks" delivered in a toothless drawl were making me a very depressed zombie. I could see no light at the end of the tunnel.

One afternoon just into the fourth week Second Lieutenant Baker poked his head into the pot shack and said, "Who did this to you?"

I said, "It ain't no biggie, sir. Just pulling a little mess duty here."

Lieutenant Baker said, "Go back to the barracks, take a shower, and get some rest." He turned to Mississippi and said, "The same goes for you, Marine."

The way it turned out, the way Lieutenant Baker got past Captain McQueen was this: everybody from the Fifth Regiment who hadn't qualified at the rifle range in less than a year was pulled off the line and sent to the range. Lieutenant Baker went to the colonel with a list of men who had not qualified from our own platoon and although it should not have been, my name was on that list. The reason I had a chevron on my collar had to do with the fact that I shot the highest score in my boot-camp platoon. That chevron separated me from being the lowest thing on the planet, a private in the Marine Corps. Being a private in the USMC is a couple of notches lower than being an untouchable in India — lower than a harijan haricot with a case of AIDS, wet leprosy, and halitosis. You could be an E-1 in the Army, Navy, Coast Guard, or Air Force but you would not be so low. In 1964 a private in the Army could just as well be some guy from Yale who just earned a doctorate in astrophysics and got drafted. A man could join the Navy and actually see the world, or a man might join the Air Force because of the food or training — but the Marines? I already listed the reasons: forced by law, insanity, and two-timed by your woman.

The next morning a troop transport left for the range at 0510 hours. Lieutenant Baker, Mississippi, and myself were on that truck and as we waited for dawn in the freezing chill, huddled in our lined field jackets and blowing on our frozen fingers, a range coach came by with a carbide lamp to blacken our rifle sights and flash suppressors. As soon as the sun cracked the horizon, the field jacket came off and sweat began to bead on my forehead. Two hours later it was running down the crack of my ass. The one thing the Marines can do better than anyone is shoot. To qualify at the range you must be able to shoot in the prone position, the seated position, and in the standing offhand position. You must shoot in rapid fire, and within the context of a more relaxed time frame, at various distances up to five hundred yards. Using your rifle sling, it is possible to hold the rifle steady and draw a bead. The Marine Corps shooting technique involves four phases. Breathe, relax, aim, squeeze. This is known by the acronym BRASS. It works for just about everyone. I mean, it's got a far higher success rate than Alcoholics Anonymous. As we practiced our shooting I could immediately see what the problem was with Lieutenant Baker. He would take the deep breath, blow it out, and then aim. But instead of squeezing the trigger, he would jerk. The reason for this had to do with the BRASS technique. Just after you take a deep breath and blow it out, relax and aim, time stops. Your concentration becomes so intense that all of time stops from here to the farthest reaches of the Milky Way. From here to all hell and gone. The next part should be easy, you just squeeze, but in the millisecond of stop-time, Lieutenant Baker's eyes would glaze over as he went past the Tao of military science and entered the realm of cosmic consciousness. When his brain finally screamed for him to inhale, he would jerk off a round and miss the target altogether and then look at you with a stupid blank stare.

Mississippi, who turned out to be a pretty decent fellow after a good night's sleep, and who happened to feel rightfully grateful to escape the pot shack, tried to teach Lieutenant Baker a method of shooting he learned plunking squirrels, possum, and deer in the sloughs and piney woods of his homeland. He had Baker line his finger along the edge of his M-14 barrel, point it at the target and then let his eye follow his finger to the target. This worked very well for the officer until we got back to the five-hundred-yard line. There, in spite of his thick G.I. glasses, which were so ugly they were known as "birth control devices," Lieutenant Baker simply could not see. But he was shooting so well in the closer ranges, we figured he could kiss off the five hundred and still qualify. On that day, at showtime, Baker, who had failed so many times in the art almost every Marine excelled at, panicked and shot high, missing his target completely at the two-hundred-yard prone-position rapid fire. By the time we moved back to the five hundred, Baker was pale with the knowledge that he would have to shoot a perfect score to qualify in the least of categories, that of "marksman." No doubt he was also thinking of the refrigerator and appliance department at the Sears & Roebuck Company in Topeka, Kansas.

I, on the other hand, had never shot so well in my life. After we collected our brass cartridge casings, Mississippi drew up next to me and said, "He ain't gonna hit the broadside of a barn, boah; what say ah put five rounds through the bull's eye and y'all pick up on the other five?"

"That's a Rog," I said. "That's a definite."

I was shooting four positions to the right of Lieutenant Baker while Mississippi was directly next to him in the fire lane to the left. When the butt pullers yanked up the targets we all commenced firing. Mississippi grouped five rounds in the heart of Baker's bull's eye. Then it was my turn. I grouped three shots in the same spot then put a round low into the second ring. I cursed myself. Even if I made my last shot, Baker would not qualify. Mississippi tossed me a look of disgust. I shook my head in disbelief and proceeded to put the next round in my original group. The targets went down and came up with white paper ribbons showing where each shot had scored. The field observer studied Lieutenant Baker's target with his binoculars. "I'll be a son-of-a-bitch. There's eleven rounds in that target." There was a quick conference with the range officer, who said that someone must have shot wide, most likely Mississippi who was directly to the lieutenant's left, and who had hit his own target a sum total of four times. Mississippi was cursing, pretending like he was highly pissed with himself.

My range observer pulled a chocolate doughnut out of a white sack, took a sip of hot coffee, and said, "You could have had a nice score, Marine. Too bad you blew it." A group of nonshooters had congregated around me in the hope I might shoot a perfect score. "Nerves," I said. I had my chance to be a hero and then just like that I was suddenly just another fucked-up PFC in the Big Green Machine. I think the fact that I knew I could have enjoyed a little ego enhancement is what caused me to blow my next to last shot at Lieutenant Baker's target. I was a victim of ambiguity.

Then the range officer announced that Baker would *not* — roger, *he would not* — have to repeat the five hundred. Because of the tight grouping in the heart of the bull's eye, the range officer deemed the eleventh shot on Baker's target to be a stray and qualified the man.

When it dawned on the lieutenant that he passed, when he realized he would be promoted to first lieutenant and could re-enlist and go to Vietnam where the life expectancy of a platoon commander was about eighty-nine seconds, he became the happiest man on earth. Everybody was whooping it up and slapping him on the back, even me. You go a year without smiling or experiencing a single endorphin passing through your brain, a smile can be a very exhausting exercise. I had a sore face for three days but in my heart I was glad because I did what every Marine would do, I helped a buddy. All the guys in our platoon threw a little party for Baker when he got his silver bars. We chipped in and bought him a new rifle-cleaning kit. Never saw Baker after that party. Much later, when I got to Da Nang, somebody told me he got greased the second week he went out on the line. You might think selling appliances in Topeka, doing anything in Topeka, Kansas, would have been preferable, but Baker, who was assigned to the rear echelon, volunteered for the line. I believe he died happy. I do not suffer from guilt for helping him get there without proper marksmanship skills. Topeka would have been his pot shack. Would have turned him into a Haitian zombie.

Captain McQueen continued to carry a hard-on for me. Most of your run-of-the-mill assholes have better things to do than sustain a grudge but McQueen was the king of assholes. Not only was I off the boxing team, I lost my gig as a typist in S-2. Got sent to the grunts along with Mississippi where I began to go through the Brasso and Kiwi dark brown at an accelerated rate. Mississippi got his three teeth pulled and was fitted with his first set of government-issue dentures. With teeth in his mouth he was altogether impossible to understand but one night when his gums were bleeding and he pulled his dentures out, he told me the story about his tattoo. He said he had no recollection of getting it and had no idea who or what "Nudey" was, but whatever, he didn't like it.

Mississippi's real name was Homer Haines. "Homer" of course was a fighting word right up there with "Nudey." The grunts who knew Mississippi called him "Bud."

In the infantry, I soon humped my gut off and in the process I learned that there were officers that were such nitpickers they made Captain McQueen seem like a pure candy-ass. Mississippi said he had him a mind to join recon. It was bad there but it was fair. I was young with less than a year in the Corps and more than three to go. Time was dragging heavy on my ass. So when I ran into my old buddy Jorgeson, my mainline man from the Island, and he too said there were openings in recon, where they take awful to a whole new level, I introduced him to Mississippi. We all got good and drunk at the EN Club, talked about jumping out of airplanes and shit, and then as soon as we ran out of beer money, we went over to headquarters company and signed the transfer papers in a hot second. A *hot* second, bro.

I'm not stupid, and I'm not pleading drunk. I don't like awful. But awful awful can sometimes be very interesting.

I Need a Man to Love Me

H ER PHONE WAS one of those black, old-time heavy jobs with a Bakelite dial, the base made out of ceramic or something — granite maybe... lead. It was like, heavy-and-a-half, an anvil. Seemed like a moron's phone if you don't know her, since in her condition she could barely lift it and it was getting all but impossible to dial. The left hand was super bad. No fast-draw Billy the Kid hand; it had no strength whatever. When it worked, when all was optimal, it was a cold blue claw and she could hook things with it. Captain Hook. People saw her Mickey Mouse around with the old phone and there was no sympathy.

The right hand was a little stronger. Not a lot, but it was her bread-and-butter hand. As the years passed it also got weaker. She wasn't Stephen Hawking yet, or like that guy with the left foot, Christy Brown, but close. That's why she liked to keep everything about her the same — the environment the same. This house, this home, her all-her-life home, forty-seven years in a shotgun shack. Okay, don't get morbid — the once cheerful, and still not such a bad...bungalow, was home. Period. The doors and windows were now secured with metal bars, a little crack action down on the corner but, hey! — that's New Orleans for y'all. Two bedrooms, a full basement, the add-on front porch done when her father was still alive. Busy beaver with a paintbrush and flower gardens was he. Her dad, Corliss, had a mania for tidiness, and her mother, too, which made the latter hell on wheels when the diagnosis came through; when they learned that she would be crippled for life. Turned her mother into a pisser.

First memories. Let's see...she could remember walking when she was maybe four. Just a little, you know. Ugly prosthetic shoes. Then the wheelchair. Oh Lord, your bony ass could get sore in one of those, day after day, even on a pile of lambskin. So how could a mother not love her only kid? Well, it wasn't that Lou Ann didn't love her, it was just that with Lou Ann being a perfectionist and all — there was a certain ambiguity, and when you have to wait on somebody hand and foot — a certain amount of resentment and you start feeling like a slave. You start feelin' that way because it's true. Corliss rose to the occasion and Lou Ann did, too, after he passed on. Finally! Lou Ann *finally* accepted the situation and tried to make the best of it. On top of everything else there was all the stress and strain of an adult daughter living with a mother, but what are you going to do? Then Lou Ann ups and dies. Her face looked like a fried prune in the coffin. A face like dried goat shit. A final accusation...like, "See what you *did* to me!"

Her dad had been a concentrated good guy, had a different temperament, but Lou Ann really never could take it. Corliss was dead now fourteen years — Lou Ann, three, leaving her to get by with daykeepers. Quite unlike her temporal home — her scrawny, dilapidated body — the house was still in good condition. You take a normal human body, you could abuse it with drugs, alcohol, tobacco, and junk food and still it would last longer than practically anything. It would last longer than a Westinghouse can opener, a pair of Levi's, or a Panama parrot. The average human body lasted longer than just about everything you laid eyes on except a house. A house could last...this house. But not the puny body that was hers. The house was still going strong. Sell it and she'd have two years in a nursing home and then indigent — a ward of the state. What happened then? You probably went down pretty fast. Some night, hooked up on a heart monitor, you know, one of those Jamaican nurse aides — *Fuck dis shit, I'm going out for a cig'rette. A Parliament cig'rette. Yeah, I want to have me a Parliament cig'rette. You could let dis here bitch die in the meantime. So what. World gonna miss her? I doesn't think so, daddy. Seriously doubts it.*

Mabel? Have you been out smoking again?

No, sir, I sure hasn't been smokin', I been right here, honey, like I s'posed to be. Turn my back an' she stroked out, thass all I know.

She would be under clover and the house would still be going strong. It was a waste of money keeping the yard so perfect. Putting on the vinyl siding — whew, she got jobbed on that one, but the salesman was so nice — man, that motherfucker *poured* out the charm. Oh well. It did look good. The roof needed work. Maybe next year. If there is a next year, huh? There wouldn't be any tomorrow if she could implement the plan, but she was an ol' scaredy-cat in regards to the plan.

Anyhow, there was the illusion of safety in keeping everything approximately the same. Better the old phone than something new. A brand-new, glossy, plastic featherweight phone would be a kind of formal acknowledgment, open up a two-lane highway from the pineal gland and pump out the death hormones. Dead wasn't so bad but dying like this was a bitch. A real live sumbitch and then pfffttt! So much for this incarnation. "Dear God, what was I supposed to figure out forty-eight years in this wheelchair?" Forty years plus of staring at the ceiling in silence, looking out the window, staring at the wallpaper, listening to classical FM radio, and looking at her face in the bureau mirror — a pretty face once, now not so hot, not with all of the makeup in the world. Bust the damn mirror. Stare at the ceiling, stare at the floor. Drink gin and watch TV. She never got out much but she knew life all too well, this life this…shadow cave and from her life she could extrapolate. Nobody but nobody was happy. They might think so, but they were wrong. When you got right down to it, they would rue the day they were born. Ho, ho, ho. Don't believe it? Wait and see. Ain't nobody escaped dying. Yeah, everybody wants to go to heaven, but ain't nobody wants to die.

Bobby was back in town. A blast from the past. Just out of prison and he lays a diamond necklace on her, a little trifling he picked up. He barely hits the streets and he's stealing again. Came over that afternoon, hardly says hi, and suddenly he's on the phone trying to buy her a new refrigerator 'cause the one she's got is "too loud." Whoever heard of such a thing? Too loud. That was pure Bobby. "But I spent a lot of money on that refrigerator. It's not even a year old."

"Yeah," he says, "and it just goes to show ya, they've been making refrigerators for years and listen to it. How can you even think? It's loud in jail, let me tell you, but that refrigerator is a killer. Good heavens, child, that machine is putting out Richter waves. What we gonna have to do here is go with the foreign made. Japanese."

"What, a Panasonic refrigerator?"

"Along those lines, darlin'. All I know is they don't take over the damn house. Believe it. I'm a thief. I'm in a lot of kitchens in the dead of night and I hear refrigerators of every make and description, and at these times I'm glad they are loud, but I didn't come over heah to steal and that thing is overbearin'. It's *audacious* and it's jes' a kitchen appliance. An object. So where does it get off? What right do it have?"

Bobby hopped on the phone and started making calls. Placed "on hold," he craned his neck around the corner and said, "America cannot make a refrigerator anymore. What are they but a damn box, a compressor an' some shelves and trays? People graduating from Harvard with degrees in engineering — you would think they could make a better refrigerator! Somebody ought to look into it and develop a whisper-quiet line of kitchen appliances. That fridge you got is loud, darlin'. The German ones are much better an' the Italian ones does look peachy but for a combination of quiet and style, my personal preference is Japanese. You know, the president of Japafreezor over they in Tokyo will bring every new model home and live with it. He will ask questions of the family. Say to the old lady, 'How you liking this fridge, baby?' Say to the kids, 'How you liking this fridge, honorable son, honorable daughta?' And these are not crude people, we dealin' with. They won't march directly forward with a bald statement lest they give offense. It's like a damn tea ceremony gettin' a straight answer since they are very civilized people. That's the way of doin' when you got seven million to the square mile. Maybe the son will get bold and say, "Why, it's not a bad refrigerator, suh, but the ice does tastes like dishwatah, they is mold on the *cheddar*, the Popsicles is gooey, an' the damn thing *hums* too much.' 'Just as I thought,' Mr. Japafreezor will say before he hops into his Lexus supreme dream and drives back to the factory at eleven o'clock at night, rolls up his sleeves and gets down to business. He is wishin' someone would invent a pill so he never has to sleep; so he can work twenty-three hours a day. Make it better. Make it better! No ice in the Jell-O, no mold on the cheddar cheese. Make it quiet. Get the *texture* of the Popsicles right. Make it pretty. None of those avocado paint jobs that looked all right in 1968 but became the worst color in the world a year later. The only American that clever, industrious, and hardworking is yoah dope fiend with a two-thousand-dollar-a-day heroin habit."

Bobby gave her a look like, "I've been in jail for almost four years, but even I know that one," and then suddenly he's talking turkey with a sales representative. Oh yeah — the automatic defrosters cause all the racket. They've got side-by-side doors or over-and-under. Gallon jug capacity in the door. Egg storage, also in the door. Colors. Cubic footage. Automatic ice maker.

In less than an hour, a delivery truck showed up and Bobby and the delivery men, smiling Asians in neat blue uniforms, tore the packing box apart and transferred all her food from the old refrigerator to the new one. There wasn't much — lettuce, baloney, milk — the usual. Bobby watched them with intense interest. "We Americans underpower our motors, don't you think? On a hot day, that ol' thing is huffing constantly. It's sufferin' from emphysema as we speak. The poor Little Engine that couldn't. Soundin' like a D-6 Cat with a Kotex in a Coke can for a muff-a-ler. Ever since I walked in the door it has been causin' me great psychic duress. I believe that my nerves are more than slightly frayed. That I am a bit edgy. Forgive me for rattlin' on so. I'm somewhat overcome. Perhaps I should make the switch ovah from regular coffee to a decaffeinated brand."

A worker plugged in the new refrigerator and flipped on the power settings for the freezer, the meat drawer, and the main compartment. It was virtually impossible to hear the motor but Bobby placed his hands in the freezer and proclaimed that it was working. "Black is a' ace of a color, don'cha think? Pretty *cool*, huh?"

He paid the delivery men with a roll of crisp one-hundred-dollar bills. "Thanks evah so much, fellas," he said, handing them each an extra hundred. "Here is a little kiss goodbye for such fast and courteous service. The world needs more people who take special pains to get things right." He gave them a hand in gathering up the packing materials and then as they rolled the old refrigerator out to their truck, he waved goodbye.

Geez! The size of Bobby's roll made her paranoid. He had to be printing money again. Thirty-four months in prison and he comes out and starts committing serious federal crimes. He would never learn. The diamond necklace — bought with phony money or stolen outright? Don't ask. It was merchandise. It gave her a small thrill to wear it but she really didn't want the damn thing or the new refrigerator either. Ultimately it would be nothing but guilt and depression.

It was sad to see Bobby do this but there was no need to drive him off with a lecture. And she had to get in the rest of her Carl and Maizie story. Those two were under her skin like bugs but it was hard to talk about it with all of the refrigerator stuff going on. Her story was rambling and incoherent but Bobby was quick; he got the gist of it. She felt better to get it out, and he listened with empathy. He kissed her tears away and carried her to bed, pulled back the sheets, white satin sheets, and Bobby remembered. Said, "White satin sheets and an ultra-firm Posturpedic. One hundred percent goose-down pillows. I often thought of you in these delicious circumstances while I was racked out in jail. You here, me there. Muslin sheets, a foam pad, and a steel slab are hard to take in your middle age; one develops delicate sensibilities as the years go by. Don't you find this to be true?"

It had been so long since a man touched her she practically came when he picked her up. He brought her to orgasms that were like epileptic seizures and dropped her into a deep and peaceful slumber from which she hoped never to return. Daykeeper #2, Lucille, came by to cook supper and help her with her toilet. After an hour of TV, Lucille put her to bed where she discovered a note from Bobby.

He promised to call back around nine and he did call, exactly at nine. "Hello." Somebody actually, finally did something they promised they would do.

"Hi."

"What are you playing? What's that music?"

"Mozart."

"Mozart? How *long* since Mozart? Time gallops anymore, even in jail. A year is a day." She heard him flip his Zippo, click the little carbon wheel and heard the small dull *bap* of ignition, a small explosion. She could picture the orange and blue flame. Then she heard him click the lighter shut and take a deep drag off a cigarette, exhale, and then fuss with his mouth, picking small strings of dark brown tobacco off his tongue. Bobby smoked straight Gauloises. He said, "Has what's-huh-name gone? The helper."

"Yes."

"Yes?" Puff. He really sucked on a cigarette. Really liked to smoke. He said, "Ain't it frightenin'? All alone for the night?"

"No, this is the best time. Why did you rush off? Why did you leave?"

"I hate to admit it, but whenever I am at liberty, it seems I am ever on the prowl for hard narcotics. When I am thusly focused, Hercules, Gilgamesh, Sir Galahad — none of them boys has got nothin' on me." Bobby sucked on his cigarette. He said, "This guy, your gentleman friend, Carl, sounds a bit *snakey* if ya ask me. I'm truly appalled by the way things have gone funny since I've been away. You just can't trust anyone anymore. Even your square johns are becoming dangerously unpredictable."

"Oh God! I'm so messed up I can't think straight," she said.

"Your best friend runs off with your boyfriend. I would guess you would be messed up. I don't blame you, darlin'. I thought you said he was married — Carl was married. Tell me about his precious wife?"

"She hasn't got a clue. She's just *out of it*. Doesn't know a thing."

"They always know. What do you mean, doesn't know? They always know. I mean you can't imagine it because you're in love with this rat-tler snake. You are not bein' objective. You're blind to the whole deal."

"I can hear you smoking. Aren't you supposed to quit smoking when you've got diabetes?"

"Yes; it's one hundred times worse. I cannot drink. I cannot eat so I'm going to smoke, take the narcotic and defile myself in all other ways pos-sible. I *am* a rebel, you know."

"The Leader of the Pack," she said.

He laughed at this and went off on a rap. "Kind sir, your leathers, Levi's, an' your motorcycle boots are quite nasty; your tattoos look like Haitian voodoo, your hair is all greasy and that beard is a fright. The very smell of you is revoltin' and if looks could kill, I do believe I would be dead. Everything is quite in order, we are all of us conformists of one sort or another, but tell me, whyever did you get a foreign-made chopper? How are you going to be a bad ass-kicker on that high-windin' Japanese piece of shit?"

"You inflicted that refrigerator on me and now you're Jap bashing!"

"Truly, darlin', a two-cycle engine is an offense to the human ear. Your Harley-Davidson rumbles in the lower ranges. Whenever I steal a bike for a job, I search out a Harley. They have become utterly dependable in recent years, an' if you are spotted in the commission of a crime, the heat will fall out on the biker groups, not yours truly."

She said, "What kind of drugs did you get? I've got downers. You could have asked me. I miss you."

"I called to discuss your heartthrob, Carl. Being a dangerous criminal sociopath has given me insights and advantages in the field of human dynamics. With a complete lack of moral values I have an edge over just any ol' Tom, Dick, or Harry. I can read deep into the human heart, darlin'. I have a few helpful pointers for ya to consider. I am about to *elucidate*. But let us first recap the situation: Carl just tells you that he doesn't like havin' such a 'limited' relationship. Although he will always love you and carry a special place in his heart for you, he can't bear to lay eyes on you again — "

"And Maizie is in love and I have to listen to her because I'm still dependent on her. I have to listen to her 'goo goo' crap. God! I just want to strangle them both. Somebody ought to take that cocksucking bitch out in the bayou and set her on fire."

"She's 'goo goo' 'cause he took her to heaven."

"Burn them! I'm serious."

"I believe you are. Your whole life, you have to be genial and pleasant. From day one you have to be nice, but you aren't a dependent person really...actually, if you could move around, if you were mobile and could ambulate at high speeds, you would be more like a barracuda. A muncher operatin' outside the boundaries of conventional morality, wreakin' havoc and mayhem."

"You got it. I have to play nice. I'm sick of it."

"When I came by I was a trifle drug sick and somewhat inattentive to your concerns. Set 'em on fire? Out in the desert? Why, I don't shock easily, darlin', but I'm still blushin' over the phone at those profane words you have spewed out in such a poisonous and vitriolic fashion. Mercy! You had mah ears flamin'. But you don't let people walk on you. You get it back. I hear what you're saying."

"God, Bobby, I'm sorry! I've never been like this. I'm so full of hate. I am almost afraid of all the hate and meanness I have inside."

"Remember that time out in the backyard when I had — I think, I had drunk around the clock and showed up drunk and we drank that whiskey, and then we went and got more? We went down to Shannon's Tavern together and you kept pissing about how I was going to dump the wheelchair, but I had presence of mind. I wasn't that drunk. You were pissed. I saw 'set 'em on fire' that night."

She sighed. "That was a great night. A starry summer night. Van Gogh's *Starry Night*. Alcohol and I'm-in-love LSD. I think about that night all the time. I don't remember anything about getting pissed."

"That was 'Light My Fire' night. I remember details. That was the night that *defined* my life. Actions proceeding from that night set me on a course from which there was no turning back. When I was in the joint I used to play Robby Krieger's guitar riff from the middle of 'Light My Fire.' The cut from the Doors' *Double Live Album*. When I was in the joint I played it several hundred thousand times on my Walkman and in it discovered the true meanin' of life. I know all about *the thing in itself* which exists in all things — this evil thing, this will to live on a planet where all is so blamin' nasty. Pain is the positive thing, the essential thing. Dear me, I *do* get carried away — so much for philosophy. You ever see Carlos, or Way-out Willie anymore? Hey, c'mon, baby. Say somethin'. Hello dere? Hello? Hiya... my name Jose Jimenez. He he heh. My name is... Walter, the performing Walrus. Ork! Ork! *I'm gonna love ya, baby... all night long.* I hope my mustache isn't too stiff and that you don't find my breath offensive at close quarters. Hello dere? Excuse me, missy, do you have a breath mint? A bottle of Scope perhaps? I may be a greasy-ass walrus but even I find a steady diet of mackerel and codfish repulsive to the palate. Ork! Hello dere, ladies 'n' gentlemen. I'm Wally the performin' Walrus and, gee, hey, isn't this a great night? Are dey *many here among us who feel that life is but a joke?* Oh yeah, y'all a bunch a existentialists, ain'tcha?"

"Oh, Robert, cut it out."

"You didn't even know 'Carl' and we had our laughs. We had good times. He wasn't even in the picture. This big hurt is going to pass off, believe me."

"Carlos is in prison," she said. "Willie...I don't know." She heard the Zippo click again and could picture him with the cigarette perched in the center of his mouth. "Yeah, Carlos is in the slammer and Way-out Willie took a powder." Bobby said, "Is that so? I figured them to be dead by now. They have exceeded my most extravagant expectations."

She took a sip from her bedside wineglass, popped down a couple Dramamine along with four Stelazine tablets. Robin's-egg-blue pills chased with more wine. She thought of Carl. Carl was a square, there was no denying.

Bobby said, "You're at that point where you don't think you can get over it again. You can do it once, twice, three times and then you lose the stomach for it. Does that make any sense?"

"I don't know — " she said. "I don't know if I can make it anymore."

"To give someone trust or credibility, you listen to them and then buy into what they tell you. When you know what they say is true, insightful, and that it feels right, over a period of time — as you come to know them, when they become your friend, you take on faith whatever else they may be pushing. As a criminal psychopath I learned that this is a vital, an essential truth. In the beginning what you had with Carl was really all on the level. Then they start lying and you believe them because you need to believe. That's why suckers buy snake oil, baby. That's why life is so damn tricky. It's the reason people get paranoid. They've got good reason. If that was his picture in your room, the man is involved in real estate. Razor bumps and halitosis. White on white tie. Diamond rings on his pinky finger. Why, I can scarcely bear to picture such a gross and horrible presentation of vulgarity. How could ya fall for a straight john like that? A pigeon like that? Well, that is water over the bridge. He's your boy. Then suddenly — whoa! This other passion is cooking for Maizie. Come to think of it he's having fantasies about her for a time and vice versa — subliminal, can you dig? Until there is some event where the two of them are alone together, one thing leads to another and they are both fuckin'. Let's not call it 'making love,' let's call it what it was, all right? Fuckin'. Probably did it in the missionary style the first time. That's how it usually goes, no improvisations or anything too darin'. All that exotic fuckin' — all of that comes later. Anyhow, he means no harm up to a point and then he has a choice to make. They're probably surprised to know you got hurt feelings! I mean they are so much into themselves."

She finished off her glass of wine and felt it warm her, it was a subject she was sick of, yet obsessed with, and this was another perspective. Nice of Bobby to try and cheer her up, but she was just so sick of it...all.

Bobby continued. "I mean, he's probably got an old condom in his wallet. Just in case. They commit the intimacy. Maybe precede it with some fellatio and cunnilingus. They are really feeling 'up' because they are doing something clandestine — naughty, sneaky. What a thrill! I mean now he's cheating at least two ways and this is really exciting. Are you feeling angry?"

"That," she said, "but more objective than usual. Disgusted."

"Fucking like a couple of dogs in heat. Get out a hose. You know, everybody does it, but they don't want the world to see it. And the reason they don't want the world to see it is because love manifested on this vibration is of a low order. It really isn't love, it's just lust, one of the cardinal vices in the Buddhist scheme. Don't you just envy them?"

"God, no! What are the other...cardinal vices?"

"Anger, avarice, and indolence. The cardinal virtues bein' chastity, generosity, gentleness, and humility. Plato's celebrated virtues would be justice — "

"Valor, temperance, and wisdom."

"Very good. I thought propriety was in there but you may be right. The prison library is rather inadequate. That's neither here nor there. Carl and Maizie. Together they feel as one. This is rapture in the back seat of a car. You feel like you're missing out on something? Smellin' kinda funky in that back seat."

"What are the Christian virtues?"

"What is this? You tell me."

"Faith, love, hope — "

"I'm not a Christian, but it seems to me that if you can have sympathy for another human being, the walls break down."

She took a deep breath and swallowed hot salty tears. "He *took her to heaven*. And you're right, she acts like she *is* in heaven, remember? Don't try to give me aversion therapy — 'it stinks in the back seat.' "

192 · SELECTED STORIES

"You say you wanna set them on fire out in the desert — that's the downside of all this shit. Part and parcel. That's all I'm saying. Think of them like dogs in heat, it's easier that way. And never, but never, get involved with a married man."

"My options are very limited," she said. "I always imagined being carried away by the passion. Swept up in kisses. You're wrecking the whole deal for me."

"This is not *Gone With the Wind*. This is a couple of dogs in heat. These two are bad. Give me the match. Has Carl got kids?"

"Three."

"That's splashing bad karma all over the place. Poor Carl, he needs *this* and he needs *that*. Fucks his kids, fucks his wife, fucks you — he's a *sorry motherfucker*. And you feel guilty crapping around with a married guy, right? *Why* would you mess around with a married man? You are not without blame, here. I get caught boosting and I do my time. I know the rules."

"You're right," she said absently. "He always needs this and that."

"And he didn't have the balls to come right out with it. He's doing it incrementally. I could go over there now and shoot him right between the eyes if you have an aversion to flame. He won't know what hit him. Where does he live?"

"I'd like that. In a way I'd like that, but — "

"You're a barracuda. I'm not lying. Little Anthony and the Imperials. 'Tears on my pillow, pain in my heart; that ain't you. The female Steven Seagal, I'm not lyin'. Where does he live? I'll get him tonight. I got my ball point and paper ready and I'm in possession of untraceable firearms."

"No, Bobby," she said wearily. "It wasn't nothin' no more than an everyday two-timin'. I jes' been down, I guess. Robert, it's so good to hear your voice. It doesn't seem like four years, it seems like yesterday."

"They were troubles yesterday. We always got troubles. Walk around on this planet and you're gonna have troubles. Only the mind does amazing things. It forgets the pain. You see pictures of people in the death camp — some guy points a camera at them and they smile, or somebody shows you a picture of Johnny and he's smiling and somebody says, 'Yeah, we took that photograph four days before he blew his head off with the twelve-gauge.' Life is tricky that way. Fools you. I could do it, you know. I could blow my head off. Once you make your mind up to end it, they say you feel incredibly peaceful and infinitely wise."

"When Johnny gets on the other side. What happens?"

"Nothing."

"You say 'nothing.' Like before you were born?"

"Just like that."

"What if Johnny gets over to the other side and finds himself in a pile of shit. A pile of shit he can't get out of?"

"No, baby, this is it. What you see is what you get. You get this. So anyhow, Johnny with his twelve-gauge. Maybe somebody says a certain thing and he don't take out the shotgun but three years later gets cancer of the pancreas. Don't have the nerve to die *now*. Don't got the balls for it anymore. Suffers excruciating pain. Termites eatin' outcher insides. Ya know? Johnny should have shot himself *then*. The part of him that can see in the future told him *then*. I'm not saying you should always follow your heart, but these unconscious drives are probably more correct than we will ever know."

She took the heavy receiver and shifted it to her other ear, cradling it against her shoulder. Poised on the edge of her bed, she reached over with her right hand and poured herself another glass of wine. She opened the drawer of her night table and pulled out the rest of her stash. She couldn't believe what she was doing. The plan. Her grand inspiration was fast becoming a reality. She never thought she could pull it off but she was doing it, taking charge.

"I could never shoot myself," she said.

"It's the fastest way out," he said.

The Dramamine had hit her fast behind all that wine. She picked up four more Stelazine tablets and swallowed those with more wine. Like Dramamine, Stelazine had an antinausea effect; it would keep her from puking. Plus, it could really make you blotto. She looked at her pills: her cache of Librium, glossy black and green capsules — five hundred or more; Valiums in blue; Xanax all pearly white; red and gray Darvons; Ludiomils in good-morning-sunshine orange; tricolored Tuinal in red, redder, and baby blue; drab brown Triavil in the 4-10 proportion; there were pastel orange methadone diskets (just two); some chalk white meprobamate in the generic — wipe-you-out-for-sure; multicolored Dexedrine spansules, passionate purple Parnate; there were her Nembutals, and the sea green, let's-do-the-job-up-right Placidyl gel caps (Baby Dills) — the pills and capsules suddenly became an object of immense beauty, a treasure. It was better than unearthing a pirate captain's sea chest filled with glittering gold doubloons, shimmering jewels: emeralds, rubies, diamonds, and chips of anthracite coal — better because pills did things. Drugs altered sensations. They could alter the worst sensation — permanently. They would do so…presently. All you had to do was swallow. What a relief to commit. To finally end it. She felt the richness and depth of color of the pills down to the roots of her hair. Pills so beautiful they made her hurt down to the roots of her hair.

Maybe it was the wine. No, really, it was the pills hitting home. Taken with wine on an empty stomach, they probably dissolved in seconds. She would have to make fast work of the cache and after she asked him what his plans were, she began swallowing the various pills and capsules with wine, ten at a time. It was like working on an assembly line and her hand began to tire. She got down thirty and had to rest a moment. She poured another glass of wine and was quickly back at it. This was her job. Her last job.

She heard the Zippo go off again. He was smoking. Thinking. There was too much of a dead space. He didn't know what to say. He was trying to psych her up and was out of gas himself. He didn't realize that he had made the final act possible. She was proud of herself. Your friends do sometimes come through. "Isn't that some bad shit at the refugee camp in Zaire?" she said merrily. She grabbed at the pills as the colors suited her mood.

"Yeah, bad. But if I'm laying in the gutter shitting and puking my guts out — and I have laid in gutters and done that, baby. Nobody comes along — no foreigner comes along with an IV tube to save my black ass. I ain't even expecting it."

"Geez, you sent me a postcard from Kinshasa, Zaire. What a great stamp. I got that card and I couldn't believe it — the Congo. He's in the Congo having an adventure and I'm stuck here. I used to wait for your letters, and the mailman, he was always so nice — when he came down the street — I'd be in the sun porch, he could see me — he'd give me the high sign when he had one of your letters. One week you were in Africa and the next week it was Finland. I thought, What is that boy doin'?"

"*That boy* got fucked up on some bad dope in Africa actually. Pretty postage stamps is all they got in Kinshasha, believe me. Man, twenty lifetimes ago; but that's how life tricks you. You're thinking he's in Africa having an adventure and it's horrible in Africa — back home watching the Atlanta Braves by the air conditioner is where it's at. Everybody always thinks they're missing out. It's an illusion."

She felt a surge of resolution and finished off the fourth handful. She could see that it was impossible to take all of them but at least the barbiturates were in, the methadone was in, most of the Valium. Her stomach felt like a bowling ball. But she didn't feel *that* fucked up, only just a shade past mellow. When is it going to hit? Why hasn't it hit? What happened? *When is this fucking show going to end?* She pulled a half pint of Gordon's gin out of her nightstand drawer and grabbed another handful of poison. It was time to get serious. You could never be too sure. Then a big wave hit her and suddenly she felt like she was blowing out to sea. It was a good feeling. It involved a long expanse of time.

She heard a voice. From far away. It was Bobby. Sounded like he was a million miles away. His voice rang with a subtle twang of desperation. "I said, 'You really sound fucked up.' What kind of downers did you say you had?"

She said, "I didn't say."

"I'm asking."

"Fifteen years' worth," she said.

Shut up! Don't let the cat out of the bag now. Medic I. Stomach pumped. Is that what she wanted? Was this just a hysterical gesture?

"Fifteen years' worth. Are you serious?"

"Why?"

"Just let me in alone in the pharmacy with a grocery bag and five minutes. That's all I ever asked of God."

It was hard to judge, but Bobby sounded scared. Her head swirled.

Bobby said, "I just called to say goodbye, darlin'. I'm about to shuffle off the mortal coil. I'm headed fo' Boogalousa where all is ultimately bound and from whence none return."

"That's why you scored?"

"Yes. To get the nerve up. Ever since I committed to the idea, a curious sense of calm *has* descended on me and I have felt somethin' like happiness for over a week or more, but now, however, the stark reality of the act has me alive with fear. If I take your meanin', you on the same path over some damn man. That's foolishness, abominable folly. I would not have announced my intentions. I was going to tell you I was headed for Chile but you let the cat out of the bag. I will not dissuade ya."

"It's too bad about the refrigerator. No one's going to use . . . it's not Carl. It's — "

"It's just a whole string of *Carl*, ain't it, darlin'?" He lit yet another cigarette. She could hear ice cubes rattling in a glass. Bobby said, "I can't hear you, darlin'."

Another wave swept over her, leaving her calm, unafraid. It seemed like a long time had passed. An eon. She weighed ten thousand pounds. "Are you on the nod?" she said.

"Shot some scag. Mozart . . ." he said. "You paralyze the high cerebral processes and mortality ain't such a biggie. No! Let me rephrase that: You paralyze the *alligator* brain and the higher cerebral processes engage in an ultimate clarity and *then* you can overcome the will to live which is seated right they-ah at the base of ya skull; you see the thing in itself in its true colors. Nay! Indeed, you feel it in the very core of your bein'. Forgive me, my thinkin' is gettin' sloppy. It's all very simple. You anesthetize and the decision to live or die ain't a whole lot harder than choosin' between chocolate ice cream and butter pecan. I have been practicin', but I must confess, I'm a trifle shaky whenevah I try shovin' the barrel of this nine-millimeter in my mouth. Th' taste of gun solvent an' cold blue steel is rather vile. I wonder how those fellas in the classical literature and the history books could fall on they-ah swords without the benefit of narcotic. Was they valiant? Why, I hardly does think so."

There was another long pause. She punched the stereo remote a dozen times. It was becoming too much of an effort to speak. The CD changer clicked and suddenly the Moody Blues were doing "Nights in White Satin." A very long time before it had been *their* song. Now he was back into the Doors and what did she have beyond *The Best of the Doors*? And how could she possibly find it in this kind of fucked-up condition? Or get to it? Even now she was still doing her whole ineradicable thing, running her game: trying to please someone other than herself. She let the phone drop next to a stereo speaker. Bobby was Wally the Walrus again.

It took considerable effort but she was able to gulp down a last few swallows of gin and edge over away from the side of the bed. Some of the liquor rolled off her chin down her neck, over her satin pillowcase. Her special crystal nightcap goblet fell to the hardwood floor and smashed.

Shit. Bobby spent half his life behind bars and what did he know really? She knew what it was like to fall back into the inner darkness of the self. To implode nights and come to every morning like reconstituted misery. Come crawling back in the day cell of the puny withering body. She knew all about the black holes of the self. She knew all about prison, about clocks and calendars. She knew single soul-crushing seconds that lasted months of Sundays. She knew sixty-second hand sweeps that *were* life plus ninety-nine; hours of agony like twenty lifetimes of Methuselah; weeks that tormented like furnace years on the surface of Mercury, months of frozen black solitude like lost ages on the icy black moons of Pluto. All the while thinking about "why me?" and "poor me." She had heard the sound of the sun and the silence of the crystal moon reflected in still mountain lakes and that did not change a thing. Nothing was altered. It was a very bad deal and then on top of everything else, you had to die. *Why has God done this thing to me?*

She was no Helen Keller. She had never been up for any of this. Thanks to all of the pills and booze there was, at last, that wonderful sense of detachment. She could take the scissors and cut the thread any time now. Should have done it years ago but *finally*...the sentence was almost completed. Some people work in that damn gold pit in Brazil, some people sharecrop, some go to jail and...some contract muscular dystrophy. That's how it was. From the telephone receiver, Wally the Walrus was singing "Hookah tookah my soda cracker? Does your mama chaw tobacco?" Then his voice snapped sober and he said, "Oh, fuck all! *Let us stop talkin' falsely now, the hour's getting late.* Are you there, sugar? Or are you not there? Are you they-ah?"

She was too fucked up to speak. It was getting difficult to breathe. That's what happened when you OD'd. Your lungs filled up with water and you drowned. She thought you fell unconscious first. You were supposed to. Oh, well, at least it didn't hurt.

Bobby recited Bob Dylan, *"Outside in the cold distance, a wildcat did growl; two riders were approaching and the wind began to howl!... Yeeowwww!"*

She heard the report of a gunshot. God! Bobby! She tried to call his name but was so stoned she was cross-eyed. Floating on the ceiling she was, looking down on the scene, looking at herself. She could hear her father, Corliss. Oh, Daddy, she thought. Daddy! My daddy!

It was just a neurological illusion. A psychic defense against the ultimate fear. A Freudian defense mechanism — denial. Apparent reality.

"Nights in White Satin" was still playing on the CD. She had hit the replay button at least a dozen times, so she couldn't gauge time by counting the cuts on the disc. Her vision was too blurry to see the clock, but she could see the colors of the music stream out of the stereo speakers like streaks of red, white, yellow, and blue neon. Each note shot out into the air like a colored needle that compressed itself as its flight was spent, and then crystallized into a bright filigreed atom before it popped with a sharp electric snap and disappeared. *Electricity cost less today, you know, than it did twenty-five years ago! A little birdie told me so.* What *was* electricity?

The plan called for Mozart but... Bobby. Shit, Bobby. In the long run, take a friend, a really good friend over a lover any day. And if not a friend, then a dog. Maybe when she hit the other side, it would be like spirits and stuff and she and Bobby would meet and be together again with fresh, young healthy bodies. After all, they were checking out together. Practically within the same hour. She hoped he had the soul strength to hold it together and wait for her. Some of them just evaporated and disappeared and some others turned into angels. How did she know that? Suddenly she knew that. "Hiya, fancy meetin' you here." She and Bobby could walk hand in hand into the promised land. Not that physical bodies could reconstitute.

God! What if she ended up in a horrible pile of shit on the other side? An eternal pile of shit. Another truth hit home. The only hell she would ever know was about to end. In fact, it was over. She felt warmth and love. She wondered if there was a heaven. Seemed very likely now, contrary to what common sense had previously deemed. Hey, you see all this shit through the glass darkly until checkout time. She felt light; soul on a string — a mere seven and one-half ounces. Truffles. Fluffy perfumed lace hankies. She felt warm. It was good. Bliss. Finally.

All she had to do now was wait for the next wave, wait for it to heave her up and carry her away. Just let go and ride out that breaking white crest into eternity. She was waiting for the next wave. Emerald wave, surfer girl.

Hang ten!

Sonny Liston Was
a Friend of Mine

As soon as the turquoise blue Impala pulled in the driveway, Kid
Dynamite was out of the back seat, across the lawn, into the house,
and dancing out of his wool pants and tie as he vaulted up to his
room. Sunday services at St. Mark's Lutheran, when communion was
offered, were very long affairs. Sit down, get up, sit down again; up-
and-down, down-and-up in a flesh-eating wool suit as voracious as a
blanket of South American army ants. Out in the car, Cancer Frank
had barely turned off the ignition switch. Kid Dynamite was already
in his gray cotton sweatpants and boxing shoes. Church, man! If the
boredom didn't kill you, the everlasting sermon could have you snoring in a bolt-upright position. Add to that six or seven hymns where
otherwise harmless old ladies howled like they were hell-bent on shat-
tering more than nerves — they were out to break celestial crystal.
So were the small babies who screamed protest against the stagnant
oxygen-deficient air and the stupefaction of body heat. What a relief
to be done with it. The only reason he consented to go at all was for
the sake of his grandmother, Mag.

As Kid Dynamite carefully taped his hands in his bedroom, he heard
Cancer Frank's heavy wingtips scraping up the front steps. There was
the snap of his stepfather's Zippo and the clatter of an ashtray being
placed on the piano. In his gray sharkskin and brown felt snap-brim,
with a Pall Mall draped from his lips, Cancer Frank was the Hoagy
Carmichael of Aurora, Illinois. Kid Dynamite laughed to himself thinking that C.F. endured the services in nicotine withdrawal — served the

chump right, too! As soon as his hands were wrapped, Kid Dynamite slipped a hooded sweatshirt over his head and was down the back stairs and out of the house. Out. Clean. Gone.

Kid Dynamite stepped through the wet grass in his boxing shoes, threw his shoulder into the side door of the garage, and stepped inside. It was cold and damp, smelling of musk. He snapped on his transistor radio. WLS was running a shitload of Sunday advertisements cheerfully promulgating the American life of living death. Kid Dynamite peered out the window where he spotted his mother, "the Driver," still sitting in the car preening in the rearview mirror. For the Driver (one trip to the Buy Right with her behind the wheel and you *would* get down on your knees and pray), church services were just another place, as all places were to her, where you went to show off your good looks and your latest outfit.

Kid Dynamite slipped on his bag gloves. It was early March and the wind was blowing hard. It had been raining off and on. Three of the garage windows were broken and the roof leaked, but the floor was made of smooth wooden planks. As Kid Dynamite did some side twists to limber up, he looked through the window again and saw his mother finally get out of the Chevy and walk into the house where there were bigger mirrors. He wondered what she had been thinking looking in that rearview. "How did I *go over* today?" No doubt.

Kid Dynamite spent a lot of time in front of a mirror himself, but only to examine his body alignment and his punching form. He was himself a good-looking young man but a realigned nose, a little scar tissue beneath the brows, and a cauliflower ear were beginning to make any comparisons with the Greek gods unlikely. Poker-faced, he threw a jab at the double-ended bolo bag and gave it a quick head slip when it bounced back. Slipping punches was the most accomplished means a boxer could employ to protect his face but also the riskiest. Kid Dynamite tattooed the bag and continued slipping punches until he began to sweat. Then he started moving in and out on the bag — started using his legs. In another few moments he was gliding around the greasy floor planks, the air so cold he could see his breath. Shadowboxing, he worked his legs, moving about the floor in a bob-and-weave style, watching himself in variously positioned mirrors. His Sunday afternoon workouts belonged to him alone and he used them to cover contingencies that had been skipped over in his regular gymnasium workouts. The old man once told him, "There are at least a thousand things that can go wrong in a fight, and how many of them can you think of — fifty?" As with most fighters, Kid Dynamite's *things going wrong* invariably involved the problem of fear. As the old man had said, "Control your fear and you are cooking with gas, baby."

At 147 pounds, Kid Dynamite fought as a welterweight. He had recently advanced through the semifinals in the open class of the Chicago Golden Gloves, but made the finals only just barely. Two of these victories were split decisions. In his last fight on Friday, he suffered a slight cut under the left eye. The opponent had pushed him to the limit and he knew that from here on in the competition would get much rougher. Four of the boxers from the Steelworkers' Hall had made it to the finals. They were all sky-high that night, driving back to Aurora on the Eisenhower Freeway in Juan's junky-ass Cadillac. But after Juan dropped Kid Dynamite off and he came into the house with his gym bag, Cancer Frank was lying on the couch watching TV and didn't bother to even look up at his stepson. The Driver was already in bed and it was too late to call his girlfriend, Melanie. So he went upstairs and woke up the Driver. "I won. I got him good," he said.

The Driver's face was covered in a luminescent green mask. "Did you knock him out?" she said wearily. There was a bath towel on the Driver's pillow and flecks of cracked green paste dropped from her face as she spoke.

'Jesus. The creature from the Green Bog," Kid Dynamite said.

"It's a wrinkle mask. Did you knock him out or what?"

"My guy? No, I won on points. Chubby knocked his guy out. I won on points. Cuba and Eloise Greene won."

"What about your homework?" she said.

"What *about* it? It's Friday night. Man, I was feeling so right tonight. It was the best thing. I'm going to win the tournament," Kid Dynamite said.

"You're just like your father and where is *he* now? He's in the nuthouse. You've got to study. You've got geometry problems."

"I'm talking to a lima bean. Screw geometry. When was the last time you had to whip out a slide rule to solve one of life's problems?"

"You hang out with those lowlife boxers and you act crude. What will you do with your life? How can you hang out with such scrums?"

"They're my friends. Jesus! I come in here feeling great. Can't you just say, 'Good, I'm glad you won. You've made me a happy lima bean.' Is that too much to ask?"

The Driver stuck her hand out groping for the alarm clock. "I've got to get up at the crack of dawn, what time is it?" she said.

"Midnight. I'm going to take an aspirin. I've got a headache. Shit!"

As he left the bedroom his mother said, "I don't want to take the wind out of your sails, but you better pass or you'll end up in the gutter."

Kid Dynamite stepped into the bathroom and closed the door. She said, "I *am* glad you won. But don't stay up all night doing push-ups; I need quiet. My nerves are shot."

He didn't bother to reply. Instead he leaned against the sink and examined the cut under his eye in the medicine cabinet mirror. It wasn't that bad, but the tissue under his eye was swollen and tender. A couple of jabs, one good solid punch could easily burst it open. He went downstairs and got an ice cube, passing Cancer Frank on the stairs. Neither uttered a word in passing. Kid Dynamite wondered if C.F. even knew he was fighting. Suddenly the elation of reaching the finals returned to him full blown. His recent win was not merely a stay of execution. This time, one way or another, he would take it all the way. Back in bed he let the ice melt over his eye, feeling the water roll down his neck onto the pillow. He could hear Cancer Frank talking to the Driver. "He'll never get past the next round. He drew Louie Reine, the redhead that nailed him last year. It was three days soaking in Epsom salts after that — "

"Who knows," his mother said. "Maybe he's better now, he's bigger. He sure thinks he's going to win," the Driver said.

Cancer Frank said, "Not even if you tied one of Reine's hands behind his back does he win."

Kid Dynamite waited in the silence of the night for this defense attorney to speak up for him. For a long time there was nothing, then came the familiar animal sounds. Christ! The two of them were having sex in spite of her stiff green wrinkle mask. Kid Dynamite rolled over on his stomach, covering his head with a pillow, but it was useless. He felt *compelled* to listen. When it was over he heard light feet squeaking on the linoleum tile, followed by intensive Listerine gargling, a hard scouring toothbrush, then footsteps back to the bed. Next Cancer Frank's heavier feet could be heard padding into the bathroom. Kid Dynamite heard his stepfather take a long horse piss and do some Listerine gargling of his own. In a moment he was back in the master bedroom where body positions were assumed, covers were adjusted, and things finally became quiet. Then he heard the Driver say, "I don't know. He was in the paper again, fifteen in a row. Knocking them out left and right."

Cancer Frank spoke matter-of-factly, without rancor or malice. He said, "Those were prelims. Kids that don't know how to fight. This other fighter, Reine, has his number. The kid is scared. He isn't going to win. He'll blow it."

Kid Dynamite was suddenly up on the edge of the bed in a rage. He pounded his fists on the tops of his thighs. Through clenched teeth he said, "You don't know *shit!*"

Cancer Frank heard him and said, "Hey!" The voice that had so terrorized Kid Dynamite for so much of his life stabbed him now like a punch to the solar plexus. Stepfather or no, the man was supposed to guide and encourage him, not run him down and disparage his every move. Cancer Frank was the original and main source of his travail in the world thus far. Kid Dynamite imagined him poised up in bed next to his mother. C.F. said, "Watch your goddamn mouth or I'm coming in there!"

Kid Dynamite got up and crossed the hallway to the master bedroom saying, "Well, come on then, you son of a bitch. If you want some, come on!"

The Driver leaped out of bed, rushed to the door, and locked it with a skeleton key just before he got there. "God! I knew this was going to happen."

Kid Dynamite grabbed the door handle and shook it. Then he began pounding the door with the balls of his fists. His hands were already sore from the tournament. This only intensified his rage. He threw his hip and shoulder against the door. It was an old door. Solid oak. "I'll knock down the wall," he screamed. "I'll kill that cock*suck*er!"

The Driver's voice was a vicious rasp, "You get the hell out of this house!"

In the middle of a coughing spasm, Cancer Frank choked out the words, "Call the police!"

Kid Dynamite stood at the door and listened to his stepfather cough. From the sound of it, Kid Dynamite knew he was overdramatizing. He shouted, "Go ahead, call them, you car-selling motherfucker. I hope you *die!*"

He gave the door a last thump and went back to his bedroom where he dropped to the floor and pumped off two hundred push-ups. He knew the police would not be called. But someone would be brought in to straighten him out. Uncle Mikey, a seriously bad guy and a notorious overreactor. Since the onset of Frank's disease, Uncle Mikey had more than once dragged his nephew out of bed, kicking his ass all the way down to the basement. He came early, too, when the kid was most vulnerable. He was like some Eastern European goon squad in that regard. It would be better if the police were called — better they than Mikey.

Kid Dynamite lay awake all night in rage and anticipation. Mikey didn't show up until noon. He was wearing a suit and tie, an indication there would be no violence. At forty, the former heavyweight champion of the Seventh Army looked like he could still fight at the drop of a hat. Unlike his brother, Kid Dynamite's old man, Mikey did not become a professional fighter; he was too smart for that. Instead he went into sales and had become the most materially successful member of the family. As far back as Kid Dynamite could remember, Mikey had the best cars, houses, clothes — the best of everything. It was Mikey, however, who had introduced Cancer Frank to his mother, and the kid's admiration for him was severely mitigated by that factor. In his suit and tie, on an early Saturday afternoon, Mikey was very solemn. Kid Dynamite knew grave matters would be discussed and threats would be issued. Compromises and concessions would be few.

After shooting the bull with C.F. and the Driver, Mikey politely invited Kid Dynamite for a drive in his new Mercedes convertible. It was a nice car and Mikey was proud of it. He talked about the virtues of German engineering as he took the river road and drove south toward Oswego. Kid Dynamite fell into a pout and nothing was said for a few miles. Then Mikey looked over at him with mounting irritation and said, "What the fuck is the matter with you? Why are you giving Frank such a hard time? He has cancer, for Chrissakes. What are you busting his balls for?"

Kid Dynamite looked straight ahead and said nothing. His body was coiled to dodge a side-arm blow, but better that than surrender his pride.

Mikey looked over and said, "I know what it is. It's Mag — your goddamn grandmother. She's been poisoning your mind against him, hasn't she?"

Kid Dynamite kept his eyes straight ahead. "No. She doesn't poison anybody. In fact, she pays Frank's bills," he said.

"Don't get sarcastic with me!" Mikey said. "I'll pull over and give it to you right now, you stupid little fuck!"

Kid Dynamite removed the wiseass from his voice and said, "It's true. She pays."

Mikey shook his head and sighed. He removed his Italian sunglasses and threw them on the dashboard so he could rub the bridge of his nose. "Okay, I'm thinking...let me think. You're in over your head in this boxing tournament. 'Hard' Reine is going to fall all over you, is that it? I saw a piece about this motherfucker in the *Sun Times*. The same guy that got you last year. He ran over you like a freight train."

Kid Dynamite was sullen. "I'm better now. But how would you know? I haven't seen you at any of the fights. Personally, I'd rather be me than him. In fact, I feel *sorry* for the guy. Frank was out of line badmouthing me. It wasn't called for. That's what the whole beef is about. I don't know what they told you, but I didn't do anything except raise my voice a little."

"Raise your voice a *little?*" Mikey said. He pulled the car over to a gravel culvert where two men in bib overalls were fishing with stink bait. Kid Dynamite braced himself as Mikey switched off the engine. The big man took a deep breath and exhaled. Nephew and uncle sat watching the river for a moment. Each of the fishermen had a can of Budweiser in hand. "The beer drinker's *stance*," Mikey said. "They always stand that way. Isn't that something?"

"Nothing in there but carp and bullheads. How can you call that fun?" Kid Dynamite said. "They ought to get off their asses and do something more active. You can *buy* fucking fish."

Mikey laughed, "The problem I'm having here is that I *like* you. You act like a spoiled little brat. No harm in that. I'm trying to get past *that* so I can help out. As troublemakers go, you're just a pissant. I was worse. Shit. There was a depression. It was different. It took the law of the fist to salvage me. Is it the same with you? I treat you decently, things are okay for a while and then you start in on him. Look," Mikey said, pointing his finger in the kid's face. "I'm on your side on this one. But you can't terrorize him in his own home. You scared the fucking shit out of him."

"I'm not a scary person," Kid Dynamite said. "I'm mild-mannered as all hell."

Mikey laughed again. He reached over and clapped his nephew on the shoulder. "Loosen up, kiddo. You're tighter than a drum."

Kid Dynamite shrugged. "I'll win the fight. I trained. I'm in shape. Once we start exchanging punches, I'll know what to do."

"Your dad had balls. He was half my size and would take on anyone. But the thing that makes you good in the ring is the very thing that makes life outside the gym impossible. I was hoping you would end up more like myself than your crazy father." The glare of the sun bounced off the river, and Kid Dynamite used his hands for an eyeshade. Mikey replaced his sunglasses and said, "You're *sure* Mag hasn't been ragging on Frank?"

"Yeah, I'm sure. She knows he's sick. She doesn't rag on him. In her way, she's trying to help him."

"He's *dying!* And he's cracking up a little bit, too. I mean, why else would he be going to church three times a week? Would you like to walk in those shoes?"

"Fuckin' wingtips, not me," Kid Dynamite said. "I don't think he's going to die, either. Two packs a day. The two of them are screwing night and day — "

Mikey spoke abruptly, "You call off the dogs, okay? I don't want to hear the piss and moan."

Kid Dynamite shrugged. "They fuck like animals; it's disgusting; I got to hear it — "

Mikey raised his hand like a stop sign. "I don't want the 'wah wah, boo hoo.' Confine your violence to the ring or you're going to end up in the bughouse, like your father, a paranoid freak. The world is not that bad a place."

Kid Dynamite turned his palms up in exasperation. "I'm not a violent person. I'm a *shy* person. What do I *do*? I don't drink. I don't smoke. I *work*. I *help* around the house. You don't see my name on the arrest reports. I'm still a virgin. I don't even jack off. Fuck, I'm a super guy. The only black marks against me are that I flunked geometry three times in a row and I've got a filthy mouth. You gonna come and see the fight? I'm going to *pretend* this guy is Frank and I'm going to kick ass!"

Mikey patted his nephew on the cheek just a little too hard. He laughed and said, "All right, kiddo. In the meantime, stay out of his way for a while."

"Serious, Uncle Mikey! Are you coming to the fight?"

"I'll be at the fight. If you don't kick the guy's ass and make it worth my while, I'll be coming after you when it's over. Deal?"

"Hey! I'll kick his ass all right."

Mikey laughed at this and exchanged seats with his nephew. South of Oswego, Kid Dynamite found a straightaway and got the Mercedes up to 130 mph. It didn't seem as if the car was doing more than sixty. "German engineering," Uncle Mikey said. "Hard work, attention to detail, and a willpower that never quits." He gave his nephew a punch on the shoulder and said, "You're lucky to be a German. Who knows, someday you might conquer the world."

In spite of the cold garage, Kid Dynamite quickly broke into a full sweat. After the assault of advertisements, Dick Clark popped on the air with "Big Girls Don't Cry" by the Four Seasons and then Paul Revere and the Raiders. Kid Dynamite expected a full day of "suck" radio and he was getting it. Still, any music was better than nothing. The kid was working hard now, gliding around the floor with his hands carried high at the sides of his head and his chin tucked down. The plank floor creaked as he moved in and out on the bolo bag. It rebounded with such speed and velocity and from so many unexpected directions that he had to concentrate intently to avoid having it slap him in the face. He did flunk geometry and that was ironic. Boxing acumen involved calculating angles. The angles of the ring, Kid Dynamite understood perfectly. He would show Louis Reine angles aplenty.

Kid Dynamite had boxed him beautifully for two rounds the year before. He had fast hands and could hit Reine at will. Listening to Lolo was the mistake on that one. Reine was discouraged and out of gas after the second round. Lolo told Kid Dynamite to stay on the outside and box his opponent, "Take this one on points." So he followed the advice and boxed at long range. Then as Reine recovered his wind, Kid Dynamite got trapped on the ropes, where Reine went to work on his body. As soon as Kid Dynamite dropped his elbow to cover his liver, he got clocked along the jaw and after that it was essentially over.

This year Kid Dynamite was in shape, but he didn't actually have any better plan for Reine than before. He wasn't going to slug with him, he was going to give him angles and box. He was the superior boxer, and he was stronger than he had been the year before, if he saw a clear shot he would tee off, but he definitely wasn't going to go in trading. Although Kid Dynamite had earned a small notice on the *Beacon's* sports page, as his Uncle Mikey had said, Louis Reine was touted in the *Chicago Sun-Times* as the premier fighter of the tournament. At eighteen, he had won forty-two fights and lost none. He had been fighting stiffer competition from the South Side and the paper said he was likely to go all the way to the Nationals.

Kid Dynamite had more fights than Reine but had suffered, in all, seventeen losses in CYO, AAU, and Golden Gloves competition. He had also got his ass kicked in a half-dozen street fights. He had been knocked cold three times, hospitalized twice. His family doctor prevailed upon his mother to make him quit after the loss in the finals the year before. But Kid Dynamite had had the fight with Reine in the very palm of his hand and he knew it. Too often, after a fighter took a single solid beating, he did not come back to the gym. Or if he did, he wasn't the same. He was gun-shy. The test of mettle was to come back with burning desire, which Kid Dynamite had done. He had not lost a fight since. He tried to explain this to his girlfriend, Melanie, the first time he saw her after the initial loss to Reine. It was a conversation that happened a year before. A tall brunette with perfect posture, she stood waiting for him at their usual rendezvous point on the corner of North Avenue and Smith Street. Melanie's ankles were squeezed together and she held her schoolbooks clutched against her breast. She was a beautiful young girl and Kid Dynamite was still something of a mess. He had a sore neck, a broken cheekbone, a black eye, and swollen purple lips. He was somewhat mystified by her tears, since his appearance had improved considerably since the fight and he had prepared her to see black and blue. Still, there were tears. He tried to reassure her. "It's not as bad as it looks," he said. "I'm just sore is all."

Light snowflakes fell on her shiny hair. Melanie had high cheekbones, a well-shaped nose to set them off, and a resolute but nice chin to better complement her heart-shaped face. She had a wide mouth and full lips, and she was quite beautiful. Her sparkling green eyes were the feature Kid Dynamite liked most. He learned to read her moods by watching her eyes. She had been the only girl he had ever cared about, and the two had been seeing one another since junior high school. Melanie was thin with frequent acne flare-ups but this bothered Kid Dynamite very little: she easily was one of the best-looking girls in the entire high school and one of the most loyal. Melanie was enough to make him believe that God was looking out for him. She approached him, reaching out to his cheek with a fuzzy woolen glove. Kid Dynamite gave her a gentle hug.

He stepped back and said, "You look so beautiful this morning. I never get tired of looking at you. It's so good to finally get out of the house and actually see you again."

"Oh, boy," she said cautiously, "are you okay? What happened?"

Kid Dynamite started to laugh but the pain of it stopped him. "He hit me so hard every tooth in my mouth rattled. But with you standing here in front of me, I'm an ace." Melanie wore a navy car coat with bone-colored toggles over her cheer-squad uniform. He said, "Why have you got the uniform on?"

"Basketball in Joliet tonight. We have a morning pep assembly. I don't want to go. I want to be with you."

They embraced again. Kid Dynamite kissed Melanie's slender neck. He could feel an erection coming on and tried to back away but she clutched him tighter. He gave in and let her hold him completely. Students were walking by, the late ones. He felt her tears rolling down his neck. "Baby, my ribs, careful!" he said.

She said, "I'm not going to the game tonight. I want to be with you."

Kid Dynamite felt hot tears of his own. He pulled his head back and kissed her. "You smell so good, you look so pretty. What you just said was the nicest thing anyone has ever said to me."

"Oh God," she said. "If it wasn't for the basketball team, I *would* have *been* there."

"You would have just seen me get creamed," he said. The procession of students hurrying to school began to thin out. Suddenly five black students came out of Fiddler's Grocery. Fid himself came out after them. He was a short heavyset man in a white apron. He stood on the wooden porch and took a final drag off his cigarette before flipping it out into the street and going back inside.

Kid Dynamite recognized the students, one of them was his friend, Eloise Greene, the club's middleweight. Jarvis Jackson packed a wet snowball and fired across Smith Street. It hit the top of the corner mailbox. Kid Dynamite tossed Jarvis the "bird" and Jarvis Jackson cried, "Hey, motherfucker! You can suck my *motherfucking* dick, man!"

Kid Dynamite dropped his books and packed a snowball of his own. He aimed it at Jackson, but the snowball didn't even make it across the street. It felt like one of his ribs had broken loose and punctured a lung. He bent over, clutching his side, as the students who had stopped to light cigarettes laughed at his pathetic toss.

Kid Dynamite looked up at Melanie and said, "I'm okay! I'm okay! Just sore and glad I missed. Jarvis a bad mo-tah scooter."

They watched the blacks proceed down Smith Street hill toward school. Kid Dynamite dried his hands by sticking them in his pockets. There was a brisk wind and he pulled his watch cap down over his ears. Both sides of North Avenue were lined with oak and maples, barren of leaves. It was a gray morning and the pristine snow was fouled by the black smoke of coal fires coming from the chimneys of the homes. Kid Dynamite stepped into a yard and snapped a small branch from a pussy willow, the first sign of spring. He traced a furry blossom around the edges of Melanie's mouth. He used his finger to trace the tears rolling down her cheeks. She wiped a wisp of tear-drenched hair from her face. She said, "My parents are at work. We can go back to my place."

Melanie's parents were both cops. Her stepfather, Vic, had been a boxer himself, a heavyweight from New Jersey who fought in club fights as a teenager. He still followed the sport and took an interest in Kid Dynamite's career. The summer after Kid Dynamite lost in the finals of the Golden Gloves tournament, Vic drove Melanie and the Kid out past the North Aurora Downs Race Track to watch Sonny Liston train for the first Patterson fight, which was set for September in Chicago's Comiskey Park. Kid Dynamite watched Vic shell out twelve bucks to get into the old Pavilion dance hall, where a gym had been set up for Liston's camp. Kid Dynamite had never actually been inside before, but the Pavilion was the site of a number of his father's professional fights before the Second World War.

There were few spectators in the Pavilion. Vic led them to some front-row padded loge seats. The world's number one heavyweight contender was in the ring working with a very fast light heavyweight. Although his size made him seem as ponderous as a water buffalo, Liston was in fact faster than the sparring partner. He worked on cutting off the ring, something he anticipated he would have to do with Patterson, who was lightning fast and a fine boxer as well. Time and again Liston trapped the light heavyweight along the ropes. Liston threw light punches and let him go, only to trap him again. After two rounds of this, a bigger man gloved up and got into the ring. A number of handlers in gray sweatshirts with "Sonny Liston" crudely stenciled on them bustled about. One of the men simply sat before a small phonograph and played "Nighttrain," over and over again. Kid Dynamite sported two fresh black eyes incurred when his doctor had to rebreak his nose to set it right, and because of this as many people were looking at him as were watching Liston.

At the first exchange, Liston knocked his new sparring partner down with a body shot. It didn't look like much of a punch but the pain was very real. The boxer writhed about the canvas in agony. In the end he could not continue. Disgusted, and out of sparring partners, Liston climbed out of the ring and began banging the heavy bag. This went on for three timed rounds.

As the workout ran down, Liston gave a rope-skipping exhibition on the solid maple floor of the depression-era dance hall. The record player continued to blare "Nighttrain" as Kid Dynamite looked about the sparse crowd. Most of them were reporters jotting notes on press pads. Kid Dynamite heard one of the trainers tell a *Life* magazine reporter that during training Liston ate nothing but rare steak, carrot juice, goat's milk, and vegetables. He said Sonny Liston was the only private citizen in America to own a carrot juicer.

Kid Dynamite was amazed at Liston's speed and by the compactness and economy of his movements. After watching so many amateur fighters, this look at a professional heavyweight left him awestruck. Liston had a left jab that would decapitate anyone with less than a seventeen-inch neck. His display on the big bag was frightening, was light-years beyond what Kid Dynamite imagined possible. Vic gave him a nudge and said, "Bet the farm on this man. Patterson is dead."

Liston had surprisingly fast legs and was doing double crossovers with the skip rope. Kid Dynamite looked at the fighter's feet, and when he looked back at Liston's face, he discovered Liston's baleful stare was locked in on him. Charles "Sonny" Liston was the most frightening person Kid Dynamite had ever seen, and at this moment Charles did not seem very happy. He met Liston's gaze but found it almost impossible to sustain eye contact. Soon it became an exercise in the control of fear. Sonny Liston gave Kid Dynamite the slightest hint of a smile and winked. Vic nudged Kid Dynamite again, and leaned over, whispering, "Your eyes. He's looking at your eyes."

Kid Dynamite had forgotten about his black eyes. Vic laughed and said, "I almost shit in my pants before I figured it out. That is one mean nigger."

As soon as the workout concluded, a handler tossed Sonny Liston a towel. He mopped off his face, which was glistening with Vaseline and crystal droplets of sweat. Another handler helped him into a terry-cloth robe. The towel man cut off Liston's bandages. His hands were like hams. On his way to the shower, Liston stopped just short of Kid Dynamite to sign a few autographs. He paused briefly to talk with sports writers and then looked back at Kid Dynamite. He said, "What are you, kid, a lightweight?"

Kid Dynamite jumped back as if he had been shot with a forty-five. His voice squeaked. "No sir, I'm a welterweight."

In a sissy voice, Liston said, "No sir, I'm a welterweight."

The writers roared and Kid Dynamite's cheeks flushed. Sonny Liston motioned to one of the handlers, who handed him an 8 × 10 black-and-white glossy. He said, "What's your name?"

Kid Dynamite seemed dumbstruck. Finally he said, "Make it out to Melanie."

"I thought you was going to hem and haw forever." Liston looked at Melanie. "Is that you?"

"Yes," she said.

"Looks like you thumped him pretty good," Liston said. There was another roar of laughter. A press photographer rushed over and staged a picture of Liston, Melanie, Vic, and Kid Dynamite. In the end, Liston had signed a picture for each of them. As soon as the fighter turned away and headed off to the shower, a man in a gray sweatshirt demanded two dollars each for the photographs. Vic paid gladly enough. "That was nice. He didn't have to do that."

Giddy with excitement, they compared inscriptions. Kid Dynamite's photo was signed, "To the Kid, from your friend, Sonny Liston."

Kid Dynamite beamed at the inscription like it was the writ of God. "Sonny Liston is a *friend* of mine," he said.

Kid Dynamite applied himself to boxing with renewed vigor. In the summer as he recovered from his nose surgery, he worked as a lifeguard at the city park. He would come in an hour early each day to swim. This was after he did a full morning workout in the garage. He bought a set of Joe Wielder weights. In the garage he did extra neck bridges and he lifted weights, then he ran to work and swam. For the rest of the day he rotated along the pool stations with the other lifeguards. Sitting in the hot sun in a white pith helmet, with a whistle in his mouth, he felt completely at rest.

After work Kid Dynamite would meet Melanie at the Dairybar across the field from his house. Melanie served ice cream there in a blue-striped seersucker frock. One night after closing up, they sat outside under the blue bug zapper. Melanie was an only child and although, like Kid Dynamite, she was raised by a stepfather, she did not know her own father at all.

"Maybe it's just as well," Kid Dynamite said. "Vic is really nice. My real father was nice, but he just wasn't around much. He used to take me to the gym when I was a kid. He thought I was a sissy. Took me to Chicago where I met big-time fighters. Joe Louis, Ezzard Charles, Tony Zale, Ernie Terrell — guys who were his actual friends. I don't know what I'll do when it's all over. I'm not good at anything." Kid Dynamite poked a straw in a clump of ice cream at the bottom of his milk shake.

Mikey had somehow patched up the mess with Cancer Frank. It seemed to Kid Dynamite that it was one of those rarest of occasions where he had managed to skate on something. Frank did not speak to him but neither did he criticize him. Kid Dynamite pretended that his stepfather was invisible and vice versa. Fortunately, their schedules did not converge that much. Kid Dynamite was up at four A.M. most days to run. On Monday morning he awoke with a pleasurable sense of anticipation. It would be the last run before the Reine fight. One more solid run and he would be ready. He had omitted nothing; if he lost it would be because Reine was the better fighter. On the edge of his bed, he clocked his resting pulse. Forty beats a minute.

This time around Kid Dynamite wasn't listening to any more of Juan's bullshit advice. By now he felt he knew his body better than anyone. And while he rested, the other fighters would be playing catch-up. For them it would be too little, too late. Kid Dynamite got into his sweats and combat boots in the dark. He walked quietly downstairs and out the door, falling into an easy jog across town to his grandmother's store. Since North Avenue was lit with orange tungsten streetlights, this was the route of choice; this was no time to sprain an ankle in a dark pothole.

Kid Dynamite picked up speed after the first mile. The homes along the lower part of North Avenue were three-story Victorians. Only in a few could he see the amber glow of lightbulbs. It was early, but as he passed the Burlington railroad station, he spotted commuters scouting parking spots for the trip to Chicago. As he crossed the Fox River bridge, a squad car passed and a cop waved at him. Kid Dynamite ran past the gas company and a number of factories, most of which looked like chambers of Dickensian horror. He used to like looking in the windows and seeing men at work on the graveyard shift. He had come to recognize many of them. How they could stand in front of a machine, a spot welder or a punch press, night after night was unfathomable to him. Did they suffer as he did in a high school classroom? Kid Dynamite knew that he might well end up in such a place himself. He did not deem himself college material, and he knew enough about boxing to know that his prospects as a professional were nil, just as they had been for his father. There was always someone bigger and better. Yet he was caught up into boxing and could think of little else. As he ran, the looks on the workers' faces were neutral, reflecting neither agony nor pleasure. By the time Kid Dynamite got to Lake Street he was in a residential area again. Here the houses were not so nice. He came down the hill, passed under the viaduct, and sprinted the last two blocks to his grandmother's store.

Mag was standing at the cash register going through bills. A bare sixty-watt bulb hung on a frayed wire above her. For the past few years, Kid Dynamite came in to do all of the heavy lifting for her — moving bulk cases from the basement up to the shelves. Shuffling milk and pop bottles, sacks of flour, bags of potatoes. He loaded the stove with coal and then joined Mag in the kitchen, bolting down a couple of egg sandwiches with black coffee. He opened the cupboard where Mag always had a homemade pumpkin pie. Kid Dynamite sliced a piece and shoveled it in his mouth. Mag asked him if he needed any money, and Kid Dynamite shook his head no.

The sun was coming up as he headed out, and as light flooded into the store, he saw that Mag had the "Kid Dynamite" article posted on the cash register for all her customers to see. On a shelf behind the counter she kept Kid Dynamite's boxing pendants and trophies like a miniature shrine. He waved good-bye and headed out the front door. It was a four-mile run back to the house, most of it uphill. He sprinted the entire way.

Of the four fighters the Steelworkers' Boxing Club sent to the finals, Kid Dynamite was considered the most likely to win. And as the lightest fighter from the club, he was the first to go up. He hadn't slept the night before the fight, but then he never did. As soon as Lolo taped his hands, Kid Dynamite began to shadowbox. After fifteen minutes of this, Juan forced him to sit down on a folding chair. The coach pulled a chair adjacent to him. "You know the game plan?"

Kid Dynamite nodded. He was dripping with sweat.

Juan looked at him intently. "Louie Reine had trouble making weight. Five hours in the steamroom, and three trips to the scales. Don't make your move until the end of the second round. If he's still strong then, wait until the third. Are you listening to me?"

"The old man called me. He said I should jump all over him."

Juan, normally implacable, registered disbelief, "Your old man, who's in a mental hospital two thousand miles away, told you this?"

"Yeah," Kid Dynamite said.

"Well, what do you think you should do?"

"It doesn't matter, Juan. I'm going to win tonight. I can *feel* it. I don't care what he does; I'm going to kick his motherfucking ass. I've been waiting a year to get this cocksucker."

"So you're going to do a job on him? No plan, no nothing! Just kick ass!" Juan shook his head in dismay. "Well, I hope you do. Just remember, the crowd will be with him tonight. It won't be your crowd."

Kid Dynamite got up and started twisting his neck from side to side, bouncing up and down. Lolo ducked into the locker room. He grabbed the spit bucket and water bottle. "Let's go, Kid, you're up."

Kid Dynamite entered the arena and climbed up the portable wooden steps to the ring. Louis Reine was already in the opposite corner, his red hair shorn in a buzz cut. There wasn't a drop of sweat on him. He looked the same as he had the year before. Kid Dynamite turned away, bracing his gloves against the ropes as he rubbed his shoes in the resin box. He flexed his neck and bounced up and down in his corner trying to shake off the butterflies. The referee called both fighters to the center of the ring, reminded both fighters that they had received their instructions in the dressing room, and wished them both luck.

Kid Dynamite returned to his corner, where Lolo held out his mouthpiece. He set his teeth in it, clamping down hard as he slapped himself on the forehead a few times to make sure his headgear was tight. Then he turned and looked across the ring with a blank stare as he waited for the bell. As soon as it rang, Louie Reine came rushing across the ring to engage, and Kid Dynamite did the same. Just before contact Kid Dynamite spotted his grandmother, Mag, the Driver, Mikey, and Cancer Frank seated in the third row next to Melanie and Vic. The only time in his life that Kid Dynamite could remember Mag leaving the store for more than an hour was the day she had her teeth pulled. The store was open seven days a week including Christmas Day. It had always been that way. He was so shocked to see her out of context he had to look twice to make sure he was seeing things right.

Reine gave him a Walcott stepover to switch angles, and threw a left hook that just barely grazed the top of his head. Kid Dynamite heard it whistle as he ducked under it and watched Reine's elbow sail by. He came up off balance and started a left hook of his own, aimed over Reine's right hand. Reine's punch landed first, catching Kid Dynamite high on the forehead. Because his feet were too close together, and because Reine was so strong, the force of the punch was sufficient to send Kid Dynamite reeling backward into the ropes. Reine then tagged him with a double jab and a straight right hand to the side of the jaw, and suddenly Kid Dynamite was sprawled facedown on the canvas. It seemed that the floor had flown up and hit him in the mouth. His whole body bounced hard. The canvas was as rough as concrete, and his face, elbows, and knees stung with abrasions. He had gone down like he was poleaxed, and the crowd went into a frenzy. Knockdowns, at least spectacular ones, were relatively rare in amateur boxing. The boxing reporter from the *Sun-Times*, the prophet who picked Reine to go to the Nationals, was on his feet scribbling in his notebook. It was the first thing Kid Dynamite saw as he raised his head.

His face burned. Pinwheels spun behind his eyelids, and he shook his head hard. Looking over to his corner he saw Juan frantically motioning him to stay down and take the full eight count. Meanwhile, the referee was having a problem getting Reine to a neutral corner. Kid Dynamite distinctly saw a smile flash across Cancer Frank's face. Mag was on her feet screaming in German for him to get up. Never in his life had he heard her speak in her native tongue. Her face was red and she was pounding her cane on the floor like a savage. Kid Dynamite felt he was in a dream. Reine's corner was furiously shouting instructions, but Reine wasn't listening. His chest was puffed up and he looked supremely confident. Kid Dynamite shook his head again, trying to clear out the cobwebs. The noise of the crowd seemed very far away. He managed to get his right glove up on the lower ring rope.

Off in the seventh row Kid Dynamite focused on a big man with a fleshy bulbous nose and frosty white hair. He watched him raise his hands to his mouth and shout encouragement to Reine. For such a big man, the sound Kid Dynamite heard was diminutive, but he could hear the man's harsh South Chicago accent. Kid Dynamite wondered if his eardrum had been broken. The man continued to scream. He was well built, and wearing a plaid flannel shirt. Kid Dynamite noticed that the threads on the man's second shirt button had unraveled into tan and brown sprouts, and he thought, "Mister, take that shirt off and put it on three more times, and the button is gone." Kid Dynamite wanted to go down into the crowd and warn him. For the man to lose his button seemed like a cosmic tragedy.

The referee picked up the count from the timekeeper. He was look-ing in Kid Dynamite's eyes. "Five...six," he cried. The smile on Cancer Frank's face widened. Melanie had her face buried in her hands. Vic was on his feet shaking his fist in the air. Vic had a heavy beard and always seemed in need of a shave. Kid Dynamite was certain he could smell English Leather coming off of Vic. He could see the fine black hairs on the backs of Vic's fingers. Next to Vic he could see the redness in Mag's face. Her skin thinned to parchment with age. She was dressed in a thick gray overcoat and pearl pop beads. Kid Dynamite had given them to her because her arthritis made ordinary clasps impossible. A six-dollar purchase. From directly behind, he heard a fan's disembodied voice say, "Don't worry, this kid is tough. He'll get up."

Time began to hurtle along again. He got up on one knee and shook his head. Goddammit if something wasn't wrong with his eardrum.

The referee cried, "Seven." Melanie lifted her head from her lap. "Eight!" the referee cried. Kid Dynamite was standing. The referee looked in his eyes and rubbed Kid Dynamite's gloves clean. "You okay?" Kid Dynamite nodded. His legs felt full of Novocain. The referee stepped back and signaled for the fight to continue.

Reine marched across the ring in a straight line. He gave the kid a real cool dip and roll, feigning a left as he fired his best punch, the straight right. Kid Dynamite anticipated this, and with the over-confident Reine walking in, he countered with a picture-perfect left hook to the point of Reine's chin. It was the best punch Kid Dynamite had ever thrown, but Reine did not go down. It was no reason for discouragement. Reine had not gone down, Kid Dynamite knew, because Reine still had hope. His job now was to erase it. He set about to do this, busily circling Reine, setting his body, and throwing punches in combination. Reine wobbled but didn't go down. The cheers of the crowd fueled Kid Dynamite's enthusiasm, but he kept his head and fought carefully. By the end of the round a frustrated Reine bulled forward, punching recklessly with both hands. Kid Dynamite returned to his corner rubbing blood out of his left eye. Juan didn't even bother with the mouthpiece, he was too busy pressing adrenaline swabs in the cut.

During the next round Kid Dynamite withstood an onslaught of sharp combinations. He methodically outboxed Reine, who began to tire and lose his composure. As Reine started throwing desperate punches, Kid Dynamite found a home for his right uppercut. By the end of the round, Reine's fair skin was marked with red welts. In the corner Juan encouraged him to go after Reine with both hands, but Kid Dynamite was exhausted as well. His lungs felt scalded by the smoke in the arena. His legs seemed as if they had never recovered from the knockdown. Juan told him Reine might have twenty seconds of gas left over after the minute's rest, to lay back and let him throw his bolt. But Reine had no gas at all. He came out arm weary and Kid Dynamite was there to pepper him with left hands. Then he moved inside, confident of his ability to slip Reine's punches. He straightened Reine with the right-hand uppercut and then threw a left-right combination, dishing out all of his mustard. It turned Reine sideways, but it did not knock him down. Reine pulled his gloves up and used his huge forearms to ward off further punishment. It was tantamount to giving up, since Reine did not mount another offensive rally. Kid Dynamite moved in and out, working his jab until the bell sounded ending the fight.

As he waited for the judges to compile their scores, Kid Dynamite chided himself for not pushing it harder when in fact he had given his all. The referee announced a split decision in Kid Dynamite's favor. Juan barely had time to pick him up and swing him around before the ring doctor jumped into Kid Dynamite's corner and pressed a gauze bandage under his eye. In the excitement of the fight, Kid Dynamite hadn't felt the cut, hadn't been bothered by it after the first round. But now the doctor shook his head, and said, "You won the fight but your tournament is over. That's a seven-stitch cut." Louis Reine came over and slapped Kid Dynamite's glove. "Good fight. I'll see you next year." Kid Dynamite felt an overwhelming affection for Reine. "Thanks," he said. Reine, who had turned away, looked back and said, "Next time I'll get you."

The only other fighter from the Steelworkers' Hall to win that night was Eloise Greene, the club's middleweight. Greene, the cigarette smoker, caught fire and waltzed through the finals, winning the open title. For this he received a trophy, a powder blue silk jacket, and his own headline on the *Beacon's* sports page.

Kid Dynamite did not go in with the other fighters to watch the subsequent bouts. He did not even go back to the Steelworkers' Hall to clean out his gym locker. Boxing was finally over and the real world, which had seemed so very far away all these years, was upon him.

The Roadrunner

THE EAGLE WOULD fly on Friday and except for the assorted shitbirds, and certain vital N.C.O.s, Captain Barnes issued First Recon ninety-six hours of liberty. Until that it had been nothing but humping the boonies. All we knew was the field. Six months of that shit, and nerves were strung tight. Now we were awaiting orders to ship out for Da Nang. Since Captain Barnes didn't want us to start a brawl in Oceanside, he gave us ninety-six hours and told us to take all that tension south of the border. "Go fuck your brains out in T-Town, that is an order!"

No sooner than we collected our pay we were packed into L. D. Pfieffer's '51 Chevy, a car that needed three quarts of oil at every fill-up. We chain-smoked Camels and split a quart of gin on the trip down Highway 101.

We crossed the border and hit a strip club on Tijuana's main drag. A stripper with a gold tooth had just whipped off her G-string and shimmied her cooch into a sailor's face. Half the crowd was cheering this swabbie on, like, "Go for it — eat her out." Others "pretended" they would never do such a thing but it was like, "So go to a Rotary Club Meeting, and get lost, motherfuckers!" First Recon wanted nothing short of Mexican Caligula.

Gerber sidled right up to the bar and said, "She's got a snatch on her like Bert Parks's toupee."

Sergeant Ondine said, "Either the bitch likes it or that sailor boy has got massive *salivary* glands."

L. D. Pfieffer, our machine-gunner, said, "Man, I'd like to stick my whole head up her pussy."

Felix Toliver, a radioman from Connecticut, eyeballed Pfieffer and said, "With a pinhead like yours it would fit like a glove." Toliver was 6'5" tall and accordingly thought of himself as a badass, and well before the fun started these two marines locked eyeballs. Sergeant Ondine stepped in and told them to knock it off, but Toliver had this nasal Connecticut accent and said, "Stay out of this, Clarence." There were two things you didn't do in First Recon — you didn't get on the wrong side of L.D. and you didn't call Ondine "Clarence." I figured Toliver must have a death wish, but just then a big whore came along, took L.D. by the hand, and turned him around. Pretty soon she's running her fingers up and down his thigh, squeezing his meat. Gerber handed me a beer and guided me to the back of the club where some of the classier whores sat. He was saying, "I'm in love, Hollywood. You should see this babe." But when we got to the back, Gerber's prostitute was nowhere to be seen. I suddenly found the love of my own life, negotiated a price, and went upstairs. A half hour later I was back. The stage show was over and it was all jukebox. The Mar-Kees were cranking out "Last Night."

Ondine and Pfieffer were at the bar slamming down overpriced shots of tequila. Sergeant Ondine was a lifer. The Marine Corps was his career, but he was an all-right guy. With Vietnam on his mind, he was deep into his rap where the essential secret to being a good soldier was first of all to concede your own death. "If you do that, you can do anything. No one can outsoldier you. No one can take a run at you and live to tell about it. No one can take you out. You can do seven-mile forced marches in full field gear with a poncho over your head and call yourself a tough guy, but if you aren't ready to give it up, you're nothing."

I had heard all this before and didn't take it too seriously. I didn't want to concede my own death. I wanted to be a hedonist — drink, screw girls, and experience vast earthly pleasures. I didn't even want to talk about death; it was something that just wasn't going to happen for a very very long time. I ordered a beer and noticed that Pfieffer was really lit. He was a heavyset guy and heavy on his feet. Not coordinated. The bartender kept setting out shot glasses of tequila for him and he would migrate from the dance floor back to the bar, where he would down another shot and then go back to the dance floor, doing some kind of dipshit hula dance. He looked like a big, stupid, happy fat guy, but if anyone laughed or got into a critique about the finer points of dance, Pfieffer would flash them his goofy grin and then biff them on the nose with the meat of his fist. I watched him lay a few on a mouthy sailor. The man's head jerked back like he didn't know what to do. Tears were running down the guy's face and L.D. stood in front of him with his goofus smile. The sailor got uppity and Pfieffer let him have another one, drawing blood this time. "There he goes again," Ondine said. Very soon a wild and woolly brawl rolled through the crowded joint in waves. I hadn't put a single beer in me before a bottle came sailing across the bar and struck me under the eye. The fight spread out into the street while the Mexican police forced their way into the front door.

All of First Recon managed to get out without getting arrested. We packed into the Chevy and spent the next hour trying to locate a whorehouse that Ondine favored. We ended up lost and stopped at a depressing little cantina to fuel up, drinking 150-proof rum. The bartender's "wife" and "sister" came downstairs and in no time we reconvened to the living quarters in the back of the building. One of the women filled a plastic bread bag with ice cubes for my swollen eye.

Waiting for your buddies to get laid is right up there with hanging out in a dentist's office. After Pfieffer got laid, I saw one of the prostitutes hanging back in the bedroom as she took a swath at her crotch with a sex towel. Then she dipped her fingers into a large tub of Vaseline containing pubic hairs of various colors and texture. This Vaseline jar brought home the true meaning of the term "sloppy seconds." But Felix didn't give a shit and he joined her in the room and soon a lot of bedboard-thumping sex was going on.

I said, "L.D., man, did you get a load of that Vaseline jar?" He was already three sheets to the wind and waved me off and said, "I'm so horny I could fuck a rattlesnake."

"You just did," Ondine said.

Pfieffer made like he was going to biff Ondine on the nose, but the Sergeant had his hands up and the two started grab-assing until the bartender came around back and threatened to throw us all out if we didn't promise to calm down. In the meantime, the bedbumping and loud groans in Felix's room were like the high drama of a full-fledged exorcism. Gerber was performing oral sex on the other prostitute on a cramped love seat in the little room without having "officially" negotiated a price. In addition to the black eye, I had that burning prostate sensation that sometimes accompanies an orgasm that is followed by heavy alcohol consumption. Every three minutes I felt compelled to go to the bathroom, even though I wasn't putting out more than a few drops of urine per visit. It felt like blue flames were coming out my dick. Then I would walk back into a room that smelled so badly of funky pussy I could have done a backflip.

The rum after gin had hit me pretty hard, and although the night was fairly young, I was already seeing double. Afraid that I was going to puke, I went outside. I saw some lights about a half mile down the road and started off in that direction. A bunch of Mexicans were sitting along a curve in the road, and just before I reached them, I fell fully into a six-foot hole in the ground. The fall almost knocked me cold. I heard the Mexicans roar with laughter and I was so pissed I wanted to kill every one of them, but by the time I had managed to crawl out of the hole, I was muddy and covered with sweat. When I got over to the tree where they sat, one of them passed me a bottle of wine and another passed a joint. I could see that I wasn't the only victim. Two of the men were grunts from the Seventh Marines and they had taken the fall together. "Some kind of road construction, man, and no warning signs either!"

Pretty soon we were all laughing when L.D. came strolling down the road. We hushed up and watched as L.D. took a dive. Then we roared. I was probably laughing harder than any of the rest until I could hear him curse me by name. With that I thought it would be a good idea to make myself scarce.

I teamed up with the two grunts and that was the last thing I remember until I came to in a Pasadena motel room, alone. I did not know how I got to Pasadena from Mexico. A motel manager with beefy forearms and a cigar clenched in his teeth pounded on the door and demanded money for another night. I didn't have a dime. Not only was I broke, I did not have my wallet nor my military I.D. What I had was a short afternoon to get back to Camp Pendleton. I took a quick shower, then guzzled cold water from the tap, and when I looked up in the mirror I saw a red and blue USMC bulldog tattooed on my left deltoid. Above the bulldog was the name "Shab." To this day I have no idea what it means. It's right up there with Stonehenge and Easter Island in the mystery department.

Acutely sick, I hitchhiked back to Pendleton. Two hours AWOL, I was greeted by a look of all-encompassing, universal disapproval. The First Sergeant could make you feel less popular than a burrito fart. For AWOL, I was put on report, had to undergo a series of punishments that were immediate and highly unpleasant, but in the end I suffered less, overall, than my drinking companions, most of whom acquired a case of the crabs or the clap or both. I had a black eye and the tattoo, but these guys were pulling giant red bugs from their drawers.

They were right on the cusp between being able to stand it and seeking medical aid. Gerber thought he could make it go away by taking aspirin, but just before we pulled liberty, he put a new combination lock on his footlocker and promptly lost the combination. He tried to pop the lock using an entrenching tool and after a couple of minutes of this everybody was taking turns. The lock was very durable but the footlocker was soon destroyed. Ondine told Gerber to diddybop up to supply to get a new footlocker before the First Sergeant got back. Supply was located on one of the low foothills just across from the company motor pool. When we got there Gerber gave the corporal in charge a fifth of whiskey for a new footlocker. It didn't take long before the bottle was getting passed around and I felt a wonderful sense of respite. The bunch of us had been counting the minutes until 1600 hours when we could go over to the enlisted men's club and get some hangover relief. It was a hot day at Pendleton and the sun was like a blast furnace. Felix rousted a roadrunner from a clump of brush and soon we were chasing the bird as it darted from spot to spot, zigzagging, impossible to catch. But Felix kept at it. I had never actually seen a roadrunner; it was a small drab-colored bird, and it didn't seem to have a great deal of stamina. Felix managed to ding it with a rock. He carried the bird back to the shady side of the supply shack and went to sip whiskey. The bird panted in exhaustion. Somebody said we should get a cup of water for it. The supply clerk filled an old coffee can with water and presented it to the bird, but the roadrunner wanted none of it.

Felix was itching so badly from the crabs the supply clerk made a joke about him playing with himself. Felix reached in his drawers and pulled out a crab to show to the corporal. It was a fearsome bug, out of all proportion, as terrifying as the roadrunner had been unimpressive. The clerk was a southern boy and said, "You know what you do for crabs, don'cha? Just wait right here," he said. He took a coffee can and walked over to the motor pool where he had it filled with gasoline. In a moment he was back and handed the gas to Felix. "Here, pour some of this in your drawers. It will kill them right now," the clerk said. Felix did as he was told and in moments a look of relief washed over his face. About forty seconds later, he busted away from the supply shack like Superman heading for a costume change. Gerber followed him to the head and returned to tell us that Felix was sitting in a wash basin running cold water over his balls.

Gerber cracked up and did a little war dance, "Aiee aiee chi chi wawa!"

By the time Felix came back, the supply clerk was gone, and Felix was not one bit happy. He was a new guy, half bad — no one knew what he would do. Start a fight? Scream? We just didn't know. People in recon were capable of anything including mayhem and murder. Suddenly he picked up the gasoline and doused the ailing roadrunner. None of us said anything. I think we were too shocked to say anything. The bird hunkered down miserably as its eyes began to blink in rapid fashion. Next Felix pulled out a matchbook and started flicking lit matches at the bird.

Again, no one made a move to stop him. I'd like to report that we were about to do something, but the bird was pretty much written off as dead by that time. Finally Felix lit half the book and immolated the bird. His accent was pure Connecticut, completely new to me. He thumped his chest and said, "They-ya, you cocksuckah. Bo'ne to kill! Arroo-gah!" The bird hunkered down into the crouch of death. Sickened, Gerber hoisted his new footlocker on his shoulder and started down the hill back to the barracks. One by one, the rest of us followed him, each one of us alone with the guilt of our own complicity. It was exactly one week after that when we shipped out to Vietnam.

A Run Through the Jungle

W ITH TWO COBRA gunships leading the way, Chief Warrant Officer Elroy rendezvoused with Second Recon at LZ Juliet Six. It was the alternative pickup zone and it was getting chewed to shit from NVA mortars until the Cobras began to lay down suppressor fire. Things on the ground had been hairy for the marines for some time. Three days previously they had blown cover and had since been experiencing something like an ongoing Chinese gangfuck thirty klicks into Cambodia. The NVA was on them like stink on shit, and if it hadn't been for the monsoons, they would have been dead on the first day. Charles had the team surrounded and was sweeping the area with tracking dogs. Fortunately the heavy rains that delayed the rescue effort also washed away the smell of the Americans. When the weather finally broke, Officer Elroy received last-minute orders to abort the mission. Headquarters maintained that radio contact had been lost and the marines were presumed dead. Elroy wasn't so sure. When the team first called for a dustoff chopper, he had been committed to go in; and no matter what the high command thought, there was no way the Americans could sneak out fast enough for Charles *not* to know that they had crossed the border in the first place. What pushed the flight commander forward was the fact that he knew he wouldn't be able to live with himself if he had left these grunts to hang out to dry. Yet he could only take this line of reasoning so far. I could see by the look on his face that Elroy was thanking his lucky stars that he was not a member of our insert team. We were packed in the back of the overloaded Huey like so many *killer* sardines with bad attitudes and a whole lot of personal firepower. Felix T., our own radio man and the tallest soldier in-country, pulled out his .45 as the orders to abort came through. Team Break on Through was no more going to allow him to abandon Second Recon than Elroy would have done himself. It was a crass move; Elroy's courage was well known and Felix had been a cowboy from day one. His mind was locked and loaded in the gung-ho mode; jammed up on amphetamines and pulling out a sidearm was a bad idea, but we all knew what he was thinking. While it was a mind fuck of an order, what we heard over the radio surprised no one. Unlike the grunts in the army, with superior logistical support and better equipment, marines were marines. We weren't used to hot meals, adequate gear, or being treated very well in the first place, but we were cranked up and ready to engage.

As soon as Elroy brought his bird down, Break on Through hit the ground running. It was an exercise known as a "flip-flop." Charles sure enough knew there was going to be an extraction, but he wasn't expecting an insertion on the same flight. Ondine and I helped the Second Recon corpsman load two wounded Montagnards onto the Huey while the rest of the Break on Through laid out a quick perimeter. One of the Yards was squirting blood from his femoral artery while the other had a sucking chest wound. Both appeared to be in shock: their dark faces were ashen, and both seemed to be beyond the realm of pain. I knew they would both be dead before they got back to Da Nang and exchanged a look with their babyfaced corpsman, a kid who didn't look old enough to be in the war. Still, he looked a good deal older than the prisoner the team had grabbed on their "snatch" mission. The young NVA's hands were secured behind his back with wire, and whenever he looked up, a powerful marine poked him in the mouth with the flash suppressor of his M-16. "Get used to it," the marine said. "It's called the Flavor of the Month, motherfucker."

I knew it was the first of many new exotic treats in store for the prisoner and was thinking that if it were me, I'd jump out of the bird as soon as they had some suicidal altitude. Over the wash of chopper blades, the corpsman was telling Ondine that the rest of the Second Recon ran for another LZ. "Make no mistake," the corpsman said, "Charlie has got spotters and fuckin' bloodhound dogs. You boys just bought the green wienie. Chuck is going to come looking presently."

"I can dig it," Ondine said.

"I'm glad you can," the corpsman said. "Because, *man*, I cannot. No shit, man! I'm getting too short for any more of this bullshit. I'm getting seriously flaky. I don't know if I can hack much more."

"Sounds like you got a personal problem," Ondine said.

As the chopper lifted off, Elroy gave Ondine the thumbs-up signal. The pilot banked the Huey sharply to the west and as soon as he started to gain altitude, small arms fire erupted from the tree line. The door gunner answered immediately with his .60. Break on Through crashed through the narrow stand of elephant grass at a low crouch. As soon as we hit the tree line, we fanned out into the jungle, fading so effectively that when a company of NVA regulars diddy-moued over to the LZ site, they ran right past us. I allowed myself a small smile of satisfaction. The flip-flop had worked and getting into the bush was a whole lot like being back in the saddle again. I felt lucky. The team was luck all the way in recent weeks, and the sense of omnipotence was intoxicating. I was ready to infiltrate Hanoi, grab Uncle Ho by the goatee, pull off his face, and make a clean escape. Cambodia did not seem like a biggie in any way, shape, or form. The NVA didn't know we were there, didn't have a clue. In our tiger-striped fatigues and war paint, Break on Through was invisible.

As soon as the enemy troopers rushed by, Ondine took the point until the team reached a fast-moving stream. He knelt down and shook a canister of CS powder along the banks to discourage dogs. As he did so, Dang Singh set an M-14 toe-popper under a pile of wet leaves and dropped a Baby Ruth bar next to it. It was pure meanness, what Singh liked to call "outchucking Charles," and across the Cambodian border where there was officially no war at all, it seemed like exactly the right thing to do.

At Ondine's signal, I picked up the point and continued moving north directly up the streambed. The team moved swiftly and silently. Eventually the stream dried out and its rocky bed converged near an NVA speed trail. I flashed an arm signal freezing the squad as three NVA soldiers toting howitzer rounds cruised past on Chinese bicycles. I could have sworn one of the slopes had eyeballed me and had been too cool to make a move. As I played with this in my head, Ondine moved forward and asked what was wrong. I told him, and Ondine resumed walking point while L. D. Pfieffer, who was covering the rear, sprinkled red pepper in our wake to foil the dogs Second Recon had been having such a shit fit over. The team picked up the pace, putting distance between ourselves and the speed trail. In another half hour we reached a bamboo thicket. There was no further hint of the enemy. Break on Through was what you called down and happy. Ondine whispered something to the shooter, Pink, and smiled. Felix T. looked at Dang Singh. "What did the sergeant say?"

Singh looked at Felix and said, "Man say, 'Welcome to Cambodia.' " Singh removed a bottle of bug juice and squirted it on a thick leech that was attached to the side of Felix's neck. When he showed it to the tall marine, Felix recoiled in horror. Singh snapped the blood-engorged leech in half and grinned. Like Felix and the rest of the team, he was curious about the shooter, a small Chicano–Native American with an angular face and a pair of cheekbones sharper than razor blades. Pink showed up at Camp Clarke wearing Spec Five insignia and an Air Cav pink team badge just two nights before the patrol. Word circulated that Pink was a sniper from Special Operations. After Pink had lunch with the Colonel and Captain Barnes, he dumped his gear in Break on Through's hooch, and broke out a manila envelope bearing grainy photographs of NVA Brigadier General Deng. Everyone knew about Deng — he was an unorthodox NVA strategist and major pain in the ass dating back to the battle of Dien Bien Phu. By all rights, Deng should have been in an old age home in Hanoi, not out in the field wreaking terror and mayhem. He had been *old* during the French occupation. There was no way he could still be in the field; it was supposed to be just another rumor. But then, too. You never knew. These motherfuckers didn't quit. Shit, they didn't know the meaning of the word.

Just before the mission got under way, I saw the shooter pass the pictures to Ondine. As soon as he handed them back, Pink pulled out his Zippo and torched them. Pink was giving Ondine some respect with this preview. A little r-e-s-p-e-c-t, so he doesn't come off like some fucking new guy, I told this to Dang, who said that Captain Barnes had stonewalled Ondine, saying that the shooter had a target all right, and Ondine would be informed on a need-to-know basis. As far as Ondine was concerned, the team's main mission was cartography. Intelligence knew Charlie was running wild in Cambodia and they wanted B-52 targets. When I saw Pink burning the pictures and became part of the secret, Ondine told me to procure an M-14 from the armory. I was one of the better marksmen on the team, and if special ops thought they needed to send us some lame-ass dogface for an assassination, Ondine was going to prove there was no need. Anyone on the team was up to it. Ondine was resentful that Captain Barnes had so little faith and to tell you the truth, Pink was not that impressive — he was a wiry little motherfucker, making the rest of the team look like Clydesdales in comparison. Actually, wiry wasn't such a bad condition. Ondine had been in a pisser of a mood — restless, edgy and full of bitterness. I didn't think it mattered. I still believed that luck was with us. At least until I saw the dink on the bicycle. I was sure I locked eyeballs with the cocksucker and now felt like my luck was all used up. I was conflicted as all hell.

After we set up for the night, Ondine broke out a map and conferred with Pink in the fading light. Early the next afternoon we skirted the bunker where the snatch had been made. An hour later the team was poised on a hill overlooking a huge NVA base supply camp that was a beehive of transport and supply activity. Buried in a narrow valley, the camp was surrounded on three sides by mountains. A well-guarded single-lane road hidden by triple canopy jungle allowed truck traffic into the camp from the north, while narrow speed trails, too small for trucks or tanks, fed into I Corps to the south. Not only was the NVA able to move fresh troops and resupply into Vietnam, the base had a hospital complete with doctors, nurses, and sterile operating rooms. There were dozens of women, in fact. Undoubtedly the base served as a safe haven for the troops to R&R after excursions into I Corps. Judging by the look of relaxation on the faces of the NVA, it did not appear they had been receiving much in the way of harassment. Pink used his own binoculars to scout the surrounding valley. He marked possible target positions on Ondine's map with a red pencil. He was lining up shots at three, five, and seven hundred meters. The shot he liked best he penciled in last. It was a spot approximately one hundred meters behind the hospital. Ondine shook his head, like "no way!" Pink pointed to the heavy cloud cover and made hand signals to indicate rain and fog. We were far enough from the base to break out a hi-fi and have a party, but Pink was cautious to the point of paranoia. He was so quiet in fact that everyone on the team was beginning to get spooked. Not only had Ondine been acting strange, no one was overly thrilled with the fact that we were in Cambodia. Normally you could blame this sort of weirdness on the new guy, but while Pink may not have been an impressive physical specimen, he certainly had his shit together. While Ondine began to diagram a plan to provide Pink with diversionary fire, the rest of the team contented themselves passing the binoculars back and forth. We saw a pair of dog teams come into the compound followed by an NVA assault team. Felix T. nudged Ondine and said, "Look, Sergeant, those are *our* gooks!"

A few seconds later, General Deng stepped out of a fortified bunker, one that Ondine figured to be an ammo dump. "There he is," Felix said. "Goddammit, motherfucker!"

The General wore a tan uniform with no insignia but it was clearly Deng. He was a man in his early seventies, with thinning gray hair that he wore in a swept-back fashion. His smile was warm and revealed a great deal of gold dental work. Deng walked with a limp. His left foot was shorter than his right by several inches. This was not from a war wound but rather a hereditary condition. With aides on either side of him, Deng leaned on his cane and spoke to the commander of the tracker platoon, who pointed back at the jungle. L. D. Pfieffer mimicked the sort of lame excuse he imagined the platoon commander must have been reciting to General Deng, who had to be very concerned with the knowledge that the Americans were in Cambodia and had *made* their camp. You could barely see their lips moving but Pfieffer supplied the dialogue. "Oh yes man! We lit a fire under their ass, General. You betcha! Jar-head took a number one run through the jungle."

Pfieffer twisted his head to the side, screwed up his face, and took on the part of Deng. "What! You mean you let them escape! You *bungling* fools! B-52s come now. Boom Boom! Efferybody, get down and give me fifty. Very bad. Very bad."

Singh and I cracked up until Pink shot us a look and then Ondine raised his head and told Pfieffer to knock it the fuck off. Felix T. pointed his M-16 at the General and kept it trained on the officer as he moved back into the bunker. "He's a motherfuckin' ant." With a scope, the shot was doable from where we stood; it was just that we would have been pinned down on the same ridge where Second Recon had caught hell. We were out in the open.

Ondine was highly p.o.'d and said, "Put that weapon down and quit fucking around, Felix. That goes for everybody. Now listen up." He flattened out the map on a boulder. We gathered around Ondine's map. He said, "We recon the valley first, but I think we should place our shooters here and here," he said, pointing to the red Xs on the map with his forefinger. "Hollywood doesn't take his shot unless Pink is compromised. He's got the M-14, and if he shoots, he gives away his location. After Pink takes out the General, we detonate nightingales at the north end of the valley while the team runs south. That should give us time to boogaloo. Two escape routes," he said, pointing down to the valley. "Right there along the streambed or straight out of the valley on the high-speed trail. They won't be expecting it. Once we get clear, we fade into the bush, circumvent the bunker, and make our pickup. Felix calls in the coordinates on the camp and while we beat a retreat back to Camp Clarke, the carpet team comes in and levels our good buddies. They've got a lot of people down there, but we'll catch them with their pants down. It should be easy. Any questions? Sound like a plan?" Ondine said. "Okay. Break out your chow; we're going down into the valley in twenty minutes."

Dang Singh could second-guess Ondine better than anyone. "*That's the plan?*" he said.

Ondine said. "Shoot 'n' run."

"Keeping things simple," Singh said.

"I'm open to suggestions," Ondine said. "I'm always glad to hear a brighter idea. We can't make the shot from up here. We've got an ideal vantage but we're too far to make the fucking shot. I can't think of another way."

"Why don't we walk back, real careful like, and let the air force take care of General Deng?" Gerber said. "You got the coordinates. As soon as the shooting starts the gooks are going to hunker down. This is a job for the bomber pilots. Why can't the air force handle it?"

"Because that would be the smart thing to do," Ondine said. "Anybody else?"

We were quickly out of the rucks and tearing open C-rats. Everyone ate without saying much. Pink ate not at all. He took a swig from his canteen, swished it around in his mouth, and swallowed. While the marines carried three canteens each, the shooter carried only one. Also, while the marines carried the maximum amount of personal firepower, Pink only had a single-shot bolt-action carbine. The end was tapped for a silencer and there was a scope mount on the rifle. He carried his ammunition in a single pouch on his cartridge belt. He wore a bush hat and no flak jacket. While the marines ate, he pulled a small copy of the New Testament from his pack and read a passage from the Book of John. Then he spread a fresh application of greasepaint on his face. While Pink wore no dog tags, he carried eight morphine syrettes around his neck. I didn't really blame him. I had been captured once and it had been one time too many. Eight syrettes would certainly do the job.

As soon as it got dark, we slipped through the bush and infiltrated the valley with little trouble. A cold rain began to fall, and after we established a rendezvous point, Ondine went over the plan with everyone again. After Pink got his shot off, he would beat feet to the second shooter's position. That was me. I would be stationed south of the hospital where I had a clean shot at the General's quarters. Together Pink and I would double-time to the rendezvous point. The rest of the fire team would be planted back in the bushes waiting to lay down cover fire. If necessary they could run an IM drill, where each member of the team would jump out into the speed trail and fire his weapon at full automatic. As soon as a man shot off a magazine, he would run to the back of the formation. like a quarterback that had just passed off the ball to a running back. The next man would step onto the trail and shoot, followed by the next and so on. Within thirty seconds a squad could put out the concentrated firing power of a fully armed infantry company. It invariably confused and frightened the enemy and gave the team our one chance to run. After running the drill, ammunition would be essentially gone. The element of surprise would be gone, and if the rain were to stop, the dogs would be all over us.

The quickest way out of the valley was by using the same speed trails the NVA were using to ferry supplies into Vietnam. The jungle leading out of the valley was thick, as we had already seen, and it was going to be quite a run to the LZ. If there was a major fuckup, we could take our chances in the bush. It was a bad option; it was the one Second Recon used. Ondine knew if we blew the pickup, we were in serious trouble. It wasn't like him to gamble in this fashion. There was an alternative LZ, but nobody even wanted to think about it. The Invisible Man couldn't make it to the alternative LZ.

Pink attached the sniper scope and silencer to his carbine. He removed two mesh screen devices known as nightingales from his ruck. These were simply screens wired to a web of firecrackers and cherry bombs and hooked to a detonator. Each would give off a five-minute explosion simulating the heavy weapons and M-16 fire of a full company. The rest of the team took positions along either side of the main trail and planted their claymores before huddling down in the bush establishing their fields of fire. The nightingales were covered with sheets of plastic to protect them from the rain. He gave one to me, along with a long coil of thin wire and a detonator. The rest of the team hunkered down and prepared themselves for the uncertainties of a long wait, while Pink and I slipped into the bushes, keeping away from the trails. It took several hours to get in position. I never saw a soldier more cautious than Pink. While my mind was jamming with amphetamine and the hot blood of fear, Pink was as cold as a snake.

We picked out positions and then moved north with the com wire, toward the feeder road. The trail coming down into the valley had a guard patrol and a pair of dogs, but the security was fairly lax. We set up the nightingales, camouflaging them with tent-shelter halves, and then returned to our positions and spent the night in a bone-chilling rain. It was so cold I could see my own breath. My feet, ears, and fingers were numb. I wondered how a puny guy like Pink could take the cold since I had body fat and he did not. My teeth began to chatter and I was practically into hypothermic shock by dawn. I popped greenies and wolfed down Nestlé's chocolate bars. The mission was beginning to feel like some major suck. We didn't need to do this. We could walk out of the valley and let the B-52s take care of the situation. Headquarters, had they been there to see it, would have known for themselves. I guess they wanted Deng no matter what happened. He was a slippery guy, and people wanted confirmation.

A low fog clung to the camp and it didn't begin to lift until noon. I saw General Deng for a half a second, but suddenly he thought of something and returned to his bunker. I wondered what Pink was doing. There was no way of knowing if he had his shit together or not. I was determined to make the shot the next time I laid my eyes on Deng's skinny ass. I wanted to get out of that place before I froze to death.

At 1530 hours a truck carrying rockets rumbled into the camp and a number of people emerged from the bunker to inspect it. Finally, General Deng came hobbling out of the headquarters. The sight of the rockets seemed to give him a great deal of pleasure. As his face cracked into a wedge of a smile, a glimmer of sunlight reflected off of the General's gold bridgework. I drew a bead on his narrow chest and waited. Suddenly the General took a half-step back on his short leg and then dropped without a sound. The NVA aides standing with the General were busy inspecting the rockets. Deng collapsed of old age. One of the aides knelt down to lift the General's head when he saw that most of it was gone. The aides scurried, and in seconds a warning siren went off. I knew that in moments the woods would be crawling with NVA. But then came the sound of the nightingales exploding to the north of the transport truck. It sounded like a small war was coming down into the valley, and the NVA did just what anyone would reasonably do. They hunkered down before their guns and poured out a "mad moment" in the direction of the nightingales. By luck, a loose RPG round hit the truck, setting off an explosion that rocked the earth. By this time Pink and I were highballing down the speed trail. A two-man NVA security team stepped out of a small grass duty hut; but our machine gunner, Pfieffer, cut them both down with short bursts from his .60. I hated the fact that he was making noise, but it had to happen. More NVA began to appear, but the team was all up and moving now. In a moment a series of small explosions was heard as the claymores the team had planted were tripped. As we continued to run we heard the anguished squeals and high-pitched bellowing of dogs along with the more familiar cries of grievously wounded men.

Pink was ahead of me running alongside a pair of unarmed NVA who had just dropped a container of rice. Both of the men wore thick tortoiseshell spectacles and were clearly noncombatants. I watched the three run in unison for a second, then, in spite of my heavy gear, broke past them like a man hell-bent on the finish line. A few seconds later both of the dinks passed me with a look of terror on their faces. Mother-fuckers looked like dinks with Down syndrome. As they increased their lead, Pink raised his carbine and placed two rounds into the base of each man's skull. It was the best kind of one-handed "John Wayne" shooting I had ever seen.

Then Ondine was up running alongside me, laughing his ass off. "Man, what kind of stupid-ass shit was that?"

"They were unarmed," I said, panting for breath. "It didn't seem right."

"Tell me the last time Charles cut you a line of slack," Ondine said.

"Tell me the last time Captain Barnes cut us any," I said. "Everybody in this for-shit country is out to fuck us, Ondine. I mean fucking everyone."

"Tell me about it," Ondine said.

In moments the team gathered at the streambed that led back to our primary LZ. Everyone was accounted for except for Felix. The sound of small arms fire from behind began to pick up. Suddenly Felix T., with his long stride, came galloping down the rocky creekbed. In addition to his rifle and gear, he was packing a PRC-25 radio and two bandoliers of .60 ammo. As he passed by, Ondine began to laugh hysterically again. I said, "Christ, Ondine, what's so goddamn funny?"

Ondine was hysterical, which wasn't like him. I wondered if Ondine was going to maintain or not. He was pointing at Felix. "Yeah," I said, "the retard Olympics. It's a regular side-splitter."

Up ahead Felix slipped on a mossy rock and went sliding down the wet rocky bed. He looked like a man trying to make a hook slide into home plate. Suddenly there was a flat, muffled explosion and Felix T. gave out a sharp piercing scream. A white phosphorus grenade attached to his web gear had become unpinned as he fell. By the time Ondine and I reached him, he was holding on to his chest. Blood was spurting from his uniform. Ondine pulled his shirt back. "Lung," he said.

"I'm fuckin' burnin' up," Felix said through gritted teeth. The white phosphorus continued to burn within his flesh. Ondine looked him over, not knowing where to start. Felix was covered with holes. He cried, "Burnin' up, *do* something! Get me a fuckin' medic, Jesus!"

I pressed my field dressing against Felix's chest but all that did was send a gusher of blood from his nose and mouth. Felix's teeth began to chatter and in another moment he was dead. He was truly lucky. It was over in less than three minutes.

Ondine wasn't laughing anymore. He stripped the radio off Felix and handed it to me. "This is yours," he said as he hoisted Felix over his shoulders.

'You aren't going to try to carry him all by yourself?" I said.

Ondine said, "Greenie power," and his black eyes flashed amphetamine. He took a few steps down the creek before he stopped and dropped the body and frantically began brushing burning pieces of phosphorus from his shoulders. Singh and Gerber caught up and without saying a word helped carry Felix's large lanky body forward. Overhead we could hear the sound of Cobra gunships and in the clearing ahead I spotted smoke grenades in the LZ. Pink and L. D. Pfieffer came back to help with the body. We got into the slicks in a hurry, remembering how Charles had locked in on Second Recon's pickup zone with mortars. Everyone braced to receive enemy fire but in moments the slicks were airborne and headed back to Camp Clarke. Singh turned to Pink and in a necessarily loud voice said, "Did you make the shot?"

Pink, the diminutive speaker, raised his voice in a shout to be heard over the helicopter noise. "It was a perfect shot. One of the best I ever made."

"All right!" Singh said. Relief was written all over his face. His expression spoke volumes for the adrenaline euphoria of war. Once the perils of a situation have been escaped, the good times roll. It's a lot like hitting yourself over the head with a hammer. It really feels good when you stop, and beyond that there's no point or moral lesson to be learned whatever. Singh was Mr. Happyface. I suppose I was, too.

"Sorry about your man, Tall Paul. What happened?" Pink said.

"Felix liked to keep the pins on his grenades straight," Ondine said. "Like fuckin' John Wayne. Well, take heed. The cat rolled a willy peter."

"Jesus," Pink said.

"Uh huh!" Pfieffer said. "You remember that bird he torched back at Pendleton? That fucking roadrunner?"

"I *do*. That was some sick shit," Gerber said. "A low deed."

"Well, that's all I'm saying, man," Pfieffer said. "What goes around, comes around!"

"Man!" I said. "Don't start with that! One doesn't lead to another, like that. It just doesn't work that way."

Pfieffer looked back at me with a wide grin on his face. "I can't fucking hear you, man. What did you say?"

I didn't want L.D. inadvertently inflicting "boonie voodoo" upon the team by establishing prophecies, or a train of thought that made such prophecies seem logical. But I didn't have the strength to shout over all of the helicopter noise. I looked down at my hands, which were sticky with Felix's blood. My rough palms were blackened like charcoal from white phosphorus burns. They were little black bore holes, the very opposite of white. Beyond those I had to thank God that I made it through another mission without suffering great physical harm. I cared not at all for Felix, never had — and who could the stupid fuck blame except himself? Had it been anyone else, it would have bothered me. I watched smoke coming from the little bore holes in my hands. Adrenaline aside, they really did hurt, but it was the sort of hurt that almost felt good. Christ! I was alive. Soon I would be guzzling beer and smoking reefer. Maybe Barnes would give us five days of out-of-country R&R. Bora Bora was supposed to be very good. I could feel the smile muscles begin to activate but couldn't help but wonder if Pfieffer wasn't right with his boonie voodoo theory. Maybe Felix T. had hexed us when he torched that fucking bird back at Pendleton. For all the smiles, something felt wrong, and we all knew it and felt guilty for not stopping him when he set the goddamn thing on fire. I pulled a small jar of Vaseline from the medical ruck and used it to cut off the oxygen supply to the white phosphorus burns on my hands. As soon as the rest of the team saw the Vaseline, they begged for me to pass the jar around. I wasn't the only one suffering from internal combustion. Wisps of rancid smoke were steaming from little pinpoint vent holes off of just about everybody.

40, Still at Home

THE GREEN ROOM would never make the pages of *Better Homes & Gardens*. The carpet was old pea-green shag. Originally, it matched the green velvet cover of the springworn Slumber King, but somewhere during the Jimmy Carter administration the velvet dyes had broken down. Now, the bedcover, canopy, and the two sets of heavy green velvet drapes had lightened to a garish shade of lime. The room's textures and color schemes were a fright, like the marriage of Transylvania and Graceland. Margo Billis could no longer bear looking at it. The plan had been to renovate this atrocity as she had done with the rest of the house, but that had been B.C., before the cancer. The future seemed worthwhile. No longer was this so.

Yet it was Matthew, her son, who seemed to be the one dying. One Sunday evening after he had logged in twelve-plus hours of continuous sleep, anger forced her across the threshold into his hovel of a room. Matthew twisted his pale round face away from the blue light of the television, arched an eyebrow, and like a demented Charlie Brown, he said, "What are you doing?"

Margo jerked back. Her son's movement's, in the ghostly light of the TV, looked sickeningly macabre — the combination of a cartoon and a ventriloquist's dummy act; the Rod Serling version of "Peanuts."

She regained her composure and said, "What does it look like? What do I ever do, except pick up after you?" Her voice was hoarse and she had to sag to one knee as she hacked off a series of painful dry coughs. To Matthew's tender sensibilities it seemed that a crew of

Northwest lumberjacks were ripping through California redwoods with seven-horsepower Husqvarna chain saws. He knew that if she didn't leave soon, he would awaken fully, long before his body rhythm was prepared for anything so hideous as consciousness. His mother continued to cough with one hand poised on her very tender lower back. The last thing she needed to do was throw out her back.

Finally Matthew effected a sit-up and turned on her, "God*damn* it! Do you always, *without fail*, have to come crashing in here like some deranged fiend when I'm trying to sleep?"

A back spasm stabbed Mrs. Billis and she was seized by a cramp in her foot. She had to hobble upright so she could put weight on the foot. The doctor told her the cramps had to do with a potassium imbalance or something. And the back pain! She thought that with all the morphine she was taking it was unfair that she would suffer back pain or any pain at all! The foot cramp eased but she took a few tentative steps to be sure. "*All* you do is sleep," she said.

Sensing weakness, Matthew boomed, "Baloney! I've been sending out résumés and you *know* it." His round cartoon mouth twisted into an "O" of hatred as he spit out these last words. Leonardo couldn't have drawn a more perfect circle than those formed by Matthew's pale lips.

Margo made three attempts to clear her throat before she said, "If you think sending out résumés is going to get you anywhere, *buster* — you're crazy. Nobody reads them. When are you going to get a job, dammit? I've totally had it with you." She brought her fist to her mouth and coughed.

Matthew's moon face sank back on the pillow as he raised an arm and clawed at the air helplessly. "Oh, God! Stop with that coughing, will you, please? Use your inhaler or something." His anger quickly dissolved into a vapid puddle of self-pity and he spoke in a gasping whisper, "Just quit *torturing* me. I've got endogenous depression. If I don't sleep, I'll be dead by Friday."

Matthew's room was cold, and Mrs. Billis huddled in her red terry-cloth robe, drawing it closed tightly against her neck. "Everybody's got depression," she said. "It's part and parcel of the human condition."

These words aroused Matthew's general sense of contempt for the world. He said, "No, they don't. Not like *mine*. People get a mild case of the blues and brag about taking Prozac or St. John's wort, but they're lightweights. They go to work, they do things. My case is worse than anything to precede it in the annals of recorded medicine." Prematurely awake, and racked with exhaustion from head to heel, Matthew let his arm flop along the side of the Slumber King, producing a visible little puff of dust before the raybeam coming from his television. Matthew's speech had given his vocal cords too much of a workout and now his throat was raw. If he was in for another bout of strep, he decided he would just kill himself now and be done with it. He was utterly without codeine and couldn't face a sore throat without narcotics. A strep sore throat was akin to having your tonsils out by the Inquisition's ace torturing squad — red-hot irons and pincers and a holy relish for their gruesome duties.

Mrs. Billis said, "You *talk* depression, but it's just a game with you. People who are really depressed kill themselves. Suicide has never even crossed your mind; all you want is the life of Riley!"

Matthew rolled his head in his pillow and said, "I'm too depressed to kill myself. Jesus! Everybody knows that you can get too low to commit the deed! When I get better, I'm going to for sure," he said. "Mark my words! I'm getting off Zoloft and getting back on Nardil just to that end. I have to go two weeks cold turkey because you can't mix conventional antidepressants with MOA inhibitors. When I make some therapeutic progress, then I'll really be dangerous. In the meantime, if you have the least shred of feeling or compassion, leave me alone to lie here and wallow in my misery and self-loathing…please, oh God, make her go. If I'm getting strep again, just shoot me. Fuck!"

"Knock it off with that crap," Mrs. Billis said. "Get your ass out of bed, get a job, and go out and find yourself some cute girl! You are your own worst enemy, and mine, too! Lying in bed isn't going to solve anything. Look at me, I've got cancer and I'm not crying the blues. I'm seventy-three and I still get up and work like a dog!"

Matthew felt he might weep. Surely he was having a nervous breakdown. He said, "Why do you always have to come busting in here with tough guy tactics when I'm ready for shock treatments? Do you time my cycles and plan on coming at the worst possible moment? You don't know what *hell* looking for work can be. Capitalism is the worst evil

244 · SELECTED STORIES

ever devised by man. Hustle, hustle, hustle until you can't go on. I can't do it anymore. I can't hack it out there in middle-management hell. If you only knew how heartless those bastards are now. In your day people were still human. I'm telling you, it's criminal and no one will stop them!"

Margo Billis barked off several shallow coughs. Her relationship with her son had come down to little more than late-night arguments. Mornings, daylight hours weren't so bad, but the nights were killers. When she could no longer control the anxiety over her impending fate, she would burst into his room on any pretext. "Be glad you aren't living in a car," she said. "Be glad you aren't trying to cut it in North Korea with beriberi and a tablespoon of rice per day."

Matthew's throat was aflame. He pitched his voice higher to work an unused portion of his larynx and Margo recoiled. He sounded perversely like Mickey Mouse. Helium-voiced, this cartoon son tossed out his hand and said, "Depression is worse than any painful disease — cancer, starvation — whatever you got — *any*thing. I've seen more than a hundred shrinks. I've taken every antidepressant under the sun. Engineering is all wrong for me. I need another *venue* to express my peculiar point of view. I mean if I have a contribution to make to the world, I need to go another road." Matthew was proud of his vocabulary choice but when he saw that it failed to impress his mother, his thin neck finally gave out and his heavy round head fell back on the Slumber King. His voice was piercing. "I can't take any further interrogation. What you are doing to me is against Geneva Convention rules." He folded a king-size pillow around his head and then stretched into the full layout position and executed a body roll-and-a-half toward the east wall. In one adroit, well-polished move he not only escaped the sharp light from the hallway, he also muffled the harsh gravel rasp of his mother's incessant nagging.

By now, Mrs. Billis had worked herself into a state of furious indignation. This unleashed a full convolution of organic trauma, but her anger was greater than fear. She swung Matthew's door shut with her lambskin slipper and stalked into the kitchen with his breakfast tray. "Lazy-ass son of a bitch! He's *worth*less! Forty years old and useless! I've had it. I'll kill him!"

She stabbed at the fried-egg mess on her china plate with a soap sponge. The eggs were harder than rocks. She wondered why she cared. Soon she would be six feet under. Then what would he do? Then what "road" would he find? She whirled around and in another moment she was back wresting the blankets away from him. Matthew had already dropped off to sleep again and clung to the blankets desperately. She backed away and turned to his closet. "I'm going to take all of this shit, throw it out on the lawn, and have the locks changed! I can't take anymore. *I'm* the one who's sick! You can just get the hell out!" She screamed as she began ripping Matthew's clothing out of the closet. Matthew leaped from the Slumber King and forced her out into the hallway. During the struggle he snagged his baby toenail on the dresser, half ripping it off. "Goddamm it," he screamed. "You're totally nuts! Just leave me the fuck alone. You're a maniac!"

Mrs. Billis pushed at the door but Matthew had the full weight of his body pressed against it. "If you aren't out of here in one hour, I'm calling the police!" she screamed. "I am sick of waiting on you, picking up after you, and paying your bills. I want you out!" She sounded like Linda Blair in *The Exorcist*.

Although his mother weighed scarcely a hundred pounds and was dying of cancer, Matthew had to use every ounce of his strength to hold her off. It felt like Lucifer bucking the other side of the door. As soon as the pushing stopped, he clicked the lock shut and returned to bed. His pulse was racing and he felt short of breath.

Out in the kitchen she began to cough again. Little poppers. *Kaff kaff kaff!* He heard the hiss of her medicinal inhaler and seconds later the coughing stopped entirely. Why didn't she pick it up at the first tickle? *Why? Because she was a fiend and coughed simply to torment him with guilt! And Jesus Christ, did his toe ever hurt!* Matthew reached for the flashlight and sat on the edge of the bed examining his bloody nail. He needed to rip the thing off but lacked the courage to do so. Instead, he resumed the full layout position and began to practice hatha yoga breath control. He wasn't doing it right, just operating on the basis of some half-remembered instructions from a meditation book one of his many counselors had laid on him.

His toenail throbbed. He flipped on the flashlight again, gritted his teeth, and pulled the snagged edge of it loose and then flopped back in the position. Such a small few micrometers of tissue and such a great pain. A perfect metaphor for life! Fuck it, going to sleep now would be impossible!

On television he saw a report about twelve hundred people drowning in Bangladesh. He reached for the remote and turned up the volume. There were scrawny women in saris sitting in trees, shots of people on rooftops, and pictures of skinny white cows floating in the muddy floodwaters. When the camera panned through a major city, Matthew took great satisfaction in seeing that the floodwaters had submerged two-story buildings. That twelve hundred drowned in a far-off land somehow comforted him. Better they than he. In fact, when God reached out like that, *He* got something off His chest — some level of celestial wrath that just as well might have been directed at Matthew. It was like an Aztec sacrifice or something. A good way to blow off steam.

Oh, it was too true that *all* was *one*, and that if he personally knew any of the drowning victims, he would be heartbroken by their plight, but suddenly his mind had been delivered from his troubles and he could feel himself about to drift asleep again. A few more hours of sleep would complete his REM cycle, fostering revival. And he was close to snoozola. He was on the verge. He could *almost* get it. But then he had to piss with a vengeance, and to piss meant leaving the sanctuary of the Green Room. Go out; venture forth with the fiend of Fordham Avenue on the loose. Shit! Suddenly Matthew found that he had to squeeze his legs together to hold his urine. There was a nerve in the bladder, a kind of natural gas gauge like the one located on the dashboard of a car. Once it hit the danger mark, the signal became hard to ignore. But to go out there? She would be on him like a peregrine falcon. Suddenly Matthew spotted a discarded Burger King coffee cup in his wastebasket. It was a pretty seedy thing to do, but he retrieved the cup and let go. He had to piss so badly his eyes were watering.

"Take a memo," he reminded himself. "Empty cup at the first opportunity." Heh heh. Man, how low can you go? Well, lay around unemployed for two years and you could always *limbo a little lower, now* — *hey dere! Heh heh heh.* Suddenly the cup was filled to the brim and warm in his hands. He didn't know where to put it. Finally he set it along the wall next to his bed. With that done, he assumed *the position* and within moments was in deepest slumber.

Matthew awoke at seven the next morning clinging to fragments of a disturbing dream — a virtual night terror. Still, no matter how bad it had been it wasn't as bad as the scourge of raw dawn. He found himself in a tight fetal ball but rolled over. His stomach roiled with the corrosive acids and bile of inhuman stress. He might have to vomit. He had a nuclear meltdown of a hiatal hernia — either that or this was it. The big one. Heart attack at forty. The American Way. Goddamn them!

Matthew closed his eyes again and tried the deep-breathing exercise. No need to get in a shithouse panic. If he did that, he would start generating beta waves in his brain pan and once that happened the adrenaline would begin to flow. He'd wake up for sure. Peace, brother. *Just back off and try a little more of that free-floating action. Come on, man. Don't freak; just slide back into slumber. Breathe.*

Frightful thoughts raced through his brain. He was certain that the pain in his upper chest was heart pain, particularly when he recalled the shortness of breath he experienced after the struggle with his mother. His saliva tasted peculiar and he wondered if pus was festering in his throat or if he had brought about a bleed from so much screaming. He endured an age of agony and managed to fall asleep nonetheless.

Matthew awoke at four-thirty in the afternoon. He came to in the full layout position and stretched luxuriously, arching his feet as he scissored his limbs and made little snow angels under the covers of the Slumber King. Except for the interlude with his mother, Matthew had pretty much put together a near-twenty-two-hour package of sleep from the last twenty-four. A commendable feat! He continued to savor little dream fragments as he walked into the kitchen for coffee. His pride and self-satisfaction vanished when he saw that the carafe under the Mr. Coffee machine was completely empty — treason and high tyranny on her part. Shit! As Matthew fumbled through the cupboards looking for coffee filters, the memory of their argument last night came back in rich detail. It had been an ugly scene. Still, it wasn't like her to hold a grudge or not have some coffee going. When he finally found the filters and the package of ground Starbucks, he filled the machine and hit the switch.

He put the biggest cup he could find under the fount since he didn't want to wait for an entire pot to fill before he got some caffeine in him. He could do a quick switch once his cup was loaded. Jesus, what a hassle! He wasn't the kind that could casually wait for coffee. When he had to have it, he had to have it. Furious over this inconvenience, he impatiently drummed his fingers as he waited for the coffee. Then Matthew spotted a full bottle of morphine tablets sitting across the room next to the Cuisinart — morphine tablets that his mother *always* kept locked up in the three-hundred-pound safe in her bedroom.

Matthew took a deep breath and listened for the least hush of sound. Suddenly thought and action were one. He closed the distance between himself and the drugs with the stealth and silence of a trained Mohican stalker. He quickly dumped a dozen of the tablets into his palm, shook the bottle to fluff it up, and then returned to his station next to the coffee machine. The entire action was completed faster than Superman making a phone-booth costume change. He had been reckless with the morphine tabs on earlier occasions. The rustle of pills was a sound both mother and son were attuned to, and as careful as Matthew was, the twelve morphine tablets sliding into his hand sounded exactly like what it was — drug theft. A herd of buffalo storming through the living room would have been more subtle. Matthew felt exposed — caught red-handed — yet to his astonishment, the quiet held. Un-fucking-believable! Making casual, he walked back to the Green Room. In his excitement to stash the pills, he bumped the Slumber King and over-turned the brimming cup of urine. He scarcely gave it a thought — hell, it would dry on its own practically without an odor. Well, maybe. Anyhow, this was no time to worry about a little spilled piss.

Matthew hurried to his mother's bedroom and peeked inside. When he saw her form under the covers, he went back to the kitchen. God! What a score! That fluffing-up procedure was amazing. He rubbed his hands together in delight. The perfect crime. He watched the Mr. Coffee machine sputter. Molasses in January. He had half a notion to unleash his expertise as a design engineer one last time and make a six-second Mr. Coffee, but the world that had treated him so badly didn't deserve such a prize.

Suddenly Matthew realized that he had *under*stolen. An opportunity like this came once in a blue moon. He slid across the room and shook out another twenty tablets. The container held 200 count. Twelve and twenty — that was thirty-two total — hell, round it out to forty. At forty, the fluff-up job looked suspicious. Reluctantly he returned four tablets to the pill bottle, replaced the lid, and went back to the coffee station. He wondered if he had gone too far. His moves were mechanical and the word *guilt* was written all over him. He needed to get back into the Green Room. His coffee cup was three-quarters full when he made the switch-over to the pot. He quickly opened the fridge and poured some half-and-half into the cup and knocked down four of the morphine tablets. He *needed* morphine. His baby toe was throbbing like a bass drum. In a more humane society, pain would be treated in a less Calvinistic fashion. Jesus! He took the remaining pills back to his bedroom and hid them with the others. With his coffee he took two Xanax from his stash and swallowed them to accentuate the high that was about to come any time soon. He slugged the coffee down to dissolve the pills faster and then got on the Slumber King and assumed the position. It was like being at the opera or some gala affair awaiting the greatest production of pleasure life could deliver. Ensconced in the Slumber King, Matthew Billis, who had been so tormented by relentless depression, who had come to feel so bad that not even taking a shit felt good, and who was bereft of a single endorphin, waited for the buzz of a lifetime. It was a buzz with a wow factor of ten. He bore witness to a glorious lotus blossom of joy opening in his stomach that sent out radiant orange tidal waves of orgasmic ecstasy — waves that pulsed up through the base of his brain, to the roots of his hair, and back down his spine to his arms, legs, fingers, and heels. In every fiber and place of his being, Matthew felt bliss — bliss that he realized had been lying in wait all along. Oh! Whoa! Daddy!

Suddenly he felt he was on to the whole game of existence, and what a great inward laugh he laughed as he thought of it all. *Love.* Bathed in a shimmering white light and healed of every ailment and affliction, physical or psychological, he knew at last that love *was* the answer. It had seemed so...far away, but there it was, right in front of him — all about him, in his every pore. In and out, he breathed it. It existed in himself and in all things, for all things truly were one. Matthew had been those women left like driftwood in the trees of Bangladesh. He had suffered their suffering but, fuck, what did it matter now? Now everything was double jake. Sooooper Fraj-A-Lizzz-tik-X.B.-Al-eh-doe-shuz! All right now! Yah-sir! Hahaha. He hovered peaceably under the lime green canopy of the Slumber King for the next hour and a half sending out love vibrations — not only to the drowning in Bangladesh, but for souls that suffered everywhere. It never occurred to him to beam one out to his old lady.

By and by Matthew became hungry. He found himself magically padding out to the kitchen with another *four and two* (four morphine tabs and two Xanax). He gulped these down with coffee and then started rooting around in the refrigerator. He soon whipped up a tray of steaming biscuits and a cheese omelet with green onions. Fucking-A, was it ever delicious. Even doing the dishes was fun. After he had them squeaky clean he began to wonder about his mother. Shit, where *was* she? Surely not in bed still, she was the insomniac of all time. Funny though, her car was in the driveway. When he got the paper he noticed that she had not brought in the mail. That wasn't like her at all! He went back to her bedroom and quietly opened the door. "Ma?"

She didn't move. Matthew moved closer. "Ma, yo! What are you doing? Are you *okay*, babe?"

He moved closer, sensing something was terribly wrong. There was a splatter pattern of blood and sputum on her pillow. He pulled back the covers and reached for her neck, to pull her up. It was too late. She was cold and blue, and as dead as a doornail. It was odd, he thought, standing there, her condition seemed neither good nor bad; dead was just what it was. Nothing more and nothing less. He wondered if he was in some egoless state of Nirvana. Beyond his mother Matthew spotted the door of the three-hundred-pound safe. Jesus H. Christ, it was wide open. He turned on the bedside lamp and pulled it to the floor for a look inside. There was another bottle of 200-count morphine tablets and an 8-by-14 canvas sack. He unzipped it and dumped the contents on the mattress. Fifty- and one-hundred-dollar bills floated to the bed. He soon counted out a sum of fourteen thousand dollars. In addition to the cash there were several stock dividend checks and a social security check, all signed and ready to be countersigned. Matthew got down on his knees to see what else was in the safe and was shocked to find a half-carton of Lucky Strike cigarettes. Mrs. Billis, to his knowledge, had not smoked in years. He threw the cigarettes to the floor and looked for more secrets. There were several cloth-wrapped Hummel figurines — her treasures. Crass stupid-ass junk really. As he was removing these from his safe a recent prescription for 200-count morphine fluttered to the floor. A script for morphine! Lord, have mercy! What a stellar find!

He took the cash, the pills, and the prescription back out into the kitchen and set them on the table next to the mail and the newspaper. Did she know that she was dying and leave the safe open on purpose? With all of that blood on her pillow, it was unlikely. She had simply died of natural causes.

Matthew's initial sense of objective detachment began to deteriorate. He turned to the Rolodex and began to spin through it looking for her doctor's number when it dawned on him that she didn't need a doctor, not really. Not anymore. Well, who to call then? There wasn't much family left, just cousins. Fuck them. He went back to the room and studied his mother's body. A look of horror was affixed to her face. She had seemed to diminish in size a good 20 percent. He pushed her mouth closed. Her limbs were still pliable. He wondered how long she had been dead. She had somehow scrunched down low in the bed, and when he pulled her forward, her mouth dropped open and a gush of blood oozed out. Matthew quickly rushed out of the room and went to the kitchen sink to wash the cold and slimy blood from his hands. Suddenly he was into hand washing in a big way. Lady "Matthew" Macbeth.

At last he opened the phone book and turned to the yellow pages looking for mortuaries. Did you just call them, or did you inform the doctor first? If he informed the doctor, he wasn't going to be able to cash that script for morphine. It would be null and void. A waste of ambrosia. Man, she was still pliable! She must have somehow been hovering, clinging to life until only just recently. Matthew wasn't sure how long it took for rigor mortis to set in. He could drive to the drugstore now, cash in the script, and then make phone calls. Who was to know? He took another four-and-two combination and went back to the safe. He removed a pack of Luckies from the carton and sat in the kitchen, smoking cigarettes, drinking coffee as he thought things over. Matthew quit smoking when his mother first came down with cancer and now he wondered why. It was such a *pleasure* to smoke. It was pure enjoyment. That she was able to sneak cigarettes behind his back seemed amazing to him, but then, given his sleep habits, it wasn't surprising at all. But why did she sneak around about it? To fool herself! Yes, that was it! Denial. His analytical powers were most acute.

An inspired plan evolved. Matthew finished his coffee, snuffed out a cigarette, and retrieved his old Boy Scout sleeping bag from the spare closet. He unrolled it on the bed next to his mother. It had a musky smell. He reached under her arms and slid her body over onto the bag, careful not to let her head slump forward. Once he had her in the bag, he zipped it shut and then hefted her up, carried her out to the garage, and placed her corpse inside the freezer. Fit was not a problem as the freezer was only half full. He returned to the bedroom and got her Hummels. He placed these into the freezer with her in case she might need them in the Happy Hunting Grounds — she had plenty of frozen food, that was for sure. Heh heh.

One of the Hummels depicted a small boy with a beagle. Matthew had given it to her when he was eleven out of money he had saved mowing lawns. He remembered that the statue had cost thirty-five bucks. It had been a lot of money at the time, but he wanted her to have it. He wanted her to have something really nice. Jesus, what kind of shit was he pulling here? He didn't know, he was just playing things by ear. He went back into the kitchen and pulled some candles out of a drawer. He set them on the freezer and lit them in her honor. The morphine was kicking in nicely now. Matthew said, "Look at it like this, babe: you aren't really dead until I thaw you out and call the doctor. In the meantime, as long as I can forge your signature, I've got all the job I need."

He thrust out his narrow chest and began to strut before the freezer, his movements suddenly fluid and rhythmic. Released from the morass of his neurotic fears, he was suddenly a kinetic art form as he popped his fingers and jived about in the garage. The Panasonic was airing a commercial in which a phalanx of ants was carrying off a bottle of Budweiser: "Do a little dance; make a little love; get down tonight! Get down tonight!"

Matthew was in a "get down" mood. He said, " 'Get a job'? Who, me?

Baby, you' talkin' to the kid! Get a job? Shee-it, man! Anyhow, why in God's name should we drag this through probate and take it up the ass from the government? Those fascist bastards! Why?"

Yes, why? Matthew retrieved a Diet Coke from the refrigerator in the garage. Back in the Green Room he shook out another four-and-two combo and slugged it down with Coke. Then hopped into the Slumber King and assumed the position. *Dateline Monday* was coming on and Matthew Billis felt absolutely, positively, right-on-the-money cap-*ee*-tal.

Tarantula

JOHN HAROLD HAMMERMEISTER arrived at W. E. B. Du Bois High School with grand ambitions. Harold loved to work, thrived on challenge, and could scarcely contain his excitement at the prospect of a new and difficult assignment.

Postings such as these were like the great wars: they provided one with opportunities for distinguishment. There was another thing, too — hard work took Harold's mind off the inner turmoil resulting from so many recent life changes. He had been racking up big numbers on the Hans Seyle Stress Scale. In less than two years he had weathered a divorce, suffered the death of both parents, and then, with the last of his inheritance, had come down from Canada — come down to Detroit to polish off the course work on a Ph.D. Now everything was done except for the thesis. It was just one last detail. A little trifling. Why, he would have it out of the way faster than you could say John Harold Hammermeister.

The principal who hired Hammermeister was scheduled to retire in a year, and Hammermeister, with his doctorate all but finished, had a "feeling" that the principal's job was his. All he needed was to whirl like a dervish for one year, a mere two hundred and twenty-six school days — dazzle them senseless — and the kingdom from on high would be his. And Harold was most definitely in contact with the kingdom. Before falling asleep each night Hammermeister tuned into the Universal Cosmic Broadcast. He was a psychic radioman who not only transmitted but received. He was connected, on the inside. It was beautiful, wonderful, mar-ve-lous!

Yeah, eyes closed at night, in red flannel pajamas, Hammermeister lay in the ancient Murphy bed of his studio apartment and *created* the future — and in that future he saw himself in the principal's office, in full command, in one year's time, a mere two hundred and twenty-six school days. The principal's office was just a little pit stop on the way over to district office proper, and he would most certainly ascend the ladder there. From the Murphy bed he created glorious visions of supreme success. He watched himself climb from the modest position of junior vice-principal all the way up to the summit of State Superintendent of Public Instruction! Why not try *that one* on for size? Heh heh.

The old Murphy bed was Harold's magic Persian carpet from which he could encompass the "big picture." He plotted his moves and savored future pleasures. Harold saw, smelled, felt, and practically *tasted* the smooth, dove gray leather seats of the burnished black Lincoln Town Car that would replace his ancient Ford. A car so quiet, the only thing he would ever hear was the ticking of the clock. In their gold-plated frames, the Lincoln's vanity plates would read: HAMMER!

In the mind-movie there was also a second wife, a newer and better model than the first. Beauty, brainpower, and refinement ("behind every great man...."). When she wasn't supporting him in his Machiavellian schemes, number two would be a well-rounded person in her own right. *Yeah, she gon be so fine!* And the school district administration center would be Harold's seventh heaven of joy — secretaries in short skirts with a little piquant bantering among them by day. A little bit of hanky-panky, while nights and weekends involved a walled country estate with polo, fox hunting, and high society available at his pleasure. Yes, a *walled* estate! Wasn't that how the rich did the world over? They put up buffers and walls against the detritus of the everyday life. It was every man for himself in the swinish cesspool of the twentieth century. And why not be absolutely selfish? Was not beauty more pleasing to the eye than ugliness and squalor? To think of this new beginning, to think that it would all take off from a place like Du Bois High School — a veritable war zone, a sinkhole of black despair, a continuous scene of barbarous violence! Well, no problem, Harold would soon have it all squared away. They would have to do a double segment on *60 Minutes* to showcase Harold and the new reformation revolution in American schools. Du Bois would become the exemplar ghetto success story. Hope would replace despair. Yes, fairy tales could come true. Harold was going to turn things around on a dime. Only fair that he should reap the rewards.

The bestseller that his thesis would become would provide the means. Written in the snappy, popular vernacular, it would be a multifaceted jewel. Americans would read Harold's terse, spellbinding prose with a curious admixture of horror and astonishment. The *All-New Blackboard Jungle: An American High School in 1999*. Probably make a movie, and playing the role of the visionary reformer — the only actor capable of playing real-life John Harold Hammermeister — may I have the envelope please? — *ta da!* Ladies and gentlemen, the only actor with sufficient authority and range to catch the infinite subtleties — with the scope, the voice, intelligence, maturity, the physical presence — ladies and gentlemen, I present to you…yet another gifted Canadian, Mr. Donald Sutherland. Was it Sir Donald? Well, it would be. The Queen Mother could hop off her ass and beknight the man. The dear fellow. It was high time. Just 'bout time, all right.

Boy oh boy, what the mind could behold, the mind could make real. Hammermeister gave the kids a watered-down version of his visualization techniques whenever it was time to light a fire under somebody's dead ass. Take pride! Pull yourself up by your bootstraps. It was always in one ear and out the other; they didn't have a snowball's chance, but you had to try. Professional ethics required one to take the idle stab.

Nobody but nobody knew anything about elbow grease anymore. People were so friggin' lazy. Work like a German! It was the golden key to riches and prosperity beyond imagining. Most American educators were shell-shocked, blown. In the trench warfare of public schooling, one needed to concentrate, work hard, confront problems and wrestle them down. Engage the mind. Work! In the trenches, friends, family, and personal recreation were inexcusable diversions. Insipid fuckfiddle. You could pick up on that action later. Climb the ladder and then harvest the bounty…in the meantime, later, alligator.

In Hammerstein's office, on the left side of his desk in a small glass cage — the bottom covered with pea gravel, the top fixed with a warm-

ing lamp — Hammermeister kept a tarantula named Lulu. Hammermeister waited a few days before he brought the spider in. He wanted to
get the lay of the land first. Lulu was a statement, and he wasn't totally
sure how to "play" these Americans. A big-ass hairy spider could get to
be *too much*, but then, with his pleasant, affable good looks, his Mr.
Nice Guy demeanor, Hammermeister wanted to establish a darker aspect of himself — a presentation of danger. If it gets down to it, boys and
girls, *if it comes down to it,* I'll fuck you up in a second! I'll mess up yo'
face!

Did he really *say* that?

No, but he *conveyed* it just the same. He put out the vibe. When a
recalcitrant student was sent to his office, Hammermeister liked to rock
back in his executive's chair, tapping the edge of his desk with a number
one Dixon Executive pencil, affecting a debonair Donald Sutherland
style, and say, "You aren't getting through to me, my friend." Tap, tap,
tap. "You aren't getting through." It got to even the baddest of the bad —
the sneaky quiet malefactors, the toughest thugs, the sulkers, wrongdo-
ers of various shapes and descriptions. Hang a leading question on the
guilty soul and he spills his guts. It never fails.

Hammermeister was the first administrator to show up in the morning and the last to leave at night. He attended the football games, the
band, orchestra, and choir recitals — plays. He even showed up at girls'
B-squad volleyball games. He wanted everyone to know that he was at
the school and of it, and that because of him and through the sheer
force of his personality, the school was going to get better, improve,
blaze into the heavens — and the plan was working. A man has to have
a plan, and Harold had a righteous plan. Beautiful, wonderful, *mar-ve-
lous!*

The students and discipline were his forte. He soon had them all under control — the wild-ass freshman girls, the dopers, the gang bangers;
the whole spectrum of adolescent vermin. It didn't have to be "I'll fuck
you up!" It hardly ever was…really. With Lulu on the desk he could
focus totally.

The principal complimented him often about how well he handled
the whole arena of discipline, but when Hammermeister asked for more
responsibilities, Dr. White put him off.

"Not just yet. Why don't you settle in for a while, huh-huh-huh-Harold? Don't want to burn out, do you? Meltdown by May. That happens to the best of us, you know, even when things are guh-guh-guh-going well."

Christ, you could stand there for an hour to hear the motherfucker deliver one complete sentence.

"Seriously, Dr. White, I want to learn everything I can. I want to know this school inside and out. I'm part of the team, and I don't like sitting on the bench."

"Okay then. There is one little trouble spot that seems to duh-duh-duh-defy our coping skills: the cuh-cuh-cuh-custodians. They're yuh-yuh-yuh-yours."

Hammermeister quickly scheduled a meeting with all thirteen of the men. He had pizza brought in to foster conviviality, but instead of the friendly get-together he envisioned, all thirteen janitors started in on him at once: the year had never been off to a worse start! It was terrible! There was a group of squirrely freshmen, and they were carrying food to all ends of the building — spilling pop on the rugs, spitting chew, sunflower seeds, and peanut shells. A particular bone of contention was a type of hot pink, new-wave chewing gum. This stuff didn't freeze when you applied aerosol-propelled gum hardener to it — freeze it so you could smack it to pieces with a putty knife, pick up the cold little broken shards, and throw them in the trash.

A red-faced custodian named Duffy harped on and on about the gum hardener. "For one thing, it erodes the ozone layer, and for another, it makes this fuckin' gum melt and soak *deeper* into the fiber of the carpet. Opposite of the very role for which it was intended, man. One piece of gum, fuck! One kid, thirty-two teeth, give or take, and one wad of gum equals twenty-five minutes of *my time*, which translates into almost nine dollars of the district's money. One piece of gum! I could *ignore* it, let the rug go to shit, but I take pride. *I take pride!* For Chrissakes, why doesn't somebody tell that jerkoff that fills up the vending machines to quit putting chewing gum in — huh? Or at least use a normal kind. I tried to talk to the man. I don't know what you have to do with that guy. I can't get through to him. Mastication of the South American chicle plant is against the law in Singapore, Harold, did you know that?

I tell this guy that selling gum is against the law in Singapore! They got their shit squared away over there. I tell this to Vend-o-face, an' he ain't hearin' it. He's one of them passive-aggressive sons of bitches who likes to drive fifty in the passing lane or who will *hang up* an express line at the supermarket jacking around with a checkbook, buying lottery tickets, and asking questions when others are in a fuckin' life-and-death hurry. Forgive my digression, but are you getting the picture? I never met anyone like him before; he's just an absolute asshole. You know the character, John Waite from *The Nigger of the Narcissus?* That's this guy. There's just no other way to describe this human piece of shit."

Hammermeister was so shocked by Duffy's stream of invective that his face went pale. In Canada, a man such as Duffy would be fired on the spot. What gross insolence! That Duffy had the nerve to speak to him in this fashion — obviously, there were different rules of engagement going on. Detroit, shit, what a very strange energy inhabited the city where such scenes were commonplace. Harold was almost certain he could smell alcohol on this man's breath. "John Waite?"

"Waite from *The Nigger of the Narcissus.* For God's sake, you're a college man, aren't you? Read the book. Don't teachers have to read in college?"

Another of the custodians chimed in. "Hey, the man is right. He knows what he's talking about. This vending guy is Johnny Waite! He should be banned from the fuckin' building."

Throughout this all, an enormous black man with a shaved head, a silver nose ring, and studded earrings locked a hard stare on Hammermeister, like a heat-seeking missile. At last he said, "Hey! I'd like to get something off my chest. You called us all in here for a meeting, and nothing will change or get done as we all know. You have the secretary call me up to come to a fucking meeting at two-thirty in the afternoon when I work graveyard. Doesn't anybody have any consideration? I need to come in and hear all of this Mickey Mouse piss and moan. *The Nigger of the Narcissus!* Watch your mouth, Duffy! I don't even want to hear you *thinkin'* 'nigger.' You don't have the right, motherfucker! I'm the one's paid dues." Roused to a fury, the large custodian wheeled on Hammermeister and stuck a finger in his face. "How would you like it if I called you up and told you you had to come to work at three in the morning? *Three in the morning*, because that's what this is for me, god-dammit! Plus, I'm sick tonight. Call me a sub. You done fucked up my circadian clock! I don't know when it will come back to normal, I'm still fucked over from fucking daylight savings back in May or when-ever the fuck! Foolin' with Mother fucking Nature. God! Great God! Goddammit, son of a bitch!" With that, Centrick Cline kicked a metal folding chair out of his way and stormed out of the room.

Mike, the head custodian, got up, ostentatiously glanced at his watch, and said, "There's a volleyball setup in the gym. Let's go. We're already two hours behind. Lord, we got to boogie, folks, or we're going to be here *awl* night long."

Hammermeister watched the custodians file out of the conference room. He looked down at the untouched pizzas, sixty dollars' worth leaking warm grease onto the limp cardboard containers. He picked up a piece smothered with sausage, pineapple, olives, and onions and ate it in four bites. It was his first meal of the day.

All the screaming had caused Rider, the senior vice-principal, to pop his head in the door and catch Hammermeister in a state of panic — catch him in a situation over which he had no control. An abominable scene. Janitors...Dr. White had been right. They defied the usual... well, hell, they were out of control. He would call them in one by one. Isolate them. Break them down. Turn them into lapdogs.

They did have a point, however, the school did look like hell. The next afternoon Hammermeister got on the p.a. and told the students of W. E. B. Du Bois High School that while the year was off to a great start, food, candy, and pop were not permitted in the halls and class-rooms. The following afternoon he repeated the message, shifting from the insouciant Donald Sutherland to the rather arch Donald. When Hammermeister continued to notice litter in the halls and classrooms, he ordered the pop and candy machines shut down for an unspecified period.

Hammermeister called the head custodian into his office and told him of this decision. "I want to help you guys out. We couldn't run this school without the custodians," he said with an ingratiating smile. "Any-thing you need in the way of supplies, or whatever, just let me know. And one other thing, the district has asked me to address the problem of sick-leave abuse. Du Bois is the worst school in the district in this regard."

No sooner were the words out of Hammermeister's mouth when Mike, the head custodian, proceeded to tell Hammermeister that his daughter had chicken pox and that he needed a sub for the rest of the week — moreover, Ralph, the day man, needed a sub for Monday because he was going in for some blood tests. And, oh, somebody else, too — he wasn't sure, well, yes, it was Ray. Ray had tickets for a rap concert and wanted to take a vacation day.

"So...Mike...at least talk to the guys. Can you do that much?"

"Yo," the head custodian piped as he turned and walked away. For a head custodian, Hammermeister felt the man had a very bad attitude in regard to chain of command. *Well, wait a minute. Mike. Come on back here, my friend. Perhaps that's too much to lay on you all at once. Maybe you ought to go home and rest. Take a year off for mental health. I'll watch your area for you and make sure all your checks are mailed...r'hat on time, bro. Izzat cool or what? I mean, I'm hip to all the problems you guys go through. I know your job...ain't no day at th' beach. I'm in full sympathy. Really. You don't think I got a heart? I gotta heart. I got a heart.*

A week after the pop and candy machines were shut off, the associated student body complained that they were losing the revenue from these machines and made it plain to Hammermeister that this revenue was the lifeblood that bought band uniforms, sports equipment, and other essentials. Hammermeister was shocked when he learned the figures. The students at Du Bois consumed enough fluid ounces of Coke, assorted beverages, and refreshments to half fill the swimming pool in a week. The Hammer didn't allow anything sweeter than fresh fruit back at the juvenile facility in Canada, and what a difference. There weren't any sugared-out junior gangsters like here, and the behavioral considerations, repercussions etc. were extremely...interesting. Well, it would all be in the thesis. Soon the wide world would know.

In less than a week there was heavy pressure to turn the candy machines back on. Hammermeister lost his cool and exchanged heated words over the matter with senior vice-principal Rider. He came back later and made a cringing apology, explaining that he wasn't used to making so many compromises, having come from a detentional facility where his word had been "law"; that he was grinding out his thesis and so on and when he reflected over the apology, it occurred to him how weak and desperate he had sounded — effete and obsequious. A wipe-out migraine could do that to him, turn him white. The pop machines went back on, and the school instantly became a pit.

Waiting for a pair of codeine #4s to kick in, Hammermeister dropped a succulent white grub into Lulu's cage and watched the spider attack it with such speed and ferocity that Hammermeister jerked back in his leatherette executive chair. He thought, "What if I were that worm? Lulu would show no mercy. And I wouldn't expect any."

The pace of the activities at Du Bois began to pick up. Hammermeister was getting hit with building requests from the science people — brainy types in Kmart jogging shoes, who wore pen packs and watches with calculators on them and who, generally speaking, displayed the whole range of absentminded-professor types of behavior. They were exasperating when you were trying to get from line "a" to line "b" within a certain time frame and didn't want to screw around with their spacey weirdness.

Worse than science were the special-education people, they were the most eccentric bunch on the entire faculty. Do-good, granola freaks in Birkenstock sandals, who came in with problems of every description. Stories from left field. All Harold could do was sympathize. He knew their burnout rate was high, and he wasn't good when they came in weeping, half crazy... they would shed hot, salty tears over virtually anything! But there was no one to foist these people off on, and he sat with a number one Dixon tap-tapping. *I have never heard of a student openly masturbating in a classroom. This is a mental health issue. Let me make some phone calls.* When they left his office, he would mechanically open his top drawer and pop two Extra-Strength Excedrins, a couple of Advils, and a deuce of Canadian 222s.

The people who taught social studies and history were coaches, mostly, and their minds were seldom on innovating the curriculum. They wanted to do everything by the numbers. One thing they could do — they could *read* the sports page.

The teachers in language arts complained that they had too many papers to grade. Harold hired part-time college English majors as assistants and fed as many student teachers into the language-arts program as he could. The math and business people, Hammermeister found dull. But dull could be good; it had its advantages. These people were undemanding and caused few problems. They were pure gravy in terms of his own job description. Ditto with the vocational-education types.

The group he cultivated most, although he had little interest in high school sports, was the coaches. The coaches who were P.E. teachers didn't count so much as those who taught academic subjects. P.E. teachers tended to be happy with the status quo. It was the latter bunch, the so-called academic teachers, who were ambitious, who would eventually give up the classroom and move into administration where there was more money.

Coaches had popularity not only with the students and the general public but with the administration. Winning teams meant high student morale and coaches were very important. With these imbeciles Harold laughed, drank, farted, and clowned. Whenever the conversation turned to the gridiron, all Hammermeister had to do was listen intently, carefully orchestrating his body language and throwing in a line like, "Geez, you really know your football, coach. I'm impressed. I never *saw* it that way before. That's absolutely brilliant. No wonder the students love you." He despised coaches, but collectively they had more juice than any other group in the building.

It was only with the women in the administrative office that Harold could let his hair down and be himself. He could tell they found him attractive, and before long, as a joke, he had everyone in the office saying "a-boot" in the Canadian style rather than "about." He wondered if they had Peter Jennings fantasies about him.

Sex was something for the next lifetime. It was tough learning the new job, but since he lived alone in a tiny apartment and required little sleep, Hammermeister was able to throw himself into his work, body and soul. He longed to get out of this rough-and-tumble high school and into the cozy air-conditioned district office building with the two-hour lunches, plush carpets, and countless refinements and amenities as soon as possible. He saw himself there. And sex was for then. He was a dervish, and he was whirling this year. Things were poppin'. There was suddenly so much to do. He had forgotten almost entirely about the janitors.

Then one day the activity director received a shipment of folding chairs for a district-wide choir recital slated for the gymnasium, and of the thirteen custodians in the school, only four were on hand after school to unload the chairs and get the gym whipped into shape. The activity director was highly agitated, and not realizing how little real clout the man actually had, Hammermeister became hysterical as well. When Harold saw the head custodian, he demanded to know where all of the other janitors were.

Mike was either in his fool-in-paradise mood — or "high." He stood before Harold and scratched his head for a moment. Well, three custodians were out sick and no subs were available. There were the two who worked graveyard: somebody or other had driven off to pick up a prescription, yet another had not acknowledged the "all call," and finally, still another, the very one who worked the gym area, did not report to work until five. Hammermeister listened to this, all the while his headache picking up steam and mutating into a kind of epileptoid craziness. Still, he managed to maintain his composure, and said, "I want that man in at two like all the swing-shift people, have you got that?"

Later that afternoon this very janitor, Duffy, walked into Hammermeister's office and caught him writing notes on his thesis. "Can't you knock?" Hammermeister asked. Duffy, who was red with anger, made a perfunctory apology. Hammermeister saw Lulu stir in her glass box. Duffy's eyes followed her movement.

"Shit, man, a bug! Weird! *Goddamm*it!"

"It's a spider, Mr. Duffy. Tarantula. Now what can I do for you?" Tap, tap, tap.

Duffy nervously stroked his mustache and short beard. He looked at the spider and then back at Hammermeister. "Mike told me you changed my hours."

"That's right, Duffy. Did he tell you why?" Tap, tap.

"He said something about unloading chairs for the concert. Only four guys were here or something."

"Yes, exactly. The next time this kind of thing happens there will be five, minimum." Tap.

Duffy took a deep breath and shook his neck to loosen up a bit. "Can I say something, Harold? I want to say this: I've been here for ten years and this is the first time that anything like this has come up. It almost never happens. If I have to come in at two, there's nothing I can clean. The gym and the upper gym are in use, the locker rooms are in use — there's nothing I can do."

"I'm sure you'll think of something." Tap, tap, tap.

"Plus — after the game, like tonight. Tonight there's football. The team won't be out of the locker rooms until a quarter to eleven — everything will be muddy, a total mess, and I'm supposed to have gone home fifteen minutes previous — "

"On game nights come in at four. How's that?"

"Look... Harold. The reason I took that gym job was so I could babysit until my wife gets home from the auto plant. She gets home at four-thirty. If you change my hours, I'm going to have to hire a babysitter — "

Hammermeister rocked back in his chair, steepling his fingers. "I am familiar with your union contract, and I can change your hours to suit the needs of the school. Is that clear?"

"All right, we can play it that way. I tried nice, but we can take this motherfucker to the union, and we can sit in hearing rooms... *by the hour!* I know you got lots of homework. It's going to be fun. You can really make progress on that thesis of yours. Or maybe you can read a little Joseph Conrad. It would do you good, Harold. Give you a little insight, Harold, into the ways of the world. I'm *filing.*"

"You pay union dues, and I encourage you to use the union," Hammermeister said evenly. He swiveled his chair away in a little half-twist and busied himself with a file folder, dismissing the custodian with a wave of the hand. He wasn't going to let the man scream or give him the satisfaction of making eye contact. Anger — for a lot of people, it was a hobby. They liked it. Why play their silly-ass game?

Duffy slammed the door so hard a draft of air lifted Hammermeister's thin, fluffy, light brown hair, which was combed forward to cover a receding hairline. He zipped open his drawer, popped two Excedrin, two Advil, swallowed a double glug of Pepto-Bismol, and then hunched over his desk and restyled his hair using a comb and hand mirror.

A few days later Hammermeister got a note from the district custodial coordinator stating that because of activities scheduling, Duffy's shift would revert back to the original 5:00 P.M. to 1:30 A.M. semi-graveyard shift. Hammermeister got on the phone and talked to the man, one Bob Graham, who told him Sean Duffy was one of the better custodians in the district and that he was not going to stand still for any aggravation. Furthermore, Graham characterized Duffy as one of the nicest, most easygoing people he knew. *Right! White was black, and black was white! What perfect logic!*

Whenever Harold needed time to "think," or to let his various headache medicines kick in, he would take a stroll over in the area of the gym and look at Duffy's work. It was hard to fault, but Hammermeister was quick to jot down "dings" with a retractable ballpoint — especially if he found them two or three days in a row. He would leave notes to Duffy. Pin them on the custodians' bulletin board for all of the classified staff to see. "To S. Duffy from H. Hammermeister: Black mark on benches, boys locker room. Why?"

When basketball season started, Hammermeister grabbed Duffy by the arm and pointed out a spilled Pepsi under the bleachers. It was the first thing you saw when you walked into the gym, and he told Duffy to go get a mop and clean it up. It was an eyesore. "Hurry up, there, chop-chop!" Hammermeister said, with heat in his voice.

Later that night, at halftime, when Duffy was giving the basketball court a quick sweep, the drill team came out, and Hammermeister made a theatrical throat-slashing gesture for Duffy to get off the court. Duffy waited at the opposite end of the gym, his face blazing scarlet with bilious fury, and after the drill team finished its routine, Hammermeister noted with satisfaction Duffy's embarrassment as he finished the job. Duffy was an aneurysm waiting to blow.

Well, there were the teachers, too, who were slackers — a good number of them. Hammermeister made note. They were easy to spot. They liked to show films or assign book reports and theme papers blocking out days at a time in the library. They followed the same curriculum year in and year out. Playing one clique off the other, Hammermeister ascertained who the lazy ones were and, if they were not coaches, he gave them heat, too.

Woodland, down in the portables, for instance. He dressed like some kind of Salvation Army bum. Beard right off a pack of Smith Brothers'

Cough Drops. When Hammermeister caught Woodland smoking one day after school, he reminded the man that he was a master teacher and wondered out loud what his future goals were.

"I used to be gung ho and *all thangs*, but now I'm getting short. Have you got a problem with that, Hammermeister?"

"I'm not saying you need to wear a suit and tie. But you have to remember you are still on the job and you are a role model, Woodland. You are a senior teacher. Where's your self-respect, man? You want to be a good teacher, then work at it. You're *getting paid*, aren't you?"

As he walked down the ramp from Woodland's portable, he turned back and saw Woodland flip him the "bird." Jesus, look at them wrong and an American could get a hair up his ass and lose it. This Woodland had murder in his heart. There was less free-floating hostility at the prison back in Canada, which was tame by comparison. Hammermeister locked eyes with Woodland, but before violence was done, he abruptly turned and stalked back to the main building with his pulse pounding. He could feel the surge of it in his neck and temples. He already had a Tylenol #4 headache over that one, but you had to give them a little jab, to let them know who was running the show. He had given Woodland a jab, and the man had showed him as much disrespect as that custodian, Duffy — well, these people would be excised. Duffy sooner and Woodland later, when the time was right... in a bloodless Machiavellian style. For some short-term revenge, Harold managed to "lose" a work order Woodland had recently put in to have his air conditioner fixed. He balled it up and slam dunked it into his wastebasket. The next thing he did was write a note reminding himself to call Woodland into his office, on Harold's turf, where he could reverse any notions the teacher had about blowing him off. He would feign consideration, all the better to ultimately crush Woodland to dust. Hah!

W. E. B. Du Bois was far from an ideal school, and the more he got to know it and was dragged down by the inertia of it, the more Hammermeister was inclined to jab these slackers or to outright get in their faces. But he had to watch himself and keep it under control, at least for this first crucial year. He really belonged in the district office, and he would be there when he whipped this place into shape. He had done well at the detention facility in Canada; he would do well here. Working in a low-morale school where so many of his colleagues were just going through the motions made Hammermeister shine like a red, white, and blue comet streaking through a night sky of blackest India ink — so, in a way, it was all to the good. *Blackboard Jungle 1999* was coming along, and in the meantime, the dervish continued to whirl.

Once the buses arrived and students started filing in, there was heavy action. Metal detectors going off. Fights picked up where they had left off the previous afternoon. Open drug transactions. Before you knew it, they were calling Hammermeister to put out one brushfire after another and another and another — all day long. Although he thrived on adrenaline, the pace of events at Du Bois was getting to be relentless. Harold was racking up some more big numbers on the Hans Seyle Stress Scale. Points that took you beyond the limits of human endurance! His stomach had become a volcano from all of the aspirin he was swallowing, and his tongue was black with bismuth from the cherry-flavored Pepto-Bismol tablets that he constantly chewed.

The high school was overcrowded, and after the first few weeks of timidity, the students mostly threw their good intentions ("*I be goin' to Princ'sun!*") out the window. The joint became as bad as it had been advertised: *The Lord of the Flies.* The chaos at Du Bois made it seem far more dangerous to Harold than his well-regulated penal institution back in Canada, where Hammermeister had fond memories of courteous and compliant murderers, rapists, and stick-up artists. These American kids were savages. And those candy machines — all of that refined sugar was just adding fuel to the fire. It was in Harold's thesis, the magnum opus; you could read all about it there, or you could wait for the movie. Heh heh heh. Harold didn't know if he would have all that much say-so in the casting, but he needed to throw a glamorous woman into the picture — a kind of gal Friday. Something along the lines of a...Whitney Houston, say. Janet Jackson would be a stretch but...maybe Gloria Estefan. Or you could get a tough bird. Oprah Winfrey? He wondered if Whoopi was lined up with commitments.

Sean Duffy was giving the head custodian a hard time about Hammermeister, the custodians' new boss. Who *was* this asshole? Who did the motherfucker think he was? "Just because he's a vice-principal, does he think he's running the place? And Dr. White is letting him get away with it. That's what really riles me!" Duffy said. "White's going to retire, and he just doesn't give a shit anymore."

Mike knew that Duffy was hitting the juice pretty hard, but he could never quite catch him with liquor on his breath. Not that he really cared to — not as long as the man did his work. Was Duffy drinking vodka or something odorless? He always looked fairly fresh on Mondays, but as the week wore on, Duffy would get red-faced, with bloodshot eyes. Increasingly, he would launch long tirades against Hammermeister — tirades that went beyond normal fury. Tirades inspired by alcohol.

One night after the swing-shift custodians left and the school was all but vacant, Centrick Cline started complaining to Duffy about Hammermeister. Hammermeister didn't like his nose ring and earrings, was a racist motherfucker — "Hey, man, why didn't they hire Alec Baldwin for the job? This geek motherfucker said he comes by at three A.M. and he better not catch me in the weight room. I *clean* the weight room," Centrick Cline said, "an' I ain't 'posed to be in the weight room?"

Duffy's own latent anger flared. They stood together and pissed about Hammermeister for forty-five minutes. Then Duffy took a customary inspection of his area, making sure he had not left a beer can on a desk somewhere before turning out the lights. When this was done, it was close to one A.M. and Duffy slugged down two quick cans of Hamms, lit a Gitane cigarette, and furtively entered Hammermeister's office. He stood before the tarantula cage a moment and then lifted the lid. He took another puff on the Gitane and blew it on the spider.

The hairy spider shocked Duffy somewhat by setting itself down. But rather than confirming his worst fear by jumping, it froze. Duffy removed a long pencil from Hammermeister's desk and nervously positioned it over the spider's thorax. Closer and closer until suddenly Duffy thrust down at it, and the large body of the spider exploded like an egg, spurting yellow matter all over the room. When Duffy let go of the pencil the spider sprang straight up in the air and landed on his shoulder. He batted the spider down and scrambled out into the commons area, grabbed his coat, and fled the building.

Hammermeister came in Friday morning, and the first thing he noticed when he stepped into his office was that the lid of the tarantula cage was ajar. He hastily closed the door thinking that the spider had escaped, since he didn't want it to bolt out into the main office. Somehow he knew something like this was going to happen. He had a funny premonition.

Lulu lay dead on the seat of his executive chair, impaled with a number one Dixon. The Gitane butt was there, but Hammermeister was struck dumb with grief and all he noticed as he looked about the room was the gruesome egg-yolk splattered essence of Lulu on his seat, the walls, and the ceiling. When he finally composed himself, he stepped out of his office and told the secretaries that the spider had been stabbed (already he had a pretty good idea which students did it), and that it had crawled up to his chair to die. This peculiar detail had Hammermeister on the verge of tears. He wrung his hands to no purpose. His face fell as if he were the comic Stan Laurel confronted with some absurd calamity. Hammermeister's favorite secretary, Cynthia — the nicest-looking woman in the building — put both of her hands on his shoulders and said, "Are you okay, friend?" Hammermeister said that he was and woodenly made his way back into the office. Not fast enough for Rider to miss the tail end of the scene, however. Harold had a four-star migraine, but his gut lining was shredded from too much aspirin. He slammed down three Tylenol #4s and chased them with a Diet Coke. As he wiped the spider splatter from his chair with paper towels, the enormity of this personal loss caused his thighs to wobble. Harold gently lifted Lulu's corpse from the chair, neatly wrapped it in his handkerchief, and deposited the body in his top desk drawer. He sat at his desk with his head in his hands, wincing, waiting for the codeine to kick in, waiting possibly to just *blow*, perish, succumb to...internal spontaneous combustion! None of these things happened, and Hammermeister didn't get any worse. But he didn't get any better. He was alarmed to find that he stayed just the same for some time. At the foot of his chair he noticed a peculiar butt. It was a manufactured cigarette, but the tobacco in it appeared to be almost black. He picked it up and examined it. No doubt it belonged to the assassin. He shoved it into an envelope for evidence and placed it in his top desk drawer, locking it.

The secretaries were so moved by Hammermeister's "nervous breakdown" that on the weekend they went to a pet shop and bought a replacement spider for fifty-five dollars. They pasted a little note on the cage that said, "Hey there, big boy, Lulu's back in town!"

On the following Friday Lulu number two was found murdered in the same fashion as number one had been: impaled with a number one Dixon. In evidence was another cigarette butt. A vile-smelling thing filled with blackish tobacco. This one was not a Gitane, but it was unfiltered and it was foreign. Harold noticed such butts in an ashtray in Centrick Cline's janitor's closet. And what a place that was. There were militant anti-white slogans pasted on the wall, posters of Malcolm X and Huey Newton, and an accumulation of what seemed to be voodoo paraphernalia. Cline was not known to be a smoker. Yet most of the staff who smoked had keys to this closet and would sneak cigarettes there. Throughout the remainder of the day, Harold made hourly checks to see if any of the teachers had smoked such a cigarette during their prep periods. There were none to be found. But then there were none in the morning after the janitors' shift either.

Because of the pace and the pressing events of the school, Hammermeister found himself playing catch-up. This alarmed him, since he was no procrastinator and was devoting every waking hour to his job. On a number of occasions the senior vice-principal came down hard on him, implying that his Ph.D. would have to wait until summer; there was a school to run. Hammermeister's objective "breath of fresh air" — the Canadian jet stream — was getting stale. Harold heard the talk and could only hope another burst of energy was available, and with it some new inspiration. When he was state superintendent of education, when the book was made into the movie and he was pulling in fifty-thousand-dollar speaking-engagement fees, Rider would still be on his fat, *Ahm a soul man, sweet potato pie* ass, forever mired deep in the middle of Detroit's blackboard jungle. In the meantime, not only was the staff all over him, but the students were becoming impossible to control. Harold was now somehow frightened by them — frightened terribly, and they could tell. Without Lulu next to him exuding encouragement, Harold grew scared and was overreacting. When he started nailing students with suspensions over petty grievances, Dr. White hit the ceiling.

White scheduled a personal one-on-one conference with Harold after school. He was far from courteous when he told Harold of the conference, and he did not stutter. The motherfucker was on the rag! Hammermeister staggered through the day, certain that he was about to be fired. But it wasn't that at all. White dumped a book challenge on Harold. At issue was John Steinbeck's *Cannery Row* — it had been called "filth" by an irate parent. White told Harold to handle it without saying exactly how. White just didn't want to get his hands dirty, that was all. There was a levy vote coming up and "how" had to mean: get the library to pull the book. Or did it?

After thinking the matter over, Harold went upstairs and spoke with the head librarian, who was horrified at the suggestion that the book be pulled. She vowed to "go to the wall." Hammermeister thoughtlessly warned her that librarians were a dime a dozen. It was the codeine talking. At least there were no witnesses.

That night Hammermeister left the building well after dark, and when he got to his car he discovered that all four tires were flat. Later, after a tow truck had hauled the car in, Hammermeister was informed that the tires were okay. The party that flattened them had simply removed the valve-core stems, then after the tires were deflated, poured Krazy Glue into the valves. The culprits didn't pull the valves and run, they were brazen enough to wait until the tires went flat and then carefully squirted glue into the valves. They even took the trouble to screw the valve caps back on. Professionals! The valves were of a type that wasn't available at that hour of the night. The car would be ready tomorrow afternoon.

Head down, hands in pocket, Hammermeister furiously strode the three miles to his apartment through a biting *Nanook of the North* sleet storm. Just as he cut through the back entrance, where the covered parking stalls were located, he heard the abrupt rustling of leather jackets. He barely turned his head when a large tawny palm engulfed his face like an eclipse of the sun. The mighty hand snapped Harold's head back and firmly cradled it between the abductor's solid chest and a rock-hard biceps muscle. As his face was getting squashed Hammermeister suddenly felt his shins getting pounded with fierce woodpecker rapidity. The *tonk tonk tonk* sounds were those of an aluminum baseball bat. Hammermeister sagged halfway to the ground, but the large hand held him firmly like he was some kind of rag doll, and Hammermeister was not a small man. He stood over 6'2" but with all of the recent stress, he was down twenty pounds from his normal weight of two hundred and twelve.

The powerful hand that encased his face forced Harold's mouth to open in an "O" as a thick, wet, balled-up sock was rammed inside, a smelly cloth was placed over his eyes, and then, as Hammermeister heard the quick rip of duct tape, the stinking rag was adhered to his face like a layer of fast-drying cement.

There were two of them. The woodpecker with the bat continued to expertly peck at his legs, knees, and elbows, while the powerful strong-armed man spun him around, cranked a solid punch into Hammermeister's solar plexus, and then let him free-fall to the ground. For the next moment Hammermeister was kicked and pounded mercilessly. He wondered if it was murder. The woodpecker was batting him in the head now but not with massive, clobbering blows. It felt like he was being poked with the knob end of the bat. Hammermeister felt himself sinking into the black vortex of hell, but then the shower of stars abruptly stopped, and in the frigid night air he heard his assailants' cold, rasping breaths tear through his brain like the sandpaper tongue of a lion. It occurred to Hammermeister that the dictum "when you lose your sight you become all eardrums" was profoundly true. Hammermeister could distinctly hear the different ways the two men breathed. If he lived to be a thousand, he would never forget the way these men breathed.

The stronger man grabbed his wrists and pulled them behind his back. As a knee came down on his spine, Hammermeister heard the sound of duct tape being unreeled and torn again, and soon his hands were bound as tightly as if he were displayed in a pillory. Then, with a suddenness that was frightening, he felt himself being lifted like a suitcase and lugged away from the lighted parking stalls to a very dark place. Even though his eyes were masked, he had been able to see shadows — now nothing. All the while the hollow bat rapped away at him. Neither of the abductors said a word. Hammermeister attempted to scream through the sock, but it was a scream that just couldn't get off the ground.

The pain in his shoulders felt like a crucifixion. Harold emitted a high-pitched scream through his nose as he was hauled off into yet a deeper forest of blackness. After what seemed like an interminable voyage, he was dropped roughly to the pavement, where he wet his pants in abject terror, waiting for the mechanical action of some sort of firearm — the rotation of a revolver cylinder, perhaps.

Both of the unseen men were panting heavily. Before they shot him, they were waiting to catch their breath. After a moment he felt their rough hands pulling at his pants, ripping them down to his knees as they turned him over on his stomach. Harold let his legs kick out wildly, and this only made the men laugh.

Suddenly there was a jolting, searing-hot pain in his right ass cheek. Hammermeister could smell his own smoldering flesh. The whole focus of his being gravitated to the burn.

The other pains were gone, he was nothing but a single right ass cheek. He writhed with the vigor of a freshly landed marlin. Then he felt himself lifted like a suitcase again. The two men heaved him up, and by the smell of things, Hammermeister realized he had been cast into the garbage Dumpster before he even landed. His body was greeted by cardboard boxes, nail-embedded two-by-fours, metal cans, offal — the slime, grit, and stink of coffee grinds and cat litter, rib and chicken bones, and cigarette butts.

There was a loud clang as the two men dropped down the metal door. There was the sound of the metal lid reverberating, followed by the squeak of sneakers peeling across the snowy pavement of the back drive, as the thugs made a New Balance getaway.

The pain of the burn was incredible. It gave Hammermeister superhuman strength. In just seconds he was able to wrest his hands free from the tape. In another few seconds he pulled the tape from his face and spit out the sock that was choking him. By the time he slipped out of his bindings and pushed up the lid of the Dumpster, the men were gone; the sleet had turned to snow, and a soft white blanket was laid about him like a kind of Currier and Ives/Edward Hopper Detroit. The Motor City.

Harold hastened to his room. After four tumblers of straight bourbon and a handful of Tylenol #4s, Hammermeister, still trembling, stood before his phone imagining what he would say to the police. When he finally called 911, a dispatcher answered with a disaffected tone and

Hammermeister quickly replaced the phone in its cradle, afraid that his call would be traced and an aid car would be sent to his building.

He staggered into the bathroom and looked at the burn. It was hideous, his buttock exuded a watery yellow fluid, yet the letters KKK were crudely apparent. They had somehow taken him to a prearranged spot where the hot iron was cooking. This sort of vicious calculation made him think of gangs. Of gang planning. Somebody really was playing hardball. Not kids. Not janitors. But who else except fucking kids and fucking janitors? Funny that they didn't steal his wallet or shoot him. Rip-off artists shaking down a random victim in a parking lot would go for the money. Kids and janitors had access to a high school metal shop where branding irons could be made.

Hammermeister went back to the phone to call an ambulance and was once again struck by indecision. It had been a warning. Maybe it would be best not to get the police involved. After all, how would he explain it to Dr. White?

One of the legs of his pants had been torn off completely. His legs were swollen with red and purple abrasions yet no bones were broken. He hurt all over, yet he really wasn't that hurt except for the searing pain on his buttock, which was an agony unlike anything he had ever known. Twenty minutes later, the burn seemed a thousand times more painful. Hammermeister took a warm shower and carefully soaped his wounds. It helped to take action. After he dried himself, he applied some antibiotic cream to his right butt cheek and placed a nonstick dressing on it. There was only one such dressing in his medicine cabinet that would fit it, a super jumbo — hell, in Detroit you would think that gun-trauma kits would be fast-moving items at every drugstore. After Hammermeister put on a pair of clean Jockey shorts, he went back to the phone where he found himself again paralyzed with indecision. As the booze and dope kicked in, Hammermeister felt a magical sense of relief. Suddenly he was packing his suitcase. He would drive back to Sondra in the morning. He missed her and the kids more than anything. God, he had been a dick. Sometimes it took a real shocker to bring you back to your senses. Well, this night had been an epiphany. The booze and the codeine were so good, so nice, he was thinking straight for the first time in years. He had a proper sense of perspective again.

In the morning Hammermeister abruptly came to in a world of pain. The burn felt more like a chemical burn, like a deep burn — like a *real deep* burn. He couldn't look at it. Instead he immediately dosed himself with vodka and codeine, and then, when he realized that his car was in the shop, he wondered about his plan for claiming the vehicle and driving back home after all. You could not drive when you could not sit down. Canada — shit, the bridge had been burned. He really hated his wife, and while he loved his kids in a way, it was one of those deals like "out of sight, out of mind." There was no going back.

Nipping from the pint of vodka, Hammermeister laced up a pair of heavy weatherproof brogues and walked to work, stopping at McDonald's for two Egg McMuffins and a large coffee to go. He was going to the school where he would confront Duffy and Cline. He wouldn't even have to ask a question, all he would have to do is listen to them breathe.

It was a zoo day. The place was a zoo. First period the head of the English department — tough, smart, and formidable — came into his office and told him there was no way in hell her department was going to see John Steinbeck banished from the school. Hammermeister told her it was a matter between himself and the librarians, and she closed the door, took three powerful strides over to his desk, where he stood looking through his memos. "Now you just wait here, buster!" In casting this role, Harold was suddenly thinking in terms of Bette Midler or Cher on a tirade.

Boy! Twenty-five Hans Seyle stress points for that one. Hammermeister had tried to appeal to her sense of reason. "We've got a levy coming, we don't need this right now. What will you say if I tell you we can't buy new language-arts books this fall?" His voice was hollow. His legs, the shins especially, began to hurt more than the burn on his ass. He gulped down more codeine with the last of his cold coffee. Why in the hell had he come back to this hellhole? To nail Centrick Cline and Sean Duffy, that's why — and from the stack of morning memos he could see that both of them had already called in sick. His secretary gave him their numbers, and he called them both at home. Neither of the malefactors answered their phones. Off somewhere together, drunk, sniggering in iniquitous delight.

Later that morning he was forced to phone the parent who had raised the hullabaloo about *Cannery Row*. She was a real kook. What the fuck! Yet Hammermeister deferred to her, sympathized and told her off the record that he was in full agreement with her. It was necessary to placate this woman. Dr. White had insisted upon it. Hadn't he?

Events quickly came to a head when the issue was thrown in at the tail end of the monthly board of directors meeting the next evening. The librarians throughout the district were on hand, as were librarians from nearby school districts. The word spread fast. "Oh God," Hammermeister thought, "a cause célèbre." He had to go home and crash before the meeting, and then, heavily medicated, he overslept and showed up looking like Howard Beale coming in to deliver the news in that old movie *Network*. Harold's buzz cut was sticky with tape, he needed a shave — he looked like a madman. But he was high and didn't care. He had not prepared for the debate; he had decided to just "wing it." Sometimes it paid to be spontaneous and genuine. You were walking on thin ice, but sometimes it did work.

The W. E. B. Du Bois High School librarian was dressed like a model of propriety. Armed with a thick packet of note cards, which she hardly ever seemed to look at, she gave a convincing pro–First Amendment presentation. This was followed by an eloquent statement by the head of the English department. Then Hammermeister suddenly found himself on his feet making counterarguments, all weak and vapid. The beneficial effects of the nap were short-lived. He was strung out from too much booze and Tylenol #4, and as he scanned the room looking for a sympathetic face, the fact that there seemed to be none inflamed him with hollow fury. This was a setup. The board members, the superintendent, and his own principal looked at him expectantly. The formality of the room was hard, as were the faces of the people sitting in the gallery. A press photographer snapped photos of Hammermeister, and as he did so, a feeling of depersonalization overcame the Canadian. Exhausted by the previous evening, the present onslaught was too much for him. He found himself saying, over and over again, that he was about to receive a doctorate in education, as if that were germane to the situation at hand. He said something about how a society that was too liberal became soft and festered with decay. Harold said something about the rightness of trying to change society for the better turning to "wrongness" when everyone focused on gender, sexual entitlement, and the color of skin. Whatever happened to genuine achievement leading to entitlement? You couldn't play center for the Tigers just because you were white. No! You had to be the best center fielder in Detroit. So what was the problem? What did sex or color have to do with genuine achievement? Why did society have to allocate prizes and create heroes out of sex perverts and deluded, talentless know-nothings, be they black, white, or brown? Why did they have to hand the keys to power over to fools? The right-minded liberal inclination to make the "all men are created equal" utopia had led to ruin. Utopia-building, good in theory, simply did not work anymore. It only led to ruin, decay, and dispersion. It was time to resort back to the police state. Like Duffy had said — Singapore!

Somewhere in the back of his brain he realized it was the codeine talking — a medicinal "misadventure" — yet Hammermeister could not stop himself. He told the audience that America was going down the sewer as it coddled weaklings and slackers. He began to talk of racial polarization and the subway shooters, until finally the superintendent, aghast at Hammermeister's presentation from the first, shot him a withering look and cut him off. "That will do, Mr. Hammermeister. Thank you for your views."

In the morning, Dr. White was sitting in Hammermeister's chair reading through Hammermeister's thesis when Harold came in. He looked up at the Canadian and said, "We'll pay your salary through the year, but don't ask for any job recommendations. You aren't gonna want my recommendation. I'm sorry for you, huh-huh-huh-Harold. There are people of cuh-cuh-cuh-color out there who can dance circles around your qualifications. It's my fault for letting you buh-buh-buh-bullshit me during the interview. I wanted to hire a white man. I wanted some diversity. I wanted you to succeed, but you're a buh-buh-buh-bad person!"

"I didn't bullshit you. I can do this job. I can *do* this job!" Hammermeister began to spill his guts about the janitors, his beating and abduction. Dr. White drew his head back in alarm.

"You don't believe me, do you?" Hammermeister shouted. He pulled down his pants and showed the man the burn on his ass and the bruises on his legs. "It looks like Kaposki's or whatever they call it." Hammermeister began to spin his theory that the custodians — Duffy and Cline, the weight lifter — had beaten him, gang bangers had stabbed his spiders...and so on.

"That's the most preposterous thing I've ever heard. For one thing, those spiders were ridiculous, and for another, Duffy has been with us for ten years and I've never heard a single buh-buh-buh-bad word — "

"Bullshit! He's an alcoholic! He's a drunk! Everybody knows it. Where have you been?"

"He hasn't taken a sick day in the whole ten years," the principal said incredulously. "The buh-buh-buh-best attendance record in the district, sh-sh-sh-short of my own."

"Alcoholics are *like* that. With their low self-esteem, they overcompensate at work. Have you ever read *The Nigger of the Narcissus*, Sidney? Do you know the character Waite? That piss-and-moan, do-nothing crybaby! Well, *that's* who Duffy is. *Duffy is Johnny Waite!* And if you haven't read the book — judging by that vacant look on your face, I dare say you haven't — then by God you should!"

"Harold. I don't know what happened to your legs or how you got that burn, but the alcohol fumes in here are bad enough to knock a person down. I think you should check yourself into...a facility! The district has a progressive policy — "

"Duffy and that burrhead in the gym, Cline — that's what you call a bad nigger."

"That's it! I've heard enough — you've got fifteen minutes before I call the police!" Dr. White said, standing up. "Puh-puh-puh-pack your stuff and get out."

"Fine," Hammermeister said. "Fifteen minutes. That's just fine. 'The custodians are a little trouble spot,' remember? 'They seem to defy our coping skills,' remember? Shit, why did I have to be born white! It's a curse!"

The principal walked out of the room, shutting the door behind him.

Hammermeister began slamming his personal supplies into a box. There wasn't much. He picked up *Blackboard Jungle 1999* and began to read. There was the truth. The American public would be shocked if they came to these schools and observed. Something very dangerous was going on inside. Well, the public did come. They were invited to come with open arms, but only to well-orchestrated events with canned speeches, lies, bullshit inspiration. If America really knew what was going on, it would be shocked. If they could see the school, day in and day out. The quality of education was an abomination!

Harold began to dictate into his personal recorder. "The school-board system: you've got a superintendent. What is his job? Why, he goes to a meeting now and then. He gets a haircut. Plays golf. Around levy time he sweet-talks some newspaper people. The taxpayers would be better off if they let the district secretary run things! When I came into this field I thought that by hard work and determination I could make a difference, but I have been swallowed up in chaos and futility. The American public has been greatly deceived! It is not only your hard-earned tax dollars that I am concerned about, it is our youth and the future of this once great nation! We need parental involvement. You can't send them to us for seven hours and expect us to undo. They're going loco. We need more metal detectors in the school. We need drug testing. We need a crime-prevention program. There should even be AIDS testing and quarantine like they've got over in Cuba. Are we going to let the rotten apples spoil the whole barrel? Goddammit, democracy just isn't cutting it anymore. Someone has to step in and get the fucking trains running on time again or it's closing time in the gardens of the West!"

Two uniformed police officers in squeaky leather jackets stepped warily into Hammermeister's office. Harold looked at his watch. Fifteen minutes? "It hasn't been fifteen minutes."

"It's time to go," one of the police officers said.

Hammermeister looked at the box. He threw his thesis in it. He attempted to place Lulu's glass cage in the box but it was too large. He set it back on the desk. He would have to carry the cage under one arm, and the box with the thesis, the Dixon pencils, coffee mug, Pepto-Bismol, aspirin, Tylenol #4s, Advil, his spare sports coat and neckties, etc., under the other arm. Except that now he was so spaced from the codeine and round-the-clock vodka drinking that he knew he would never manage it.

"Let's go," the officer said.

Hammermeister stuffed his pockets with the codeine #4s, then on impulse flipped the thesis into the wastebasket, dumping the remainder of the box in after it — the pencils, coffee cup, neckties, spare sports jacket, everything. He was dizzy with rage. He had a crazy impulse to dash over to the office safe and grab the nine-millimeter they recently pulled off a drug peddler and fire off a few rounds. If Sean Duffy and Centrick Cline were not there, he'd just shoot…whomever. Get Rider and White first. Instead, he flung the cardboard box aside and placed Lulu's empty cage on top of his wastebasket. He raised a pebble-leather, oxblood brogue over the cage and then stepped down several times, crunching the glass.

The police officers braced for action, but then Hammermeister sagged. The only picture that came to his mind now were those of the flattened tires of his Ford. Gone was the movie, the new and better wife, the Lincoln, polo, and country clubbing. His shoulders slumped and he turned to them defeated. "I'm ready," Harold said with a melodramatic flourish, presenting his hands for cuffing. "Read me my Miranda and let's clear out of this place."

The police officers, one short, one tall, exchanged a significant look. The short one said, "No need for the handcuffs, sir. They just want you off the grounds. It's a routine eighty-six, that's all. They just want you to leave."

Hammermeister seemed disappointed that he was not under arrest. He felt cheated but let the police officers lead him through the party of "concerned" but not entirely unsympathetic office secretaries. They led him out into the throng of students who had heard the sound of smashed glass and had gathered to witness what they intuitively knew was a very strange and very bad scene. Several of the students wondered out loud as to what was going on. One of these, a student who had once been mesmerized by Hammermeister's power of positive thinking spiel, and who had a certain affection for the former junior vice-principal, asked, "Wha'chew got, man?"

Hammermeister looked over his shoulder and cried, "Murder one."

And with that he was led out to the parking lot to a squad car, driven to the bus stop, and dumped off. He had never taken a bus in America, didn't know how, didn't know when one was coming, and when he could no longer stand the cold, he gulped down a couple more codeine tablets with a slug of vodka and surveyed the landscape before him. Hammermeister realized he was the only Caucasian in the neighborhood, and he began to feel conspicuous. A couple of thugs, also brown bagging, joined him at the bus shelter. One carried a ghetto blaster. Clarence "Frogman" Henry was singing, "I'm a lonely frog, I ain't got no home." Hammermeister watched as the man inserted a rock in a crack pipe and took a hit off of it before passing it to his companion.

Moving from the shelter of the Plexiglas bus stop, Hammermeister dropped his head down against yet another *Nanook of the North* sleet storm. A mere pedestrian in the heart of the Motor City, new citizen John Harold Hammermeister caught the shoe-leather express back to his apartment.

Mouses

Rodents infiltrated my place at the first hard frost of the fall. I had a minor premonition that this would happen, and then, lo, it happened. For a couple of days it was in the back of my mind, in the twilight area where minor worries flourish — no big alarm bell rang, because most of the stuff you worry about never comes to pass. But then came the evidence, the irrefutable fact that not only did said perpetrators (previously unknown to me) claw and chew through a box of Wheat Thins, they defecated at the scene of the crime, leaving sizable pellets behind. Apparently "Don't shit where you eat" isn't in the rodent codebook. Hygiene is not a big concern with them. At first, I was in a state of denial. My place is sealed as tight as a drum. How could they get in? Also, I was thinking, I don't need this now. I really *do not* need this. I was facing problems at work. There were rumors of a cutback at the plant. In spite of my seniority — I've been an engineer for ten years — I knew I was high on the shit list. I'm a convenient target. Why? Because I'm very short in stature. Five feet nothing. And I have a slight spinal deformity — a hump. No matter what goes wrong at that hellhole, I get blamed. "Anson, the midget, did it." A computer goes down, blueprints get lost, milk sours in the lunchroom refrigerator: "The midget did it!"

So at first I buried my head in the sand. I had woken up late that day, no morning coffee, and my feet had barely hit the floor when I saw the chewed-to-shit Wheat Thins box. What a sight! It looked as if a wolverine had gone through it. There I was, standing in my pajamas in a state of complete disbelief. This was no time to conduct a full-scale pest investigation. I was late for work.

That night in bed, when fears are greatly magnified, not only was I worried about my suck-ass job, I began to think that the intruder might be a big black rat with an appetite for human flesh. Jurassic. The Wheat Thins box looked like it had been blasted by a shotgun and, as I said, the waste pellets were mighty big. For all I knew there could be a whole pack of vermin running around my place bearing disease and pestilence. Off a ship from Africa or something. Can you get rabies from *proximity*? That's what I was thinking. About 3 A.M. a miasma of moldy rodential air came wafting into my bedroom. I hadn't noticed *that* before. Somewhere, unseen, these vermin were stirring about, revved up into a state of high activity, giving off odoriferous secretions.

The next morning I was up early to see what dirty work had occurred during the night. I entered the kitchen with a heavy brogan shoe in my hand, and it was just as I thought: they had been at it again. Bolder than ever! I had thrown out the contaminated food, and closed the cupboard tight, but — hey! — no problem: the culprits had gone to the breadbox! Its lid was ajar, a good inch and a half. Had I closed it? You'd think you'd remember a pertinent detail like that, especially if you're in a batten-down-the-hatches frame of mind. And what if I *had* closed the breadbox? This rodent must be very strong. This rodent might very well be a rat — a rat that bench-pressed No. 3 vegetable cans and probably played tackle for the local ratball team. Black Bart, the Norway power rat. Fangola from Borneo.

On no sleep, work that morning was an ongoing hell. I had to sneak out to my car at lunch and catch a nap, but I woke up three hours later not in the least refreshed: it wasn't a nap, it was a damn coma. The boss called me in: "Yeah yeah, ying ying, ya ya, where in the *hell* have you been?" Put the fear of God in me. I stayed late working on the annual report, which made no sense to me anymore. I was just sitting there, "pretending," which is a lot harder than actually working. You could chop logs all day, stack thirty cords of wood, and not get as tired. When the boss bagged out, I waited five minutes and then left. My back was killing me. The hump veers toward my left shoulder. It was all hot and knotted up like an angry fist. Just complete agony.

I stopped at the supermarket for some Advil and asked a stocker where the mousetraps were. Evidently, there'd been a run on rodent traps. "Cold weather," he said.

I said, "You haven't been selling *rat* traps?"

"Rat traps, yeah, sold a few," he said, pointing them out. They were huge rectangular slabs of pinewood with monstrous springs and rectangular clap bars made of heavy-gauge metal. Big enough to snag a Shetland pony.

"Whoa, man!" I said. "I hope I don't need one of those."

"Where do you live?" he asked me, and I told him the neighborhood and he said no doubt my problem was mice. Rats don't frequent upscale places, he said. They go for the shitholes where people leave garbage around. He couldn't guarantee it but he was ninety percent sure. Then he left me alone in the aisle to inspect the merchandise. I chided myself for being melodramatic. No rats, just some mice. And others were having the same problem. I was reassured. I was fortunate to be able to get any traps at all. There were only five left and I bought all five.

I thought of using poison, going for complete and certain eradication, but I wanted to see the corpses. Your mouse poisoner is like a bomber pilot flying miles above a war zone — the bloodless battle. That's cool, but sometimes you hear of poisoned mice dying in parts of the house that are inaccessible to the homeowner and giving off a horrible smell. People start yanking off drywall panels to get to the smelly things, knocking down chimneys, tearing up the foundation.

Vacor, for instance, a rodenticide that looks like cornmeal, destroys the beta cells of the pancreas, causing instant diabetes, followed by chest pain, impaired intellect, coma, and finally death. A diabetic mouse with severe hyperglycemia will develop an incredible thirst and head outside to look for water — you don't have to tear your house apart tracking down odors. Strychnine is another possibility. An overdose of strychnine destroys the nerves and causes convulsions. The sick rodent cannot bear noise or bright light. It dies a prolonged, agonizing death of utter torment. That kind of mouse wouldn't opt for the hustle and bustle of the outdoors. That's a hide-in-the-drywall mouse.

All in all, the trap is more humane. But I was so angry at the inconvenience I had been through — disturbed sleep, fright, the loss of snack foods — that the thought of a mouse writhing in pain out in a field some-where did not bother my conscience in the slightest. The opposite was the case. It gave me satisfaction. Die, suckah!

I set three of the traps in the kitchen using peanut butter as bait. I put another in the bedroom and one behind the living-room couch. That night, moments after I turned off the lights, I heard one of the kitchen traps go off. *Wap!* Man, I almost hit the ceiling. I wasn't sure if I heard a shriek or not. It all happened so fast. In the blink of an eye, an execution.

I'm embarrassed to admit that I was a little afraid to confront the consequences. But what could I do? I picked up my heavy shoe and went out. The victim was a gray mouse with broad, powerful shoulders, prickly chin whiskers, red beady eyes, and a short stumpy tail. Its mouth was open, exposing a crimson tongue and sharp yellow teeth. Ahggh! The trap had snapped its neck. I picked up the trap and quickly tossed it in the garbage. How that mouse had so totally destroyed the Wheat Thins was beyond me, but such are the mysteries of life. There, I'm thinking. Done! Half an hour later I was sawing logs.

In the morning I got up and went to the kitchen to make coffee and I saw another mouse, this one still alive, with one paw caught in a trap. It was trying to drag-ass out of there. I got my work gloves out of the garage and picked up the trap, the mouse hanging down from it, wriggling. I put the mouse in a coffee can, and then — I don't know what made me do it, maybe because Christmas was coming — I punched some holes in it for air. The mouse's foot was smashed, but otherwise it was okay. I set the can in the garage and went off to work.

I was tired again, with moderate-to-severe hunch pains. Except for short-lived bursts of activity when my boss passed by with a scowl on his repugnant face, all I could do was sit at my desk and "pretend" all day. Even though I'd got some sleep, I was thrashed, body and soul.

When I got home I threw some wood shavings into an old aquarium and put the mouse in there. If it was in pain, I couldn't tell. I gave it a little dish of water and some cornflakes. The thing was this: I couldn't stand having an invisible invader prowling around in my house at will, but with the animal caged and me in full control, I could tolerate it. I mean the mouse was just trying to get by like the rest of us. I named him Al.

After a few days, Al's foot turned black and fell off. He wouldn't eat for a while. I think he had a fever. A close call with death. I put out some whole-wheat bread with peanut butter on it. He loved that. He was going to weather the crisis. He started to gain weight. I found a hamster wheel at a garage sale and the guy just gave it to me to get rid of it.

That's when Al began his rehab therapy. Without his foot, he got by hobbling, but his whole left shoulder was weak. On the wheel, he struggled and became disoriented. To encourage him, I put his favorite treat, a Hershey's chocolate square, in a little box in front of the wheel. Stick and carrot. Pretty soon Al was running his ass and lost all the weight from his peanut-butter days of convalescence. With treats to motivate him, he'd put in five hours a night on the wheel. One night, just as I was getting him his Hershey's square, he hopped into my palm and let me hand-feed him. It was a momentous transition. Suddenly this little wild animal was on the road to domestication. He trusted me. I felt like I was in tune with the universe. But not for long.

The next day at work, the boss stuck his ugly face inches from my own. "You're terminated, Anson. Clean out your desk! You have one hour."

The heartless bastard. I'd known it was coming, but I was devastated just the same. He couldn't wait until after Christmas. I immediately drove to the unemployment office. Filled out the forms. Stood around and waited. Geez, what a seedy stink-ass joint.

If you're an engineer, a job in these times is the hardest thing in the world to find. There are thousands of engineers.

I put together a résumé and scanned the want ads. There was nothing. One of the no-jobs at the unemployment office told me that nobody hires during the Christmas season, so just chill out.

At night I watched TV. It was me and Al, with him crawling up my arm and on top of my head and whatnot. Once in a while out slipped a mouse pellet but what are you going to do? Al is my friend, so it was no biggie. I wondered if he missed his life in the wild. I wondered if he was bored. If I let him go in the spring, with no foot, what would happen?

One night after a futile and discouraging day of handing out résumés,

I popped over to the pet shop and bought a companion for Al. A pet mouse cost a dollar and eighty-nine cents. I got a female and named her Angela. I put her in with Al and they sniffed each other out for a bit, but when I turned my back they started fighting. Angela was kicking ass. She bit the piss out of Al and he was left bleeding all over, especially from his stub. I broke up the fight, stuck her in the coffee can, and put her in the dark garage for punishment. Then I put hydrogen peroxide on Al's wounds. If it wasn't for the incredible cardiovascular reserve he'd built up running the wheel, I think she would have killed him.

I took to hand-feeding Al again — I had to — and he eventually came around. He seemed to like the mouse chow I got him. I figure that animals have body wisdom and will eat the right thing if you provide it for them. Pretty soon Al was on the wheel again, and we were watching TV together at night, and everything was just hunky. He padded around on my scalp with his three little paws, up and down my arm, with no fear at all. It was like we'd been pals in some previous lifetime. Bosom buddies.

I fashioned a divider panel for the aquarium and took Angela out of the punishment can. But I was still hating her. I gave her nothing but peanut butter. I denied her access to the exercise wheel. And in a couple of weeks she was a disgusting tub of lard. Meanwhile, Al, on his good diet, exercise regime, and nightly entertainment, was the very picture of health. Angela was practically eating her body weight in peanut butter every day. She ballooned up. I started weighing her on a postal scale, and one time she bit me. She didn't break the skin, but after the infraction it was three more days in the punishment can.

By now I had been to every fucking engineering firm in the city. Nobody was hiring. If you're a senior engineer, forget it. They hire a guy out of college, pay him a substandard salary, and get him to do the work of ten people. I reformulated my résumé and started looking for a job as a technician.

Angela was still eating peanut butter by the tablespoon. One day I came home and she was lying on her back with four feet in the air, stiff. Heart attack. In just six weeks' time. I enjoy peanut butter myself. I had been carrying peanut-butter sandwiches in my briefcase as I canvassed the city looking for work. I switched to low-fat turkey. It costs a fortune and, hungerwise, it doesn't satisfy, but I got to thinking of all the stuff I had eaten in my life, the whole pile of it. In peanut butter alone, there would be a warehouse. Cigarettes? Truck trailers full. After what I'd seen happen to Angela in six weeks, I felt lucky to be alive. I squared my diet away.

I got some Just for Men and colored my hair jet-black. I began to figure that my age was another handicap. But then one of the no-jobs at unemployment asked me if I'd lost my mind. "Anson, you look like Bela Lugosi!" Another said, "Man, that's a dye job you can spot a mile away." Some skaters on the street asked me if I was the singer Roy Orbison. Maybe they said this because I was wearing a pair of shades, or maybe they were just dicking with me. I said, "No, man, I'm Junior fuckin' Walker."

When I got home and checked myself out in the mirror, I saw that the no-jobs were right about my hair. It was too dark and it made my skin look pale. It was almost green. I looked like an undertaker. Plus, I'd lost weight, and my clothes were too big. Overnight, I had metamorphosed from a Stage One no-job to a Stage Three. Up all night with pain, I finally dropped off and didn't get up till four in the afternoon. Too late to go out. I didn't shave. I was thinking, What's the point of looking? They don't want to hire you. Capitalism sucks. The big companies just want to get rich. I got to hating everybody.

I drove over to the pet store and bought two dozen mice and a separate wire cage for each. You read stuff in medical reports about how a certain drug or vitamin did something in some study but it will be five years before the general public can get it. Or you read that something has produced miraculous results in chickens but they haven't tried it on humans yet. I'm the kind that figures, hell, if it works on a chicken it's going to work on everybody. I mean, if some guy spots mold on bread and turns it into penicillin, why not me? If I can't get a job, maybe I'll just go out and win the Nobel Prize.

I put the mice on a variety of diets and subjected them to various stresses. I kept a control group and fed its members the same mouse chow I fed Al. Other mice — eating a diet similar to my own, drinking a proportionate amount of coffee, and keeping the same hours — were dead in five weeks. Challenge, a momentary adaptation to stress, then exhaustion and death. I accepted the results with equanimity. I knew what was in the cards for me; once again I had evidence. Maybe I was lucky to have been canned. What I needed now was a plan: I wasn't going to be a victim anymore.

At 3 A.M. I took off my white lab coat, washed my hands, and called up my ex-boss. *Brrringgg! Ding-a-ling! Brrringgg!* When he answered, I hung up! Ah, ha, ha, shit! I then had a snack and about twenty minutes later — just when he'd fallen back to sleep — I called again. Ha, ha, ha, fuck! I pictured him lying there seething.

I put another batch of mice on a regime mimicking my old schedule, but I fortified their diets with vitamins. They died in just *under* five weeks, confirming something I always suspected: vitamins, especially the kind that have a strong smell, not only make you feel bad but can hasten your demise! The result held even for the mice that had the antioxidant cocktail: flavonoids, soy, red-wine extract, beta carotene, etc.

To some mice I gave huge amounts of coffee. Coffee mice became very aggressive and would often bite me. For each attempted bite, it was no coffee and three days in a punishment can. It skewed the validity of the experiments, but I already suspected the ultimate outcome. They say coffee is pretty much harmless, but after studying a coffee mouse's brain at autopsy I calculated otherwise. Shrunken thymus glands, a swelling in the cranial cavity, and a shriveling of the adrenal glands. They could run the most complicated labyrinths I constructed, but they were burning it at both ends.

One night I called my ex-boss and he fucking *made* me. He said he got caller I.D. and knew it was me on the line. He threatened to turn me in to the police. I didn't say boo, man. I just hung up. I worried until dawn. I could hear my heart thumping in my chest. Was what I'd done a jailable offense? So much for the job recommendation.

And then, lo, one of my hundreds of résumés bore fruit! I got a call from a large electronics firm, went in, and took some grueling tests involving math, calculus, even physics. I was interrogated by a panel of hard-ass guys with starched white shirts and stern faces. At the conclusion, they said I was one of fifteen people being considered. Two hundred applicants had already been rejected. They told me that em-ployees were subject to random drug tests. They said they would do a background check. Then they'd call me.

The hardiest of my mice turned out to be the swimmers and walkers. The walkers were put on exercise wheels equipped with speed governors and forced to march at a nine-mph pace eight hours a day. Along the bottoms of their cages were metal grids wired to give them an electric shock if they decided to hop off the wheel and shirk their duty. A few rebelled, but the rebellion was dealt with easily: I merely dialed up the electricity. This made me realize the folly of my so-called punishment cans. A nice dark spot in a quiet room was not "punishment." True punishment, such as that reserved for recidivist biters, now took place in a proper punishment room with hot bright lights and severe jolts of electricity. A yoga mouse that I happened to take a dislike to, a little Hare Krishna crybaby who couldn't handle the nine-mph pace, died after thirty-four hours of continuous exercise. The shock burns on its feet, tail, and stomach were secondary to cardiac arrest. Hey! I'm sorry, but it's survival of the fittest. My tests demonstrated that a reasonable amount of hard physical labor each day produced health and content-ment. Bodies are made for work, not idleness.

Man, what else could go wrong? I was standing on a corner, minding my own business, and this no-job I knew, a Stage Three, came along and of-fered to buy me dinner at a Greek restaurant. I said sure, thinking some windfall had come his way. We did a fair amount of drinking and then had this big meal, several courses, with rounds of ouzo for the house. Then he got nervous for some reason. When he reached the register, some drastic thought passed through his brain like a dark cloud. He said to me, "Have you got any money?" I told him I had about sixty cents, and he stood there for a moment. He looked up, down, over his shoul-der. Suddenly he yelled "Run!" and bolted. I was standing flat-footed. A couple of waiters took off after him. So did the cook, with a fifteen-inch blade. What a shocker! Too late, I ran the other way, and the older waiters started after me. Six long blocks they chased me. The no-job got away. Me, I was arrested. The police handcuffed me, shoved me into a patrol car, and whipped me off to the precinct station with their lights flashing. I spent the weekend in jail and finally arranged bond on Monday morning. To cap things off, when I got home I found Al in his aquarium with his three feet in the air, stone dead. I won't lie to you. It was very upsetting. I burst into tears. The lady living above me heard my raking sobs and knocked on the door to see if I was okay.

Hannibal was a well-exercised gladiator mouse. He had a piebald coat, white and tan. I fed him a diet of meat, vegetables, and grain. I gave him testosterone injections from ground-up mouse testicles. He got little boils at the injection sites, but he also became supermuscular. Hannibal won the first annual Gladiator Mouse Championship, killing in succession two swimmers, two walkers, a coffee mouse, and the remaining population of yoga mice — seventeen victims in all. I just kept throwing them in, one after another, getting more and more excited by the ferociousness of the battle. I felt like Caligula. Oh, man! It was too much.

Hannibal's capacity for work and his resistance to the usual stressors, including the punishment sessions, exceeded that of any of my previous specimens. His entire torso was pure muscle. The discipline he showed on the wheel, in the maze, in the pool, or defending his life in the gladiator pit, his appetite for work, and his willingness to meet any challenge made him my most interesting success. I knew I was on to something huge if only there was some way to dampen his murderous impulses, his relentless aggression, and his compulsive sexuality. To be able to harness all that drive and latent productivity. What a challenge!

I was able to farm more testosterone, and I injected it into female mice. The results were dramatic — similar to those which had occurred with Hannibal. But the female supermice, with a natural supply of estrogen, were more tractable. I was at a crossroads in my research. Was this the answer? A female named Cynthia defeated Hannibal in a tooth-and-nail gladiator bout. Yet she stopped short of killing the former champion. I removed his battered body from the little arena and administered adrenaline to his wounds, and then Hannibal bit me on the quick of my fingernail. Yeowza! What happened next was a blur. I slammed Hannibal against the wall like Randy Johnson hurling a ninety-eight-mph fastball. He bounced off and started scrambling around on the floor. I gave chase and stomped him to death in my stocking feet. What an ingrate! And after all I'd done for him.

A few weeks later I was at the university veterinary school, checking out some books on mouse anatomy, when it seemed to me that people were purposefully avoiding me. It went beyond the normal thing you get from being little. Was my fly open? Did I have something in my nose? As I walked up to the checkout desk, I smelled B.O. I put two and two together and realized that the B.O. was coming from me. I tested my breath by licking the back of my wrist and smelling it. It was awful. How far had I sunk? I had a brief panic attack outside and quickly made for home. After I'd had a long bath, the episode passed off.

With the help of the textbooks, I started harvesting other mouse hormones, even though the organ systems were often so tiny I felt I was performing microsurgery. It was also frustrating. The boils Cynthia developed from growth-hormone injections turned into large hard lumps that eventually proved fatal: upon autopsy, I discovered that these were tumors. Cynthia's liver nourished tumors as well. One by one, all my female supermice developed the same symptoms. Another dead end.

I never got the call from the firm that interviewed me. A month had passed, so, taking the bull by the horns, I called the firm and said that I had enjoyed our meeting and would be grateful for a job. I knew it was too late, and it made me angry. Just because I'm five feet tall! I hinted at the possibility of a discrimination suit. A vice-president got on the line and told me that my size had nothing to do with it. They were impressed by my qualifications. I had the job in the bag, but my former boss had given me a poor recommendation: he said I made harassing phone calls at three in the morning. The man said I could have even skated on that charge, but he'd noticed an item in the police blotter involving an incident at a Greek restaurant. I was so shaken by this disclosure that I said it must have been someone else with the same name as mine. A transparent lie. Despondent. I went out and bought two six-packs of beer. The next day I couldn't get out of bed. Nor on the following. I got a violent, three-day hangover and vowed never to drink again.

Court. Oh, God! The very thought of it. I went over to the restaurant and offered full restitution. Nothing doing, they said. I tried to explain what had happened but they made furious Greek gestures at me — God knows what they meant. They said, "See you in court, haffa pint! Broke-a-back. Shorty pants!"

Well, wait a minute, I said. It was the other guy's fault. I gave them the whole story. They said, "Tell us who the other guy is and we'll drop the charge." Actually, I don't know the guy. I mean I "know" him, but he told so many lies I don't know if up is down with him. At one point he told me he was an actor and had been engaged to Catherine Deneuve. He was a smoothie, and handsome — I half believed him.

I threw myself on the mercy of the court and got reamed with a two-hundred-and-fifty-dollar fine, court costs, six months' probation, and a hundred hours of community service. Plus, now I've got a record. Also, I got hit for a hundred and fourteen in unpaid traffic tickets.

After court I lost interest in the mice and fell into a deep, Stage Five no-job depression. The Nobel Prize? Screw it. I went to a clinic and got prescriptions for antidepressants and anti-anxiety drugs. On them, all I wanted to do was sleep. Twenty hours? No problem. It was a pleasant escape. After years of insomnia, I was in heaven.

But the medicine made me fat. Bloat weight. I gained back all that I'd lost. Pretty soon I couldn't get into the clothes that had once been hanging on me. I got a huge gut, a pair of thighs like twin water heaters, and a fat ass that stuck out like a clown's. I'd never thought that I could sink this low. I resorted to wearing sweatpants.

I started setting my alarm clock for late-afternoon appointments and even then I missed about half of them. I wondered how I would ever reassimilate myself into the mainstream of American life. I felt so low and so bad I didn't want to talk to anybody. The landlord came by: people were complaining about a smell. I didn't want him to see my mouse lab. The way things were going it would have been a federal bust — Dr. Mengele Nabbed At Last! I told the landlord I was taking care of a pair of hamsters for a friend, don't worry, I'll deal with the smell. He said, "Man, Anson, you gained weight." Well, no shit, Sherlock!

I cleaned out the mouse cages, replacing the soiled sawdust with fresh cedar shavings. Then it occurred to me to put the mice on this antidepressant that was kicking my ass so bad. Whenever I tried to get off it, I got this full-body pulsar buzz, and everything began to vibrate until I took another pill. I calibrated doses and started medicating the mice. Within three hours all of them were out. Dead? I couldn't tell. But it turned out no, they weren't dead — they were in comas. I wondered if that's what I looked like at night. One slept for two days and didn't change positions: frozen in one posture. I put another on the punishment wheel, and it was oblivious to the shocks. Blue sparks were popping off its paws and it ignored them.

I mentioned earlier that most of the bad stuff you worry about never comes to pass. But sometimes, I was now discovering, it does. You fall into a kind of Bermuda Triangle of hard-ass reality. How long was this going to go on? I asked myself. I finally managed to get off the drugs by taking smaller and smaller doses. And slowly the bloat weight came off. I phoned for an interview for a technician's job at a factory less than a mile from my building, and I was hired that very day. I couldn't believe it. The job was a piece of cake, too. I went in and read the paper and drank coffee for an hour before anyone got ambitious. There were numerous breaks and good camaraderie all the way around. Even so, it was hard to get through a day. I didn't have the stamina. Coming back from Stage Five was tough business. In the annals of no-jobdom, it's rare. Almost unheard of. I had pulled off a big one.

Pretty soon some of the design engineers were hanging out with me, asking my advice on projects and so on. One thing led to another, and I was promoted to senior engineer and making a third more than I got at the last place. It was easy duty, this job. I got into the work and — zing! — the time just flew. I never had a job I *liked* before. I didn't think such a thing existed.

The mice, as they died off, I buried in little toilet-paper tubes. They have a life expectancy of three years. I didn't replace them. Ashes to ashes, dust to dust. What I did was pretty unconscionable. Absolute power, as they say. I'm not proud of my behavior. I had been living without checks and balances. The crap I pulled makes me think of what the space invaders will do to us if they conquer the world. Make slaves of us, eat us, flay us alive and torture us, do every kind of sinister thing in the book. There's a dark side to intelligent beings, an irrational craving for war, personal defilement, and reckless destruction, even if we know better. So if aliens are out there and they do come down I don't expect good things. Aliens aren't out there flying around on errands of mercy or benevolence. To them, we're just so much protein. We're calories. When the space invaders take over, it's the end of the human era. Before that happens, I want to get in a few good times — travel to Ireland, learn how to dance, take tuba lessons, who knows. Happiness is like the gold in the Yukon mines, found only now and then, as it were, by the caprices of chance. It comes rarely in chunks or boulders but most often in the tiniest of grains. I'm a free-floater now, happy to take what little comes my way. A grain here, a grain there. What more can you ask for?

Daddy's Girl

P A LIKED TOOTIE the best. We were three girls, and then Hubert died at six weeks of whooping cough. Pa always wanted a boy, and when Tootie came along, number four, she was as close as you could get. Tomboy. Followed Pa everywhere. Out in the garage all the time with the mechanics was Tootie. Tootie could fix cars. She knew how they worked, and when something went wrong with one she could diagnose its troubles. All I knew of cars was to get in and go. When I was fifteen, I said to Pa, "Pa, when you going to give me a car?" There was an old Ford in the lot and he said, "You can have that Ford, Junk," and he tossed me the keys. He always called me Junk, which is not to say he didn't love his kids, but he didn't like women, and this is one way it slipped through, by calling me that name. Pa was good to me and although he was what you would call a ladies' man, he really hated women. He treated Ma awful. He would go with floozies and buy them diamond pendants and then tell Ma about it and make her nuts to the point where she would almost faint. He would get her so riled me and my sisters would have to put a cold rag on Ma's head at the back of the store in the kitchen where no customers could see. She would go back in the kitchen and nearly faint because of the way he would throw it in her face.

Anyhow, Pa gave me the keys to an old Ford that was parked under the oak tree back behind the car shop. It was a convertible, and me and Barbara Carpenter drove it down Lake Street past the stockyards, glad to stir up a little breeze, it was such a hot day. Of course, I didn't know how to drive and we smashed into a fire hydrant in Montgomery. No one was hurt but we had to walk home along the side of Lake Street, which was so hot that day the tar was melting and the heat of the pavement burned through our saddle shoes. The dog days of August. I told Pa what happened and he didn't get mad or anything, he just told one of the mechanics who had some spare time to take me out in a new Chevrolet and learn me how to drive — that's what he sold, Chevrolets — and when I learned how to drive, I had a new car. Pa was good that way. When my sister Ida wanted to play tennis, he had the tennis courts built and Ida got fancy tennis clothes, but after a few weeks she got tired of it. I think Pa just built them to show off because at the time all of the rich people were putting up tennis courts. Pa had them build two courts and put a big fence around them so no one would have to run down tennis balls. They still have morning glories growing on the fence. If my arthritis isn't too bad I like to go and look at them and smell the lilacs when they bloom.

Tootie could play tennis and beat anyone in the whole south end of town. Grown men she could beat, but when she played Pa she would let him win even though Pa was pretty bad at tennis apart from the fact that he was a big and strong man.

Pa had this punching bag in the basement and he liked to punch on it and show off, and all the kids in the neighborhood got pretty good at it. Because he liked kids and knew how to fool with them, all the kids in the neighborhood thought Pa was swell. I could punch the bag like all the kids, but Tootie could actually box and would box with Pa. She could beat up any of the boys, even the ones that were quite a bit older. This went on until she was about thirteen and she got her period, which was normal but really threw Tootie for a loop.

You know, Pa could play the fiddle and dance and call square dances. Everybody liked Pa. The mayor and big shots in town, the poor people — just about everybody liked Pa. He had Ma pack lunches for us in a straw basket so he could take us kids out on summer picnics, usually to the gravel pit for swimming. In the fall he liked to take us out bird-watching and got binoculars for everyone and would point out the birds. There was all kinds of different ones in those days. The best present he ever gave Tootie was a book on tropical birds, and she used to tell Pa she was going off into the jungle someday to see birds like this. Ma never went along on the picnics — she always worked the store — but she was glad for us to go.

All of us girls were pretty, but Tootie was the best. She looked like a movie star. She looked like Rita Hayworth. All the boys was after her. She cut her hair short and dressed like a boy, but her beauty came through; you just couldn't hold back that kind of beauty. Pa was drinking bad by then, losing money, giving it to women, ruining his business, taking money from Ma. She kept her store money in Dutch Master cigar boxes or White Owl boxes, and he would get to drinking and just take it from her until she got to hiding it. One time he pulled out a .32 pistol and stuck it in her neck up in the bedroom because she wouldn't give him any money. She was pregnant with Moonie at the time and nearly lost her. Pa called Ma filthy names and kicked her down the steps. It was terrible, but in those days things like that was common, Pa being drunk — scenes like that you used to hear about regular and think nothing of it. That's just how life was in those days.

When Pa pulled out his .32 that was the only time he ever laid a hand on Ma, but he had done worse things. All of us girls had to run the store while Ma laid there in bed worried about Pa and went into labor. No sooner did Ma give premature birth to Moonie, the fifth girl, than Pa came home sick to death. They brought him home because he had gone blind drinking bad moonshine booze. It was Prohibition times and he ruined his liver. I remember the doctor said there was nothing they could do. Pa screamed something horrendous and vomited blood all over the bedroom for five days before he died. We girls had to take care of him. Ma was busy with Moonie and wouldn't have anything to do with him, and he laid there and died in the same bed where his youngest daughter had just been born.

Really I was the main one who had to take care of Pa and look after Moonie and run the store to boot. I was the oldest and stuck with all of the responsibility.

Sometime after the funeral a lawyer man came and told Ma that they were going to take the property away because of all the debts Pa had left. Ma got another lawyer and told him that if she could keep the store she would pay him back all the money Pa owed, which was $63,000. In those days that was like millions. But Ma worked the store day and night and paid back the money.

Of all the girls, Ma didn't show any favoritism except maybe for Moonie. When Moonie was little, she had curls and looked like Shirley Temple. All of the customers in the store would come in and rave about her and make a fuss. It wasn't Ma so much as it was the customers. Moonie seemed even prettier than Tootie because she liked being feminine and liked clothes and dressing up, but whenever Tootie halfway tried to look like a woman, she was gorgeous. She had the most beautiful shiny red hair like you see on those Irish. Beautiful smoochy lips, a pretty face — there's no denying. She just couldn't hide it.

When Tootie was about sixteen, the boys got after her something awful. She wouldn't go out with them. She would play baseball and basketball with them and horse around with them because she was still this awful tomboy, but she wouldn't "fool" with them. Tootie got sick headaches like Ma — they had that in common — and we would have to go up in her room and put ice packs on her head. It didn't seem like Tootie to get sick, because she was so tough — because she was such a toughie and could go without sleep and work like a man — but when she got headaches she saw lights dancing in her brain and talked to angels. Sometimes she talked to Jesus. All of these headaches came after her first menstruation.

Everything Tootie did had to be just so. She did good in school because of this. She was the valedictorian of the high-school class. She went off to college and studied to be a doctor. One time she came home for Christmas and told me the men in college was after her and she didn't want any fool man. This is because she was her daddy's girl and no man in the world could be like her Pa for her. Pa was far from perfect but he was Tootie's pal, and whenever you told her how Pa kicked Ma down the stairs and pulled out his .32, Tootie would walk away or she would defend Pa. Once she hit Ida in the face over a quarrel about Pa and broke her nose. Tootie could hit like a man. It was a curse that she was so beautiful, and at medical school she got fat to cover it up. She went into a fat period. Tootie was the first woman doctor in all of town. Ma helped — it was the German way to get education and better yourself in life. Tootie won scholarships and went to the University of

Chicago, which is where all of them intellectuals went. She inherited Ma's spunk and wasn't afraid of nothing.

Ma sent me to secretary school, but I was running with Chunky then and quit after three months. Ida married Harry and he was good to her, although he liked to run with women and cheat. Harry got rich and moved them to De Kalb, and we didn't see that much of them after that. Moonie married Tom when she was eighteen; then after the war he left her for some floozy and she had a nervous breakdown and we had to look after her and the baby until she got over it and married Wilson.

Mary Lou, the second oldest and the one most like Tootie, got married to Monk and moved to Oswego. Ma ran the store on her own except there were always grandkids to take the clinkers out of the furnace and shovel coal, stock the shelves, and do all of the heavy work, and we girls was never far away. Moonie never did much to help in the store. She was the opposite of Tootie. She was crazy for men. Happy-go-lucky whenever one came around.

I can remember the way Ma used to stand behind the counter in the store and talk to customers. She had a way of standing, her legs one in front of the other but spread wide. She always wore a cotton dress with an apron, and when she would talk to customers she would always say, "Ain't that swell?" No matter what they were telling her it was always "Ain't that swell?" She had a big belly and little stick legs. She was left-handed too. Ma was pretty when she was young, but when she got older she lost her looks. She looks like George Washington in the last picture I have of her, and her little stick legs look like Babe Ruth's.

Chunky and I lived in the house across from the store. Chunky was a weakling and never kept a steady job. He was sickly. He was always seeing Tootie about some ailment, and she made him feel better. If she couldn't kid him out of his troubles she gave him some pills. What they were was sugar pills. We all had to laugh because we knew, but Chunky was in the dark and said those pills made him feel like a new man. Tootie liked Chunky and would listen to him after he got religion. Tootie was interested in religion since the time she got her headaches and saw the dancing lights of heaven and talked to the angels. One day she came home and told Ma she had joined the Catholic Church. We were Lutherans, German Lutherans, and Ma just about died. I remember there was a big fight about it in the store. And while the fight was going on there was a terrible thunderstorm with lightning. Lightning hit the walnut tree, which sat just outside the window near the cash register. Scared me enough to kill me. It sounded like the world coming to an end, with a smell like I never knew.

When Ma was a kid living out on the prairie, one of thirteen kids, she was sitting by a Franklin stove when lightning struck through the stovepipe and knocked her out. That's why she had lightning rods on the store — three of them. There was one on the gas station. Three on the garage. Two on the little house. One on Weasie's shack. One on the back house. Two on the barn, but none on that blame walnut tree. Boom! It sounded like the world cracked in half.

Ma always got upset during a thunderstorm; she would get to shaking, and she was doing this during the fight with Tootie. I remember the electric went out and I was lighting candles in the store when she and Tootie got into the fight about the Catholic Church. Ma was almost as upset as the time Pa pulled the pistol on her. The storm and the fight all at once. Ma's cat was so scared it started tearing around the walls until it was running on the ceiling through the power of centrifugal force. Nobody believes me, but that cat was running on the ceiling, completely upside down, or so it seemed to me. Maybe I was wrong.

It began to hail the size of grapefruits. They always say when it hails that it was the size of golf balls or grapefruits, although if you were to see it, you would see that it hailed the size of BB's. But I was there, and it hailed the size of grapefruits! Smashed up the roof on Mrs. Idoc's house. Tootie left in her doctor's Buick, which got dented on top from all that hail, and I had to help Ma upstairs and put ice packs on her head.

A week later we got a letter from Tootie — she had gone and joined the Catholic Church and they made her a nun. About a year after that we got a letter from her from Africa. All these beautiful stamps on an envelope that looked like wax paper. Tootie was a doctor in a leper colony. She said she was happy serving the Lord.

Because of Chunky, I left the Lutheran Church and became a Baptist. Chunky was a street-corner preacher. He worked odd jobs when he could. Then he died of heart trouble at thirty-one. The last thing he said to me was, "I told you I was sick, Junk. But now I'm going to a better place."

After Ma died, blind with diabetes, and the money was split up, Tootie wrote a letter to Ma's lawyer and said she wanted all of her money to go to the mission to buy medicine for all of them lepers. Mary Lou tricked the lawyer — she was smart and had a head for figures. Of all of the girls, Mary Lou was closest to Tootie and wrote to her in Africa every month telling her about her life with Monk and raising Pug and Barney and so on. It was a happy life. Mary Lou didn't have to work because Monk made good with his welding and so on and eventually became the plant manager at the Durabilt. So Mary Lou wrote her happy news and told her what everyone in the family was doing, not mentioning the bad things that happen in all families. Mary Lou tricked that lawyer and held money back for Tootie, and it was a good thing.

When Moonie called to tell me Mary Lou had cancer, she just said, "Mary Lou called me and said 'The doctor told me I've got cancer in my breast.'" Just as plain as that. Moonie said that Mary Lou didn't seem that worried about it. She said she'd had a lump for two years and tried to make it go away by practicing Christian Science. When Monk found out about it he took her to the doctor and they took off the breast. Monk was pretty upset. He could count on Mary Lou. Mary Lou and the kids were all he lived for. They took off the breast and Mary Lou went home. She used to tell me, "I haven't got cancer anymore. I can just tell." But it went to her lungs. They had to put her in the hospital on oxygen, but she finally suffocated. I hope I don't die that way, and with diabetes I probably won't. Diabetes gives you a heart attack; Chunky said it feels like a truck driving on your chest. Real bad pain, but it's over in ten or fifteen minutes. Ain't that swell, the way we have to live and die and suffer on this earth?

It was a relief to see Mary Lou's suffering end, but still, after the death, Monk was left with a hole in his life. He didn't want another woman, although Pug and Barney tried to tell him that it would be a good idea. Then his dog died and Monk went through a drinking spell. Nobody wanted to be around him. That's how the family is about drinking — down on it. Ma drilled that into us pretty good.

304 · SELECTED STORIES

Then Tootie comes home from Africa in her nun clothes. She isn't pretty no more, she's almost fifty years old. Her face is pinched and white, though you'd think it would have been tan — as black as the ace. It's a hard life over there in Africa, with bad food and constant work, she says. "The futility of it all," she says. "Such...futility." She talked like the world was coming to an end, and that wasn't like Tootie, even with her headaches. Futility, I had to look the word up in a dictionary. It means hopeless.

The Catholic Church gave Tootie a leave, and so she gets Monk straight off the booze and puts me on insulin shots. She didn't come home for Ma's funeral or for Ida's funeral after Ida died of kidney failure, but aside from Pa, Mary Lou was her closest friend and she flew home on a jet plane.

I asked her if she seen all of those birds in the jungle, and she said she did. I said, "Tootie, you look bad. What happened to you?" She said a big mamba snake, nine feet long, went crazy and bit five Africans and some goats. Tootie cut off its tail with a hoe, but that only made it mad and it chased after her and bit her too, over there on the Dark Continent. Her life and health was bad ever since. Still she gave me hell because of what I eat, and I told her that if the Lord wanted to take me, I was ready to go. I would go up to heaven and see Chunky again and Wilbur, my second husband. Since Tootie was a nun, I asked her who I was supposed to be married to — Chunky, my first man, or Wilbur? Tootie told me she didn't believe in God. I said, "Tootie, you are a nun, and when you was little and had your headaches, the angels talked to you and Jesus talked to you," and she just laughed a bitter laugh. She told me that being a nun was no different than if she had stayed in Aurora and lived a normal life with a man. She said there wasn't nothing to it and for sure there was no God. It was all just make-believe. But Tootie took Monk to the AA. She had a power over people and could make them well without giving them shots or medicine, she believed in herself so. Every day for ninety days she drove Monk to the AA, sometimes two and three times a day. In this she was a hypocrite, because she didn't have any more belief in God, but she could still lay it out pretty good, and for Monk this was the cure, not the AA. She even got him to quit smoking.

One night Tootie came by in her car and caught me eating fried pork rinds and peanut brittle. It made me guilty but I told her, "Tootie, you can talk to me until you're blue in the face; I ain't going to change. I'm too old for it. A person has to eat."

She gave me hell upside and down and then drove me down to Oswego to check on Monk. After Mary Lou died, he'd kept everything in the house the same — we walked in through the back porch as always, and Monk was fixing himself something to eat in the microwave. It was like old times. He was glad to see us and he had a lot he had to get out. This was before his son Barney died and he gave up hope altogether. We went and sat in the living room, and Monk looked at Tootie and she looked at him, and I saw real love between the two of them. The love of two friends. Monk had the emphysema and it was hard for him to talk. He said, "All that welding in bad conditions with no ventilation, three packs of Chesterfields a day. Coming up in the depression, it was hard. I had this old Oldsmobile — I was just a kid and it was my first car. It had a split windshield and the left side was broken out and, I don't know, it must have been January. I remember I went over to my girlfriend's house in that car and drank Coke and we played the player piano — 'It's a Long Way to Tipperary,' 'Happy Days Are Here Again,' 'The Dark Town Strutters' Ball' — when it started to blow real hard and I realized how late it was and I had to get home. I had to be to work the next day. The dagblam Oldsmobile overheated. We didn't have antifreeze in those days but ran alcohol through the radiator, and the closer I got to town, the hotter the car got and the slower it was going until I finally made it downtown and stopped at the Strand. A Chinaman there gave me some water for my radiator. I practically had to beg for it, since it was midnight and they were closing. No gloves. Twelve below. Lightweight coat. No hat. By the time I got to the store the car was overheating again, and it kept going slower and slower until I had to downshift into first gear as I drove out Jericho Road toward my mother's house. Finally the old car lugged to a stop and smoke started pouring out of the engine. I flipped up the hood and fire was coming out of the carburetor, so I ran over to the side of the road, scooping up frozen snow with my bare hands alongside a barbed-wire fence — can you imagine that? — trying to put it out. But that didn't work, so I beat the flames with my jacket, and that caught on fire, and by the time the fire went out I was crying because I knew the engine was ruined and I just wanted to die. I was out there on Jericho Road by Blackberry Creek and I saw a light go on in Bobby O'Neil's house and saw a face come up to the window and wipe away the steam. Bobby made a cup with his hands to look out — I can see his face now with that stupid look of his; he was half crazy — but then the light went out, and I was too ashamed to go knock on the door and ask for help, so I got in the car and huddled down, and before long I was in and out of sleep and realized that if I didn't get up and do something I was going to freeze to death. Tootie, the wind was blowing so hard I had to walk home backwards! I thought the wind was going to cut me in half. Three miles of this. Frostbite ears, frostbite feet. My mother soaked them in cool water and put me to bed covered with wool blankets, and I just passed out, didn't get to work on time, and was fired. There I was. The girlfriend two-timed me a day later, my car was shot, and no job. People don't know how hard it was in those days." This is what Monk said. Tootie and I got nuts the way he was telling the story, and we was laughing so hard we practically wet our pants. I hadn't got nuts and laughed like that since Ida was alive. Ida could be fun and get you nuts — make you have a good time.

This guy I saw on the *Donahue* show said if you laugh all the time you can heal yourself from fatal diseases and that some guy healed himself by watching the Three Stooges and the Marx Brothers. Well, I guess I'll just have to die, because I could never laugh over something so stupid as that. Really, Monk knew what he was doing and made the story funny to make us laugh like that — he was always a kidder. But after Barney died right after the dog and Mary Lou, Monk caved in. All that good stuff he learned at the AA about the higher power, which helped Monk quit drinking and smoking, the higher power Monk chose to call God — it all quit working. Monk was no dummy. He could see Tootie was just practicing the Hippocratic oath with no real feeling. Although she tried to cover it up, Tootie went into a depression, too. She didn't feel right at home and she didn't want to go back to Africa. She put up a front, but Monk could see through it. No matter what Tootie did for him or what Pug did for him, he just sort of dried up inside. Pug was with him when he died. Pug was with Barney when he died and with

Mary Lou. Three in five years. Pug said Monk was rational right up to the end. He didn't say nothing about Jesus taking him to heaven. What he said was, "Ain't this a bitch?" After he said that, Pug said he rolled over and died. Maybe Pug saw it wrong. Maybe Monk closed his eyes and prayed for his own salvation, for the forgiveness of his sins. Late at night when I can't sleep, I think of Monk up in heaven with Barney and Mary Lou and the whole family short of Pa, who died cursing God.

My doctor gave me an operation because my lower eyelids were growing up and going into my eye. The pain was horrible. Tootie did the operation over, to get all of the eyelid roots out, but they still sprout up and stick me in the eye and I have to tape my eye open, put drops in it, and take aspirin. Sometimes the pain is so bad I just have to lie on my bed and hold a picture of Jesus to my heart and pray for Him to come and take me, or pray for Him to save Tootie's soul. She has done good things for the world, but only through the grace of Jesus are we saved. Our righteous acts are as filthy rags. Everybody knows that one.

Tootie quit the Catholic Church and used the money Mary Lou held back to start her own doctor practice. Dermatology. In the daytime she cures pimples on teenagers and at night she goes out with men and lives the fast life. Her looks are gone. She dresses wrong. She doesn't know how to act right after all of those years in Africa. She comes on too independent. Maybe being around those lepers and those African drum dances put Satan in her life. Satan made her forget how Jesus sent an angel to save her from an elephant stampede and another time from getting shot by those rebels in Angola, or how He saved her from her snakebite. Satan is the prince of this world and his powers are strong. He prowls the earth like a hungry lion looking for souls to devour. He knows his days are short, and he's trying to make hay and catch every sinner in his net of evil. I never thought he could get Tootie, though.

Or maybe Tootie's troubles was because of Pa. Tootie was her daddy's girl, and that can be too much of a good thing. I do believe that a Catholic can go to heaven, but not unless they accept the grace and salvation the Lord offers us. It's so easy. It's so simple. Tootie don't think it's rational, and it isn't rational. Lions playing with lambs and eating straw sounds ridiculous, I guess, especially if you've been to Africa and seen how they do and have been bit by a nine-foot mamba snake…who am I to judge? It's not rational; it's what you call a paradox. You have to believe like a little child. Believe it because it's impossible. There's no need for holy water or praying to a lot of saints when you can talk to Jesus direct. When I think I can't take it no more, I hold my picture of Jesus against my breast and pray for Tootie and my family and for all of the lost souls in the world. I say, "Jesus, I cry my bleeding heart out every day for you; come down to earth and forgive them all, *for they know not what they do*. Come down and give us a thousand years of peace like you said you would and throw Satan down in the pit where he can't get at us no more." When I do this the grown-up in me dies and I'm like a little child and can see the world fresh again. *Born again*. Sometimes I don't really believe in no life after death, but I do believe that Jesus has saved me. Other times I believe it all — tigers eating straw, the water turned to wine, the Red Sea parting, the Tower of Babel, and a thousand years of peace on earth with our Lord and Savior, Jesus Christ.

I am ninety-two years old and I had to get this in before I go.

NEW STORIES

Night Train

JACK BUFFMEIR, AS far as I knew, being a little kid, didn't seem to have a real job or any work history whatsoever. On occasion he made birdhouses, and if he couldn't sell them to people, he just gave them away. They weren't all that hot. Something a simpleton would knock together. In addition to this, Jack raised a few chickens and grew vegetables. My grandmother felt sorry for Jack and let him live in a shack on the back of her property. It was just a one-room affair with an outhouse behind it.

What interested me most about Jack was his black-and-white bull terrier, Oyster, a rarely seen breed of dog, then as now. I coveted the dog, but Oyster would rarely give me the time of day. As far as Oyster was concerned, his oddball master was the sun, moon, and stars. With a full-time religion like Jack, the dog did not have any time for little boys.

Jack could play the fiddle, and when he was in good humor, he liked to dress up in his white suit and play "Turkey in the Straw" at the back of my grandmother's store. In the middle of the song he would set the fiddle on the pop case, pull out a soup spoon, and cavort around dancing as he clapped the spoon against his cheeks. He would pick up carving knives from the meat block and flash them around with the authority of a samurai warrior while clog dancing in his two-toned brown-and-white shoes. Meanwhile, Oyster would do back flips, roll over, and dance about on his hind legs with Jack. There was no television, and people found their entertainment in peculiar ways.

All you had to do to get a meal or a place to flop from my grandmother was to offer to pluck the "clinkers" from her coal furnace down in the store basement and haul them out back to the barnyard. A mental defective, hobo, or dangerous bum off the streets could come in and accomplish bed and board for this small chore. Boy Cleatus, a black of fifteen, used to do the job for a quarter. The clinkers were heavy sizable things, like fossilized starfish. How the little pellets of coal clumped together during incineration was something I never understood. Whenever Boy Cleatus got in trouble with the law and was sent to the reformatory in St. Charles, the clinkers were mine to haul for no quarter. Since the firepit was small, I often opened the furnace door and poked at these spiky formations. When the bulk of the fuel had burned, they became hollow, like fragile shells, and it was fun to mash them down before I threw more coal into the pit. The cold clinkers from the bottom of the ash pit I put in a laundry tub and carried out back. It paid to wear gloves when handling clinkers, although I seldom bothered; I mainly wanted to get the job over with as soon as possible, so I tolerated minor burns and ashen splinters. I learned to shovel coal and haul clinkers at an early age, but Jack Buffmeir, who lived scot-free in the shack, never dirtied his fingers in this fashion.

He was a thin, dapper fellow who preferred a suit and a vest to ordinary clothes. He neither drank nor smoked. I had heard that he had been gassed in the first war and had somehow gotten out of mortal combat early. My grandmother disputed this story and told me that Jack had been struck by lightning and never served in the Great War. When he wasn't in his turkey-in-the-straw mood, Jack was a quiet, suspicious man preoccupied with his health. It was one extreme or the other with him, glaring, contrasting differences like the opposing colors of his two-tone shoes.

Buffmeir could swing into states of highest agitation, constantly pulling his watch from his vest pocket and flipping it open like a man who kept an urgent, variegating schedule. He was continually going to doctors. My grandmother was given to believe that his aches and pains were imaginary, but I wasn't so sure. Because I was a kid, he seldom paid attention to me; I could observe his unguarded visage, which was often that of a man in severe pain. His face took on a sour countenance and he would sometimes buy packets of fizzing stomach powders, which he mixed in a glass under my grandmother's kitchen spout. Like Napoleon in a white suit with a straw boater, he would insert his hand under his jacket and press it against his side, stoically waiting for fast pharmaceutical relief. Oyster positioned himself close enough to Jack so that he could look up at his master and gauge his moods while he stood vigilantly braced to defend the old man against a 360-degree perimeter of incoming evils.

Jack demanded complete and unwavering loyalty from the animal, yet he hardly bothered to feed the dog, and never once did I see him deign to kneel down and pet the animal or even bother to say a kind word. This lack of gratitude toward Oyster did not surprise me.

One cold day I stood out in front of the store waiting for the *Aurora Beacon-News* to dump off their afternoon bundle of papers, when I spotted a stray feral cat. I wanted a pet more than anything in the world, and I went for the tortoise-colored female. I managed to pick her up as she worked my face over with her front paws slashing like razors. She was a bundle of compressed fury, but I managed to stumble up the stairs with her, bust in the door, and drop her on the floor. The cat dashed off for the basement, and after my grandmother treated my scratches with Mercurochrome, I took a bowl of milk to the basement. I looked all over for the cat to no avail; but a cat can hide, and the basement was a warehouse of stock.

There were cases of cereal, toilet paper, coffee, Campbell's soup, Dinty Moore beef stew, sardines, potted meat, SOS scrubbing pads, and various and sundry goods. I ran about pell-mell looking for the animal, but it seemed to have vanished. Several days later I saw her purring in contentment on the white batting that insulated the coal furnace. The cat, which had given birth to six kittens my grandmother later drowned in the cistern, nonetheless found a home in the store as a mouser. Like Oyster, she spurned my attempts to befriend her.

Then a more hopeful time arrived. Jack Buffmeir saw an osteopath who convinced him to become a full-out vegetarian. The diet produced instant and miraculous benefits. Buffmeir left off wearing his dandy suits and plowed an additional two-acre garden behind the shack. He claimed he felt like a new man and would talk endlessly about the virtues of organic produce to anyone who would stand still and listen to it. Not only that, he put Oyster on a vegetarian regime and claimed that

the luster and sheen on Oyster's harsh black-and-white coat was a result
of nutrients from the life-giving soil. The earth was rich and productive
Illinois black topsoil and under the blazing sun and with an attentive
watering schedule, Jack grew tomatoes, rhubarb, potatoes, corn, peas,
carrots, and beans. Once these were in the ground he began tending to
the trees on my grandmother's property, trees he had planted earlier in
life under my grandmother's instruction. There were fruit trees and a
couple of black walnuts, an arboretum of sorts, albeit long neglected.

Buffmeir believed in the healing properties of nuts, which were rich
in proteins. He also stepped up his egg production, selling what he
didn't eat at my grandmother's store. These were in the milk and butter cabinet with a small sign in front of them that read JACK BUFFMEIR'S
MAGIC EGGS, FRESH DAILY. The eggs, which had brown shells, were fertilized by the fuckingest rooster on the south end of town. They cost a
nickel more per dozen than regular eggs, and my grandmother was constantly besieged with questions about exactly what was so damn special
about Jack Buffmeir's eggs. Jack said that he fed his chickens a special vitamin-enriched diet. I heard claims that they were good for your
hair and nails and could even cure baldness. Even though Jack had no
woman he produced a convincing argument that the zinc in them improved flagging sex lives. I didn't precisely know what a sex life was, but
one day Jack grabbed me in a headlock and gave me a Dutch rub that
really hurt, saying that if I wanted to grow big and slug home runs I
should eat two of his eggs for breakfast every day. I was used to eating
Dolly Madison chocolate doughnuts dunked in coffee for breakfast, but
soon I had my grandmother frying egg sandwiches for my lunch.

The deleterious effects of cholesterol were unknown in those days,
and eggs were fairly sensible nutrition. But Jack did not come into full
glory until he broke from his osteopath's guidebook and, all on his
own, discovered nature's true miracle food — the peach. He ate peaches
morning, noon, and night. Illinois peaches were small, hard, and sour.
Jack admitted as much, but ate them anyway. In an astounding burst
of industry he planted hybrid peach trees and hybrid apple trees. He
cultivated mulberry, pear, and sour-cherry trees. He revived the long-
neglected grapevines that grew alongside my grandfather's old Chevrolet garage, which, by then, my grandmother had rented out to a German

machinist. Jack was constantly pruning trees, watering them, fertilizing them, and splicing hybrid branches on them like artificial limbs. But Jack refused to cut the grass; that job was left to Cousin Eustace, a head-injury victim.

There were a lot of birds when the fruit got ripe. Buffmeir killed flocks of crows and blackbirds with his shotgun (Oyster would finish off the wounded with a few quick snaps of the neck). Buffmeir would let me collect the bird bodies in a cardboard box, on the outside of which he would tally his kills before we tossed the dead birds into the trash burner. I was always being told that there were hungry people in the world, but I grew up in a store and all I ever saw was food. I had the good fortune to be born after the trees had matured. Jack had worked these trees back to vigor. For me, they were just there for easy picking. The only *tree* tree on the property was an oak that had gotten the jump on Jack — it was there in manifested maturity before he could do anything about it.

My grandmother liked flowers. I used to collect morning glories from the vines that grew up along the high fencing behind the garage. In the salad days, when my grandfather ran the prosperous Chevrolet dealership, he constructed a concrete tennis court behind the garage. There was a patch of grass back there that Cousin Eustace also cut, and from there I could collect wildflowers to add to the bouquets of morning glories I presented to my grandmother. Even if you got them into a glass of water, they were only good for a couple of hours. Having seen Jack Buffmeir raise vegetables, I planted nasturtiums and petunias, but just as the seedlings began to sprout, Eustace would hack them down with the push mower. My grandmother refused to intervene, since mowing the lawn seemed to be my cousin's only reason for being. Cousin Eustace was a diabetic, only a few years older than myself, but as my mother had dropped him on his head as an infant, he was feebleminded in a more straightforward way than Jack Buffmeir. I'm fairly sure that any psychiatrist worth his salt would have diagnosed Jack as a paranoid schizophrenic with a propensity to manic depression. This was particularly evident when he started in on a food jag. His views shifted.

Pretty soon peaches were just okay, but the real healing miracles involved carrots and foods with violent colors like eggplant, green and red peppers, tomatoes, and watermelon. The peach, the mainstay of his diet, well, cut into one and what did you see but anemic yellow flesh. Jack started eating carrots like there was no tomorrow. He also went to the library and brought home an exotic book about yoga in which very thin, dark, little people twisted themselves into knots, their faces composed into visages of radiant inner peace.

There was a punching bag in the basement of the store. It was an inflatable speed bag that hung from the ceiling. One morning Jack set to work on the bag at five A. M., shortly after my grandmother opened up. I could hear the bag popping from my bed on the second floor. Since my father was a professional boxer, the sound of the bag filled me with the hope that he had sobered up and come to pay a visit. When I got my clothes on and rushed down to the basement, Jack Buffmeir was doing a headstand in the rag bin, a small closet where my grandmother tossed the gunnysacks the red and white potatoes from Idaho were shipped in. Jack's face was redder than a fire hydrant. I said, "Where's my dad?" But then I looked at Jack's knuckles and saw that they were scuffed raw. Oyster must have mistaken my intentions, for he rushed me and began ragging my pantlegs. Jack said, "Oyster, leave off!"

I rushed upstairs and asked my grandmother what Jack Buffmeir was doing a headstand in the rag bin for? She looked up from doing her bills. "Getting a stroke," she said.

A few days later I was sitting out on the back porch drinking chocolate milk and reading comic books with the Marzuki brothers when Jack asked us if we would like a boxing lesson. We demurred, but Jack insisted. Soon Butch Marzuki was standing in the gravel parking lot with a pair of sixteen-ounce pillows on his tiny fists. Jack Buffmeir was wearing the other pair. With a suddenness that verged on cheating he said, "Okay, box!" He was dressed in a glen plaid suit and wore a vest with a watch chain and that pair of two-toned brown-and-white shoes. He danced around Marzuki, cuffing his ears until they turned red. Marzuki, who barely came up to his waist, launched a right, and Buffmeir's left hand cracked over it and bloodied Marzuki's nose. Tears followed.

"Defend yourself at all times, boy. You had that one coming," Buffmeir said, dancing about the lot as he tossed his head side to side, keeping his neck loose. He looked very pleased with his victory, adding, "And quit that sniveling, you big sissy."

Buffmeir looked at me and said, "You're next."

"I ain't fighting," I said.

"Why not? Are you scared?"

My grandmother came out to the back porch with a pail of dirty water and a mop. I noticed that Jack's face flushed with color at the sight of her. "Just teaching the boys the manly art of self-defense, Mag."

"Leave them be," she said. "They fight enough as it is."

"They asked me to show them," he croaked.

"No, you forced us," David Marzuki exclaimed.

"Did not."

"Yes, you did!" Marzuki said.

"Ingrate!" Buffmeir said. "Liar."

"Am not," Marzuki said.

Shortly after this episode Jack Buffmeir fell into deep black moods. When they came upon him, he couldn't even bear the companionship of his dog, Oyster. After the dog killed Jack's rooster, a mean bird, and most likely Oyster could have claimed self-defense, Buffmeir took after him with a horsewhip. Some of the factory workers from the Durabilt were eating sandwiches on my grandmother's front porch when he set upon the animal. A dark, muscular man with a cut of plug in his cheek set down his sandwich and snatched the whip out of the man's hand. "No way to treat an animal. Shame on you."

Furious, Buffmeir walked though the front door, exited to the back, crossed the parking lot, and went into his shack. The dog was still waiting for him on the front porch late the next morning. My grandmother said, "The dog thinks Jack is in the store."

I coaxed the animal inside and he walked up and down the aisles, even went down into the basement looking for his master. When he could not find him, he waited for the next customer to come through the front door and returned to his post on the porch.

That night Mag lured Oyster inside with some leftover pot roast. The dog followed us upstairs to bed, but he did nothing but pace and whine the entire night. Finally she had to let him out to wait on the porch for Jack, who showed up the next day and reconciled with his pet.

A few days later Buffmeir abandoned the dog on the back porch. He walked through the store with a sack of carrots and didn't return until dark. My grandmother was getting ready to close when Jack appeared and said, "I walked up to Batavia and swam naked in the gravel pit." Batavia was seven miles away.

When my grandmother recounted the story to Cousin Eustace and his father, Pug, Pug said, "Damn, he should have kept right on going until he got to Elgin." Elgin was the city north of Batavia that housed the state mental institution, just one city beyond St. Charles, which housed the Boys' Reformatory where Boy Cleatus was incarcerated.

Cousin Eustace leaned against the pop machine, mimicking his father's body language. He had a strained, high-pitched voice and a pasty complexion and too much weight. "He should have kept right on going to Elgin, Mag," Cousin Eustace said.

"Hell, yes," Pug said, waving a sweaty bottle of Green River.

"Hell, yes, he should," Cousin Eustace said. "That man is full of bunk."

"He's a damn nut!" Pug said.

"Sure he is, Dad, a damn nut! Lock him up and throw away the key."

Each day as Jack Buffmeir took his carrot-fueled excursions, Oyster waited on the back porch. I tempted the dog with succulent cuts of beef from the meat locker, and while he would eat them, he refused to give in and play with me. He would not fetch. He would not wrestle. He tolerated my hugging him, and once when I got into a screaming and cussing rock fight with Carl Smith, Oyster leapt from the porch and chased Smith out of the yard and clear over to Bowditch Avenue to the Smith hovel. Shortly thereafter Carl Smith came back with reinforcements, the Tinsley and Calhoun brothers: big, tough, and mean-all. I was caught flat, but the dog sensed their sinister intentions immediately and soon had the entire pack racing for Bowditch Avenue. A few days later I saw Carl Smith at the playground and shoved him to the ground, pulling his arm up behind his back for the goose egg that one of his rocks had inflicted on my forehead a few days before. The playground supervisor quickly broke up the fight and not only sent me home for the afternoon, but kicked me off the junior softball squad. Dejected, I returned to the store. I parked my bike along the side of the garage, and when Oyster came off the back porch to greet me, I was mildly astonished. I sat near a pile of leaves that had blown alongside Pug and Vera's place and hugged the dog, who let me cuddle next to him for warmth. A burst of sunlight broke through the clouds and warmed us and almost instantly I fell into a deep and wonderful slumber. It was cold and nearly dark when I awoke. Oyster had abandoned me for his position on the porch. I dusted off my clothes and went inside.

Oyster would not fetch or wrestle, but he liked to play tug-of-war with a rope. It was virtually impossible to beat him at this game and Jack exploited the dog's power in these demonstrations to help sell his canned produce. Oyster was eighty pounds of pure muscle. Another thing he liked to do at Jack Buffmeir's behest was jump at inflated balloons, a comical sight that caused the customers to stop and watch in wonder. Oyster possessed incredible vertical leaping ability. It looked as if he were playing basketball. He timed his jumps so that each time his snout hit the balloon, he seemed to hang in the air a moment. Jack could sell several cartons of fertilized eggs whenever he put his wonder dog into action. But this seldom happened once the black moods befell him.

The long, introspective, carrot-nibbling walks continued. The heels of Jack's two-toned shoes were worn down. He stuffed them with cardboard, though the cheapest shoemaker in town had a shop just across the street.

Jack was letting his dandy image slide. His skin was stiff and yellow. He looked like a cadaver. My grandmother asked him what was wrong, and Buffmeir shook his head gravely. "Cancer, Mag. It's all in my liver. I just seen a doctor in Chicago. I got six weeks. Who's going to take care of my dog? Who's going to mind the trees?" Jack Buffmeir didn't wait for an answer. We watched him walk down the back steps and cross the parking lot to his shack with his dog behind him. His right hand was pressed firmly under his ribs, an area which pained him greatly; his thin jaw was set hard.

My grandmother had a huge medical reference book with illustrated pictures in her bedroom. I looked up liver diseases and saw a patient looking every bit as bad as Jack. Worse, I saw what cancer did to the liver. The human liver looked much like the liver in my grandmother's meat cooler. With cancer, it was infiltrated by orange, unnatural-corded knots that sought to strangle it. I quickly slammed the book shut and prayed to God that never would such a fate fall upon me. Jack Buffmeir was a goner!

The night crew at the Durabilt had thirty minutes for lunch. Mag would slice cold cuts for them and dish up salads. They liked to congregate around the pop cabinet, comb back their slick ducktails, smoke, and posture while the Italian girls from the neighborhood came in wearing their shorts in hot weather. Or, if the men weren't scoping, they would sit out on the front porch talking sports or playing grab-ass.

The factory was set along a trunk of the Burlington Railroad that supplied Aurora with industrial transport. Just beyond were the main rails for the fast Burlington Zephyrs that bolted from Seattle to Chicago and back. I liked to stand and wave at the passenger trains and catch glimpses of the dining cars or the sleepers that seemed like compartments of Pullman pleasure. This was particularly true at night when a passing tableau of scenes was presented by the illuminated compartments. With every need attended to, the passengers had the leisure to read, smoke, eat and drink, or converse. They were often finely dressed and had destinations — places to go and things to do; it was mysterious, romantic, and enchanting. I also loved counting freight cars and spotting hoboes. I most eagerly awaited the passage of the caboose, which would sometimes display a railman asleep in the upper loft while another was preparing coffee in a blue enamel pot, or sitting at a little table drinking it while reading a magazine by a kerosene lantern. I watched wistfully as the clacking and banging of the train receded, and the caboose disappeared; and suddenly I was back in my own world of Lutheran restrictions and sameness.

But the trains came often. The day-and-night bump-and-rattle of trains was a given. The tracks also provided footpaths to the west end of town. One Friday night at about eight o'clock, Pug and Cousin Eustace were waiting for the dinner crew to disperse and for Vera to get off from the plant, where she worked as a bookkeeper. I was helping box up some groceries for a young Polish girl and her mother who lived on the far south end. The girl was a skinny blond with buckteeth, and, like others in this account, she was said to be a bit feebleminded. It seems that

Boy Cleatus and a couple of his friends had taken advantage of her. My grandmother's term for it was "molested." I wasn't at all sure what that meant. I did know that the girl, whose name was Lois, was very poor, but by all accounts her mother was honest and hardworking. Lois didn't make eye contact much, but the more I looked at her, the more I was certain that I was in love with her. My grandmother was giving them food, which meant staples like bread, potatoes, and dried fish. I swiped a couple of Chunky bars, a Three Musketeers, and a Snickers, and put them in the box under a bunch of bananas when Vera came running up the front porch screaming, "Jack Buffmeir is out on the train tracks, and the train is coming!"

"Well, hell, didn't you pull him off?" Pug asked.

"I tried that and he slugged me," Vera said. "He just yelled, 'Fuck all and leave me alone!' Then he set that dog on me and I ran here."

I was out the front door like a shot. Away from the neon signs of the storefront, it was dark. I could hear shoes scuffling in the dark, heavy breathing, and men slipping and falling in the gravel as they raced to the tracks. I had fallen twice and my knees and palms stung with abrasions. My lower lip was swollen and bleeding, and I had chipped a tooth, but I got up running both times. Suddenly the Burlington rounded a curve as it crossed the Lake Street viaduct and straightened out. At that point the train's mighty spotlight picked up Jack Buffmeir, who had laid himself directly on the main rails. He had walked north toward the curve so the engineer would have little time to see him, let alone stop. I bolted down the track bed in the direction of the blinding light. The train's horn was blaring and the iron wheels started screeching as the engineer hit the brakes. Jack was now on his hands and knees trying to push Oyster away from him. For once the dog refused to obey — he seemed to realize that his master was bent on suicide and he couldn't let that happen. I didn't care about Jack Buffmeir, but I had come to think of Oyster as my dog. I ran the tracks as fast as possible and could hear heavy breathing behind me. Just as the train hit Buffmeir one of the factory workers grabbed me and pulled me to safety. I heard two quick thunks and saw Oyster flying through the air like he was shot from a cannon. It was a freight train with over seventy cars.

I ran down to the viaduct, crossed underneath it, and came back to the point of the collision and began searching for the dog. I found Buffmeir's right forearm and hand severed almost bloodlessly. Then at the bottom of a sloping grass hill, I spotted Oyster. He was unmarked, but dead just the same. I lifted his head to my lap and talked to him, but his body was limp. I thought that maybe if I could get him back to the store, somebody there could do something to revive him. As I said, he seemed unmarked. I tried to lift him but he weighed more than eighty pounds. I tried pulling him up the grassy slope by his rear feet, but I kept slipping and falling down. I dragged him for a ways across the gravel, but that was undignified and unbefitting to such a fine animal.

I heard frantic voices, police sirens, and saw a good number of flashlight beams combing the area under the train. And then I heard even more frantic voices calling my name. I was the subject of an intense manhunt. I said nothing in reply and, instead, wrapped my body alongside that of the dog, holding him much the way I had held him months ago on the patch of oak leaves that had blown along the side of Pug and Vera's bungalow.

The accident drew a banner headline in the *Aurora Beacon-News*. People who never heard of Jack Buffmeir attended his funeral. You would have thought Rudolph Valentino had died. To add to the pathos, the engineer insisted that he saw Oyster spending his last moment on earth trying to drag his master to safety and paying with his life.

A few days after the funeral I followed my grandmother out to Jack's shack. She seldom left the store, and when she did, she had to walk with a cane. She removed a key from her apron pocket and opened the door. There wasn't much inside. A bed and a dresser. A small kitchen table. There was a pantry filled with canned vegetables and fruit. Jack Buffmeir did not have a refrigerator, but an icebox. There was a bottle of sour buttermilk inside. As I sniffed it, I saw a cushion on the floor, and above it, on the wall, two paint-worn footprints. I had located the site where Jack did his hour-long daily headstands that were meant to defeat the pernicious effects of gravity on the human body.

There was a small closet filled with his dandy clothes, and, on the top, a box containing his birth certificate, a number of medical books, and an honorary discharge from the U.S. Army. In addition to this was a Purple Heart and Jack's wallet, which contained four dollars. My grandmother handed me the box of papers, and after she locked the door, we walked back to the store together.

The next afternoon my grandmother mailed Jack's four dollars to his osteopath. A few days later the doctor called her. I could see consternation on my grandmother's face, and I was shocked at the length of time she spent on the phone — some four or five minutes. When she hung up, I asked her what was going on. She said that Jack Buffmeir didn't have cancer after all. His liver was fine. The doctor in Chicago said the reason Jack turned yellow was from all the carrots he was eating. He was healthy as a horse.

Later that night, when I had finished sweeping up, I moved to the front of the store, where my grandmother sat in a folding chair, dozing. Once a week or so during this time, I would clip a few gray whiskers that grew on her chin. She was the least vain person I ever knew, but she always put on a show of being greatly pleased by this ritual. When she awoke I said, "Gram, are you sad about Jack Buffmeir?"

"Sad? No. I'm not sad. He wasn't really fit to live. He was not right. Never. They were drawing up papers to send him to Elgin," she said.

I thought those would be her last words on the subject, but as she looked at my yearning eyes she had one further pronouncement: "In the end the fool got what he really wanted — hit by a train and out with a great splash. And who was stuck paying for his funeral? Me!" She looked at the wall clock. It was eleven-thirty. She said, "Come on, now. Let's lock up and go to bed."

It was a hot night. After I brushed my teeth, I lay in bed waiting for a car to zoom past on Lake Street to stir up a little breeze, but there was no traffic. My grandmother rubbed her legs with liniment and picked up her prayer book. I wanted to ask her if Oyster was in heaven. I was pretty sure Jack Buffmeir was in hell, and I knew what her answer would be anyway. When you are dead, you are dead, unless you were very bad, in which case you were in hell. If by some off chance there was a heaven, less than ten souls inhabited the place.

The blare of a distant night train resonated from the southeast. In less than an hour people from Washington, Utah, Montana, Nebraska, North Dakota, and Iowa would be disembarking at Union Station in Chicago — to do what? I guessed they would be tired and eager to get into the safe cars of relatives: either that or they would have to flag down cabs to find hotel rooms. Soon they would be ejected from the comfortable haven of the plush coach cars and scrambling for shelter in a big and mean city. As my grandmother shut off the night-light, I waited for the rattle of steel wheels on iron rails. It seemed the train would never come. But when it did, I began counting cars by the sound of wheels rocking over the spliced rails.

Volcanoes from Hell

S HE WAS A petite brunette with a high forehead, beautiful sparkling blue eyes, hair pulled back in a ponytail, waiting for a bus in the rain. I liked her from the get-go. Just the way she was standing there. She had those large warm eyes, plump rosy cheeks, and a nice nose, neither short nor long. Hers was a kind face but her eyes sparkled with mischief. It was raining fairly hard and her trench coat, made of cheap materials, was drenched. Something about that cheap coat broke my heart. No umbrella and that coat. She looked downtrodden, woebegone, in need of care. I felt like I needed to step into her life and help her out, inject a ray of sunshine. Christ, the rain! All about her was a bunch of bad boys in 211 nylon running suits. They were just hanging, nothing to do, nowhere to go, throwing gang signals, acting bad, making her nervous. Let me tell you, it was some real bad action. I knew this as Blackstone Ranger territory, a notorious crack cocaine zone, and you could see that these jungle bunnies were too hopped up to be affected by the weather. They had their chests puffed out, going about their *bid'ness*, putting on a show. I gave them a severe look to back them off and one of them says, "Man, who are you?"

Still another pipes in, "Motherfucker look like a hairdresser to me. A hey-*dresser*."

They all laughed their asses off, but I ignored this shit and eased up to the girl with my umbrella and in a baritone whisper sang, "*Hello, I love you, won't you tell me your name?*"

She laughed a little and looked me over. I could see a sense of relief roll over her like a wave. "Judith," she says with a cockney accent. "Judith Smith. Who would you be, then?"

I extended my umbrella over her head and told her my name. She called me a real gentleman. Something she was unused to in these parts. I said, "Judith Smith, you look like you could stand to dry out. Look, I'm hungry. I don't wish to sound forward or menacing; I'm a straight guy. Would you care to grab a bite?"

She braced herself and thought it over for a minute and then said, "Sure. I'm famished. I believe I could eat a horse."

I hailed the next cab and as the driver whisked us away from the gangbangers, I told him to take us to Some Like It Hot. It was cold, and steaming with humidity in the taxi. I figured she could do with something spicy and the restaurant was in the general neighborhood. It was a fairly classy place, with a doorman in a red wool overcoat and a pair of white gloves waiting for us under a green canvas canopy. It was a slow night and we were escorted to a table overlooking the street. I made a pretense of looking over the menu but I knew what I wanted. I ordered the Szechuan Chicken No. 5. The way I see it, there are people who climb Everest, ballplayers who strive to hit ninety homers a year, runners trying to crack the three-minute mile, and people who eat five-power Szechuan. The waitress could barely speak English, so when I says, "Number five," she goes off running and a second later the manager comes over in his blue tuxedo and extremely deferential he says, "Mr. Marzuki, you must be mistaken. Number five is *velly huat*. Not just for average Joe-man, Tom, Dick, and Harry."

"That's how I like it," I says. "Hot stuff, babe — can't *get* enough."

Judith E. Smith tittered at yet another appropriately laid-in golden-oldies citation. Heh heh. I was doin' good. I like to work song lyrics into my conversation. My court-appointed shrink says it's a schizophrenic trait but chicks go for it. Meanwhile this restaurant manager is looking at me like I'm crazy. "Number five?" The guy had gone from yellow jaundice to pure white. Chinese Johnny Winter. He was a skinny guy but his hands were plump and he kept stabbing at the menu with his stubby finger. He says, "No, please, sir, this one velly big... *misunnerslandish*." I held firm and away he went in a major Chinese tizzy. He disappeared into the bowels of the restaurant.

Out came the manager's son, who spoke perfect English. We repeated the same conversation. "Number five?! Number *five*? Oh God, oh God, oh God!" I could tell Judith was impressed. She had slid out of her raincoat and started fussing with her hair. Preening behavior. Pretty soon the whole sinister Gang of Four surrounded our table, all of them excited. "*Velly* hot, *velly* hot! Not *adwisable*."

"Calm down, boys. I am Louis E. Marzuki and I can eat anything you throw my way — ground glass, granular Drano — anything. I'm a responsible adult and I'm walking into this with my eyes wide open." I was also going to add that I served in Manchuria with the Second Marines during that protracted conflict. I was going to lay that one in but I didn't want to come off like a braggart.

Judith was impressed. She was in the palm of my hand. I could tell by her body language.

Given the gravity of my request the Gang of Four didn't seem to catch the subtleties of my humor. They agreed to give me No. 5 but made me sign a consent form, in triplicate, absolving them of all responsibility. Had it notarized by the bookkeeper. Turns out they had never seen a common occidental eat authentic five-power Szechuan. Either I was completely insane or some kind of rough customer who was nonetheless charming, polite, charismatic, good-looking, et cetera — the list is long. Judith said, "If they don't want people eating number five, then why is it on the menu?"

It felt good to get out of the rain, but an aura of tense expectation surrounded our small table. We had scarcely placed our order before the waiter appeared with our food. Judith got the spinach island with prawns at No. 1. She took two mouthfuls and had to put down her fork. Tears squirted from her big blue eyes. I asked her what she thought and she said it was like eating a volcano from hell. But then she has to be thinking, *If this is a one and Louie orders a five, what other superpowers must he possess?*

I dug into my Szechuan Chicken and was instantly transformed into a fire-breathing dragon. My throat slammed shut but I didn't let on. I watched Judith Smith swallow a full glass of water and attempt another go at her spinach island. It was too much for her. Her neck spun in concentric circles and she goes, "Louie, I'm on fire!"

"Drinking water makes it worse, luv. Clear your palate with plain rice." The words were barely out of my mouth when the second volley of delayed-action Szechuan chicken heat struck home. The sensation of a flaming napalm conflagration I felt at the back of my throat and oral cavity rose ten thousand degrees into a white phosphorus combustion; from a superficial burn to deep-tissue ignition. Like Judith, I was assailed by a fierce thirst. I gulped green tea, which only made it worse. By the time they got me to the ER, I was almost comatose. Instead of an evening of connubial bliss with the fair lady, I got an ice bath in the hospital hydrotherapy room. Then the ER doctor says, "Mr. Marzuki, your blood pressure is 260 over 195. And your blood work is not good. Your cholesterol is 409 and the triglycerides beyond measure. I'm putting you on Lipitor." With Judith standing there wringing her hands, I forced myself to laugh. "Doc, I'm under a lot of pressure at work but, hey, I'm Louis Edmund Marzuki and I didn't get to where I am in the world by sweating the small stuff. Don't be such an alarmist."

The doctor asked me what sort of work I perform. I think he was just making small talk so he could ogle Judith. I told him that I make hospital deliveries for Rado Labs. "Perhaps you've heard of us. My job is to convey radioactive materials to hospitals in the greater Chicago area. When you get riddled with cancer and all hope is gone, Rado can give you a single radium injection that gives you three months of health. Enough time to get your affairs in order and then...well, brother, then it's all she wrote. You just bought the farm! Our sojourn on this fair planet is brief. Heh, heh, heh."

But what I said was true, I was under pressure. Those motherfuckers at work are always expanding my area because the other drivers can't cut the mustard. They go to old Mr. Reliable but how much can one man stand? I had made two late deliveries that week. From their point of view, you've got a cancer patient on the table and the surgeon and techs all in lead aprons and the conveyer and conveyance are unavoidably tied up in Chicago traffic! After I explained the situation, the ER doctor said, "Mr. Marzuki, I mistook you for an eminent physician, not a deliveryman."

I just shrugged. "Well, Doc," I says, "it's a long story of coulda beens. You see, I had a misspent youth and did a lot of drugs and drinking. I was out there ripping and running. One time I took twenty hits of LSD and went into McDonald's when the ghost of Jim Morrison came up to me, pointed his finger in my face, and said, 'Louis, *never* take drugs again! Take it from one who knows.' I told the Lizard King I would quit — gave him my word! We conversed for about an hour, talked about the Twelve Step Program and so on and then I said, 'Jim, tell me something; what's it like *on the other side?*'

"James Douglas Morrison thought this over for a moment and said, 'It's really great, Louie. You wouldn't believe. I mean, it's totally far out. Completely radical. *Très bien,* man. *Très bien.* But this is no time for you to *break on though to the other side,* Lou. Work your program, man.'"

The doctor said, "Was Mr. Morrison bloated, bearded, and twenty-seven, just as he died?"

I said, "No, he was at the zenith of health, thin, but dressed in sixties garb."

Both Jude and the doctor were blown away by this little vignette, as it not only confirmed their hope for a better world after this one, but also demonstrated my special status with a legend of rock music.

The doctor looks at me and says, "That's amazing! Bizarre, but it has the harrowing ring of utter truth. What else did he say?"

"Well, you know, not a constant chorus of infernal hymns or anything boring but a true garden of luxury where the lion layeth down with the lamb. Pretty much how I had it figured. This was back in '93 and I haven't touched drugs since, that is except for my lithium and the Mellaril. I can get a little cranked up without that therapeutic combo. Boy!"

The ER doctor shook my hand and then he shook Judith's hand and told her, "Mrs. Marzuki, your husband is one of the most intelligent and fascinating persons I have ever met."

Of course Judith wasn't Mrs. Marzuki *then.* It was our first date. I hardly knew her. She was wearing a white blouse and because it was partly wet you could see through it. She had thin shoulders and large breasts — just a humongous set of ta-tas. I couldn't wait to get my hands on them, but of course you never know. Sometimes a woman will look great in clothes and then you get her bra off and find cellulite or something and it's all you can do to go through with the act. This is especially true of redheads. Their pussy hair is weird. My first wife, Shaundra, was like that. If the truth be known, I only married S. because I felt sorry for her.

Shaundra, man, back in those days I was a chef at Never on Sundays and Shaundra was making her way as a waitress. One time she came back to the kitchen in tears. She was extremely distraught. I said, "What is wrong, Shaundra?"

Well, it turns out that Gary Payton when he was still with the Seattle SuperSonics came into town to play the Chicago Bulls. Now he was in her section acting rude and saying insulting things, she said. I have good common sense and am known for my ability for handling difficult people in touchy situations. I said, "Shaun, you go back out there and *demand* an apology." Two minutes later she comes back crying even harder. She *tried*, but it simply didn't work. She didn't have the nerve to pull it off, the ego strength. Disgusted, I stepped away from my chores and said, "I'm going to just have to take care of this myself." And man, did I ever. Here's what happened: I marched out into the restaurant and confronted the high-scoring but often troublesome point guard *mano a mano*. I told Payton that just because he was a celebrity he had no right to act rude to any person be they big or small. I patiently and firmly reminded him that he was a role model for a lot of children and that it wasn't right for him to come into a public establishment and start in with his vulgar trash talking. And he soon saw the error of his ways. By the time I was finished his head hung low in shame and tears were forming in the corners of his eyes. I thought maybe I went too far and because I didn't want him to break out sobbing in the establishment, I demanded that he and his party leave immediately, which they did, chastened to the max! Needless to say, everyone was super impressed. Shaundra later changed the story of this incident to where she was no mere waitress but the *hostess*. And I wasn't the chef but the *dishwasher* and Gary Payton wasn't really Gary Payton but just some "tall black guy emaciated from crack cocaine and AIDS." I mean I can tell a big-ass motherfucking lie like anyone, but my version of the story is what *really happened*. I was benching 380 in those days. Well, fuck her and the horse she rode in on — and she was a horse! Shaundra's ankles were always too strong and her legs were only passable in high heels and sheer stockings. You can sure get sick of a chick coming at you with legs like a Clydesdale. Having her home in on you like a linebacker, bearing down hard — not pleasant.

But I digress. Rado's been all over me not only for two "lates" but also for a series of driving violations. This guy in a red BMW convertible, some kind of olive-skinned camel jockey, pulled in front of me on Lake Shore Drive the other day and when I caught up with him, I took my hands off the wheel and you know, I don't like being crude or anything, but I double-flipped him off. Bingo, a motorcycle cop pulls me over and starts writing me up for reckless driving. Real calm, I said, "Officer, I want you to understand that the man in that red BMW almost caused a five-car collision. He is the true psycho and a menace of the roadway. A road-rage classic, an angry and bitter maniac!"

"Is that right?" the trooper says, a big wiseass.

"Yes," I said. "You know, last night in bed I was reading Cicero where this guy comes along and says, 'And yet, Prometheus, I think you know that reason may be doctor to your wrath.' And Prometheus says, 'Yes, if it chooses well the time for treatment and does not probe the wound that is inflamed.' Perhaps you take my meaning, Officer."

He did, called me a regular philosopher. He put away his ticket pad as I informed him that I was a commercial driver with a priority order of radioactive material for a VIP cancer patient. "As we sit here and banter a sick man lies on the table, dying." The officer looked in the back seat and saw the radioactive cautionary signs on the lead box and said, "Mr. Marzuki, say no more. I'm human and capable of mistakes like any man." He handed me back my license and took off on his motorcycle. I was greatly relieved because another violation and my license would be suspended. Five miles north I saw him writing a ticket to the shitheel in the BMW. I honked as I passed and the police officer gave me the thumbs-up signal and flashed a big smile. Little good it did. I was twenty-eight minutes late and placed on probation by the chief pharmacist at Rado. "Fuck up one more time, Marzuki, and your lazy ass is on the street," he says.

Charles Bronson, the actor, is a good pal of mine. You know, it's probably no secret but Charlie likes the ladies as I do. We like to go down to Mexico and party with Hollywood starlets, in the nude. Charles is eight inches hard and my wanger is ten. We have really great times in Mexico and we've been doing this since God knows when. Sometimes he will just pop by to talk about philosophy or to pick my brain about world events and the meaning of life. A great chess player is Charles. Not my caliber but damn close! Judith calls this all a "Walter Mitty fantasy." I won't lie, we went through some tough times after that romantic first date and she quit believing in me.

Sometimes Judith can be harder than nails and she will just *ride my ass*. She let herself go after we got married and put on some major poundage. It is my bane! Seven wives and all of them fatsoes! The fat gave her energy — turned into a carping fishwife, a highly dominant woman of the sort who can only respond to men that are stronger than her. Men who are confident at every level of thought and action. Hugh Hefner and I have had many discussions on this very subject. Hef has made a life study of the opposite sex. Ordinarily I can chill Judith out with a love poem and five or six dozen roses, but when we went to the Marzuki family reunion in Skokie last week, my stupid brother, Calvin, threw food in my mother's face. Jesus, what a dick! Well, he was completely out of control on Pabst Blue Ribbon. I had to do something so I hopped on the bastard, threw him out the window, and then ten cop cars show up. It took eighteen officers to pull me off of Calvin. Eighteen, and that is no lie. During the bloody scuffle, the officer in charge said, "Louis, please listen to reason; you're going to kill him and go to jail. It's not worth it for a man of your caliber to throw it all away over a senseless weekend beef." He was right.

They wanted to cuff me and chain me in leg irons but when I gave the officer in charge my word to behave, I was taken to the station without restraints. In fact I rode to the precinct building with the homicide detective, who said he never saw such a display of martial arts short of a Jackie Chan flick! Eighteen officers on one man! Judith followed along in the Morris Minor to bail me out. She reminded me that this was the fourth straight Marzuki reunion that had ended in a brawl. (Okay, I'm one-fourth Native American and sometimes I forget my own strength and fighting prowess *and* sometimes I forget my medication.) After I posted bail, I took Judith to Vito's. I was formerly the head chef there and in all modesty I must confess that my Alfredo sauce put them on the map — made them famous! (They stole the patent on it but hell, that's all water under the bridge. I let bygones be bygones.) At Vito's Judith ordered a mai tai that was too sweet and the next thing you know, I'm behind the bar fixing drinks. I'm a pretty good mixologist. (Hef used to love what I could do with rum and Pepsi, begged me to come work at the mansion back in the old days, but I was writing my novel at the time and had to turn him down.) So, as I said, I got pretty creative behind the bar and, meanwhile, Judy got laced. Alcohol was the bridge that led her into a really bad, high-dominance mood. There are times when you realize that your very marriage can slip into eternal ruin if you do not immediately say or do the exactly right thing. Like *duh*, I got some big experience there? Well, that night at Vito's, after the brawl and the jailing and her sitting alone drinking solitary mai tais — this was one of those moments. I reached deep down into the heart of my Marzuki soul. I did not come up with lyrical poetry. Words were simply not sufficient; like the samurai that I am, I chose action. The next thing you know we were back at Some Like It Hot. I told her I lost four hours' time on the job with Rado. She's all pissed, worried I'm going to get canned. But, man, I don't even know what happened. One minute you're fine and the next, four hours is gone! Twilight Zone gone. What happened to the time? Weird. I just remember coming to on Lake Shore Drive. I had a dull headache and my face lay against the steering wheel of the Morris Minor. One minute it's 8 A.M. and the next thing you know it's high noon. I missed a shitload of deliveries. This is what I tell Judith. She lit up a Marlboro Light and narrowed her huge eyes into angry little razor slits. She gets this bored sarcastic voice and says, "Tell your boss it was a UFO abduction." This is not as ridiculous as it sounds. In fact, it was highly likely. I sort of remember a probelike object being stuck into my liver by these little dudes in silver suits with big eyes. Ho, you say! But it's true! I don't embellish or self-aggrandize. I show my warts. The court-appointed shrink says I have borderline-personality disorder that occasionally slides away from hard reality into the dark world of psychosis. He heard my story and seemed to think I flipped out and lost four hours to madness, not a UFO. Was I on my meds? "'No? Well, sorta?' Aha, Louis! Proof positive! I hope you haven't been drinking again!" Goddamn it, the bastard. I only see him because of the court order, though I must confess the last time I shit-canned the lithium, some very bad things happened and I got a look at the dark pit of my soul. Here is how it went down, years ago: I maxed out my Master Charge and got a sound system installed in the Morris Minor. Top of the line. I parked it in back of the kitchen. This is back in the days when I *was* washing dishes. I just got through cleaning out the grease trap, stepped outside for a smoke, and there sat the Morris with four flat tires, my sound system gone, and a pair of smashed headlights in the bargain. I had to hump it home that night, six miles. Six miles through the South Side of Chicago. Right through the heart of Blackstone Ranger territory. I didn't give a shit, the way I was feeling I wished a whole pack of them would try to attack me! Let's get it on. I was ready to rumble.

Well, I had to pass through this war zone before I got to my neighborhood. It was early fall and I took a little shortcut through some abandoned projects. Anyhow, I'm going along wondering where in the fuck is my Higher Power? Why is life so goddamned hard? Why was I born? You dig? Why wasn't I *consulted*? I'm having thoughts of this nature when I see a light on in a window. There's no electricity but when I get near there I look inside and see a guy sitting at the table reading the Big Blue Book by a gas lantern. He was a skinny guy in a grungy singlet. Just kicked off a pair of greasy boots. Holes in his socks. Like me, just off work. I see they got a big kerosene heater in there. A woman who looked like she just woke up was cooking over a propane stove. She was frying eggs, Spam, and potatoes. I saw a jar of Tabasco sauce on the table. Lightweight fare but it caught my interest. I just stood there on the sidewalk and watched. The guy lit an Old Gold and closed the Blue Book. His arms were covered in tattoos and I could see track marks over his veins. The woman, who was stabbing at the eggs with a spatula, didn't look like a user to me. She could have been, I don't know. The man got up and poured himself a cup of coffee. He had a fresh heart-shaped tattoo on his left deltoid that read BOBBY AND LAURA, ETERNAL LOVE. As Laura (?) was dishing out the food, Bobby got up, scratching his balls. He walked over to Laura and kissed her on the back of the neck, giving her a little pat on the butt. Then he flipped on a little black-and-white TV that was hooked up to a DieHard battery. A condemned building, at least one ex-junkie, and both of them were carrying some hard miles but you could also tell they loved each other. What an unlikely but well-ordered love nest they had fabricated! When I passed the building in the light of day their apartment showed no signs of life whatever. There was a padlock on the door. I wondered if I had dreamed it all. Crossing through those projects was like taking a trip through Chernobyl after the meltdown. It was the site of utter desolation, but the next night at two in the morning I saw the light again and looked in on another compelling domestic scene. Bobby had got his boots off again, and sat at the table eating his Spam and eggs. For the first time I noticed a little red-and-white-checkered oilcloth on the table. A single candle burned in an empty Chianti bottle. Bob had his left hand on the Big Book and was reading an uplifting passage to his eternal love, Laura, who sat right at his side smoking a cigarette. He looked up from the book and said something in addendum that made her laugh. Then she reached over and patted his forearm. There I was, the loneliest guy on the planet, just standing there watching them. I realized that I was pulling for them so hard that my heart was near to bursting. And just like that I found myself sobbing. I haven't cried since I was eight years old. I guess I was feeling sorry for myself because I wanted what they had and also I was feeling sorry for every miserable creature in the world, thinking that if they might be laughing now, riding high or whatever, it will all turn to shit in the end. I appealed to the God of Rock and Roll but I got no hour-long shit session this time. I got no consolation. I got zip. I looked up in the sky, railing at heaven, "Jimbo! Morrison! Hey, man, check it out. We are all working the program down here. They got the Big Book out. How about a little help for your boy, Louis?" Nothing. I made a choking sound and Bobby got up and looked out the window. I quickly made off. Why couldn't I find a woman who loved me like that? Why did it always go so bad? I know I'm half nuts but you would think there would be someone out there. It had been five years since I found Judith standing in the rain waiting for the bus. But for all of it, I only *knew* Judith those first few moments when I offered her my umbrella. Now at Vito's I found myself desperate to reconnect with her. I'm all jacked up feeling impossible notions roiling up from deep down inside me and I can't turn them off. I can't shut them down. Cannot exercise a reasonable amount of disaster containment. Talk about your volcano from hell! What kind of low-self-esteem asshole pulls the sort of shit I do? How can I see myself truly one moment in a light-year and then "through a glass darkly" forever after? One bright flash of insight and then a century of blackness. Why does nothing float up from the depths other than bad? Why can't we reach the Truth as the crow flyeth? Why must I traverse the underworld roaming in *such a wilderness of pain*, Jimbo, how about a little help?

The Gang of Four came out to greet me and Judith. "Long time, no see. How very good to have you back. What a delight! Whatever you want is on the house, Mr. Marzuki." After all, Louis Marzuki was pretty much legend, come to think of it.

Suddenly all my bad thoughts vanished. It was as if I had been invited back into the brotherhood of mankind. They were just some Chinese waiters but it didn't matter, I espied visions of glory. Wow! Snap your fingers. It can happen that fast. Sir Edmund Marzuki. I slipped into the men's room and coated my throat with a little olive oil I purloined from Vito's. When the waiter brought our food, not only the Gang of Four but a good many patrons hovered nearby to see me patiently savor the palate-blistering goodness of the No. 5 Szechuan Chicken.

"*Heut* enough, Mr. Marzuki?" the manager inquired.

"Fair," I said, pulling a bottle of Mongolian Fire Oil from my jacket. I shook a copious quantity on a spring roll and devoured it in two bites.

Hard-as-nails Judith thought some sort of fakery was going on and asked for a sample bite. She barely got it down before she dropped her chopsticks and violently cocked her head to the side as her fingers reached up for her neck. I heard something pop like she broke her collarbone or cervical spine. She seemed frozen in this posture, looking like a woman dangling from the gallows in a hanging gone awry. "Wah!" she goes, like Jackie Gleason in some skit from *The Honeymooners*. Another volcano from hell! Ah ha ha ha!

"Louie, you ain't taking your lithium," she says in a gasp. And then she's out in a Szechuan stupor.

Before we carried her out to the car I saw a glimmer of recognition in her eyes that acknowledged, yes, I was a Marzuki through and through and that the entree was, in fact, the No. 5 Szechuan. It was an unguarded look of real affection and I'm delighted to report that Judith has subsequently made a complete recovery. Also, I might add, to this day I have not heard a single cross word from this woman. It's been a day shy of a week and nary a peep. In the medical world that's pretty much considered a complete and total cure. Tra la. Heh heh. I got the world on a string. Seven times is a charm.

A Merry Little Christmas

FROM: tj34
TO: CC14
DATE SENT: December 23, 1998
SUBJECT: Re: Have Yourself a Merry Little Christmas!

Feliz Navidad and just what in the fuck are you trying to pull here? Christ! Calling me at my house?!!! Drunk on your ass?!!! Two in the morning?!!! Right after the bars close?!!! What were you thinking? What can I do after someone pulls a number like that except change the phone number and sever all contact? Crazy-ass bitch. Goddamn it, I don't care how fucking drunk you get, that's something you just do not do *ever* no matter what happens. Never! Ever! It's not permissible. I was fucking ready to fucking kill you. Now I have to memorize two new phone numbers, and for this old dog new tricks come hard. So tell me, are you proud of yourself? Did you actually think you could win me back with a caper like that? Stupid fucking psycho bitch. If I was lovesick no matter how bad, I would never do what you did. There are rules. I'm not going to wreck *your* marriage, suck marriage though it may be. This is absolutely my last contact with you. This is absolute and unequivocal. I'm closing your ignominious file today; it's over!

You must realize that after that drunken-ass screaming insane bullshit phone call waking up everyone in the fucking house, I

can never trust you again — you crossed the line. I do *like* you and think of you fondly — it's just over. Anyhow, the whole affair was bullshit. I was really going after your pal, Lisa, the psychiatrist. She was the one I was chasing and you kind of interjected yourself. I really hate it, the way you did that and then got all fucking clingy dependent. How was I going to come on to Lisa after that? Your whole insecure jealousy thing is virtual paranoia. You should take Thorazine or something. I'm serious. So long, pretty baby — and Feliz Navidad. Have a holly jolly Christmas,
As always, I remain your sweet potato,
Xxxxs
Maximilian Schell
P.S. Please delete this email message immediately.

TO: CC14
RE: Lisa Knows About Your Tawdry Unnatural Desires
DATE SENT: December 26, 1998

I can't believe you told Lisa I was hot for her. Shit! Why did she break up with that asshole? Don't tell me. What else did she tell you? I want to savor every detail. I'm in Oxford, MS. Staying in Faulkner's well-preserved house. Wm. never was much of a screenwriter and I don't know a soul who's read his books. Overrated, doncha think?
Love,
Uncle Ho

TO: CC14
RE: Have Yourself a Merry Little Christmas!
DATE SENT: December 31, 1998

Look, perhaps I did go too far, but you have to stop making these crazy threats. And calling up Lisa was not a good move. True, I did kiss her, but it was just one of those one-time things. Maybe you should tell her how you called me up at 2 A.M.: "Motherfucker! I hate you, you fucking cocksucker! I don't care if I wake up the whole fucking house — I hate you. You ruined my life!" Tell Lisa that. Tell how you stormed and raged like a fucking maniac. You don't think people in bed next to someone can't hear screaming over a telephone? Jesus! Talk about uncalled for.

Nonetheless I'm slightly sorry. I do have a measure of empathy and compassion. But you knew what I was when you got into it with me. You were forewarned. Now you say you're dicking Seth Holmes, that cornball anesthesiologist? You better watch out. You'll get caught and Bob will slap divorce papers on your ass before you can pull your panties back on. Really. You're a fucking amateur, babe. You don't want a divorce, believe me. So cool your jets. Okay? And don't try to track me down again through the studio. My agent informed them never to disclose my whereabouts. Chill! You'll be fine,

Sonny Barger

TO: CC14
RE: Oh Yeah! Well, You Can Kiss My Ass!
DATE SENT: January 26, 1999

Hey, babe, calm the fuck down. I didn't say you were insane per se. It's just a figure of speech. Screwing a new guy? You're playing with fire. Didn't I tell you to watch your ass? Of course Bob *suspects* something. You *changed* your look. You are *never* home. That "on call" bullshit only goes so far. You are violating your pattern and you don't know how obvious it is even to the unthinking dullards of the world. You wanna know something else? The way they really can tell you're fucking somebody? Sex is different, that's how. You can keep the same schedule and so on but it's different. That's the giveaway beyond. But it's not conclusive eleventh-hour Perry Mason courtroom testimony. Bob doesn't want to believe it. It's your job to allay his fears. Whatever you do, admit to nothing. Deny it! He isn't going to go anywhere. He's just blowing off steam. It will pass. Just play it cool, okay?

Yours,
Dr. Zarkov

TO: CC14
RE: Ace, Man, You Are One Stupid Asshole!
DATE SENT: January 29, 1999

Look, if the little Bobcat interrogates you, gets a little rowdy, and smashes some furniture, a few priceless antiques — it only means that he loves you. Whatever you do, don't confess and don't knuckle under. I know you're guilty, feel like Hester Prynne and all of that, but don't let it show. For Christ's sake. Just tell him to go fuck himself. He hasn't got aerial photography. It's all paranoid conjecture. The green-eyed monster has got Bobby-boy in its clutches, but cool out. He's a dependent personality. He won't leave you. Guaranteed. You can take that one to the bank.

Hang in,
Xxxxs
Ace

TO: CC14
RE: He Did It! He Packed the Samsonite and Blew Town!
DATE SENT: February 2, 1999

Hey, babe, so sue me, I was wrong. But he'll be back. Three days max. And this is your story: You were having a late snack with a colleague after a long shift. That's *all* it was. Perfectly innocent. Give Bob shit for following you. What kind of crap is that, anyhow? Who is this new guy, anyhow? You said he was a resident. How old is he? Is he hot?

Zarkov

TO: CC14
RE: One-Night Stand
DATE SENT: February 4, 1999

A one-night stand. Right! Well, I told you that you would get caught if you weren't careful — but here's the good news: You weren't really caught! How many times do I have to tell you this?

342 · NEW STORIES

342 · NEW STORIES

It's like talking to a brick wall. You deny everything. All you were seen doing is having a snack. You weren't holding hands in the restaurant, were you? No. You're just sitting there with stars in your eyes. Well, that's not getting caught, baby. Is this new one a surgeon? How tall is he?

James Douglas Morrison

TO: CC14
RE: Jealous
DATE SENT: February 7, 1999

No, I am not jealous, and if that's what is motivating this bullshit hanky-panky, you can forget it! What does Lisa think? Are you giving her the blow-by-blow? What kind of shit-for-brains shrink is she, anyhow? Use that high-priced intellect of yours. Be logical.

Meanwhile, I've been getting back into my novel these last few weeks. Novel? Sonnets? Corporate advertisements? — all of these things are preferable to scriptwriting.

Ming of Mongo

TO: CC14
RE RE RE: Happy Valentine's Day!
DATE SENT: February 14, 1999

Baby, this is ridiculous. I *couldn't* read all your emails. You just hit me with the whole Library of Congress! I didn't write back not because you are pathetic but because each time I write back, you fucking flip.

Yours truly,

Captain Torch

P.S. Do not scan photos and send them to me. It's obvious that your new look is an attempt to transform yourself into a second Lisa. You're not her. You looked fine the old way. This new look *is* pathetic. I mean (LOL) — it's not you. Dig? Assemble your senses and quit pulling crap.

TO: CC14
RE: Malicious Slander
DATE SENT: February 16, 1999

In no way, shape, or form do you appear in the book, I swear!
And Lisa neither. Jesus, baby! How crass do you think I am?
Xxxs
A.

TO: CC14
RE: Touching Reunion
DATE SENT: February 17, 1999

I told you Bob would come back and I also told you you
would despise him if he did. But look at it like this — you were
totally freaked when he walked — a fucking basket case. I don't
know how you can be so cool in the ER and such a hysteric
in real life. You should take a lesson from Benjamin Franklin
and eradicate jealousy from your list of emotions. If you can do
that, great deeds await you, babe. As for this resident you're dicking — it's simple infatuation and it will pass. The only way for
two people to live happily ever after is for them to get killed in
a car crash on their third date. I mean, name the happy couples
you know — you can probably count them on one hand. Falling
in love is extremely hazardous. Just don't expect anything from
people and enjoy them while it lasts. As for Bob — fuck Bob.
He's a loser. Divorce him.

Hey, last night I fucked a blond lawyer. Harvard grad. Patrician.
Not bad for a greaseball, huh?
Yrs,
Da Fonz

TO: CC14
RE: Nice Reviews, Tiger
DATE SENT: February 22, 1999

Yeah: *Time, Newsweek, People, USA Today, Boston Globe* — all raves. Nielsens are good. Another Emmy? Well, don't be surprised, I won't be. Anyhow, thank you, my dear. One irksome development: Did you see the *LA Times* review? The script got trashed. Reviewers? Some asshole who wants to be a scriptwriter and can't hack it, pissed off at the whole world. Well, fuck him! I just might go look up the cocksucker and inject a little terror in his life. Or hire some thugs to do it for me.

    Yrs,
    Wild Bill

TO: CC14
RE: Now What Do I Do?
DATE SENT: February 28, 1999

    Jesus, not another one! Well, don't let the resident know. You have to keep your victims isolated. Remember: *You* are the center of the universe and they are mere satellites. Isolate him. Magnetic Seth and the fresh resident must never meet. And yes, it is a wicked web, but you're an energetic little spider. Go out there and repair that web on a daily basis. Keep the victims isolated and keep that net in good repair. Fun, isn't it? I'm proud of you. Just watch out for space debris — comets, meteor dust, and the rusting hulks of Citroën Deux Chevaux.

    So we're shooting in Miami this week and it is hotter than a motherfucker. The Diet Pepsis in my bar cabinet are like only ten ounces at four bucks a crack! I can drink five at once. I dunno, I feel guilty drinking fifty dollars' worth of soda before lunch. Apart from screwing starlets, what I like best about location shooting is the sound of that room service cart jingling down the hall, you know? The clatter of bone china and the aroma of fresh coffee. Here comes one now. Gotta go.

    Xxxs
    Richard # III

TO: CC14
RE: Bob Thinks I'm Fucking Lisa!
DATE SENT: March 4, 1999

LOL — babe, it's better that he thinks you're a dyke, believe me. A whole lot easier on his ego. Personally, I think he just went to the lawyer to blow off steam. He is hurt and he wants to strike back. It's the oldest story in the world. No matter what, he's not going to divorce you. And so what if he does? I don't know why you are so hot for that old house anyhow; it's nothing but work, and you're never there. Get yourself a little fuckpad and pay back your medical school loans. Power to the people, babe. I gotta go.
Eldridge

TO: CC14
RE: I *Am* Fucking Lisa!
DATE SENT: March 5, 1999

You, a dyke? No way. Jesus, give me a break! Look, I know you're stressed out. These things happen. It doesn't mean you're some hard-core lesbian. Trust me, I know you better than you know yourself. But just the same: My God! Is Lisa a good fuck?
Your partner in crime,
Ace
P.S. What are the kids at the Foxhead saying about the show?

TO: CC14
RE: Three-Way Sex: Are You Up to It, Sport?
DATE SENT: March 6, 1999

Whoa! Are you *shitting* me? Yeah! I'm up for it. Boing! Way up! LOL. Señor Caligula is up for most anything. A three-way sounds absolutely great! Tell me, though, what are Lisa's tits like? She hasn't got tobacco-brown nipples, has she? That just makes it impossible for me. It ruins everything. She's very fair-skinned, so I doubt this will be a problem. But please advise me at the first possible opportunity.

Ready and Rarin',

Yrs,

Suckman

TO: CC14

RE: C Cups, Pink Nipples

DATE SENT: March 7, 1999

God! C cups! Pink and well formed! I thought so! I thought so! Goddamn. Man! I'm in heaven! Crack out the Viagra. Heh heh. And well formed, too! Boy! Shit. Usually at thirty, they start to sag. Well, maybe she had a tit job. Didn't she run with a cosmetic surgeon for a time? Jeez, this sounds too good to be true. I can't wait. Just tell me this: If you two are such dedicated lesbians, why do you want to fuck me? You said she gives you multiple orgasms. I didn't give you multiple orgasms. What's the deal, comrade?

V. I. Lenin

TO: CC14

RE: Divorce Papers

DATE SENT: March 8, 1999

Babe, you're better off without the sorry-ass motherfucker; good riddance! Bob was nothing but "poor me." Dump him. Put the house on the market and get on with it.

Your loving crisis counselor,

Maynard G. Krebs

TO: CC14

RE: Ovulation

DATE SENT: March 9, 1999

I knew there had to be a catch. And I can't believe Lisa, either. How did this plan get hatched? You suddenly want me to knock you both up so you can be single parents? Is Lisa stealing drugs from the meds cabinet? Anesthesiologists will do that — and she hangs with your guy Seth. He's probably got a shitload of good stuff. Or have you both lost your minds? Flipped out completely? Goddamn! I think those long shifts in the ER are taking their toll on you. Burnout. Get a grip on yourself, woman.

Zamboni, King of the Kongo

TO: CC14
RE: Contracts
DATE SENT: March 11, 1999

Look, I'm going to be in town one night. Even if by some miracle of chance you're both ovulating, I'm not going to get you both pregnant. It's statistically unlikely. I mean, you're the doctors. Figure. And contract or no, I'm going to know that I've got kids — kids living with lesbian parents. This is the stupidest thing I've ever heard of. I quit screwing physicians a long time ago as most of them are out of touch, fucking psychotic. What if one of you gets pissed and decides to sue for child support? I've been out there too many years to fall for this bullshit. The answer is no!

Sincerely,
Ace

TO: CC14
RE: Oh Baby, Please Please Me
DATE SENT: March 13, 1999

Okay, here are the rules: It has to be all natural. I'm not leaving sperm samples. And remember: Don't let my good looks fool you, writers are crazy. These kids are going to be getting some fucked-up genes. And you are no paragon of mental health either, dear heart. I'm not the one who has to live out the consequences; you are. Think about that. Christ, the whole idea of this reduces me to a piece of meat. It's demeaning. You're audacious, babe. You're coming up in the world. You're like...almost totally amoral. Congrats!

Rocky Balboa

TO: CC14
RE: Lisa
DATE SENT: March 14, 1999

No, I said I could have fallen for Lisa *at that time*. Things change. I'm not — look, in light of what's happened, I'm certainly not going to fall in love with her, okay? As to who gets fucked first, let's just play it by ear. I've got to run. I'm doing a radio interview. San Francisco has so many good places to eat, but try and find a parking spot. It can't be done. LOL.

Yrs,

Frederick J. Flintstone

TO: CC14
RE: The Big Day
DATE SENT: March 15, 1999

I'm at a computer room over at Stanford killing time before the flight. Four — well, actually three — chicks came on to me in Palo Alto. You know the one about the Polish chick who tried to get ahead by fucking the scriptwriter? LOL. Pure power. Anyhow, I declined some true delectables so I could get back to my room and be well rested for tomorrow night. It made me sick to do it. And then, instead of sleeping — the couple in the next room got into a fight and kept me up all night. Well, I'll do my very best to get the job done.

Love,

Iago

P.S. Give my regards to Lisa. ROFL.

TO: CC14
RE: Hey There, Big Boy, You Fucked Our Brains Out
DATE SENT: March 17, 1999

No, dear heart, the both of you fucked *my* brains out. LOL. That was a fantastic experience. I think it's Darwinian or something when you screw with the intent to have kids. Very affirming. And her tits were even better than advertised. Christ! I came six times. What a glorious night! Thank God we're in Chicago for two days. I gotta catch up on my sleep. I'm all fucked out!

Your boy,

Slick

P.S. I'm sorry I had to leave the party so early. ROFL! Heh heh.

TO: CC14
RE: Beware the Ides
DATE SENT: March 22, 1999

Shit! Back home with a deadline. That tour took it all out of me. Woe is Aceman. I feel vile and I hate everybody in the entire world including myself. Thank God the season is over.

Yrs,

Big Daddy

TO: CC14
RE: Bingo!
DATE SENT: May 15, 1999

Both on the same day? Well, you were both fucked on the same night; it only makes sense, doesn't it? I mean, in a highly improbable way. Anyhow, congrats (I guess). If Lisa gives up her practice to take care of the kids — I mean *what*? Who is the catcher and who is the pitcher in this deal? I know shrinks don't make that much relative to surgeons, but she has a bold personality. I figured she would be assertive in bed. I guess it's none of my business.

Yrs,

Chas. Manson

P.S. Screwing Bob just after I left town was a masterstroke. Now you can nail him for child support. Baby, that's cold. Way to go.

You are truly dedicated in service to the Master, Lucifer. You may even be due for a promotion soon. I'm sensing real hellish evil in you, dear heart. It's such an adorable quality. Cultivate it.

P.P.S. How can you be so sure he won't ask for a DNA test?

TO: CC14
RE: So Horny I Could Die
DATE SENT: May 22, 1999

You fucked another young buck! I didn't think you were a dedicated dyke. I never bought that. Just remember, web repair. Use your head. If you are now screwing a hot-piece-of-ass intern on the floor, be very careful. It's a small town and an even smaller hospital. Also, do not change your sex habits with Lisa. If she finds out, the whole shitting deal will go down the drain. A med student is not marriage material, babe. Also, tell me this: Do guys like dating pregnant women? The times they are a-changin'. Indeed! Befuddled. I must bring myself up to speed.

Alistair Cooke

TO: CC14
RE: Ultrasound Confirms It: Girls
DATE SENT: August 5, 1999

Hey, if you guys are happy, I'm happy. I already told you, I don't plan on being an active father. I doubt that I will ever even meet the kids. Don't give me reports. I don't want that kind of involvement. I don't want guilt and I don't want attachment. Seriously,

Josef Mengele

TO: CC14
RE: Caught!
DATE SENT: September 4, 1999

Flagrante delicto, huh? At least Lisa was cool about it. Remember how vindictive and pissy Bob was? That this guy is an intern from Salt Lake City is all to the good. Christ, he's not a fucking Mormon, is he? Anyhow, Lisa isn't going to be threatened by a teenybopper. But isolate your victims and maintain web repair. And always remember this: *You* are the center of the universe and *they* are the satellites. If you hold that thought, there is no conquest that is beyond you. Coolio, no?

Ace

TO: CC14
RE: Retaliation
DATE SENT: September 11, 1999

After the shock wave of betrayal wears off, then comes the anger, babe. Lisa wanted to get even, that's all. I wouldn't make too much of it. And listen: You weren't keeping the web under control, it's your own fault.

Hey! What's the deal anyhow — are guys suddenly into hitting on chicks that are six months pregnant? Maybe I just don't know the score anymore. Even an experienced evildoer such as myself has blind spots and makes mistakes. She'll come crawling back. Don't you worry, baby.

Johnny Ringo

P.S. I just finished a motherfucker of a rewrite job. It was a suck-ass from start to finish. The producer is always saying "Breathe some life into this piece of shit." I'm not kidding; this is the most nonglamorous profession in the world. I want to get back on the novel.

TO: CC14
RE: Encouragement
DATE SENT: October 19, 1999

Thanks, babe. It was nice to hear from you. I don't know what the fuck is wrong with me anymore. I can't focus on a single thing. My skull feels like it's got rancid malted milk balls rolling around inside it. I put my .337 in the attic, in case I get the impulse to shoot myself. It takes so long to get into the attic, I'll think better of it before I get to the pistol. Suicide really isn't me in spite of the family history. Maybe that's because I'm just a big chickenshit. Maybe it is the ultimate act of nobility. Yes, given a moment to reflect — a breather from the onslaught of life's travail — and I'm a philosophical individual.

Used and confused,
Algonquin J. Calhoun

TO: CC14
RE: Lisa
DATE SENT: November 1, 1999

Remember, babe, I actually don't know Lisa all that well. You were the one that said she was a dyke. Maybe because she's pregnant, she has an urge to have a husband suddenly. Honestly, she wasn't that hot of a fuck. I mean, to me it seemed like I was fucking a straight-out man-hating lesbian. Three-ways seldom work. They involve too much tension and jealousy unless everyone is drugged and drunk out of their minds. Or complete degenerates. Anyhow, Lisa wasn't into me all that much and — whatever else you say about me — I'm an experienced lover. Man, then she stands on her head after I came in her. That was kind of strange, no? She must really want a kid to let my greasy lips press against her own. She wouldn't French. But standing on her head? I thought I had seen it all until that one. Don't get jealous again. (Read a Ben Franklin book and eradicate that emotion from your personality.) Personally, my guess is that this is a temporary thing with her. Most men don't want to marry a woman carrying some other guy's kid, you know? This guy will get sick of her, I'm sure of it. Anyhow, keep me informed. If I didn't have such high self-esteem and such supreme confidence, she would have made me feel like a reptile. So, fuck her.

Satan

TO: CC14
RE: Tears on My Pillow
DATE SENT: November 3, 1999

Heh heh! I told you she was a dyke! She was just getting even with you and it got out of hand. That is why it is so essential that you care for and maintain the wicked web on a daily basis. Lisa is just a satellite. So don't act overly thrilled because she cried her heart out to you. Show some frost.

Yrs,

Duke

P.S. How did you give her seven orgasms? I mean, are you a couple of Chinese acrobats all of a sudden? Do you use vibrators? Butt plugs? Oral sex with Altoids? *What?* Let me mention one other thing: I don't want to introduce negatives, but consider this with an open mind: You are not a dyke. Not really. Once the motherhood thing becomes routine, don't be surprised if you find yourself pining over some guy. And if that happens, act with restraint. Ignore the mood swings and whatnot. You must always let the head rule over the dictates of the heart if you want to play this game.

Concerned,

Earl, the Duke of

TO: CC14
RE: Any Day Now
DATE SENT: December 15, 1999

The ninth month is *supposed* to suck. Quit your goddamn fucking and bitching. Hey, check it out — I think I finally found the right voice for this fucking novel. *Finally!*

A

TO: CC14
RE: Good on Ya, Sport
DATE SENT: December 16, 1999

Thanks, babe. I *am* a sportin' man. No doubt about it. And I'm really into this novel. The work. It's all about the *work*. The rest is bullshit. Man, I feel great; this is the best part. The part I really like. My fingers are scorching the keyboard. I'm just a fucking conduit now. All the angst is gone. My mind is clicking at levels unsurpassed. You might say I'm experiencing my personal best. But, really, I'm humble. I take no credit. It all comes from the Holy Spirit and all the credit belongs to God. That's no lie. Praised be his name! I'm just his servant. But shit, I wrote twelve thousand words last night. Fucking great stuff, too. Man! I am a genius! Over and Out!

Slim

TO: CC14
RE: Hannah Marie
DATE SENT: December 21, 1999

Lisa got what she wanted. And your turn is coming. Shit, I can't believe she cursed *me* through labor. I thought that Lamaze shit was a fad from the eighties or something. When it's your turn, I advise you to avail yourself of painkillers, or get a spinal block. Why suffer needlessly?

Yrs,

Dukester

P.S. Do not tell me the kid's name. I don't want to know names, remember? That was part of the deal. Don't start violating rules this early in the game. I know you're a woman and have poor impulse control, but don't fucking do it. I'm serious.

Duke

TO: CC14
RE: 19,000 Words
DATE SENT: December 22, 1999

Hey, I'm a genius, what more can I tell you? Not only that, I've got myself a new little baby — you know, a "baby." LOL. She's cute as hell. When I feel this good I have so much confidence I can pick them up in supermarkets, take them home, and fuck them on the floor while the ice cream melts in the grocery bag. Heh heh.

Nookie. To get it, you will tell any lie, do whatever — the feeling of power is so incredible. I'm totally stoked. I have never been so happy in all my life. It's like the veil has been lifted and I can suddenly see. Life is grand, babe! I'm a happy fucking guy.

Yrs,

Hanoi Harry

TO: CC14
RE: New Babies
DATE SENT: December 23, 1999

Hey, babe. *Pissy?* Don't get that way. It's just pussy. I told you that our three-way in Iowa City was all about you. Lisa was a flop. You were the one. You were the star. This new stuff is just fool's play. A diversion. Frivolous folly.

Those ugly things I said a year ago when you got crazy on me were in self-defense. They were calculated to bring you to your senses. I didn't *mean* any of it. The sex we had before you freaked out was incredible. We did it like every night for six months and never missed a night, as I recall. Are those the actions of a guy who wasn't turned on? Of a guy who wasn't absolutely crazy about you? Come on. Follow the inspiration of Buddha and waketh thou up!

Kung Fuck

P.S. Can't they induce labor? How overdue are you?

TO: CC14
RE: 10 lbs. 9 oz.
DATE SENT: December 28, 1999

Hurrah! It's over. Cesarean, huh? And on Christmas Day yet. I'm sorry it was so long, and you had to go through pain and all, but being born on Christmas has to be an upper. She will one day piss and moan because of the presents all coming on the same day, but secretly, she'll be grateful. It's a very good omen, if you ask me. Congrats, doll. I hope this makes you happy.

Yrs,

Stagger Adam Lee Huxtable

P.S. Did you get the check? I know you're too proud to ask but I got all this advance money for the new season — for once I've got *too much* money and since you don't, I wanted you to have it. You shouldn't go back to work until you are strong again, and you shouldn't pull such long shifts anymore. You have to learn how to take better care of yourself now. Pace yourself. I read that doctors have a life expectancy of sixty because of the hours they put in. Also, take note: You already know this, I'm sure, but babies that weigh over ten pounds often become diabetic. I don't want to sound like a worrywart, but feed this kid sushi and don't let either one of the girls get into junk food when they turn four and see all the other kids wolfing it down. I'm really happy for all of you. Really am. Thanks for not telling me the name. I have to go my own way and I don't want to know the name. Thanks for respecting that.

P.P.S. You didn't name her LaDonna or Chandelle or some shit like that, did you? ROFL.

P.P.P.S. My own baby (the novel) is now three-quarters finished. I've got the voice down and the characters have taken on a life of their own. I'll just see where it leads. It's great fun, only they don't like to print fat books anymore because of the paper costs. Well, it's too good not to print. I've gotten so high on this goddamn book that I know soon I'm going to get exactly that low. It's some kind of universal law. I mean, with the baby — you have hope and joy. You have unconditional love looking at you. What a great Christmas present, huh? I was secretly regretting this whole thing until I got your message today. Now I'm truly glad. I had a rare unselfish moment. Careful there, Ace. The next thing you know, you'll be volunteering at soup kitchens. LOL.

Yours, the one and the only,

Aceman

P.S. What actually did you name her? Forget what I said about not wanting to know; I want to know.

TO: CC14
SUBJECT: Love You Madly, Need You Badly
DATE SENT: December 31, 1999

Dear Carol,

Why aren't you answering my messages? Did your computer crash with the millennium bug? Total cataclysm isn't supposed to happen until tomorrow. Are you okay? What's going on? Your phone number, I see, is hereby unlisted. I called the goddamn hospital — I even called Bob, who refuses to spill. Does he know that we fucked seven ways till Sunday? Did you meet some new guy? Why are you hiding from me? I can't really, in all modesty, imagine you met a *neater* guy than me. So what the fuck is going on? Do I have to fucking drive to Iowa City and hunt you down? Christ, baby, you're making me crazy! So what is up?

Don't think I failed to sense a shift coming. Actually, I expected you to pull some shit like this.

I know you, and I know your nature. You will be crawling back on your hands and knees. And that's what really frosts me. Because as I write this, I'm disgusted with you. In two weeks, I will have forgotten that you ever existed. And when you see yourself in my book, when you see how deftly I captured your pathetic essence — then, dear heart, you will be the one who is devastated, humiliated, and utterly destroyed! You will suffer agonies that you have never imagined — you thought last time was "excruciating"? Baby, you don't even know the meaning of the word. You are one stupid fucking bitch! And you'll find there's *nothing* you can hit me with. My wife *read* the book; she knows my proclivities all too well. You cannot get back at me this time. I am the victor. In two mere weeks — fourteen days — (that's right, sugar pie, the clock is already running) you will be nothing but a long-forgotten memory. I won't know you anymore. Two short weeks and you are forever dead to me. I've got better things to worry about than your sorry ass. The "novel," if you dare read it, will fill you with impotent rage. I held back nothing. Slap your $24.95 on the table. This whole thing was a setup, a hustle: Lisa, the babies — everything. You may ask your-self why? Why am I such an evil cocksucking bastard? That's a fair question, dear heart, and the answer is this: Even I don't know the true extent of my evil genius. I just am and I revel in what I am. You want to escape notoriety when it hits the bestseller list, move to Albania or wherever. That's right, go ahead — feel free and just have yourself a happy little New Year's. You know something, Carol? I hate you and you can suck my motherfucking dick.

As always, I remain your obliged humble servant.

Farouk, King of the Assholes

All Along the Watchtower

CLIFFORD HOMER GRIMES JR. got the interview thanks to an uncle on his mother's side of the family. Harry was a bottom-feeder in the Daley machine who had just enough bite to foist his wayward nephew onto the city's Department of Transportation. He did this reluctantly, only after his sister Martha got down on her knees and begged. But Uncle Harry came through. After announcing the good news, Harry sat in her living room fingering his pencil-thin mustache as he awaited a token gesture of thanks. Clifford being Clifford, none was forthcoming. Harry moved to the bay window and saw a cop stick a parking ticket under the wipers of his Oldsmobile. He was out the door like a shot. It was all a blur to his groggy nephew, who was recovering from a stupendous hangover. Moments later Harry was back, holding an orange ticket. "Too late, goddamn it, but I know people in Traffic. I'll have it squashed. The sons of bitches."

Harry had been worn down by his sister's appeals. His nephew was a fucked-up mess, and when (not if) he was canned, Harry's good deed would generate only scorn downtown. It was an idle stab, but Harry handed Clifford a paperback copy of *How to Win Friends and Influence People*. He had done his best; his nephew was hopeless. All he wanted to do was hang out with those faggots at the gym and lift weights. He looked like a goddamn freak. Then Harry put on his trench coat and stepped outside. He noticed a couple of kids running away from his car. The Olds hadn't been on the street more than fifteen minutes and it had been zapped by the parking ticket and a pair of quick-ass hubcap thieves.

Clifford dragged himself into the bathroom, brushed his teeth, and left for the gym. Interview in less than a day; he was terrified. After his workout he went home for a nap.

At eight-thirty P.M. Clifford got up and hit the bars. He favored silk shirts, gilded chains, a zircon pinkie. As his main man Winston liked to say, "Who's goin' get the booty, muh fuck? I'll tell you: the chief peacock, not that ugly drab-ass uncle!" When Clifford told him about the interview, Winston hopped around Casey's Bar and Grill singing, "*After breakfast every day, she never fail to say, Get a job. Sha da da da, sha da da; yip yip yip yip, mum mum mum, get a job.*" Clifford proceeded to get hammered.

When he came to the next day, the last thing he remembered was puking in the alley. He glanced at his watch. Shit, it was late. He got dressed and was out the door with barf still on his breath. The battery in his beat-to-shit Morris Minor was dead. He looked at his Timex again — shit, eleven-thirty — and made a dash to the El. He chewed his fingernails and paced. The train came at last, packed to the gills. By the time he showed up for the interview, his iridescent blue satin shirt was stained with sweat. The chain around his neck was a major mistake. This was a suit-and-tie interview, and he looked like a damn greaseball. He tried to slide his pinkie ring off, but he couldn't get it past his second knuckle. He reeked of booze, vomit, and cologne.

There were no preliminary courtesies. The three-person panel immediately began firing questions. Flop sweat rolled down Clifford's face. He reached for his handkerchief, a crumpled yellow rectangle of cloth, and shook it open; the members of the panel recoiled. The three huddled over his résumé, speaking in whispers. Clifford heard snatches of muted questions.

"Fired? A drywall hanger? What's this here, mortuary assistant? Well, what is it, mortuary or exterminator? Both? Fired from both? Oh my God, a paperboy! Thirty-three years old and a paperboy?"

Clifford struggled to compose himself. Having heard enough, the assistant deputy commissioner of the Bureau of Bridges and Transit tossed his half-frames on the table and rocked back in his chair. He locked his hands behind his head and leaned back, revealing two muffs of nasal hair. The smirk on his face was enough to make Clifford want to pound the bastard to the ground.

A man resembling Joseph Stalin poured a glass of water. He took several small sips, straightened his tie, and began, "Mr. Grimes, it says here you served in the armed forces. Tell us about that."

Clifford told the panel he had won a Silver Star during Operation Desert Storm. A broad grin lit the assistant commissioner's narrow face. He leaned forward, picked up his glasses, and said, "Your recent work history points in the opposite direction, Cliff. Things just don't seem to jibe here."

Clifford wiped down his face and said, "Look, I can do this job!"

"An orangutan can do the job. That's not the point."

The heat of the room was unbearable. Clifford rolled up his sleeves, revealing a tattoo that read JULIET AND CLIFF, TRUE LOVE SPRINGS ETERNAL. He saw six eyes fall upon it. He could scarcely breathe. He said, "Gulf War. Sergeant in the Green Berets. Some heavy shit went down, and — "

The third member of the panel interrupted Clifford. She was a dour woman of fifty, her hair in a salt-and-pepper bob. She had a snub nose as bad as Lon Chaney's in *The Phantom of the Opera*. The woman waved a copy of Clifford's service record and said, "Bad-conduct discharge. Private. No Green Beret, but a four-month stretch in the stockade."

Clifford hadn't thought about a background check; this job was supposed to be a shoo-in. He turned up his palms in a gesture of wonder. "You must have the wrong Clifford Grimes." He swallowed hard, and his Adam's apple bobbed up and down like an elevator. His larynx was tight, dry, and strained. He sounded like Tweety Bird with his cartoon nuts in a vise. The interview was blown.

The assistant commissioner replaced his glasses and scanned Clifford's service record. "These are discharge papers for a Clifford Howard Grimes at 1187 South Sullivan in Chicago. Is this your address, Cliff? You listed it as such on your application. Are we meant to believe there were actually two Clifford Howard Grimeses in the U.S. Army?"

"It does seem a little far-fetched," Clifford said. "I don't under — "

"I've heard enough bullshit for one day," the commissioner said. "Let's cut it off here. Thanks to your uncle Harry, you are hired, effective next Monday. Report to personnel at nine A.M. sharp, and be advised that all new hires work on probationary status the first six months. If you slip up, if you can't cut the mustard, you'll be out on your ear."

"I'm a hard worker. I never get sick, and I will do a terrific job; you will be glad you took me."

"Enough! Get the hell out of here!"

As he staggered from the building his silk shirt was soaked. Oh man, Disasterville! But at least they didn't know he'd been thrown in the brig for impregnating the colonel's daughter, Juliet, an epileptic, fourteen years old, with an IQ of 64.

The bridge-tender job was simple. All Clifford had to do was sit in the bridge house at Cermak Road and push a red button to let a ship pass through. Still, Clifford pissed and moaned because they stuck him on the graveyard shift. Harry said, "What do you expect, sonny boy? You're the junior tender. You're lucky to get the job. Goddamn it, I'm not God! What more can I do?"

"Graveyard sucks. Why do you think they call it graveyard? It fucks up your body rhythms. You don't get any melanin, which leads to cancer, which leads where? I'll tell you, Uncle Harry, it leads to the graveyard!"

"Oh, fuck you, you son of a bitch. You don't want a job. You just want to lift weights. You look like a cocksucking faggot. I'm done with you!"

Harry was wrong; Clifford liked girls. Nights he prowled the neighborhood bars in a relentless search for pussy. Like Cinderella, Clifford now had to cut things short to punch in before midnight. Not many ships went by during his shift, and, half drunk, he often slept on a coffee-stained futon when things were slow, which was almost always.

The two retractable leaves of the bridge opened like the jaws of a crocodile and could clamp down with surprising speed. With the push of a red button it was up or down, up or down. It was Clifford's bad luck to come in drunk on a night when traffic was brisk. Up, down, up, down, until he was ready to die. As the booze wore off, the familiar black cloud draped over Clifford's brain. He was worthless. Go out drinking? Never again!

He felt better after the first month on the job. One night when things were especially slow he picked up *How to Win Friends and Influence*

People. The book was a blueprint for moral renovation. Clifford bought a fresh copy and pressed it on Winston with the fervor of a street-corner evangelist. His buddy backed away. Clifford was coming on like some sort of twelve-step freak working his program. Who wanted to hear that crap? Clifford accepted this without resentment. His old life was shed like a snake's skin.

Back at the bridge house, Clifford set to work like a human tornado. He cleaned the windows with old terry-cloth towels and Windex. They were covered in pigeon shit, and it took all night. Next he hauled out the floor scrubber and removed what seemed like fifty coats of wax from the floors. He put down new wax and buffed it to a diamond-hard shine. After tearing off aged pinups, he painted the walls powder blue. The day man, Cotton McCormick, was not happy. The next day he came tramping on the fresh wax with his galoshes. He carried a bag filled with replacement centerfolds and tacked them to the walls.

Clifford cleaned the refrigerator, an old-timer with the motor on the top. It was filled with rancid food and warmer than a swamp cooler. Clifford dumped everything, including a partially eaten tin of sardines. He took a screwdriver and attacked the glacier of ice in the freezer like a Gila woodpecker. Near the back Clifford discovered a Hungry Man meat loaf dinner, two Nutty Buddies, and a frozen rabbit. He pitched the lot into the river, then scrubbed the fridge interior with Mr. Clean. When he plugged the fridge in again the temperature dropped to forty degrees in the space of two hours.

Cotton hit the ceiling when he discovered his "perfectly good sardines" missing. To make amends Clifford replaced them with three fresh cans of Pride of Norway sardines. The day man put on his reading glasses and studied the label suspiciously. Rather than thank Clifford, he took the sardines to the garbage can and slammed them to the bottom. "Those sardines are packed in soybean oil. Goddamn it, did you ever eat sardines packed in soybean oil? Soybeans are what they feed to pigs. The whole mess tastes like transmission fluid."

"I don't eat sardines. I didn't know."

"There are a lot of things you don't know, Clifford. A whole lot. Keep your goddamn hands off a man's food! And what's this crapola coming in with a pierced ear and that stupid turban?"

"It's a do-rag, Cotton, not a turban. Winston gave it to me."

A blue vein throbbed on Cotton's neck. "You come in looking like a damn jungle bunny. Now you're talking like one. And tell me this: How can you man your post if you're cleaning all the time?"

"Hey, dude, I'm sorry about the sardines. I'll get you a can of King Oscars and a box of saltines, okay? Meanwhile, what is so bad about clean? If you think I'm trying to make you look bad or rat you out, tell people I'm the lazy ass and you're the one doing the cleaning."

Cotton had no retort, but Clifford felt himself take a swan dive into the dark abyss of his former life. You could only read *How to Win Friends* so many times before the chickens came home to roost.

Not only did he continue his workouts at Gold's Gym, he brought his own weights to work, where he spent another two to three hours pumping iron. To make up for lost ground he skin-popped huge doses of steroids and human growth hormone. In a matter of weeks he was a giant. The drugs brought to the fore long-buried primal urges.

He called his old girlfriend, Suzie Q. Suzie had a low-slung ass, but her ta-tas were looking fine. After Clifford dicked her one afternoon, she told him to ditch the cologne. "It's worse than chloroform. While you're at it, lose those gold chains. You look like Iceberg Slim."

He felt like saying, "And you can lose that cellulite, you fat-ass bitch."

She had more corrective advice. "Those muscles make you look like some kind of S&M fairy. Back off on the weight training."

"You liked me better when I was a geek?"

"Oh yeah," she said. "Definitely. You were smoking pot and mellow. Now you're fucking scary!"

He sent Suzie Q a dozen red roses the next day with a note that read "Dear Suz, I'm real sorry about last night, babe. You're a real Georgia peach. XXX's, Cliff."

There were attacks of roid rage. Once he clenched his teeth so hard he cracked a molar. The dentist who pulled the shattered tooth gave Clifford a script for pain pills. That night at work, while goofing on Percocet, Clifford picked up his high-powered binoculars and scanned the six-story Hudson & Swain lofts.

Clifford spotted a brunette working on a clay sculpture. She was a newcomer to Hudson & Swain. She had a cigarette in her mouth as she removed her smock and washed the clay from her hands. She disappeared from view, and Clifford shifted his binoculars to another floor. Suddenly the brunette returned to the window nude except for a white towel around her head. He could see each and every detail.

She stood at the window extracting another Gauloise from a blue packet as she raised the sill for a little air. Jesus, what a set! Thirty-four-D cups with no sag factor. She lit her cigarette with a Diamond-brand kitchen match. She took a deep drag as she shook out the match. She must have been about twenty-five, and she was absolutely gorgeous. She set the cigarette down on a white Martini & Rossi ashtray and removed the towel covering her hair. She leaned forward, running her fingers through her shoulder-length hair, and straightened up, flipping it back. Clifford's dick was hard in an instant. It pressed against the inside of his Levi's like a pole.

As she picked up the cigarette, Clifford pulled out his cock. The girl snuffed out her smoke and turned away. She had a hot fucking ass. Suddenly the lights went off, causing Clifford to wonder if it had all been a dream. A moment later the low-watt bulb from her refrigerator blinked on. Baby was now attired in a long black Metallica T-shirt. He watched her stand before the open refrigerator eating yogurt with a plastic spoon. When she finished she threw the spoon and the empty cup in the garbage. She shut the fridge. The show was over.

The nighthawks in Hudson & Swain knew how to put out quality entertainment. Dopers in black leather jackets occupied the third floor. Clifford trained his binoculars on them. A pair wearing paper face masks sat chopping dope in the small kitchen, while others packaged it into glassine bags. Junkies came and went, fifteen in the space of an hour. They laid cash on the table and retrieved thirty or so bags of powder. A huge brute of a black dude Clifford dubbed Big Boy stood by the door. Periodically, Big Boy peered through the peephole and opened the door to most of the same street hustlers Clifford had seen twenty or thirty minutes before. A few came in, made their buys, and retired to a shooting gallery in back. He couldn't see what was going on in there; the windows were covered with foil.

Clifford aimed his binoculars at the choppers again. On the table before them sat two handguns and a pile of cash. When the pile grew high, Big Boy stuffed it into a safe. Shit, it was quite the operation. If any window deserved a layer of foil it was the one where the choppers worked. Yet who other than Clifford had a vantage? Still, they were careless as all hell. The amazing part of it all came from the throbbing rap sound of DJ Screw on the boom box. Why not just call the narcs and tell them what was going on? Clifford was sure he knew where the second-shift man, Johnny Magill, scored. Magill regularly came to work half baked. It was a wonder he could function at all.

The next night at Hudson & Swain was a repeat of the night before. And so it went. Night after night Clifford nearly creamed his jeans watching Baby.

One night a skinny pothead wearing an army jacket and White Sox cap turned up with Chinese food and a video. Baby demonstrated a certain amount of affection toward him, but he made no moves. Possibly he was her brother. Both of them sat on a torn couch, smoking dope, adept with their chopsticks as they ate, and watched the blue light of the TV. Looking through the binoculars gave Clifford a blinding headache. He shook four Percocets from the dental prescription bottle and swallowed them with mineral water. When they kicked in half an hour later he was back on the watch.

Now Baby was holding hands with the skinny guy. What was the deal with that? Nothing more than a little hand-holding. Maybe the guy was a homosexual suffering from AIDS. It seemed likely. When the stupid little fairy finally left, Baby took her shower and made her appearance before the window. She stood caressing her breasts a moment or so. This was new. Was it some kind of weekly breast exam? She lifted her arms as she removed the towel covering her hair. This provided a five-star view of those incredible breasts. Clifford trembled as she caressed her belly and the tops of her thighs. Christ, she was turned on. She was going to go frig herself off!

Instead she repeated her Gauloise ceremony. Four deep drags before snuffing out the butt in the Martini & Rossi ashtray. Looking out into the black void, Baby had no idea that the king of voyeurs had her in his crosshairs. He watched her stretch her arms and let go with a long, luxurious yawn. She did the perky ass pivot, killed the lights, and the show was over. It was a no-yogurt night. No doubt she was frigging off. As she went to bed with rock-hard nipples, what other explanation was there? He wanted to bust the door down and say, "Look, I can see you're jerking off, no doubt fantasizing about cock. I got a hard-on. What say we get it on, baby?"

Suddenly Clifford heard air horns from the river below. He hit the button and watched a salt barge clear passage. He hit the button again, and in less than a minute the car traffic resumed. It had snowed through the night, and he watched fluffy flakes spin through the air, no two alike; another miracle from the magical universe that wasn't so magical without Percocet.

When his shift was over Clifford walked to his apartment and abused himself twice before he closed his eyes and watched Technicolor cartoons play out on the back of his eyelids. He was amped up on Percocets and the delirious chemicals of infatuation. No matter, he would take what he could get. Oh Christ, she was beautiful!

He woke up at three the next afternoon feeling like death warmed over. He took three Percocets with a cup of instant coffee and within fifteen minutes was back on top of the world. He rushed over to the Hudson & Swain building to scan the mailboxes for her name. Maura Michaels, had to be Maura Michaels. Clifford walked nine blocks to the House of Roses. He tried to order four dozen long-stem red roses for her loft. The florist told him his MasterCard was maxed out. There was enough money on his Visa card to cover three dozen roses. "Okay, fine," Clifford said as he penned a note. "To Maura with love. Your secret admirer."

By the time he got to work he was kicking himself for writing such a lame piece of crap. "Your secret admirer," what kind of shit was that? He began scanning Baby's apartment the second Johnny Magill punched out, but it remained dark clear through dawn, when he heard Cotton's heavy feet tread up the stairs to begin the morning shift.

That bitch! No doubt she was out fucking some sleazebag on the assumption the roses came from him, or whoever she had been banging last, or maybe the guy before that. A thousand or more! What a slut!

He might have known. Christ, what an idiot he was! He gives his own mother a four-dollar bouquet from Dominick's along with a "Sorry I'm late" birthday card, and he sends three dozen roses to a whore.

His mother, Christ. The last time she bailed him out he had promised to shovel her walk whenever it snowed. Clifford felt a pang of guilt over that one but not enough to make concessions or amends. Bridges were burning, but he was running nonstop on the hamster wheel of life. All of his pocket cash went for injections of testosterone and that fountain of youth — human growth hormone. To get the amphetamine rush from the stuff, he had to use more and more, until he was exceeding the recommended dosage two-hundred-fold. He couldn't drop it cold turkey, and his efforts to wean himself were in vain. Shit, he was spending more on hormones than a junkie with the biggest habit on the South Side. One minute things were under control, and then suddenly the whole shithouse came down. He felt like a supersonic jet pulling ten Gs in an all-out screaming nosedive. Like a doomed rocket manned by Daffy Duck. He could feel himself smash through the earth's crust, bore through layers of packed sediment and superheated rock until he came to a grinding halt at the planet's core. Steroids. Juice.

Maura was not home the next night either. Sitting alone in the bridge house while she was out cheating on him was almost more than he could bear. Heartbroken, he scanned the third floor of Hudson & Swain. The bloods had DJ Screw going strong again. The door to the cutting room was wide open and so was the door of the safe. DJ Screw. The fucking shit was driving Clifford nuts.

It seemed like an out-of-body experience. He patted the blackjack he carried in his side pocket. From on high he watched himself stalk out of the bridge house determined to exact retribution. He crossed the street, and then it was up the cigarette-and-syringe-strewn stairway to the drug den. Ding-dong. He saw a shadow cast over the peephole. Big Boy asked, "What is it?"

"Your pizza," Clifford said.

"We didn't order no goddamn pizza. Plus, I don't see no pizza in your hand, gray boy."

"Okay, motherfucker, make that fried chicken."

Big Boy opened the door with a gun in his hand. "I'll pop a cap in your ass right now," he said.

"Go ahead, do that. Every cop, SWAT team, and National Guard will burn you to the ground."

"Get the fuck out of my face! I ain't goin' tell you twice. Get lost!"

Big Boy dropped his vigilance for a second, and Clifford clocked him across the skull with the blackjack. Rage was packed behind the blow, and now the motherfucker was stretched out on the floor bleeding.

Two of the dopers at the cutting table reached for the Glocks lying no more than an arm's length away, but Clifford hit the room like a thermite grenade. He grabbed both cutters by their thin junkie necks and smacked their heads together. The cutters sank to the floor as if they'd been shot. Clifford heard the frantic scuffling of shoe leather. He grabbed both guns and went back to investigate. He found nothing but an open window and shadows of junkies running over the Cermak bridge. They were running over his bridge!

He returned to the cutting room, where he scooped up a bag of cash and two bags of powder. On his way out he fired five rounds into the ghetto blaster, putting an end to DJ Screw.

Back in the bridge house his ears rang from the gunfire. Still, he heard a pair of boats blaring their air horns from the river. He pushed the red button. The air horns gave way to the sound of sirens and the screeching tires of squad cars, blue lights flashing as they surrounded Hudson & Swain. Clifford secreted the Glocks, dope, and cash behind a trick door he'd discovered when he painted the walls, the stash hole where Magill hid his marijuana.

It took three hours for the police to clear the crime scene. Thanks to DJ Screw, Big Boy was going to pay through the nose for a lawyer and a bail bondsman. Well, he had it coming. You don't fuck with the kid and live to tell about it.

When the cops were gone, Clifford went back to the stash and pulled out the dope for a taste. He'd started sorting the cash in piles of tens, twenties, and fifties when a euphoric glow replaced the adrenaline rush occasioned from his violent rip-off. He was calm for the first time in months.

The cash added up to $19,000. His rash actions had provided a way out of his financial bind. He took another taste of heroin, ran to the bathroom to puke, and then lingered with his head on the toilet seat. He closed his eyes and found himself in seventh heaven.

It was nearly eight A.M. when he emerged from the toilet. He quickly stashed the dope, guns, and cash in his backpack. He heard Cotton trudge up the stairs, punch in, and pour coffee into a mug his granddaughter had given him for his fifty-eighth birthday. He took a sip and spewed coffee from his mouth like Oliver Hardy in one of the old Laurel and Hardy farces. He said, "This coffee tastes burned. Why didn't you make fresh? It's not like you've got anything better to do. Hey, what's so funny, bub? You look like the cat who swallowed the canary."

"I did, Cotton. I swallowed the yellow bird whole."

The next afternoon Clifford deposited $3,000 into his checking account. He wrote checks as partial payments to the three credit-card accounts. He paid Winston his growth-hormone debt in cash and then breezed down to the House of Roses. It was eight degrees out, but the old neighborhood felt like paradise. He sent six dozen red roses to Baby and a dozen yellow roses to his mother. He shucked out limp and greasy junkie-handled bills in payment. Yeah, the money was greasy, but even that was righteous. He didn't give two shits about the petty day-by-day. After another snort of heroin he puked twice (hey, now, is that cool or what?), and then he flipped WLS on the radio and bopped around the kitchen in stocking feet. Goddamn it, muh fuck, let's get down!

That night at work, kicking back on H, Clifford caught the next episode of the Baby show. "You lookin' fine, girl. I'm goin' make you mine, girl!" He flashed on the dope den. It was black and devoid of action. *Oh ho ho haw!*

Clifford called in sick the next day. He caught a cab over to Michigan Avenue and got a $100 haircut. So much for the mullet. He hadn't even known it was a mullet until the stylist told him. He bought an Italian suit, size fifty-two, and gave the tailor an extra $200 to rush the job. He bought a pair of shoes, a $300 dress shirt, and a $400 silk tie. He paid for these in greasy junkie bills. He bought a carton of Gauloises and a $900 solid-gold lighter, a steal. The lighter generated a superheated laser beam, and according to the salesman it was fail-proof in hurricane-velocity winds.

What Clifford liked most was the lighter's car-door-sounding click. It was irresistible, and it took a blister on the thumb to stop him from clicking. Late the next morning, clicking his new lighter left-handed, Clifford called in sick again. He Michael Jackson–voiced it. "Hi, Gloria, it's Cliff again. I don't know what's wrong with me. Boy, if it wasn't February I'd swear I have West Nile," he said.

"There's a lot of flu going around," she said. "Take all the time you need, and you be careful, big boy."

Big Boy! *Ah ha ha ha.*

Clifford taxied downtown and tried on his new suit. He looked great in it. Soon he was climbing the steps to Baby's loft. Bolstered on heroin, he rapped on her door. The door opened, and there she was, alive and in living color.

She wore a black turtleneck and black leotards under a short gray skirt, a beatnik outfit. She was taller and more beautiful than he'd expected.

"Hi, Miss Michaels, my name is Cliff Grimes," he said. "A pal of mine in the art world has been raving about your formal introduction, but he got me so excited, I just had to drive over."

"Who is your friend?" she asked.

"Mick Magill. He's a collector."

"How come I don't recognize the name? I know everyone in the Chicago arts community."

He looked past her and said, "You've got a lot of flowers in there."

Maura lit a Gauloise and said, "I take it you want to come in and look at my work."

"Sure," he said.

"Did you just get out of prison?"

"Prison?"

"You're huge. Only men in prison have enough time to cultivate big muscles like yours."

"Maura, come on."

"Never mind," she said. "Take a look around."

Clifford stepped inside, shaking a Gauloise out of a blue packet of his own. He flashed the gold lighter and with his sore thumb torched the Gauloise with a red laser beam. "Looks like we smoke the same brand," he said.

"People in my business all smoke them," she said. "We conform in our eccentricities."

He studied her pieces with fierce concentration, nodding his head once in a while. Best not to open his big mouth. Soon Maura was talking about her work, her inspiration, her hopes and dreams. He didn't look at her legs, tits, or ass. He focused on her eyes, her forehead, and her eyes again. He listened. He smiled now and again. She began to preen. They shared a couple of laughs. After Clifford bought four ridiculously inept sculptures, he asked her out for dinner. Maura replied that she should take him out to dinner given the magnitude of his purchase. Dinner, Saturday night. Settled. How much better could this tumultuous hell on earth get?

He ordered a town car and took her to Rush Street. He let her pick the restaurant and, as they ate, let her do most of the talking. Her parents had been well-to-do. Once as a girl they had taken her to Europe on the *Queen Elizabeth II*, then they flew home on the Concorde. A month later her father and mother were killed in a car wreck on the way to church. A back-seat human projectile, Maura had been launched through the windshield.

Maura began to sculpt by carving bars of Ivory soap in her hospital bed. Simple stuff — a duck, a camel. She joined two moistened bars of soap ("a big innovation for a kid") to form a block. She sculpted busts of her parents as she remembered them. She told Clifford that if she focused her attention on the figures she was making, the pain of life couldn't intrude into her consciousness. She said she had never given the full version of her tragedy to anyone before. Clifford nodded sagely, then said, "Sometimes it's easier to tell a stranger."

"That's so true!" Maura said. "It seems like I've known you all my life. Are you a Sagittarius?"

Maura kissed Clifford that night. She let him cop a feel on the second date. By the third date she took him to her bed, where, thanks to the heroin, Clifford couldn't get it up. Maura gave him a hand job. From the sculpting, her hands were as rough as a construction worker's. When he didn't respond she squeezed his cock as if she were choking a chicken. With that kind of action he knew he wouldn't come in a million years. She went down on him like a professional dick sucker. Just before he came she begged off, claiming her jaw hurt and she had drunk too much wine. As she began to snore Clifford went into the bathroom to facilitate himself.

After he got back to the bridge house, her apartment remained dark for eight days. He left phone messages that were not returned. Finally he showed up at the studio one afternoon, catching her home at last. He gave her the gold laser lighter she so admired. Why not? He hated smoking. She was so pleased, she asked him if he wanted to lie down.

"Lie down?"

"Yeah," she said, taking his hand as she led him toward the bed. He couldn't get it up despite the Viagra. She said she felt congested and asked him to eat her pussy. After twenty minutes of this, she said, "More pressure."

"Huh?"

Now she was exasperated. "More pressure. You're a big guy, use more pressure. Jesus Christ!"

He was a big guy, but he couldn't do push-ups with his tongue. He really didn't know what he was doing down there. His limited access to air made him snort like a hog. At last she came from the friction of his nose rubbing against her clitoris.

Back at work the next night, he'd hoped to scope out the Baby show but saw the fey dude in her Metallica T-shirt wave Maura over to a telescope! He was too stunned to move. Suddenly she was staring back at him. She flipped him the bird and killed the lights in her loft.

It took Clifford a week to get the nerve to call her, but he just got a phone-company recording that said the number had been disconnected. He went across the bridge and knocked on her door. Nothing. He half knocked it down and still nothing. "Goddamn it, son of a bitch, motherfucker!"

He started down the stairway and was dealt a concussive blow on the back of his head. He got the full star show as he tumbled down the stairs. Soon the blue-steel barrel of a .44 was working over his head, while his body was being kicked by a total of six combat boots. Then everything went blank.

When he came to, Clifford found himself bound in a chair in a dark room. His mouth was covered with duct tape. A tall man wearing a ski mask pointed a Mini Maglite in his face. "I want the money, the guns, and the good," the tall man said. "Where is it?" He ripped the tape from Clifford's mouth.

"I got the guns and most of the dope, but I spent the money."

"Wrong answer. I want to hear the right answer."

"I told you, I blew the money."

Two sharp blows to the face. Clifford swallowed a tooth with a mouthful of hot salty blood.

"I don't want to hear that fucking shit. I want the good, brother. The good."

"There's a way," he said. "I know a way."

"You find the way, you give us the good, and you can go back to your strange little life."

He was led outside and pushed into the back of a gray Mercedes. They drove him to his apartment and collected the dope and guns. Next stop was his mother's house. The old woman, fresh from chemotherapy treatment, got the bad news. She sat next to her son in the back of the Mercedes as they drove to the bank. She took out a second mortgage on her house, converted it to cash, and handed the tall man $19,000.

Driven to the driveway of her twice-mortgaged home, Mrs. Grimes staggered into the house, locked the door, and wet her pants on the hardwood floor.

Meanwhile, the thugs dropped Clifford in the hospital parking lot. Two days there and he was shipped to detox. From there it was in-house rehab. He had full medical, so the stay cost him only seventy dollars, which he had to borrow from his mother. He had more than exhausted his sick leave, but given the nature of his situation, other tenders contributed to a sick-leave pool on his behalf. He lay in his mother's house watching *Oprah*, drag-assing between the couch and refrigerator until the end of June, a full three months.

In July he returned to his post on Cermak, though he could hardly stand. In between button pushings he rested on the floor. The wax was fragrant still. One nice thing, he had done a good job on the floor. He felt as if he would die. Day after day it was the same routine. By midsummer he was feeling a little better, though he was unable to reestablish contact with the higher power. It was a bleak and godless universe.

In early August, Cotton had a hernia operation, and Clifford filled in for him. He wasn't used to bright sunshine and the heat of summer. He sat in the bridge house with his binoculars. There had been three jumpers that month, there was a full moon, and he was told to be on the lookout for anyone gathering his nerve. The advice was ironic, since Clifford wanted to jump himself.

The river smelled of rotten carp. Clifford needed to hit the floor again, but a barge was coming downriver. He could lie down and get up in five minutes, but that would entail doing a sit-up to right himself. So he stood waiting on frail, toothpick legs. Since he quit the juice, and since he had been away from the gym, he'd lost so much muscle mass that he was just a gray bag of skin. He pushed the button, and as the cement barge chugged through the oily waters, Clifford spotted three dead dogs in its wake, bloated like sausage boiled to the point of bursting. They were medium-size dogs, one black, another gray, and the third — whew, the third! — a rotten blob of golden fur without shape or form. In the dogs Clifford saw dimensions of death no mortal was meant to see.

Meanwhile, horns blared on Cermak, punctuated by psychotic screams of murder. The sun shimmering off the chrome bumpers and trim was blinding. Drivers stepped out of their vehicles and shook their fists at Clifford, who stood at his post in the watchtower feeling nine inches tall. The air was saturated with misery; the room spun, the dying carp gasped. Clifford pushed the red button.

Diary of My Health

APRIL 2. HOMER, my UPS guy, drops off three cartons of Medco pharmaceuticals. Homer is an okay guy if you steer him clear of religion and all talk of hell, but I slipped up today and got him going. "Hell?" he says. "You're looking at bad shit before your feet hit the ground, before you even get there. Man, they got these close-quarter holding cells at the farthest edge of the earth, little concrete anterooms where they soften up the condemned before transit. Bones are crushed. Sinners are pounded, gassed, drawn, quartered, lashed up and down. Then you're deloused with carbolic acid, and all the while they play Grateful Dead albums. Have you ever really listened to a Grateful Dead album? Actually listened? It's only the beginning! Charon, a terrifying monster in his own right, proceeds to ferry the doomed across the river Styx. Weeping and wailing like a pack of howling wolves. Begging forgiveness, gnashing teeth. Are you with me?" he says with a celestial fire in his eyes. "I don't think so, Thomas. I don't think you're paying close attention, but you should because it gets much worse. Up here hedonists like yourself frolic and sin as they have for centuries, pushovers for Satan and his lies! Hell is no cartoon; it's a real place. Cross the river, baby, and you got H-E-double-hockey-sticks for all of time. Abandon hope all ye who enter! First thing, they roast you on a spit while Satan reads you the rules and regulations. He's a fast talker with that split tongue, but still, it takes nine days to complete the job, and all this time you're roasting on a skewer. Once the grave implications of your situation sink in demons cool you off with liquid nitrogen and send you out to mop and wax a football field, side by side with the likes of Joseph Stalin and Ivan the Terrible. When that's done, thirty centuries later, you get five minutes to write a sixty-page term paper with a pencil nub or a melting beige Crayola crayon before some other hideous torment." Along with my pharmaceutical boxes, Homer picks up a smaller package from his hand truck. He looks at it and shakes his head in dismay. "Thomas, you are still getting packages from *Playboy* magazine. Why do I stand here wasting my breath?" Homer glances at his watch. Thank God he's running behind. He hops back in his brown truck and peels rubber out of my driveway. I carry three boxes of drugs to my little pharmacy just off the kitchen and begin to restock the shelves. Okay, what have we got here?

Box one: a. Lamictal, Neurontin, and Klonopin for epilepsy. (I hit my head on a rock the first time I went over Niagara Falls in a barrel.) **b.** Elavil, Prozac, Mellaril, Tegretol, and lithium for bipolar disorder. (Take lithium for a while and you're a Haitian zombie, no Niagara Falls pioneer.)

Box two: a. Six bottles of Humalog insulin in bubble-wrapped cool packs. I store those in the fridge. **b.** Blood-sugar strips. A brittle diabetic, I have to test fifteen times a day at eighty cents a strip. **c.** Glucose tablets for hypoglycemia. **d.** Glucometer batteries. **e.** Lancets, alcohol swabs, insulin reservoirs, and soft-set infusion kits.

Box three: a. Lipitor, cholesterol. **b.** Atacand, blood pressure. **c.** Nitroglycerin cream for cyanotic toes. **d.** Provigil for narcolepsy. **e.** Crap for my sleep apnea ventilator (two blow-dryers up the nostrils work just as well).

April 6. I read the Bible today. I don't know where Homer comes up with this shit. The only part of the hell scenario I can confirm is the "weeping and gnashing of teeth." Jesus. I already gnash my teeth. That's why I wear a plastic tooth guard at night.

April 7. Is it just me, or am I correct in thinking that the only time people have any semblance of fun is when they're on dope or hard liquor? I was a little kid the last time I had natural fun. Aurora, Illinois, July 25, 1954. The top of the ninth. White Sox versus Boston, the first game of a doubleheader, a partly cloudy, cool day, 26,068 fans. Jack Harshman on the hill mowing them down. Now with an 0-and-2 count, he shakes off the catcher. I am across the street at Pike's Dairy, throwing waterlogged baseballs, three pounds each, against a rusty milk truck when my mother calls me in to put on my pair of wool pants and go to church. I am thence sucked into a vortex of darkest gloom from which I've never been released.

April 14. Los Angeles. A table reading of my fifth film script. Not a good time for a Crohn's disease flare-up. I tough it out with butt cheeks so tight that coal could be squeezed into diamonds. The reading goes badly. In a CAA men's room, butt cheeks give way to Hershey-squirt diarrhea. Back in my hotel room, more of the same. On the three-hour plane ride home, a botched attempt at sneaking a fart leads to an episode of explosive diarrhea. I disembark (without underwear) and, in the safety of home, endure the usual agony while I wait for the Lomotil to kick in. I failed to stuff the medication into my portable pharmacy. It was the grave omission of a shock-treatment memory-loss fool. On top of everything else, the script gets shelved.

April 16. I've been out of sorts lately, flat-out depressed. That's why I decided to pick up my health journal again and record my last days. Sometimes I want to eat a quarter pound of barbiturates and various supplementary poisons, chased with absinthe, and then relax to Rammstein in the closed garage with my Citroën 2CV full throttle.

April 21. Does an ant have a soul? Do good ants upgrade into a higher life-form? A lobster, say? Endless reincarnations suck. Every female I have ever met tells me she used to be Cleopatra. I was a yak tender of no distinction living on the steppes of Mongolia, where there was nothing to eat except clay.

April 25. Most Americans don't know it, but noise is a leading cause of strokes and heart attacks. People get used to noise, but it kills them all the same. A person in an inner city can sleep only to the lullaby of sirens and gunfire. At five in the morning I hear fucking birds chirping, crows cawing, while a woodpecker tattoos the aluminum rain gutter just outside my bedroom. My Dutch neighbor Elsa says somebody has been vomiting outside her window at five in the morning. It's probably her neighbor, who used to attend two AA meetings a day. "Why would someone vomit outside?" she asks me. "It makes a mess. You could just puke in the toilet and flush it." Elsa says she was about to go outside to investigate but saw a large wolf looking at her through her sliding glass door. "Thom, he just wouldn't quit staring at me."

April 29. The UPS guy knows I don't exactly work, so he asks if I can drop by in the morning to help move his wife's grand piano up to the third floor. "While we're in the attic, I'd like to move my anvil collection from upstairs down to the basement. If there's time, I want to knock down a chimney. Bring a respirator." If I piss Homer off, he'll throw my pharmaceutical shipments off a bridge into the river. The fish will begin doing odd things. They could grow feet and walk around town like thugs. Who knows?

April 30. Goddamn it. My fucking back is killing me, and I squashed my thumb trying to haul two anvils at once. No "under the spreading chestnut tree," just a busted thumb.

May 4. Killer back pain.

June 6. Oh, for Christ's sake, not only is my back still killing me, I've got a whopping summer cold!

June 7. Raw throat, fever, and nasal congestion. A seven on the Thom Jones Misery Index.

June 8. Cold worse. I have to lay all day.

June 10. Canker sore on right tongue edge. My tongue looks like elephant leather.

June 11. Now a cough. I knew this would happen.

June 12. Took five hundred mikes of mescaline and am examining the crevice in my tongue when it suddenly turns into a Komodo dragon and chases me out into the yard. I come down at midnight and can't find my tongue. Dope paranoia forces me to hide under the bed, where I discover a box turtle with halitosis. I come down a little and carefully creep downstairs, secure all door and window locks, double-check same, and then watch a Pee-wee Herman flick on HBO, all the while standing on the balls of my feet, filled with terror and great apprehension.

June 13. Find tongue under the Citroën. Superglue it back on.

June 14. After stocking the shelves of my pharmacy I make for the health food store to pick up a few bottles of vitamins and snake oil remedies:

a. Vitamins: complete 50-milligram Bs, vitamin C, folic acid, dissolve-under-tongue B12, pantothenic acid, vitamin E (natural mixed tocopherols), biotin, and vitamin D. **b.** Minerals: selenium, calcium citrate, magnesium, biocitric copper, chromium, and Kreb's "Transported by the Fuel of Life" zinc. **c.** Antioxidants: alpha lipoic acid, lutein, ly-copene, grape seed oil, pine bark extract, Q10, Essential Greens 3000, curcumin, etc. **d.** Herbs: saw palmetto, hoodia, pau d'arco (I can't remember what it's for), hawthorn berry. **e.** Amazon River tropical frog skin.

Have I already mentioned that my memory is shot? I don't remember.

June 15. As a kid I experienced instances of natural fun whenever the Gypsies came to town. My grandmother saved the burlap bags potatoes came in and each year gave them to the Gypsies, who in turn sharpened all her butcher knives and fixed a coffeepot with a broken handle. What a life! Roving caravans, dancing around a campfire to accordion and violin music. Crystal-ball visions of the future. One of the Gypsy elders took a shine to me and invited me to join up.

"Join up? Tonight? Let me think about it. I'm only five years old."

"Yes. Escape the ball and chain and come with us. It's a slacker lifestyle. The women do all the work."

I didn't go. I should have. Every time I think of it I kick myself in the ass.

My grandmother paid the fortune-teller fifty cents to tell her where she misplaced a cigar box filled with cash. The fortune-teller hit the nail on the head. It was a two-for-one deal. While my grandmother retrieved the cigar box, the Gypsy told me I would be jailed four times, fired from a number of jobs, mental hospitals, ambulances called, squad cars, and ultimately twenty-two years as a custodian. Boy, did she ever hit the nail on the head.

June 16. Cough much worse. *Kaff, kaff, kaff,* damn! It's not the cough of acute bronchitis, which I have experienced seven times. It's a dry cough, which rules out pneumonia and cystic fibrosis. It's not lung cancer, with its telltale wheeze, lobar atelectasis with mediastinal shift, diminished expansion, dullness of percussion, and loss of breath with pain and loss of weight. It could be Hand-Schüller-Christian disease. You will have a dry cough when you get that.

June 17. Dizzy. Head spinning, eyes whirling like pinwheels, smoke coming out of my ears. It feels like getting off the carnival Rock-O-Plane after a corn dog, a jumbo birch beer, and a haystack of pink cotton candy.

June 18. Woke up okay. Blood pressure 115/64. Pulse 57. Blood sugar 89. The fever is down, but the cough dogs me. What if it is lung cancer? Fuck. Had to lie on floor and breathe into a brown paper bag.

June 20. Eat a bowl of alfalfa to bolster my waning immune system. Man, I'll never do that again. Decide to just fuck everything and ingest a large dose of ketamine. Paralyzed, I lie on the floor and watch my soul leave my body and fly to remote galaxies in outer space. Get real scared and try to reel my soul in. A bad scene ensues. I am chased by a fleet of spaceships from the planet Mongo. Captain Torch at the wheel of the lead rocket ship. (Man, he hasn't aged well.) He shakes his fist at me, and I flip him the bird. Then I turn invisible, which is really draining. I bump into the Hubble Space Telescope and bruise my hip smashing the auxiliary lens into a thousand pieces.

June 22. I wake up with three ### floaters in my eye. When the nurse hands the phone to my ophthalmologist I overhear him saying, "What's wrong with poor Thom today?" I say I think little elves are in my eye typing on the back of my retina with an old portable Smith Corona typewriter. "Like with a faded ribbon," I tell him. When I explain this to him over the phone, this is what he says: "Look, Mr. Jones. You call me drunk at two in the morning. You call in the middle of Thanksgiving dinner. How many times have I found you sitting on the curb in front of my office as I drive in to work? Before I put the car into park you're banging on my window with some new bullshit symptom. I don't want to be your doctor anymore. Don't even come close to my office. I'm filing a restraining order against you, and I'm having my phone number changed."

June 28. I just noticed how yellow my teeth are getting. I brush them with Comet for a gleaming white smile.

June 29. Gums hurt. Scurvy? I eat four lemons and get a sour stomach. I take a Tagamet, Nexium, and drink an entire $2.95 bottle of Pepto-Bismol.

July 1. Constipated. Respite from diarrhea caused by Crohn's disease, finally.

July 5. Insomnia.

July 6. Insomnia. Completely hagged out.

July 7. I just can't sleep. Lie in bed and worry.

July 8. Toss, turn, and mash pillows all night. Insomnia.

July 9. Will it never end? "The healthy man," writes E. M. Cioran, "only dabbles in insomnia: He knows nothing of those who would give a kingdom for an hour of unconscious sleep, those as terrified by the sight of a bed as they would be of a torture rack."

July 12. Twelve nights and not even a wink.

July 14. Haggard beyond belief. There is a variant of mad cow disease (bovine spongiform encephalopathy) that induces fatal insomnia. Dead in four to twelve months! Boy, I've eaten my share of burgers.

July 19. What if I were to fly to Africa, to a heavily infected tsetse fly zone, and contract sleeping sickness to counterbalance my affliction? Book a flight to Africa.

July 26. Try to read *Ulysses* and fall into a five-day coma. Why didn't I think of that in the first place? I feel great!

July 27. Depressed again. Antidepressants should be called what they really are: hammers of despair. You can't sleep, you can't fuck, and your head feels like it contains seventeen pounds of aluminum.

Labor Day. Tossing a football with my brother, I jump to catch a high pass and feel a lightning bolt shoot through my arm. Shoulder hurts so bad I can only tightly squeeze my elbow to my rib cage. Can't put on a shirt by myself.

September 5. Frozen shoulders are so rare, most people seldom hear of them. Twenty percent of the diabetic population gets them. A frozen shoulder is no day at the beach.

September 6. Insomnia again. The same old routine.

September 7. Born to suffer.

September 12. Acupuncture for shoulder. No go, nothing, zip. Just a big waste of time.

September 14. Rolfed by some Wavy Gravy chick who talked aromatherapy, e.g., the catfish flower.

September 16. Deep-tissue massage. Yet another flop.

September 20. The orthopedic surgeon attempts to break the shoulder-capsule adhesions under anesthesia. "I couldn't do it," he says later. "I thought I was going to break your arm. Go to a pain clinic."

September 24. Pain clinic dispenses narcotics. "Not enough to get you high," the nurse says with a smile. Meanwhile, "the shoulder will only get worse. There is an osteopath you might try."

October 9. Facedown on the treatment table. Dr. Coors, osteopath and Spanish inquisitor, pulls my arm mercilessly. There are loud pops as he breaks the adhesions in the shoulder capsule. The pain is so bad I think my hair will catch fire. Coors says, "Come back tomorrow."

October 11. Facedown on the table, I bite a hole through the Naugahyde, swallow a rusty spring and three wads of horsehair stuffing. Coors says, "We're beginning to get somewhere. We're making progress."

October 24. Lying in bed the evening after my third treatment, I suddenly notice something. My God! For the first time in months my shoulder doesn't hurt. Ecstatic for a moment. Then I realize there's a disaster I'm currently unaware of that will announce itself with a thunderclap.

October 25. Boy, I sure hope I don't get bird flu.

October 26. Shoulder a lot better. Nothing to report except a hangnail on my anvil-crushed thumb. By and by it begins to feel like a cobra bite.

October 27. Slept until four P.M. Thumb still bad. Why are we here? Just to suffer?

October 29. Elsa calls and says she saw the wolf again, hunkered down behind her woodshed. "It's an evil beast. Thom, I am so afraid. Why won't he leave me alone?"

October 30. Prostate trouble and a searing pain in my urethra. I take an OxyContin and soak in a hot bath to relax.

November 1. Elsa tells me the five A.M. puker is still at it.

November 2. Took some Advil for my thumb. The Advil ignites a nuclear fireball in my stomach. Heartburn. The Channel 7 weatherman said there would be a meteor shower tonight. Outside for an hour and all I see are fizzlers. As a result, I get a sore neck and have to dig through the garage to find my cervical collar.

November 5. Elsa caught the dawn puker. Her immediate neighbor "just couldn't take it anymore."

November 9. I spring out of bed at noon, determined to accomplish great deeds. I tackle a raft of dishes, and through the kitchen window I see the farmer who lives behind me chucking fallen branches from his side of the fence over to mine. With him is the gray Norwegian elkhound Elsa has mistaken for a wolf. It is medium-size, about fifty pounds, and wagging its tail to beat the band. I thank the farmer for the logs and tell him that with all that lumber I can finally build a meth lab. He looks at me and says, "You can kiss my ass!"

November 12. My diabetic toenails have evolved into hooves. Square them away with a rat-tail file.

November 15. Decide to use the business-class plane tickets I bought to Africa during my insomnia phase. They cost a small fortune; best I use them. All day packing. Wide-eyed and fearful. Another ghastly trip. What was I thinking?

November 16. Dawn limo to Sea-Tac, five hours to New York, two-hour layover, then an all-night flight to Heathrow, nine hours to Nairobi, drinking shooters. Arrive drunk. A pickpocket lifted my dummy wallet with my old driver's license, an expired library card, and two bucks. Thank God for money belts, though mine was purchased during the Jimi Hendrix era. The psychedelic colors will be a big hit in Zambia.

November 17. Hitch a ride to the tsetse fly zone on the back of a sorghum truck. I arrive with my face pasted with red dust. Prostate trouble, a blowtorch in my dick, all fifteen inches of it. Hop off the truck in a mud-and-wattle village. No hotel, no B&B, no TV, no McDonald's. Nothing.

November 18. Late afternoon. Fucking Christ, is it ever hot! I rent a room in the back of the OD Macaroni Factory.

November 19. I hate Africa.

November 20. I dug out a flea that had somehow burrowed under my thumbnail. There is a small fan over at the button factory. I rent a stall there. Mealie meal for breakfast, lunch, and dinner. At least you don't get caught in a menu quandary.

November 21. The night watchman introduces me to Charles, a university student from Ethiopia who quickly makes himself at home in the stall across from my own. Charles shares a bucket of beer with me. In the light of a kerosene lantern we play cards all night. Lions roar in the distant jungle.

November 23. Bucket-of-beer hangover persists. Charles constantly sprays himself with DEET. "Tsetse flies, man. Can't be too careful."

November 24. Drunk on palm wine at nine A.M. I buy a fish, oranges, and a banana at the outdoor market. While the saleswoman bundles my purchase, I drop her baby and momentarily pass out on the road. Thankfully, the baby broke my fall.

November 25. Tonight at dusk, as I walk back from the market, I step off the road to take a leak and, forgetting I am in Africa, disturb a jumping pit viper (*Porthidium nummifer*). It's a sturdy, short-tempered snake. This one strikes with such force, its husky body leaves the ground. It shoots past me faster than a left jab and sails deep into the roadside undergrowth. I pick up its Bolivian passport and wallet. Inside there's a picture of the snake's wife and children. There is also a letter. "My darling Estella, Africa is very bad. I have lost weight living on mouses. I miss joure shovel-shaped head, joure hort-shaped face, you gleaming fangs. Do you miss me at all? Why have you run off with Kenny Stabler?"

November 26. Oh God, I promise, I swear I will never drink palm wine again. Save me!

November 29. Venture into the bush with Charles and a new acquaintance, Sylvester. Chased by warthogs.

December 2. My stomach hurts low down. Sylvester says it's roundworms. "Eat a cigarette and it will die," he says. I wolf down a Pall Mall and become sicker than a dog.

December 3. I void a nine-inch tapeworm. That's odd. No wonder I'm so thin. Sylvester wants me to sponsor him to America. "Sell tapeworms to college girls," he says. "They can eat all they want and stay thin. Make us millionaires."

December 11. Charles takes a Magic Marker and points a stake west to Seattle. The sign reads HOME SWEET HOME THOMAS. I doubt I will live to see Seattle again. Another warthog runs through the village at dusk.

December 14. How come everything feels so much better when you're lying down? I'm really growing to love my little pallet at the button factory.

December 16. Sylvester won't lay off the tapeworm scheme. Now he's got Charles hot for the idea. I say, "American women, no matter how fat, won't swallow a thick white worm." "Yes they will," says Sylvester. "They will! What do you know anyhow?" Charles pipes in, "No worm to swallow, just a small vacuum-packed worm capsule. Just the ticket, man."

December 17. Charles drives me to a three-hut village packed with victims of sleeping sickness. They all look pale, like Michael Jackson. They aren't so much sleeping as they are "out of it."

December 19. The button-factory watchman tells me Charles and Sylvester made off with my passport. My mini-pharmacy? "Long gone, man. Fat man Jimi Hendrix belt gone too." I fall to the ground and kick at it and beat it with both fists. I chip a tooth on a rock. Send me a helicopter, God, and I swear I will never harbor a mean thought for the rest of my life.

December 23. Home just in time for Christmas. Three days in the Slumberking riding out a case of sandfly disease.

December 24. Christmas Eve. A stabbing pain in my foot. I hobble around bowlegged all day, like a busting-bronco cowpoke. I wrap Christmas presents. I can't get to the Slumberking fast enough. Beyond awful. I wonder what it's like to die. I'm sick all the time, but the final agonies must be worse. Yet so often I see old people smiling. Putzing around their yard, smiling. Horseshoes and lawn bowling between chemotherapy, and still smiling. What is with that? They croak and an influx of new ones rushes in to replace them. On the plane home I saw a woman eight months pregnant, and she had a big-ass smile on her face. Was she just putting on a good show? Was she really thinking, "Why did I ever fuck that ex-con mentally retarded lowlife? Having this kid of his is going to hurt like hell, and I'll be a walking stretch mark. On top of it all I'll have a screaming kid on my hands night and day, living on welfare the next twenty years while the old man luxuriates in the penitentiary without a worry in the world. Man, could I ever use another hit of methedrine."

December 25. Birds chirping. The distant sound of puking in the bushes. Merry Christmas!

December 29. All I do is sleep. Jesus, I used to have time to do things, but now life revolves around Crohn's disease, prostate trouble, heartburn, epilepsy, a hundred million problems.

January 27. Feel deathly ill. I spend the entire day on the Slumberking. Every once in a while I have to sit up and look at the callus on my foot.

January 28. I pick at the callus with a small knife. The pain is unbearable. I can't get anything done. I just hobble from one room to the next looking for stuff I have misplaced. **January 29.** A sharp triangle of glass begins to emerge from the callus. I finally dig it out with my knife. It is a dime-size piece of amber beer-bottle glass. My senior year in high school I was wading in Aurora's Mastodon Lake and stepped on something sharp. The foot bled copiously. The next day red streaks were working their way up my leg. My doctor gave me antibiotics. From then on, touching that spot with a fingertip sent me flying through the ceiling. It was a lot like stepping on a punji stick. Glass doesn't show up on X-rays. I had to order custom-made shoes from plaster of paris molds. The shoes looked like Frankenstein boots. People ridiculed them openly. I learned how to find normal shoes that would accommodate the sore spot. After forty-two years the glass works its way out. Amazing! **February 5.** No matter how you cut it, it hurts to die. Asphyxiation is usually involved. With type 1 diabetes I will most likely have a stroke or fatal heart attack. Get out of the easy chair to take a whizzer and "Ah-hhh!" *Ka-plop*. Two weeks later firemen will break inside trying to find the cloying odor that has the neighborhood up in arms. "Jesus, will you look at that? His head is bigger than a pumpkin! I wonder how they will ever squash him into a coffin."

So there you have it. The aeons of nonexistence, birth, Shakespeare's seven ages of man (which boil down to years of suffering in various forms), dreams that seldom come true, and just enough good stuff to keep you going. Then death and the foreverness of all eternity, painless and carefree. No more problems. No demonic tortures. Just nothing, pure and simple. How can you top that?

HERE LIES THOM JONES RIP
HE PACKED 2,000 YEARS OF AGONY
INTO THE SUBSTANDARD 62

The Junkman of Chengdu

Go to china and you really don't want to drink the tap water. It's the biggest no-no going. Highly inadvisable. Nowhere in China can you take a sip from the tap and live to tell about it. You could be dying of thirst but still, it's a no-go. You can dump a ton of halazone into this murk and you still got poison. Detonate a small germ-busting nuclear bomb the size of a pinhead in your cup, feel the tiny "flash burn" on your face, and with sunglasses watch the miniature mushroom cloud erupt before your eyes like a five-petaled lotus flower. Still there's no guarantee all the bugs are dead. So unless you're a camel whizzing through the country with a seven-day stash of Perrier in your hump, you're going to need safe and palatable drinking water. I say palatable, as a fresh and delicious taste is also a consideration.

What to buy? All-natural Ice Dew brand springwater comes in convenient twelve-ounce bottles and it's fricking delicious. If you're planning to stay awhile and set up residence, you install a home dispenser and get the five-gallon Culligan-size water jugs. What you do is rustle up some friend/boyfriend handyman type, which for me is where Marcello comes in, hire a cab, and go on a water run. Pick up a ten-kilogram sack of white rice while you're at it. Marcello is a professional soccer player and he's in excellent physical condition. A jug on each shoulder is no problem for Marcello. I get him to lug fresh water jugs up six flights of stairs into my place and set a fresh jug in the water dispenser. The five-gallon jugs of Ice Dew come in opaque, dark-blue glass bottles. I've got a groovy blue neon light behind the dispenser, the whole setup is very art deco, very sleek; I couldn't be happier. It's too cool for words. You find yourself drinking extra water just for the fun of it.

I brush my teeth with Ice Dew. I wash my hair with Ice Dew and Bright and Shiny shampoo, and then I rinse with Ice Dew alone. You get that squeaky-clean feeling. Pinch the wet hair with your fingers and it really does squeak. An hour later, on the polluted streets of Chengdu, you are a walking grease pit again. But at least you had that hour. That's the way I look at it.

I also make my tea from Ice Dew, though in China there are these water heaters all around, in the hall, in the kitchen, in almost every conceivable locale. The cookers are like television sets in America — everywhere, in every nook and cranny, just everywhere. But most of the older cookers do not boil. They cook tap water just to the brink of boiling. Let me hazard an educated guess on the water temp as about 210 degrees Fahrenheit. That's unreliable because I don't trust the water cookers and don't use them in the first place; it's like Russian roulette. I'm just trotting out a number. But certain bugs thrive in 210-degree water. Those extremophile bacteria that live near volcanoes in South America for instance. I mean you might get Ebola or Guinea worms from drinking that shit.

I won't go on about this like some obsessive. I'm not a germ freak, just a careful, prudent person. The almost-boiled tap water is probably sterile but you can see things floating around in it, spooky things, and I just can't go that route. There is heavy sediment that sinks to the bottom of the cup, like sand and gravel; there are indecisive mid-mug floaters that don't know up from down and so just hang suspended there; and finally there's a scummy layer of frothy debris at the very top. It rests there in a layer of foam. I'm not a microbiologist but I would imagine there are millions of invisible things, too. So boiled or not, why take the risk? Not only is Ice Dew a cheap alternative, it's guaranteed bug-free. I have emailed this information to my father, back in the States, and he thinks I go too far with it. He's tired of hearing long digressions about water. He warned me about going to China in the first place.

My dad prefers hearing various other horror stories, stories with an element of danger, and then he writes me warnings he's gleaned from the *Lonely Planet* guide to China. Like when I wrote I was going on a side trip to Urumqi, he wrote back, *"Danger! Red Alert!* Avoid west gate into city! It is filled with a congregation of pickpockets and aggressive robbers who like nothing better than to get you from behind, slash your backpack with a razor, and you are none the wiser as they truck off with your worldly goods." I'm like twenty years old and I'm getting this. I passed through the west gate at midnight and it was completely tame, a cakewalk.

One more point about the water. I drink a lot of tea now but (here's the funny part) I was never a tea drinker until I came to China. You can't avoid the stuff over here. To this day a sip of coffee has not passed my lips. I had a narrow escape at the Helsinki McDonald's in Finland. Here's the story: I was given a small cup with a $29.52 Happy Meal. I opened the lid and ugh — COFFEE! I gave the damn cup to a drunk. I got no Red Alert on that one and I was so tired at the time I almost drank it. I wasn't in my right mind.

I like to travel. One day I may pass through Seattle, where thugs like to tie you up, blindfold and handcuff you, and then force coffee down your throat with a funnel: espresso, French roast, Starbucks breakfast blend, and so on. You need to hire a bodyguard in Seattle or in all of Washington State for that matter. They can put a gun to my head, but I won't drink coffee. One mere cup and you're an addict for life! Not for all the tea in China would I voluntarily drink coffee. That volatile liquid is like rocket fuel.

"All the tea in China" is a worn-out expression sliding out of the American lexicon. It's remembered only by Depression-era seniors and their baby-boomer offspring (like my very own father), who were brainwashed with this phrase, who have heard their parents opine time and time again. Twenty times a day they hit you with "Not for all the tea in China will I do this or that." It's hyperbole, meaningless cackle.

It's not just water in China that presents perilous health hazards; food is dangerous as well. I've seen what happens to careless eaters over here. People possess accurate information about suspect foods but they eat it anyway and thus learn the hard way. You're in the country for three months for instance and you drop your guard, you think you're acclimated to the national germ array. But let me tell you the deal: eat tainted food and it's three days of puking into a squat toilet. Oh ho! Not so immune after all, huh?

The Chinese squat toilet is a horrible affair where greenbottle flies the size of bumblebees fly blind with their Saran Wrap wings, seduced and entranced by the magical aroma that calls to them like the Sirens of the Cyclades Islands. They furiously circulate the stall, knocking their heavy bodies against the wall — whap, whap. Whap. Whap, whap, and whap. It takes three days for them to get tired but eventually they succumb to exhaustion. As I said, my dad loves to hear such accounts of unspeakable, but nonlethal, horror.

Not only do you contend with flies, there are roaches and other prowling vermin at Squat Toilet Ground Zero. Rats love a squat toilet. Home sweet home. They're all too happy to sink a fang into you, and the rat carries plague fleas. Twenty-nine percent have rat fever. I mention this to impart a feel for the romance of travel in exotic climes. You hate it when it's going on but years later you look back on the experience with fondness. Or so they say about Peace Corps gigs, etc.

Many of the girls in my exchange program are anorexic binge-purgers. Trying to match the prepubescent, rail-thin physique of the Chinese ideal damsel. Catch one puking and they cop the bad-water or food-poisoning defense when in fact bulimia is the more likely villain, especially among repeat offenders. My roommate, Elizabeth, is a puker and she barely tries to hide it. She will starve herself for days. She will live on air for eleven days and then comes the binge. By then her stomach has shrunk to the size of an English walnut, but on Day Eleven she starts pounding the food down. Day Eleven you come home and find everything in the cupboard scarfed, ingested, devoured, and done away with like Mother Hubbard's bare cupboard and her faithful but starving Great Dane.

In the hotel room of Elizabeth's alimentary track, checkout time is eleven A.M. "Huh-rooga!" she goes. "Oh God! Oh God! Oh God! Huh-rarf!" You can hear her in the "ce suo" with a greenbottle fly providing a backbeat to her puke music. When Elizabeth plays the whale in the squat toilet I somehow feel compelled to wait and listen, like I've been paid to bear witness. I stand there and listen to see what comes next. Elizabeth actually believes that if she tapes up her thin-lipped cakehole and makes the magical 90-lb. mark, she'll bag her Prince Charming. A handsome dog along the lines of Matt Damon, Ryan Gosling, Jake Gyllenhaal, or some combination thereof. If not one of them, and she's feeling grandiose, she dreams of landing her very *fave*, Brad Pitt. Like that is so not going to happen, but when it comes to Brad Pitt, Elizabeth is *in* love.

Elizabeth is Chinese-American but she hates the look of Chinese men, utterly despises them. She bitches about them constantly. E's got big bones and huge shoulders and she actually looks better heavy. She looks best as a middle linebacker. Sumo E. No matter how thin she gets the other girls call her "The tanker, Ms. Exxon Valdez." When E drops fifteen, her inflated Miracle-Gro pumpkin head looks even bigger. It's monstrous in the first place and with the weight of this hydrocephalic water-on-the-brain head of hers combined with weak neck muscles, the head flops around like some kind of rag doll, or it will loll to the side depending on which way the wind blows. It's a damn watermelon. She looks like Oprah Winfrey whenever that international billionaire TV mogul takes her own diet to the starvation level, when she has twice-daily workouts with a personal trainer, or so they say in the tabloids. It's all a crying shame since Oprah is not a bad-looking woman. Oprah looks far better with a little meat on her bones, at least in my opinion.

However, it is well known that you can't reason with anorexics; they can never get thin enough. When it comes to body weight a puker is supremely deluded. Puker stories abound and no healthy American woman can fail to read the horror tales of anorexia/bulimia with anything less than astonishment, fascination, and smug self-righteousness. "There goes that walking skeleton now. Look at her, two months ago she was fatter than a hog! Thank God it isn't me!" My favorite anorexic story is the tragic account of Karen Anne Carpenter who, if I'm not mistaken, may have been on a macrobiotic diet. They wrote a whole book about it. What utter depravity! If Elizabeth doesn't watch her ass, she sure as shit is going to end up burning a hole through her esophagus. Her teeth will rot to nubs. Note: I don't swear in front of my dad; it's disconcerting to him, though he sure enough likes to cut loose with the foul language. With him it's always "Motherfucker this," "cocksucker that." "Shit, fuck, piss, goddamn it, Jesus Harrison Christ," and so on. He listens to Samuel L. Jackson swear and imitates him, *Pulp Fiction*–style. I've heard this sort of trash talking from Day One.

The hard-core anorexic lives on air and bottled water, the aforementioned Chinese tea, and now and then an occasional baby carrot or a ketchup packet. I have made an objective and impartial study of the yo-yo dieter. For a layperson I pretty much have my finger on the pulse of this problem. I got eyes. I can see.

When Elizabeth goes long enough without food she becomes positively evil. Once after a Valium-and-beer suicide attempt, she confessed to me that an eating binge gives her a pleasurable sugar rush comparable to getting trashed on Tsingtao beer.

So I stand near the toilet and listen. "Tomato skins and corn? Good God! I don't remember eating tomatoes and corn." After a big chunder in the squat toilet she eats a low-cal spinach salad and feels virtuous.

Elizabeth grew up speaking Chinese in her Nevada home, where her family spoke Chinese and Chinese alone. Like after twenty years in America, her parents still can't speak three words of English. Which means Elizabeth knows the Chinese language well enough to get straight A's in introductory Chinese-language classes. She doesn't have to open the book. Meanwhile she basks in the glory of her professor's high praise. So there you have it, two felonious crimes! Not only is Elizabeth a puker, she also pretends to learn Mandarin Chinese when in reality she already knows it forwards and back. She has even tricked herself into feeling proud over this pathetic non-accomplishment. I'm a Caucasian taking advanced Chinese courses, doing the work of fifty Sabine slaves and forty horses, and still, B's are not unknown to me. I believe that a report card with inflated A's is as dishonest as a puker's thin frame. I'm not some evil bitch. I feel empathy and compassion for Elizabeth, I truly do, and I don't report her secret life to anyone. Mainland China has thrown many a young American around the bend, but enough of my tiresome clichés.

Chengdu, where I live and go to school, is in Sichuan Province. It's a city of ten million. I'm one of the hundred or so Caucasians in this sunless, three-packs-a-day, air-pollution nightmare of a megalopolis where the sky is perpetually white with ozone-dense smog and where, as I have briefly mentioned, the tap water is undrinkable.

When you are out and about roaming the drab streets of Chengdu you drink Ice Dew bottled water only after carefully checking the aluminum-sealed bottle caps for tampering. A bottle of Ice Dew drinking water goes for less than two yuan, about twenty cents. In the little street stalls these beverages are mostly warm, though the shop proprietors sometimes keep a bottle or two of Ice Dew water in the ice-cream freezers.

I give the empty Ice Dew bottles, which are refundable, to a junkman who sits in front of five trash bins outside my apartment complex. This is what the man does for a living. My father loves junkman reports and inquires after him at every opportunity.

If you are a puker like Elizabeth you can drink Ice Dew or tea for appetite-suppressing liquid bulk and you are one step closer toward recovery. Elizabeth is such a frequent barfer the enamel of her teeth is coming off. Her grandfather left her a trust and she plans on spending every dime to beautify herself. She wants to take a little trip down to Tijuana, where she can go eyetooth to eyetooth for one of those Gary Busey 750-watt smiles. In Tijuana she can also get her crooked pugilist stump of a nose streamlined. Then, with a blinding smile and an irresistibly beautiful nose, her big head notwithstanding, Elizabeth will be swept right off her size 12, triple-X wide feet by Prince Charming. Once she bags her man, she will never have to lift another finger.

"You foolish girl," I told her after suicide attempt number four, "consider how seldom things turn out the way we expect them to."

Meanwhile Elizabeth makes do with Quinny, who stands in at five foot two, carrying one hundred and eleven pounds of nervous energy. As you may have guessed, Quinny is no Brad Pitt. His flat snake eyes are as black as obsidian and color-coordinated to go with his black upper-incisor cavities. He's got extra-special bad breath because he's always dipping his food into some rancid fish-sauce concoction. This is breath that can buckle your knees at a distance of fifteen yards. It could fell a herd of oxen.

Quinny is the antithesis of Prince Charming. He's a hyped-up ADD, Adderall-doesn't-work, walking nervous breakdown. What a pair they make, the alpha and omega of social dysfunction. Late into the night I hear them screwing on Elizabeth's futon, stopping in the middle of it so Quinny can tie her up and spank her fat ass with a stolen rec-center Ping-Pong paddle. But I shouldn't complain. For so many highly strung types, sexual release is the last of the bleed-off valves. Without sexual relief, both of them would sink into the black psychic abyss of manic psychoses and probably take me with them, as insanity can be infectious. Both of these nutcases are on maximum-strength Paxil. Sometimes their shrill craziness permeates the humid rice-paper walls of the cramped apartment, infiltrating even the synthetic fibers of the shag rug that smells like a wet dog. E's got dirty clothes lying all over the place, dirty dishes, laundry hanging to dry on strung-up ropes, and on top of that there are a hundred fifty Quinny messes as well. I sometimes want to take a knife to both of them. Or maybe just get my hands around their necks, bonk their pumpkin heads together, and then just shake the living hell out of them both. And to think I actually "liked" Elizabeth back in the States, before we came to Chengdu as roommates.

In her weight obsession, E says all Chinese women are bulimics, that's why they all take chopsticks to the bathroom after every meal. E's mother and sister — both born in China — are pukers too. It's all in the fam. A waif frame is part and parcel of being a Chinese female. Not only that, but due to the heavy air pollution obscuring the sunshine, the Chinese girls have flawless white complexions. On a green air-quality-index day, however, when the sun peeks through the smog, you won't catch a Chinese woman without a parasol. There is mastery in the art of bicycling one-handed with an umbrella in the other. But what really drives a Chengdu female crazy and makes her most insecure is a short stature. You read the lonely-hearts classifieds and it often goes something like this: "Tall Chinese male, 5'3", seeks Chinese girl, 5'4"–5'9". GIRLS WITH SHOELIFTS OR COWBOY BOOTS NEED NOT APPLY!"

When her parents can afford it, a short Chinese teenager will have an orthopedic surgeon break her shin bones and then install ratchet devices on either end of the broken bones. The patient will then pretty much lie in bed for two years eking out a millimeter or two of bone length each week with an Allen wrench. Remember that China is the country that put foot binding on the map. So you can acquire six centimeters of shinbone growth by this method and, with luck, meet your Chinese Prince Charming. You might even bag a European guy and effect a permanent escape from this grimy hellhole. Always industrious, the Chinese girl will spend her long convalescence mastering English, French, German, Spanish, Italian, Arabic, Euclidean geometry, physics, chemistry, Kantian philosophy, or something roughly approximate. She will acquire violin and trombone expertise, and when the whole show is over she will have a typing speed of seven hundred words a minute.

At the university level they all want to learn English. The girls will take you out to dinner or to some awful karaoke bar. They flatter you and blow smoke up your ass just so they can practice their English. We call them English sluts. On the other hand I can earn a hundred yuan of under-the-table income to teach a one-hour class in English. Really simple stuff. *"Put your right foot in, you put your right foot out; you do the Hokey Pokey and you shake it all about. Shake 'em up, baby!"* My Chinese friends, intellectuals for the most part, beg me to order them copies of *Reader's Digest*, that very paragon of literary excellence and sophistication. Like watching American films and *Bonanza* reruns, *Reader's Digest* helps students cement the basics of English.

Their next move is to go out and buy some new clothes. Small fortunes are put out for a wardrobe full of qipaos. Chinese girls will take out loans and surety bonds just to follow the latest trend, complete slaves of fashion. For all the book learning, not an iota of common sense.

I'm five foot six and when I walk the back alleys to Sichuan University or tool over there on my Flying Pigeon bicycle, people will point and stare. "There goes the round-eyed barbarian. No doubt she's a Western spy."

I'm not fat by American standards, but they call me fat here, follow me and gawk at my foreignness. They chant "fatso" in the local dialect, Sichuanhua. They don't know I speak Chinese until I turn around and lower the boom with "Cao ni ma!," which translates into "Fuck your mother!" That little bon mot never fails to get a rise out of them. Often they retort something to the effect that I'm a cheap American whore, when in fact I'm the very model of propriety. To keep the men off me, I wear a plain gold wedding band. I tell them, "My husband got out of prison yesterday and as we speak, he's on a flight to Chengdu. And brother, let me tell you, he's a bad motor scooter, jealous as hell. So you better look out; he'll nail your ass to the nearest tree." Of course, since the Chinese have cut down every tree in the country you would have to go to Finland for a tree. My father knows nothing of this.

When pressed on matters of nationality, I claim to be Canadian. The Chinese love things American but hate America. As for Canada, they think it's a city in southern Ecuador. Americans in China take a lot of heat over Iraq and our honorable president, George W. Bush. I learned not to admit to being American after the third or so cab driver yelled vehemently at me for voting GWB. Shit, I wasn't even old enough to vote yet when he was elected. And good luck explaining the Electoral College to a stranger in Mandarin. Not worth the effort, so Canadian I became.

China is one of the few remaining places on earth where material goods are still cheap, though there are two prices, prices for locals and prices for foreigners. You have to bargain them down or they have contempt for you. In America you bargain down the price of a house or car, but you don't go into a supermarket and haggle over the price of canned peas. I let Elizabeth handle this. At least she's good for something.

They don't have dental floss in Chengdu, so my father sends me seventy-five-foot dispensers of waxed floss in every care package. No tampons here either, but I don't ask him to send me those. Also, the children don't wear diapers. Instead there is an open gap at the back of their trousers from which they piss and shit in the streets. Even little toddlers are adept at this revolting habit. In this regard they are totally lacking in shame. You get used to seeing it by the third day and realize that it's normal. Once I saw a woman put cabbage leaves out to dry on a piss-and-shit road.

In Sichuan the food is so hot with spices and fiery oils that it can raise blisters on the roof of your mouth, your inner cheeks, tonsils, and uvula. This hydrochloric-acid diet causes pieces of flesh to hang off the oral cavities like string, like you just ate a McDonald's hot apple pie straight from the sizzling French-fry cooker. My father also sends me bottles of selenium, which he claims is deficient in the

Sichuan soil, and the lack of which is rumored to cause stomach cancer. At his behest I take selenium and zinc.

Until my nineteenth year I lived on junk food. China has made a vegetarian of me not only for my health but also for ethical reasons. What right do we have to so demean animals as to reduce them to food? What kind of sadistic Adolf Hitler insanity is that? Come to think of it, Hitler was a vegetarian.

Twenty years ago people still thought smoking was glamorous. I can't give the exact date, but I foresee that one day eating animals will become untenable. Meanwhile not only do the Chinese eat cocker spaniels and Chihuahuas, they've got restaurants that serve broiled rats. A damn rat ran across my foot with comic-book ferocity at the hair salon. This on my third day in-country. Its sharp paws scraping across the tile floor sounded like fingernails on a blackboard. I just about peed my pants. And the rat knew what he was doing; it was a calculated act of malevolence because after he ran past, he turned his head over his shoulder, bared his razor-sharp teeth, and caught my glance with his red squinty eyes. He didn't squeal with pleasure. No, he had a low baritone voice like James Earl Jones and kinda went, "Huh, huh, huh." Like some cartoon rat. Daddy loved that incident, though he was concerned that I might come down with rat fever.

Our first weeks here, Elizabeth and I wanted to see everything in China, every square inch. We went to the panda research center and it was a stone bore. Ten red pandas that are not impressive at all; they look like raccoons. There are about ten giant pandas and a bunch of guys with thick glasses in white coats with clipboards. And you can't just go anywhere, as half the place is restricted from tourists. For years you hear pandas are sacred and lovable but then you stand there and watch them and they won't do a single interesting thing. A brain no bigger than a BB. I got rapid-fire mosquito bites one after another. The whole ordeal was a total bust.

Next we took a trip to the mountains and were warned by guides not to get fooled by the cute act of the monkeys along the trail, that they most definitely would harass us and bite. I came back from that journey with mosquito welts the size of quarters and a festering monkey bite in the web between my forefinger and thumb. I think Chinese mosquitoes have antifreeze inside them. The only effective bug repellent is pure DEET and five tablespoons of DDT taken orally four times a day.

In Tibet I saw an Alley Oop–looking dude eating a raw shank of yak meat and washing it down with tea and a splash of yak milk. The fat content of yak milk is 16 percent. I am a lacto vegetarian but I draw the line at yak milk. Instead I put soymilk on my cornflakes. It tastes awful but like anything, you get used to it.

Once on a forty-hour train trip to Beijing I saw a bucket of dead eels by the train toilet. That night cooked eel was served in the first-class dining car. Newly vegetarian, I couldn't face cooked eel and ate a chocolate bar for dinner. Chinese chocolate is bitter like a combination of cooking chocolate and Dial soap. It was good for another Daddy report. He wrote back asking for "every detail."

You get a sleeper coach with a first-class train ticket. It had always been a dream of mine to sleep in a plush Pullman sleeper. Click clack, click clack as the steel wheels rock along iron rails, the most comforting sound in the world. In China the train beds are narrower than a balance beam and about as hard. Cigarette smoke like gas warfare. Every Chinese male over the age of eight smokes at least two packs a day. Boy, my hopes were dashed on that one. Top it off, I got the gastro and spent the whole ride balancing over the squat toilet, conveniently located at the hinge between train cars. Nothing like a little polluted air blast to the ass when you're good and sick.

At the site of the world's largest Buddha I met some nice Danish girls who asked me what was I doing in China when I didn't have to be there without some compelling reason. We traveled to Outer Mongolia together and slept in the same yurt. The Danes told me they'd hit China by accident and were bugging out for the nearest border, which I recollect was Siberia. This was just after SARS raised its ugly head. At the height of SARS hysteria Chengdu appeared to be a ghost town, the crowded streets empty except for lone individuals in face masks making panicked runs to the nearest pharmacy or grocery store. People in our program would get drunk on Tsingtao beer, and with beer bravado they vowed long and loud to stick it out until the end. A day later you would hear they'd lost their nerve and in the dead of night had caught the first flight home.

The weather in Chengdu is so variable that you can almost die of heatstroke one day and on the next you're wrapped up in a mummy sleeping bag by the electric heater with your teeth clacking like a pair of joke-store dentures. On cold nights you can see your breath. It forms into ice crystals that look like diamond dust. They hang in the air a moment and then tumble to the floor with tiny silver-bell tinkles. Antarctica.

As for the cockroaches, you get so used to them you learn to stab them to death with your index finger. Early on, the Chengdu roaches were so terrifying to me that at the first look I would bust down walls to effect an escape. What really got to me were those razor-sharp jaggedy things on their legs, and those wispy thin whip antennas. See one coming and I would go on a rampage like a twenty-ton elephant that had just seen a mouse and was convinced the harmless little rodent would climb up its trunk and accomplish a suffocation. Quinny says that for the elephant a field mouse is akin to a small but highly visible SARS molecular virus. He said it's all a matter of proportion, a matter of scale. And it's all completely irrational. "Like how many people worldwide have died of SARS, three hundred? That's just a stupid superstition!" But the next afternoon his crap was all gone and Elizabeth informed me that Quinny had caught the eleven A.M. flight to Vancouver. What a piker!

During my first months in Chengdu the streets were so thick with the confusion and disorder of human traffic, the city's every corridor so crowded, that I scarcely knew where I was going. You just got caught up in riptides of the frantic hoard. I would get so lost I had to take cabs home at extravagant prices.

Once I had my bearings, I bought a Flying Pigeon model bicycle off the black market. Daddy loves Flying Pigeon stories. The Pigeon had bald tires and bad brakes. Still, it was a deal — the only commercial transaction in which I came out ahead in a lifetime of shopping. Well, there I am riding the Pigeon when a truck shot past me and knocked over an old man who was riding a bike without a seat. The accident left the poor man sprawled out on the road, an unconscious bloody wreck. No ambulance came. The man began to have convulsive seizures and turned blue. No police came. People stopped to stare at the injured man but no Good Samaritan lifted a finger to help him out. Sometimes I think the residents of Chengdu are positively evil, all ten million of them. I'm not from Samaria but I helped the man to a teahouse and from there I hired a pedicab to take him home. I offered to take him to a hospital but he said he was okay and wanted to go home.

When the brakes on my Flying Pigeon went out, I bought a new set that cost twenty cents installed. The bicycle repairman later fixed a flat for an American dime. Elizabeth called me a fool and told me the bike guy totally ripped me off. How do you get ripped off over a dime?

I give as much every week to the rotating watchmen at our apartment building, although the prevailing fee is less, a single tenth of a yuan. These men guard bicycles for a living. That's all they do. A week after the old man was struck by the truck, my Flying Pigeon was stolen from a bike rack near the post office. Bike thieves carry commercial lock cutters. There is simply no percentage in owning a nice bicycle; it's just going to get stolen and with a new bike you have to get it licensed at the police station and take a bike-riding test. Since the Pigeon got taken, I've lost three crappier bikes. The Pigeon 2 was a rust bucket but it did have a basket and a bell, each of which was stolen on separate occasions within a week. Next the square foot pedals were stolen and I was left pedaling on thin pegs. Then someone stole the seat cushion, leaving an exposed seat spring that was determined to munch a hole in my ass. I told my dad about it. My father hears "rusty spring" and he fears tetanus. He hears "monkey bite" and fears rabies. Mosquito bites: malaria, Japanese encephalitis, and dengue fever. You don't even want to know what he feared when he first heard of the SARS epidemic. Obviously no way in hell did I consider telling him that Marcello was a black soccer player from São Paulo, Brazil, eleven years my senior.

The Danish girls had it right. Life in China is so arduous, there's never a single day when I don't wish I were somewhere else. Bad things happen on a daily basis. But I don't necessarily want to go home. I'd happily join a wandering Gypsy horde in Romania or travel the Australian desert with a tribe of Aborigines. My big fear is that I will return to an America unknown to me, an America where I will face plasma TVs with impossible remote controls, an America with a new jacked-up level of road rage, with an indecipherable new wave of computer software. I will return as Jennifer Crusoe. Or Rip Van Jennackal. This is what often happens to Peace Corps volunteers, or so I've heard.

Chengdu is such nonstop noise. Bulldozers and stuff. We had a water pipe in the bathroom burst and the whole bathroom had to be remodeled. You had to step over the construction workers when you came and went since the workers sleep at the job site. They sleep, wake up, drink a cup of tea, eat a bowl of rice, and then work for hours on end. Smoke two packs of cigarettes, go back to sleep in the stairwell, on and on they go twenty-four hours a day, seven days a week, every day the carbon copy of the day before. Chinese *Groundhog Day*. Building and construction work gets done quickly but it's highly dangerous employment. People doing manual labor, people who work in factories or in coal mines, are constantly getting maimed or killed on the job. You don't want to be a doctor or lawyer in China; a janitor has more clout. The highest-status job goes to the engineer or computer geek or an entrepreneur versed in American business know-how.

My junkman is always standing by the garbage cans like a prostitute on a street corner. He's short even by Chinese standards and he likes to clasp his hands, swinging his arms back and forth while whistling to himself or smoking hand-rolled cigarettes. My father is greatly amused by this man of mystery but there is so little to say I have to make things up. One of my goals for China was to get to know the common man but this is impossible because of class differences and the fact that the Sichuan dialect is pretty much impenetrable.

My dad doesn't get that. In every email or every calling-card phone conversation home he interrogates me about the junkman. "What kind of clothes does the junkman wear?"

"A charcoal sports jacket with gray slacks, suspenders, and a pair of Nikes with white spats."

"Oh, ho ho. There you go again but really, a sports jacket? Like a businessman, a stockbroker? A lawyer? Does the junkman have a family? How old is he? What career path did he follow before he was reduced in circumstances to the five garbage cans?"

My father sent me a Mariners ballcap and I gave it to the junkman, who wears it with tremendous pride. Or so it seems. Once I gave him what was left of a phoned-in pizza. The deliveries of pizzas, incidentally, are made by bicycle with little hot boxes on the rear fender. Rather than thank me for the pizza, the junkman sneered and tossed it into a garbage can. He didn't smile at me for a week after this incident. I wondered what unfathomable line I had crossed to offend him, but beyond that I didn't really care.

My father says that if I'm making a hundred a pop teaching English to junior high school kids, just think what kind of windfall it would be if I gave the junkman five bucks now and then? Wouldn't it be similar to giving the character Pip in *Great Expectations* an ersatz trust fund? Wouldn't it confer unto me a sense of power, grace, and entitlement? This was something that never really crossed my mind and when the junkman disappeared overnight, I had to confabulate more junkman anecdotes for my father, who often seemed more interested in the junkman than in me.

I was curious about his fate as well. He just vanished into thin air. People get sick and die overnight in China. Sometimes you see them lying dead in the streets. I wondered if maybe the junkman had crawled off somewhere and died in a gutter. It seemed likely.

At the university my research project is water pollution. And as I said, Chinese tap water is most definitely not Ice Dew. The rivers are polluted by sewage, factory runoff, human and animal wastes. People like to commit suicide in the rivers and think it highly romantic. So the rivers contain poison in many guises and the surface is covered with a white sudsy foam that looks like washing detergent. The chemical oxygen demand in most rivers is high. What's weird is the fact you can always see people fishing along the riverside. They catch fish with tumors, extra fins, or faces like Jay Leno. The lantern-jaw thing.

The cheapest, most rudimentary form of pollution control is both simple and practical. You round up a little manpower in a city where labor is almost free. You get them to dig cisterns in the channels that lead to the rivers. The cisterns temporarily contain the water, where the force of gravity allows the fecal sediment to settle on the bottom. Then you permit the relatively clean top water to enter the river systems. It's affordable and very much a step in the right direction. Another pollution fix-up in coal-powered China, with its bad air, is the Three Gorges

River Dam Project. The dam will soon replace countless coal-burning generators, supplying pollution-free electricity. In this regard China is on the verge of a legendary historical event. The world's largest hydroelectric dam!

To see the last days of the Yangtze River Valley, Marcello, Elizabeth, and I took the three-day ferry trip downriver. The cliffs are so high you get a sore neck looking up toward the top. Our tour guide pointed to the 170-meter white painted stripes on the Yangtze Valley's granite cliffs. That's how high the floodwaters would reach. Looking up, I felt like I was having a Jack and the Beanstalk adventure. One hundred and seventy meters is a trip into the clouds.

Flooding the plain will not only fill the river gorges, it will displace millions of peasant farmers. It will bury the Panda Cave, the Suspending Coffins, the Bright Temple, and Fendu, a ghost town where malevolent spirits are thought to dwell, and more — much more. The Chinese government seems not to worry about this, pointing out with pride that the world's fastest-emerging economic power will soon boast the world's largest dam. Early on, engineers and project managers realized that three separate dams would provide more power than one, and would disperse the available electricity over a greater and more expansive area. But why drive a Beetle when you can drive a Cadillac?

With most of the passengers seasick, we disembarked at Double Dragon Town to recover our land legs. In Double Dragon Town the citizens were literally removing every stick of furniture, every brick and stone, chipping away with pickaxes, hoes, and tiny hammers, and lugging all this stuff to the high ground, where they were reconstructing the whole city. And here comes the kicker: in Double Dragon Town, whom do I find but my junkman. It was the Mariners ballcap that first caught my view and sure enough it was him. Geez! Talk about finding a needle in a haystack! The junkman was wearing his charcoal sports coat and his gray trousers, which were now torn at the knees because of his new occupation. His knobby knees were thick with grime, scuffed and bloody. I chased a pair of Dramamine tablets with a bottle of Ice Dew and, having done so, I handed the empty bottle to my old friend. He gave me a toothless smile of recognition. Because the whole story would delight my father, I gave the junkman a pair of one-hundred-yuan notes, a sum of approximately twenty-five dollars. Money enough to buy a good deal more than a new pair of pants.

The junkman took my money but he didn't exactly seem thrilled to have money. You would think he would be; my father would think that. I mean here he is working like a dog, and it can't be for his health, you know what I mean? In that sense the junkman was like the David Carradine character Caine, in the TV series *Kung Fu*, above such trifling worldly concerns as m-o-n-e-y!

He didn't say, "No thanks, Grasshopper, you keep the money," but he did something that showed where his heart was. When the junkman saw that I was shivering from the cold he reached into a big sack he had with him and gave me an extra-large, olive-green, ankle-length quilted Mao jacket, an item that is next to impossible to find these days. After the Cultural Revolution ended, Mao jackets were soon as scarce as passenger pigeons. I'm sure the junkman knew the value of such a jacket. They are dandy as all get-out, a hundred percent cotton, nice and roomy, excellent in rain and raw weather, not all that stylish but a veritable fortress. I was cold and the junkman gave me a coat. I was completely blown.

My year in China didn't exactly teach me to go with the flow, to experience the eternal Tao, which, like the water behind the Three Gorges dam, will conquer all things. You can freeze the water, poison it, boil it into steam... all of that is true. But relax your life and follow the Tao where it leads you? Choose nonaction over action? They compiled that philosophy thousands of years ago. In this day and age you pull a number like that and every graduate program in America will turn your lazy ass down. Law school? Forget about it. You pull that shit and you'll be serving coffee at Starbucks. Try that one and what you've got is a lifetime "career" in coffee.

Bomb Shelter Noel

MICKEY BOUGHT ME a goldfish he named Seven Cent. He's got an orange streak along his lateral line running from forehead to tail. His dorsal fin is as black as night and appears to have been chewed. Otherwise he is albino in coloration except for his tail, which is translucent. You can see clear through to the bone. Me personally, I would have named him X-Ray, but you can't judge a book by its color. Seven Cent is a showman, a gifted performer, and he's got some pretty smooth moves.

He swims the perimeter of his little fish tank hugging the side of the glass with one eye, in full presentation for effect. He swims around in concentric circles with his mouth going open-close, open-close like a normal fish until he begins to pump his gills and then shoots himself skyward, partially breaking the surface, where he executes a well-timed flip, wagging his tail for propulsion, right down to the bottom, where he shakes things loose.

When you are on the Highway to Death, like me, everything is interesting. Everything is important. You see different, taste and smell different; everything has wonder written in it. Things you have done six million times seem new, and likewise you run into a seven-cent celebration of life in its otherwise impenetrable glory.

As Doomgirl I host a show called *Bomb Shelter Radio* broadcast at 147.859 MHz. The program is directed to survivalists. Mickey roped me into doing it because I have a pleasantly low voice. It's his radio, and he rigged up an antenna, which bounces radio waves at a communications satellite so the show can be heard worldwide. I play classical music and do some astrology, but the show is mostly about survival.

Mickey taught me a lot of survival stuff and this is what the listeners tune in to hear. I can build an igloo in frozen Antarctic wastes or a cozy tropical shelter poised to withstand apocalyptic tornadoes and hurricanes. I can read a compass, hunt, fish, forage edible roots high in vitamin C, and I have helped Mickey construct our bomb shelter, which is A-1 deluxe.

Watching Seven Cent, I sometimes feel like I'm drifting through the icy rings of Saturn, sight unseen, far far away, safe and secure amid grains, flakes, and pieces of smashed comets. Chunks of rock the size of trucks are there, to be sure, but mostly it's snow and ice. Who knows? I feel like those odd people reading your fortune at the carnival when I begin to speculate on things unknown. When I told this to Madame Rosa she threw back her Roma head and laughed like a hyena. Madame Rosa is a tarot reader with advanced paranormal skills. She asked me, "What's your blood sugar? Ten?"

I am a type I diabetic with hypoglycemic unawareness. Because of this I'm on a first-name basis with every paramedic in town. "Laura! Laura! Can you hear me?"

You wake up with an IV in your arm, totally spaced. Every coma I have is different. When I have a rock-bottom seizure I come out of it feeling pretty good. It's the light stuff that contains the most terror. They are the realm of the Bone Crusher and his dancing Salvador Dalí demons. You come out of those ice-cold and soaking wet. I follow my diet religiously, eat in a timely fashion, and test my blood sugar on the hour. People think you just go around like a reckless fool. "Here comes that dopey girl with her big bag of Halloween candy."

Last night in the warm glow of my Aladdin kerosene lantern down in the bomb shelter, I was reading about a family in Ulaanbaatar, Mongolia. Ulaanbaatar is the coldest capital city on the planet but only 3 percent of the population over the age of twenty is diabetic. Three percent in a world where 8 percent is average! Many among the rural population of Mongolia, the prosperous ones anyhow, live in snazzy yurts. The people of Ulaanbaatar eat mutton dumplings, tinned herring, and cabbages. They smoke L&M cigarettes. Ulaanbaatar is like any other city except for the extreme cold.

At the dialysis center some of the day patients brought in a Christmas tree. Someone wrote "Christmas is just around the corner" on the green chalkboard at the well-lit entryway. Dixie Platte picked up a piece of chalk before a treatment and added, "Have a Holly Jolly Christmas!"

Dixie is one year and seven months older than me, like that makes her the final word on subjective topics. Dixie is a lap dancer at the Zebra Club. She says the dialysis fistula planted under her wrist looks like a 1965 portable phone from Botswana. Dixie gets by on a cadre of older customers who don't look at her wrists.

A dialysis fistula is a special tract placed under the skin of the forearm connecting an artery and vein to provide access to a dialysis machine. Without the surgically created fistula, a patient's blood vessels would quickly break down altogether.

A few people on the midnight-to-four-A.M. shift still have jobs. They will sleep, read, or maybe engage in a little lighthearted banter while the techs hook us up. Occasionally someone will have a mini-nervous breakdown. Some of the dementia patients are screamers. There is an adjunct room in the back, but you can hear them anyhow. You wonder why they never get hoarse.

Mickey and I used to drive to the hospital emergency room on Friday and Saturday nights as well as nights of the full moon, since there are so many drunken automobile and motorcycle accidents, and drive-by shootings, random shootings, knifings, etc.

This is how Mickey got his new pancreas and kidney, from a twenty-five-year-old man, blood type O, cause of death unknown. Mickey wanted me to get them but the man's organs were too big, or I'm just a little shrimp. I didn't know it at the time but a donated organ has to fit or it won't work right. Mickey takes prednisone so his immune system doesn't destroy the new kidney and pancreas. He's got a swollen face, but apart from the pills, he's cured. He tells me over and over that he wishes I got the cure, not him. He said he would die to save me. He said he will protect me from any harm that might befall me and that I'm the only person he can trust.

When I turn seventeen we are driving to South Carolina and getting married. Dixie helped me pick out lingerie to wear on my wedding night. When we were at the laundromat she told me that my underwear was too "utilitarian." Personally I think her thongs, bustiers, and other sexy garments are uncomfortable-looking. She badgered me into buying a black ruffled petticoat. It's not the kind of thing any girl in Ulaanbaatar would ever put on.

I can fell an edible crow with a blowgun or drop a hefty vulture with a boomerang. I can practically start a fire under water. Ha-ha. Additionally I can handle .50-caliber machine guns, crush a villain's trachea, or knife him through the heart even though I don't like seeing people get hurt.

Hen Pierson sits in the geri chair across from my own. He was a diabetic at twelve and has been on dialysis nineteen years interspersed with two short-lived transplants. His albumin-creatinine ratio (ACR) at 3.4 is better than my own.

Hen is sixty-four. His brother was thrown in prison for murder, and while he sat many a long year in his death-row cell, the weight of his crimes weighed heavily upon him. Hen asked his brother for a kidney but his brother wrote back, "Why should I give you a kidney? Nobody ever gave me anything worth having."

A week later Convict Pierson, age fifty-seven, was stabbed to death in the prison infirmary. Madame Rosa said she knew this was going to happen. "It was plain as day."

She said she was glad it happened. I think her lumbago puts her in a bad mood sometimes. She is not a mean person. I have seen her read the Bible from time to time.

Hen came to treatment looking pretty down after the incident at the prison. He wanted the kidney, sure, but he loved his brother and he was always loaning him money or paying off lawyers, money he could have spent on himself.

He was wearing a suit that looked three sizes too big on him. He removed his jacket and rolled up the sleeve of his left arm, exposing his arterial fistula.

The dialysis technicians were coming down the line, hooking everyone up, but when they got to Hen's chair, I heard a terrible scuffling of shoes against the tile as Hen stumbled out of his chair and started to fall. The clinic nurse hurried down the aisle and helped him gain his balance. "Are you okay, Mr. Pierson?"

Hen's face was white with fear. "I'm done," he said. "I'm just going to go home."

The long room fell dead with silence. When Hen realized he was the center of attention, he tried to put a good face on things and said, "I want to thank everyone for being a pal for so many years. I sincerely wish you all the best."

Hen approached my geri chair, where I lay with my lower lip trembling. I was crying big tears, snot coming out of my nose, choking. I just couldn't control my feelings. I was so ashamed. I didn't want him to feel still worse. It felt like someone stuck a spoon in my heart and twisted it. Hen always looked after me. He knew me since I was little. We were solid. He gave me a hug and said, "Don't you worry about a thing, sugar britches. Everything is going to be all right."

I said the same stupid thing to him I always said after dialysis. "See you later, alligator."

The ultrafilters on my machine took three liters of water out of me after that. I can't urinate; the machine does it for me. Losing all that water at one go is a shock to your body. I had cramps, my knees hurt, and I itched everywhere, but I put on my winter coat and staggered to the bus stop. Dixie and Vera T. Bailey, who is slightly retarded but nice, offered me a ride home. I should have taken it. I should have gone back to the clinic. People actually get angry with you if you don't ask for a stupid ride. They all seemed like mechanical people to me. Machines and robots like the damn Tin Man in *The Wizard of Oz*, who was so fake he wrecked everything in that movie. What a bozo.

The next day Mickey and I bought a four-gallon BiOrb aquarium at the Goodwill. It looks just like a crystal ball. It came with a filter, bubblers, air stone, and magnetic algae cleaner. It was just too cool for words. I was so happy, I couldn't wait to get home and fill it.

Mickey said, "Looks like Seven Cent got him a fifty-five-dollar crib."

I hugged Mickey and kissed him until some Goodwill shoppers told us to "go get a room."

"We don't need a room, what we need is a mortgage," Mickey said.

Ha-ha.

The BiOrb was the talk of treatment; at the clinic, twelve midnight to four A.M., I went on and on about it. Finally Dixie said, "Most of the stuff you get for Christmas is crap you don't want, just stuff you have to get rid of, a used piano or something. An anvil."

Ha-ha.

A young man named Jerome now sits in Hen's geri chair. He's tall, thin, and good-looking, from New York City. He's got a crush on Dixie and won't leave her alone. Dixie told him to zip his lip, but it only heightened his ardor. Pretty soon Dixie has a big crush on Jerome, and listening to their crazy infatuation talk was almost scary. They begin to sound like mental patients in their heated excitement. By that I mean they can be talking about normal everyday stuff and something insane will pop out like a jack-in-the-box. *Pow!*

Dixie started in with a story she read in the *National Examiner* about an ostrich that swam from Nelson Mandela's prison island to Cape Town, South Africa.

"Why would an ostrich go to the trouble?" I said.

Dixie said, "I don't know. To pull rickshaws or have chariot races. They got the legs for it."

Jerome said, "An ostrich is no more than a giant chicken, too heavy to swim or fly. All they can do is the fifty-yard dash."

Normal non-in-love people don't talk at length about things no one else cares about, fighting over nothing. Mickey is the love of my life, but I have never broken into this sort of gibberish pining over him.

"Jerome, you are just an ignorant fool," Dixie said. "All you do is lay over there acting gangster. You should go back to New York City and live in the 'hood again."

"I was starting to like you, but now I have changed my mind," Jerome said.

Dixie lay back in her chair. She said, "I'm right and you know it."

I used a commonsense voice with levelheaded humor and said, "Let me get this straight, jobless ostrich braves howling winds, tenebrous currents in search of work, ha-ha —"

Jerome wheeled on me in a fury. "Why don't you just shut the fuck up? You aren't funny. You think you are but you aren't. I am not gonna lay here for four hours three times a week, twelve hours total not including the fucking goddamn Mickey Mouse of coming and going, only to get ha-ha'ed to death by you."

Super Huge Hudson, a dialysis technician and martial artist, came thumping down the aisle on his size-fourteen feet. He pinched a muscle on Jerome's neck, paralyzing him. "I don't want to hear another word out of you, Jerome, ever again, so long as you live. Do you follow? I am back there at my desk trying to read *The Girl with the Dragon Tattoo*, and I don't want to hear another word come out of your filthy mouth."

Jerome didn't so much as say "Ouch," but later I could hear him sniffling. What was he thinking about? This fresh humiliation? The rigors of dialysis?

I felt bad for him, I who cried bitter tears across the aisle from him over Hen Pierson, who was never coming back. Hen walked out with a clear mind. He knew without dialysis he had a week, maybe ten days.

One night when Super Huge Hudson was out sick, I was lying in my geri chair, half flaked, and I could hear Jerome crying again. I said, "Jerome, I know that normally you are a nice person —"

"No I'm not!" he shouted back. He leaped forward at me with such blinding speed I thought he would rip the tubes to the fistula loose. Instead he half toppled his machine, screaming, "If I could get away with it, I would kill you right now, today!"

Dixie looked over and said, "Put a lid on it, dorkhead. You aren't supposed to talk. Jesus H."

I spoke to Jerome in low confidential tones. "Down deep inside you are a nice person, Jerome. Down deep you are wonderful and I love you."

None of what I said was true, but why hit someone when they are down? I was freezing cold. It felt like a Jack Frost crew of half-inch Eskimos had infiltrated my machine with sacks of dry ice over their shoulders. My blood sugar was so low that I fainted amid a room of fellow sufferers. Dixie said, "That's the third time this month."

The skies cleared and it got colder. I went back to the Goodwill store, where I saw a coat that wasn't too bad. More importantly it was lined with sheepskin. Like some hand-me-down from Cinderella. I like a coat with loose sleeves. I wear long sleeves even in the summer to hide my fistula. For knock-around activities I wrap an Ace bandage around it.

Damn! Look at the lovely bride wearing a black ruffle petticoat with a large conspicuous fistula bulging out of her arm. Isn't she lovely? Ha-ha.

I was at the bus stop and along comes Hannes Smit, another type 1 diabetic, and he's back to drinking again. He's on the list for his third kidney. He won't get one; he's sixty-two years old. He was some kind of part-time janitor.

"You live in a dangerous neighborhood," he said. "Let me walk you home."

"Naw, the bus is good."

Hannes said the whole world would end before dawn, and being gay, could he fuck me since he never had sex with a woman before? Tell me what chick hasn't heard that come-on a thousand times?

We were on a long desolate street inhabited by empty shops and failed restaurants. Down the road I watched the approach of the yellow Union Street bus, bumping and squealing along on a leaf-spring suspension and razor-thin drum brakes, its headlights imperceptible.

I hopped on and moved to a seat with an open window. Outside Hannes was having an argument with the parking meter I had been hanging on to moments before. At least I knew that it was a parking meter.

I wanted the bus to get going but the driver sat behind the wheel trying to light a wet stub of a cigar, and outside Hannes had now turned his vitriol on a fire hydrant. Hannes wasn't right in his mind from a stroke he had. Once he split his pants and I saw he was wearing aluminum foil underwear.

Mickey and me live kind of far out, and when I got off the bus the sidewalks were extra slick. I unlocked the iron gate surrounding the house and struggled up the incline to the front door. I could hear the low rumble of the diesel generator.

There were three access portals to the shelter, all sealed with blast-proof doors. There was one in the basement, another in Mickey's shed, and the third out in the field covered with thorny blackberry bushes. Mickey called it "hiding in plain sight."

He was down in the basement shoring up a section of a narrow tunnel. He crawled out and wiped the grime off his face and hands with a clean rag. He was sweating in spite of the cold.

I asked him why he had the generator going.

"Air movement," he said. "I just put in a backup filter. Now we got two."

A strong current of air came out from the tunnel, which was constructed with a lot of ninety-degree turns designed to block the forward path of nuclear radiation.

"As long as the generator is going," I said, "I'll go do twenty minutes of my show. I don't feel like it, but I'll do it anyway."

"Have you sketched out a script?"

I shook my head no. "I know what I'm going to do." He shrugged his shoulders. I knew he wanted to get back to his project. I went to the radio shack, where I had a hidden six-pack of lime Diet Coke. I had been sneaking one too many only to pay the piper on the ultrafilters. Back at the bus stop I swore up and down I would never do such a thing again. But I was so thirsty I guzzled an entire can and opened another.

I put on the radio headset and adjusted the microphone.

"Good evening, all and sundry. Welcome to another fabulous hour of *Bomb Shelter Radio*. This is Doomgirl and you are dialed in at 147.859 MHz. Hang on to your hats; this is going to be a truly fantastic show."

The words coming out of my mouth were hollow, but I pressed on. "I'm sort of rattling things off the top of my head, but there is this young man, Jerome. I wish to dedicate tonight's show to Jerome. I hope you are okay, buddy. I just want to tell you that you are not alone in thinking your stalwart plans will only vaporize and disappear in the weak rays of light. I have Mickey and Seven Cent and all you out there listening, but can someone tell me why life is so hard?

"I want to ask about loneliness and tears, about frustration, lots of frustration, about my head exploding, about how I ache for love, unconditional love that will last and last, about how hopeless I feel no matter how much I know, of how I will die soon, about how I have so few friends, about all the bad things I've done, about how afraid I am of dying in pain, about how I am such a disappointment to those who love me, about how slow I am, about blood coming out of me, about the places I go and don't come back from, and really, Jerome, for all this the only thing I have to offer is the first tune of the evening, the Waltz in C-sharp Minor, op. 64, by Frédéric Chopin, the man who wrote poems with the piano, who wrote for Saturn's icy rings and Ulaanbaatar, for Madame Rosa and beautiful Hen and Dixie in her thongs, here we go. I love you all out there in Radioland. Stay warm. Merry Christmas."

Acknowledgments

On Thom's behalf, we would like to extend our deepest gratitude to Richard Fisher, Don Fotheringham, Troy Young, Will Conroy, Braxton Pope, Lee Froehlich, Candida Donadio, and Patrick Keller for their inspiration and many, many years of loyal friendship. For their selfless devotion and canine companionship, eternal thanks to Boxer, Shelby, Manny, and Sugar. May you all look after one another in heaven. For their infinite patience and many, many prescriptions, thank you to Doctors Samuel Coor and William Bradford. Additional thanks to the Olympia Public Library for the ever-revolving supply of books (apologies for the snack stains), and thanks to the Olympia Fire Department and Emergency Medical Services for the countless hypoglycemic revivals. Finally, an enormous thank-you to Ben George of Little, Brown and Jin Auh of the Wylie Agency for this magnificent collection and remembrance of our favorite literary genius, husband, and father.

— Sally and Jenny Jones

These stories originally appeared, sometimes in different form, in the following publications: "Pot Shack" in *Buzz*; "Night Train" in *Double Take*; "Daddy's Girl," "I Need a Man to Love Me" (published as "Nights in White Satin"), and "I Want to Live!" in *Harper's*; "The Black Lights," "Cold Snap," "Mouses," "The Pugilist at Rest," "Sonny Liston Was a Friend of Mine," "Superman, My Son," "Way Down Deep in the Jungle," and "A White Horse" in *The New Yorker*; "All Along the Watchtower," "Bomb Shelter Noel," "Diary of My Health," "A Merry Little Christmas," and "Pickpocket" in *Playboy*; "Mosquitoes" in *Story*; "Volcanoes from Hell" in *Tin House*; "Tarantula" in *Zoetrope*.

"The Pugilist at Rest," "The Black Lights," "I Want to Live!," "Silhouettes," "Mosquitoes," and "A White Horse" were previously published in *The Pugilist at Rest* (Little, Brown and Company, 1993). "Cold Snap," "Superman, My Son," "Way Down Deep in the Jungle," "Pickpocket," "Pot Shack," and "I Need a Man to Love Me" were previously published in *Cold Snap* (Little, Brown and Company, 1995). "Sonny Liston Was a Friend of Mine," "The Roadrunner," "A Run Through the Jungle," "40, Still at Home," "Tarantula," "Mouses," and "Daddy's Girl" were previously published in *Sonny Liston Was a Friend of Mine* (Little, Brown and Company, 1999).

"The Pugilist at Rest," "I Want to Live!," "Cold Snap," and "Way Down Deep in the Jungle" were selected for *The Best American Short Stories* in 1992, 1993, 1994, and 1995, respectively. "I Want to Live!" was also selected for *The Best American Short Stories of the Century*. "The Pugilist at Rest" and "Tarantula" each won the O. Henry Prize and were included in that anthology in 1993 and 1998, respectively.

About the Author

Thom Jones, who died in 2016, was a National Book Award finalist, O. Henry Award winner, and the author of three story collections: *The Pugilist at Rest, Cold Snap,* and *Sonny Liston Was a Friend of Mine.* He received an MFA from the University of Iowa in 1973 and thereafter worked an array of jobs, from copywriter to janitor, until he was published for the first time, in *The New Yorker,* in his midforties. His stories went on to be published in other magazines such as *Harper's, Esquire, Playboy,* and *Story* and were reprinted numerous times in *The Best American Short Stories.* John Updike chose his story "I Want to Live!" for *The Best American Short Stories of the Century.*